THE PRENTICE-HALL SERIES IN ACCOUNTING

Editor: Charles T. Horngren

ADVANCED MANAGEMENT ACCOUNTING, *Robert S. Kaplan*

A NEW INTRODUCTION TO FINANCIAL ACCOUNTING, Second edition, *Robert G. May, Gerhard G. Mueller,* and *Thomas H. Williams*

AUDITING: AN INTEGRATED APPROACH, Second edition, *Alvin A. Arens* and *James K. Loebbecke*

AUDITING PRINCIPLES, Fifth edition, *Howard F. Stettler*

BUDGETING: PROFIT PLANNING AND CONTROL, Fourth edition, *Glenn A. Welsch*

COST ACCOUNTING: A MANAGERIAL EMPHASIS, Fifth edition, *Charles T. Horngren*

CPA PROBLEMS AND APPROACHES TO SOLUTIONS, Fifth edition, *Charles T. Horngren* and *J. Arthur Leer*

FINANCIAL ACCOUNTING: PRINCIPLES AND ISSUES, Second edition, *Michael H. Granof*

FINANCIAL STATEMENT ANALYSIS, *George Foster*

FUND ACCOUNTING, Second edition, *Edward S. Lynn* and *Robert J. Freeman*

INTRODUCTION TO FINANCIAL ACCOUNTING, *Charles T. Horngren*

INTRODUCTION TO MANAGEMENT ACCOUNTING, Fifth edition, *Charles T. Horngren*

KOHLER'S DICTIONARY FOR ACCOUNTANTS, Sixth edition, *William W. Cooper* and *Yuji Ijiri*

LONG LEASES

1. **Operating Lease**

Rent expense	1000	
Cash		1000

   Nothing on B/S

2. **Capital Leases**
   1. Transfer of ownership
   2. Lease contains bargain purchase option
   3. Lease term ≥ 75% estimated economic life
   4. PV lease payments ≥ 90% MV of property at time of lease

Measurement

Value = PV (Lease payments)

To record lease

Leased asset	7980	
Leased liability		7980

To record payment

Interest expense (8% × 7980)	638	
Lease liability (2000 − 638)	1362	
Cash		2000

Depreciation

Dep expense	1596	
Acc Dep		1596

Payments Schedule

Payment	Interest 8%	Principal	Balance
			7980
2000	638	1362	6618
2000	529	1471	5147
⋮	⋮	⋮	⋮
2000	148	1852	0

B/S Disclosure

Assets

Fixed Assets
- Leased Assets 7980
- − Acc Dep 1596   6384

Liabilities

L-T Liabilities
- Lease liability 6618

or

Current Liabilities
- Current portion of L-T lease 1471

L-T Liabilities
- Lease liability 5147

2nd edition

A NEW INTRODUCTION TO FINANCIAL ACCOUNTING

ROBERT G. MAY
University of Texas at Austin

GERHARD G. MUELLER
University of Washington

THOMAS H. WILLIAMS
University of Wisconsin—Madison

 Prentice/Hall International, Inc., London

Library of Congress Cataloging in Publication Data

May, Robert G
   A new introduction to financial accounting.

   (The Prentice-Hall Series in accounting)
   Includes index.
   1. Accounting. I. Mueller, Gerhard G., joint author. II. Williams, Thomas Howard, joint author. III. Title.
HF5635.M454   1980   657'.48   79-28471
ISBN 0-13-614859-X

This edition may be sold only in those countries to which it is consigned by Prentice-Hall International. It is not to be re-exported and it is not for sale in the U.S.A., Mexico or Canada.

Interior Design by Barbara Alexander
Editorial-production supervision by Patricia Lewis
Art Director: Lorraine Mullaney
Manufacturing Buyer: Edmund W. Leone

©1980, 1975 by Prentice-Hall, Inc., Englewood Cliffs, N.J. 07632

All rights reserved. No part of this book may be reproduced in any form or by any means without permission in writing from the publisher.

Printed in the United States of America

10 9 8 7 6 5

Prentice-Hall International, Inc., London
Prentice-Hall of Australia Pty. Ltd., Sydney
Prentice-Hall of Canada, Ltd., Toronto
Prentice-Hall of India Private Limited, New Delhi
Prentice-Hall of Japan, Inc., Tokyo
Prentice-Hall of Southeast Asia Pte. Ltd., Singapore
Whitehall Books Limited, Wellington, New Zealand
Prentice-Hall, Inc., Englewood Cliffs, New Jersey

ACCOUNTING FOR OE PROPRIETORSHIPS ; PARTNERSHIPS ; CORPORATIONS

PROPRIETORSHIP

Closing the books

Revenues	20,000	
Expenses		8,000
P. Capital		12,000
P. Capital	6,000	
Drawings		6,000

Statement of Changes in OE

P. Capital (Beg. Bal)		xx
+ Add'ins	xx	
+ Net Income	xx	xx
− Losses	xx	
− Drawings	xx	xx
P. Capital (End. Bal)		xx

PARTNERSHIPS

Entries reflecting cost   Entries reflecting Market

Cash	5000	
Land	4000	
X - Capital		5000
Y - Capital		4000

Cash	5000	
Land	5000	
X - Capital		5000
Y - Capital		5000

TO OUR CHILDREN

CORPORATE FIRM

+ ability to raise capital
  ease of transferring ownership
  perpetual existence
  limited liability of owners

− subject to numerous state & federal laws
  Earnings subject to double taxation
  Loss of control by original owners.

Types of capital A/c's

1. Capital stock
2. Add. paid-in capital
3. Retained earnings

Common Stock

+ Voting rights   − Residual claims to π
  rights to residuals   Residual claims to Assets

Preferred Stock

+ Prior claim on π   − No vote
  "   "   " Assets   Fixed return

Par value

a. est. firms min. legal capital
b. determines the amount of premium recognized on the sale of capital stock

ISSUANCE OF CAPITAL STOCK

CASH	507,500	
P/S		5,000
Premium on P/S		2,500
C/S		100,000
Premium on C/S		400,000

Balance Sheet

Stockholders Equity

5% P/S, par $10 auth 1000 Sh., issued & outstanding 500 Sh	5,000	min legal cap
C/S par $1 auth 200,000 Sh issued & outstanding 100,000 Sh	100,000	
Premium on P/S	2,500	
Premium on C/S	400,000	
RE	100,000	
Total Stockholders Eq.	607,500	

TREASURY STOCK

Buyback of shares

eg ABC reacquires 10k shares for $5, issued for $5

Treasury Stock	50,000	
Cash		50,000

B/S

Stockholders equity

C/S $1 par issued 100,000 Sh outstanding 90,000 Sh	100,000
Premium on C/S	400,000
RE	100,000
	600,000
− Treasury Stock	50,000
Total SE	550,000

Contra OE a/c

DIVIDEND PAYMENTS

closing entries

Revenues	XX	
Expenses		XX
Net Earnings		XX
Retained Earnings	250	
Div payable		250
Div Payable	250	
Cash		250

Contents

PREFACE   xi

I   FINANCIAL ACCOUNTING CONCEPTS

1. Accounting, Decision Making, the Economic Environment, and the Business Enterprise   3

2. Present Value Approach to Investment Decisions   36

3. Conventional Accounting: An Investment Decision Perspective   72

4. Conventional Accounting: Framework, Recognition of Economic Events, and Periodic Statements   104

5. Conventional Accounting Income Measurement: Some Elaboration   147

x CONTENTS

    6. Resource Flows and Statements of Changes in Financial Position   184

    7. The Financial Accounting Information System   222

II CONVENTIONAL ACCOUNTING MEASUREMENT ISSUES

    8. Revenue Recognition   265

    9. Revenue Recognition Refinements   300

    10. Expense Recognition and Related Asset Valuation Issues   337

    11. Expense Recognition and Related Equity Valuation Issues   387

    12. Valuation and Income: Some Further Issues   435

III ALTERNATIVE FINANCIAL ACCOUNTING MODELS

    13. Alternative Financial Accounting Models: Modifications for General Price-Level Changes   495

    14. Alternative Financial Accounting Models: Current Entry Prices (Replacement Costs)   543

    15. Alternative Financial Accounting Models: Current Exit Prices (Market Values)   593

    16. Financial Accounting Models in Perspective   627

IV CONTEMPORARY FINANCIAL REPORTING ENVIRONMENT

    17. Capital Market Institutions and the Accounting Policy-Making Process   673

    18. Dissemination and Content of Corporate Financial Reports   710

    19. The Audit Function in Financial Reporting   759

INDEX   786

Preface

This second edition has afforded us the opportunity to extend and refine the material presented in the first edition. We have selected a different chapter sequence and have altered our approach to a number of individual topics and yet we have retained the philosophy and overall approach of the first edition.

Thus, it is appropriate to reprint the following paragraph from the first edition Preface.

> In this book we introduce the student to (1) accounting as an intellectual discipline having a primarily utilitarian as opposed to purely esthetic orientation; (2) accounting as an information specialization in society, having professional-level achievement in status as one of its many manifestations; and (3) accounting as a social force, having policy implications that affect the welfare of virtually all citizens. We use the vehicle of financial accounting subject matter to accomplish these goals. At the same time our objective, in terms of specific skills, is to develop financial statement "literacy" rather than technology only.

Six major changes characterize the new edition relative to its predecessor.

1. Conventional double-entry bookkeeping procedures and the financial accounting system are now introduced in Chapter 7 (Part I) rather than in an appendix. This material is not only expanded from the first edition, but—starting with Chapter 7—it is referred to and utilized wherever appropriate.

2. The Chapters on alternative accounting measurement models appear in Part III of the new edition rather than Part I. Part II is an expanded and more readable version of the prior material on how conventional accounting concepts are applied to specific revenue, expense, asset, liability, and equity measurement problems. The new sequencing gives the beginning student a better grounding in conventional accounting and, therefore, a better perspective from which to examine alternatives.

3. The statement of changes in financial position is introduced in Chapter 6 (Part I) rather than later as a special financial accounting issue. This earlier sequencing augments the discussion of the income statement and the balance sheet as basic financial statements and yields a better understanding of output objectives for the student working through various issues, standards, and measurement procedures.

4. The former general introductory Chapter 1, as well as the financial-institutions-related Chapter 10, have been greatly shortened. The materials removed from these chapters are incorporated in appropriate chapters throughout the book. In contrast the chapter on revenue-recognition was expanded to two chapters in the second edition, as was the chapter on current costs and market prices as alternative accounting measurement models. In all, the first edition had 17 chapters and an appendix, and the second edition has 19 chapters.

5. The entire manuscript has received considerable additional editing. The result of this effort should be both tighter presentation and greater readability.

6. Professional aspects of financial accounting have received even greater attention in the second edition. More actual case materials and excerpts from published financial statements have been interspersed throughout the text and a number of new exercises have been added.

Without relisting all the names of colleagues around the world and officials of the Price Waterhouse Foundation whose contributions to the first edition were properly acknowledged there, we reiterate our grateful appreciation for their many efforts in helping to bring this text about in the first place. Several of these individuals have conveyed thoughts and comments which proved helpful in preparing the second edition. At the University of Washington, Professors Robert Bowen, William L. Felix, Jr., and Eric W. Noreen gave us specific suggestions which we utilized. At other universities, Professors Lowell Bourne (Syracuse University), William T. Geary (DePaul University), E. Dee Hubbard (Bringham Young University), Mohamed Onsi (Syracuse University), J.M. Smith (Brigham Young University), Christopher Taylor (Natal University, Durban, South Africa), Ann Rich (University of New Haven) and Robert K. Zimmer (University of Minnesota) reviewed the manuscript for the second edition and provided much appreciated helpful comments. Quite a number of informal comments were also received from Ph.D. students utilizing this text in undergraduate classes—and this source of help is also acknowledged thankfully.

Ms. Sylvia Christensen, Administrative Assistant in the Department of Accounting at the University of Washington, managed the manuscript production of the second edition. We are doubly indebted to her, since she also served as production manager of the manuscript for the first edition.

As is customary for projects of this type, the co-authors accept full responsibility for all errors of commission and omission. To those who have used the book in the past we say thanks. Special thanks to those who made possible the successful launching of an international edition of the book. We also would like to take this opportunity to invite comments from all those who choose to use our second edition.

ROBERT G. MAY

GERHARD G. MUELLER

THOMAS H. WILLIAMS

FUNDS STATEMENT

- initial funds statement = balance sheet
- Income statement explains ΔOE
- Funds statement explains Δ(balance sheet)

Uses

1) how are π employed
2) how were investments financed
3) why dividends not paid despite high π
4) how could dividends be paid in the face of losses

Definition of FUNDS

1. CASH
2. WORKING CAPITAL = CURRENT ASSETS — CURRENT LIABILITIES

Major sources & uses of funds

major sources & uses of funds (= WC) relate to operating income & changes in non-current items

$$CA + FA = CL + LTL + OE$$

$$CA - CL = LTL + OE - FA$$

$$\Delta(CA - CL) = \Delta LTL + \Delta OE - \Delta FA$$

Sources

1. income from current operations + non cash expenses or losses
2. increase in Long-term liabilities
3. Sale of fixed assets
4. Sale of common stock

Uses

1. payment of dividends
2. retirement of long-term liabilities
3. purchase of fixed assets
4. reacquisition of common stock

Statement Format

Sources of funds
   Operations:
      Net Income   xx
      (+) Dep^n xx   xx
   Sale of Fixed Assets   xx
   Increase in L-T debt   xx
   Sale of capital stock   xx   xx

Uses of funds
   Purchase of fixed assets   xx
   Repayment of L-T debt   xx
   Reacquisition of cap stock   xx
   Payment of dividends   xx   xx

Net change in working capital   xx

Cash definition of funds

$$Cash + Other\ CA + FA = CL + LTL + CE$$

$$\Delta Cash = \Delta CL + \Delta LTL - \Delta Other\ CA - \Delta FA + \Delta CE$$

Sources
as before +
  5. Increase in current liabilities
  6. Sale of "other" current assets

Uses
  5. Repayment of current liabilities
  6. Purchase of "other" current assets

Methodology

1. Construct a comparative BS of net increases or decreases in each current asset + current liability item to determine the net increase or decrease in WK

2. Analyze changes in each non-current A/c beginning with BS
   1. WK changes   xx   xx
                                     Analyses
   2. Working paper   xx   Debit   Credit   xx

FINANCIAL STATEMENT ANALYSIS

Limitations
1. oriented towards past
2. quantitative vs qualitative
3. historical cost vs market values
4. assumes purchasing power constant

Analyses
1. trend
2. % change
3. Common size
4. Ratio Analyses
   - Absolute stds
     - rules of thumb
     - budgets
   - Historical o Industry Standards

LIQUIDITY

$$\text{current ratio} = \frac{\text{current assets}}{\text{current liabilities}}$$

$$\text{ACID TEST ratio} = \frac{\text{current assets} - \text{Inventories} - \text{prepayments}}{\text{current liabilities}}$$

SOLVENCY (LEVERAGE)

$$\text{Debt ratio} = \frac{\text{Total liabilities}}{\text{Total assets}}$$

$$\text{TIMES INTEREST EARNED} = \frac{\text{Net income} + \text{interest} + \text{taxes}}{\text{interest}} \quad (EBIT)$$

EFFICIENCY

$$\text{Inventory turnover} = \frac{\text{cost of goods sold}}{\text{Average inventory}} \quad \leftarrow \text{Balance sheet} \therefore \text{avg}$$

(liquidity)

$$\text{Average collection period} = \frac{\text{Avg receivables}}{\text{sales per day}}$$

Total Asset turnover = $\dfrac{\text{Sales}}{\text{Avg total Assets}}$

Period Margin on sales = $\dfrac{\text{Net Income}}{\text{Sales}}$

FINANCIAL ACCOUNTING CONCEPTS

Return on total assets = $\dfrac{\text{Earnings before interest \& taxes}}{\text{Avg total assets}}$

a good measure : $\dfrac{EBIT}{\text{Avg Assets}} = \dfrac{EBIT}{\text{Avg Liabilities + OE}}$

ie earnings on funds provided by creditors, owners & govt.

Return on Stockholders Equity = $\dfrac{\text{Net Income - Preferred Dividends}}{\text{Avg common stockholders equity}}$

Price Earnings Ratio = $\dfrac{\text{Market price}}{\text{EPS}}$

Transnational Reporting Practices

- Translate language only
- Lang + currency
- Lang + Slipsheet domestic GAAP
- Lang + Restate earnings to US GAAP
- Lang + currency + acc princ + audit

Accounting, Decision Making, the Economic Environment, and the Business Enterprise

WHAT IS ACCOUNTING?

Accounting is a language. It is used to communicate financial and other information to people, organizations, governments, and some technical information processing and storage devices.

Accounting information is used when one applies for a mortgage loan at a bank or when a candidate for political office wishes to make public some formal statements about his or her financial situation.[1] Business enterprises use accounting to plan and control their business activities and to report the results of these activities to stockholders, creditors, labor unions, and governmental agencies. Organizations not organized for profit—for example, churches and private hospitals—also use accounting for planning, conducting, and finally reporting their activities.

Governmental units do likewise. Local school districts or fire districts must organize their financial affairs as efficiently as possible, and accounting helps to do this. Larger governmental units like the U.S. Department of Health and Human Services have the same problem. In fact, accounting plays a vital role in international government agencies like the International Monetary Fund or the World Health Organization. Hence we can readily agree with the authoritative definition put forth by the American Institute of Certified Public Accountants

---

[1] In general "he" and "his" are used alone throughout this book rather than "he or she," "he/she," "person," or any other "balanced" pronoun configuration. This is done for the sake of *convenience* and *readability* only.

(AICPA): "Accounting is a discipline which provides financial and other information essential to the efficient conduct and evaluation of the activities of any organization."

Accounting information is thus used at all levels of organized society. To underscore this theme, a brief comment is offered on those who use accounting information about (1) individuals, (2) business enterprises, (3) nonbusiness organizations, (4) social programs, and (5) units of government.

Information about Individuals

Accounting information about individuals is used by other individuals. This occurs, for example, when individuals plan to organize partnerships or small corporations. Individual credit is typically extended only after the prospective borrower has furnished a reasonable accounting of his private financial affairs. In recent political history there are examples of candidates for major office making public various accounting statements about their respective income and wealth positions.

Organizations are also interested in the summarized accounts of individuals. This applies to income tax collectors, since the largest share of annual income taxes collected by state and federal governments comes from individuals. It also applies to banks evaluating applications for home mortgages or for other forms of consumer credit. It even applies to scholarship committees of colleges and universities when they seek to evaluate the financial need of a student applicant.

Information about Business Enterprises[2]

Those who have or contemplate having a direct economic interest in business enterprises can benefit from having accounting information about those enterprises. This group of users includes (1) owners, (2) creditors, (3) suppliers, (4) management, (5) taxing authorities, (6) employees, and (7) customers.

In addition, those with indirect concerns about business enterprises include (1) financial analysts and advisers, (2) stock exchanges, (3) lawyers, (4) regulatory and registration authorities, (5) financial press and reporting agencies, (6) trade associations, (7) labor unions, and (8) the public at large.

These parties continually evaluate business firms and make decisions about them or on their behalf. This includes the entire range of the life span of an enterprise—from raising funds and other resources necessary to organize it to steps leading to voluntary or involuntary dissolution.

Information about Nonbusiness Organizations

Nonbusiness organizations like churches, hospitals, the March of Dimes, the Boy Scouts of America, the YWCA, the Red Cross, a political party, and trade

---

[2] Based on the AICPA's *Statement of the Accounting Principles Board No. 4*, "Basic Concepts and Accounting Principles Underlying Financial Statements of Business Enterprises," 1970.

or professional associations cannot get along without preparing accurate accounting information about themselves. Users of such accounting information are similar to those listed for business enterprises.

As a special party at interest, the general public wants to know enough about the financial status of such organizations to determine whether it should make private contributions to them and, if so, in what amount. One major foundation, when seeking public contributions, learned that public support for it was dwindling rapidly. Its most recent financial statements had shown that more than 50 percent of all the funds collected were spent on administration!

Information about Social Programs

The conduct of massive social programs is a relatively recent phenomenon in U.S. society. Program administrators face the challenge of adequately reporting on the success or nonsuccess of entire programs or separate program components. This is still a frontier area in accounting.

The information needed is generally referred to as cost-benefit information, that is, the systematic assessment in terms of dollars or other measurements of the relationship between resources expended and program benefits achieved. Public agencies are a major user group. Congressional committees and elected, as well as appointed, officials are also potential users. There are even instances where official delegations from other countries are eagerly studying reports about the cost-effectiveness of certain social programs now in force in the United States.

Information about Units of Government

The leaders of virtually every governmental unit use a wide variety of accounting information. A local property assessor cannot assess and collect property taxes without statements about property value and ownership. Sales tax collections cannot take place without appropriate records of sales, and income tax collection certainly depends completely on adequate accounting for income tax purposes. Moreover, tax policy at all levels of government cannot be evolved reasonably without good accounting information about present and potential tax bases within the particular jurisdiction. For instance, the probable impact of a certain tax structure on property ownership, business formation, or employment levels cannot be estimated without underlying accounting data.

National income and gross national product accounts are needed to measure the productivity of the total economy and the distribution of economic resources that exist or become available. This type of information supports the formulation of national economic policies, the stimulation or curtailment of a nation's money supply, and most certainly its foreign trade and investment policies. Government officials use accounting information to administer sweeping price and wage control programs or less-sweeping direct foreign investment control programs. More importantly, on the same type of information, individual citizens (voters) may ultimately base their judgment of the ability of certain public officials (at all levels) to discharge their responsibilities.

A Caveat

Let us conclude this general introduction with a caveat. It appears that the widespread and often intensive use of accounting information throughout society cannot be denied. Nonetheless, accounting information is typically only a part of all the information that decision makers use. Few decisions are or should be made on the basis of accounting information alone. At the same time, most decisions with financial or economic implications presumably can be improved with the use of accounting information.

FOCUS ON FINANCIAL ACCOUNTING

We have described accounting as a field of knowledge concerned with information that is useful for a broad range of decision making. The task now at hand is to introduce the reader to the ways and means by which accounting and accountants perform their respective roles in society.

External Accounting. In beginning this task, however, it is necessary to acknowledge a limitation. We simply cannot deal with the full range of accounting activity and, at the same time, achieve any depth of understanding. So we are prepared to confine discussion initially to one avenue of the broader topic of accounting in society. That avenue is the concern with providing information about various kinds of accounting entities for use by external parties. To be precise, the two groups we are interested in may be defined as follows:

Accounting Entity. An accounting entity is any individual or organization that (1) is involved in using economic resources to achieve a purpose, (2) has an identity of its own, and (3) is of interest to one or more individuals for decision-making purposes.

External Users of Information. External users of information concerning an accounting entity are those interested parties whose decisions relate to the entity, but who are not employed by the entity to direct its activities or utilize its resources.

Accounting Entities. The concept of an accounting entity is purposely encompassing, again expressing the breadth of applicability of accounting in human activity. Individuals, governmental units, corporations, a charity fund drive, and a household are all obvious examples of accounting entities. But there are other, more subtle forms of accounting entities as well. If a man or woman is in business, if a housewife does ironing for neighbors, if a corporation administers its employees' pension fund, these *segments* may, themselves, be considered accounting entities, as may be the larger entities that contain them. Why? Because they are of decision interest in and of themselves and because their activities can be distinguished from the activities of other segments of the larger entity for decision-making purposes.

Entry Point: Financial Accounting. Although the broad definition of an accounting entity seemingly throws the discussion wide open again, we reconfine it by limiting our attention to only one major class of entities—business enterprises.

Because of their preeminence as organizational units in the productive activities of a so-called market economy, business enterprises are of particular significance. They control the bulk of productive resources at the disposal of many of the economies of the world, including our own. For this reason we introduce external accounting in the context of accounting for the business enterprise. In traditional accounting terms, *external accounting* is a synonym for *financial accounting*.

Financial Accounting. Financial accounting is that branch of accounting thought and practice concerned with generating useful information about business enterprises for external decision makers.

Decision Making and Enterprise Contexts. We could proceed by describing for the reader, in catalog style, the many concepts, principles, and procedures that make up present-day financial accounting practice. But the purpose of this book is to enrich the introduction to the subject matter, insofar as possible, with a knowledge of the context in which it exists. To this end, the chapter is devoted to three important contextual relationships: (1) the relationship between decision making, information, and information specialties like accounting, (2) the role of the business enterprise in a market economy, and (3) the decision-type interests (in business enterprises) of external decision makers. The remainder of the chapter is divided into three sections, each attending to one of these topics.

DECISION MAKING AND INFORMATION ECONOMICS—IN BRIEF

The Resource Allocation Dilemma: Motive for Economic Decisions

The most fundamental force leading to uses for information (like accounting information) is people's basic resource allocation dilemma. The human race (collectively and individually) is faced with virtually unlimited wants and needs. But, unfortunately, the means to satisfying those wants and needs, the things we call resources, are in very limited supply indeed.

Unlimited Wants and Needs. Although it is difficult to prove rigorously, it is intuitive that people have unlimited wants and needs. We can assure ourselves that this assertion is warranted by first thinking of reasonable categories or classes of wants and needs and then asking ourselves whether all individuals or groups we can think of are entirely satisfied within each category. It is impossible to answer yes, whether the category of needs is the most sophisticated (e.g., the individual's self-realization) or the most primitive (e.g., people's physiological requirements for survival—food and protection from the elements).

Scarce Resources. It is also obvious today that the resources at our command are quite limited in supply. Traditionally we classify resources available to human beings into the somewhat rough classes of land, labor, capital, and enterprise:

Land. The world *land* when used to refer to supplies of resources includes all the natural resources of the planet Earth and its atmosphere.

Labor. Labor as a resource category is the capacity of the individual for mental and physical output.

Capital. Capital consists of any implement, technology, or learned technique that improves the output of the available supply of the primary resources, land and labor. Unlike land and labor, capital is usually considered by economists to consist of resources *produced by people* as opposed to resources provided by nature.

Enterprise. Enterprise or entrepreneurial ability is a very special resource consisting of (1) the creative and leadership capacity possessed and employed by certain individuals to organize other individuals and resources to produce products and services that satisfy individuals' wants and needs, and (2) the willingness to take the risk that the prices those products and services finally bring may not equal the cost of production plus a reward to the organizer for his or her efforts.

Incidentally, it should be noted that "cash" is purposely omitted from the list of resources. As individuals, we all count the cash we have as a resource because it represents a means of securing available land, labor, capital, and so forth, through exchange. But for an economy as a whole, cash is only a medium of exchange, not a resource *per se*.

Resolving the Dilemma—The Decision-Making Process

Faced with unlimited wants and needs and limited means to satisfy those wants, the individual must do something to resolve the conflict. We call the process used to resolve this conflict decision making.

Decision Making. Decision making is the process of choosing from among alternative courses of action, conclusions, and so forth, according to some criterion or criteria adopted by the decision maker.

It should be stressed that according to the above definition, decision making is, above all else, a process. But the definition also implies that the decision-making process will usually comprise certain features or stages similar to those that are illustrated in Exhibit 1-1 and elaborated below.

Notice that in Exhibit 1-1 the separate stages of decision making are set out across a single continuous arrow with only dashed lines separating them. The intention is to emphasize that decision making is a process and to emphasize

Exhibit 1-1

STAGES IN THE DECISION-MAKING PROCESS

| NEED FELT | PROBLEM IDENTIFIED | INFORMATION SOUGHT ABOUT ALTERNATIVES | ALTERNATIVES EVALUATED | CONCLUSION OR ACTION SELECTED | ACTION TAKEN IF APPROPRIATE | OUTCOME REVIEWED; NEW NEEDS EMERGE |

the artificiality of describing any complex process in terms of a set of discrete stages.

The process of decision making is sufficiently important and complex to warrant extensive discussion elsewhere. Here we are only interested in producing sufficient insight to facilitate an introduction to accounting as a discipline that provides information for decision making.

Example 1-1

> Betty and Gerald Adams are a young couple who have just decided to abandon city life in favor of farming. Although both were well on the way toward promising professional careers as attorneys, they found less and less satisfaction in the hectic and often stressful routines of their respective big-city law offices. So they pooled every resource they commanded and purchased (with the aid of a big mortgage from the U.S. Land Bank) a multiple-crop, medium-sized farm. Proudly they named their property the BGA Farm.
>
> In addition to the land itself, the farm consists of many different pieces of machinery and equipment and various sheds and buildings. It is located near a small town and its soil is quite good. Naturally, the Adamses face the upcoming planting season with some trepidation. They must decide what to plant and how to cultivate their crops. The previous owner had always planted the same things over a simple crop-rotation cycle of several years. While this was a convenient approach, prices of the crops traditionally produced were in a steady decline. The Adamses agreed to make the best effort possible to achieve the highest attainable yield from their farm.

Betty and Gerald Adams's situation clearly fits into the mold of the resource allocation dilemma outlined earlier. They have quite a large package of new and unfulfilled wants. At their disposal is a limited amount of land and capital goods, plus their own (and possibly hired) labor as well as their enterprise ability. The combination of unsatisfied wants and limited resources motivates them (causes them to feel a need) to make a conscious and systematic effort to do their best with their BGA Farm. This means that they must decide on the best course of action available to them under the circumstances.

Identifying the Problem

If simply feeling a need were all that successful decision making required, we would have scarce reason for this discussion. The felt need is really only the stimulus to decision making. The process does not start in earnest until the problem is identified.

Problem identification is an organizational step. In defining the problem, the decision maker arrives at the criteria that he must eventually have in mind in order to favor one course of action over another with the expectation of satisfying his need. One way to establish the criterion or criteria that can be used to choose between alternative courses of action is through a set of related statements commonly referred to and defined as follows:

> **Statement of Objectives.** A statement of objectives is an expression of the decision maker's preferences in terms of the consequences of potential courses of action.

Constraints. Constraints are statements of the limitations within which the decision maker must work in making a choice. To be feasible, an alternative course of action must not violate the constraints faced by the decision maker.

Example 1-2

The Adamses have expressed the need to make the best use of their land, labor, capital, and enterprise in the coming season. Obviously, though, they may face certain limitations, either by choice or otherwise. They may reason (1) that it is too late to order new equipment and have it delivered on time; (2) that it is too late to learn complicated agricultural techniques or hire competent help this season; (3) that it is too late to lease additional land; (4) that they must stick to crops that are reasonably suited to the soil on their land; (5) that the cost of seed, fertilizer, labor, and other inputs cannot exceed the cash on hand plus what they can borrow from the bank, pending ultimate sale of their crops, and so forth. All of these conclusions, whether in the back of their minds (implicit) or brought to the fore (explicit), constitute constraints that any crop must meet in order to be a feasible alternative for this season.

Concurrent with the identification of constraints facing their farming activities, the Adamses can construct a statement of objectives that will indicate feasible alternative courses of action which will best satisfy their needs. For instance, as with many farmers, the produce that the Adamses grow for their own consumption is insignificant in terms of total potential production—thus attention can be focused on all other wants and needs. The Adamses will have to purchase virtually all of the goods and services that they consume, in exchange for cash. Therefore they are likely to want to concentrate on the cash-related aspects of each feasible alternative. They may conclude that the crop or crops that will bring the greatest excess of cash receipts upon sale over the cash paid out for seed, fertilizer, labor, and so forth, will most satisfy all of their wants and needs. Thus the Adamses have a statement of objectives that indicates the positive (cash from sales) and negative (cash paid out for production) contributions that alternative crops can make. They may even have an indication of which crop would be preferable (maximum cash inflow in excess of cash paid out).

For the decision maker, defining the problem as we have defined it in the example provides two valuable inputs to the remainder of the decision process:

1. The set of constraints and the statement of objectives provide a framework for the evaluation of alternatives leading to a choice.
2. The terms of the constraints and the objectives statement prescribe what information will be relevant to the decision maker.

Evaluation of Alternatives

Ignoring for a moment the information-gathering stage of decision making, consider the question of exactly how the definition of the problem can assist in the process of evaluating alternatives. Assuming that all relevant information is in hand, the problem definition can be used in the evaluation process in two ways:

1. The objectives statement and constraints tell the decision maker how to

combine facts and measurements about an alternative into tests of its desirability.

Example 1-3

> As stated in Example 1-2, the definition of the Adamses' selection problem tells them that if the description of the soil requirements of a particular crop is out of line with the soil composition of their land, the crop must be rejected as an alternative. It also tells them that the expected cost of seed for a crop is one of the items that should be subtracted from the expected proceeds of sale in order to determine its expected overall contribution of cash, and so forth.

2. Knowledge of the stated objectives and constraints can be used to devise time-and-effort-saving strategies for evaluation.

Example 1-4

> In the BGA Farm situation, for instance, one might easily fall into the trap of choosing an overly straightforward approach to evaluation by assessing the cash contribution and conformity to all constraints *for every "cash crop"* that might be grown in the area. But this approach could lead to unnecessary time and effort spent in evaluation. A better way might be to first measure the conformity to the constraints for each crop and then measure the expected cash contribution of only those that pass the test of all constraints. A still more efficient technique might be to apply the constraints in some order, rejecting immediately any crop that fails to conform to a constraint, thereby constantly narrowing the field of alternatives undergoing continued evaluation.

Regardless of their sequence of application, the constraints and the stated objectives form a basis for the most important role of evaluation—that of choosing the best alternative within the limitations faced by the decision maker.

A Common Index of Merit, or "Common Denominator." Although defining objectives and constraints provides the necessary guidelines for evaluating decision alternatives, it does not necessarily guarantee that the final choice will be unambiguous or easy. Indeed, one of the most perplexing dilemmas in decision making is that of facing two or more alternatives, each of which promises more of one desirable attribute and less of other desirable attributes than the other decision alternatives. In such cases it is often worthwhile to spend additional time, while defining the problem, in looking for a single index of merit, or comcom denominator. Different decision outcome attributes can then be translated into this common denominator for greater ease of comparison.

Example 1-5

> In the case of the BGA Farm, we have already intuitively defined the Adamses' objectives in terms of a common scale of merit, cash flow. Think of how difficult it would be for them to decide among several crops that all satisfy the applicable constraints, if the expected sacrifices required to grow and harvest the crop and the benefits from its production could not all be measured in terms of cash paid or received. The Adamses would perhaps have to weigh mentally one crop that is superior on a scale measuring labor effort, against another that is superior in its low-fertilizer requirements, against still another that

promises more benefits from harvest, but none of which dominates all others in every respect.

Having a common scale of merit reduces all the relevant considerations (within the constraints of the situation) to a single score or index of merit for each alternative. The choice problem is thereby simplified to selection of the alternative with the highest score among those that satisfy all constraints.

Quantitative versus Qualitative Scales. In searching for common scales of merit on which to evaluate decision alternatives, the characteristic of quantifiability can be of great help, and sometimes of great hindrance as well. By *quantifiability* we mean the ability to represent, *in the form of a numerical score,* the degree to which a particular characteristic is possessed by a decision alternative. Qualitative characteristics are those that cannot be readily expressed in terms of numbers. One great advantage of quantifiable characteristics is the possibility of applying well-developed mathematical operations to manipulating numerical scores, once those scores are assigned to alternatives. This often facilitates the reduction of many measured attributes of alternatives to a single score on a common scale of merit.

Example 1-6

In the BGA Farm case, quantification of certain crop characteristics will clearly help to arrive at the cash flow to be expected from each crop. On the positive side, for instance, the Adamses will find it convenient to have estimates of the *number* of bushels of expected yield per acre from each crop and the number of dollars per bushel expected price from each. Having these two numerical inputs, they can *multiply* the separate scores of each crop on the two different scales (yield and price) to get a single score measuring expected benefit from the crop (expected cash yield per acre)—a score that is measured on the same scale (money) as many other relevant characteristics of the crop.

Although quantification of attributes of decision alternatives is a powerful tool of decision making, it presents a hazard as well. Because of our ability to manipulate quantitative scores, we tend to place too little emphasis on relevant aspects of decision alternatives that are not easily quantified. Such a tendency can lead to disastrous results.

Example 1-7

The Adamses, in dwelling on the cash-flow aspects of each crop, may ignore a relevant property of farm crops like "disease resistance" which is not readily translatable into numbers. Perhaps they might inadvertently choose the worst of their alternatives if they do not bear this important attribute in mind.

Upon reflection still other advantages and hazards of quantification will occur to the reader. One additional advantage that is of importance to accountants is the increased transferability of understanding that can often be achieved when attributes are quantified. For instance, if individual A wishes to describe the intelligence of individual B to individual C, the words "highly intelligent" may give C only a vague understanding of B's intelligence. An IQ score of 155 may convey much more precise understanding in C's mind. But, again, there is a hazard related to the hoped-for increase in transferability brought about by quantification. The hazard, clearly evident in the case of IQ scores, is that a score that measures only one aspect of an abstraction like intelligence will eventually become a substitute for the abstraction itself. The reader is no doubt aware of other instances of this phenomenon.

The Role of Information

In the preceding section it was assumed, for the sake of elaborating the evaluation stage of decision making, that "all relevant information is in hand. . . ." We can now gain some perspective on the information-gathering stage of decision making by dropping that assumption.

After defining a problem, the decision maker should have some idea as to the characteristics of alternative courses of action that might impinge upon his constraints and contribute to or detract from his objectives. But usually he will not be able to predict exactly the extent to which various alternatives, if adopted, will exhibit those characteristics. This condition is known as uncertainty.

> **Uncertainty.** Uncertainty is the condition of not knowing at the time of decision precisely what the outcomes of relevant future events will be, that is, not knowing precisely the consequences of alternative courses of action.

Uncertainty can never be eliminated altogether. But its effects can be lessened by such things as keeping options open and entering into contracts to ensure that others *intend* to perform certain actions. The effects of uncertainty can also be lessened by acquiring information.

> **Information.** Information is any item of intelligence that improves the decision maker's understanding and predictions of the outcomes of uncertain future events.

The decision maker is essentially interested in the results or consequences that will be forthcoming from the selection of a given decision alternative. With more and more information, in any given situation the *expected* level of satisfaction from a decision usually becomes better and better. But, interestingly, this does not mean that more information is always better for the decision maker.

The Economics of Decisions and Information

The last statement above, which implies that more information is not always better for the decision maker, is seemingly in conflict with the one that immediately precedes it, which implies that more information improves the expected outcome of a decision. But the two statements are not in conflict at all.

Defining a decision problem explicitly indicates what features and characteristics about each alternative must be known in order to make the best choice *as the problem is defined.* Thus a particular problem definition prescribes that information which is decision relevant.

Decision Relevance. Information is said to be relevant with respect to a particular decision situation if it may be expected to improve predictions of outcomes of future events of concern in that decision.

But it may not be economical for the decision maker to go to unlimited lengths to gather decision-relevant information in order to make the best choice. This is illustrated by one aspect of our earlier example, which we have ignored so far.

Example 1-8

In the Adamses' crop selection problem, the objective spelled out was to select the crop that had the expectation of contributing the most cash upon sale in excess of the cash paid out for seed, labor, and so forth, required to produce it. To make the best selection, then, the Adamses would technically have to know a great deal about each crop's growing habits and cultivation requirements, such as average yields per acre and average labor hours per acre required under expected conditions. They would also have to estimate the wage rates they would have to pay, and the price per unit of output that they would get at harvest time.

As newcomers to farming, Betty and Gerald Adams are probably ignorant of most of these decision-relevant features of each crop. Furthermore, left strictly to themselves, they may not be able to come up with technical information, like the expected yields of various crops in the BGA Farm's type of soil. Moreover, the needed information may not be available on a timely basis for this season's crop selection. Without any expertise the Adamses might have to experiment with small plantings of many different crops for several seasons before they could predict expected yields. But such a strategy might also mean that they would face greatly reduced cash flow from the crops for those seasons because they would be spreading themselves too thin (for example, by changing cultivation techniques and implements too frequently to be efficient).

In essence, this extension of the Adamses' crop selection problem into the stage of information gathering emphasizes a feature of all but the most trivial decision situations: *the decision-making process, particularly the information-gathering stage, consumes resources.* Virtually every decision situation contains a trap that most of us avoid intuitively—the possibility that spending too much of our precious time, effort, and other resources on the decision might reduce our ability to undertake desirable courses of action. This leads us to two related conclusions:

1. Successful decision making is *not* simply a matter of choosing the most desirable of several alternatives but is a much more complex process of finding the most rewarding combination of (*a*) the expected decision outcome and (*b*) the level of resources expended in making the choice.

2. Information has value (depending on its decision relevance) in that it improves the expected outcome of a decision. But information is costly, as well.

The latter conclusion is of particular significance to accountants because it is at the root of why information specialists like accountants are in demand in every economic system. To see this, reconsider the Adamses' position with respect to the highly technical information about crop yields that they would like to have.

Example 1-9

> If Betty and Gerald Adams had to develop complete crop-yield data for their soil type for all crops they might consider, the prospect of gathering the information would appear very costly. They might, therefore, justifiably conclude that they would be better off scrapping the whole business of crop selection and, instead, spend their time growing any crop that the BGA Farm history indicates will be worth more than the cost to produce it. In doing so, they will sacrifice the prospects of getting the highest cash production from the land, but they will also avoid the possibly prohibitively greater cost of achieving the improved productivity.
>
> But suppose the Adamses can buy information about expected crop yields for their type of soil. If they can buy it for less than the increase in cash that they expect from selecting the best crop, they surely may wish to do so.

Information Specialists

Fortunately for the Adamses and other decision makers facing the same type of decision, there exist sources that can produce the kinds of information they want at much less cost than they can on their own. We call such sources *information specialists.*

> **Information Specialist.** An information specialist is an individual who devotes his resources to producing decision-relevant information for use by others.

Example 1-10

> In the BGA Farm's case one way to acquire crop-yield information for its particular soil would be to hire an agronomist, who specializes in field-crop production and soil management. Whereas it might take the Adamses several years' experimentation to develop crop-yield information for their soil, the agronomist ought to be able to estimate expected yields after spending much less time. And, although his hourly fee may be high, his total fee to the Adamses may be low because of his efficiency.

The agronomist illustrates the key reason why so many people make their living providing information to others. Division of labor, leading to specialization and the development of expertise or facility in providing a particular product or service, usually results in higher productivity and/or lower cost. Where large numbers of individuals make decisions involving the same or similar courses of action, there is room for division of labor. For example, one or more individuals may specialize in providing information (or techniques for gathering information) for everyone. Information thus produced has value to many decision makers, provided it is decision relevant. Since the specialist can provide it at a lower cost (price) than would be incurred by the others in developing their own information (or information-gathering techniques), some will willingly pay for his services. Those decision makers will be able to achieve greater expected satisfaction from their decision outcomes with more information at lower cost, and the information specialist will be able to employ his talents and other resources more fully than perhaps in any other occupation. Everyone benefits, in an economic sense, from the division of labor.

Besides the benefits of division of labor inherent in information specialization, there is sometimes an additional bonus. Many individuals may find identical information to be decision relevant. In such cases the benefits of information specialization compound.

Example 1-11

> Suppose that the Adamses' land is similar in soil composition to the land of a dozen other farmers in the same vicinity. In addition, suppose that they are all aware of the same four crops as the set of possible cash crops for their local market. If each evaluated every crop for its yield potential, fifty-two crop evaluations would be required (thirteen decision makers times four alternatives). But if they pooled information, or more likely, if they had a common source of information (an information specialist), only four evaluations would have to be made—one for each crop.

This added bonus that comes from common or universal decision relevance of information can be particularly compelling under some circumstances. For instance, even with the greater efficiency in producing information that can be achieved by a specialist, sometimes no single individual will find an item of information of sufficient value to pay for its production. Only if a number of decision makers share in its cost can it be economically produced—whereupon all will benefit from its availability. Examples include such things as weather maps and predictions, handbooks of all kinds, mathematical and statistical tables, and census reports.

In considering the multiperson (or "social") benefits of information, however, one must always be aware of the possibility of falling into the trap known as the "fallacy of composition." That is, in many cases it is not true that what is good for one is good for all. This is sometimes true of information.

Example 1-12

> Suppose that the Adamses and their dozen neighbors with similar soil hired an agricultural economist to rank each of the four cash crops traditionally grown in their region in terms of its expected cash yield per acre. It would be natural to expect each farmer then to select the number-one crop. Although this makes sense individually, it could lead to unfortunate results for the group. A drastic increase in the local supply of that one crop could cause a sharp decrease in price—possibly bringing financial disaster on everyone.

On the other hand, there is no reason to conclude that the fallacy of composition obviates any potential for information to have value to many users. But it is obvious that information suited to given individuals' objectives *will not always* be similarly valuable to many individuals—even if they have similar objectives. Although the design of information for use by the many may begin at the individual level, ultimately its desirability for the many must be assessed according to its consequences *for the many*.

Accounting—An Information Specialization

Accountants, like agronomists, journalists, advertising copywriters, financial analysts, attorneys, and many others are information specialists. *Accounting is above all else an information specialization.* Our discussion of decision making and information specialization to this point indicates that the existence of any information specialization like accounting depends on several conditions—

1. That there exist classes of decision makers with common decision problems;
2. That there are identifiable kinds of decision-relevant information of value in solving the common class or classes of problems; and
3. That to produce information relevant to the common class or classes of problems efficiently and effectively, one must become expert in applying a specialized body of knowledge or expertise.

In the remainder of this chapter and in Chapter 2 (as well as at intervals throughout the book), we will explore the first two of these conditions as the threshold to understanding accounting. That the third condition applies to accounting will become obvious as our discussion leads us into a fuller exploration of the kinds of information that are relevant for the classes of decisions served by accounting.

THE BUSINESS ENTERPRISE IN A MARKET ECONOMY—IN BRIEF

The major emphasis of this book is on the role of accounting in supplying information to several of the classes of decision makers concerned with the business enterprise. To establish clearly (1) the identity of these classes of decision makers, (2) their common decision problems, and (3) the information that they might regard as decision relevant, we will briefly review the role of business enterprise in the context of a so-called free-enterprise, or "market," system.

The Business Enterprise and the Enterprise Function

Given the aggregate demand for goods and services in a market economy, certain individuals, called entrepreneurs or enterprisers, in the aggregate determine what products and services will be produced and in what quantities. Enterprisers respond to the aggregate demand in the economy for various products and services by (1) organizing factors of production in order to produce specific goods and services and (2) taking the risk that the price of the goods or services sold may not exceed the cost of factors of production used. Presumably, enterprisers are motivated by the expectation that sales prices will exceed factor costs by a sufficient amount (profit) to justify the effort expended and the risk taken.

In performing their dual role of organizing and risk taking, enterprisers usually work within the facilitating framework of a business enterprise.

Business Enterprise. A business enterprise is an organization composed of one or more individuals, capital goods, and other resources, directed toward the purpose of producing specific products or services for sale.

As organizational units, businesses have a significant impact on our economic life. The business enterprise facilitates the enterpriser's activities in a number of ways:

1. The business enterprise is a means of separating the production activities of individuals from their consumption activities. In this sense an enterprise structure benefits even the individual in business for himself.
2. The business enterprise is a means of coordinating the activities of individuals engaged in (*a*) complex production processes and (*b*) large-scale production with a high degree of division of labor and specialization.
3. The business enterprise is a means of dividing or sharing, among many individuals, the enterprise function itself.

The first of these contributions needs no explanation. The second, though not so obvious, is characteristic of human activity under any economic system. Each individual can, in theory, work independently—supplying completed products or services to others. But few complex products or services can be produced efficiently "from the ground up" by a single individual. To become proficient in a highly technical process one must narrow the scope of the undertaking, that is, specialize. In most cases, however, it does not pay to have hundreds or thousands of individuals—each specializing in very limited tasks—buying thousands of partially completed products, performing one or two specialized tasks on each, and then selling them to someone who performs the next specialized production step. Transfers and exchanges would consume too much of everyone's time and resources. A single organization coordinating the efforts of specialists in all stages of production is usually the most efficient answer. Essentially it is a means of breaking down a large and complex opportunity for production into coordinated individual opportunities.

Example 1-13

> The automobile industry started out in the United States with many individuals and small groups "custom" building cars. But few really prospered, since they produced at such a high cost that only a few wealthy people could afford their products. The industry did not really prosper until many of the smaller manufacturers were consolidated into a few large organizations. And, of course, the price of the automobile was finally put within reach of large numbers of people through the efficiencies of the assembly line, introduced by Henry Ford. The assembly line was as much an organizational innovation as it was a technological innovation.

Sharing the Enterprise Function. The third contribution of the business enterprise, that of facilitating the division of the enterprise function, is really a special case of the second contribution. But because of the importance of the enterprise function, it deserves separate consideration. When an enterpriser sees an opportunity for profit in the efficient production of a particular product or service, he must do two things to exploit the opportunity. First, he has to secure the necessary factors of production. Second, he must organize them and set them in motion producing and selling the product or service to others.

To accomplish these two steps, the enterpriser must have considerable resources at his disposal initially. The reason is that before the sale of products or services starts to bring in cash, the enterpriser may have to pay for buildings, equipment, and other capital goods, as well as for material and wages. Furthermore, long after starting in a particular line of business, the enterpriser will still find it necessary to acquire and pay for factors of production before or at the time they are committed to production, with some time lag before the sale of products and services brings in cash. This requires the ongoing commitment of money capital, which typically involves risks as to future outcomes of production ventures.

> **Money Capital.** Money capital is the cash committed (or the cash equivalent of other resources committed in lieu of cash) to a business enterprise or other venture in order that it may procure and meet its obligations to pay for capital goods, labor, material, and so forth, as needed.

The provision of money capital and the acceptance of the attendant risk that the proceeds of sales may not cover the outlays for factors of production are an integral part of the enterprise function.

But individual enterprisers may not possess adequate money capital to complement their ability to identify opportunities for profit and organize production. Faced with an imbalance, enterprisers may (1) borrow money, if they can, in exchange for fixed interest payments, or (2) arrange for others to share the enterprise function with them as owners or part owners of a business, contributing money capital in exchange for a share in profits to be earned. In either case, the business organization is a means of breaking down a large opportunity for profit that the individual cannot exploit by himself into a number of smaller individual opportunities.

Kinds of Business Enterprises

There are three traditional kinds of business enterprises—proprietorships, partnerships, and corporations. All are recognized by accountants as economic units or entities separate from their owners. But they differ in a number of respects that influence the extent to which they offer the advantages described in the preceding section. In particular, they differ in legal status, arrangements for ownership and management, extent of risk or liability associated with ownership, duration of life and dissolution, and transferability of ownership interest. The differences between the three types of business enterprises with respect to these features are summarized in Exhibit 1-2 and briefly elaborated below.

Proprietorships. A proprietorship is an inherently personal business. It is formed unilaterally by a single individual. It serves as an organizational identity for his production activities, to separate those activities and the resources that he devotes to them from his private life. Legally, however, a proprietorship is not a separate entity. It is identical with the owner and, therefore, cannot be involved in any legal relationship or action except in the name of the owner. If, in the conduct of the business, some person or his property is harmed, the proprietor may be held responsible (liable) not only to the extent of the resources committed to the business but for everything else he owns as well. A proprietorship may be dissolved by the proprietor more or less at will. It will, however, dissolve upon his death if he does not dissolve it sometime earlier.

Partnerships. Partnerships are similar to corporations in one respect. They involve more than one owner. In other respects they usually resemble proprietorships. A partnership is an association of individuals, not a separate legal entity. Like a proprietorship, a partnership cannot engage in legal activity separately. Instead it enters into legal relationships or actions in the names of the partners, usually jointly. Unless otherwise agreed, each partner is entitled to a voice in the conduct of the business and the use of its resources. Each partner can usually legally bind the partnership by his own actions. Furthermore, although some partners may be able to limit legally their liability for damages to others brought about by the partnership, one or more partners are always liable to the full limit of their personal fortunes.

A business partnership is formed when two or more individuals implicitly or explicitly agree to combine their efforts or other resources in an activity aimed at generating profits, and to share the resulting profits between them. A partnership dissolves upon the death, withdrawal, or bankruptcy of any partner. A partner cannot usually transfer his interest in a partnership without consent of the other partners.

Corporations. Corporations, in contrast to proprietorships and partnerships, are legal entities separate from their owners. Legal actions can be conducted by or against the corporation in its own name. The owners, called stockholders or shareholders, do not have a direct voice in the conduct of the business, cannot directly use or possess its resources, and cannot bind it legally by their actions. Rather, the stockholders have the right to vote in the election of the directors who manage the corporation and to share in the profits generated by its activities.

In exchange for limited involvement or power over the resources of the business or its management, owners of corporations have a certain flexibility and immunity not enjoyed by partners and proprietors. First of all, since shareholders do not enter into personal arrangements with or become dependent on each other with respect to the business (as partners do), their shares are usually transferable without the consent of other shareholders. Thus the corporation can have a perpetual existence, with ownership (and management) passing from person to person. Second, shareholders cannot be held liable for the actions of the corporation, except to the extent of their share in the resources of the corporation and the profits derived therefrom.

These latter features of limited liability and transferability of ownership are ideal for serving the purpose of division of the enterprise function between those who recognize production opportunities and direct activities (management) and those who take the risk associated with supplying money or physical

Exhibit 1-2

COMPARATIVE FEATURES OF TYPES OF BUSINESS ENTERPRISES

Type of Business Enterprise	Legal Status of Business Entity	Owner-Management Relationship	Risk of Ownership	Duration of Life	Transferability of Ownership Interest
Proprietorship	Not a separate legal entity	Separation of ownership and management only by owner choice	Owner's personal fortune at stake	Expires by owner choice or death of owner	If proprietor sells his interest, the business is reconstituted under new ownership
Partnership	Not a separate legal entity	Separation only by partnership agreement	At least one partner's personal fortune at stake	Expires by choice or withdrawal of partners	Partnership share cannot be sold without agreement of other partners; new partnership is formed
Corporation	Separate legal entity	Separation of ownership and management; owners influence management indirectly	Limited to loss of interest in benefits of ownership	Indefinite life span; possibly unlimited	Usually transferable

capital (owners). Why? Because those who contribute money capital but not management talent to a business are limited in the degree to which they can protect their own interests in the business's activities. They would be much less willing to back enterprising and creative managers if they could be held liable for corporate actions and responsibilities to the full extent of their personal possessions. Furthermore, if some owners disagree with courses of action taken by management but are in the minority among all owners, it is better for everyone if they can liquidate their interest by selling it, rather than calling for dissolution of the whole business and distribution of the proceeds. The greater amounts of money capital that can be raised to complement management skill, as a result of the appealing features of corporate ownership, have made the corporate form of business preeminent in organizing large-scale production in modern market economies.

DECISION MAKERS AND DECISIONS RELATED TO THE BUSINESS ENTERPRISE

Earlier in this chapter we mentioned a number of types of users of information about the business enterprise. The list consisted of (1) owners, (2) creditors, (3) suppliers, (4) management, (5) taxing authorities, (6) employees, and (7) customers. We also noted that information specializations like accounting spring up where such groups exist, if they have common decision problems and demand identifiable information that can be prepared more efficiently for them by experts or specialists. With the brief background in the preceding section about the role of the business enterprise in society, we can now begin to identify some common classes of decisions shared by members of the above groups. At the outset, however, we will recognize a distinction that separates two major classes of decisions concerning the business enterprise.

Internal and External Decision Makers

We can separate all decision makers concerned with the business enterprise into two groups, internal and external, according to how their individual decisions relate to the enterprise. To distinguish internal users of information from external users (defined earlier), we have the following definition:

> **Internal Users of Information.** Internal users of information concerning the enterprise are those individuals who are employed to direct the activities of the enterprise (managers) or to utilize its resources to fulfill the goals of the enterprise (other employees).

Unlike internal users, external users generally are not employed by the enterprise to directly affect its activities or the deployment of its resources.

The relationship to the enterprise of the employee group known as management is entirely made up of decisions that affect the direction and activities of the enterprise and the deployment of its resources. Therefore management is clearly in the internal group. Other employees may also be classified as internal users of information when they are making decisions about the conduct of their respective tasks within the enterprise. But employees may be external users of information about the enterprise as well.

When an employee is trying to make decisions about such things as his long-run job security with his employer, or whether he should change jobs, he is really an external user of information considering features and characteristics of the enterprise that are of interest to him but which he probably is not empowered to alter by his actions alone. Similarly, present and potential owners and creditors of large businesses (particularly corporations), taxing authorities, governmental regulatory bodies, suppliers, and customers all may have an influence on the conduct of a business as groups, but they are not employed within the enterprise to affect its operations directly. Instead they are usually concerned with whether or not to enter into some exchange or other relationship with the business entity as a whole, or to ensure its compliance with government policy or the provisions of a contract.

We can draw a definite distinction between the decision interests of internal and external users. The former are interested in choosing among decision alternatives or opportunities available to the business enterprise itself, while the latter view the business enterprise as a source of decision alternatives or opportunities available to them. With this strong distinction in decision interest between the two groups, it is easy to see why a distinct subdivision of accounting thought and activity has responded to the needs of each—managerial accounting for the internal group, financial accounting for the external group. Although many of the accounting concepts, tools, and approaches applied to problems of the two groups are the same, the differences in the decision interests mean that quite different information outputs usually result. Thus for purposes of study, as well as accounting practice, it is often useful to deal with these two branches of accounting separately—a custom we follow in this book. *The focus of the book is accounting for the business enterprise from the perspective of decision interests of external decision makers.*

Classes of External Decisions

The decision interests of external users of information about the enterprise can be further subdivided into two fundamental classes. One class of decisions consists of investment decisions. The other class includes quite a variety of decisions that have to do with the distribution of the current benefits resulting from the enterprise's operations.

Investment Decisions. Roughly, we can define investment decisions as those involving exchanges of present resources for rights to resources in the future. Present and prospective owners and creditors have a common investment-decision interest in the business enterprise. For this reason we typically refer to present and prospective owners and creditors of a business, together, as "investors." Two avenues are available to investors to acquire the rights of creditors or owners. They may either (1) contribute money capital (or other goods and services) directly to the business or (2) buy the *transferable* rights of present creditors or owners.

Either way the *creditor* receives an implicit or explicit contractual obligation on the part of the business to (1) pay a specified amount of money, called the principal amount, after some time interval, along with (2) a specified amount or rate of interest on the principal amount. The *owner* receives ownership interests in all rights and properties owned by the business enterprise in proportion to his ownership percentage. In addition, he receives the right to share proportionally in (1) the distributed profits of the business (e.g., dividends from corporations), and (2) the proceeds remaining after sale of the business's resources and discharge of the obligations, in case of dissolution.

In addition to acquiring rights as creditors and owners, present owners and creditors may view the reverse process as an economic opportunity. That is, they may decide to sell their rights in the business for cash or other consideration, provided the rights are transferable. In the case of nontransferable ownership interests in partnerships, the same thing can be accomplished by dissolution of the partnership and settlement with the withdrawing partner.

Both the acquisition and the sale of creditor and ownership rights in a business may properly be called investment alternatives, since they always involve an exchange of present resources (the capital contribution or price paid or received) for rights to future benefits—interest and principal payments for creditors; ownership interests, dividends, or withdrawals for owners. *Together, present and prospective investors in businesses constitute an important class of external users of information about businesses.* And their decision problems are sufficiently interesting and challenging that we devote the next chapter to a model (logical structure) for making investment decisions. The model later serves as a basis for discussion of the types of information about a business enterprise that are thought to be decision relevant to investors.

Distributions of Enterprise Benefits. At the time of deciding about or reconsidering an investment in a business, present and prospective owners are concerned with the future benefits expected from ownership. As time passes, though, owners will be interested in receiving some of those expected benefits. Since owners are residual beneficiaries of the business, they have a natural interest in a periodic assessment of the achievements or accomplishments of the enterprise, as well as its ability to distribute money or other resources to them.

Residual Beneficiaries. Residual beneficiaries are parties whose rights and claims remain after all existing statutory and contractual rights and claims (e.g., bills, wages, taxes) have been satisfied.

Interestingly, other groups share the owners' interest in the accomplishments of the enterprise and its residual benefits. These groups include

1. Management
2. Taxing authorities
3. Regulatory authorities
4. Employees

In one sense these "other interested groups" compete with owners—they share or hope to share in the residual benefits of the enterprise. But in the sense that all benefit from increases in those benefits, their interests and the interests of the owners are complementary.

Management's interest in measuring the accomplishments of the enterprise stems largely from its sharing the enterprise function with owners. Owners take the risk associated with supplying money capital to the enterprise, which is then deployed by management in pursuit of profit opportunities. To safeguard their interests, while not interfering with the management of the enterprise, owners often find it useful to reward management with a share of profits available (if any). In pursuing their own rewards, the managers therefore presumably do what is best for the owners as well.

Where the federal, state, or local government has deemed it desirable to grant exclusive rights (monopolies) to a single enterprise to provide vital products or services (like electrical power), regulation is usually considered necessary to ensure that both the public interest and the interests of the enterprise are served. Regulation of this type of enterprise often takes the form of limiting the prices or rates charged by the regulated monopoly to the minimum level necessary to provide a "fair" reward to all suppliers of the resources required to provide the product or service to consumers. Thus regulatory commissions are almost always interested in the profits generated by the regulated enterprise at a given level of rates or prices (along with other information, such as the quality of service provided).

The currently pervasive income tax is intended to be a nonconfiscatory tax in which government simply shares in residual benefits with owners and management. That is, by only applying to profits, the tax authority never takes away from an economic unit the stock of resources with which it operates. The income tax has been likened, in this respect, to harvesting fruit from an orchard. Only the fruit is picked; the trees are left intact to produce another crop. The income tax authority is clearly interested in periodic assessments that separate the new growth (profits) from the original stock of resources of an enterprise.

Finally, whereas employees other than management are not usually compensated on the basis of profits or growth of the enterprise, they collectively often have an interest in assessment of profit and accomplishment. Their interest is often one of determining whether the benefits of production are equitably divided between labor, management, and capital contributors to the enterprise.

Thus it is clear that a number of the external groups share a common decision interest in the assessment and distribution of the residual benefits of the enterprise. After we have discussed the nature of the investment decision in the next chapter, and begin to introduce the decision-relevant accounting information for that purpose, we will come back to a concurrent consideration of information relating to the distribution of residual benefits of the business.

SUMMARY

The substantive content of this chapter reaches beyond the typical general and introductory nature of a "Chapter 1." First we defined accounting and specified several of its more common uses in society. Then we focused on financial accounting for business enterprises and its specific relevance to external decision makers. This gave us a framework for step-by-step development of a reasonably rigorous context for the book as a whole.

A first building block in the development of the desired context was the relationship between decision making, information, and information specialties like accounting. Exhibit 1-1 shows the various stages in the decision-making process. By building an illustrative case around the evaluation and planning of the operations of a family farm, we were able to demonstrate not only the basic elements of the decision-making process but the role of information in this process. Then an *information specialist* was defined as "an individual who devotes his resources to producing decision-relevant information for use by others." Accounting, it was asserted, fits the mold of an information specialty.

The second building block utilized was a synopsis of how the business enterprise works in a market economy. We noted the separation of production and consumption activities, the coordination function for complex production and distribution factors, plus the need for and the nature of the enterprise function itself. Exhibit 1-2 portrays the principal features of the three traditional kinds of business enterprises—proprietorships, partnerships, and corporations. Money capital is needed to operate any business enterprise, but especially the large-scale operations of the modern, complex corporation. And since monetary expressions of all types of business activities are fundamental to decisions about utilization of money capital, another connection to accounting is built.

Our third and final context-building device was the role between decisions to be made and those making decisions in the setting of the business enterprise. While we recognized the need for both internal and external decisions on behalf of enterprise processes, we reiterated our initial focus on "accounting for the business enterprise from the perspective of decision interests of external decision makers." These decision interests were divided between investment decisions and those having to do with the distribution of the current benefits resulting from the enterprise's operations. The former involve creditors and owners; the latter (in addition) such diverse groups as management, taxing authorities, regulatory agencies, and employees. All use decision-relevant information which accounting can supply—at least in part.

Questions for Review and Discussion

1-1. Define:
   a. Accounting
   b. Statement of objectives
   c. Constraints
   d. Uncertainty
   e. Information
   f. Decision relevance
   g. Information specialist
   h. Business enterprise
   i. Money capital
   j. Internal users of information
   k. External users of information
   l. Accounting entity
   m. Financial accounting

1-2. Who might use accounting information about individual persons and for what purpose?

Accounting, Decision Making, the Economic Environment and the Business Enterprise 27

1-3. List ten different parties who benefit from having accounting information about business and public organizations. Also specify individual benefits as you perceive them.

1-4. What motivates the production of goods and services in a market economy?

1-5. What is the role of the enterpriser in a market economy? Why would an enterpriser undertake this role? What methods or devices do enterprisers employ to raise sufficient money capital for their business endeavors?

1-6. What is an information specialist? Why do information specialists exist, that is, what function do they serve? List five types of information specialists and indicate some justification for the existence of each.

1-7. What is the role of a business enterprise in a market economy?

1-8. Why are governments in so-called free-enterprise economies heavy users of accounting information? Express your thoughts in a short essay.

1-9. Describe the three traditional forms of business enterprise. Why is the corporation the dominant form of business enterprise (in terms of resources controlled) in a modern market economy?

1-10. Distinguish between internal and external decision makers. How do their individual decisions relate to the business enterprise? What are the two major classes of decisions about the enterprise made by external parties?

1-11. In general, what is the advantage of quantification in producing or using information for decisions? What are the disadvantages?

1-12. Various governmental agencies have an interest in business enterprises (as external users of information). Describe some of these interests and the kinds of information that might be relevant to them.

1-13. Give an example in which a particular kind of information is valuable (worth its cost) to an individual *and* to a group or class of individuals. Give an example in which a particular kind of information is valuable to an individual but not necessarily to a group. Give an example of information that is valuable to a group but not worth its cost to an individual.

1-14. *Decision making* is defined as the process of choosing among competing alternative courses of action according to some criteria adopted by the decision maker.
   1. Given that a decision maker is faced with a problem, can the decision maker elect not to make a decision regarding the problem?
   2. Must the decision maker always obtain information prior to making a decision?
   3. Should the decision maker always obtain information prior to making a decision?

1-15. Is the traditional grade-point scale used in most educational institutions an example of a common scale of merit? A quantitative scale? How are grade-point averages used? What do they measure?

1-16. Give three examples of quantified scales of merit that are often used in society today but which omit significant nonquantified information.

1-17. Decision makers *need* good information to make economic decisions. Do you agree or disagree? Defend your position.

1-18. More information is always better than less. Do you agree or disagree? Defend your position.

Exercises

1-1. When Does Accounting Begin? Lauren Berg, a college professor, has always wanted a small apartment house. He has never had any excess funds to invest but for years has studied building costs, maintenance costs, rental rates, and many other economic and legal factors pertaining to apartment house ownership.

In 19X0 an uncle he had never met bequeathed to him the sum of $24,000. Even before these funds were transferred to him, Mr. Berg consummated an earnest money agreement in the amount of $500 from his savings for the purchase of a lot suitable for construction of a small apartment house. An architect friend prepared, cost-free, six preliminary sketches of a building that might be erected on the property selected. Armed with this preliminary information, Mr. Berg began tentative negotiations with a construction company. He had estimated that he would be able to finance a building project at a total cost of $250,000.

After the construction company assured Mr. Berg that his building project was feasible, he commissioned the architect to prepare blueprints. At the same time, Mr. Berg contacted two commercial banks, three savings and loan associations, and several insurance companies to obtain financing for his project. He also signed a conditional purchase contract for the building site in the amount of $22,000.

After the blueprints were finished, and three competitive construction contract bids obtained, it became clear that Mr. Berg's credit was insufficient for financing the contemplated apartment project. Two weeks later he received his uncle's legacy and compensated the architect for his services. He then bought himself a new automobile and made a down payment of $15,000 on a duplex building which he intended to offer for rent. At what point should the accounting process start for Mr. Berg's real estate investment project? Defend your opinion in a short essay.

1-2. Accounting Measurement Problem. Green Lake is a large lake in Queen City. Its beautiful beaches and parklike setting make the surrounding residential area very attractive. After much negotiation, the Urban Development Company obtained a building permit from the City Planning Commission to erect a six-unit apartment building directly adjacent to and partly protruding out over Green Lake.

Construction began immediately. At this time, a lawsuit was filed by several neighborhood residential associations and environmental groups to have the building permit declared void because the planned structure would obstruct views of existing property owners and generally deface the immediate environs of the lake.

After the Urban Development Company had invested about $300,000 in the Green Lake apartment project, a court held with the plaintiffs and ordered demolition of the construction project as well as restoration of the site to its original condition. Demolition and restoration would cost approximately $100,000. On appeal, a higher court upheld the lower court's decision.

How might accountants measure the economic worth of this project on the day before the legal decision? What difficulties do you foresee in making such measurements? Who sustained the loss in the situation described?

1-3. Accounting Information Effects. Select three large corporations whose stock is traded on the New York Stock Exchange. From information sources available in your Business Administration Library, list the high and low price quotes for these stocks for each of the last three years. Has the average quoted price increased, decreased, or stayed the same for each stock?

Would you expect accounting information made available to stockholders to have influenced the quoted prices? If so, what do you think is the nature of this influence? Attempt to support your answer with facts as best you can.

1-4. Units to be Accounted for. Sears, Roebuck and Company is headquartered in Chicago. It operates many retail stores, a large mail-order business, and scores of warehouses and certain production facilities. Also, many manufacturers produce merchandise under a Sears label through various licensed production contract arrangements.

In several metropolitan areas, Sears has as many as a dozen retail stores. Its sales territories are divided into regions, and the company operates subsidiary companies in Canada, Mexico, and South America.

List three parties each of whom would benefit from accounting for (1) each individual store, (2) all stores in a metropolitan area, (3) all stores in a region, (4) all stores in the United States, (5) the mail-order segment of the business in the United States, (6) production and licensing activities in the United States separated from all other operations, (7) all business in the United States combined, and (8) total combined worldwide business. What is the most appropriate unit of accounting for Sears, Roebuck and Company?

1-5. Duality in Bookkeeping. Keeping track of items of wealth is the first step in the bookkeeping process which serves as a major tool of accounting. List ten items that you feel might constitute the property (or resources) of a small manufacturing company. Also list ten claims (or obligations) that various parties might have against the company. (*Hint:* Machines and cash-in-bank are examples of property; sales taxes payable and stocks sold to the public are claims.)

1-6. Limitation of Short Periods. The Northern Smelting Corporation operates a large phosphorus smelter in Poca, Idaho. During 19X4 several scrubbing towers and other pollution control equipment are installed to reduce the phosphorus content of emissions from the smelter's smokestacks. The equipment costs $5.4 million; the installation and test costs amount to $0.6 million. Engineers estimate that the new equipment will have to be replaced twelve years later.

The management of Northern Smelting prepares an annual accounting information report for its shareholders. Should the entire $6 million expenditure be allocated somehow over the next twelve years? If so, how? State five reasons why *annual* business reports seem desirable, and also five reasons why they might be undesirable.

1-7. Purchase of Information. The *Wall Street Journal* is a major weekday business newspaper in the United States (like the *Financial Times* in the U.K., etc.). Aside from its asserted usefulness for managerial and economic policy-making purposes, it is advertised as being a source of direct benefits for personal money management and financial planning.

Required:

1. Propose a numerically expressed scheme according to which a family could evaluate whether it should subscribe to (i.e., purchase the information contained in) the *Wall Street Journal.*
2. Like other publications, the *Wall Street Journal* has special low-cost student subscription rates. As a university student potentially interested in such a subscription, is the evaluation scheme developed under requirement 1 above also applicable to yourself? Why or why not?

1-8. Cost and Value of Information. The Department of Accounting at State University has received two scholarship grants. Either one of the grants can be awarded this year, with the other to be awarded next year. The first grant provides that the recipient is to receive $1,500. The second grant is in the form of securities and other valuables to be sold by the trustees of a deceased benefactor's estate. If the proceeds exceed a certain amount, then the scholarship will be $2,000. If the proceeds fall short of the minimum, the scholarship will be only $1,000.

The Scholarship Committee of the Department of Accounting has selected Student A, who ranked first among all applicants, to receive this year's award. Since one of the fellowships is uncertain in amount, the committee further decided to give Student A a choice as to which scholarship she would like best. Unfortunately, it must award the scholarship before the trustees are scheduled to sell off the property of the deceased benefactor's estate.

The committee has informed Student A of its decision and has allowed one week for Student A to make a choice. In addition, it has informed Student A that the trustees of the deceased benefactor's estate (who are experts in handling estates) have estimated that there is a fifty-fifty chance that the estate's property will sell for more than the minimum amount. They indicated that they could say definitely one way or the other, but only after making a complete appraisal of the estate. Since such an appraisal was not called for in the will, however, they would have to charge the appraisal fee to whoever requested the information. The committee did not request the appraisal because the fee would then have to be paid out of the scholarship proceeds, making less available to the recipient.

Required:

Put yourself in Student A's position and satisfy the following requirements:
1. Without any additional information, can you decide between the two scholarships? If so, which would you choose? What factors make you prefer your choice?
2. Might you be willing to request an appraisal of the value of the estate's property? If not, why not? If so, what is the maximum you would be willing to pay?

1-9. Quantitative Scales. The Pratfall Chair Company produces two lines of office chairs, standard and deluxe, both of which have been selling very well in recent years. This led the company to undertake a factory expansion and the employment and training of additional workers. Previously the factory had capacity for 100 workers (in three shifts), each of whom put in 2,000 hours per year. With the factory expansion 20 more workers have been added to the work force. All workers are paid at the same rate of $5 per hour.

A standard chair, which sells for $65, can be made in 3 hours. A deluxe chair takes 5 hours to make and sells for $100. The other costs of production associated with each type of chair are as follows:

	Standard	Deluxe
Materials	$20	$22
Hardware	5	8
Other costs	5	5

Now that the factory expansion is complete, Pratfall management is trying to decide how much of each kind of chair to produce. It has been producing and selling 30,000 standard chairs and 22,000 deluxe chairs. Management intends to produce at least as many as before of each chair so as not to disappoint faithful customers of either line. It also feels that at present prices it cannot sell more than 10,000 additional deluxe chairs or more than 20,000 additional standard chairs. Beyond these levels, prices would have to be drastically reduced.

Required:

1. On what common scale of merit should additional production of the two products be compared?
2. How much of each product should Pratfall produce? Support your answer with appropriate calculations.

1-10. Quantitative versus Qualitative Factors. Harold Bevan is the owner and manager of a filling station. His operations have been greatly complicated by a recent (presumably temporary) gasoline shortage. He has been receiving 20,000 gallons of gasoline per month from the refinery—only about two-thirds of what he normally sells. When the gasoline is delivered each month, he must decide how much to allocate to his "regular" storage tank and how much to "premium." There is no difference between the gasoline pumped from the delivery truck. Instead, Harold pours certain "additives" into the premium tank after each delivery. During the shortage, Harold has been allocating 10,000 gallons of his monthly supply to each of the tanks.

This month, just before his monthly delivery, Harold received word from the refinery that he could have 5,000 additional gallons of gas in his next delivery provided he agrees to certain conditions: (1) he must allocate at least as much gas as last month to each tank (regular and premium), and (2) the amount of one grade of gas that he sells may not exceed 130 percent of the amount of the other grade.

Harold knows that he can sell all he wants of both grades at the present government-controlled prices of $.90 per gallon of regular and $.99 per gallon of premium. However, he has tried to maintain some fairness among his customers who demand about equal amounts of premium and regular gas. So far, no one has been able to have all the gas he has wanted.

Required:

Assuming that Harold pays $.80 per gallon for gasoline and that the additives cost $7.00 per pound and are added to the basic gasoline to get premium in a ratio of one pound per 100 gallons, how should Harold allocate his next delivery? Restrict your answer first to only quantifiable factors. Defend your answer. Are there any nonquantified factors that Harold should consider? Describe them.

1-11. Cost and Value of Information. Betty and Gerald Adams, whose case is described in Example 1-1 in this chapter, have asked you for your help with a decision they face. After talking with them and consulting with their neighbors, you determine that—
   a. The best crop to plant would be either corn, wheat, or green beans.
   b. Growing more than a single crop on their 100 acres at this time is not feasible because of higher cultivation costs.
   c. Measured in bushels per acre, the expected yield from corn ranges from 60 to 120 bushels; from wheat, 90 to 100 bushels; and from green beans, 80 to 200 bushels.
   d. The yield depends largely on the composition of the soil. However, you do not know the actual composition of the soil, and the soil of the neighboring farms varies from farm to farm.

Required:

1. Given the above information only, can a decision be reached? Explain the basis of your answer.
2. What choice would you recommend if you expected that the net price per bushel (selling price minus production costs) for the three crops was approximately $.75 for corn, $1.00 for wheat, and $.50 for green beans? Support your answer.
3. At this point what kind of additional information might change your answer to number 2?

4. A local consulting firm will examine soil samples for a fee of $500. Its past record indicates that it can provide an extremely exact projection of the yield per acre for any crop.
    a. Could the more exact information alter the Adamses' choice of crop?
    b. Can you categorically recommend that they buy the information from the consulting firm?
5. Suppose now that you have reliable information that only one of two soil conditions exists in the region of the Adamses' farm and the chances are fifty-fifty that their farm could have either condition. One condition would mean a definite wheat yield of 100 bushels per acre and a bean yield of 180 bushels. The other condition would mean a wheat yield of 90 bushels and a bean yield of 200. Should the Adamses pay for a consulting report costing $600 that will indicate exactly which condition exists in their soil? If the report would only cost $300?

1-12. The Tale of the Ancient Taxpayers. (Adapted from the "Sheepherder's Game" by Warren Higgins, University of Connecticut.) Once upon a time there was a tiny mountain kingdom of Cascadia, ruled by a fierce but well-loved king, Tamalpias III. Cascadia had a strictly pastoral (barter) economy, with no money ever changing hands. Instead, the principal products of the kingdom were cattle, cheese, and hides, which the residents traded among themselves and with the surrounding lowland kingdoms in exchange for produce, clothing, building materials, and so forth.

Taxes were assessed each year by the royal tax collector. According to royal decree, each person's tax was to be proportionate to how well off he was, relative to everyone else in the kingdom—in the royal tax collector's judgment, that is. Unfortunately, the royal tax collector was corrupt and accepted occasional bribes from a few, instead of their just contribution to the Royal Treasury. When King Tamalpias discovered this, he stripped the man of his position and all of his possessions and had him thrown into the dungeon for life.

In place of the royal tax collector, King Tamalpias III decreed that henceforth each of his subjects was to assess and pay his own *just* tax, based on how well off he was. The tax rate was set at 5 percent to be applied as of New Year's Day each year.

Of course, the king was no fool. He knew that not all of his subjects could be counted upon to fairly assess and pay their own tax. Some penalties for failure to comply were necessary. But most of his subjects were simple people, and the king himself abhorred complicated laws. So, being an accomplished poet (in his own opinion, at least), he penned the following limerick and had it read publicly and posted throughout the kingdom:

> There once was a citizen, Faber,
> Who was twice as well off as his neighbor,
> But he paid much less tax
> For which he was lax,
> Now he's making it up at hard labor.

Well, the limerick had the desired effect. It struck fear (and a modicum of honesty) into the hearts of most subjects. But it also caused much puzzlement among the citizenry as to how to assess the tax. As the new year approached following the decree, two old friends, Roland and Buford, were "sharing a cup" in their village pub and comparing notes. Buford was a tanner and very good at his trade. His only source of dissatisfaction in life was due to the tanning process, which gives off an obnoxious odor. Because the odor clung to him and permeated his cottage, none of the kingdom's eligible maidens would think of marrying him and moving into his cottage. Roland was a dairyman, happily married. He enjoyed his dairying very much. In past years, Roland and Buford had often argued (boastfully) about which one was better off. Now they were worried about how much tax each should pay and how they should pay for it.

Buford owned mostly hides, since they were his stock in trade. For the hides on hand, 200 in all, he gave a total of 2,000 "rounds" of cheese. All of the hides were in the process of being cured, however, and when finished would bring roughly 3,000 rounds of cheese upon sale. Buford also owned five cows, a cottage with a beautiful view of a neighboring lowland kingdom that he enjoyed very much, and a donkey and cart for taking his finished hides to market. For each of the cows, he had given 50 finished hides over the last several years. The cottage was inherited from his father, who originally gave five cows for it. The donkey and cart were acquired two years ago (from the time the king's latest tax decree went into effect) in exchange for a cow plus ten finished hides.

Roland owned 20 cows. Ten were inherited from his father, who gave 600 rounds of cheese for each over a number of years. The others were acquired by Roland for an average of 700 rounds of cheese each. In addition to his cows, Roland owned 50 rounds of cheese, a cottage and a horse-drawn wagon. The cottage was built by Roland's father about the same time Buford's father acquired his cottage. Roland's father gave three cows for all of the materials. The horse and wagon were acquired by Roland for a cow plus a donkey-and-cart combination (both in good shape) that no longer served the needs of Roland's dairy operation.

Required:

Let us suppose that you lived in this kingdom at this time and that you formed a tax-consulting service for the kingdom of Cascadia. Calculate the amount of tax that Roland and Buford should pay, and indicate how they should pay it.

1-13. Problem Definition—A Highly Structured Decision. Suppose IDRA, an international disaster relief agency, has as its primary goal to be prepared to deliver all the food (needed for a balanced survival diet), clothing, and temporary shelter required by disaster victims anywhere in the world at any time. The agency can count on air transport for goods and personnel at the time of disaster from the nation concerned or sympathetic neighbors. The agency has always received ample storage space free or at minimal fees from various governments and private individuals. Its mission, therefore, is mainly to maximize the amounts of food, clothing, and shelter at the ready in its storage locations around the world. Unfortunately, it operates on a limited budget. Each year IDRA undertakes a fund-raising drive and then allocates the total amount received to the three categories of food, clothing, and temporary shelter. Then its procurement directors for each category take over from there. Assume that *you* are the procurement director for food. Assume further that no single food commodity is optimal, so the problem involves selecting an optimal mix of several basic food commodities.

Required:

1. Satisfy the following two questions as an integrated set, that is, each should be answered in relationship to the other. (See the hints below.)
    (a) What statement of objectives would you use to guide your choice of how much of each basic food commodity to buy?
    (b) What constraints are present and how would you state them in relationship to (in the same term as) the objectives function?
    Hint 1: The decision alternatives in question are alternative mixes, proportions, or sets of total purchases of each of several food commodities.
    Hint 2: A major hurdle in the problem is to find a common scale of merit for incorporation into the statement of objectives.
2. Can you suggest some procedure for efficiently evaluating alternatives and coming to a solution?
3. Indicate some nonquantifiable aspects of the problem. How do they complicate the problem definition or solution?
4. Suppose that IDRA cannot get unlimited storage space. Does this complicate the problem definition or solution? If so, how?

Present Value Approach to Investment Decisions

In Chapter 1 we noted that the investment decision is one of two major categories of decisions made by external parties who have an economic interest in the business enterprise. Starting with Chapter 3 we specify some alternate kinds of information about business enterprises that accountants can produce for investment decision makers. In this chapter we intend to give the reader some general understanding of the nature of investment decisions and how one might go about making them—to which later discussions will relate.

The chapter is divided into three major sections. The first describes investment decisions and some of their general characteristics. The second section develops a simplified (present value) model for choosing between investment decision alternatives. And the third section is an elaboration, to bring out some more subtle but important aspects of the simplified model.

THE INVESTMENT DECISION PROBLEM

The Objective of Investment Decisions and Its Implications

All economic decisions are presumably made for the ultimate purpose of enhancing the individual's well-being, that is, the satisfaction of wants and needs that the individual experiences. Investment decisions are no exception. But investment alternatives usually do not directly offer satisfaction of wants and needs. Instead, like many other production-oriented (as opposed to consumption-oriented) activities, investment decisions usually deal with the material or physical means to human satisfaction that we refer to as wealth.

Wealth. Wealth is the command over present and future goods and services owned or controlled by an economic unit as of a point in time.

Wealth is clearly not identical with well-being or satisfaction. Satisfaction may be derived from all kinds of nonmaterial, noneconomic things like friendship, esteem, and self-confidence. But, in general, economists have assumed that, other things being equal, more wealth means more well-being for the individual, since the term *wealth* embraces all *economic sources* of present and future want satisfaction.

In Chapter 1 we defined *investment decisions* as those decisions involving exchanges of present goods and services for rights to goods and services in the future. Thus investment decisions can be thought of as exchanges of wealth in one form (usually rights to present goods and services) for wealth in another form (rights to future goods and services). It is generally assumed in economics and accounting that investment decisions are made *with the objective* of maximizing wealth.

The implication of this objective is that the investment decision maker must be able to assess or measure the wealth that he is expected to give up, and the wealth he expects in return, in some comparable way. To accomplish this, he will maximize his wealth by choosing the alternatives with the maximum excess of wealth return over wealth given up. The central purpose of this chapter is to develop the methodology for making the necessary measurements. A useful first step in that direction is to be more specific (albeit briefly) about the wealth-related features of investment alternatives.

Features of Investment Decisions with Some Simplifying Assumptions

In order to be explicit about how individuals ought to go about choosing between investment alternatives, we will make some simplifying assumptions. First, we assume that all wealth given up or returned in each investment alternative is in the form of cash. Second, we ignore constraints on the decision maker and concentrate instead on methodology for determining the amount that a given investment alternative will contribute to the wealth of the decision maker. Finally, for the present, we assume that all future cash flows, whether to be paid out or received, are known with certainty at the time of decision. Each of these assumptions is discussed briefly below.

Cash-flow Orientation. Although it is a narrowing assumption that investment alternatives are composed exclusively of cash flows, it is not a particularly damaging one in view of the environment. In a modern economy virtually no one produces goods and services exclusively to directly satisfy his own wants and needs. Nearly every individual (1) specializes to a degree in producing some specific good or service, (2) exchanges quantities of that good or service for cash, and (3) uses the cash proceeds to purchase other goods and services to directly satisfy his wants and needs. Like other production-oriented activities, most investments offer *primarily* cash returns in the future in exchange for present cash commitments or outlays.

Nevertheless, some investment decisions hinge on the more qualitative (non-cash) aspects of the alternatives. So it must be remembered that the importance of cash in our discussion of investment decisions is not that it is the *only* relevant aspect of investment decisions but that it is a relevant and quantifiable feature of practically all investment decisions.

Constraints Ignored. In Chapter 1 we mentioned that a decision maker faced with a decision situation will want to define his choice problem by specifying both a statement of objectives and constraints. But in our discussion of investment decisions we will ignore constraints for two reasons. First, constraints are not usually properties of investment decisions *per se* but rather are limitations that are imposed on the decision maker, for example, having a limited budget. Whereas the constraints faced by the individual may be unique to him, the objective of wealth maximization seems to apply widely across decision makers and investment alternatives.

Second, as was pointed out in Chapter 1, constraints can be applied in sequence before or after the decision maker has considered an alternative's promised contribution to his decision objective. Whatever choice or ranking we make between investment alternatives, based on their contribution to the objective of wealth maximization alone, it may later be altered when the constraints faced by the decision maker are brought to bear.

Certain Cash Flows. In Chapter 1 we defined *uncertainty* as the condition of not knowing at the time of decision precisely what the outcomes of relevant future events will be. Because investment decisions involve future flows of resources (usually cash), they are complicated by uncertainty. But precisely because uncertainty complicates investment decision making, we ignore it for the present. However, we will return to the matter of uncertainty in a later section of the chapter because it is an important aspect of most investment decisions.

Investment Decisions under Certainty

Having made the foregoing simplifying assumptions, we can be specific about the features of investment decisions with which the decision maker must come to grips. We can now describe investment decisions as decisions involving cash-flow alternatives that may differ with respect to (1) magnitude and (2) the times, present and future, at which cash inflows and outflows take place.

Example 2-1

An individual has two possible investment alternatives, investment A and investment B, each requiring an initial outlay of $100 but promising different cash inflows (returns) at the end of each of the next five years, as shown in Exhibit 2-1

Exhibit 2-1

	Initial Outlay	\multicolumn{5}{c	}{Returns}	Total Returns
		\multicolumn{5}{c	}{At the end of year:}	
		1	2	3	4	5	
Investment A	−$100	$40	$35	$30	$25	$25	$155
Investment B	−$100	$25	$30	$30	$35	$40	$160

Which alternative should the individual choose? It is technically impossible to answer at a glance. We may come to the hasty conclusion (after some mental arithmetic) that investment B is better, since it promises $160 over five years in return for $100, whereas investment A promises only $155 in total. Such a conclusion implies that the $10 and $15 *greater* inflows in years four and five promised by investment B are worth more in combination than the $15 and $5 *greater* inflows in years one and two promised by investment A. But individuals would not unanimously agree to such a conclusion.

One person may prefer the later, but greater, excess inflows of investment B over the earlier, but lesser, excess inflows from investment A. Another person may have the opposite preference. In either case, the individual needs to determine which of the two different sets of promised inflows will leave *him* better off.

The present value model of investment decision making developed in the next section specifies how an individual can make such a determination in cases where one alternative does not clearly dominate all others in every respect. But understanding the model depends on the three "building-block" concepts of (1) time preference for money, (2) compound interest, and (3) present value. These concepts are developed in turn below.

THE PRESENT VALUE MODEL FOR INVESTMENT DECISIONS

Time Preference for Money

Most individuals value the opportunity to have a specific amount of money now higher than the opportunity to have the same amount, no more, no less, at some future date. We call this phenomenon an individual's *time preference for money* and define it more explicitly as follows:

> **Time Preference for Money.** An individual's preference for possession of a given amount of cash now, rather than the same amount at some future time, is called "time preference for money."

Two basic reasons account for most individuals' time preference for money. First, money is the means by which individuals acquire most goods and services.

And most people prefer present consumption to future consumption of the same goods and services, either (1) because of the urgency of their present wants or (2) because of the risk of not being around to enjoy future consumption. Second, there are usually opportunities to put present cash to work earning additional cash. For instance, an individual offered $100 now or $100 one year from now can usually take the $100 now, put it in a savings account, and withdraw that amount plus $5 or $6 interest in one year. Thus, if he wishes to maximize his wealth, the opportunity to save leads him to prefer $100 now to $100 one year hence.

Time Preference Expressed as a Rate. Generally, an individual's time preference for money can be characterized for convenience by an interest rate, with the aid of a simple mental game. The individual merely asks himself, "If I am offered either possession of $10 today or the right to have some greater amount one year from today, at what greater amount would I be exactly indifferent between the two opportunities?" If the answer to this question is $11, for instance, it implies that $11 to be received one year from now is equivalent in value (personal satisfaction) to having $10 in hand right now. This in turn implies that the strength of the individual's time preference for money can be designated by the 10 percent per year differential (*time preference rate*) that was added to get $11. Similarly, if it only takes $10.50 to be received one year from now to make the individual indifferent, his *time preference rate* for money is only 5 percent. (Note: A commonly used synonym for time preference rate is the term *discount rate*.)

Using the Time Preference Rate. How does knowledge of a specific time preference rate help the individual in his investment problems? It permits the individual to translate different amounts offered at different times of possession to amounts of *equivalent value* to him at present. A common point of reference (the present) is thus established.

Example 2-2

Consider an individual with a time preference rate of 10 percent. If someone offered him a chance to have $1,155 one year from now in exchange for giving up $1,000 of his dollars today, would he take the offer? The answer is yes. When the individual determines that his time preference rate is 10 percent, he is saying that he is indifferent between any amount today and 110 percent of that amount one year hence. He would obviously favor more than 110 percent of the amount one year from now, but if the amount offered one year from now were less than 110 percent of the immediate payment, he would retain the immediate payment. Now we can ask the question: Between what amount today and $1,155 one year from now would the investor be indifferent? The answer is that amount of which $1,155 is exactly 110 percent. Dividing $1,155 by 1.10 we get:

$$\frac{\$1,155}{1.10} = \$1,050,$$

or more than the $1,000 that the individual is asked to give up today. This means that if the individual had been asked to give up $1,050 to get $1,155 back after one year, he would be indifferent—not really caring whether he took the offer or not. Since the actual offer calls for him to give up only $1,000 to get $1,155 back after one year, he will take it. He only has to give up $1,000 to get something that is equivalent (in value to him) to having $1,050 in his possession right now.

Time Preference, Consumption Levels, and Alternate Opportunities. Before leaving this introductory discussion about time preference for money, some additional subtleties need to be brought out. Primarily it should be noted that, at any point in time, an individual's time preference for money may be conditioned by a number of things. Among the important conditioning variables are (1) the present level of consumption enjoyed and (2) the attractiveness of opportunities available.

To see intuitively that the present consumption level enjoyed conditions time preference, consider the contrast between an individual existing at the subsistence level versus one who is very wealthy. The former is not likely to be able to think of a rate high enough to make him forgo present survival (present consumption at the subsistence level) for opulence in the future. On the other hand, the latter may be willing to forgo additional present consumption at a fairly low rate, simply because he already "has everything."

To see the influence of other opportunities on the individual's time preference rate, consider a brief example.

Example 2-3

Suppose an individual is currently consuming well above the subsistence level, that is, postponement of present consumption is feasible. Also, suppose initially that he can place cash in a savings bank that will return $105 after one year for every $100 deposited. Assume that the 5 percent rate of return implied by the savings bank deal is just sufficient to make the individual decide to save some of his money. But before actually depositing the money, he becomes aware of a chance to place $450 in an investment club that guarantees a $470 return in one year. The question is: Is the investment club deal attractive to the individual? The answer is no. As long as the investor can receive $105 for each $100 of consumption forgone for a year, he can actually receive $472.50 from the savings bank at the end of a year for forgoing $450 in present consumption. He would not want to receive less than the amount afforded by the best available opportunity.

The example can be generalized to any investment alternative. An investor will be indifferent to an investment alternative if it promises a return equal to his opportunity rate.

Opportunity Rate. An investor's *opportunity rate* (of return) is the rate he can earn on his best known investment alternative.

An investor will favor any new alternatives promising returns higher than his present opportunity rate. New alternatives offering less than the opportunity rate of return will be rejected. Thus the investor's time preference rate *is his opportunity rate*, assuming he has passed the threshold of deciding to forgo present for future consumption.

The Rationale for Compound Interest

So far, we have only worked out sufficient logic for deciding between cash inflows and outflows that are separated by one period, such as one year. What about more complicated investment opportunities of more than one period's duration, like the unresolved choice between investments A and B in Example 2-1? We need to extend the logic developed above and thereby make it more flexible.

Let us continue to work with an individual who has determined that it takes a 10 percent premium to make him indifferent to inflows or outflows of cash one year apart. The question now is: How should he arrive at comparative values of inflows and outflows two, three, or any number of years apart?

Once an individual has determined his personal time preference for money for any single period of time (like one year), we can determine the relative difference in amounts that he would require for postponing possession of cash for any longer period. A two-year period, for instance, is nothing more than two successive one-year periods. If the individual first agreed to give up $1 for one year, he would have $1.10 back at the end of that year in exchange for the original $1. If he recommitted the whole amount for an additional year, he would demand 110 percent of the whole amount, or $1.21 ($1 × 1.10 × 1.10) at the end of the second year. Notice that for any time after the first year he will insist on receiving a premium on the first-year premium as well as a premium on the original amount. When the premiums are called interest rates, this concept is described as *compound interest*.

The same reasoning can be extended to a third year. We now know that an individual with a time preference of 10 percent would be indifferent between $1 today and $1.21 ($1 × 1.10 × 1.10) at the end of two years. And, having $1.21 at the end of the second year, he would be indifferent between holding it or giving it up for one more year for a return of $1.21 × 110 percent, or approximately $1.33 ($1 × 1.10 × 1.10 × 1.10). In other words, he is really indifferent between $1 now and $1.33 to be received at the end of three years. We could continue to work out amounts for four years, five years, six years, and so forth, but it has already become awkward to continue verbally. Besides, a formula can be used to represent symbolically the amount that an individual would demand after any number of years in return for $1 given up initially at any rate of interest.

The Future Value of One Dollar. Let r represent the decimal equivalent of the individual's time preference rate for one period (0.10 per year in the above discussion). And let n be the number of years before payoff. Then the future value (amount of cash) an individual would require in return for $1 given up for n years at r rate, represented as $FV_{(n,r)}$, is equal to

$$FV_{(n,r)} = \$1 \times (1.0 + r)^n$$

Example 2-4

To show that this is so, consider the example used in the discussion above; r is 0.10, so the term in parentheses would be 1.10. To represent the inflow from a sacrifice of $1 for three years, we raise 1.10 to the power $n = 3$:

$$FV_{(3,0.10)} = \$1 \times (1.10)^3$$
$$= \$1 \times (1.10)(1.10)(1.10)$$
$$= \$1.33$$

We get the same amount that was computed earlier using verbal rather than symbolic logic. The advantage of the formula is that it characterizes the same logic for any interest rate and any number of years.

The Future Value of any Amount. As a final comment on the generality of the above formula, it should be pointed out that what we calculate as future value for a sacrifice of $1 for some number of years can easily be used to determine the future value for any number of dollars initially sacrificed.

Example 2-5

The inflow for a sacrifice of $9 for three years at 10 percent is simply nine times the inflow for $1, or

$$9 \times \$1(1.10)^3$$
$$9 \times 1.33 = \$11.97$$

Symbolically, if the number of dollars to be sacrificed for n years is represented by S, then the inflow at the end of n years can be represented by

$$S \times FV_{(n,r)}$$

Or

$$S \times (1.0 + r)^n$$

Recalling the original motivation for this discussion, it may now be observed that we have the power in the concept of compound interest to compare cash inflows and outflows that are separated *by more than one period,* given an individual's time preference rate *per period.*

Example 2-6

If an individual with a time preference rate of 10 percent per year were offered an opportunity to pay out $55 now for a return of $68 after two years, should he take the offer? The answer is yes. He would be exactly indifferent between having $55 now and having $55 $(1.10)^2$, or 55×1.21, two years from now. Since the latter amount, $66.55, is less than the payoff offered, $68, the individual would willingly give up $55 now to get the return of $68 two years from now.

Present Value

Whereas we can now translate any amount of present cash into an amount of cash equivalent value to be received at the end of any number of future periods, it is often convenient in investment decisions to be able to work in the other direction. Hence we turn next to the appropriate technique for working from future cash flows to their present values.

Present Value. The present value of a future cash inflow or outflow is the amount of current cash that leaves a decision maker indifferent between it and a specified amount of cash to be received or paid at a future date.

Once we have concluded that an individual with a time preference rate of r per year is indifferent between $1 now and $(1.0 + r)$ one year from now, or $(1.0 + r)^2$ after two years, or $(1.0 + r)^3$ after three years, and so forth, we can ask a set of related questions. How much would the same individual give up now to get a payoff of $1 at the end of one, two, or three years? The answer in each case is a matter of proportionality.

Consider the one-year case. Assuming a time preference rate of 10 percent, the *present value* today of $1 to be received at the end of the year must bear the same relationship to the $1 inflow as a $1 sacrifice today bears to an inflow of $1.10 after one year. We can state this algebraically as a set of related ratios with the symbol $PV_{(1,0.10)}$ representing the present value of $1 to be received in one year at a 10 percent time preference rate:

$$\frac{PV_{(1,0.10)}}{\$1} = \frac{\$1}{\$1.10}$$

Or, solving for the present value:

$$PV_{(1,0.10)} = \frac{\$1}{\$1.10} = \$.909$$

This means that with a time preference rate of 10 percent, the present value of $1 to be received after one year is 90.9 cents. To see that this is consistent with the individual's expressed preference rate, we only need to note that one dollar (the promised inflow) is 110 percent of 90.9 cents.

The present values of one dollar inflows at the end of two- and three-year waiting periods can be worked out similarly. Since the individual with a time preference rate of 10 percent is indifferent between $1 now and $1.21 after two years, he is also indifferent between 82.6 cents now and $1 after two years:

$$\frac{PV_{(2,0.10)}}{\$1} = \frac{\$1}{\$1.21}$$

$$PV_{(2,0.10)} = \frac{\$1}{\$1.21} = \$.826$$

The same individual, indifferent between $1 now and $1.33 three years from now, must also be indifferent between 75.1 cents now and $1 three years later:

$$\frac{PV_{(3,0.10)}}{\$1} = \frac{\$1}{\$1.33}$$

$$PV_{(3,0.10)} = \frac{\$1}{\$1.33} = \$.751$$

Naturally, the same type of calculations can be worked out for any individual for any number of years and any time preference rate.

The Present Value of One Dollar. The general form of the foregoing present value calculation technique can be represented symbolically as follows:

$$PV_{(n,r)} = \frac{1}{FV_{(n,r)}} = \frac{1}{(1.0+r)^n}$$

Notice that the present value of $1 to be received at the end of n years at r rate is simply the reciprocal of the future value to be received from investing $1 for n years at r interest rate.

The Present Value of any Amount. The advantage of knowing the present value of $1 by applying the formula above is that the present value of an inflow of any number of dollars, represented by P, can be found by simply multiplying the present value of $1 by P. Symbolically:

$$P \times PV_{(n,r)} = P \times \frac{1}{(1.0+r)^n}$$

This formula tells us how much current cash we would consider to be equivalent in value to, say, $100 to be received three years from now ($n = 3$) if the time preference rate (r) is 10 percent. The term $PV_{(n,r)}$ tells us that the present value of each of those dollars is

$$\frac{1}{(1.0+0.10)^3} = 0.751$$

Therefore the total is worth 100 times that amount (100 × 0.751), or $75.10.

Present Value and Future Value Tables. Once the notion is understood, a good deal of efficiency can be achieved in finding the present value (to an individual with a given time preference rate) of any amount of dollars promised at the end of any number of years. How? By constructing precalculated tables of present values of $1 to be received at the end of any reasonable number of years (say, one to thirty) at any reasonable interest rate (say, 1 percent to as much as 20 percent). Table 2-1, in Appendix A to this chapter, is just such a table. To use Table 2-1, one needs to read off the present value of $1 to be received at the end of n years at r rate as the number at the intersection of the nth row of the column labeled r rate in the table.

To confirm this, recall that earlier we computed the present values of $1 to be received at the end of one, two, and three years for a time preference rate of 10 percent. The amounts computed were $.909, $.826, and $.751, respectively. The same amounts are shown at the intersections of the .10 column of Table 2-1 and the first row (one year), second row (two years), and third row (three years), in turn. The same convenience is available in Table 2-2 (also in Appendix A), which is organized in the same way for future values of $1, at the end of n years and at r rates of interest. In taking advantage of the convenience of the tables, however, one must never lose track of the logic behind the numbers that appear there.

One additional convenience of precalculated valuation factors, available in special cases of so-called annuities, is described in Appendix B to this chapter—along with the related table of annuity values.

Relationship between Present Value and Future Value. The compound interest effects of both present value and future value calculations can also be demonstrated graphically.

The following points of reference are plotted on the graph in Exhibit 2-2:

b. $\$100 \times FV(1, 0.10) = \$100 \times (1 + .10)^1 = \$100 \times (1.10) = \$110$

c. $\$100 \times FV(2, 0.10) = \$100 \times (1 + .10)^2 = \$100 \times (1.21) = \$121$

d. $\$100 \times FV(3, 0.10) = \$100 \times (1 + .10)^3 = \$100 \times (1.33) = \$133$

a. $\$133 \times PV(3, 0.10) = \dfrac{\$133}{(1 + .10)^3} = \dfrac{\$133}{1.33} = \$100$

b. $\$133 \times PV(2, 0.10) = \dfrac{\$133}{(1 + .10)^2} = \dfrac{\$133}{1.21} = \$110$

c. $\$133 \times PV(1, 0.10) = \dfrac{\$133}{(1 + .10)^1} = \dfrac{\$133}{1.10} = \$121$

Exhibit 2-2

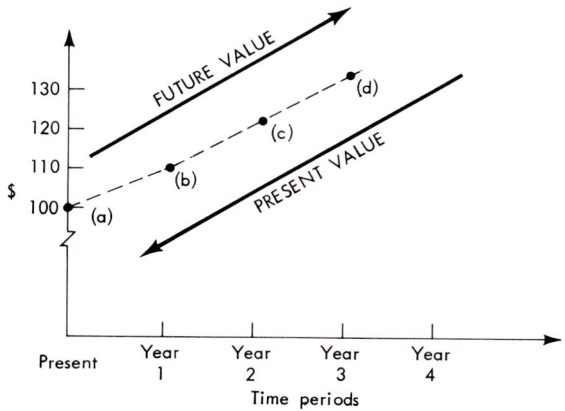

Exhibit 2-2 highlights and summarizes our earlier discussion of the consequences flowing from people's time preference for money. Note in particular that (1) the compound interest effects are the same for present value as well as future value calculations, (2) present value arithmetic is but the reciprocal of future value arithmetic, and (3) any time reference point may be reached in a number of different ways. For example, point c in Exhibit 2-2 may be reached with $\$100 \times FV(2,0.10)$, that is, starting at the present. But it may also be reached by going to point d with $\$100 \times FV(3,0.10)$ and then applying $\$133 \times PV(1,0.10)$ to move back to point c. The reader may wish to contemplate still other ways of reaching point c or, for that matter, any other reference point plotted on the chart.

Net Present Value: A Model for Investment Choice

With the aid of present value tables like Table 2-1, an individual who can specify his time preference rate for money can determine the amount of dollars today that would be of equivalent value to him of any given future cash inflow or outflow. With little additional effort, these individual present values can be combined to get a single total present value for each investment opportunity.

Example 2-7

Again assume a time preference rate of 10 percent *and* recall the unresolved choice between investments A and B in Example 2-1. Because a decision maker can assign a present value to any single dollar promised in any future year, he can assign total present values to all the promised annual cash flows of investments A and B, as shown in Exhibit 2-3.

Calculating Net Present Values. Looking just at investment A, the decision maker has recognized that, to him, the receipt of $40 one year from now is equivalent to receiving $36.36 today. Likewise, the receipt of $35 two years from now is "worth" the equivalent of $28.91 today. Similar calculations apply to the other three years' payoffs.

If the $40 at the end of year one is worth $36.36 today and the $35 at the end of year two is worth $28.91 today, it is sensible to conclude that any opportunity combining $40 at the end of the first year *and* $35 at the end of the second would be worth $36.36 plus $28.91, or $65.27 in total today. Each of the two promised cash flows has been measured on the same numerical scale—present dollar value. Thus we can generalize that *the total present value of a set of promised future cash flows is the sum of the present values of all of the individual periodic cash flows.* When an investment opportunity promises both future cash inflows and outflows (as in any case requiring an initial outlay), we can sum the present values of the inflows and the outflows separately and find the difference between the sums.

Net Present Value. The sum of the present values of the future cash inflows minus the sum of the present values of the present and future cash outflows is the *net present value* of an investment opportunity.

Exhibit 2-3

	Initial Outlay	Returns At the end of year:				
		1	2	3	4	5
Investment A:						
1. Promised cash flows	-$100	$40	$35	$30	$25	$25
2. Present value of one dollar at 10%	1.00	0.909	0.826	0.751	0.683	0.621
3. Present value of promised cash flows (line 1 × line 2)	-$100	$36.36	$28.91	$22.53	$17.08	$15.53
Investment B:						
1. Promised cash flows	-$100	$25	$30	$30	$35	$40
2. Present value of one dollar at 10%	1.00	0.909	0.826	0.751	0.683	0.621
3. Present value of promised cash flows (line 1 × line 2)	-$100	$22.73	$24.78	$22.53	$23.91	$24.84

Example 2-8

Returning to investment A, we can conclude that the total present value of the inflows is

$36.36 + $28.91 + $22.53 + $17.08 + $15.53 = $120.41

The total present value of the outflows is $100, namely the amount of the solitary (initial) outlay. The net present value of investment A is therefore $120.41 - $100.00 = $20.41.

Interpreting Net Present Values. The interpretation of this net present value number is very useful for decision-making purposes. The present cash value of the outlays required to enter upon investment A as a course of action is $100. The present value of the benefits (cash inflows) from doing so is $120.41. Therefore the act of paying out $100 to enter upon investment A is *equivalent* to paying $100 and immediately receiving $120.41 in return. The gain is $20.41, the net present value of investment A. The investor would obviously find this an attractive course of action unless some other course of action, like investment B, promises an even greater net value (or cash-equivalent gain). To find out if B is more attractive, we follow the same procedure as with the calculation of the net present value of investment A.

Example 2-9

The present value of the outflows for investment B is equal to the $100 initial outlay, as with A. The total present value of the inflows from B equals

$22.73 + $24.78 + $22.53 + $23.91 + $24.84 = $118.79

The net present value of B is therefore $118.79 - $100.00 = $18.79. To undertake investment B *is equivalent,* to the decision maker, to receiving an immediate gain of $18.79.

We surmise that the decision maker would prefer investment A to investment B, since we can be reasonably sure that he would prefer an immediate gain of $20.41 to a gain of $18.79, the net present values of investments A and B, respectively. In other words, calculating and comparing net present values provides a basis—a decision model—for choosing between complex investment alternatives.

Summary of the Net Present Value Model. In summary, any individual who can specify his time preference rate for money can specify a present value or amount of current cash that is of equivalent value to him of any specified (certain) amount of cash to be received or paid at the end of any future period. From there it is a matter of only three additional arithmetic steps to compare *net present values* of complex investment alternatives. The total sequence of steps in the process is

1. Specify the cash inflows and outflows for each period associated with each investment alternative.
2. Calculate the present value of each individual cash inflow and outflow associated with each investment alternative.
3. Aggregate (sum) the present values of all the positive and all the negative cash flows for each alternative.
4. *Find the net present value* of each alternative by calculating the difference between the total present value of the positive cash flows and the total present value of the negative cash flows.
5. Finally, choose that alternative or combination of alternatives with the largest net present value.

These five steps, represented schematically in Exhibit 2-4, constitute our simplified model for investment decisions. They have been illustrated by Examples 2-7, 2-8, and 2-9. Now it remains for us to show that the net present value technique is a means for choosing between investment alternatives consistent with the assumed objective of wealth maximization.

Present Value and the Concept of Wealth

At the beginning of this chapter *wealth* was defined as the command over present and future goods and services owned or controlled by an economic unit as of a point in time. *Investment decisions* were described as those decisions involving alternative commitments or sacrifices of current forms of wealth that are expected to lead to greater quantities of goods or services in the future, that is, greater wealth. The discussion then proceeded to the development of a decision model that called for choosing from among all investment alternatives the alternative (or set of alternatives) whose net present value is greatest. In adopting this criterion we implicitly accepted present value as a means of measuring the abstract concept, wealth.

Let us look again at the individual choosing between investments A and B. With a time preference rate of 10 percent, he would choose investment A over

Exhibit 2-4

NET PRESENT VALUE MODEL

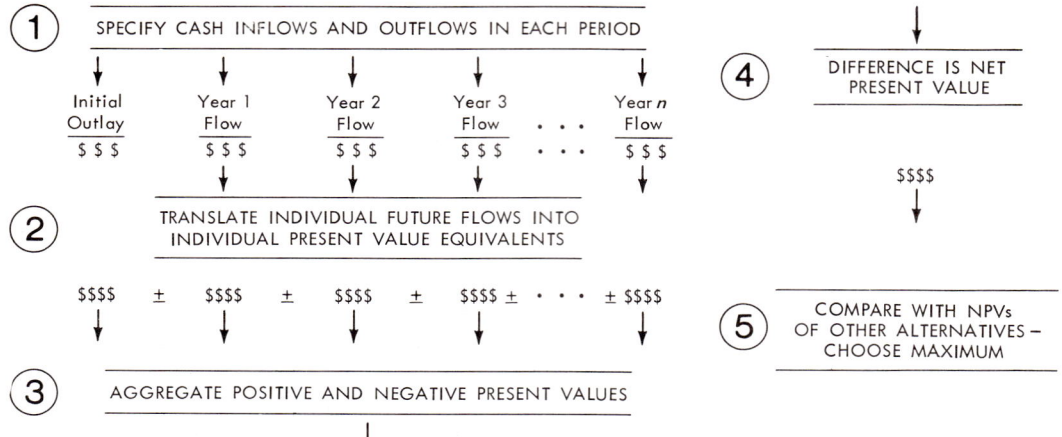

investment B because A has a *net* present value of $20.41 as opposed to B's net present value of only $18.79.

Prior to selecting investment A or B, the individual presumably has wealth in the form of $100 in cash. After selecting investment A and paying the $100 initial outlay, investment A replaces the $100 cash. But how do we assess the meaning to the individual of his wealth prior to and subsequent to his decision? Technically we cannot. Only the individual can "feel" the satisfaction that he gets from owning $100 in cash or the "feeling" he gets from owning the rights to investment A.

Because cash is the medium by which an individual in a modern economy acquires goods and services (the components of wealth), we can make an inference about the individual's feelings of wealth from holding cash. For instance, we can say that when the individual has $100 cash he feels as wealthy as the goods and services he can command with $100 cash can make him feel. More cash will always make him feel more wealthy (because he can command more goods and services), and less cash will always make him feel less wealthy. So we say that an individual with $100 cash has $100 of wealth. Now what about possession of an item like investment A? How wealthy does that make the individual? We have already answered this question.

In assessing the present value of A, we said that an individual with a specified time preference of 10 percent per year would value investment A exactly as he would value $120.41 *in cash* today. Thus we can conclude that possessing investment A makes him feel as wealthy as possessing $120.41 in cash, the (total) present value of A. Hence the wealth of an individual can, in a sense, be measured (quantified) as his current cash on hand *plus the present value* of the future cash inflows and outflows that he will receive from all of his noncash wealth items.

As a final thought, it should be emphasized that present values are not wealth *per se* but rather are valuations of wealth (or wealth items).

Valuation. Valuation is the measurement (quantification) of wealth (or wealth items) in money terms.

Therefore any valuation (like present value) may be used interchangeably with wealth, but with qualification. The qualification is necessary because the individual can use present value (for instance) as a means of quantifying his wealth only insofar as he can translate his wealth items into equivalent cash flows for which he can then calculate present values based on his time preference for money. In the case of investment A this is easy. It promises no *direct* want-satisfaction, as we have described it. Its only physical property is a stream of future cash flows. But other types of wealth items, art objects for example, obviously possess significant noncash want-satisfying properties. Recall, however, that we have purposely excluded consideration of such items through our initial assumptions.

Net Present Value and Wealth Maximization

Having established that present values can be thought of as a means of quantifying or valuing wealth, we can reflect briefly on the relationship between the net present value decision-making criterion and the objective of wealth maximization. This is the final step in introducing the net present value model as a simplified but plausible way of approaching investment decisions.

Returning to the example, we can look at investment A's *net* present value of $20.41 as being composed of two parts: (1) a negative component amounting to the present value of the wealth that the individual gives up, in this case $100, and (2) a positive component representing the present value of the wealth that the individual gets in return, in this case $120.41. Thus *the* **net** *present value of an investment opportunity may be thought of as the improvement in wealth (as measured in terms of present value) that will result from selecting the opportunity.* Choosing investment alternatives on the basis of maximum net present value improves the wealth position of the individual to the fullest, that is, it maximizes wealth as measured in terms of present values at the time of decision.

PRESENT VALUE METHODOLOGY—SOME ELABORATION

In the preceding section we developed a simplified model with which decision makers who have the objective of maximizing wealth can approach investment decisions. This section is devoted to some features of present value methodology. Each of these additional topics will either strengthen the reader's grasp of the basic model or extend it in a direction that will be relevant to discussion in later chapters.

Sensitivity of Net Present Value to Time Preference Rate

A most important feature of the net present value model is its dependence on the time preference rate selected. Without preselecting a time preference rate, we cannot accomplish the step of translating cash flows of various future periods into cash equivalents of a common point of reference, the present. Furthermore, the outcome of a decision can be highly sensitive to the magnitude of the rate selected. Although we may calculate net present values of several decision alternatives based on one rate and conclude that an individual who selects that rate would unequivocally choose one alternative above all others, we cannot always conclude—without repeating all the calculations—that another individual selecting a different time preference rate would choose the same alternative. To see that this is so, consider Example 2-10.

Example 2-10

Two investors, X and Y, are considering the same investment, a corporate bond that is selling for $963. The bond has a face, or principal, value of $1,000 and will mature in one year, that is, the principal of $1,000 will be paid in exactly one year. The bond pays 5 percent interest per year on the principal, including the year of maturity. Thus in one year the bond will pay $1,000 principal plus $50 interest for the year to anyone who presents the bond for redemption at that time.

Of the two investors, X has selected a higher time preference rate, 10 percent; Y's rate is only 8 percent. X has decided not to buy the bond based on present value calculations, whereas Y has decided to buy—also based on present value calculations. At his 10 percent time preference rate, X values each dollar to be received in one year as if it were $.909 in present cash, that is, .909 is $PV_{(1,0.10)}$, according to Table 2-1. Hence the present value of $1,050 to be received in one year is $954.45 to X ($1,050 × 0.909), somewhat less than the $963 price of the bond. For Y, with a time preference rate of 8 percent, the present value of one dollar to be received in one year is $.926. The present value of $1,050 in one year to Y is therefore $972.30 ($1,050 × 0.926), or somewhat more than the $963 selling price of the bond. Thus Y finds the bond an attractive opportunity; X does not.

Although it is a special case, the example highlights a phenomenon that holds in general. It is always true that an individual who places a higher time preference rate on money will assign a lower present value to a given number of dollars promised in the future than will an individual with a lower time preference rate. The present value formula supports this reasoning:

$$PV_{(n,r)} = \frac{1}{(1.0 + r)^n}$$

Since r, the time preference rate of the individual, appears in the denominator of the formula, we know that the greater r is, the less will be the present value of each dollar promised in any future period. This makes sense, of course, since an individual who has a high time preference rate expresses a stronger immediate demand for money, either because of the urgency with which he wants to consume or the attractiveness of his alternate investment opportunities. Naturally, such a person will be less patient about waiting for a given amount of money and will therefore value future money less.

Present Value and the Hicksian Concept of Income

A well-known economist, J.R. Hicks, proposed a concept that he called *income*, which is, by definition, tied to the concept of wealth. Income in the Hicksian sense is of obvious interest to all wealth holders and wealth seekers—as will be apparent from the following definition:

> **Income (Hicksian).** In the Hicksian sense, income is the maximum amount of wealth that can be disposed of by an economic unit during a period of time without reducing its remaining wealth below the level of wealth held at the beginning of the period.

Hicksian income, in the abstract, is the total increase in wealth that is experienced by the economic unit during a period of time. It is therefore a measure of accomplishment, and, as implied in the definition, it is also the maximum amount that an individual would want to consume or a business to expend if it were interested in preserving its original wealth position. For this reason we refer to Hicksian income as *disposable wealth,* a more descriptive term and one that will not be confused with other economic and accounting uses of the term *income*.

Perhaps the definitional properties of Hicksian income are intuitively obvious. What is less obvious is the dependence of any assessment of Hicksian-type income on the prior assessment of wealth at the beginning and at the end of a period of time. Although an individual can perhaps "sense" how much his wealth position has increased or decreased over a period of time, a business cannot "feel" its wealth. And even an individual may find that he is better able to decide how much he can spend on consumption and reinvestment if he periodically measures his wealth and income in terms of dollars and cents.

Calculating Income Based on Present Values. In later chapters of this book we return from time to time to the dual concepts of wealth and Hicksian income (disposable wealth) to see how they may be represented using alternate valuation or assessment techniques. For now, since we have already established that the present value technique may be used to assess wealth in terms of money, we illustrate the calculation of income by using present values as the means of measuring wealth.

Example 2-11

> For convenience we again refer to the individual with a time preference rate of 10 percent and the choice between investments A and B. Assume that he has already paid $100 in exchange for investment A. His wealth at this point in time (the beginning of the first year of investment A) is $120.41—the present value of investment A as recalculated in Exhibit 2-5.
>
> Now suppose that the first year goes by and we are interested in measuring the individual's wealth at the end of the first year and his income during the year. Let us assume for simplicity that he continued to hold investment A and realized, as expected, the first annual cash flow of $40. His wealth items would then consist of $40 cash plus investment A with four years' cash flows remaining. His end-of-year-one wealth can be assessed using present values, as shown in Exhibit 2-6.

Notice that each cash flow promised by investment A is worth more at the end of year one than at the beginning. The reason is that each promised cash flow is one year closer to receipt. The first promised cash flow of $40, which one year ago had a then-present value of 0.909 per dollar, or $36.36, is now actually in hand, so it has a present value of a dollar-for-a-dollar (or $40). The

Exhibit 2-5

WEALTH POSITION—BEGINNING-OF-YEAR-ONE VALUATION

Cash flows promised:		Beginning of year one:	
At the end of year	Amount	$PV_{(n, 0.10)}$	Present Value of Cash Flows
1	$40	.909	$ 36.36
2	35	.826	28.91
3	30	.751	22.53
4	25	.683	17.08
5	25	.621	15.53
Total present value			$120.41

Exhibit 2-6

WEALTH POSITION—END-OF-YEAR-ONE VALUATION

Cash flows promised:		End of year one:	
At the end of year	Amount	$PV_{(n, 0.10)}$	Present Value of Cash Flows
1	$40	1.00	$ 40.00
2	35	.909	31.82
3	30	.826	24.78
4	25	.751	18.78
5	25	.683	17.08
Total present value			$132.46

$35 promised for the end of year two is now only one year away and so is worth 0.909 end-of-year-one cash equivalent per dollar promised (as opposed to 0.826 per dollar one year ago). Similarly, the $30 year-three cash flow has a present value as of the end of year one of 0.826 per dollar—and so forth through the fifth year's cash flow.

So, as can be seen from the total of the last column of Exhibit 2-6, the wealth of the individual at the end of year one is $132.46. Since there was no disposal of any wealth during the period, calculating income is a relatively simple matter. The difference between end-of-year-one wealth ($132.46) and beginning-of-year-one wealth (120.41) is the amount that he *could* dispose of immediately and still be as wealthy at the end of the year as at the beginning. His income, therefore, is $132.46 - $120.41 = $12.05. (Note that if for purposes of determining income we wished to include in the year the instant in which the investor purchased A, his income would be $20.41 greater, i.e., it would include the gain experienced from purchasing A. Income in that case would be the difference between the end-of-year present value of $132.46 and the prepurchase beginning-of-year value of $100.)

Time Preference and Other Determinants of Income. Not surprisingly, the investor's income (excluding the initial gain) is approximately 10 percent of his beginning wealth (but for rounding error it would be exact). This is a direct reflection of his time preference for money! After all, the only thing that has happened in the one year is that he is one year closer to all the cash flows embodied in investment A and therefore values them all at 110 percent of their values at the time of decision. But we have assumed that (1) the individual's time preference rate did not change during the year, and (2) all future cash flows will occur as expected.

Of course, in a real-world situation, neither of these assumptions necessarily holds. By the end of the first year of investment A, any one of several unexpected changes might take place. None of the changes will alter beginning-of-year value, because as soon as the new period starts, that value becomes a matter of history. But by altering end-of-period value, the changes we are concerned about also alter the measured income for the period. Three types of possible changes stand out:

1. The individual's time preference for money could change during the period. If the rate of time preference increased, end-of-period value and, therefore, income would be less than otherwise; if it decreased, end-of-period value and income would be greater. (Note: To affirm the effects of different time preference rates on present value calculations, refer back to the section of this chapter entitled "Sensitivity of Net Present Value to Time Preference Rate.")

2. The actual cash flows of the current period can be more or less than the cash flows expected at the beginning of the period. If the actual cash flows are greater than expected, end-of-period value and income for the period will be greater, and conversely if actual cash flows are less than expected.

3. The individual may revise his expectations of remaining future cash flows as of the end of the year. If his revised estimates are greater than previously, end-of-year value will be greater, and conversely if end-of-year estimates are less than previous estimates.

Each of the three types of changes can take place by itself or in combination with the others.

Uncertainty and Risk Assessment in Investment Decision Making

Uncertainty was defined in Chapter 1 as the condition of not knowing at the time of decision what the exact outcomes of alternative courses of action will be. Under uncertainty, the best the decision maker can do is to choose alternatives that he *expects* will provide him with the greatest satisfaction. After choosing, though, he may be disappointed in that the alternative selected may perform less well than his expectation at the time of decision.

For simplicity, we have ignored the problem imposed on decision making by uncertainty as we have developed the rationale for the net present value criterion. But since uncertainty is a most compelling problem facing any decision maker, we cannot ignore it entirely. Hence we will introduce the related concept of risk and illustrate some means by which the decision maker may compensate for risk within the present value model. *The reader should recognize, however, that we are concerned only with understanding the basic structure of the investment decision problem, including uncertainty, and some of its implications.* Once again we proceed via an example.

To keep things manageable, we will simplify matters. First, we assume that the individual is only interested in investing in one investment at a time. Second, we concern ourselves only with opportunities to invest for one period at a time, meaning that we only have to work with a single initial outlay and a single actual inflow at the end of one period for each alternative.

Example 2-12

An individual wishes to invest as much as $1,000 in a single investment opportunity for one year. His time preference rate for any *certain* cash flow is 8 percent. An opportunity, C, is available, but it does not promise a certain return at the end of a year. Instead, there are several possible returns associated with it, each having some probability of occurring. Investment C can therefore be represented by a table of possible returns like that shown in Exhibit 2-7.

Exhibit 2-7
INVESTMENT C

Possible Cash Flows	*Probability of Cash Flows*
$1,250	.25
1,000	.50
750	.25

The probabilities in Exhibit 2-7 indicate that if an individual were to choose investment C time after time for a virtually unlimited number of turns, he would receive $1,000 at the end of a year about 50 percent of the time, $1,250 about 25 percent of the time, and $750 about 25 percent of the time.

Expected Cash Flows. Clearly, uncertain investments like C, which offer more than one possible cash flow at the end of a period, are more of a challenge to evaluate than those offering a single certain return. One way of dealing with the extra complexity is to use a single number as "representative" of all of the several possible cash flows from such an investment. Then one can arrive at present values for uncertain investments in the same way as for certain investments by using the "representative" cash flow for each period for each investment. A single number that might be used for this purpose is the mathematical expectation from the investment, or, simply, the *expected* cash flow.

Expected Cash Flow. The expected cash flow for a period from an investment is the sum of the products of (*a*) each possible cash flow, times (*b*) its probability of occurring.

In other words, the expected cash flow is the amount that an individual would receive *on the average* at the end of a year from a particular investment if he entered into that investment over and over again.

Example 2-13

Drawing on the possible cash flows and their probabilities from Exhibit 2-7 for investment C, we can calculate its expected cash flow, designated $E[C]$:

$$E[C] = .25(\$1,250) + .50(\$1,000) + .25(\$750) = \$1,000$$

Risk Associated with Uncertain Investments. Now that we have arrived at a "representative" cash flow for investment C, the question is, How can the individual value that amount in terms of present value methodology? Should he apply his 8 percent time preference rate for certain cash flows to the expected cash flow from an uncertain investment? The answer is no. Most individuals would not consider the expectation of $1,000 equivalent to the certainty of $1,000. A *risk* is associated with the $1,000 expected cash flow of uncertain investment C.

Risk. With respect to investments, risk is the potential that less-than-expected cash flows will result from a particular investment.

Since, for any given investment in C, there is a 25 percent chance that the cash flow will be $250 less than $1,000, C is a risky investment. Most (but not all) people are *risk averse,* meaning that they would respond to this risk negatively. They would consider C to be less attractive than $1,000 certain—even though there is an equal probability that C will yield $250 in cash flows greater than expected. The reason is that most individuals consider a dollar loss or penalty to be more undesirable than an equally probable dollar of bonus is desirable. Furthermore, the greater the probability of less-than-expected cash flows and/or the more they depart from expectations, the more negatively the individual will react, other things equal.

Assessing Risk with Present Values—One Approach. Although we would not want to apply the time preference rate for certain cash flows to the expected cash flows from a risky investment for the reasons given above, there are some simple and logical alternatives. One is called the *certainty equivalent approach.*

The certainty equivalent approach requires that the investor play a mental game. He must suppose that he is just about to receive the cash flow from a risky investment at the end of some future period but does not know precisely how much it will be. Then he must pose the question, If someone offered to pay me a *sum certain* in exchange for the rights to the cash flow, how much would it take to make me indifferent between the sum certain and impending, but uncertain, cash flow? The answer is called the *certainty equivalent* of the uncertain cash flow.

The certainty equivalent is an alternate "representative" number for the uncertain cash flow. It is likely to be less than the *expected* cash flow for risky investments for reasons already stated—namely, that the individual responds negatively to the risk associated with the expected cash flow.

Unlike the problem encountered with the determination of the present value of the *expected* cash flow, *the individual can apply his time preference rate for certain cash flows to the certainty equivalent* of an uncertain cash flow to get its present value.

Example 2-14

The individual considering investment C *might decide* (based on his own risk preferences) that even though it has an expected cash flow of $1,000, the risk associated with the possible payoff of $750 more than offsets the good feeling he associates with the possible payoff of $1,250. Thus *he considers* an investment in C to be equivalent to an investment in a sum certain of, say, only $950. To get the present value of investment C, the individual finds the present value of $950 to be received at the end of one year at 8 percent, his time preference rate for certain cash flows.

Risk and Present Value—Summary. Although there are other methods of incorporating risk assessments into calculations of present values for risky investments, the foregoing illustration covers the essentials and suffices for the present purpose. Regardless of which of several recognized methods is used, the same two conclusions about the risk and the present value of uncertain cash flows (risky investments) can be drawn:

1. Risky investments will always have less net present value to the risk-averse individual than an investment in certain cash flows equal to the expected cash flows from the risky investment.

2. If any two risky investments have the same expected cash flows, the risk-averse investor will assign a lesser present value to the more risky investment.

It is important to bear in mind that to arrive at present values of risky investments in the way described above, the individual must consider how he personally feels about the risk associated with the expected cash flows promised by the risky investments. But, having made such an assessment, he can arrive at a single present value of the future cash flows from a risky investment that can be compared with the certain present outlays (using certainty equivalents or some other technique). Thus, although we developed the net present value model under the simplifying assumption of certainty, it can accommodate the problem of uncertainty inherent in most investment decisions.

APPENDIX A

Table 2-1

PRESENT VALUE OF ONE DOLLAR

n/r =	.01	.02	.03	.04	.05	.06	.07	.08	.09	.10	.12	.14	.15	.16	.18	.20
1	.990	.980	.971	.962	.952	.943	.935	.926	.917	.909	.893	.877	.870	.862	.847	.833
2	.980	.961	.943	.925	.907	.890	.873	.857	.842	.826	.797	.769	.756	.743	.718	.694
3	.971	.942	.915	.889	.864	.840	.816	.794	.772	.751	.712	.675	.658	.641	.609	.579
4	.961	.924	.888	.855	.823	.792	.763	.735	.708	.683	.636	.592	.572	.552	.516	.482
5	.951	.906	.863	.822	.784	.747	.713	.681	.650	.621	.567	.519	.497	.476	.437	.402
6	.942	.888	.837	.790	.746	.705	.666	.630	.596	.564	.507	.456	.432	.410	.370	.335
7	.933	.871	.813	.760	.711	.665	.623	.583	.547	.513	.452	.400	.376	.354	.314	.279
8	.923	.853	.789	.731	.677	.627	.582	.540	.502	.467	.404	.351	.327	.305	.266	.233
9	.914	.837	.766	.703	.645	.592	.544	.500	.460	.424	.361	.308	.284	.263	.225	.194
10	.905	.820	.744	.676	.614	.558	.508	.463	.422	.386	.322	.270	.247	.227	.191	.162
11	.896	.804	.722	.650	.585	.527	.475	.429	.388	.350	.287	.237	.215	.195	.162	.135
12	.887	.788	.701	.625	.557	.497	.444	.397	.356	.319	.257	.208	.187	.168	.137	.112
13	.879	.773	.681	.601	.530	.469	.415	.368	.326	.290	.229	.182	.163	.145	.116	.093
14	.870	.758	.661	.577	.505	.442	.388	.340	.299	.263	.205	.160	.141	.125	.099	.078
15	.861	.743	.642	.555	.481	.417	.362	.315	.275	.239	.183	.140	.123	.108	.084	.065
16	.853	.728	.623	.534	.458	.394	.339	.292	.252	.218	.163	.123	.107	.093	.071	.054
17	.844	.714	.605	.513	.436	.371	.317	.270	.231	.198	.146	.108	.093	.080	.060	.045
18	.836	.700	.587	.494	.416	.350	.296	.250	.212	.180	.130	.095	.081	.069	.051	.038
19	.828	.686	.570	.475	.396	.331	.277	.232	.194	.164	.116	.083	.070	.060	.043	.031
20	.820	.673	.554	.456	.377	.312	.258	.215	.178	.149	.104	.073	.061	.051	.037	.026
21	.811	.660	.538	.439	.359	.294	.242	.199	.164	.135	.093	.064	.053	.044	.031	.022
22	.803	.647	.522	.422	.342	.278	.226	.184	.150	.123	.083	.056	.046	.038	.026	.018
23	.795	.634	.507	.406	.326	.262	.211	.170	.138	.112	.074	.049	.040	.033	.022	.015
24	.788	.622	.492	.390	.310	.247	.197	.158	.126	.102	.066	.043	.035	.028	.019	.013
25	.780	.610	.478	.375	.295	.233	.184	.146	.116	.092	.059	.038	.030	.024	.016	.010
26	.772	.598	.464	.361	.281	.220	.172	.135	.106	.084	.053	.033	.026	.021	.014	.009
27	.764	.586	.450	.347	.268	.207	.161	.125	.098	.076	.047	.029	.023	.018	.011	.007
28	.757	.574	.437	.333	.255	.196	.150	.116	.090	.069	.042	.026	.020	.016	.010	.006
29	.749	.563	.424	.321	.243	.185	.141	.107	.082	.063	.037	.022	.017	.014	.008	.005
30	.742	.552	.412	.308	.231	.174	.131	.099	.075	.057	.033	.020	.015	.012	.007	.004

Table 2-2
FUTURE VALUE OF ONE DOLLAR

n/r =	.01	.02	.03	.04	.05	.06	.07	.08	.09	.10	.12	.14	.15	.16	.18	.20
1	1.01	1.02	1.03	1.04	1.05	1.06	1.07	1.08	1.09	1.10	1.12	1.14	1.15	1.16	1.18	1.20
2	1.02	1.04	1.06	1.08	1.10	1.12	1.14	1.17	1.19	1.21	1.25	1.30	1.32	1.35	1.39	1.44
3	1.03	1.06	1.09	1.12	1.16	1.19	1.23	1.26	1.30	1.33	1.40	1.48	1.52	1.56	1.64	1.73
4	1.04	1.08	1.13	1.17	1.22	1.26	1.31	1.36	1.41	1.46	1.57	1.69	1.75	1.81	1.94	2.07
5	1.05	1.10	1.16	1.22	1.28	1.34	1.40	1.47	1.54	1.61	1.76	1.93	2.01	2.10	2.29	2.49
6	1.06	1.13	1.19	1.27	1.34	1.42	1.50	1.59	1.68	1.77	1.97	2.19	2.31	2.44	2.70	2.99
7	1.07	1.15	1.23	1.32	1.41	1.50	1.61	1.71	1.83	1.95	2.21	2.50	2.66	2.83	3.19	3.58
8	1.08	1.17	1.27	1.37	1.48	1.59	1.72	1.85	1.99	2.14	2.48	2.85	3.06	3.28	3.76	4.30
9	1.09	1.20	1.30	1.42	1.55	1.69	1.84	2.00	2.17	2.36	2.77	3.25	3.52	3.80	4.44	5.16
10	1.10	1.22	1.34	1.48	1.63	1.79	1.97	2.16	2.37	2.59	3.11	3.71	4.05	4.41	5.23	6.19
11	1.12	1.24	1.38	1.54	1.71	1.90	2.10	2.33	2.58	2.85	3.48	4.23	4.65	5.12	6.18	7.43
12	1.13	1.27	1.43	1.60	1.80	2.01	2.25	2.52	2.81	3.14	3.90	4.82	5.35	5.94	7.29	8.92
13	1.14	1.29	1.47	1.67	1.89	2.13	2.41	2.73	3.07	3.45	4.36	5.49	6.15	6.89	8.60	10.70
14	1.15	1.32	1.51	1.73	1.98	2.26	2.58	2.94	3.34	3.80	4.89	6.26	7.08	7.99	10.15	12.84
15	1.16	1.35	1.56	1.80	2.08	2.40	2.76	3.17	3.64	4.18	5.47	7.14	8.14	9.27	11.97	15.41
16	1.17	1.37	1.60	1.87	2.18	2.54	2.95	3.43	3.97	4.59	6.13	8.14	9.36	10.75	14.13	18.49
17	1.18	1.40	1.65	1.95	2.29	2.69	3.16	3.70	4.33	5.05	6.87	9.28	10.76	12.47	16.67	22.19
18	1.20	1.43	1.70	2.03	2.41	2.85	3.38	4.00	4.72	5.56	7.69	10.58	12.38	14.46	19.67	26.62
19	1.21	1.46	1.75	2.11	2.53	3.03	3.62	4.32	5.14	6.12	8.61	12.06	14.23	16.78	23.21	31.95
20	1.22	1.49	1.81	2.19	2.65	3.21	3.87	4.66	5.60	6.73	9.65	13.74	16.37	19.46	27.39	38.34
21	1.23	1.52	1.86	2.28	2.79	3.40	4.14	5.03	6.11	7.40	10.80	15.67	18.82	22.57	32.32	46.01
22	1.24	1.55	1.92	2.37	2.93	3.60	4.43	5.44	6.66	8.14	12.10	17.86	21.64	26.19	38.14	55.21
23	1.25	1.58	1.97	2.46	3.07	3.82	4.74	5.87	7.26	8.95	13.55	20.36	24.89	30.38	45.01	66.25
24	1.27	1.61	2.03	2.56	3.23	4.05	5.07	6.34	7.91	9.65	15.18	23.21	28.63	35.24	53.11	79.50
25	1.28	1.64	2.09	2.67	3.39	4.29	5.43	6.85	8.62	10.83	17.00	26.46	32.92	40.87	62.67	95.40
26	1.30	1.67	2.16	2.77	3.56	4.55	5.81	7.40	9.40	11.92	19.04	30.17	37.86	47.41	73.95	114.48
27	1.31	1.71	2.22	2.88	3.73	4.82	6.21	7.99	10.25	13.11	21.32	34.39	43.54	55.00	87.26	137.37
28	1.32	1.74	2.29	3.00	3.92	5.11	6.65	8.63	11.17	14.42	23.88	39.20	50.07	63.80	102.97	164.84
29	1.33	1.78	2.36	3.12	4.12	5.42	7.11	9.32	12.17	15.86	26.75	44.69	57.58	74.01	121.50	197.81
30	1.35	1.81	2.43	3.24	4.32	5.74	7.61	10.06	13.27	17.45	29.96	50.95	66.21	85.85	143.37	237.38

APPENDIX B: PRESENT VALUE OF AN ANNUITY

Situations are frequently encountered in which it is desirable to determine the present value of a series of identical periodic future cash flows. Such series, called annuities, can be valued in a straightforward fashion in the sense that the present values of each of the individual flows can be determined as described in the body of this chapter. Then the present value of the series can be determined by summing the present values of the individual flows. However, because an annuity consists of a stream of identical flows, a certain arithmetic convenience can be achieved in determining its present value.

Example 2-15

Suppose we wish to determine the present value of $1,000 to be received (or paid) at the end of each year for three years and that the appropriate time preference rate is 10 percent. The straightforward calculation is as follows:

Year	Cash Flow	$PV_{(n,0.10)}$	Present Values
1	$1,000	.909	$ 909
2	1,000	.826	826
3	1,000	.751	751
		2.486	$2,486

The present value of the annuity of $1,000 for three years at 10 percent is the sum of the present values of each of the $1,000 installments at 10 percent. That is, the present value of the annuity is the sum of the individual products of (1) the present value factor for a given year in the annuity and (2) the constant cash flow. Since the multiplier (annual cash-flow amount) remains con-constant, we can algebraically sum the present value factors and then perform a single multiplication upon such sum. The result is the same:

$$\$1,000 \times (.909 + .826 + .751) = \$1,000 \times 2.486$$
$$= \$2,486$$

Furthermore, since the sum of the present value factors will be the same for any annuity involving a given number of years and a given time preference rate, annuity factor values are precalculated and made available in tables such as Table 2-3 in this Appendix. Notice, for instance, that in Table 2-3 the value of $1 to be received at the end of each of three years at 10 percent (i.e., $n = 3$, $r = 0.10$), is 2.49, approximately what we calculated in the above example (but taken to only two-decimal accuracy).

Table 2-3

PRESENT VALUE OF AN ANNUITY OF ONE DOLLAR

n/r =	.01	.02	.03	.04	.05	.06	.07	.08	.09	.10	.12	.14	.15	.16	.18	.20
1	.99	.98	.97	.96	.95	.94	.93	.93	.92	.91	.89	.88	.87	.86	.85	.83
2	1.97	1.94	1.91	1.89	1.86	1.83	1.81	1.78	1.76	1.74	1.69	1.65	1.63	1.61	1.57	1.53
3	2.94	2.88	2.83	2.78	2.72	2.67	2.62	2.58	2.53	2.49	2.40	2.32	2.28	2.25	2.17	2.11
4	3.90	3.81	3.72	3.63	3.55	3.47	3.39	3.31	3.24	3.17	3.04	2.91	2.85	2.80	2.69	2.59
5	4.85	4.71	4.58	4.45	4.33	4.21	4.10	3.99	3.89	3.79	3.60	3.43	3.35	3.27	3.13	2.99
6	5.80	5.60	5.42	5.24	5.08	4.92	4.77	4.62	4.49	4.36	4.11	3.89	3.78	3.68	3.50	3.33
7	6.73	6.47	6.23	6.00	5.79	5.58	5.39	5.21	5.03	4.87	4.56	4.29	4.16	4.04	3.81	3.60
8	7.65	7.33	7.02	6.73	6.46	6.21	5.97	5.75	5.53	5.33	4.97	4.64	4.49	4.34	4.08	3.84
9	8.57	8.16	7.79	7.44	7.11	6.80	6.52	6.25	6.00	5.76	5.33	4.95	4.77	4.61	4.30	4.03
10	9.47	8.98	8.43	8.11	7.72	7.36	7.02	6.71	6.42	6.14	5.65	5.22	5.02	4.83	4.49	4.19
11	10.37	9.79	9.25	8.76	8.31	7.89	7.50	7.14	6.81	6.50	5.94	5.45	5.23	5.03	4.66	4.33
12	11.26	10.58	9.95	9.39	8.86	8.38	7.94	7.54	7.16	6.81	6.19	5.66	5.42	5.20	4.79	4.44
13	12.13	11.35	10.63	9.99	9.39	8.85	8.36	7.90	7.49	7.10	6.42	5.84	5.58	5.34	4.91	4.53
14	13.00	12.11	11.30	10.56	9.90	9.29	8.75	8.24	7.79	7.37	6.63	6.00	5.72	5.47	5.01	4.61
15	13.87	12.85	11.94	11.12	10.38	9.71	9.11	8.56	8.06	7.61	6.81	6.14	5.85	5.58	5.09	4.68
16	14.72	13.58	12.56	11.65	10.84	10.11	9.45	8.85	8.31	7.82	6.97	6.27	5.95	5.67	5.16	4.73
17	15.56	14.29	13.17	12.17	11.27	10.48	9.76	9.12	8.54	8.02	7.12	6.37	6.05	5.75	5.22	4.77
18	16.40	14.99	13.75	12.66	11.69	10.83	10.06	9.37	8.76	8.20	7.25	6.47	6.13	5.82	5.27	4.81
19	17.23	15.68	14.32	13.13	12.09	11.16	10.34	9.60	8.95	8.36	7.37	6.55	6.20	5.88	5.32	4.84
20	18.05	16.35	14.88	13.59	12.45	11.47	10.59	9.82	9.13	8.51	7.47	6.62	6.26	5.93	5.35	4.87
21	18.86	17.01	15.42	14.03	12.82	11.76	10.84	10.02	9.29	8.65	7.56	6.69	6.31	5.97	5.38	4.89
22	19.66	17.66	15.94	14.45	13.16	12.04	11.06	10.20	9.44	8.77	7.64	6.74	6.36	6.01	5.41	4.91
23	20.46	18.29	16.44	14.86	13.49	12.30	11.27	10.37	9.58	8.88	7.72	6.79	6.40	6.04	5.43	4.92
24	21.24	18.91	16.94	15.25	13.80	12.55	11.47	10.53	9.71	8.98	7.78	6.84	6.43	6.07	5.45	4.94
25	22.02	19.52	17.41	15.62	14.09	12.78	11.65	10.67	9.82	9.08	7.84	6.87	6.46	6.10	5.47	4.95
26	22.80	20.12	17.88	15.98	14.38	13.00	11.83	10.81	9.93	9.16	7.90	6.91	6.49	6.12	5.48	4.96
27	23.56	20.71	18.33	16.33	14.64	13.21	11.99	10.94	10.03	9.24	7.94	6.94	6.51	6.14	5.49	4.96
28	24.32	21.28	18.76	16.66	14.90	13.41	12.14	11.05	10.12	9.31	7.98	6.96	6.53	6.15	5.50	4.97
29	25.07	21.84	19.19	16.98	15.14	13.59	12.28	11.16	10.20	9.37	8.02	6.98	6.55	6.17	5.51	4.97
30	25.81	22.40	19.60	17.29	15.37	13.76	12.41	11.26	10.27	9.43	8.06	7.00	6.57	6.18	5.52	4.98

Questions for Review and Discussion

2-1. Define the following terms:
a. Investment decision
b. Well-being
c. Wealth
d. Time preference rate
e. Opportunity rate
f. Compound interest
g. Future value
h. Present value
i. Net present value
j. Expected cash flow
k. Risk

2-2. How does the concept of wealth relate to the concept of well-being?

2-3. What justification is there (if any) for the assumption that investment alternatives offer strictly cash inflows and outflows as opposed to flows of wealth in other forms?

2-4. In developing the net present value model, the chapter ignores constraints on decision makers (such as limited budgets). What justification is there for ignoring such constraints, which are often present in real-world investment decisions?

2-5. Most individuals seem to exhibit a time preference for money. Give the reasons that presumably explain such a preference.

2-6. An individual's time preference for money may be expressed as a rate. Explain.

2-7. What relationship (if any) exists between an individual's time preference rate and opportunity rate?

2-8. Explain in words the economic significance to an individual of the following:
a. The present value of an amount of money to be received at a future date
b. The present value of an obligation to pay an amount in the future
c. The future value of an amount invested or consumed today

2-9. The *net* present value of an investment opportunity is the cash equivalent of the gain (loss) experienced by the investor in undertaking the opportunity. True or false? Explain.

2-10. List the five steps required to apply the net present value model.

2-11. Explain in words why investment decisions based on the net present values of alternatives may be different if different time preference rates are used.

2-12. Explain in words why income (disposable wealth) under the present value model is equal to beginning-of-period value times the time preference rate assuming everything works out as expected.

2-13. Most (but not all) people appear to be risk averse. What does this mean?

2-14. Given a future cash flow and an individual's time preference rate, what is meant by the statement that the individual is indifferent between the present value of the future cash flow and the future cash flow itself?

2-15. What must be specified before one can determine the net present value of an investment opportunity?

2-16. What is the effect on the first year's expected income if at the end of the first year of an investment—
   a. the individual's time preference rate has increased?
   b. the actual cash flows of the current period are greater than the cash flows expected at the beginning of the period?
   c. remaining future cash flows are expected to be less than previously expected?

2-17. Present value (and therefore *net* present value) is an example of a common scale of merit. Do you agree or disagree? Explain your answer.

2-18. As an investor you are faced with an opportunity that provides an expected cash flow of $25,000 at the end of each of the next three years. You are concerned with the risk associated with these uncertain cash flows and consider these uncertain cash flows to be the equivalent of a certain cash flow of $20,000. The time preference rate you consider satisfactory for certain cash flows is 8 percent.

While you are considering your investment decision, another investor offers to purchase the investment opportunity at a much higher price than you would be willing to pay. Why should this other investor be willing to pay more for the investment than you would be willing to pay?

Exercises

2-1. **Future Values of Amounts Invested.** Determine the following future values utilizing an opportunity rate of 8 percent:
   1. The future value of $5,000 to be invested now for a period of five years
   2. The future value at the end of three years of an investment of $4,000 now and $4,000 one year from now
   3. The future value at the end of eight years of an investment of $6,000 at the end of each of the first four years and a withdrawal of $5,000 per year at the end of years five through seven.

2-2. **Present Values of Future Cash Flows.** Compute the present value of each of the following cash flows utilizing an opportunity rate of 12 percent:
   1. $1,000 cash outflow immediately
   2. $2,000 cash inflow one year from now
   3. $2,000 cash inflow two years from now
   4. $1,000 cash outflow three years from now
   5. $3,000 cash inflow three years from now
   6. $2,000 cash inflow four years from now

2-3. **Net Present Value.** Calculate the net present value of the total cash flows in problem 2-2 utilizing an opportunity rate of 12 percent.

2-4. **Net Present Value of an Opportunity.** Determine the net present value of a business opportunity that costs $1,000 initially and generates cash inflows of $2,000, $2,000, $3,000, and $1,000 at the end of years one through four, respectively. An additional outlay of $1,000 for maintenance will be necessary at the end of year three. The salvage value of the opportunity at the end of year four also equals $1,000. The appropriate discount rate is 12 percent.

2-5. Investment Opportunity Evaluation. You have an opportunity to make the following three investments:
   a. You can buy a piece of property for $4,000 today. At the end of four years you can sell the property for $6,000.
   b. You can buy a copying machine for $3,500 today which will generate a cash inflow of $1,500 for each of the next four years.
   c. You can invest in a business that will require investments of $2,000 now and $2,000 at the end of the first year. You will receive $5,500 from the business at the end of the fourth year.

Required:

1. Calculate the net present value of each of the three investment opportunities—using a time preference rate of 8 percent.
2. What is the income for the first year for each of the three opportunities?

2-6. Future Value of a Replacement Fund Program. The William Corporation is currently using equipment that will become obsolete in five years. To provide the necessary funds for replacement of the equipment, the company plans to invest $40,000 in U.S. securities now, $50,000 at the end of each of the next two years, and $60,000 at the end of each of the two years after that. If these securities will pay an after-tax rate of return of 4 percent, compounded annually, what amount will be available at the end of the fifth year?

2-7. Future Adequacy of a Saving Fund Program. Mr. E.K. Roarke wishes to provide for the college education of his six children. He estimates that each child will require $6,000 for each of the four years of college payable at the beginning of the school year.

The triplets are fifteen years old and will start college in exactly three years. The twins are fourteen and will start college in four years. The youngest child is seven years old and will start college in eleven years.

If Mr. Roarke deposits $100,000 in a savings account that pays an annual interest rate of 6 percent, will he have provided for the college educations? What is the exact amount Mr. Roarke should deposit now to provide for the college educations?

2-8. Sensitivity of a Decision to Time Preference Rate. The Hobard Cattle Company needs grazing land for its cattle operation. It can either purchase the land outright for $160,000 or lease it for $10,000 per year on a fifteen-year lease. The rental fee is payable at the beginning of each year. In either case, the company must pay all taxes and maintenance costs. The land will be needed for fifteen years, at which time it would be salable for $200,000. If the company required a before-tax rate of return of 8 percent for this type investment, which alternative should it choose? If it requires 6 percent?

2-9. Present Value of an Investment in Common Stock. Mr. Ronald Downs wishes to invest $10,000 for a five-year period. He is considering the purchase of Buford Company common stock, which currently pays an annual cash dividend of $2. Mr. Downs expects that this dividend will be paid each year for the next five years and that the stock at the end of the five-year period will be selling for approximately $30. If investments of comparable risk yield a before-tax rate of return of 10 percent, what is the maximum amount Mr. Downs should be willing to pay for a share of stock?

If the stock is currently selling for $25 per share, should Mr. Downs be willing to purchase it?

2-10. Present Value of an Investment in a Promissory Note. A promissory note is offered for sale on which the yearly payments are $45. There are ten payments still due, with the first one due one year from now. The principal amount, $1,000, is to be repaid at the end of the tenth year. What is the maximum amount an investor would pay for this note if he wished to earn at least 8 percent on this type investment? If he wished to earn 10 percent?

2-11. Present Value of a Taxicab Business. You have an opportunity to invest in a taxicab business. The business owns one cab and has made the following estimates of future cash flows. Assume that these cash flows take place at the end of the year and that you consider them to be realistic.

- a. Passengers pay $.76 per mile for cab service.
- b. Gas, oil, tires, and other operating expenses are $.20 per mile.
- c. The driver is paid $.16 per mile plus tips.
- d. The present owner expects that the cab will carry passengers a total of 50,000 miles per year for the life of the automobile, which is three years. After three years the car will be worthless.
- e. You have decided to invest if you can earn a before-tax rate of 10 percent on your investment.

Required:

What is the maximum amount you would pay to acquire the business? What is the amount of net income (disposable wealth) you expect to earn for the first year's operations? Explain.

2-12. Evaluating an Offer for the Taxicab Business. Assume you have purchased the taxicab business described in problem 2-11. At the end of the first year, after you have withdrawn the cash receipts, you are approached by an investor who offers you $36,000 for the business. Should you sell?

2-13. Effects on Income of Changes in Expectations and Preferences. Assume that you have purchased the taxicab business described in problem 2-11. Instead of paying the driver $.16 per passenger mile as originally projected, you had to pay $.20 per mile.

Required:

1. What would the first year's income have been if no change in costs had occurred?
2. What is the first year's income, given the change in cost?
3. What is the first year's income if there is also an increase in your time preference rate from 10 percent to 12 percent?

2-14. Determination of the Implicit Time Preference Rate. Mr. Curtis Driver owns a ferry service which carries workers to and from an offshore drilling rig. The rig will be operational for three years. When it is shut down, Mr. Driver plans to liquidate his business and retire. The contract under which the business operates pays a flat sum of $100,000 every year at the end of the year. Expenses amount to $75,000 per year. Mr. Driver withdraws $25,000 every year and expects to be able to sell his equipment for $30,000 when he retires. At the end of the first year, Mr. Driver is approached by an investor who offers him $68,192 for the business. Should Mr. Driver sell? (*Hint:* At what time preference rate would he be indifferent?)

2-15. Uncertainty Factor in Present Value Calculations. National Steelmakers, Inc., is in the business of manufacturing sheet metal for car bodies. Unfortunately, it is also a heavy polluter of the atmosphere. Consequently, it expects the EPA to force it out of business in four years. Until that time it anticipates that the following cash flows will occur:

End of Year	Cash Inflows	Cash Outflows
1	$280,000	$200,000
2	300,000	250,000
3	320,000	270,000
4	350,000	300,000

Required:

Given a time preference rate of 10 percent
1. Calculate the wealth position of National Steelmakers at the beginning of year two (assume net receipts are withdrawn at the end of each year).
2. Calculate income for year two.
3. You realize that these cash receipts and disbursements figures are just estimates and may differ from actual results. List two ways that you, as an individual owner, could adjust your calculations to account for this uncertainty.

2-16. Net Present Value: Sensitivity to Time Preference Rate. The company you work for, Starr Cutter, is a medium-size tool and die company that is interested in expanding its line of services to its customers. The company has decided to provide one new service that requires the purchase of a new machine. Two brands of the machine needed are available, brand A and brand B.

The machines differ only in the way they affect the "other" costs of providing the new service to customers, that is, they have different break-in periods, rates of physical deterioration, maintenance requirements, and so forth, but they will provide the same output capacity. As a result, the following patterns of cash flows have been estimated for the two machines:

	A	B
Initial price of machine	$20,000	$21,500
Annual net proceeds:		
At the end of year		
1	$10,000	$ 5,000
2	10,000	10,000
3	10,000	10,000
4	5,000	10,000
5	5,000	10,000

You are asked to choose the best machine for the company to buy. Your first impulse is to compute a net present value for each machine, but you have run into a problem. The treasurer of the company thinks the time value of money to the firm is 10 percent (compounded annually), but the president insists it is more like 15 percent.

While they are debating the question, you decide to compute net present values at both interest rates, hoping that maybe one machine will prove better regardless of which rate is used.

Does the same machine prove to be "best" for both interest rates? If not, explain.

2-17. Investment Opportunity Evaluation. You have an opportunity to invest in a joint venture of five years' duration. The venture consists of initially buying a building that a company has constructed for its own use and then leasing it back to the seller. The joint venture requires that any number of partners put up a total of $100,000 at the outset to buy the building. Net cash flows (rent less taxes, insurance, etc.) projected for the venture equal $20,000 per year for each of the five years. At the end of five years the original seller has the right to buy back the building at $55,000. This option is expected to be exercised because the price is less than the expected market value after five years and the building is essential to the original seller's business. All amounts received are to be split and distributed each year according to each partner's contribution to the initial outlay.

You are considering buying a one-fifth share in the venture. Assume that your opportunity rate for investments of equivalent risk is 12 percent.

Required:

1. What is the maximum amount you would be willing to pay for a one-fifth interest in the venture?
2. What is the net present value of the opportunity to buy at $20,000 *and* how does this net present value relate to your assumed investment decision objective of wealth maximization?

2-18. Analysis of Risk. You are confronted with two uncertain one-year investment opportunities, A and B. Their possible payoffs in one year are as follows:

A		B	
Probability	Payoff	Probability	Payoff
.3	$110,000	.3	$105,000
.4	100,000	.4	100,000
.3	90,000	.3	95,000

Required:

1. Would you value A over B, or B over A, or value the payoff of A equal to the payoff of B? Explain.
2. What is a certainty equivalent? Would the average person accept a certainty equivalent of $100,000 for payoff A?

2-19. Risk and Relative Value. An investor has two uncertain one-year investment opportunities, Y and Z. Each calls for an initial outlay now and promises possible payoffs in one year as follows:

Y		Z	
Probability	Payoff	Probability	Payoff
.20	$40,000	.20	$35,000
.60	50,000	.60	50,000
.20	60,000	.20	65,000

1. How would you value Z relative to Y, that is, "greater than," "equal to," or "less than"? Would you expect most people to apply the same relative ranking? Explain the rationale for your ranking.
2. Would your answer to number 1 differ if Z promised the following payoffs in one year? Why or why not?

Z	
Probability	Payoff
.25	$40,000
.50	50,000
.25	60,000

2-20. Present Value Analysis for Social Programs. The primary objective of the Space Shuttle is to reduce the cost of space operations substantially and to provide a capability designed to support a wide range of scientific, defense, and commercial uses. Following are some preliminary estimates of the costs of achieving these objectives (amounts in millions):

	Space Shuttle	Conventional Launch Vehicles
Useful life	20 years	20 years
Development costs	$10,000	$100
Ground facilities	$ 500	$ 20
Annual labor and maintenance costs	$ 100	$500
Annual operating costs (fuel, vehicles, etc.)	$ 200	$500
Risk level	High	Medium

Space Shuttle advocates argue that since the government is simultaneously undertaking many projects, the overall risk of government projects is low.

Required:

1. Which project is the less costly when high-risk projects are evaluated using a 10 percent time preference rate and medium-risk projects are evaluated using a 7 percent time preference rate?
2. Which project is the less costly if the Space Shuttle advocates' argument is accepted, and low-risk projects are evaluated using a 5 percent time preference rate?
3. Which anlysis (1 or 2) do you prefer? Explain why.

2-21. Comprehensive Present Value Exercise. Tri-Cities Tours is a small business that is up for sale. The business is well known in the Tri-Cities area and has enjoyed consistent success. The company operates out of a small rented office. Its only substantial assets are *two* touring buses, each in good working condition. You are interested in buying the business and have been given access to all of its financial records for purposes of determining what you think it is worth. Based on your investigation you have made the following estimates:

    a. *Each* of the buses will be operated for a total of 1.5 million passenger miles per year.
       (1) The average cash fare per passenger mile will be about $.05.
       (2) Fuel, lubricants, and routine service will run about $.01 per passenger mile.
    b. Other yearly costs of operating the business are expected to be:

Rent	$12,000
Wages and salaries	60,000
Bus overhauls	18,000
Insurance	10,000

    c. The buses will no longer be suitable for the touring and charter business after three more years of operations. However, each is expected to bring $10,000 upon sale at that time.

Assume, unless otherwise stated, that the appropriate time preference rate is 10 percent.

Required:

1. What is the maximum amount you would be willing to pay for the company?
2. Suppose the asking price of the owner is *less* than the amount you calculated in number 1. List the factors that could each, independently, account for the difference. (Assume real-world conditions and take into account the direction of the difference between the two amounts.)
3. Assume that you bought the business at the amount you calculated in number 1.
    (a) How much income (disposable wealth) would you *expect* to report in the first year? Explain the source of this income.
    (b) Indicate, for each of the following changes in circumstance during the year, whether the effect on income would be an increase or a decrease relative to your answer to *a*. Explain your reasoning.
        (1) Fuel costs less than expected.
        (2) Your time preference rate increases.
        (3) Your assessment of the risk of the business lessens.
4. Assume that you bought the business and your time preference rate changed from 10 percent to 12 percent immediately after purchase. What would happen to (*a*) the future value of the business and (*b*) the present value of the business? Explain in words why the effects you have indicated would occur.

Conventional Accounting: An Investment Decision Perspective

Business enterprises, as described earlier, are organizational units that employ factors of production in producing specialized products and services for sale. Often a business organization is necessary in order to exploit certain production opportunities efficiently, particularly those that require complex production processes with a highly specialized division of labor, and those that require large-scale physical capital. To serve their purpose, often business enterprises must secure and control large blocks of money capital. Typically, in the case of large corporations, the necessary money capital is supplied by investors who, for the most part, are not directly involved in the operations of the business.

Prospective investors who supply money capital to business enterprises are interested in selecting the best employment for their funds among the many opportunities available. Relevant information about alternative opportunities is presumably valuable to them in making the best choices. Considering the large numbers of business enterprises available as potential investment opportunities, however, the cost of collecting and evaluating relevant information about every alternative is probably prohibitive. Since it is possible for many potential owners and creditors to have an investment interest in any given business, there is a good deal of potential for duplication of effort. But as was pointed out in Chapter 1, such potential duplication of effort is good reason for one group, in this case accountants employed by the enterprise, to provide information about the business for use by the many interested parties. It must also be recalled, though, that to succeed in eliminating wasteful duplication in information gathering and dissemination, there must be identifiable kinds of information that are decision relevant to many of the potential decision makers.

The remainder of this chapter (1) examines more closely the decision situation faced by investors in business enterprises, and (2) introduces some alternate kinds of information about business enterprises that might be decision relevant to present and potential investors.

Investments in Business Enterprises

Prospective owners and creditors who supply capital to a business do so in return for expected future cash returns to themselves. For instance, a creditor (e.g., an owner of a corporate bond) acquires contractual rights to specified future payments of interest and principal amounts. A purchaser of a share of corporate stock, on the other hand, acquires the right to share proportionately with all other shareowners in the residual cash flows generated by the corporation. Therefore the decisions of shareowners and creditors as to which of many enterprises to invest in fit into the context of the net present value model that was introduced in Chapter 2.

In order to choose to invest in a particular business, both the creditor and the owner presumably want to assess the present value of the rights that come from investment and compare that present value with the amount they will have to pay to receive those rights. They can then compare the net present values of investments in various businesses in determining the investment or set of investments they will undertake.

Valuing Investment Opportunities. The nature of the decision to invest in a business, as described above, is simple in principle. In practice, however, it is a formidable challenge. The process of arriving at present values, as described in Chapter 2, begins necessarily with the step of specifying the cash flows expected from an investment in future periods. Of course, other elements, such as selection of the appropriate time preference rate (opportunity rate), are necessary as well. But the valuation of a particular investment opportunity cannot proceed without a projection of the expected stream of future cash flows.

For the prospective owner, the step of projecting or forecasting future cash flows is quite open-ended. For the prospective creditor, the step is simplified somewhat, as the expected cash flows from his investment are usually specified in a contract. On the other hand, in the real world (the world of uncertainty) both the creditor and the owner will want to assess the risk associated with expected future cash flows. The greater the risk associated with a given expected future cash flow, the less it will be valued by either a creditor or an owner, other things equal. (See the discussion in the Chapter 2 section entitled "Uncertainty and Risk Assessment in Investment Decision Making.")

But risk assessment means that in addition to forecasting potential future cash flows, some thought must be given to the likelihood that the forecast flows will (or will not) actually materialize. Thus investors face the task of looking into the future and making some fairly complex predictions or forecasts about the amounts and probabilities of the cash payments the enterprise will be able to make to them in fulfillment of their rights as owners or creditors.

The Business Enterprise as a Net Producer of Cash. To gain more insight into the forecasting or cash prediction problem facing investors, we can suppose that investors view the business enterprise as a generator of net cash flows. The cash-flow generation process in a business is based on a strikingly simple operating sequence which is descriptive (in the abstract) of virtually all business enterprises in a market economy. This operating sequence comprises the following steps:

1. The enterprise usually begins its life with an initial endowment of cash contributed by owners and perhaps creditors, e.g., banks.

2. *The enterprise acquires control or possession of the factors of production* necessary to provide a particular product or service. In exchange, it gives immediate cash payments or promises to pay cash at some future date.

3. *The factors of production are committed* as needed to the process or processes used to generate the enterprise's product or service.

4. Finally, *finished products or services are provided* as demanded by customers, in exchange for cash or promises to pay cash to the enterprise at some future date.

Forecasting Future Cash Flows. One reasonably promising way to attempt to predict future cash flows from a particular business is to approach the operating sequence described above in reverse. First, future prices and quantities demanded are estimated, with some attention given to variations that might occur due to competitive pressure, changing tastes and preferences, and so forth. Expected sales, along with probable payment terms, then lead to estimates of the amounts and timing of cash inflows. The quantities of resources required to satisfy demand are determined, based on knowledge of the ratios of inputs to outputs inherent in the production process. Finally, the prices and payment terms for various resources enter into estimates of probable amounts and timing of cash outflows to support operations. The difference between estimated cash inflows from sales and estimated cash outflows in support of operations is the estimated net cash inflow or outflow of the enterprise for a given future period (assuming no additional capital contributions from owners or dividend payments to them).

Example 3-1

Sports Equipment Sales Corporation (called S.E.S.) was founded a number of years ago to merchandise a variety of sports equipment to retail customers. There are 10,000 shares of S.E.S. stock outstanding at present, owned by approximately five hundred people. The company grew rapidly in its early years, but now management believes, on the basis of market research, that it has reached its limit as far as increased activities are concerned.

For at least the next thirty years, though, it expects to maintain an annual level of cash receipts from sales of $500,000. Costs of merchandise sold at that level of activity are expected to be $400,000 per year. The company has a thirty-year lease on its retail store building calling for annual rental payments of $10,000. Wages, salaries, maintenance, and miscellaneous outlays are expected to be $37,500. The company has just renovated the interior and exterior of the store and purchased new display equipment. But it expects to have to repeat these outlays every ten years until it gives up the lease on the building. This means that major outlays of $50,000 for renovation are expected around the end of years ten and twenty, in addition to all routine outlays connected with merchandising operations in those years. Finally, to raise additional money capital a few years ago, S.E.S. issued fifty corporate bonds with face values of $1,000 each, on which it must pay a total of $2,500 interest annually. The bonds are due to be paid off at the end of thirty years at face value, $50,000.

The cash flows to be generated by S.E.S. Corporation over the next thirty years are shown in Exhibit 3-1.

Some Impediments to Investor Forecasting. Now the forecasting procedure described earlier is straightforward enough. Unfortunately, to follow it is by no means easy or inexpensive. For, as described in Chapter 1, investors in large corporations are essentially "outsiders." That is, they do not take part directly in the operations of the enterprise. But the "outsider" status of investors is not, itself, a problem. As described in Chapter 1, it is actually desirable that large numbers of investors be able to *delegate* the operations of large businesses to a specialized group of insiders known as "management." As a result, however, investors individually and as a group typically do not have ready access to parts of the information, especially about production processes, factor costs, and so forth, that would facilitate the kind of forecasts that they would probably find most useful. *This obviously creates a dilemma.*

The dilemma in question is one of several stimuli that explain the continued presence of financial accounting as a medium through which managements of enterprises provide certain financial information to investors. Before proceeding to the kind of information that currently characterizes financial accounting practice, we first consider briefly some idealized possibilities. Although not in widespread use, these alternative reporting possibilities are receiving growing attention. Furthermore, they provide a ready-made context in which to introduce conventional financial accounting.

Exhibit 3-1

S.E.S. CORPORATION

Thirty-Year Estimated Cash Flows

Years 1 through 30		
Sales receipts		$500,000
Merchandise costs	$400,000	
Rent	10,000	
Salaries, etc.	37,500	
Interest on bonds	2,500	450,000
Net *annual* cash flow		$ 50,000 *per year*
Year 10		
Renovation costs		$50,000
Year 20		
Renovation costs		$50,000
Year 30		
Bond redemption		$50,000

Forecast Information Supplied by Management of the Enterprise

One alternative to consider is that the management of each enterprise should issue public forecasts of future cash flows for everyone's use.

Management Forecasts. Although public issuance of forecasts of future cash flows has been the exception in recent corporate financial reporting, the idea is gaining some support for a number of reasons:

1. Estimates of future cash flows are of direct interest to investors.

2. No one is in a better position than management to assess (*a*) the demand for an enterprise's products, (*b*) the input requirements for its production processes, (*c*) the input and output prices in the industry in which it competes, etc.

3. Only management can fully assess the future implications of *its own internal decisions* regarding the course that the enterprise will follow.

4. For its own internal use, management will have projected future cash flows anyway, so that making them public involves relatively little additional effort.

5. Since internal management forecasts exist, they should be made public (at least in the case of large, publicly held corporations) lest they be "leaked out" to a privileged few who could then exploit them to special advantage.

There are, of course, equally valid reasons why management forecasts of expected future enterprise cash flows should not be published routinely. These reasons include possible loss of competitive market advantages for a company's products and services, possible reduction of management's willingness to assume business risks, and likely institutionalization of forecast economic conditions (because of publicized commitments thereto) even if subsequent events warrant deviations. We return to the topic of problems with cash-flow forecasts by management later on in this section.

Still, management has a tremendous comparative advantage over outsiders in projecting future events and relationships on which forecasts of cash flows can be built.

Valuation of the Enterprise—a Further Refinement. Given that (1) the management of an enterprise has a comparative advantage in projecting future cash flows, and (2) the investors are interested in the value of those cash flows, it has been suggested that the ideal information to be provided to outside investors by management is the present value of the enterprise.

Example 3-2

Based on the projected cash flows in Exhibit 3-1, and assuming that the management of S.E.S. Corporation feels that 10 percent is an appropriate discount rate, the present value of S.E.S. can be calculated as in Exhibit 3-2.

Exhibit 3-2

PRESENT VALUE OF S.E.S. CORPORATION

Years	Cash Flow	$PV_{(n, 0.10)}$	Present Value of Cash Flows
1-30	+$50,000/yr.	9.430*	$471,500
10	− 50,000	.386	− 19,300
20	− 50,000	.149	− 7,450
30	− 50,000	.057	− 2,850
Present value of S.E.S. Corporation			$441,900

*Note that since $50,000 is the annual cash flow expected for every year from year one through year thirty, we have taken the convenient computational shortcut of using the present value factor from Table 2-3 of a thirty-year annuity at 10 percent. See Appendix B to Chapter 2 for an explanation of annuities and the use of Table 2-3.

Perhaps it is intuitively appealing to have management actually provide a ready-made present value of the enterprise (as opposed to only providing cash forecasts), on the grounds that it would be a further savings of effort for investors. Management would, after all, have possibly complex cash forecasts reduced to a single number. On the other hand, if management only provided its valuation of the enterprise to outsiders in place of the underlying forecasts of future cash flows, certain objections come to mind.

One reason for not substituting a present value of the enterprise for forecast future cash flows is that the value of a possible investment interest in the enterprise might not be directly inferred from the value of the enterprise as a whole. For instance, in Example 3-1 it was noted that S.E.S. Corporation has 10,000 outstanding ownership shares. In Example 3-2 the present value of S.E.S. was calculated based on an assumed 10 percent time preference rate. Does that mean that to an investor the value of one ownership share is $44.19, that is, the present value of the enterprise ($441,900) divided by the number of shares outstanding (10,000)? Not necessarily. Except in the special case where all cash inflows in excess of required outflows are paid immediately to owners, there will probably be significant differences in timing between cash flows to the enterprise and cash flows to the investor.

Another reason for not substituting a present value for a set of forecast cash flows is that individual investors may vary as to their assessments of the risk associated with management's forecast cash flows (including possible forecast error or bias). They may also differ in the way that they take this risk into account in placing a value (i.e., individual time preference rate) on the cash flows. To deny them access to the actual forecast cash flows would therefore deny them certain potentially relevant inputs to their individual valuations.

Some Problems with Management Forecasts. In view of the objections raised above, it is not surprising that present-day financial reporting does not consist of public issuance of present values of the many business enterprises in the economy. But given the comparative advantage possessed by management, it is perhaps perplexing that management forecasts of future cash flows are rarely made public. Let us examine the reasons that make the dearth of management forecasts more understandable, particularly from management's point of view.

One key reason, as already noted, is that forecasts would reflect the latest management decisions as to competitive strategy, production method, and so forth. Such disclosure would not only help investors but might inform the "competition" of management's strategies, making their success (and implementation) less likely.

Another reason for the dearth of management forecasts is that the estimates of future cash flows expected to be generated by the business are just that—estimates. Although the accountants working for the business may be best qualified to make such estimates, they may err. Indeed, in an uncertain environment, actual experience may depart from prior expectations by chance alone. Furthermore, the managements of business enterprises have vested interests in investors' decisions. That is, investors decide whether or not to place money capital at the disposal of managers. Therefore there may be a temptation for management to bias estimated future cash flows in order to influence investor decisions.

One can visualize, then, what the results would be if many investors relied upon the accountants' expert opinions, in the form of forecasts of future cash flows disclosed by managements of various enterprises, only to be disappointed by later experience. It would be difficult to separate those cases in which the accountants had erred or were purposely biased and those in which uncontrollable events intervened. It is for this reason probably more than any other that in today's environment business enterprises have not provided forecasts of future cash flows for use by present and prospective investors.

The Outlook for Management Forecasts. At this writing, the role of management forecasts in the financial reporting practices of large, publicly held corporations is in a state of potential change. It is widely acknowledged that such forecasts have certain advantages for present and prospective investors but that they also have disadvantages for present owners and management. To date the decision to issue forecasts has been at the discretion of management. Hence it is understandable that few forecasts extending very far into the future have been issued. But the balance could shift at any time.

Relevance of Past Performance in Forecasting

In moving from a discussion of management forecasts to other currently more practical information alternatives, two implications of the foregoing discussion carry over. *First, the nature of the investor's decision problem is unchanged, whether or not management issues forecasts of future cash flows.* That is, presumably investors want to arrive at valuations of investment opportunities based on the expected future cash flows and expected risk that they associate with those opportunities. Knowledge of management forecasts simply offers some potential for arriving at better expectations with perhaps less expenditure of time and other resources in the process. *Second, whether or not management issues forecasts, some more factually based types of information about the enterprise are relevant to investors.* As was noted above, one of the major objections to management forecasts is that such forecasts may be in error or even purposely biased. To give investors some basis for acceptance, rejection, or modification, management forecasts should be accompanied by other financial information portraying the present and past operations of the enterprise, against which the forecasts can be compared. Moreover, in the absence of management forecasts, such information will serve the same function with respect to investors' own forecasts.

In considering financial reporting alternatives, either as substitutes where management forecasts are not forthcoming or as complements where they are, it follows from the preceding discussion that we want to consider alternatives that (1) are not as susceptible to bias and error in reporting as forecasts, and (2) can nevertheless be employed in forecasting uncertain future cash flows by investors. To be less susceptible to bias than management forecasts, the "other information" reported by the enterprise to investors must be based more on facts—on the actual events and activities experienced by the enterprise. To be employed by investors in forecasting, the "other information" presented must bear some discernible (logical) relationship to that which is of interest—namely, future cash flows.

Past Performance Related to Future Cash Flows

The notion that information about events and activities already experienced by an enterprise could be relevant to the estimation of future cash flows is based on an assumed continuity of events and activities engaged in by the enterprise. That is, although many aspects of an enterprise's activities (like its product lines, production processes, etc.) may change over time, many important aspects remain constant or change slowly. Thus the immediate past provides a context in which to consider future possibilities. The further various future possibilities depart from the immediate past, the less credible or probable they usually are.

The idea of continuity of events can be applied to the enterprise as a generator of cash flows. For instance, recall that earlier the enterprise was described in terms of an operating sequence that included (1) acquisition of resources for immediate or future cash payments, (2) conversion of resources into products and services, and (3) sales of products and services in exchange for immediate or future cash receipts. For most enterprises this sequence or process of generating cash flows is more or less continuous. Furthermore, an enterprise will usually tend to be engaged in all steps simultaneously.

Enterprise Performance. Assuming that there is some continuity in the cash-generating process, a portrayal of the enterprise's present "performance" in that process is surely relevant to investors who are interested in future cash flows. By "performance" we mean the rate at which the enterprise is generating cash inflows in excess of cash outflows. Such a rate can be thought of as representing the enterprise's *cash-generating ability* or *cash-generating capacity per unit of time.*

Periodic Net Operating Cash Flow as a Measure of Performance

With the above discussion in mind, we are prepared to discuss some alternative measures of enterprise "performance," in the "cash-generating-ability" sense. An obvious first choice for a periodic performance measure is the net cash flow from business operations of an enterprise for a given period, such as a week, a month, a year.

Net Operating Cash Flow. Net operating cash flow is defined as the excess of total cash received by the enterprise during a period of time over total cash disbursed during the same period of time, but excluding dividends or withdrawals paid to owners or contributions made by owners or long-term creditors.

For the sake of convenience, we abbreviate the term "net operating cash flow" to "net cash flow" throughout the ensuing discussion.

Advantages of Net Cash Flow. As a measure of performance, net cash flow has some definite advantages that make it attractive for periodic reporting to outside investors:

1. The amounts of cash taken in and paid out by an enterprise are largely factual data—not matters of estimate.
2. The computation of periodic net cash flow is identical to the computation of the cash flows of future periods that are of interest to investors.

Disadvantages of Net Cash Flow. But net cash flow has at least one distinct disadvantage. When measured over short periods of time (really, any period short of the full life of the enterprise), it may seriously misrepresent the *cash-generating ability* of the enterprise for several reasons:

1. Many of the larger cash expenditures in a particular period are made to acquire resources like buildings and equipment that will be used to produce the products and services of many future periods' operations.
2. Often resources are acquired on credit and are used to produce products and services in a particular period, for which payments are not made until later periods.
3. Much of the cash received in a particular period may be payments from customers for products and services provided by the firm in earlier periods on a postponed-payment basis.

Thus there is no necessary association between the measure of effort (total cash expenditures) and the measure of accomplishment (total cash receipts) embodied in the performance measure, periodic net cash flow. With no such necessary association, there is only limited usefulness of net cash flow *by itself* as a measure of performance for outside investors to use in judging future cash-generating ability of the enterprise.

In a period in which the enterprise is actually very efficient in producing products and services of great value to its customers, its net cash-flow performance might look bad simply because it makes an expenditure for a new piece of equipment that will help induce efficient production for many months or years to come. Whereas the act of buying a piece of equipment may be good for future cash-generating ability, it will have a negative effect on the measure of the current period's performance of the enterprise. Similarly, in a period in which an enterprise's productivity declines, its net cash-flow performance may continue to look good, sustained by cash collections from customers for products and services provided in past periods. This point is illustrated in Example 3-3.

Example 3-3

Let us suppose that a small group of investors wishes to enter the retail business in several metropolitan areas likely to experience considerable economic growth during the next twenty-five year period. It commissions a market research study which projects higher-than-normal returns on investments for retailing ice cream items. Thus the investor group agrees to establish a local chain of ice cream parlors. The investors plan to start with twenty outlets. The company they incorporate for this purpose is named Fancy Flavors, Inc.

Among themselves, the investors are able to raise $150,000 in cash which becomes their stake (or, in accounting and finance terminology, their "owners' equity") in Fancy Flavors, Inc. Since the group also has exceptionally good bank connections, a five-year bank loan in the amount of $600,000 can be secured. This loan carries an annual rate of interest at 12 percent and is renewable. Thus $750,000 in cash is invested to start Fancy Flavors, Inc.—$150,000 by the owners and $600,000 by a major creditor.

Prior to August 19XX twenty store locations are found (plenty of pedestrian traffic, easy-access parking, etc.). It is expected that, at these locations, there will be a good demand for ice cream cones as well as ice cream specialties to be made to order for banquets and such. Twenty store managers are employed effective August 1, 19XX. One of these managers is appointed chief executive officer of Fancy Flavors, Inc. For ease of exposition, the twenty Fancy Flavors stores are dealt with in combination as a single unit throughout the rest of this example.

As of August 1 sufficient employees are engaged, including a number of part-time student assistants. Three months' rent is paid in advance on August 1, totaling $60,000. Various store furnishings and equipment are purchased and installed at a total cost of $600,000. The equipment will meet Fancy Flavors' business needs until it wears out in five years and then has to be scrapped. The following additional items are purchased: (1) supplies (cones, napkins, spoons, scrapers, etc.) for $20,000 cash, and (2) ice cream, $30,000, with payment due at the time of the next delivery.

Business operations commence on August 1 and proceed very smoothly. Additional operating facts for August are as follows:

1. Cash ice cream sales total $400,000 during the month. In addition, various ice cream items were provided for numerous big banquets for which payments totaling $50,000 will not be received until September.

2. Salaries and wages for August paid on or before August 31 totaled $120,000. In addition, $30,000 of salaries and wages for work done during August had not been paid as of August 31. They will be paid on the first payday in September.

3. In total, $165,000 worth of ice cream (including the initial order) was purchased from several dairy products companies. During August $130,000 was paid against outstanding invoices—the other $35,000 not being due until the first ice cream delivery date in September.

4. Miscellaneous cash expenditures were made, totaling $10,000, for heat, light, and so forth, during August.

5. An additional $10,000 worth of supplies was ordered and received in August but will not be paid for until September.

6. At the end of the month, an inventory count was conducted at each of the twenty store locations. This count determined that $20,000 worth of ice cream and $15,000 worth of supplies were on hand at that time.

Both the owners and the managers of Fancy Flavors are well pleased with the first month's operations of their business. Of course they recognize that summer months are better for the ice cream business than winter months. Good results during summer months will have to compensate in part for lesser results expected during the winter. This makes it necessary to establish, month by month, just how well the business is going.

In addition, the loan officer at the bank needs to know how likely it is that Fancy Flavors can not only meet its interest payments on the loan but also repay its principal amount in the future. If Fancy Flavors gains sufficient financial strength, its owners may be relieved from personal liability for the bank loan—at least in part.

So how do we go about representing Fancy Flavors' August 19XX business operations in a significant way? First, we might try the net cash-flow approach for the month of August to see if it gives a satisfactory representation of the business's cash-generating ability.

Total cash receipts of the business (excluding the initial investments) are the $400,000 cash sales noted above. To get the *net* cash flow for the month of August, the difference between these total cash receipts of $400,000 and the total of the cash disbursements is determined, as shown in Exhibit 3-3.

The net cash flow is -$540,000. In other words, Fancy Flavors, after being initially established, experienced a net cash outflow or drain of $540,000 in the month of August, obviously not a very satisfactory measure of "performance" in August. Why? Because there is an indiscriminant matching of dollars paid out and dollars received as if each dollar expended and received applied equally to the operations of the business during the month of August—which intuitively is not the case. The positive side of performance, the total cash receipts of $400,000, does not include $50,000 to be received in September for ice cream items *provided to banquet customers in August.* Similarly, the negative side of the measure of August performance includes the whole $600,000 laid out for equipment that will last five years, and $60,000 in rent that covers not only August but September and October as well. In addition, it omits all of the $35,000 that will be paid in September for the last delivery of ice cream that

Exhibit 3-3

FANCY FLAVORS, INC.

Net Cash Flow for August 19XX

Total cash receipts		$400,000
Cash disbursements for:		
Equipment	$600,000	
Three months' rent	60,000	
Supplies	20,000	
Salaries and wages	120,000	
Ice cream	130,000	
Miscellaneous	10,000	
Total cash disbursements		940,000
Net cash flow		-$540,000

was at least partially used in August, and the $30,000 that will be paid in September for work performed entirely in August.

Conventional Accounting Performance Measurement

While the net cash-flow measure certainly indicates some aspects of the periodic performance of an enterprise, it is clearly not an appropriate overall or total performance indicator. Thus we are led to an alternative measure of periodic performance of the enterprise included in "conventional accounting." ("Conventional accounting" is the label we apply to the financial accounting model that dominates accounting practice today.) Analogous to periodic net cash flow, the measure of performance produced by conventional accounting, called *net operating income,* is the difference between a measure of accomplishment, called *revenue,* and a measure of effort or sacrifice, called *expense.* Although the data used in conventional accounting are the same as the data used in calculating periodic net cash flow, that is, prices received for products and services and prices paid for factors of production, they are used more selectively and are allocated to the periods in the life of the enterprise in which they appear to affect performance. Most of these differences are embodied in the definitions of revenue and expense under conventional accounting.

Revenue Defined. For all practical purposes, we can define conventional accounting revenue as follows:

> **Revenue.** Generally, revenue is the sum of the selling prices (or fees) of all products sold and services provided to customers during the current period—whether or not the sales are cash sales or "credit sales." (Credit sales are sales for which the customer promises to pay at a later time.)

Notice that revenue differs from total cash receipts of the enterprise for the period of interest. Cash receipts include payments made by customers in the current period for products and services received in an earlier period. Revenue, on the other hand, includes the selling prices of products or services provided during the current period for which cash is received in a later period.

Example 3-4

> In Example 3-3 above, only $400,000 was actually received by Fancy Flavors from customers during the month of August, all from cash purchasers coming to the twenty stores. That $400,000 is the measure of total accomplishment under net cash-flow performance measurement. But there was $50,000 worth of ice cream sold to banquet customers who did not pay immediately, but rather promised to pay in September. Both the $50,000 promised to be paid and the $400,000 actually paid by customers in August are included in August revenue of $450,000. Furthermore, the $50,000 due from customers *will not be included* in revenue upon receipt in September as part of that month's total accomplishment.

The Realization Principle and Revenue. It should be noted that the above definition of revenue is somewhat simplified for purposes of present discussion. Measurement of revenue under conventional accounting requires the application of a more sophisticated criterion than the one implied by the above definition. In the general sense, conventional accounting revenue measurement is governed by the so-called realization principle.

> **The Realization Principle.** Accomplishment (revenue) should be recognized in the period when the prices to be received for products and services provided by the enterprise (1) become reasonably certain and (2) have been "earned" by the enterprise.

The term "earned" in the definition is generally interpreted as meaning that the enterprise does not face any substantial additional production barriers or steps (like delivery) before actually providing a satisfactory product or service to a customer, thus ensuring that the price of that product or service will actually be forthcoming. In a market economy, fairly strict interpretation of the word "earned" *usually implies* that a legally enforceable sale of a product or completion of a service has already taken place. Furthermore, a legally enforceable sale usually satisfies the stipulation that the price to be received from a customer be reasonably certain as well. Thus the definition of revenue in the preceding paragraph describes the result of applying the realization principle in the majority of cases in practice. We will take up discussion of the several types of special cases encountered less frequently in practice in Chapters 8 and 9.

Relationship Between Revenue and Cash Receipts. Over the whole life of the enterprise, the *sum* of all periods' revenues will equal the *sum* of all periods' cash receipts from sales of products and services. The differences between the revenue and the cash receipts of individual periods will usually only be a matter of timing. The reason is that regardless of which way the enterprise recognizes accomplishment, the price paid by a customer for a given product or service will be included in the measure of accomplishment in only one period in the life of the enterprise. If the performance measurement period is very long (say, as long as a year), a particular customer's purchase is apt to result in a cash receipt in the same period as that in which it is included in revenue anyway. So why bother with the distinction? The answer is important enough to warrant some brief additional discussion.

Measuring Periodic Accomplishment. The "real" economic accomplishment of an enterprise for a period of time is the total value that the enterprise has added to all resources (raw material, etc.) that it controls, *by all of its productive efforts.* Although this is what we would like to measure ideally, it is impossible to measure all value added in any largely objective way. For instance, if an enterprise starts raw materials into production during a period of time but does not bring them to completion during the same period, how is it to characterize what it has accomplished in any largely factual way? The partially completed goods may be worthless junk if never brought to completion. Or it may turn out that a whole batch cannot be sold upon completion because for one reason or another it does not meet acceptable quality standards.

Furthermore, in the case of many special production techniques, it may be impossible to say when a certain percentage of the final conversion of raw materials to finished goods has been completed. It usually requires a largely subjective judgment to estimate the total value added to goods and services brought to various stages of completion during the period. So even though we would like to include all "real" value added by an enterprise when measuring its accomplishments for a period, we cannot objectively do so.

The Advantages of Revenue for Performance Measurement. Among the outside events that can be relied upon to affirm economic value added, the receipt of a customer's payment in cash leaves the enterprise more certain of the value of the products it has provided than does the customer's promise to pay. Nevertheless, conventional accounting usually recognizes the "value added" embodied in an enterprise's products in the periods in which they are sold rather than in the period of receipt of cash, for two reasons:

1. Thanks to the existence in our socioeconomic system of a stable legal environment that will enforce a customer's agreement to pay, the additional uncertainty caused by recognizing accomplishment before cash is received is minimal and can often be predicted with accuracy.
2. The period in which a product is sold is almost always earlier than (or the same as) the period in which cash is received, and hence chronologically closer to the period(s) in which most of the productive activity that added value to the product took place. Thus the measure of accomplishment (and hence the measure of performance) in conventional accounting is less likely to represent productive potential that is outdated or no longer achievable.

Hence in conventional accounting we use revenue (as described earlier) as a measure of accomplishment because it is usually sufficiently more timely to offset its slightly lesser objectivity than net cash receipts. Again, several special cases of revenue recognition and certain exceptions to the general conventional accounting rules are discussed in Chapters 8 and 9.

Measuring Periodic Effort or Sacrifice. Earlier in the chapter it was pointed out that one objection to a net cash-flow concept of performance is a general lack of association between the level of measured accomplishment and the level of measured effort for a given period. In conventional accounting an effort is made to overcome this objection. But it must be noted that the measurement of accomplishment, revenue, is not conditioned upon the measurement of effort. In measuring revenue under the realization principle, we ignore some of the real economic efforts of a particular period by which the enterprise adds value. Instead of measuring value added as it takes place, we recognize in the period of sale the cumulative efforts of the present and past periods embodied in completed products and services provided to customers.

Expense Defined. To achieve the hoped-for cause-and-effect association between measured effort and measured accomplishment, measurement of conventional accounting expense for a period is conditioned upon revenue recognized for the period, as indicated by the following definition:

Expense. Insofar as possible, total expense for a period includes the costs of all resources that were sacrificed to produce the revenue recognized in the current period.

Again, this definition is a simplification of a more general and sophisticated set of criteria. The implied relationship in the definition between expense recognition and revenue recognized for a given period is a simplification of *the matching principle.*

The Matching Principle. Insofar as possible, the total sacrifices made in all periods to produce and sell a particular product or service are recognized as expense in the period in which the revenue from the same product or service is recognized.

The matching principle gives to conventional accounting performance measurement what is lacking in net cash flow—an intuitive cause (effort) and effect (accomplishment) relationship. But the matching principle as defined implies some concept for measuring the sacrifice (effort) made in producing products and services. The measure of sacrifice in conventional accounting is governed by what we call *the original transaction cost principle,* or, more simply, *the cost principle.*

The Cost Principle. The measure of sacrifice associated with the acquisition and subsequent use of any resource is the price paid for the resource, that is, its cost in the exchange or exchanges in which it was acquired.

Clearly, the definition of expense is simply a combination of these two fundamental principles—the matching principle and the cost principle.

Expense Recognition Illustrated. Expense recognition, according to the matching principle, calls for a selective measure of effort that is consistent with the measured accomplishment (revenue) of a given period. For any given period, the sum of the prices of the products and services provided to customers is the recognized measure of accomplishment. Then, ideally, in the same period the sum of the prices paid for resources used to produce *those* products and services is the recognized measure of effort.

Example 3-5

Again recalling the facts of Fancy Flavors' ice cream operation in Example 3-3, we can contrast the expenses that would be recognized during the month of August with the cash disbursements recognized earlier.

Notice that in Exhibit 3-4 there are two directions of contrast between August cash disbursements and August expenses. In the cases of equipment, rent, and supplies, the cash expenditures exceed recognized expense. In each case we are recognizing that the business paid for more of that resource in the month of August than was sacrificed to produce August's revenues of $450,000. For instance, equipment was purchased for $600,000 but was expected to supply service for five years, or sixty months. Assuming equal applicability of that service to all sixty months, the cost of the first month's use would be 1/60 × $600,000, or $10,000.

Similarly, three months' rent was prepaid at $60,000, but two months' paid-up occupancy remain, indicating that only one-third, or $20,000 worth of occupancy, was used up. In the case of supplies, $30,000 worth was received, but $15,000 worth was still on hand at August 31, as yet to be sacrificed. Thus we infer that supplies used during August originally cost $15,000.

In the case of salaries and wages as well as ice cream, the expense recognized for August exceeds cash disbursements for August. In both cases we are recognizing that the sacrifice of a resource took place in connection with production of August's revenue of $450,000, regardless of when cash will actually be paid. For instance, even though we only paid salaries and wages of $120,000 during August, salaries and wages for hours actually worked (in producing August's revenue) amounted to $150,000; the additional $30,000 will be paid on the first payday in September. Similarly, ice cream worth $165,000 in total was received from the manufacturer during August. Of that amount $35,000 had not been paid for at August 31, but only $20,000 remained unsold. We therefore infer that the cost of the ice cream sold during August was $145,000.

There are two additional items for which August expense recognition is required even though *no* related cash disbursements occurred. One is interest expense. The $600,000 loan from the bank is subject to an interest cost of 12 percent per year, or 1 percent per month. Therefore $6,000 of interest was earned by the bank during August, and Fancy Flavors should recognize (accrue) this amount as an expense related to the month's operations.

The other expense item in need of recognition is the obligation to pay federal income taxes on any corporate income earned. Accounting ramifications of income taxation are a complex subject dealt with in later chapters. For the present purpose we simply acknowledge that federal income tax rates are progressive up to corporate taxable income levels of $100,000 from which point on the tax rate is a uniform 46 percent.

Assuming taxable income of $94,000 for Fancy Flavors, Inc., for the month of August 19XX, the corporation should recognize a federal income tax expense (actually payable on a quarter-by-quarter basis) as follows:

Corporate Taxable Income	Rate	Taxes Payable
First $25,000	17	$ 4,250
$25,000 to $50,000	20	5,000
$50,000 to $75,000	30	7,500
$75,000 to $94,000	40	7,600
Total federal income taxes payable for August 19XX		$24,350
		($24,000 rounded)

Note: The progressive rates apply on an annual basis. If additional taxable income is earned September through December, 19XX, the next $6,000 is taxed at 40 percent and the remainder at 46 percent.

We do not recognize a difference between the August cash disbursement and the expense recognized for miscellaneous heat, light, power, and so forth. This implies that all such items or services were used to produce the revenue of the month in which they were paid.

Product Expenses versus Period Expenses. We have made quite a point of the association between revenue and expense brought about in conventional accounting through the matching principle—particularly in contrast to the relatively greater lack of association between periodic cash receipts and disbursements. But some qualification is in order lest we mislead the reader about what can actually be expected from applying the matching principle in practice.

To be strictly applied, the matching principle requires that virtually every sacrifice of any resource used in production in a given period (1) be specifically identified with a particular product or service, (2) have its original cost accumulated with the costs of all other sacrifices made to produce that product or ser-

Exhibit 3-4

FANCY FLAVORS, INC.

Cash Disbursements versus Expenses for August 19XX

	Cash Disbursed in August	Expense Recognized in August
Nature of the sacrifice:		
Equipment	$600,000	$ 10,000
Rent	60,000	20,000
Supplies	20,000	15,000
Salaries and wages	120,000	150,000
Ice cream	130,000	145,000
Interest on loan	—0—	6,000
Federal income taxes	—0—	24,000
Miscellaneous	10,000	10,000
Total	$940,000	$380,000

vice, and (3) be recognized as an expense in the period in which the particular product or service is sold or provided.

Even when possible, such specific identification of every resource sacrifice with some product or service is very costly. Furthermore, such scrupulous matching of resource sacrifices with products or services and later with revenue is often impossible.

Some resource sacrifices are easily traced to the specific products sold in specific periods.

Example 3-6

In the case of Fancy Flavors' ice cream operations, the ice cream used during August was the ice cream and banquet desserts sold during August.

On the other hand, some resource sacrifices simply cannot be directly associated with specific products or services provided.

Example 3-7

The managers of Fancy Flavor, Inc., may have spent most of their time in August making business contacts with restaurants and caterers in trying to promote future banquet business. But it would be difficult or impossible to discern which future sales, or how many, are a direct result of the managers' expenditure of time (the enterprise's expenditure of salaries) during August.

Hence the matching principle is rarely followed to perfection. Instead, a rather general dichotomy is usually followed in recognizing expenses for a given period.

If a resource sacrifice has been made in a particular accounting period, the accountant will consider the way in which the resource was used. If consumption of the resource can be identified or associated with a specific product or service (or batch of products and services), its original cost to the enterprise is accumulated ("attached" to the product or service) until the period in which the specific products are sold or services completed, at which time the related revenue is recognized. Product expenses are resource costs, like the cost of ice cream, that logically "attach" to products. Product expenses are recognized as expenses in the period in which the particular product is sold.

But if a resource is consumed during the period and its consumption bears no discernible relation to the production of any particular present or future product(s) or service(s), that is, it cannot be specifically identified with a unit of present or future revenue, its cost is recognized as an expense in the period in which it is consumed or sacrificed. Such costs, like the managers' salaries, are called *period expenses*.

This general dichotomy is somewhat evident in our recognition of the August expenses of the ice cream stores. The point of bringing up the distinction here is that while conventional accounting performance measurement is based on a cause-and-effect relationship between sacrifices made and resulting accomplishments recognized, in practice such a relationship is never perfectly achieved. But every effort within reasonable limits is usually made to match a cost with the specific revenue (product) that it helped to generate, before resorting to the expedient of merely treating the cost as an expense in the period in which the resource is used.

Measuring Periodic Performance. The index of periodic performance in conventional accounting is called *net operating income*.

Net Operating Income. Net operating income is defined as the algebraic difference between revenues and expenses recognized in a particular period:

Net operating income = Revenues − Expenses

Example 3-8

Since we have already calculated Fancy Flavors' revenue ($450,000) and expenses ($380,000) for the month of August, it is a simple matter to determine net operating income:

Net operating income = $450,000 − $380,000 = $70,000

We can now display the details in a sensible array called an income statement, illustrated in Exhibit 3-5.

As we would expect, the $70,000 net operating income measure of performance for the month of August contrasts sharply with the company's net cash flow of −$540,000 calculated earlier.

Because net operating income is the arithmetic difference between recognized revenues and expenses, most of its properties as the periodic performance index of conventional accounting derive from the way that expenses and revenues are measured. Hence we briefly summarize the properties of revenue, expense, and net operating income in Exhibit 3-6.

There are still many open issues concerning income measurement and the

Exhibit 3-5

FANCY FLAVORS, INC.

Income Statement
For the Month of August 19XX

Revenue from sales of ice cream		$450,000
Less expenses:		
Equipment	$ 10,000	
Rent	20,000	
Supplies used	15,000	
Salaries and wages	150,000	
Cost of ice cream sold	145,000	
Interest on loan	6,000	
Federal income taxes	24,000	
Miscellaneous—heat, light, etc.	10,000	
Total expenses		380,000
Net operating income		$ 70,000

Exhibit 3-6

SUMMARY OF CONVENTIONAL ACCOUNTING OPERATING INCOME MEASUREMENT CONCEPTS

	Definition (What?)	Conventional Timing (When?)	Conventional Measurement (How much?)
Revenue:	Value of goods and services provided to customers during the current period	Recognized when goods have been delivered or services have been rendered	Price (fee) paid or agreed to be paid by the customer
Expense:	Value of resources consumed in the past or present (sometimes the future) to provide a product or service	Recognized in the period in which the related revenue is recognized, i.e., expense is "matched" against revenue	Cost of (original price paid for) resources consumed to provide the products or services delivered during the period
Net operating income:	Difference between revenue and expense of the period	Determined as a result of recognizing the related revenue and expense of the period	Difference between the aggregate prices (fees) from products sold and services rendered and the aggregate costs of the resources sacrificed in providing those products and services

larger conventional accounting framework or context into which income measurement fits. These issues are the subjects of Chapters 4 and 5 and several other later chapters. But it is felt that one last item of elaboration on an earlier theme is worthwhile here.

Net Operating Income versus Net Cash Flow. Assuming that the agreed-to selling prices of products provided are all collected from customers eventually, the sum of the revenues recognized in all the individual periods of an enterprise's life will equal the sum of all the cash receipts over the life of the enterprise. Similarly, since expenses are recognized in terms of the prices originally paid for resources used in the business, the sum of the expenses recognized over the enterprise's life will equal the sum of all cash disbursed for resources used in production over the same period. It is therefore also true that the sum of the net operating income amounts calculated for all the periods in an enterprise's life (the sum of the revenues minus the sum of the expenses) *must equal the net cash flow over the whole life* of the enterprise (excluding payments to and receipts from owners). We ignore, for the present, gains and losses which are discussed in Chapter 5.

Thus, over the whole life of the enterprise, conventional accounting net operating income is completely consistent with long-run net cash flow. It differs from *periodic* net cash flow only in the way that it represents performance or the rate of progress in the successive time periods along the way. Hence it presumably provides *a better index of long-run net cash-flow potential* than does *periodic* net cash flow. The now-familiar reason is that matching is an attempt to relate the revenues and expenses of a *particular period* on a cause-and-effect basis, insofar as possible.

Still we must not lose sight of the fact that short-run (periodic) net cash flow also provides important decision information to management and interested external parties. Net cash flow from operations (essentially illustrated in Exhibit 3-3) is not the same as the net amount of cash receipts and cash disbursements. This difference is discussed and analyzed in Chapter 6, where resource *flows* (as opposed to income determination) receive attention. The essential contrasts between short-run and long-run indexes of business performance will come into fuller focus after the study of Chapter 6.

Questions for Review and Discussion

3-1. Define:
 a. Net cash flow
 b. Revenue
 c. Expense
 d. The realization principle
 e. The matching principle
 f. The cost principle
 g. Product expense
 h. Period expense

3-2. From an investment decision viewpoint, what aspects of the business enterprise are decision makers concerned about?

3-3. The cash-flow-generating process of a business enterprise is strikingly simple (in principle). Describe the steps in the cash-generating (operating) sequence of a business enterprise.

3-4. Give several reasons favoring the publication of management forecasts of future cash flows.

3-5. Although the potential relevance of management forecasts for investor decisions can be established, certain problems limit the feasibility of management's supplying such forecasts to outside investors.

92   CHAPTER 3

      a. What are these limitations?
      b. Does the presence or absence of management forecasts alter the investor's basic decision problem?

3-6. It has been suggested that there are significant reasons why managers prefer not to publish cash forecasts in the present environment. Give the reasons.

3-7. The scarcity of management forecasts in present-day financial reporting (and the probable usefulness of supplemental information even if forecasts were generally available) led to our discussion of net cash flows and net operating income as possible alternatives or supplements to forecasts. What criteria were used to introduce these alternatives?

3-8. Provision of historical cash flows for use by investors in making investment decisions is considered to have both advantages and disadvantages. Discuss both.

3-9. The conventional accounting performance measure, called net operating income, is based on historical events.
      a. What are the reasons for this historical orientation when investors are concerned mainly with future cash flows in valuing prospective investments?
      b. How or why can historical measures of performance be used as indicators of likely future performance?

3-10. Distinguish between:
      a. Cost and expense
      b. Product versus period expense

3-11. Over the whole life of an enterprise, net cash flow from operations will equal net operating income. Explain why this is so.

3-12. The discussion in the chapter considered net cash flow and net operating income to be alternative performance measures (primarily for exposition purposes). Do you see any potential usefulness in viewing the two measures as complementary? Explain your position.

3-13. Net operating income is not considered to be a forecast *per se*, though it is presumably relevant to investors who wish to forecast future cash flows. Under what conditions will the current period's net operating income be an actual forecast of the next period's (or other future periods') net operating income(s)? Does knowledge of these conditions have any implications for investors?

3-14. Conventional accounting net operating income can be thought of as an attempt to simulate the net cash flow from the operations of the business *as if* (1) the business acquires all resources for cash in quantities no greater than the current period's requirements, (2) all products produced (purchased) are sold in the same period *and* all products sold are produced (purchased) in the same period, and (3) all sales are for cash. Do you basically agree or disagree? Explain your position. Do you wish to qualify your basic agreement or disagreement in any way?

3-15. The timing of recognition of revenue generally determines when many expenses will be recognized. Explain why this is so. What kinds of expenses will generally not be subject to this pattern of recognition?

Exercises

3-1. **Net Cash Flow for Future Cash-Flow Predictions.** John Jacobsen and Steve Block started a small delicatessen specializing in exotic sandwiches two years ago when they were both undergraduates in business administration. The business has been very successful, and what was initially viewed as a temporary venture to defray college expenses now appears to be able to provide a good permanent income for one of them. Steve is interested in remaining in the business, and John has agreed to sell his share if they can agree on a mutually satisfactory purchase price. Steve has suggested using past cash flows of the business as an indicator of likely future cash flows. John, on the other hand, believes that past cash flows are not representative due to heavy initial cash outflows for start-up costs and relatively light cash inflows while the business was building up a clientele. Actual net cash flows for the first two years of operation were −$1,000 the first year and $6,000 the second year. They each have projected annual net cash flows as follows:

	John (projected)	Steve (projected)
Year 1	$10,000	$ 6,000
2	12,000	8,000
3	14,000	8,000
4	14,000	8,000
5	16,000	8,000
6	18,000	8,000
7	20,000	10,000
8	20,000	10,000
9	20,000	10,000
10	20,000	10,000

Required:

1. Assuming the business will last for only the ten years projected, what is the PV of the business in each case if their time preference rate is 10 percent?
2. Suppose you are John. How might you go about convincing Steve that your projections are more realistic based at least in part on the actual events and transactions of the business during the first two years?

3-2. **Feasibility of Future Cash-Flow Projections.** The Northern Construction Corporation is engaged primarily in the construction of various government projects. Over the years it has developed a management team that is one of the best in the region when it comes to working with government agencies and knowing what government construction projects are in the offing. Three years ago the management of the firm believed that the number of government projects it would be able to undertake was likely to increase substantially. Based on this premise, it projected net cash flows that were significantly larger than in the past. In the belief that this information was important to both current and potential stockholders, it supplied the following estimates of future net cash flows:

19X0	$ 60,000
19X1	75,000
19X2	90,000
19X3	120,000
19X4	125,000
19X5–19X9	130,000

Unfortunately, in the years immediately following these projections there was a significant cutback in actual government expenditures. As a result, the company's realized net cash flows stayed approximately constant at a level of $60,000. Furthermore, the company's management saw little prospect for net cash flows to increase in the foreseeable future.

Required:

1. Assume that there are a total of 1,000 shares of stock in the corporation. If the shareholders' time preference rate is 10 percent, what are the present values of the shares for the two sets of circumstances? (Assume that net cash flows are distributed in full to owners in the year received.)
2. Suppose you had purchased shares based on management's first cash-flow projections (and had paid approximately their then present value). How might you react to the revised estimates? Why?

3-3. **Net Cash Flow as a Performance Measurement.** The Green Thumb Nursery was started five years ago to raise and sell various kinds of decorative trees and shrubs. The varieties that it grows require from three to five years to reach a salable size. As a result, it has experienced rather heavy cash outflows in the first five years of operation while growing the shrubs, but relatively small cash inflows, since it has had few shrubs of marketable size. Net cash flows for these years were as follows:

Year 1	$(60,000)
Year 2	(40,000)
Year 3	(42,000)
Year 4	(34,000)
Year 5	(6,000)

Because of these heavy cash outflows, the firm is in need of additional capital and is currently attempting to attract new investors. It realizes that investors make investment decisions on the basis of prospective future cash flows, but it is unwilling to make such estimates public because of the potential legal liability if they are not realized as projected.

Required:

1. One alternative it has considered is simply presenting the entirely factual and objective historical cash flows, but it feels that they do not

adequately represent the past performance or future potential of the firm. Comment on this alternative. Why may it be inadequate information for prospective investors?

2. How might the nursery present largely factual information that would be more likely to give investors an indication of potential future cash flows?

3. What sort of criteria should be used for generating the information for potential investors?

4. If you were in a position to supply all the additional capital required, what combination of information would you request? (Assume that anything you request will be forthcoming.)

3-4. **Net Cash Flow as a Performance Measurement.** The Coastal Trading Company's principal activity is the sale of fishing equipment, supplies, food, and clothing to the Alaskan fishing industry. Its business, like the fishing industry, is highly seasonal. Outfitting boats during the months of June and July accounts for approximately 40 percent of its annual sales. As a result it uses these two months as an indicator of its performance for the year. During June 19XX it had sales of $172,000, of which $16,000 was paid in cash and the balance was sold on account. Also during June it received payments on account from May sales totaling $18,000. Merchandise sold during June included goods purchased in May totaling $43,000, goods purchased on account during June totaling $48,000, and goods purchased and paid for in June totaling $23,000. In addition, it paid accounts payable for merchandise received in May totaling $23,000. June salaries and wages, advertising, and miscellaneous expenses were paid as incurred and totaled $14,000.

In July, as the fishing season progressed, the company's sales declined to $82,000, of which $61,000 was paid in cash and $21,000 was sold on account. It received payments on account during July of $156,000. Merchandise sold during July had a cost of $52,000 and was purchased in previous months. There was no new merchandise purchased during July. July cash payments included wages and salaries, advertising, and miscellaneous expenses totaling $11,000, and payments on account for June purchases totaling $40,000.

Required:

1. Construct separate cash-flow statements for June and July based on the above information.

2. Which month's indicated cash performance is better? Explain.

3. Which, if either, is the better indicator of future performance of the company? Explain.

4. What are the problems associated with use of either statement alone as an indicator of likely future performance?

5. In August sales declined further to $63,000, of which $46,000 was cash and $17,000 was sold on account. Payments received on account from May and June sales totaled $20,000. Based on this information,

what is total revenue for the three months? What are total cash receipts for the same period? Discuss the reasons for their similarity despite the use of different principles in determining each.

3-5. The Maine Fish Company—Cash-Flow Performance. The Maine Fish Company has recently set up a new operation which will own and operate a chain of fish, chip, and chowder restaurants. It has appointed a bright young employee, Jim Robinson, to manage the operation, and realizing that it is net cash flow that is important to investors, it has decided to base his salary in part on the cash flows he generates. Specifically, he is to receive 3 percent of the net cash flow in the form of an annual bonus. But Jim does not know this.

During the first year of operations, Jim was able to open a total of four new restaurants and make final plans for an additional three. He feels that this was a rather outstanding performance and as a result is looking forward to a substantial bonus. The following events summarize his activities for the year.

a. Purchased property for the four restaurants for $80,000.
b. Signed contracts for purchase of three additional pieces of property costing a total of $65,000 but has not yet paid for them.
c. Constructed the four restaurant buildings. Total cost was $143,000, and he expected they would last about twenty years each.
d. Purchased equipment for $62,000, which he expected would last ten years.
e. Hired six full- and part-time employees for each restaurant.
f. Paid for initial advertising for the four restaurants of $7,200.
g. Paid wages totaling $37,000 for the year.
h. Paid for food supplies totaling $66,000.
i. Miscellaneous expenditures for the year totaled $4,300.
j. Received cash from sales totaling $134,000. (All sales are for cash.)

In checking over his records at year-end, Jim found that he had virtually no unpaid bills outstanding but had $3,000 in wages which were earned but as yet unpaid. Similarly, he had $2,000 worth of food supplies remaining at year-end.

Required:

1. Prepare a cash-flow statement for Jim's operations for the year.
2. How much is Jim's bonus likely to amount to? Do you think it adequately rewards him for his performance?
3. Can you suggest an alternative measure of performance on which to base Jim's bonus? How much bonus would he receive for the first year under your plan?

3-6. Analysis of Effects of Transactions. Following are some randomly selected business events of the XYZ Company:
a. The company pays off a bank loan.
b. Wages for the period are paid by the company.
c. One of the owners contributes cash to the company.

d. The company makes cash sales.
e. One of the owners uses up company supplies for personal purposes.
f. The company buys stock in ABC Corporation.
g. Credit sales for the period are recorded.
h. The company pays in advance for an insurance policy.
i. An item of inventory becomes worthless (normal spoilage).
j. A piece of equipment is sold for a price higher than the amount at which it is carried in the company's books of account.

Required:

Indicate the effects of each event (positive, negative, or no effect) on the following:

1. Net cash flow

2. Net operating income

3-7. **Revenue Recognition.** The National Manufacturing Corporation is currently compiling its income statement for the year immediately past. It is using the realization principle for recognition of accomplishment and has events as follows:

a. Signed a contract for sale to the Metal Stamping Company of $60,000 worth of machinery which it manufactures. Of this $60,000, $32,000 worth has been manufactured and delivered during the year. The balance is to be manufactured and delivered next year.

b. Sold $43,000 worth of machinery to the Northwest Metal Products Company, all of which has been delivered. However, it has not yet received payment for these goods.

c. Completed manufacture of $82,000 worth of machinery for which it has no buyer as yet.

d. Received a partial payment of $15,000 as an advance for machinery that is to be manufactured and delivered to the Water Research Laboratory next year. The total selling price of the machinery is $37,000.

e. Manufactured and sold machinery to various customers during the year totaling $172,000. At year-end, it had received payments for this machinery totaling $155,000. The remainder is to be collected next year.

f. Received payments totaling $35,000 for machinery that had been delivered to various customers in the year preceding the past year.

Required:

1. How much revenue is attributable to the year's performance for each of the above events, using the criteria embodied in the realization principle? Explain your answer in each case.

2. For what reasons does conventional accounting use the realization principle for recognition of accomplishment?

3-8. The Matching Principle. Jack's Gardening Service is a small sole proprietorship started by Jack Williams three years ago. The principal activity of the business is maintenance of residential and commercial landscaping. Prior to now, Jack has been measuring the success of his enterprise simply on the basis of cash flow. However, he realizes that cash flow alone is not necessarily a good measure of performance and does not take into account the need to replace resources as they are used. In particular, he is concerned with leaving enough cash in the business to replace his truck and equipment as the need arises. Thus he has decided to use conventional accounting net operating income as his measure of performance. He is presently concerned with matching efforts (expenses) with last month's accomplishments (revenues). The relevant facts are as follows:

   a. At the start of his business, he purchased a truck for $4,000. He estimated at that time that it would last six years and that he could sell it at the end of six years for $400.
   b. He also purchased mowers, a Rototiller, and other equipment at the outset, for which he paid a total of $1,400. He estimates that this equipment will have to be replaced at the end of the fourth year and that he will get a $200 trade-in allowance for the equipment at the time of replacement.
   c. During the past month, he paid out $72 for gas used in his truck and mowers during the month.
   d. He paid wages to employees of $800 during the month, $200 of which was for time worked in the previous month.
   e. He purchased $450 worth of fertilizer and other supplies on account. At the end of the month, he had $200 worth of fertilizer and supplies remaining. He had started the month with $50 worth of fertilizer and supplies.
   f. On January 1 of the current year, he had paid for various business licenses and insurance for the year totaling $600.
   g. At the end of the month, he paid his bookkeeper for three months' services. This totaled $165.
   h. At the end of the month, he withdrew $750 from the business to pay personal living expenses.

Required:

1. Using the matching principle, what are Jack's expenses for the month based on the above events? Explain your reasoning in each case.
2. Which of the above might be classified as product costs? Which are period costs?

3-9. Revenue Recognition. Theodora Thimble operates a women's wear shop which produces custom-made as well as ready-to-wear women's outfits. During a recent month the events listed below took place. Indicate how much revenue should be recognized for the month in each instance (including amounts implied but not directly stated).

   a. Customers were permitted to put a number of items on "layaway" for deposits totaling $200. At the end of the layaway period the customers need not buy the items, in which case they forfeit their deposits. Otherwise the deposits apply against the price.

b. A customer dropped by to try on a custom-made outfit. The outfit was satisfactory and the sale completed. The customer paid the balance of $80 between the $100 price of the dress and the deposit paid at the end of last month when she ordered the outfit.
c. Other customers were measured for custom-made outfits, with total selling prices of $3,000. At the time of measurement, when the order is accepted, customers pay 20 percent of the total price.
d. Received $2,000 for cash sales, some of which were out of lay-away with deposits totaling $200 received earlier.
e. Received $3,500 in cash payments on credit sales. The beginning balances due from customers totaled $4,000, but by month-end they totaled $5,000.

3-10. **Recognizing Accounting Principles.** Three important principles of conventional accounting have been discussed in the chapter: the realization principle, the matching principle, and the original transaction value (cost) principle. Identify the principle that is most relevant to each of the following events. (Note: More than one principle may be involved.)
a. Purchased a used truck at the end of a period at a cost of $3,000.
b. Supplies originally cost $1,500, which had been used to produce goods sold during the period, are recognized as an expense.
c. Prepaid rent was reduced by $500, representing the amount expired for the period.
d. A customer order was received for 100 of the power tools manufactured by the company (total price, $3,000).
e. Through a friend, you purchase for $450 a piece of equipment that normally costs $500. You record an increase of $450 in equipment held by you. You do not recognize revenue or income.
f. Depreciation of equipment is $600 for the period.
g. Marketable securities costing $3,000 increase in value to $5,000. No revenue is recognized as a result of the increase.
h. $500 is paid in advance to you for services to be performed by you next year. Your recognized net income for the current period is unaffected by the event.
i. Wages accrued (earned but not paid) at the end of 19X9 are recognized as expense in 19X9.
j. Interest earned, but not received, on a loan made by you to an associate is recorded as income of the period.

3-11. **Net Cash Flow and Net Operating Income Contrasted.** George Craft owns and operates a boardinghouse near a large university. He started the business two years ago when he leased a large old house for $3,600 per year payable one-half on January 1 and one-half on July 1 of each year. The house accommodates fifteen students for both room and board at a monthly rate of $100 each and provides meals only to another ten students for $60 per month each. To establish his venture, Mr. Craft had to buy both furniture and food preparation equipment. The furniture cost $3,600 two years ago, and he estimates that it will last no more than a total of six years. The food preparation equipment cost a total of $3,000, and he estimates this equipment will have to be replaced every five years.

During May of this year, he made food purchases of $970 on account and paid for April's purchases totaling $1,060. He estimated he had $240 worth of food on hand at the end of April and $190 worth of food on hand at the end of May. He employs one person who handles both cleaning and meal preparation for a salary of $650 per month. Heat, light, and other miscellaneous expenses for May totaled $73.

Mr. Craft is currently reevaluating the profitability of his investment. He is unsure whether to measure it on the basis of net cash flows or net operating income.

Required:

1. Prepare a statement of net cash flows for May for Mr. Craft's venture.
2. Prepare a conventional accounting income statement for May.
3. Which is the better performance measurement (i.e., which is a better indicator of the long-run cash-generating ability of the venture)? Explain.

3-12. Net Operating Income and Net Cash Flow Contrasted. Diver Supply Company was recently formed by Tim Wilson to manufacture a new kind of "wet suit" for skin divers. In its first month of operation, the firm was involved in the following transactions:

April 1   Tim invested $10,000 cash in the business.

April 1   Purchased wet-suit material on account for $1,700. The account must be paid by May 10.

April 1   Hired two part-time employees to assemble wet suits at a salary of $200 each per month.

April 2   Purchased equipment for manufacture of the wet suits. He paid $7,200 for the equipment.

April 5   Signed an agreement with a local sporting goods store to supply wet suits for April and May delivery (one-half delivered each month). The total selling price was $3,600, $1,000 of which was paid at the time of the order, the remainder to be paid at the end of May.

April 30 Paid employees for month of April. Counted inventory and found there was $700 worth of material still unused. Delivered one-half of the wet-suit order as scheduled.

Required:

Assuming that the equipment has a three-year life with no salvage value, that no additional materials were purchased in April, and that he had no finished wet suits in inventory at the end of April:

1. Prepare a cash-flow statement for the month of April.
2. Prepare a conventional accounting income statement for the month of April.

3. Compare the two statements. Which do you think is a better performance measurement? Explain.

3-13. Net Operating Income and Net Cash Flow Contrasted. The On and Up Glider Company was formed on January 1, 19X5, to sell supply items to glider fans. During the first month the following transactions occurred:

January 1   Owner invested $15,000 in the business.

January 1   Hired a part-time salesperson for $500 per month.

January 2   Purchased $5,000 of supply items for cash.

January 5   Purchased for cash a delivery truck for $3,500. The estimated life of the truck is five years, after which it will be sold for $500.

January 10   Purchased $2,000 of supply items using credit. First payment is due in March.

January 31   Paid the part-time salesperson the January salary.

January 31   Paid $500 of miscellaneous business expenses.

January 31   Sales receipts for January indicated $3,000 of cash sales and $1,000 of credit sales.

January 31   An inventory of the supply items indicated that $5,000 worth of supplies have *not* been sold.

Required:

1. Prepare a cash-flow statement for January 19X5.
2. Prepare a conventional accounting income statement for January 19X5.
3. List and explain each difference of items and/or amounts between the two statements.

3-14. The Matching Principle—Small Business Transactions. The Custom Sign Company is a sole proprietorship started by John Smythe during March of this year. The principal activity of the business is construction and painting of exterior signs for commercial establishments according to customer specifications.

When the business was started, Mr. Smythe opened a checking account in the name of the business. Until now, he has been evaluating his monthly performance by the monthly increase (decrease) in the balance of the firm's checking account. However, he realizes that net cash flow is not the only measure of performance and that net cash flow does not take into account the usage of equipment and services that were paid for in prior months. He has therefore decided to use conventional accounting operating income as a measure of monthly performance.

At the end of the current month (September), he is concerned with properly determining and measuring the expenses of the month. Since he has no credit customers, he feels that cash receipts (collected at the time signs are completed) are a fair measure of revenue.

Some of the notes that Mr. Smythe has made to himself include the following information:

a. On March 1, he purchased a used heavy-duty pickup truck for $2,700. He estimated that the pickup would last for five years and that he could sell it for $300 at the end of the fifth year.

b. Immediately after the purchase of the pickup, he purchased a portable gasoline-powered generator and installed it in the pickup for use in on-site sign construction and painting. The total cost of the generator was $1,200. He estimated the life of the generator to be eight years and the salvage value to be $240.

c. Other equipment purchases on March 1 totaled $540. The estimated life at the time of purchase was three years (no salvage value).

d. At the same time he purchased the truck (March 1), he paid for the city and state licenses required to operate a commercial business. The cost of the licenses totaled $400, and the licenses expire on October 31.

e. Mr. Smythe acquired an insurance policy (truck, fire, casualty, and liability) effective March 1. The policy is for a three-year period, with prepayments of annual premiums on March 1. The annual premium for the first year is $480.

f. Mr. Smythe rented a small building on April 1 for the storage of materials and equipment and for off-site sign construction and painting. The rental is $100 per month, with prepayments of three months' rent due every three months. He prepaid three months' rent on April 1 and July 1.

g. Gasoline for the pickup and generator is purchased using a credit card. During the current month he purchased $80 worth of gasoline using the credit card. He also paid an oil company statement (for gasoline purchased in prior months) for $120.

h. He purchased $750 worth of sign materials (lumber, paint, etc.) during the month. He estimated the cost of the materials on hand at the beginning and the end of the month to be $200 and $150, respectively.

i. He withdrew $450 at the end of August to pay for his estimated September personal expenses and withdrew $500 at the end of September for his estimated October personal expenses.

Required:

1. Using the matching principle, what are the September expenses for the Custom Sign Company? Explain your reasoning for each item included or excluded.

2. Which of the September expenses might be classified as products costs? Which are period costs?

3-15. Cash Flows and Conventional Accounting Income. Mary Morton owns and operates a photography shop which specializes in pictures for special occasions. She started the business last year when she leased an old house which could be converted into a studio. The rental on the house is $2,400 per year, with advance quarterly payments due on the first of January, April, July, and October. The lease is renewable on an annual basis for up to five years. At the end of five years, the lease may be canceled or renegotiated.

Before she could begin operations, Ms. Morton had to convert the interior of the house to a studio, purchase furniture and fixtures, and purchase photography equipment. The leasehold improvements (cost to convert interior to a studio) cost $1,800. If the lease is canceled at the end of the five-year lease period, the leasehold improvements belong to the owner of the house. The cost of furniture and fixtures was $4,800. Ms. Morton estimated that the useful life of the furniture and fixtures would be eight years and that the salvage value would be negligible. The photography equipment cost $2,700. The estimated life of the equipment is ten years, but Ms. Morton plans on trading in all equipment for new equipment every three years. She estimates that the trade-in value at the end of three years will be one-third of the original purchase price.

During April of this year, she purchased $600 worth of film and other photography supplies on account and paid all the outstanding statements for the prior two months' purchases in the amount of $400. She estimated that she had $200 and $300 worth of photography supplies on hand at the beginning and the end of the month, respectively.

Ms. Morton bills customers after they have ordered photographs from the proofs. During the current month, she billed customers in the amount of $2,800. She collected $2,700 from customers during the month.

Ms. Morton employs an assistant who aids in studio photography, acts as secretary-receptionist, and keeps books on a cash basis. Her salary is $700 per month. Miscellaneous expenses (including utilities) totaled $100 for April and were paid for in April. Ms. Morton withdrew $500 for personal expenses at the end of the month.

In prior months Ms. Morton had not tried to measure the profitability of the business, since she had no cash problems. However, she now anticipates a rise in the price of film and other photography supplies of approximately 10 percent, and she plans to raise the salary of her assistant to $750 in the near future. Therefore she is wondering how much effect the expected cost increases will have on profitability and whether or not she should revise her price schedules. She also is unsure whether to measure performance on the basis of cash flows or operating income.

Required:

1. Prepare a performance statement for April based upon net cash flow as a measure of performance.
2. Prepare a conventional accounting income statement for April.
3. Which is the better profitability measure (i.e., which is the better indicator of long-run cash-generating ability)? Why?

Conventional Accounting: Framework, Recognition of Economic Events, and Periodic Statements

In Chapter 3 conventional accounting performance measurement was introduced. Conventional accounting also includes a well-developed framework within which periodic determination of net operating income is accomplished. This framework is introduced and illustrated in the present chapter. Some further issues, principally concerning income measurement, are covered in Chapter 5.

There are two (perhaps more) important reasons for the development and use of the accounting framework. First, periodic income determination uses data from economic events very selectively, often requiring that information about events be recorded at the time of their occurrence for use in income determination in later periods. For instance, during a particular year a significant resource like a piece of heavy equipment may be acquired by the enterprise but not put into use immediately. Hence no expense is recognized in the current period with respect to that resource. But its cost (purchase price) needs to be recorded at the time of purchase for use in later periods to recognize the expense associated with its use in production as the products it helps to produce are sold.

Second, many economic events to which the enterprise is party, but which do not affect income determination in the period in which they take place, are of economic significance themselves—quite apart from their significance in later income determination. The piece of equipment mentioned above is a good example. Its mere possession by the enterprise may be a significant clue to future productivity—a supplement to current net operating income data in projecting the future cash flows of the enterprise. Similarly, payment of cash to discharge a loan that was originally used to finance the purchase of productive resources may prove helpful in assessing the ability of the enterprise to satisfy its creditors and therefore its ability to borrow additional funds in the future. Finally, the receipt of cash from customers for sales already included in revenues of prior periods may be significant affirmative evidence that recognition of revenue at the time of sale is not unwarranted in light of experience with collections.

At any rate, conventional accounting includes a *framework* which facilitates the determination of net operating income and which, when reported along with net operating income, conveys additional information about the enterprise's status and activities. That framework is called *financial position*. It consists of several broad classes of elements known as *assets, liabilities,* and *owners' equity*.

Building the Framework—Assets and Liabilities Defined

Until now, we have avoided much of the traditional vocabulary of accounting or have used it in the very loose way that many of its terms are often used by nonaccountants. The term *asset* is one that we have largely avoided.

Assets. Assets are resources (rights or possessions) to which an accounting entity is legally entitled and which are expected to produce future benefits.

Example 4-1

Examples of assets are easy to find, but it is important to remember that assets include nonphysical rights to benefits as well as physical possessions that can be used to produce benefits. Thus assets include such things as:

1. Cash
2. Copyrights and patents
3. Buildings
4. Equipment
5. Autos, trucks, buses
6. Amounts due from others for products sold to them

Roughly speaking, *liabilities* are the opposite of assets. They can be defined as follows:

Liabilities. Liabilities are obligations of an accounting entity to provide cash or other benefits to some other economic unit at some future time.

Example 4-2

As with assets, examples of liabilities are easy to conceive. Again, less clearly defined obligations must be included along with more obvious obligations. Thus liabilities include such things as

1. Amounts due suppliers for items delivered, for which payment has been deferred
2. Unpaid wages and salaries for work already performed
3. The services that may eventually have to be performed under terms of warranties given with products sold
4. A mortgage note on a building or equipment

Valuation of Assets and Liabilities in Conventional Accounting

The above definitions of assets and liabilities are not strictly unique to *conventional* accounting. They are common to a number of possible financial accounting models of the business enterprise, including conventional accounting and several others, to be discussed in Chapters 13 through 16. One of the principal things that distinguishes one accounting model from another, however, is the way that assets and liabilities are valued in each.

In the discussion in Chapter 2 entitled "Present Value and the Concept of Wealth," we defined *valuation* as the measurement (quantification) of wealth in money terms. Applying present value methodology, we valued any given asset or liability by assigning to it an amount equal to the present value of the future cash flows expected to be received or paid. Under conventional accounting, assets and liabilities are also assigned money values. The basis for assigning the values, however, depends on whether the item is a "monetary" or a "nonmonetary" asset or liability.

Monetary Assets and Liabilities. Monetary assets include cash plus all assets consisting of rights to *receive fixed amounts of dollars at future times*. Monetary liabilities are all obligations to pay fixed amounts of dollars at future times. Monetary assets and liabilities consist of such things as the following:

Monetary Assets	*Monetary Liabilities*
1. Cash	1. Amounts payable to suppliers
2. Savings deposits	2. Wages due employees
3. Amounts owing from customers for products delivered or services rendered	3. Taxes owed to government units

Nonmonetary Assets and Liabilities. Nonmonetary assets and liabilities, as the label implies, are all assets and liabilities other than monetary assets and liabilities. Nonmonetary assets and liabilities consist of such things as the following:

Nonmonetary Assets	*Nonmonetary Liabilities*
1. Raw materials on hand	1. Obligations to deliver products in the future (usually for which payment has been received)
2. Equipment	2. Obligations to perform services (for which payment has been received)
3. Buildings	
4. Land	
5. Copyrights, patents, etc.	

Valuing Monetary Assets and Liabilities. Because monetary assets and liabilities consist of cash and claims to specific amounts of cash, it is relatively easy to value them. For instance, most people would agree that a promise to pay $100 with virtual certainty tomorrow or next week is worth roughly the same as $100 possessed today. The exceptions, of course, are the monetary assets (liabilities) calling for uncertain receipt (payment) of cash in the more distant future, thereby making risk and the time value of money significant factors in their value. Such cases are discussed in some detail in the context of conventional accounting in Chapters 9 and 11. For the present, we ignore time value of money and risk in introducing conventional accounting valuation.

Thus, when we refer to monetary assets and liabilities in this discussion, we are concerned mainly with cash and amounts that are collectible or payable in the near future with virtual certainty. The single exception is the bank loan introduced in Example 3-3. While it is long term in nature, its amount is based on a cash transaction and therefore not subject to any special valuation problems. Assuming the enterprise operates satisfactorily, repayment of the loan at its face value after five years is also quite certain.

Most monetary assets are received in exchange for the products or services sold by the enterprise. Most monetary liabilities are owed to suppliers of resources used in the business. *In conventional accounting most monetary assets (liabilities) are valued at their nominal amounts, that is, the specified amounts to be received (paid).* In most cases of short-term monetary assets, the amount to be received (from, say, a customer) is also equal to the cash or its equivalent in products or services given in exchange for the (customer's) promise to pay. Similarly, in most transactions giving rise to a short-term monetary liability, the amount to be paid is equal to the cash or its equivalent in goods and services received in exchange for the liability.

Example 4-3

Suppose an enterprise provides services for two different customers. One pays $1,000 in cash; the other receives services worth $2,000 and pays the $2,000 before the end of the month. The enterprise recognizes the new monetary assets at the amounts received or to be received, namely, cash of $1,000 and "accounts receivable" of $2,000.

Example 4-4

Suppose an enterprise receives supplies worth $3,000 from a supplier and incurs an obligation to pay the $3,000 in thirty days. The liability "accounts payable" is valued at the amount agreed to be paid, $3,000.

Valuing Nonmonetary Assets. Relative to monetary assets (liabilities), nonmonetary assets (liabilities) are typically more difficult to value. The benefits to be derived from nonmonetary assets are determined by how they are used to produce future cash flows. If a nonmonetary asset is held for sale, the benefits from its possession depend on the price it will bring at the time of eventual sale. If a nonmonetary asset is held for use in the business, the benefits from its possession depend on the amounts of products and services it can be used to produce and the prices they will bring. To value nonmonetary assets (liabilities) directly requires the kind of forecasts of uncertain future cash flows that conventional accounting is supposed to avoid. Thus, direct valuation of nonmonetary assets is usually avoided in conventional accounting. *Under conventional accounting a nonmonetary asset generally is valued at an amount equal to the cash plus monetary assets (or liabilities) given in exchange for it.* This is justified on two grounds.

First, in most transactions in which the enterprise acquires nonmonetary assets, it gives up strictly cash and other monetary assets or liabilities in exchange. Second, it is presumed that if an economic entity is behaving rationally, then the value of what it receives in a given exchange transaction must be worth at least as much as the value of what it gives up in return. It is therefore both convenient and sensible to value the nonmonetary assets acquired at the amounts of monetary assets and liabilities given to acquire them.

Example 4-5

> Suppose a retail business acquired merchandise for resale in its stores. In exchange for the goods delivered, it paid $500 at delivery and agreed to pay $1,500 at the end of the following month. The nonmonetary asset acquired, namely, "merchandise," is valued at $2,000, the sum of the monetary assets given (cash) plus the monetary liabilities incurred (accounts payable) in exchange for it.

The reader should be aware that most, but not all, nonmonetary assets are acquired in exchange for cash plus other monetary assets or liabilities. Some are acquired in exchange for other nonmonetary assets. These cases present greater valuation problems for accountants. Discussion of such cases is postponed to Chapter 10.

Conventional Accounting Valuation—General Comments

To summarize the above discussion of conventional accounting valuation, it can be said that assets and liabilities are initially valued at their "original transaction values."

> **Original Transaction Value.** The original transaction value of an asset or a liability is the value established in the exchange(s) in which the asset was acquired or the liability incurred. Usually such exchange values are determined by the amounts of monetary items given, promised, received, or to be received, depending on the circumstances.

This general statement, although somewhat abstract, is convenient because it embraces both nonmonetary and monetary assets and liabilities. As a result, the term *original transaction value* (or the more customary *historical value*) can be used to represent conventional accounting valuation in general. Incidentally, when the idea of original transaction value is applied only to nonmonetary assets, the term *original transaction cost* (or *historical cost*) is used.

The reader should recognize that although an asset is initially valued at its original transaction value (cost) in conventional accounting, it may not persist in being valued at its full initial cost as time passes. In the case of a nonmonetary asset that is used in production, portions of its cost will be recognized as expense in periods in which products that it helps to produce are sold. Each time a portion of an asset's original transaction cost is recognized as an expense, its remaining recognized value to the enterprise is reduced by that amount, as is illustrated later. Not surprisingly, a recognized expense is often described simply as an *expired cost,* referring to the idea that expenses are portions of the original costs of assets proportionate to the amount of the asset that has been used up or has expired. Similarly, the value of an asset at a point in time (and sometimes the asset itself) is often referred to as an *unexpired cost.*

Completing the Framework—Owners' Equity; Financial Position

The owners' equity of a business enterprise is an abstraction (or concept) based on roughly the opposite economic implications of assets and liabilities. This is summarized in the definition that follows:

Owners' Equity. Owners' equity represents the owners' residual interest in, or rights to, the future (cash) benefits from the enterprise, in excess of what is required to satisfy the enterprise's liabilities.

Valuation of Owners' Equity. Owners' equity is not valued or measured directly. At any given point in time, total owners' equity is valued at the amount by which the values placed on all assets exceed the values placed on all liabilities. In other words:

The value of owners' equity equals the sum of the values assigned to all the assets of the enterprise minus the sum of the values assigned to its liabilities—which is usually simplified to: Owners' equity = Assets − Liabilities.

Financial Position Defined. Defining assets, liabilities, and owners' equity brings us to a final important definition in building the framework for conventional accounting:

Financial Position. Financial position is the financial status of the enterprise, consisting of the values assigned to its assets, liabilities, and owners' equity, as of a point in time.

The Accounting Equation. Because of the way that owners' equity is valued, financial position always satisfies the relationship implied in the following equation, called the basic accounting equation:

$$\text{ASSETS} = \text{LIABILITIES} + \text{OWNERS' EQUITY}$$

Interestingly, this equation, in expanded form, can be used as a clerical device to represent an enterprise's financial status as of a point in time. It also serves as a framework within which to recognize its performance for a period of time.

Applying Conventional Accounting Concepts within the Framework

Let us now return to the Fancy Flavors, Inc., case introduced in Example 3-3. We will trace its economic status (financial position) through the first month of operations, relying on the definitions and relations developed in the preceding discussion and using the basic accounting equation as a clerical (bookkeeping) device.

Original Investment in an Enterprise. Recall that the first event in Fancy Flavors' history was the investment of cash of $750,000. The owners invested $150,000 and a bank loan in the amount of $600,000 was secured. The effect of these events on Fancy Flavors' financial position can be represented as follows:

$$\text{ASSETS} = \text{LIABILITIES} + \text{OWNERS' EQUITY}$$

$$\$750,000 = \$600,000 + \$150,000$$

The investment has put $750,000 of monetary assets in the form of cash under the control of the business. Liabilities plus owners' equity equal total assets. The owners' direct investment plus the bank loan are the sources of the available assets (cash).

Acquiring an Asset. Let us now consider the next event in the life of the business, the purchase of equipment for $600,000. To recognize this event we need to take advantage of the clerical convenience of the financial position equation. That is, we need to expand it to include more detailed elements of financial position, or "accounts," as elements of financial position are customarily called. In this case we need only expand the assets class to handle the event involving two kinds of assets, cash and equipment. Just before the purchase of the equipment, we can think of the financial position of the business as follows:

$$\text{CASH} + \text{EQUIPMENT} = \text{LIABILITIES} + \text{OWNERS' EQUITY}$$

$$\$750,000 + 0 = \$600,000 + \$150,000$$

This represents no substantive change from the earlier representation, since the amount of total assets is the sum of all the individual asset values. But now we can represent the change in the enterprise's financial status that has resulted from the purchase of equipment as shown in Exhibit 4-1.

Exhibit 4-1

	Cash	+	*Equipment*	=	*Liabilities*	+	*Owners' Equity*
PRIOR POSITION	$750,000	+	0		$600,000	+	$150,000
Event: Purchase of equipment	($600,000)		$600,000				
NEW POSITION	$150,000	+	$600,000	=	$600,000	+	$150,000

What we have done is start with an initial position, then recognize an event (the purchase), and finally arrive at a new position incorporating the effect of the event. Notice that the "event" line simply indicates that the purchase results in a decrease in cash of $600,000 (denoted by the parentheses around the $600,000 in the Cash column) and an increase in another asset, equipment, in the same amount. When the elements of the event line are added (algebraically) to the prior total of their respective accounts, the result is a new financial position different from the original position *reflecting the occurrence of the event.*

Several additional observations can be made at this time about the procedure illustrated in Exhibit 4-1. First, the "prior position" satisfies the equality condition of the basic financial position equation—the total of the assets equals the total liabilities plus total owners' equity. Second, the "event" line also satisfies the equality condition—it represents offsetting plus and minus elements to only the *assets* side of the equation, which means that the equality condition is not disturbed. Third, as a result of these first two observations, the "new position" line also satisfies the equality condition. The total assets (cash of $150,000 plus equipment of $600,000) equal the sum of the liabilities ($600,000) and owners' equity ($150,000).

Finally, it probably seems sensible that the mere acquisition of one asset for another (cash for equipment) does not increase owners' equity. In conventional accounting this is generally the case. Remember that in conventional accounting nonmonetary assets are valued at their original transaction cost to the enterprise. Hence, in recognizing the purchase of the equipment, the value assigned to the equipment must equal the value of the assets given up (in this case $600,000 in cash). With no change in total assets (or liabilities in this case), there simply can be no change in owners' equity recognized from such an exchange.

Prepaying for a Service or Benefit. Now consider the second event of interest in tracing Fancy Flavors through its first month of operations, the payment of three months' rent totaling $60,000. Before we consider how to recognize the effect of this event on financial position, a further point needs clarification. Prepaid rent conforms to the definition of an asset given earlier. Upon prepayment of rent, the enterprise has a right to occupy buildings that can be used to produce goods and services and therefore contribute to future cash inflows to the enterprise. So in prepaying rent, the enterprise gives up one asset—cash—and receives another asset—the right to occupancy (customarily we call this asset "prepaid rent"). Since the prepayment of rent is an exchange of one asset for another asset, it has an effect on financial position similar to the effect of the purchase of equipment. That effect along with the purchase of equipment is represented in Exhibit 4-2.

Exhibit 4-2

	Cash	+	Equipment	+	Prepaid Rent	=	Liabilities	+	Owners' Equity
PRIOR POSITION	$750,000	+	0	+	0	=	$600,000	+	$150,000
Event 1: Purchase of equipment	($600,000)		$600,000						
Event 2: Prepayment of rent	($ 60,000)				$60,000				
NEW POSITION	$ 90,000	+	$600,000	+	$60,000	=	$600,000	+	$150,000

Again notice that no change in liabilities has taken place and no change in owners' equity is recognized. Also notice that both the additional event line and the new position line again conform to the equality condition. In the new position, *assets* (cash of $90,000, equipment of $600,000, and prepaid rent of $60,000) add up to the same total as *liabilities* ($600,000) plus *owners' equity* ($150,000).

Cumulative Effect of Events on Financial Position. Finally, notice that the new position shown in Exhibit 4-1, after only the equipment purchase had taken place, has been dropped from the worksheet in Exhibit 4-2. This does not change the result from what it would be if we calculated the new financial position after the equipment purchase first, and then modified *that* position further for the prepayment of rent. Furthermore, in practice it is both tedious and unnecessary to recalculate a new financial position after each event. Thus, all the events for a particular period of time are recorded in a manner analogous to the "events" lines we have used above. Then, at the end of a typical accounting period, each account is adjusted for the *cumulative effect* of all events affecting the account. This is illustrated in Exhibit 4-2 with respect to the cash account, the only account affected by more than one event so far. The new position of $90,000 results from subtracting the two reductions of $600,000 and $60,000 (or a total of $660,000) from the original position of $750,000.

Recognizing all of the Events of an Accounting Period—A Financial Position Worksheet. We now shift away from the introductory practice of finding a new position after each event in the example. Instead, we will consider the effects of all events of the first month's operations on one worksheet. A new financial position is computed as of the end of the month, taking account of all the events of the month at once—as would likely be done in practice. Exhibit 4-3 represents the worksheet for the month of August. Each event line is numbered and is discussed below with the exception of numbers 1 and 2, which are the now-familiar equipment purchase and rent prepayment events.

The reader will notice that there are a few differences in form between the expanded worksheet in Exhibit 4-3 and the earlier worksheets in Exhibits 4-1 and 4-2. First, there are a few more headings because as we consider more types of events, we need the greater descriptive power of a more detailed financial position equation. Second, there is a double vertical line separating the assets from the liabilities and owners' equity (the claims to assets). This is nonessential but serves as a reminder of the location of the "equals" sign in the financial position equation and also reminds us that as we recognize each event we should leave the equality condition undisturbed. Some of the other unfamiliar features of this expanded worksheet are explained as we discuss the treatment of individual events below. For the sake of clerical convenience, and in keeping with actual business financial *reporting* practices, three zeros (000s) are omitted from all amounts appearing in Exhibit 4-3. That is, each individual number is an expression in "thousands of dollars."

Recognition of External Events, or "Transactions"

Many "events," as we have been calling them, that affect the financial status of the enterprise are exchange transactions between the enterprise and other economic entities. For obvious reasons, such events are referred to as *external*

Exhibit 4-3

FANCY FLAVORS, INC.

Financial Position Worksheet
(amounts in thousands)

Description	Cash	+	Accounts Receivable	+	Prepaid Rent	+	Ice Cream	+	Supplies	+	Equipment	+	Accumulated Depreciation	=	Accounts Payable and Accrued Liabilities	+	Bank Loan Payable	+	Owners' Equity
Prior Position	750																600		150
1. Purchase of equipment	(600)										600								
2. Prepayment of rent	(60)				60														
3. Purchase of supplies	(20)								20										
4. Purchase of ice cream							30								30				
5. Additional ice cream purchases							135								135				
6. Payments for ice cream purchased	(130)														(130)				
7. Additional supplies purchased									10						10				
8. Sales	400		50																450 (R)
9. Miscellaneous expenses paid	(10)																		(10) (E)
10. Payment of salaries and wages	(120)														30				(150) (E)
11. Cost of ice cream sold							(145)												(145) (E)
12. Cost of supplies used									(15)										(15) (E)
13. Recognition of expired rent					(20)														(20) (E)
14. Recognition of equipment depreciation													(10)						(10) (E)
15. Recognition of interest on loan															6				(6) (E)
16. Recognition of federal income tax obligation															24				(24) (E)
New Position	210	+	50	+	40	+	20	+	15	+	600	+	(10)	=	105	+	600	+	220

113

events, or *transactions.* Besides the equipment purchase and prepayment of rent, lines 3 through 10 on the worksheet also represent the effects on financial position of transactions engaged in by the Fancy Flavors enterprise during August 19XX. Discussion of these events follows.

Purchase of Supplies for Cash (Line 3). At the beginning of its first month of operations the enterprise purchased supplies for $20,000 cash. In purchasing supplies for cash, the enterprise decreased its level of cash by $20,000 as indicated by the "(20)" in the Cash column of line 3 and established a stock of supplies that it will value at the "original transaction cost" of $20,000 as indicated by the "20" in the Supplies column of line 3. Again the effect on *total* assets is zero; one type of asset has replaced another of equal amount.

Purchase of Merchandise on Account (Line 4). Also as part of its starting-up activities, Fancy Flavors purchased $30,000 worth of ice cream. But rather than paying cash immediately, the enterprise was able to postpone payment until delivery of the second order of ice cream. Hence the enterprise incurred a liability by exchanging a promise to pay (an obligation) for an asset, ice cream. When an enterprise promises to pay one of its regular suppliers (like the ice cream manufacturer) for goods delivered, we usually refer to the liability as an *account payable.* Thus line 4 contains a "30" item in the Ice Cream column and an identical "30" item in the Accounts Payable and Accrued Liabilities column, recognizing an increase in both assets and liabilities (again, no change in owners' equity).

Additional Merchandise Purchases (Line 5). The original statement of the facts in Example 3-3 indicated that the total ice cream purchases for August amounted to $165,000, including the first purchase of $30,000 recognized on line 4. This means that another $135,000 was purchased beyond that already recognized in Exhibit 4-3. Thus line 5 shows a *further* increase in the stock of ice cream of $135,000 and an additional increase in the obligation to pay the ice cream supplier. Here we are using a *summary event* to represent probably three additional weekly deliveries of ice cream after the initial delivery but before the end of the month. To be completely descriptive, we should recognize each of the additional purchases on a separate line in the worksheet. But the final effect on financial position of recognizing several different purchases totaling $135,000 is exactly the same as one purchase for the whole $135,000. So we take advantage here of the summary transaction to eliminate unnecessary detail.

Similarly, as each new delivery was made, presumably the prior purchase was paid for in cash, eliminating the prior liability and establishing an obligation to pay for the new delivery in its place. But none of these timing differences is important as long as we do not calculate a new financial position before we have recognized the effects of all the events or transactions that affect the account in question. Note that all the individual August cash payments for ice cream deliveries are recognized in one summary transaction on line 6 of Exhibit 4-3.

Payments for Prior Purchases (Line 6). Example 3-3 indicated that of all of the ice cream deliveries received in August, only the last, in the amount of $35,000, had not been paid for by the end of the month. Hence $130,000 of the total $165,000 ice cream deliveries was paid during the month. Line 6 represents the effect on financial position of a summary transaction in which cash of $130,000 was paid to reduce the obligation to pay the ice cream manufacturer by $130,000. Notice that no change is recognized in the stock of ice cream as a result of paying the supplier for ice cream already delivered and recognized.

Additional Supplies Purchased (Line 7). Before the end of the month an additional $10,000 purchase of supplies was made "on account," that is, with a promise to pay the supplier later. Hence the line 7 treatment of the second supplies purchase is the same as the purchases of ice cream "on account" recognized on lines 4 and 5. The Supplies column contains an increase of $10,000 with a matching increase in the liability, accounts payable.

Revenue Recognition within the Financial Position Framework

Before moving to an explanation of line 8 of Exhibit 4-3, it is appropriate that we develop for the reader the relationship between the concepts involved in conventional accounting performance measurement and the framework of financial position. The first relationship, which is illustrated on line 8 of Exhibit 4-3, is the relationship between the revenue of an enterprise and the changes in financial position that are implied by its recognition.

When an enterprise (through its business operations) provides products and services to customers in a period, there is an infusion of new assets in the form of cash or promises to pay from customers. The reader will recall that the amount of revenue (or accomplishment) recognized for the period is the total amount of this inflow of resources, that is, the total prices paid or agreed to be paid by customers for products and services provided. Now consider the effect of sales of products and services (revenue) on financial position.

When the enterprise provides a product to a customer for cash or a promise to pay, the enterprise gains a new asset. But since no new obligation (liability) arises, the increase in assets is matched by an equal increase in owners' equity. Owners' equity is defined in such a way that this is always true. (Recall that Owners' Equity = Assets − Liabilities.) But it is also intuitively sensible. Revenue is the measure of accomplishment of the enterprise. And accomplishments should improve the owners' position or interest in the enterprise provided the enterprise is recognizing and meeting its obligations (liabilities). If products are provided and no new obligations are incurred, any increase in assets increases the owners' interests in the enterprise. So revenue is recognized as an increase in owners' equity at the same time (in the same period) that we recognize increases in cash and promises to pay (referred to as accounts receivable) from sales to customers. This is illustrated on line 8 of Exhibit 4-3.

Revenue Recognition (Line 8). Example 3-3 indicated that Fancy Flavors' sales of ice cream cones for cash during its first month came to $400,000. Sales of banquet desserts on credit came to $50,000, none of which had been collected as of the end of the month. Thus there has been an increase in cash of $400,000 and an increase in another monetary asset, accounts receivable, valued at $50,000. Furthermore, according to the realization principle, all actual sales, whether made for cash or for customers' promises to pay, are recognized as revenue during the period. And, as mentioned above, revenue by itself is recognized as an increase in owners' equity. Line 8 indicates an increase in cash of $400,000, an increase in accounts receivable of $50,000, and a total increase in owners' equity of $450,000. The R notation on the worksheet next to the "450" in the Owners' Equity column is to distinguish this increase due to revenue from such other possible increases in owners' equity as an additional investment of assets. No other types of increases actually take place in the first month of Fancy Flavors' operations, but the notation will later help the reader in more complicated problems.

Expense Recognition within the Financial Position Framework

If we were to draw a line below line 8 of the worksheet and compute a new financial position recognizing revenue but omitting the related expenses, the result would be nonsense. In describing revenue as the increase in owners' equity due to recognized productive accomplishment for a period, we must bear in mind that some sacrifice is always involved in providing products and services to customers. So the effect of the operating performance of a period on the financial position of the enterprise is not complete unless both revenue and expenses are recognized.

The matching principle calls for the recognition, in the period in which products are sold (and revenue is recognized), of the resource sacrifices that were made to produce the products and provide them to customers. Thus the recognition of expense means a recognition of decreases in the amounts of various kinds of assets controlled by the enterprise. Since the assets were sacrificed, not to decrease the liabilities of the enterprise but to produce products, there is no offsetting decrease in liabilities. Rather, a decrease in owners' equity in the amount of total expenses is recognized at the same time that the expense-related reductions of various types of assets are recognized. Lines 9 through 16 of Exhibit 4-3 are illustrative of expense recognition. Since the reasoning behind each item of expense of Fancy Flavors' operations for August was covered in Chapter 3, we will mainly concern ourselves here with the changes in financial position that relate to the recognition of each expense item.

Miscellaneous Expense (Line 9). Ten thousand dollars in cash was paid during August by the enterprise in miscellaneous types of expenditures (heat, light, power, etc.). Thus on line 9 of the worksheet we recognize a $10,000 decrease in cash to recognize the expenditure of some of that resource. Since the facts of the problem as stated in Example 3-3 were silent about any association between the $10,000 expenditure and revenues (sales) of future periods, we consider the whole $10,000 an expense of the current period, August. Thus on line 9 a decrease in owners' equity of $10,000 is recognized and labeled E for expense.

Salaries and Wages, Paid and Accrued (Line 10). The $120,000 wages and salaries actually paid to employees during August constitute resource sacrifices made during the month to provide ice cream products to customers, resulting in the month's recognized revenue. Unless some of the labor paid for during the month can be related to products or services of future periods, all of the $120,000 should be matched against current revenue, that is, all of the $120,000 should be recognized as expense in August.

In addition to the $120,000 in cash paid to employees for salaries and wages earned, another $30,000 was earned by employees during August but not yet paid by August 31. Unless those $30,000 in wages and salaries clearly relate to revenues of September or later months, the matching principle requires that they too be matched against August revenue as expense. So on line 10 of the worksheet we recognize not only a decrease in cash for wages paid of $120,000 but also an increase in a liability (as of August 31) of $30,000 of wages payable (in the Accounts Payable and Accrued Liabilities column). The total salary and wages expense recognized for the month of $150,000 appears appropriately as a decrease to owners' equity.

Accrual Accounting. The treatment of wages, as yet unpaid, as an expense of the period, is another example of the contrast between conventional accounting performance measurement and net cash flow. In this case the sacrifice of a resource (labor) is recognized in a period before cash is expended, whereas in the case of such long-lived assets as plant and equipment, the cash expenditure is often made first, followed by many periods of recognized sacrifice as the resource is used up in the production of revenue. In practice, many expenditures are made in periods after the period in which resources or services are used and matched against revenue. This requires the recognition in the earlier periods of obligations to eventually pay for the services consumed, such as the wages payable in the case at hand. Such obligations are sometimes referred to as *accruals* or *accrued liabilities,* from which one of the synonyms for conventional accounting derives—*accrual accounting.*

Recognizing Needed Adjustments

We have now concluded our analysis of all the transactions that Fancy Flavors engaged in during its first month of operations with economic units *outside* the enterprise. Before turning our attention to summarizing and evaluating the overall effects of this operational period, especially the determination of net operating income, we must review the current status of ongoing activities to establish whether any financial position adjustments are called for. Business processes are, by and large, continuous and therefore straddle individual accounting periods. Hence the need for review prior to any financial position "cutoff."

Financial position adjustments (typically made at the end of an accounting period—on August 31, 19XX, in the case at hand) are changes in the components of financial position that are evidenced largely by observation of events *within* the enterprise. Many of these internal observations have to do with the physical sacrifice of resources experienced in the production of the revenue recognized. Recall that because of the realization principle, revenue is generally recognized in connection with an external transaction of the current period, that is, a sale of a product to a customer. But only sometimes is an expense evidenced by an external transaction *of the current period,* such as the wages, salaries, and miscellaneous expenses in our example. In many cases expense recognition is a matter of determining how much of an asset's original transaction cost should be recognized as an expense in a period some time after the asset was acquired in an external transaction. This is what we do, based on the facts of Fancy Flavors' August 19XX operations, on lines 11 through 16 of Exhibit 4-3.

Merchandise Conveyed (Line 11). It was noted in Example 3-3 that, of all the ice cream purchased during the month of August, $20,000 worth was still in the freezers at the end of the month. Since $165,000 was purchased (received) in total, this means that $145,000 was either conveyed to customers in return for their cash and promises to pay or wasted or consumed by employees. In any case the internal observation that $20,000 worth remains tells us that a total sacrifice (expense) of ice cream worth $145,000 was made to generate the month's sales revenue of $450,000. That amount ($145,000) is therefore recognized as a reduction in the stock of ice cream with a matching reduction in owners' equity (with an expense designation) on line 11 of Exhibit 4-3.

Supplies Used (Line 12). Similar reasoning applies to the recognition of the original cost of supplies used. The internal observation that, of all supplies purchased during the month, $15,000 worth remains to be used tells us that $15,000 was used up during August and their cost should be matched against August revenues as an expense. This reasoning is recognized by a decrease in supplies of $15,000 and a matching decrease in owners' equity of $15,000, on line 12.

Expired Rent (Line 13). On line 2 we recognized that at the beginning of the month, upon payment of three months' rent in advance, the enterprise had exchanged one asset, cash, for another, the right to occupancy. But as of the end of the month, one-third of the total occupancy rights have expired. On line 13 we recognize a one-third reduction in the asset of $20,000, along with a concurrent $20,000 reduction in owners' equity for rent expense.

Depreciation of Equipment (Line 14). Earlier discussion of the net cash-flow method of measuring performance brought out that the total cost of the equipment purchased at the beginning of August should not be considered a sacrifice of doing business only in August. The equipment is expected to serve the business for five years, or sixty months. But neither is it sensible to wait until the equipment is completely worn out to recognize that its service potential has been completely consumed. Rather, in conventional accounting, some of the original cost of such long-lived assets is recognized as expense in each period of the asset's life—ideally, in proportion to the "depreciation" or decline in its service potential that is actually consumed in each period.

However, it is usually difficult to perceive how much of the service potential of an asset expires in any given short segment of its life. The usual practice is to make a reasonable estimate of how long the item will last and then choose some reasonable, systematic pattern of apportioning the original cost of the asset to each of the periods in its expected life. The simplest of these patterns is called the straight-line method, in which an equal share of the original transaction cost is apportioned to each period of the life of the asset. For the sake of simplicity this method has been adopted for purposes of our example. Discussion of other, perhaps more sophisticated, methods is postponed to Chapter 10.

Using the straight-line method we apportion or allocate $10,000 of the cost of the equipment to the first month of operations. (Based on an estimated life of five years, or sixty months, and a total original cost of $600,000, the per-month allocation is $600,000 ÷ 60 = $10,000.) Line 14 therefore shows a reduction of owners' equity of $10,000 in the month of August and a matching reduction in a column on the asset side of the worksheet—but not the Equipment column. Rather, the reduction appears in the column headed Accumulated Depreciation. Actually, the reasons for this seeming complication are rather uncomplicated and sensible.

Accumulated Depreciation—A Contra-Asset Account. First, the $10,000 expense recognized for use of the equipment for the month of August was based on an uncertain estimate that the equipment would last exactly sixty months—no more, no less. The amount of expense recognized is also based on the assumption that the business is a "going concern," that is, it will continue to operate long enough to experience all of the equipment's service-in-use potential. Either the going concern assumption or the estimate of useful life could prove to be wrong, in which case the enterprise would want to modify the effects on financial position (expense) that it has recognized based on the error. If so, it will prove convenient not to have lost track permanently of the total original transaction cost of the equipment or have to comb through old records to find it.

Second, there is the matter of portraying decision-relevant information through the statement of financial position (to be discussed more fully shortly). The financial position of an enterprise does convey information, in conjunction with periodic net income calculations, on which investors might base their estimates of future cash flows of the enterprise. In this sense it is often relevant to preserve and convey the original cost of long-lived assets along with depreciation-to-date, because often together they portray the operating capacity of the assets better than does the unexpired cost of the assets alone.

Example 4-6

> Suppose an enterprise acquired a $1 million diesel-driven electrical power generator expected to last twenty years and having a capacity in each year of its economic life that is twice that of a $500,000 generator. After ten years the enterprise, using the straight-line method of depreciation, will have offset a total of one-half of its original cost against revenues of the ten years, leaving an unexpired value of $500,000. If only the $500,000 is reported in the enterprise's financial position, it might be interpreted that the enterprise had a generating capacity equal to that of a $500,000 generator. In fact, though, the enterprise has a generator with twice the capacity per period of a $500,000 generator, but one that has served half of its expected useful life.

Hence, as a general rule, the total original transaction costs of long-lived assets are not directly reduced by the amounts of expense recognized in connection with their use. Instead, a separate, offsetting account, called a *contra-asset account*, is set up to recognize the reduction in use. The *accumulated depreciation* account of Exhibit 4-3 is just such an account. Its always-negative balance serves to modify the equipment account's balance. The two accounts are complementary in representing a long-lived asset and are never considered separately as components of financial position. Thus we recognize depreciation expense with a *decrease* in owners' equity of $10,000. At the same time, we *increase* the magnitude of the negative accumulated depreciation account by $10,000, which is tantamount to decreasing the equipment account itself. The difference is only a clerical convenience reflecting the tentative nature of recognizing the expiration of the cost of long-lived assets, and possibly portraying a more accurate picture of the production capacity of the enterprise resulting from possession of the asset.

Accrual of Interest and Federal Income Tax Expenses (Lines 15 and 16). The recognition of one month's interest expense on the bank loan is an additional adjustment related to August's operations. While the loan benefits (i.e., the availability of cash) were utilized during August, interest on the loan is not actually payable until a later point in time. Thus $6,000 is shown as an increase in Accrued Liabilities as well as a decrease in Owners' Equity on line 15.

Similarly, line 16 recognizes a future tax obligation relating directly to the enterprise's operations during the month of August. The reader is referred to Chapter 3 for the underlying calculation of the $24,000 amount of this further accrued liability. As with the entries on lines 10 and 15, Owners' Equity is correspondingly reduced.

End-of-Period Financial Position

Exhibit 4-3 shows how various elements of financial position are affected by each external transaction and each needed internal adjustment of the enterprise for the month of August. It requires only a simple additional step to arrive at a new financial position. The new level of each account is found by adding to the original level all increases indicated in the column of that account and subtracting from that sum all decreases indicated in the same account.

Example 4-7

> To illustrate, consider the cash account. Upon establishment of the business, the enterprise had a stock of $750,000 cash. During the month it experienced an inflow of cash from sales of $400,000 recognized on line 8 of Exhibit 4-3 in the Cash column. Thus $750,000 + $400,000 = $1,150,000 was the total available cash during the month. In addition, the enterprise experienced outflows of cash during the month represented by all the numbers in parentheses in the Cash column, each individually representing one expenditure or group of expenditures: Their total is $940,000 (600,000 + 60,000 + 20,000 + 130,000 + 10,000 + 120,000), which when subtracted from $1,150,000 gives the remaining stock of cash at the end of the month, $210,000, shown at the foot of the Cash column.

Applying the same logic to other columns gives the amounts shown as the new (or end-of-month) levels in all the other accounts as well.

Example 4-8

> Starting with the initial position of zero in the stock of ice cream, we add $30,000 for the initial purchase from line 4 and $135,000 in additional purchases from line 5 and subtract $145,000 of ice cream consumed from line 11, leaving an end-of-month balance in the ice cream account of $20,000.

Why bother with the new position? The answer brings us back to the overall view of conventional accounting.

The Relevance of Financial Position. First, the $20,000 stock of ice cream, like the remaining stock of $40,000 of prepaid rent, as well as the remaining stocks of all other assets, are the original costs of resources that have not yet been consumed in the production of revenues. Thus they will be recognized as expense and matched against revenue of future periods if and when the products they help to create are sold to customers. The ending financial position of one period is the beginning financial position of the next period and carries forward information for future use in performance measurement.

Second, since financial position is a way of characterizing the resources (and obligations) that are in the command of the enterprise at a point in time, it is considered to have potential, in and of itself, to convey additional information to external investors about the ongoing ability of the enterprise to generate cash.

Example 4-9

> At its inception, Fancy Flavors, Inc., borrowed $600,000 from a bank (ostensibly to purchase needed furnishings and equipment for its several store locations). In Example 3-3 this loan was stipulated to be for a five-year period—that is, repayable in full five years after its original transaction date.
>
> If repayments were due monthly on an installment basis, the bank would wish to scrutinize periodic financial position statements in order to assure itself that enough financial resources become available regularly to meet the repayment schedule.
>
> With a lump-sum repayment of the full amount after five years, the bank is no less interested in periodic financial position statements. From one statement to the next the bank will wish to ascertain that sufficient resources are building up (aside from operational needs) so that the loan repayment can in fact be made when it falls due.

The foregoing discussion leads directly to the next consideration—that of how to represent financial position of the enterprise to interested external parties.

The Balance Sheet, or Statement of Financial Position. One of the primary means of conveying information about an enterprise to outside investors is through the periodic publications customarily referred to as financial statements. One of the several statements published each period is a tabular presentation of financial position which (again as a matter of custom) is often referred to as a balance sheet.

A balance sheet (or statement of financial position) is merely an organized array of the names of the components of the financial position and the amounts of their recognized values. The balance sheet is suitably labeled to identify (1) the enterprise, (2) the nature of the statement, and (3) the *point in time* for which the financial position is being represented. Perhaps the best way to explain the statement is by illustration. Exhibit 4-4 portrays the balance sheet of Fancy Flavors as of the end of August.

Notice that the two sides of the financial position equation are presented separately—all assets first, then all liabilities and owners' equity following. Notice too that their totals are equal (they balance each other). Not surpris-

Exhibit 4-4

FANCY FLAVORS, INC.

Statement of Financial Position
As of August 31, 19XX

Assets:		
Cash		$210,000
Accounts receivable		50,000
Prepaid rent		40,000
Ice cream		20,000
Supplies		15,000
Equipment	$600,000	
Less accumulated depreciation	(10,000)	590,000
Total assets		$925,000
Liabilities and Owners' Equity:		
Accounts payable and accrued liabilities		$105,000
Bank loan payable		600,000
Owners' equity		220,000
Total liabilities and owners' equity		$925,000

ingly, this is the reason why the term *balance sheet* is often used interchangeably with *statement of financial position*.

Constructing a Balance Sheet. To construct a balance sheet at the end of any period is a simple matter if a worksheet has been constructed recording all the changes in financial position since the last statement date. Such is the case in the Fancy Flavors example. So all that is necessary, after arriving at a new position at the foot of Exhibit 4-3, is to transfer the new balance of each account to its place on the face of the balance sheet in Exhibit 4-4. The reader need only glance back at the last line of Exhibit 4-3 to confirm that each number that appears at the foot of the column of one of the accounts appears opposite that account in Exhibit 4-4.

The Statement of Income, or Results of Operations

The other statement that has traditionally been a part of the periodic accounting representation of a business enterprise is the statement of results of operations, customarily referred to as the income statement. The income statement for Fancy Flavors' August operations has already been illustrated in Chapter 3, Exhibit 3-5. We have reproduced that statement in Exhibit 4-5 for the reader's convenience, to help us make several more points about income measurement and reporting.

Constructing an Income Statement. The income statement is an array or presentation of recognized revenue and expenses for a period, along with the residual, net operating income (or loss). Like the balance sheet, the income statement is usually headed by suitable labels identifying (1) the enterprise, (2) the nature of the statement, and (3) the *period* in the life of the enterprise covered by the statement.

Given a financial position worksheet, complete with respect to all events affecting financial position for a period of time, construction of an income

Exhibit 4-5

FANCY FLAVORS, INC.

Income Statement
For the Month of August 19XX

Revenue from sales of ice cream		$450,000
Less expenses:		
Equipment depreciation	$ 10,000	
Rent	20,000	
Supplies used	15,000	
Salaries and wages	150,000	
Cost of ice cream sold	145,000	
Interest on loan	6,000	
Federal income taxes	24,000	
Miscellaneous—heat, light, etc.	10,000	
Total expenses		380,000
Net operating income		$ 70,000

statement also is a simple mechanical process. The income statement is nothing more than an array of the changes in owners' equity due to recognized revenues and expenses during the period. Glancing back at Exhibit 4-3, the reader will see that each of the numbers (labeled R or E for *revenue* and *expense*) appearing in the Owners' Equity column appears on the income statement opposite a description of the event (or class of events) that it represents. The total expenses are then subtracted from total revenue to get net operating income, the net result from operations and the index of performance in conventional accounting.

The Relationship Between Net Operating Income and Financial Position. As we have proceeded through our line-by-line explanation of the recognized changes in financial position of Fancy Flavors' first month of operations we have paused several times to explain certain important relationships and concepts. Two of these important relationships are the relationship between revenue and financial position and the relationship between expense and financial position.

In each period recognized accomplishment (revenue) increases owners' equity to reflect the increase in assets of the enterprise (cash and accounts receivable) brought about by sales of products and services. Expenses decrease owners' equity to reflect the sacrifices of assets (or increases in liabilities) made in present and past periods to produce the current period's revenue. Combined, these two effects increase (decrease) owners' equity by the amount of net operating income (net loss). Or, in other words, net operating income is the recognized net increase in the ownership interests of the enterprise that results from its productive activities—its performance. We will see later that owners' equity may increase or decrease for other reasons, for example, gains or losses (defined in Chapter 5) and additional investments or withdrawals of assets by the owner(s) during the period. *But net operating income (loss) is that portion of the total increase or decrease in owners' equity that is due to the recognized productive performance of the enterprise during the period.*

The reader should be aware, then, that the income statement is a descriptive statement of how and to what extent the recognized accomplishments (revenues) and efforts (expenses) of the enterprise altered the ownership interest in the business during a period of time (in the case of Fancy Flavors, Inc., the month of August).

Along with knowledge of any gains or losses and additional owners' investments or withdrawals of assets during the period, the income statement can be thought of as explaining the change between two levels of owners' equity—that at the beginning of the period and that at the end of the period. In the Fancy Flavors case, the $70,000 net income completely explains how the ownership interest in the enterprise went from an initial level of $150,000 to $220,000 at the end of August—since there were no gains, losses, additional investments, or withdrawals during that time. Thus the income statement bears a well-defined relationship to the ending and beginning balance sheets of the period that it covers.

Other Statements of Change in Elements of Financial Position

Even though net income, and hence the change in the owners' equity element of financial position, are of special interest, the income statement *may not be the only* statement of a change in a financial position component that is of interest. The change in the stock of cash, for instance, may also represent desirable information. Even though we noted earlier that the change in cash in a single period (net cash flow) may be a poor index of long-run cash-generating ability, it may indicate how cash, as a facilitator of exchanges (and therefore a productive factor), is being used by the enterprise.

The income statement explains the change in one particularly important component of financial position—owners' equity. To construct a statement explaining the change in *any* component of financial position, one need only follow the basic ideas described above for the income statement. That is, after identifying the enterprise, the statement, and the period covered, array the increases and decreases that appear in the worksheet column of that component of financial position opposite brief descriptions of the events that caused them.

Example 4-10

To illustrate, a statement of cash flows for Fancy Flavors for the month of August appears in Exhibit 4-6. Again, the reader will be able to trace each item to the Cash column of Exhibit 4-3.

Notice that, in the same way that the net income number explains the change in owners' equity, this net cash decrease explains the change in the cash account from an initial level of $750,000 to an ending level of $210,000. At the same time, it lists or itemizes the individual causes that made up the change.

So the cash-flow and income statements are each special cases of a more general concept, that is, *statements of the flows* (increases and decreases) that describe the transition between the beginning and ending *stocks* in a component of financial position. In chapter 6 this notion is further elaborated and still another example of a frequently reported flow statement (the statement of changes in financial position) is discussed.

Exhibit 4-6

FANCY FLAVORS, INC.

Statement of Cash Flows
For the Month of August 19XX

Cash receipts from sales		$400,000
Cash disbursements:		
Purchase of equipment	$600,000	
Prepayment of rent	60,000	
Purchase of supplies	20,000	
Payments on account for ice cream purchases	130,000	
Payments of salaries and wages	120,000	
Miscellaneous payments	10,000	
Total cash disbursements		940,000
Net cash decrease		($540,000)

The Events, or Transactions, Approach to Accounting—A Perspective

In the body of this chapter we have described for the reader the most fundamental concepts of conventional accounting and their applications to measuring the status and activities of a business enterprise. Many different themes have been woven into the single illustration. Because of the complexity of the resulting fabric, it would perhaps be helpful to the reader to have a brief summary that will serve as a mode of operation for applying conventional accounting concepts in other situations. Such a summary appears at the end of this section. Before getting to the summary, however, it is appropriate to develop some perspective on the approach to accounting measurement underlying it.

The Transactions Approach and Comparative Values Approach Contrasted. Two of the major periodic outputs of the present-day financial-accounting system are the balance sheet, portraying financial position or status as of the end of a period, and the income statement, portraying performance in productive activity for the period. In the illustration in this chapter we arrived at these end results by (1) starting with the beginning financial position of the enterprise and (2) recognizing all of the changes in that financial position resulting from external economic events and internal adjustments that affected the enterprise during the period. But it was not necessary to proceed event-by-event to determine ending financial position and measure net operating income.

Ending financial position, in principle, can be constructed at the end of the period without recognizing all of the many events that took place individually. The employees of the enterprise can count the cash on hand and confirm the amount on deposit with the bank. They can observe the amounts of supplies and merchandise on hand at year-end and determine the prices originally paid from the purchase invoices or bills sent by the suppliers. Knowing the original cost and expected lives of the long-lived assets, they can determine the amount of depreciation-to-date on each. And they can ascertain the undischarged amounts of liabilities as of the end of the period.

Having valued all the end-of-period assets at their unexpired costs and all the end-of-period liabilities at their undischarged original transaction values, owners' equity would be measured by the difference between total assets and total liabilities.

Example 4-11

In the Fancy Flavors example, the cash count and confirmation of cash in the bank, and the counts of ice cream and supplies on hand at the end of August, would show: cash of $210,000, ice cream of $20,000, and supplies of $15,000, all on hand at month-end. Examining copies of the unpaid sales invoices sent to banquet customers would indicate $50,000 in accounts receivable at the end of August. With knowledge that $60,000 was prepaid during August for rent through October, the $40,000 portion unexpired at August 31 would be determined. Similarly, with knowledge of the original cost ($600,000) and expected life (sixty months) of the equipment, after one month it would be valued at $600,000 less $10,000 accumulated depreciation.

Examination of unpaid bills from suppliers, unpaid time cards of employees, the loan contract with the bank, and federal income tax rate schedules would lead to recognition of $105,000 in accounts payable and accrued liabilities. With interest expense accrued in a separate account, the bank loan would still be valued at its original transaction balance of $600,000. Then with all assets and liabilities valued, ending owners' equity would be measured by the difference between the sum of the assets and the sum of the liabilities:

$$\text{Owners' equity} = \$925,000 - \$705,000 = \$220,000$$

The $220,000, of course, checks with the owners' equity figure shown earlier on our worksheet and balance sheet, as expected. But the process by which it was derived differs from the event-by-event process depicted in the worksheet.

Just as it is not necessary to recognize individual events and transactions to get end-of-period financial position, it is not necessary to explicitly measure revenues and expenses to determine net operating income for the period. If financial position is measured at the end of each successive accounting period, we can always take advantage of the relationship between net operating income and financial position to measure periodic net income.

We emphasized earlier that net operating income is the change in owners' equity from the beginning to the end of the period *that results from operations.* Thus we know that the change in owners' equity for a period equals net operating income plus (minus) any new investments (withdrawals) and plus (minus) any gains (losses).

Example 4-12

Fancy Flavors started August with owners' equity of $150,000 (equal to the owners' original contribution of cash). The August 31 owners' equity, calculated above, is $220,000. Since there were no gains or losses or investments or withdrawals by the owners during August, net income must be $220,000 - $150,000 = $70,000. That, of course, checks with the income statement figure shown earlier in our event-by-event illustration.

The Advantage of the Transactions, or Events, Approach. In view of the discussion in the above paragraphs, one might question why accountants in practice bother with the event-by-event approach to accounting for the business enterprise. It appears to involve more effort for the same results. The answer is that although the transactions, or events, approach may require more effort, it provides a richer and potentially more useful pool of information. Under the comparative valuation approach illustrated above, for instance, one would know the beginning and the ending balances in owners' equity plus the net income for the period, but none of the details of revenues and expenses that are forthcoming in the transactions approach would be made available to investors. Such detail is usually considered helpful in using conventional accounting net operating income as a basis for predicting future cash flows. Thus the additional effort involved in the transactions approach is usually considered worthwhile.

The Accounting Cycle—A Summary of the Transactions Approach. Although more complicated than the comparative valuation approach to accounting, the transactions approach can be summarized in a few broad steps as follows:

1. Start with the ending financial position of the prior period, that is, each account in the financial position begins the new period with the ending balance of the prior period.
2. Recognize the changes in financial position brought about by transactions entered into by the enterprise during the accounting period. In most cases, as a result of applying the realization principle, the revenue of the period is recognized in this stage of the accounting cycle.
3. Before assessing the end-of-period financial position, recognize all changes in financial position believed to have taken place during the period but which were not a direct result of a current transaction between the enterprise and another economic unit. Many kinds of expenses are recognized in this stage through application of the matching principle, for example, depreciation of long-lived assets acquired in earlier periods and accrual of liabilities for services received but not paid for.
4. Assess the end-of-period financial position.
5. Report the end-of-period financial position, net income, and other relevant aspects of the change in financial position, cash flow for example, in a coordinated set of statements. Customarily the set of financial statements includes an income statement and a balance sheet at a minimum. For larger businesses the set will include a statement of changes in financial position (to be described in Chapter 6) as well.

This outline constitutes a brief but complete statement of the process illustrated in the main body of this chapter. The next chapter continues with the discussion of conventional accounting, elaborating the concepts of income and financial position and concluding with some evaluation of conventional accounting as a financial accounting model.

Before going on with our elaboration of conventional accounting concepts, we should point out that we have resorted to a considerable degree of abstraction in this chapter to depict the essential features of the accounting cycle. The Fancy Flavors example and the worksheet format are representative only "in principle" of the accounting cycle under conventional accounting. As a practical matter one would not expect to fit on a single page all of the accounts and transactions of even the simplest types of businesses for the shortest accounting periods. Clearly a more sophisticated set of tools is required for practical applications of the accounting cycle. The financial accounting information system, including traditional bookkeeping, offers just such a set of tools, which has evolved together with conventional accounting over several centuries. The financial accounting information system is introduced in Chapter 7. The text utilizes traditional bookeeping tools in the examples, illustrations, and discussions from Chapter 7 on.

Questions for Review and Discussion

4-1. Define:
  a. Assets
  b. Liabilities
  c. Monetary assets and liabilities
  d. Original transaction value
  e. Owners' equity
  f. Financial position

4-2. What justification is there (if any) for valuing nonmonetary assets at the amount of cash or other monetary assets (or liabilities) given in exchange for them?

4-3. Owners' equity is not valued directly. True or false? Explain your answer.

4-4. Because of the way that owners' equity is valued, the sum of the values assigned to the assets of the enterprise is equal to the sum of the values assigned to the liabilities plus owners' equity. Show that this is true.

4-5. Explain the distinction between an external event and an internal adjustment. What is the significance of the distinction in the accounting cycle?

4-6. Strictly speaking, the value of the financial position framework is that it provides a clerical framework for processing transactions and calculating income. True or false? Explain your answer.

4-7. Explain in words why revenue is recognized as an increase in owners' equity.

4-8. Explain in words why expenses are recognized as decreases in owners' equity.

4-9. Give some reasons why the unexpired costs of long-lived assets are accounted for with two accounts in financial position.

4-10. Net operating income explains the difference between the beginning and the ending owners' equity of the business for a given period. True or false? Defend your position.

4-11. Since the transactions approach to conventional accounting perhaps requires more record-keeping effort than the comparative values approach, why do accountants bother with the transactions approach in practice?

4-12. In the ordinary course of events, the revenue for a period is recognized in connection with external events, whereas expenses are often recognized only as the result of internal adjustments. Do you agree or disagree? Explain your position.

4-13. In conventional accounting, when an asset is acquired it is valued at its original transaction value (cost)—the amount of cash or other assets and liabilities given in exchange for it. Does this amount represent the value of the asset to the firm? Defend your answer.

4-14. Suppose that at the end of the business year a business immediately sold all of its assets to various buyers and paid off all of its liabilities. Would the resulting cash available for the owners be equal to the year-end owners' equity figure? Explain your position.

4-15. One of the things that distinguishes conventional accounting from strictly cash basis accounting is the recognition of accruals. Do you agree or disagree? Explain your position.

Exercises

4-1. **Inventory Stocks and Flows.** Arnhem Distributors commenced 19X0 with 5,000 plastic boomerangs costing $2,500. It purchased 12,000 more boomerangs at $.75 per boomerang. By the end of the year, 3,000 of the boomerangs were left (all purchased during the year).

Required:

1. What was the cost of the boomerangs sold?
2. What would have been the cost of the boomerangs sold if the company had commenced the period with 5,000 boomerangs costing $.80 per unit? (The rest of the facts remain the same.)

4-2. **Account Analysis.** The following events are observed during 19X9:
   a. Total purchases of supplies at a cost of $450.
   b. Supplies costing $80 (purchased in 19X8) are returned.
   c. $300 of accounts payable is paid (the $300 accounts payable arose from purchases of supplies on credit during 19X8).
   d. $270 is the supplies expense for 19X9.
   e. $400 of supplies are on hand at the end of 19X9.

Required:

Determine the cost of supplies on hand at the beginning of 19X9.

4-3. **Determining Net Income.** On July 31, 19X5, Percy, who owns Pike Street Antiques, drew up a statement of financial position for his business:

Assets:			Liabilities and Owners' Equity:	
Cash		$ 4,000	Accounts payable	$ 3,500
Merchandise		8,000	Wages payable	200
Accounts receivable		1,500	Loan from finance company	2,500
Fixtures and fittings	$3,000		Total liabilities	$ 6,200
Less accumulated depreciation	(1,000)	2,000	Owners' equity	9,600
Prepaid rent		300	Total liabilities and owners' equity	$15,800
Total assets		$15,800		

Given:

a. Sales for August were $6,500.
b. $500 worth of those sales were returned by dissatisfied customers.
c. $700 was paid out for wages during August. Percy's shop assistants had not been paid for the last two days of August, which meant that $70 was owing to them.
d. The statement of financial position at the end of August showed that total accumulated depreciation of fixtures and fittings was $1,075.
e. By the end of August, only one week's rent ($150) was still prepaid. Percy had paid an additional $450 to his landlord during the month.
f. An additional $2,000 worth of merchandise was purchased during the period. $6,500 was still on hand at the end of the period.
g. Interest on the loan amounted to $40 for August. Percy paid the $40 on August 31.

Required:

Produce an income statement for Percy's business for the month of August 19X5.

4-4. **Transaction Analysis.** The 6-10 retail store reports the following financial position statements for last year:

	(amounts in thousands)	
	Jan. 1	Dec. 31
Cash	$ 10	$ 12
Accounts receivable	20	25
Merchandise	30	32
Plant and equipment	60	66
Accumulated depreciation	(10)	(14)
Total assets	$110	$121
Accounts payable to suppliers	$ 15	$ 22
Owners' equity	95	99
Total liabilities and owners' equity	$110	$121

Transactions during the year were:
    a. Cash collections from customers, $145,000.
    b. Cash payments to suppliers, $95,000.
    c. Purchases of equipment (in cash), $6,000.
    d. Cash dividends to owners, $5,000.

Required:

Compute the following:

1. Sales revenue for the year

2. Cost of merchandise sold during the year

3. Depreciation expense for the year

4. Net operating income for the year

4-5. Conventional Accounting Valuation and Income Determination in Perspective. During March 19X3 Ron Barassi Furniture Builders Company produced the following product lines:

Costs	Line A	Line B	Line C
Raw materials	$300	$250	$420
Labor costs	150	200	120
Other manufacturing costs	100	75	150
Total costs	$550	$525	$690

"Other costs" were incurred amounting to $300, but these could not be specifically identified with any of the particular products.

Beitzel Custom Builders was building competitive product lines and had the same costs, with the exception that its "other costs" amounted to $200.

By the end of March the Barassi Company had sold all the products associated with line A and line B for a price of $850 and $800, respectively. The Beitzel organization had, however, only sold the products of its line B for a price of $825. There appeared to be little doubt that the other projects would soon be sold, however, at prices of $850 for its line A and $925 for its line C.

Required:

1. Draw up an income statement for each of the two companies.

2. Based on conventional accounting valuation principles, calculate the difference in the recognized values of "furniture inventory" that would be shown on the statement of financial position of each company as of March 31 (you can assume that the companies are identical in every respect except where information has been given to the contrary).

3. Explain the reason for the differences between the two companies in income and furniture inventory.

4. Are the differences economically significant?

5. What justification can you give for the contrast between the accounting differences noted above?

4-6. Accounting Arithmetic On December 31, 19X9 the "Machinery" account represents two machines. One was purchased on January 1, 19X6, for $20,000 and the other was purchased for $10,000. The depreciation expense on these machines (both have the same estimated life) in 19X9 was $3,000, computed on the straight-line basis. Total accumulated depreciation for both machines at December 31, 19X9, was $15,000.

Required:

On what date was the $10,000 machine purchased?

4-7. Product versus Period Expenses. The Big Deal Land Developers Corporation began operations on January 1, 1980, with $600,000 in cash, contributed by a number of wealthy financiers. Two projects were commenced immediately—the Lakeside scheme and the Peninsula project. During the first three months of 1980, the following events occurred.

January   Land at Lakeside was purchased for $100,000.
          Land on the Peninsula was purchased for $200,000.

February Land surveys necessary to eventual subdivision and sale of the properties were conducted at a cost of $10,000 ($4,000 for Lakeside, $6,000 for Peninsula).

March   Contractors cleared the land at both projects.
          Cost: Lakeside $30,000
                Peninsula $25,000
          Roads and drainage were established at Lakeside at a cost of $15,000. On March 30 the Lakeside project was sold for $230,000.

During the three months a total of $18,000 was paid in wages and salaries for head office staff. Other general and administration expenses amounted to $30,000. All transactions in the period were cash transactions. During the period April 1 to June 30, general and administration expenses were $29,000, and head office salaries and wages were $16,000. Roads and drainage were established at the Peninsula project at a cost of $48,000. A new project (the Condo project) was commenced during June, with the purchase of a tract of land at a cost of $70,000. A land survey was conducted at a cost of $10,000. On June 28 the Peninsula project was sold for $350,000.

Required:

1. Produce an income statement for Big Deal Land Developers Corporation for the three months ending March 31, 1980. List the *total* assets of the corporation as of March 31.

2. Perform the same functions that you did for requirement 1 for the period April 1 to June 30.

4-8. **Applying the Accounting Cycle.**

July 1	Smith and Smythe deposited $1,000 each in a bank account under the name of the Campus Record Center. They paid $1,200 for three months' rental of a shop, and after arranging a $500 loan from the bank, spent $700 on equipment such as record racks and a cash register. The partners felt this equipment would last five years and have proceeds of $100 on disposal.
July 2	Hired Sally Swinger as salesperson at $400 a month.
July 3	Purchased records on credit at a cost of $1,500. Purchased general supplies for cash at a cost of $100. Billed by the university paper for $60 for advertisements.
July 4-12	Cash sales of records $950; paid advertising bill.
July 11	Paid $20 for insurance to the end of the month. Purchased 200 records at a cost of $2 per record (credit transaction).
July 12	Paid $500 to suppliers of records
July 12-31	Paid Sally her monthly wage. Record sales (cash) $1,000. Repaid the bank, including interest, with a payment of $510. Paid $60 for insurance to October 31. Paid $50 to a local artist for a personal appearance at the store. Paid $250 to record suppliers. Counted record stock and found stock costing $1,300 still on hand. Counted general supplies and found supplies costing $80 still on hand.

Required:

Produce a worksheet and an income statement for the Record Center for the month of July 1980. Draw up a statement of financial position as of July 31, 1980

4-9. **Applying the Accounting Cycle.** The Cruiseline professional football team started operations in September 1979.

The following activities took place during the first three months (1st quarter) of the next year:
1. Collected $50,000 from season ticket holders.
2. Occupied office space with annual rental fees of $10,000, which was paid in advance on 1/1/80 when the lease started.
3. On 1/1/80 Cruiseline borrowed $20,000 from a local bank and agreed to pay 8 percent interest.

4. Paid salaries of $40,000 on 3/31/80 for the first quarter. Players have earned an additional $10,000, but that will be paid on 4/15/80.
5. Owners withdrew $5,000 for personal uses.
6. On 3/31/80 the team bought a practice field for $20,000 cash.
7. On 1/1/80 the team bought $6,000 worth of office supplies on credit.
8. A count of supplies at 3/31/80 revealed that $2,000 worth of supplies were still on hand.

Required:

Prepare a worksheet to record the foregoing events Make sure all internal adjustments are recorded at 3/31/80. Since 1/1/80 balances are not given, do *not* attempt to calculate balances at 3/31/80.

4-10. Applying the Accounting Cycle. Five years ago several individuals got together and started a business called Copy Fast Corporation. The business consists of several part-time employees and some high-speed dry-copying equipment. Small (several-page) copying jobs are done for cash as people walk in with them off the street. Large jobs, on the other hand, are done for regular customers and on a competitive-bid basis. The balance sheet of the business as of the end of its third year is as follows:

COPY FAST CORPORATION

Statement of Financial Position
As of the End of Year Three

Assets:			Liabilities and Owners' Equity:	
Cash		$ 4,000	Accounts payable	$ 2,500
Accounts receivable		3,000		
Supplies and paper		6,000		
Equipment	$15,000			
Less accumulated depreciation	(7,500)	7,500	Owners' equity	18,000
Total assets		$20,500	Total liabilities and owners' equity	$20,500

During year four the following events are recognized:
a. Cash sales of $9,000 and credit sales of $20,000 were made.
b. Paper and supplies worth $10,000 were purchased on account.
c. Rent of $2,400 for the year was paid in cash.
d. The equipment is estimated to last five years in total and bring $2,500 upon resale at the end of that time.
e. Wages of $9,000 in total were paid all in cash.
f. At year-end $7,000 worth of supplies and paper were still on hand, and $2,000 of the total accounts receivable from customers had not been paid.
g. The business paid all but $4,000 of its total accounts payable by year-end.
h. The owners withdraw cash equal to conventional accounting net income at year-end.

Required:

Record the effects on financial position of the above events in worksheet form. Prepare an ending balance sheet and an income statement for year four as well.

4-11. **Applying the Accounting Cycle**.

January 1-5 — $18,000 is placed in a bank account entitled Chablis Enterprises by Harry Wright.

Three months' rent (amounting to $1,200) was paid by Harry for a wharf-side building to be used for a restaurant. Harry bought cooking equipment at a cost of $5,000, paying $3,000 and being granted thirty days' credit for the balance. The equipment will have a life of four years and is expected to bring a price of $1,000 on its disposal.

Harry purchased supplies costing $2,000 on credit. Harry hired cooks, waitresses, and a resident band. The total payroll of $2,000 will be paid every two weeks. Harry purchased furniture costing $6,000 for cash. The furniture will last ten years and have $1,200 salvage value.

January 6 — The Chablis Restaurant opened.

January 6-31 — Wages were paid totaling $4,000 ($700 was owed by Harry at the end of the month). An additional $2,000 was paid by him for guest performers, and $6,000 worth of supplies of food and drink were purchased on credit. Suppliers were paid $7,000 (including the $2,000 owed for cooking equipment). Harry withdrew $500 in cash for his own personal use. Supplies costing $2,200 were still on hand at the end of the period. Revenue from meals for the month amounted to $15,500 (all paid in cash).

Required:

Produce a worksheet and an income statement for January, and a statement of financial position as of January 31, 19X4.

4-12. **Levels and Changes in Owner's Equity.** Bob Menzies is the sole owner of a plumbing business—Menzies Plumbing Company. On December 31, 1979, the company's statement of financial position showed total assets to be $15,000 and total liabilities $2,000. On December 31, 1980, owner's equity was $18,000.

Required:

1. What was the owner's equity on December 31, 1979?

2. If total assets were $23,000 on December 31, 1980, what were total liabilities at that date?

3. If there were no withdrawals from the business or contributions to the business by Bob, what was the net income for 1980?
4. If Bob had contributed $2,000 in cash to the business in 1980, what would net income for 1980 have been?
5. Ignoring number 4, what would the net income for 1980 have been if Bob had withdrawn cash of $4,000 during 1980?
6. What would net income have been if, during 1980, Bob had contributed the $2,000 *and* withdrawn the $4,000?
7. Given the information in number 6, what revenue must the company have earned during 1980 if total expenses were $3,000?

4-13. Relationship between Accounting Equation and Income Statement. Partial statements of financial position for the Eckto Company show:

	12/31/80	12/31/81
Total assets	$10,000,000	$12,000,000
Total liabilities	1,500,000	1,000,000

During the 1980–81 calendar year, the total revenue generated by normal business operations was $14 million. $900,000 was received from the sale of additional shares of stock, and dividends of $200,000 were paid.

Required:

Using the information above, prepare a summary conventional income statement for the Eckto Company for the year ended December 31, 1981.

4-14. Accounting Equation Analysis. The following information is taken from the financial records of the Talisman Corporation.

Totals as of:	12/31/78	12/31/79	12/31/80
Assets	23,000	50,000	?
Liabilities	4,000	18,000	20,000
Owners' equity	?	?	?
During year:	1978	1979	1980
Net income	10,000	?	16,000
Withdrawals by owners	?	8,000	6,000
New investments by owners	12,000	5,000	10,000

1978 was the first year of operations for Talisman Corporation.

Required:

1. Withdrawals during 1978
2. Net income for 1979
3. Total assets at 12/31/80

4-15. Recognition of Effects of Events on Financial Position.

Required:

Indicate the row number, the account (column), and the amount of all numbers missing in Exhibit 4-7 (see page 138).

4-16. Recognition of Effects of Events on Financial Position. On the Jones Printing Service worksheet are entered the effects on financial position of all the external events and internal adjustments related to the start-up and first month of operations of a small company.

JONES PRINTING SERVICE

Financial Position Worksheet

	Cash	Supplies	Prepaid Rent	Accounts Receivable	Equipment	Accumulated Depreciation	Notes Payable	Owners' Equity
1.	8,000							8,000
2.	(4,000)				10,000		6,000	
3.	5,000						5,000	
4.	(3,000)	3,000						
5.	(3,600)		3,600					
6.	3,500			2,000				5,500
7.						(100)		(100)
8.			(300)					(300)
9.		(2,600)						(2,600)
10.	5,900	400	3,300	2,000	10,000	(100)	11,000	10,500

Required:

Give a description of an event or adjustment likely to have produced each numbered entry in the worksheet.

4-17. Relationship of Financial Position and Statements of Change. The following statements for John Gorton Enterprises are presented to you (page 139).

Additional information:
  a. There were no contributions or withdrawals by the owners during January 1980.
  b. No credit sales during January 1980.
  c. All merchandise was bought on credit. During January, merchandise costing $1,600 was purchased. (*Continued on p. 140*)

Exhibit 4-7

MASTERMIND ENTERPRISES—WORKSHEET

Description	Cash	Accounts Receivable	Mer-chandise	Prepaid Rent	Equipment	Accumulated Depreciation	Accounts Payable	Wages Payable	Interest Payable	Mortgage Payable	Owners' Equity
1. Prior Position	1,500	1,000	2,500	200	6,000	(1,500)	1,750	-0-	100	3,000	
2. Cash sales	1,300										2,000 (R)
3. Purchased merchandise on credit			500								
4. Credit sales											
5. Paid rent in advance				100							
6. Receipts from customers		(2,500)									
7. Payments to suppliers	(1,000)										
8. Purchased equipment with cash	(1,000)										
9. Credit sales of $1,500											
10. Paid wages	(700)										
11. Paid advertising	(300)										
12. Paid interest owing	(100)										
13. Purchased merchandise with cash	(200)										
14. Depreciation											(800) (E)
15. Merchandise used			(900)								
16. Rent expense for period											
17. Accrued wages								200			(150) (E)
18. Interest expense for period (not paid)											
19. Contribution by owner	2,000										(80) (E)
20. New Position											

138

JOHN GORTON ENTERPRISES

Statement of Financial Position
As of December 31, 1979

Assets:		
Cash		$5,000
Prepaid rent		100
Merchandise		400
Equipment	$2,400	
Less accumulated depreciation	(800)	1,600
Total assets		$7,100
Liabilities and Owners' Equity:		
Accounts payable		$1,000
Interest payable on bank loan		100
Bank loan		2,000
Owners' equity		4,000
Total liabilities and owners' equity		$7,100

JOHN GORTON ENTERPRISES

Income Statement
For Month Ended January 31, 1980

Revenue		$6,000
Less Expenses:		
Merchandise used	$1,500	
Rent	150	
Equipment depreciation	400	
Interest on bank loan	25	
Wages	600	
Total expenses		2,675
Net operating income		$3,325

JOHN GORTON ENTERPRISES

Statement of Cash Flows
For Month Ended January 31, 1980

Inflows:	Cash sales		$6,000
Outflows:	Accounts payable	$1,000	
	Rent	100	
	Interest	50	
	Wages	600	
	Total outflows		1,750
	Net cash inflows		$4,250

Required:

Prepare a statement of financial position as of January 31, 1980. *Hint:* The income statement and statement of cash flows are both "change" statements. They provide information on the month's increases to and the decreases from items in the December 31 statement of financial position given above. For example:

Cash balance, December 31, 1979	$ 5,000	(from prior statement of financial position)
Additions	6,000	(from statement of cash flows)
	$11,000	
Subtractions	1,750	(from statement of cash flows)
Cash balance as of January 31, 1980	$ 9,250	

4-18. **Net Income and Owners' Equity.** You are at the monthly meeting of the Campus Investors' Club. The club's investment in McMahon Corporation is shortly to be discussed. The club has a 10 percent interest in the corporation and receives 10 percent of any dividends that the corporation pays to its stockholders. You were responsible for bringing the 19X2 financial reports of McMahon Corporation to the meeting but have discovered that you have neglected to do so. By a stroke of good fortune you discover that today's newspaper has a brief article on the McMahon Corporation, from which you can glean the following information:

	19X1	*19X2*
Sales	60,000	65,000
Total assets	120,000	125,000
Total liabilities	90,000	80,000

Sales are the only form of revenue for McMahon Corporation.

Required (each question is independent unless otherwise stated):

1. Assuming there were no dividends paid and no contributions made by stockholders to the corporation during 19X2, calculate the corporation's 19X2 net income figure.

2. Assuming that there were no dividends paid but that the corporation's stockholders contributed an additional $10,000 (in proportion to their previous holdings) in cash during 19X2, what would be the corporation's net income for 19X2?

3. Now assume the same facts as in number 2, except that you now recall the Campus Investors' Club received a cash dividend of $2,000 during 19X2. What would be the 19X2 net income for the corporation now?

4. Using the conventional accounting net income figure derived in number 3, what would be McMahon Corporation's total expenses for 19X2?

5. You have a sneaking suspicion that the sales figure given for 19X2 is wrong. You are also satisfied that the figure for net income that you derived in number 3 is correct. If the total expenses incurred by McMahon Corporation for 19X2 were $60,000, what should the sales figure have been?

4-19. Recognition of Accountable Events. Indicate whether the following events result from adjustments (A) or external transactions (T).

  a. Recorded purchase of $500 worth of supplies on credit.
  b. From a count of supplies, calculated and recorded the cost of merchandise used as $400.
  c. Recorded $700 depreciation of machinery.
  d. Recorded the expiration of $200 of prepaid rent.
  e. Recorded payment of advertising bill of $25.
  f. Recorded withdrawal of $300 cash by a partner in the business.
  g. Recorded $300 as wages owed by business at end of period.
  h. Cash dividends earned by the business were recorded as revenue.

4-20. Recognizing Effects of Events on Financial Position. For each of the following events relating to the Antique Weavers Company, indicate the effect upon the individual accounts in the company's financial position. Treat each event *independently,* and do *not* do a worksheet. Indicate in each case whether the event is a transaction (T) or an adjustment (A). Expenses and revenues are to be identified as such. For example:

Incurred and paid advertising of $200
(T) Assets (cash)—decrease of $200
Owners' equity (advertising expense)—decrease of $200

Events:

  a. Purchased wool from suppliers on credit for $1,000.
  b. Purchased weaving machine for $5,000, paying $2,500 in cash with the bank paying the balance
  c. Placed advertisements in the local paper at a cost of $180—payment has not yet been made.
  d. Paid rent for the next eighteen months—$1,800.
  e. Paid wages owed for work done in the preceding period—$800.
  f. Paid $500 to bank in repayment of a loan.
  g. Made sales of $3,000 to a major retailer who paid cash of $1,500 and promised payment of the balance within thirty days.

h. One of the owners contributed a delivery van (market value $2,000) to the company.
i. Depreciation of equipment for the period—$150.
j. The retailer (in g above) returned some goods, claiming he was overstocked. Antique Weavers gave him a credit note for $500 (i.e., reduction in the amount payable).
k. Discovered at the end of the period:
   (1) Wool supplies used during period cost $300.
   (2) Amount of prepaid rent that expired during the period was $500.
   (3) Wages owing at end of the period were $250.
   (4) Interest owing at the end of the period was $80.
l. Paid a $500 cash dividend to owners.

Exhibit 4-8

CUSTOM SIGN COMPANY

Financial Position Worksheet

Description	Cash	Materials	Prepaid Expenses	Long-lived Assets	Accumulated Depreciation	Accounts Payable	Owners' Equity
1. Original investment	10,000						10,000
2. Purchase of pickup	(2,700)			2,700			
3. Purchase of generator	(1,200)			1,200			
4. Purchase of other equipment	(540)			540			
5. City and state licenses	(40)		40				
6. Insurance premium	(480)		480				
7. Quarterly rental—4/1/80	(300)		300				
8. Quarterly rental—7/1/80	(300)		300				
9. Purchases of material	(3,000)	3,000					
10. Withdrawals through 7/31/80	(1,000)						(1,000) (W)
11. Payment of gasoline credit card statements	(300)						(300) (E)
12. Cash receipts from customers	6,200						6,200 (R)
13. Withdrawal at end of August	(450)						(450) (W)
Position after *cash* events through 8/31/80	5,890	3,000	1,120	4,440	-0-	-0-	14,450

4-21. Recognition of Adjustments. The Custom Sign Company's financial position worksheets (Exhibits 4-8 and 4-9) contain the external cash transactions based on information available in Exercise 3-14. Also, the worksheets contain external cash transactions based on the additional information on p. 143.

Exhibit 4-9

CUSTOM SIGN COMPANY

Financial Position Worksheet

Description	Cash	Materials	Prepaid Expenses	Long-lived Assets	Accumulated Depreciation	Accounts Payable	Owners' Equity
Beginning Position—9/1/80	?	?	?	?	?	?	?
1. Purchase of materials (paid by check)	(750)	750					
2. Payment of gasoline credit card statement	(120)					(120)	
3. Withdrawal at end of September	(500)						(500) (W)
4. Cash receipts from customers	1,800						1,800 (R)

    a. Materials purchased through 8/31/80 (paid for by check)—$3,000.
    b. Cash withdrawals for personal expenses through 7/31/80—$1,000.
    c. Total of gasoline credit card statements paid by check through 8/31/80 (treated as an expense when paid)—$300.
    d. Cash received from customers through 8/31/80—$6,200.
    e. Cash received from customers during September—$1,800.
    f. Original investment—$10,000 cash.

For purposes of convenience, prepaid licenses, prepaid rent, and prepaid insurance have been grouped into one account—prepaid expenses. The long-lived assets account includes the pickup, generator, and other equipment. The accumulated depreciation account may be used for depreciation on all long-lived assets.

Required:

1. Complete the financial position worksheet as of 8/31/80 by:
    (a) Recognition of external transactions not involving cash up through 8/31/80 (if any).
    (b) Recognition of adjustments for the period 4/1/80 through 8/31/80.
2. Complete the financial position worksheet as of 9/30/80 by:
    (a) Recognition of external transactions not involving cash in September (if any).
    (b) Recognition of September adjustments.
3. Prepare a state of financial position as of 9/30/80. What is the net income for September?

(Note: *You must refer to Exercise 3-14 in order to complete this problem.*)

4-22. Recognition of Internal Events. The financial position worksheets in Exhibits 4-10 and 4-11 contain the external cash transactions based on information available in Exercise 3-15. Also, the worksheets contain external cash transactions based on the additional information on p. 146.

Exhibit 4-10

MARY MORTON PHOTOGRAPHY STUDIO

Financial Position Worksheet

Description	Cash	Accounts Receivable	Film and Supplies	Prepaid Rent	Long-lived Assets	Accumulated Depreciation	Accounts Payable	Owners' Equity
1. Original investment	15,000							15,000
2. Leasehold improvements	(1,800)				1,800			
3. Furniture and fixtures	(4,800)				4,800			
4. Photography equipment	(2,700)				2,700			
5. Quarterly rental on 10/1/79	(600)			600				
6. Quarterly rental on 1/1/80	(600)			600				
7. Salary of assistant for 11/1/79–3/31/80	(3,500)							(3,500) (E)
8. Payments on account for film and photography supplies	(2,000)						(2,000)	
9. Receipts on account from customers	10,000	(10,000)						
10. Miscellaneous expenses	(800)							(800) (E)
11. Cash withdrawals	(2,400)							(2,400) (W)
Position on 3/31/80 *before* recognition of external events not involving cash and adjustments	5,800	(10,000)	–0–	1,200	9,300	–0–	(2,000)	8,300

Exhibit 4-11

MARY MORTON PHOTOGRAPHY STUDIO

Financial Position Worksheet

Description	Cash	Accounts Receivable	Film and Supplies	Prepaid Rent	Long-lived Assets	Accumulated Depreciation	Accounts Payable	Owners' Equity
Beginning Position—4/1/80	?	?	?	?	?	?	?	?
1. Quarterly rental on 4/1/80	(600)			600				
2. Payments on account for film	(400)						(400)	
3. Salary of assistant	(700)							(700) (E)
4. Miscellaneous expenses	(100)							(100) (E)
5. Cash withdrawal	(500)							(500) (W)
6. Receipts on account	2,700	(2,700)						

a. The photography studio was opened on October 1, 1979. At that time the lease officially began, and Ms. Morton paid for the leasehold improvements, furniture and fixtures, and photography equipment.
b. Ms. Morton hired her assistant on November 1, 1979. Her salary is paid by check on the last working day of each month.
c. Payments on account for film and photography supplies from 10/1/79 to 3/31/80—$2,000.
d. Receipts on account from customers from 10/1/79 to 3/31/80—$10,000.
e. Payments for miscellaneous expenses totaled $800 for the period 10/1/79–3/31/80.
f. Cash withdrawals totaled $2,400 for the period.
g. Original investment—$15,000 cash.
h. Unpaid amounts due from customers were $700 and $800 at the beginning and the end of April, respectively.

For convenience, leasehold improvements, furniture and fixtures, and photography equipment have been lumped into one account—long-lived assets. The accumulated depreciation account may be used for depreciation on all long-lived assets.

Required:

1. Complete the financial position worksheet as of 3/31/80 by:
   (a) Recognition of external transactions not involving cash up through 3/31/80.
   (b) Recognition of adjustments for the period 10/1/79–3/31/80.
2. Complete the financial position worksheet as of 4/30/80 by:
   (a) Recognition of external transactions not involving cash in April.
   (b) Recognition of April adjustments.
3. Prepare a statement of financial position as of 4/30/80.

(Note: *You must refer to Exercise 3-15 in order to complete this problem.*)

Conventional Accounting Income Measurement: Some Elaboration

5

In the preceding two chapters we introduced some fundamental accounting definitions and concepts—assets, liabilities, owners' equity, revenue, expense, financial position, and results of operations. In addition, we introduced the basic principles that govern the way in which the concepts and definitions are applied—realization, matching, and recording of assets and liabilities at original transaction values. Finally, we applied the basic definitions, the concepts, and the principles of conventional accounting to an illustrative example. For the sake of simplicity, however, Chapters 3 and 4 were limited to the most fundamental level, exposing only the most basic (and distinctive) characteristics of conventional accounting.

In this chapter we (1) look at conventional accounting income measurement from several perspectives other than the performance-measurement orientation that was used to introduce it and (2) discuss some of the strengths and weaknesses of conventional accounting in both practical and theoretical terms.

INFORMATION FOR DISTRIBUTION OF ENTERPRISE BENEFITS

The "Disposable" Wealth of the Enterprise

In Chapter 1 we noted that besides investment decisions there is another class of decisions, involving parties outside the business enterprise, with which accountants might concern themselves. That class of decisions has to do with periodic distributions of the residual benefits generated by the enterprise to, for instance, (1) owners (in the form of withdrawals or dividends), (2) management (in the form of bonuses or other incentives), and (3) government (in the form of income taxes). As has been pointed out several times in earlier discussion, an investment decision is a personal decision. It requires that the individual determine the value *to him* of the future cash flows that he estimates will be forthcoming from an investment in the enterprise. If the value to himself is greater than the price he has to pay, he will find the opportunity attractive; otherwise he will not. On the other hand, decisions as to the distribution of residual benefits of the enterprise generally are not personal in nature. They have to do with rights of different groups that have an interest in the enterprise. Furthermore, the interests involved are often competing interests. Thus there is some potential that different information will be relevant for decisions involving distributions of enterprise benefits than that which is relevant for investment decisions.

All interests in the distribution of residual benefits of the enterprise have one thing in common: the determination or measurement of the amount of wealth of the enterprise that is actually residual or disposable at a given point in time. But *residual* and *disposable* are relative terms—they imply measurement relative to some criterion. Specifically, they imply that it is desirable to preserve some identifiable level of wealth, a "criterion level" against which disposability can be gauged. If, at the end of a period, the measured wealth of the enterprise exceeds that level, the excess may be considered disposable or expendable.

One "criterion level" that has some relevance for virtually all purposes is the level embodied in the so-called Hicksian concept of income defined in Chapter 2. Recall that Hicksian income (disposable wealth) is the amount of wealth that may be disposed of (distributed) by an economic unit during a period of time, without reducing the remaining wealth *below the level of wealth held at the beginning of the period.*

The Hicksian criterion for measuring disposable wealth is of obvious interest to owners. Dividends or withdrawals in excess of Hicksian-type income, period after period, imply a shrinkage in the wealth that remains in control of the enterprise and, concurrently, a shrinking in the interests of the owners. If it is desired that the enterprise retain its economic stature, Hicksian-type income is the maximum level of consistent distributions that should be made to owners.

With the separation of ownership and management, owners who do not control the enterprise directly often share the residual benefits of the enterprise (in the form of profit sharing) with the managers who do control its destiny. To motivate management to act in the interest of the owners, it is often considered important to tie its rewards to a basis that reflects the interests of the owners. Since management starts each period with a stock of wealth that was the result of all prior management actions (its own and its predecessors), it seems reasonable to measure *management's* performance from that initial level.

The philosophy of income taxation is to take a portion of the new wealth generated by an economic unit each period, always leaving untouched the wealth base that produced the increment. Because proprietorships and partnerships are not separate legal entities they are not taxed as such. Instead the income from such entities is taxable income of the owners (whether or not withdrawals take place). Corporations, on the other hand, are subject to a separate corporate income tax. To tax the disposable wealth of the enterprise measured on a basis other than against its beginning-of-period wealth might tend to confiscate some of the wealth base with which the enterprise operated throughout the period. Hence the Hicksian criterion of beginning-of-period wealth is consistent also with the philosophy underlying income taxation.

We should hasten to add, however, that tax policy often departs from the simplistic philosophy described above, when serving many of its special purposes—for example, as an economic incentive system. We devote part of Chapter 12 to the way that income taxes are treated in present-day financial reporting practices.

Conventional Accounting Measurement of Disposable Wealth

The concept of disposable wealth requires that some measurement or assessment of wealth be made. In Chapter 2 we called the process of measuring wealth items, and expressing (quantifying) their magnitudes in terms of numbers of dollars, the process of *valuation*. We noted then that present value is one approach to valuation.

Conventional accounting may also be thought of as an approach to valuation and wealth assessment. The basis of valuation in conventional accounting is the original transaction value (cost) of an item of wealth. It should be emphasized, however, that *the original transaction value of a wealth item is not synonymous with wealth*. At best, since it was a price willingly paid for an asset by the enterprise at the time the asset was acquired, the original transaction value is evidence that the future benefits that were *then expected* from its possession were worth as much or more than the amount paid. Presumably the enterprise would not otherwise have acquired the asset.

Since, by definition, an asset is a positive item of wealth and a liability is a negative item of wealth, the financial position (equation) of an enterprise is, in a sense, a wealth assessment. At any moment in time it includes the unexpired original transaction values of each of the assets then possessed and the undischarged original transaction values of each of the liabilities as yet unsatisfied. Intuitively, to assess the wealth of the enterprise, one would sum the original transaction values assigned to the liabilities and subtract the total from the sum of the values assigned to the assets. But this is precisely the conventional accounting definition of owners' equity (also referred to in this sense as "net assets" or "net worth"). Total owners' equity (total assets minus total liabilities), therefore, can be thought of as representing the wealth of the enterprise as of a point in time, *based upon valuation at original transaction values*.

Conventional Accounting Net Operating Income and the Hicksian Criterion. Having established that in conventional accounting the owners' equity portion of the enterprise's financial position may be thought of as an assessment of its wealth, it follows that conventional accounting *net operating income* is the measure of disposable wealth in the Hicksian sense (in the absence of gains and losses, which are discussed in a later section). We originally introduced net operating income from a performance-measurement point of view. But we went to some length in the preceding chapter to point out that *net operating income is synonymous with an advance in owners' equity*. In fact, the reader will recall that the income statement was described as an explanation of the change in owners' equity due to operations between the beginning and the ending financial position of a period.

In the absence of gains or losses or owners' investments or withdrawals, the net operating income for a period is equal to the increase in owners' equity and thus is matched by an increase in the excess of assets over liabilities. Subsequent distribution of assets to the owners in an amount equal to net income will therefore set owners' equity back to its level at the beginning of the period. Thus conventional accounting net income conforms to the Hicksian definition of income or disposable wealth given earlier, *based on valuation of assets and liabilities at original transaction values*. But perhaps the point can best be seen by example.

Example 5-1

Suppose that a group of individuals starts a merchandising business (a corporation) with an initial investment of $6.5 million in cash. At the outset the business buys equipment that will last three years for $6 million cash and an initial stock of merchandise for $1 million on account. With these initial outlays it commences business and operates for three years, each year paying cash dividends to the owners at the end of the year equal in amount to the net operating income for that year. Exhibit 5-1 gives summary facts concerning the business's operations for the first three years. At the end of the third year the equipment is completely worn out, and a salvage contractor has agreed to haul it away for whatever salvage value he can get for it.

By using the convenient clerical device of the three-year financial position worksheet in Exhibit 5-2, we will be able to assess the recognized effect of these facts on the accounts of the enterprise. (Note that to save space the last three zeros of each number in Exhibit 5-2 are omitted.)

Many aspects of Exhibit 5-2, such as the treatment of individual summary transactions, should already be familiar to the reader, so we will restrict discussion to the few additional observations necessary to make the point at hand. First, notice that the financial position as of the end of each year is the beginning position from which we work for the next year. Once we add or subtract

Exhibit 5-1

MERCHANDISING BUSINESS, INC.

Facts of Operations
(amounts in thousands)

	Year 1	Year 2	Year 3
Sales (all in cash)	$4,500	$5,000	$5,000
Merchandise purchases on account (not including initial purchase)	500	2,000	600
Payments on account	1,000	1,800	1,300
Merchandise on hand at year-end	500	1,000	-0-
Labor expense (all paid in cash)	300	300	300
Income tax expense (at 50% of pretax income)	600	600	550

Exhibit 5-2

MERCHANDISING BUSINESS, INC.

Three-Year Financial Position Worksheet
(amounts in thousands)

Description	Cash	Merchandise	Equipment	Accumulated Depreciation	Accounts Payable	Owners' Equity
Beginning Position	6,500					6,500
Year 1:						
Equipment purchased	(6,000)		6,000			
Merchandise purchased		1,500			1,500	
Sales	4,500					4,500 (R)
Payments for merchandise	(1,000)				(1,000)	
Labor expense	(300)					(300) (E)
Merchandise used		(1,000)				(1,000) (E)
Equipment depreciation				(2,000)		(2,000) (E)
Income taxes	(600)					(600) (E)
Dividends	(600)*					(600) (D)*
Ending Position	2,500	500	6,000	(2,000)	500	6,500
Year 2:						
Merchandise purchased		2,000			2,000	
Sales	5,000					5,000 (R)
Payments for merchandise	(1,800)				(1,800)	
Labor expense	(300)					(300) (E)
Merchandise used		(1,500)				(1,500) (E)
Equipment depreciation				(2,000)		(2,000) (E)
Income taxes	(600)					(600) (E)
Dividends	(600)*					(600) (D)*
Ending Position	4,200	1,000	6,000	(4,000)	700	6,500
Year 3:						
Merchandise purchased		600			600	
Sales	5,000					5,000 (R)
Payments for merchandise	(1,300)				(1,300)	
Labor expense	(300)					(300) (E)
Merchandise used		(1,600)				(1,600) (E)
Equipment depreciation				(2,000)		(2,000) (E)
Income taxes	(550)					(550) (E)
Dividends	(550)*					(550) (D)*
Ending Position	6,500	-0-	6,000	(6,000)	-0-	6,500

*See the "Three-Year Comparative Income Statements" in Exhibit 5-3 for the determination of amounts available for dividends each year.

the effects of a period's events on the various accounts and arrive at a new financial position, we need not reconsider those events in the next period.

More important, notice the relationship between net operating income for each year and the amount of the owners' withdrawal in the same year.

Example 5-2

If we constructed income statements for each year, we would get the results shown in comparative form in Exhibit 5-3.

In each year, the business distributes to its owners dividends equal in total to the net operating income for that year. (Note that the last event line for each year in Exhibit 5-2 shows a decrease in cash and a decrease in owners' equity designated with a *D* for dividend.)

Now in order for net operating income to conform to the Hicksian concept of income, the business must be left as well off at the end of a period in which dividends equal to net operating income were paid as it was at the beginning of such a period. A glance at Exhibit 5-2 (the owners' equity balance in beginning and ending "position lines" for each year) confirms that this is indeed the case.

The business starts its first year with wealth (owners' equity) of $6.5 million all held in the form of cash. It proceeds with its operations and "earns" net operating income of $600,000. If the owners are paid nothing from the business in the first year (and invest nothing additional), the net operating income of $600,000 means that owners' equity, and therefore the net assets of the business, would be greater by that amount at the end of the year than at the beginning of the year. Therefore, net operating income is the amount of cash or other assets that can be removed from the business without reducing the net assets at the end of the year below the level at the beginning of the year. Thus in year one, after paying dividends of $600,000 cash, the business ends the year with an excess of the unexpired original transaction costs of assets over the undischarged original transaction values of liabilities of exactly $6.5 million, the amount of *net assets* (assets minus liabilities) with which the year was started. However, the composition of the financial position has changed from the all-

Exhibit 5-3

MERCHANDISING BUSINESS, INC.

Three-Year Comparative Income Statements
(amounts in thousands)

	Year 1	Year 2	Year 3
Revenues from sales	$4,500	$5,000	$5,000
Less expenses:			
Labor expense	300	300	300
Merchandise used	1,000	1,500	1,600
Equipment depreciation	2,000	2,000	2,000
Income tax expense	600	600	550
Total expenses	$3,900	$4,400	$4,450
Net operating income	$ 600	$ 600	$ 550

cash composition of assets at the beginning of the year to the mixed composition at year-end. The same reasoning also applies to the second and third years.

However, by the end of the third year when (1) the equipment has become completely worn out (the negative "accumulated depreciation" balance then offsets entirely the original transaction cost) and (2) the business has not replaced the stock of merchandise sold during the year, the wealth position of the enterprise not only equals but is identical in composition to the position with which it started its economic life—$6.5 million cash and $6.5 million owners' equity. Of course, we have made the unusual assumption in the example that the enterprise has a very short life cycle. But this somewhat unrealistic assumption serves to illustrate that in using conventional accounting net operating income as a measure of "disposable wealth," *the concept of wealth involved is the money capital invested in the enterprise.*

Gains and Losses and Income Measurement

The discussion of income to this point has been concerned with net operating income, defined in Chapter 3 as the difference between revenues and expenses. We now wish to add explicit recognition of the components of income called gains and losses.

> **Gains (Losses).** Gains (losses) are increases (decreases) in owners' equity due to events or transactions that are not routinely associated with providing the primary product or service of the business to customers.

Gains and losses arise out of such events as (*a*) the sale or destruction of assets (such as buildings and equipment) which are held for use in the business rather than for sale to customers, or (*b*) the settlement of an obligation at less than its original transaction value. When a gain or loss occurs the sales price, insurance proceeds, or other compensation received as a consequence is considered *roughly analogous* to the price received for one of the enterprise's products or services (revenue). The unexpired cost of the asset lost or given up is the measure of sacrifice, *roughly analogous* to the expense incurred in providing products and services. But there is an important difference. Revenue and expense apply to the routine productive activities of the enterprise—meaning the provision of products and services to customers on a regular basis; gains and losses, on the other hand, are not directly associated with providing products and services to customers. Thus when a gain or loss occurs, we offset the insurance proceeds or other compensation received against the unexpired cost of the resource given up (lost), recognizing only the *difference* as a net increase (gain) or decrease (loss) in owners' equity. If the entity experiencing a gain or loss is a corporation (making it subject to income tax), the income tax effects of the gain or loss are also offset directly against the net increase or decrease. The result is a "net of tax" gain or loss, which is the recognized increase or decrease in owners' equity and, therefore, the amount reported in the income statement for the period. (This is illustrated below.)

Now consider the issue of whether gains and losses should be included in the calculation of net operating income, along with revenues and expenses. Net operating income is intended to measure performance in the sense of the firm's long-run cash-generating ability. Intuitively, it should therefore reflect the long-run cash-flow consequences of all those events and transactions taking place during the period that are not atypical of the long-run conduct of the type of business in which the enterprise is engaged. That is, gains and losses that arise out of events that are expected to occur from time to time in businesses of the type in question (such as sales of worn-out or obsolete equipment) are as much a part of performance in the long-run sense as the sales of products and services—even though they occur less frequently.

At the same time, gains and losses from truly unusual or atypical events and transactions should not be included in the calculation of net operating income. Their inclusion would, by definition, erode the representativeness of net operating income relative to the ongoing cash-generating ability of the enterprise. The gains and losses that should be excluded from the calculation of net operating income are customarily called *extraordinary* gains and losses and may be defined more precisely as follows:

> **Extraordinary Gains (Losses).** Extraordinary gains (losses) are changes in owners' equity due to clearly abnormal events or transactions. By "clearly abnormal" is generally meant that (1) such events are not a normal part of the operations of the business in the long run *and* (2) such events occur infrequently in the environment in which the enterprise operates.

Extraordinary gains and losses may arise out of such unusual events as natural disasters, arson, expropriation of assets by a foreign government, or condemnation by a domestic government unit.

Example 5-3

> Weather Sealing Incorporated is a small company that waterproofs basements, roofs, patios, and so forth. Its status and activities for the current year, 19XX, are represented on the worksheet in Exhibit 5-4. The first event recognized for the year is the sale of a truck, with an original transaction cost of $5,000 and accumulated depreciation of $2,000, that had been used in the business through last year. The proceeds of the sale were $3,500. Another truck has been leased pending delivery of a replacement. The $500 gain on the sale is not an extraordinary gain. The gain is taxable at the regular (assumed) tax rate of 40 percent.
>
> The last event recognized for the year is the uninsured loss of supplies with an original cost of $2,000. The supplies were stored at a job site and were destroyed when the site was struck by a freak storm. Authorities noted that such a storm had not occurred in that area in well over one hundred years. The company's insurance policy does not cover losses from such storms. Thus there were no proceeds to cover the loss. The loss is an extraordinary loss. However, the loss can be deducted from the company's other taxable income, resulting in a reduction in income taxes for the year equal to 40 percent of the loss.

The recognition given in Exhibit 5-4 to the loss due to the highly unusual storm is quite straightforward. Prior to the storm, supplies with original costs totaling $2,000 were owned. These assets were lost in the storm and therefore the supplies account is reduced by $2,000. At the same time taxes payable are reduced because the $2,000 loss may be deducted from taxable income on the company's tax return. At the assumed tax rate of 40%, the deduction reduces

Exhibit 5–4
WEATHER SEALING INCORPORATED

Financial Position Worksheet for the Year 19XX

Description	Cash	Accounts Receivable	Supplies	Equipment and Truck	Accumulated Depreciation	Accounts Payable	Taxes Payable	Owners' Equity
Beginning Position	200	1,000	2,000	10,000	(5,200)	1,000	200	7,000
Sale of truck	3,500			(5,000)	2,000			300 (G)
Purchased supplies			10,000			10,000		
Fees earned		50,000						50,000 (R)
Collections	50,000	(50,000)						
Salaries and wages	(35,000)							(35,000) (E)
Payments on account	(9,000)					(9,000)		
Supplies used			(9,000)					(9,000) (E)
Depreciation					(800)			(800) (E)
Income tax expense							2,080	(2,080) E
Storm loss			(2,000)				(800)	(1,200) (L)
Ending Position	9,700	1,000	1,000	5,000	(4,000)	2,000	1,480	9,220

the company's tax bill by $800, recognized as a decrease in the "taxes payable" account. (Note: The $2,080 income tax expense recognized in Exhibit 5-4 is the expense applicable to the income of the period *other than* the recognized gains and losses.) Since there were no other changes in financial position to compensate for the loss, the $1,200 reduction in net assets is reflected by a $1,200 reduction in owners' equity labeled L for loss.

The recognition accorded the sale of the truck in Exhibit 5-4 is complicated slightly by the number of accounts involved. Prior to the sale, the truck was represented in the financial position of the business in two accounts. Its original cost of $5,000 was included in the equipment and truck account up to the time of sale. Depreciation-to-date on the truck of $2,000 was also included in the accumulated depreciation account. The sacrifice of the truck, in the amount of its $3,000 unexpired cost, is therefore recognized by a $5,000 decrease in the equipment and truck account, offset by a $2,000 decrease in the negative balance of the accumulated depreciation account. Offsetting the net decrease in assets of $3,000 for the previously unexpired cost of the truck against the $3,500 proceeds recognized by an increase in cash gives a $500 overall increase in assets. However, this "gain" adds $500 to the company's taxable income, and, at a 40 percent tax rate, it adds $200 to its annual tax bill. This amount is recognized by an increase of $200 in the taxes payable account. The "net" or after-tax increase in owners' equity resulting from the sale of the truck is therefore $300.

Net Operating Income—Performance or Disposable Wealth Measure? We showed initially that for most purposes, net operating income (the measure of performance in conventional accounting) also serves as the measure of disposable wealth. This dual role of net operating income seems inherently sensible in that the recognized advance in wealth (net assets) of an enterprise ought to be related to its performance in productive activity.

The duality occurs as a result of the way that revenues and expenses are defined; net operating income usually represents the overall change in net assets (owners' equity) from all sources other than additional contributions and withdrawals by owners. But we must recognize that this relationship, and hence the duality of net operating income, does not hold when there are extraordinary gains and/or losses. Because extraordinary gains and losses are, by definition, not a part of normal operations, they are not a part of the operating income of the enterprise. Therefore they must be otherwise reckoned with in measuring disposable wealth at the end of a period.

Example 5-4

> From Exhibit 5-4 it can be seen that income from operations for the period in question was $3,420, that is, revenue of $50,000 plus a nonextraordinary gain of $300 (after taxes) minus total expenses of $46,880 ($35,000 wages, plus $9,000 supplies, plus $800 depreciation, plus ordinary income tax expense of $2,080). But if $3,420 cash had been distributed to owners as dividends at the end of the year, owners' equity would have been reduced to $5,800.

The fact that a dividend of $3,420 would reduce owners' equity to $5,800, an amount less than the recognized owners' equity at the beginning of the period, is important. It means that net income from operations, still the measure of enterprise performance, does not in this case qualify as a measure of disposable wealth in the Hicksian sense. Rather, the disposable wealth amount in this case consists of the $3,420 net income from operations minus the $1,200 extraordinary loss on supplies, or $2,220. The reader can confirm, by looking back at Exhibit 5-4, that an end-of-year cash dividend of $2,220 would reduce the business's net assets (owners' equity) only to the $7,000 level of the beginning of the year.

Two Income Measures. To accommodate the notion that extraordinary gains and losses are significant for disposable wealth measurement but not necessarily for performance measurement, accountants usually report two income numbers in any period in which extraordinary gains and losses occur. They can be distinguished as follows:

Net Operating Income. Net operating income (loss) is the excess (deficiency) of revenues from operations over related expenses, plus or minus ordinary gains or losses, respectively.

Net Income. Net income (loss) is defined as net operating income (loss) of the period, plus or minus any recognized extraordinary gains or losses, respectively. Net income equals net operating income when there are no extraordinary gains and losses. It is in this sense that the two are often used synonymously in uncomplicated or simplified situations.

Example 5-5

Again return to Example 5-4—Weather Sealing Incorporated. To portray both the performance of the enterprise for the year 19XX and the disposable wealth, the accountants would prepare an income statement approximately as shown in Exhibit 5-5.

Notice that since the net income figure is more inclusive, the statement works down to it after first showing the more selective (excluding extraordinary gains and losses) net operating income figure. By reporting both net operating income and net income on the same statement, the statement presumably serves both types of decision needs of outside groups (investment decisions and wealth distribution decisions).

Exhibit 5-5

WEATHER SEALING INCORPORATED

Income Statement for the Year 19XX

Revenue		$50,000
Add gain on sale of truck (net of applicable taxes)		300
Less expenses:		
Salaries and wages	$35,000	
Supplies used	9,000	
Depreciation	800	
Income tax expense	2,080	
Total expenses		(46,880)
Net operating income		$ 3,420
Less storm loss (net of applicable taxes)		(1,200)
Net income		$ 2,220

Two Criteria for Disposable Wealth

So far, we have only considered the Hicksian criterion for measuring disposable wealth and the way that conventional accounting net operating income conforms to that criterion. The Hicksian criterion seems relevant for most purposes, but in the corporate form of business another criterion is relevant for a purpose not yet discussed—determining the legality of dividends.

Corporations would not exist legally were it not for permissive legislation on the part of state governments allowing for the chartering of corporations. One of the desirable attributes of the corporate form of business is the limitation of the liability (potential losses) of the owners of the corporation to the amount of their current interest in the corporation. To protect other parties, however, the state laws governing corporations usually restrict dividends paid to owners, so that the original capital contributed to the corporation by owners remains intact (in the form of recognized net assets) to satisfy the rightful claims of other parties. That is, dividends may only be distributed to the extent that net assets exceed the money capital of the enterprise contributed by owners in exchange for shares of stock. Thus, for legal purposes, some measure of the extent to which the recognized net assets of a corporation currently exceed the capital paid in by owners is usually relevant for dividend-distribution decisions.

In the paragraphs that follow we show how conventional accounting has traditionally adapted to the legal concept of disposable wealth as well as the Hicksian concept. One word of caution, however. The economic and accounting interpretations of the original contributions by owners to the enterprise may differ from the interpretation called for by statute or handed down in court decisions. Rather than get into the complexities involved, we will assume for illustrative purposes that no such differences exist. In any case, we must recognize that *in practice legal pronouncements prevail over accounting theory in determining the legality of dividends.*

We have noted above that there are two criterion levels of wealth for decisions concerning distributions of dividends to owners: (1) the original capital contributed by owners (paid-in capital)—the criterion level generally relevant for legal purposes, and (2) the beginning-of-period net assets or owners' equity—the criterion level relevant for most economic purposes. Both of these criterion levels are usually handled simultaneously in conventional accounting through the recognition that the owners' equity component of financial position can be split into two separate parts or accounts called *paid-in capital* and *retained earnings*—just as the category *assets* is broken down into *cash, accounts receivable, supplies,* and so forth.

Paid-in Capital. Paid-in capital is the part of total owners' equity equal to the amount of money or other capital contributed by owners to the enterprise in exchange for ownership interests.

Retained Earnings. Retained earnings is the part of owners' equity equal to the cumulative excess of net income over dividend distributions to owners from the inception of the business.

Example 5-6

> Reconsider the merchandising business introduced in Example 5-1. Suppose that instead of distributing cash equal to net income ($600,000) in year one, it distributed only $300,000 retaining $300,000. Assuming that all other facts remain the same except that the subdivision of owners' equity into paid-in capital and retained earnings is recognized, the first year's operations are represented in Exhibit 5-6.

Notice the several changes from the earlier worksheet in Exhibit 5-2. First, of course, there are two accounts that together represent total owners' equity: paid-in capital and retained earnings. Second, all revenue, expense, and dividend amounts are shown as increases or decreases to the retained earnings account. The paid-in capital account is only increased when new ownership contributions are received in exchange for new shares in the business, and decreased when old ownership interests are liquidated or retired. The retained earnings account is increased to the extent of net income and decreased to the extent of dividends paid to the owner(s). The balance of the retained earnings account at the end of any period is the amount by which cumulative net income exceeds cumulative dividends.

Finally, note that since only $300,000 was withdrawn by the owners instead of $600,000, the full amount of net income for year one, there is a $300,000 balance of retained earnings at the end of year one. This, of course, is matched by $300,000 more assets (cash) than the enterprise would have had if $600,000 had been paid. Thus the $300,000 represents a growth in the money capital of the enterprise over the $6.5 million originally invested by the owners. Total owners' equity of $6.8 million ($6.5 million paid-in capital plus $300,000 retained earnings) reflects the growth in net assets.

In year two, recognized net income (in the original example, $600,000) will measure the advance in recognized net assets (resulting from operations) beyond this new level of $6.8 million. Net income will again represent the amount of cash or other assets that can be withdrawn without reducing the enterprise net asset position *below its beginning-of-year level*. On the other hand, at the end of year two, year-two net income ($600,000) *plus* the beginning balance in retained earnings ($300,000) is the total amount ($900,000) that can be withdrawn *without reducing the net assets of the enterprise below the level of paid-in capital of $6.5 million*. The reader may find it a useful exercise to show that this is true, working from the year-one ending position in Exhibit 5-6, using the facts of operations from Exhibit 5-1, and varying the withdrawal policy appropriately.

Thus, within the conventional accounting framework, *net income for a period, alone or in combination* with the beginning balance of retained earnings, provides the information that we have concluded is relevant for wealth distribution purposes. Having made this point, we will not always separate the paid-in capital and retained earnings portions of owners' equity in our examples until later chapters. The distinction is irrelevant for many of the points we will be illustrating, and the extra detail may therefore be avoided. It should be noted, however, that in practice retained earnings are customarily separated from the paid-in capital of an enterprise. Moreover, a brief statement is usually presented

Exhibit 5-6

MERCHANDISING BUSINESS, INC.

Year One Financial Position Worksheet
(amounts in thousands)

Description	Cash	Merchandise	Equipment	Accumulated Depreciation	Accounts Payable	Owners' Equity Paid-in Capital	Owners' Equity Retained Earnings
Beginning Position	6,500					6,500	
Equipment purchased	(6,000)		6,000				
Merchandise purchased		1,000			1,000		
Merchandise purchased		500			500		
Sales	4,500						4,500 (R)
Payments on account	(1,000)				(1,000)		
Labor expense	(300)						(300) (E)
Merchandise used		(1,000)					(1,000) (E)
Equipment depreciation				(2,000)			(2,000) (E)
Income taxes	(600)						(600) (E)
Dividends	(300)						(300) (D)
Ending Position	2,800	500	6,000	(2,000)	500	6,500	300

which reconciles the beginning and ending balances in retained earnings, as shown in Exhibit 5-7 (based on the facts presented in Exhibit 5-6). Such statements often appear on the same page of annual financial reports as the income statement, and sometimes are integrated with the income statement (this is accomplished by simply reversing the first two lines in the statement as shown in Exhibit 5-7, in which case it becomes a continuation of the income statement).

Disposable Wealth versus Available Cash

Before leaving the discussion of disposable wealth measurement, one final important point needs to be emphasized: the net income (disposable wealth) of the enterprise for a period may be large, but the enterprise may not be able to distribute cash dividends to owners equal to net income. The reason may already have occurred to the reader. As a disposable wealth index, net income measures the advance in assets (*of all kinds*) in excess of liabilities. Net income may be substantial, but the net assets of the enterprise may not be in readily distributable form. So most wealth distribution decisions are based on two considerations, net income and the availability of cash.

Example 5-7

Interior Designs Incorporated is a quality retailer of furniture, specializing in complete decoration of business and residential interiors. The company buys only floor samples of its furniture line. When it sells furniture, the items are delivered direct to the company's customers from the manufacturer, and Interior Designs is billed for their cost at that time. The company has just completed a very profitable year, as is evidenced on the worksheet in Exhibit 5-8.

Notice that net income was substantial; revenues of $250,000 less expenses totaling $215,000 equals income of $35,000. This of course is matched by an increase in the

Exhibit 5-7
MERCHANDISING BUSINESS, INC.

Statement of Retained Earnings
As of the End of Year One
(amounts in thousands)

Retained earnings balance, beginning of year one	$ 0
Net income for year one	600
Less year-one dividends	(300)
Retained earnings balance, end of year one	$ 300

Exhibit 5-8
INTERIOR DESIGNS INCORPORATED

Financial Position Worksheet

Description	Cash	Accounts Receivable	Floor Samples	Equipment	Accumulated Depreciation	Taxes and Accounts Payable	Owners' Equity
Beginning Position	10,000	50,000	5,000	20,000	(10,000)	25,000	50,000 250,000 (R)
Sales		250,000					
Collections	220,000	(220,000)					
Cost of furniture						90,000	(90,000) (E)
Salaries and wages	(70,000)						(70,000) (E)
Rent	(15,000)						(15,000) (E)
Floor samples purchased	(20,000)		20,000				
Payments on account	(90,000)					(90,000)	
Depreciation					(5,000)		(5,000) (E)
Income taxes	(30,000)					5,000	(35,000) (E)
Ending Position	5,000	80,000	25,000	20,000	(15,000)	30,000	85,000

excess of recognized assets over liabilities. But at the end of the period the stock of cash is far too low to pay dividends to owners equal to net income. This is due in part to (1) the purchase of $20,000 in new floor samples, and (2) the apparent buildup in the stock of accounts receivable during the period, probably because of some large sales toward the end of the year on which payments are not yet due. Assuming that the enterprise required a minimum cash balance of, say, $3,000 to conduct its transactions, the maximum end-of-year dividend that it could pay to owners would be $2,000 ($5,000 cash balance minus $3,000 minimum cash requirement).

Example 5-7 serves to illustrate an entirely predictable phenomenon. Although net income may be the measure of disposable wealth in the abstract, the stock of available cash of the enterprise is a practical constraint on the distribution of dividends at any point in time.

CONVENTIONAL ACCOUNTING: SOME QUALIFICATIONS

Uncertainty in Conventional Accounting Measurements

Although conventional accounting net income is largely factually based, that is, based on values established in actual exchange transactions, it is not wholly "factual." Conventional accounting does not require the kind of estimation of future events that forecasts or present values of enterprises require. It nonetheless requires more estimation and is therefore more subject to uncertainty than appears to be the case at first glance. Two significant areas in conventional accounting measurement that require estimates are (1) the apportionment of the cost of long-lived assets to various periods in which their service potential is used, and (2) the collectibility of prices to be received in the future from customers for products and services provided.

Uncertainty and Long-Lived Assets. Estimation is required in determining how many periods the enterprise will benefit from the use of each of its long-lived assets. The total expense over the entire useful life of any long-lived asset is limited to the original transaction cost of the asset. However, the amount that is recognized as expense in a given period depends upon the estimate at that time of how long the asset will continue to provide service. If the enterprise errs in estimating the useful life of the asset, depreciation expense will be understated or overstated, and, thus, net income will be overstated or understated, respectively.

Uncertainty from the Realization Principle. Conventional accounting net income is also subject to possible error from application of the *realization principle*. Generally speaking, revenue is recognized in the period of sale of products and services to customers rather than the period in which customers finally pay. Although for most businesses a *bona fide* sale gives sufficient certainty of collection to warrant revenue recognition in the period of sale, some accounts will undoubtedly not be collected even from the best clientele. Merchandise will no doubt have to be repossessed or perhaps will be lost altogether. Any business that makes "credit sales" faces these "facts of life." Hence revenue is usually recognized in the period of sale, but only in the amount of the total credit sales that are then *expected* to actually be collected.

If the enterprise fails to accurately estimate the amount or percentage of the total accounts receivable that will actually be collected, then later experience with collections will lead to unexpected increases or decreases. Revenue and net income will therefore originally be too high if more accounts than estimated turn out to be uncollectible, or too low if fewer defaults by customers take place than expected. In either case the effect will be the same as when a period's net income is inflated or deflated because of understatement or overestimate of depreciation expense. The specific techniques for recognizing initial estimates of uncollectible customer accounts and later recognition of actual customer defaults is covered in Chapter 8.

Implications and Adaptations to Uncertainty

What are the implications of an actual overstatement or understatement of income? Presumably, the many decisions that were influenced by reported income might have turned out differently if the overstatement or understatement had not occurred. Investors who decided to buy, sell, or hold the stocks or bonds of the company may have pursued other courses of action. Similarly, in the case of a significant overstatement, the propriety or legality of dividend distributions might have been challenged if income had been stated differently at the time. Hence, in extreme cases, when significant overstatements or understatements of income later come to light, their disclosure can result in legal actions on behalf of present and former owners and creditors for damages allegedly caused by reliance on the earlier misleading information.

Adaptation in Dividend Policy to Uncertainty. One of the most obvious and simple adaptations that enterprises have made to uncertainty in income determination is that they rarely distribute assets to owners in amounts equal to net income period after period. They almost always distribute less—thereby hedging against the possibility that when new and better information is available, it may appear that the enterprise earned less than originally recognized. Also, restricting dividends may compensate for the effects of inflation on the firm's ability to replace its assets as needed, or the owners may simply prefer to have the enterprise grow by reinvesting part of each period's earnings in the business.

Conservatism in Applying Conventional Accounting. Still another adaptation to the uncertainty involved in income measurement is a tendency in practice toward so-called conservatism in applying conventional accounting principles. *Conservatism* refers to the inclination to err on the high side in estimating expenses or losses and on the low side in estimating revenues and gains so as to consciously reduce the probability that income will be inadvertently overstated.

Revenue is recognized in the period in which a product is actually sold. Theoretically, total expense for a period is supposed to include the original transaction cost of the resources sacrificed to produce and distribute the products that were sold during the period. But as we noted earlier, a perfectly scrupulous matching of the original costs of resources with the products they served to produce is seldom fully achieved in practice. Instead, in each period, each significant resource sacrifice is scrutinized by the accountant. If the sacrifice bears some discernible relationship to the production of a particular product, it is recognized as an expense in the period (possibly a later period) in which that product is sold. On the other hand, if the sacrifice does not bear a discernible relationship to the production of a particular product or group of products, it is recognized as an expense in the period in which the resource is consumed. Hence there may be a tendency in practice to err on the "early side" in recognition of expenses.

It may have occurred to the reader that this kind of conservatism is good in the sense that when expense tends to be overstated and income tends to be understated, lesser amounts of assets will tend to be distributed to owners than otherwise. This, of course, tends to conserve the assets of the enterprise. But from other points of view, there is an element of nonconservatism when this type of biasing of net income occurs. When certain types of expenses are recognized early to depress the current period's income, the income will be equally overstated in the later period in which the expense should have been recognized. Furthermore, an investor may pass up an opportunity to invest in (or a present owner may sell) what will ultimately prove to be a very successful enterprise simply because at the time the enterprise may have been painting an unnecessarily glum picture of itself by stating income too conservatively.

If conservatism is carried too far, it can undermine the usefulness of accounting outputs, particularly operating income as a performance measure. Excessive conservatism negates the supposed cause-and-effect relationship between revenues and expenses—the feature that presumably makes net operating income representative of current productive ability.

**Conventional Accounting Income—
Relevance in Times of Changing Prices**

Income Measurement Summarized. Net operating income, the difference between revenues and expenses, measures the recognized increase in net assets from the operations during the period over and above the original costs of the assets sacrificed in connection with those operations. If net assets are reduced by distributing to owners amounts equal to net operating income (net income if extraordinary gains or losses are experienced) period after period, the recognized net assets (owners' equity) of the enterprise at the end of a period will equal the level at the beginning of the period. If this policy is followed from the inception of the business, net assets at the end of each period will always equal the original capital paid in by the owners. At the same time, net operating income presumably represents the ability of the enterprise to convert the productive resources it acquires into products and services of greater value than the cost or sacrifice made to acquire the resources.

Net operating income as a disposable wealth measure was illustrated in Example 5-1 (the merchandising business). The owner invested $6.5 million cash at the outset. Part of the cash ($6 million) was then converted into equipment that lasted three years. Each year during the three-year life of the equipment, net income was calculated and dividends were paid in that amount. When the cycle of asset replacement was interrupted at the end of year three, that is, the used-up equipment and merchandise inventories were not replaced, the enterprise actually started year four in exactly the same position as at the beginning of year one—with $6.5 million cash and no other assets or liabilities (see Exhibit 5-2).

The reason for returning to this example is that by looking at some of the options available to the enterprise at the beginning of year four, we can reexamine the relevancy in the preceding three years of conventional accounting net operating income as a measure of performance and as a measure of disposable wealth.

The Relevance of Conventional Accounting Income Measurement. As it enters year four with exactly $6.5 million cash and $6.5 million owners' equity, the merchandising enterprise has two options that are of particular interest to us. First, the business can return all of the $6.5 million cash to the owners and go out of existence. Or, second, it can replace the worn-out equipment and the required merchandise inventory, much as it did at the beginning of year one, and continue in business. A good test of the relevance of conventional accounting is (1) whether, upon returning the $6.5 million *wealth preserved in the enterprise,* the owners would be as well off in possessing that amount as when they first invested it in the enterprise, and (2) whether, upon replacing its equipment and stock of merchandise, the enterprise can continue to carry on business in succeeding years as well as it did in earlier years, *as reflected in net income of those years.* If economic conditions are static, the answer to both questions is yes. By *static* we mean that nothing in the environment changes (including the prices, the tastes, preferences, and values of the owners, the efficiency of the enterprise, etc.). But if certain economic conditions change (prices in particular), then some problems arise with conventional accounting income measurement. The problems introduced by changing prices are described below.

Changes in General Purchasing Power. Because of the relationship between cash and wealth, the owners would be as well off upon return of their $6.5 million as they were with the same amount at the start of business only if the prices of goods and services have not increased or decreased significantly in the meantime. The $6.5 million cash preserved in the business has no intrinsic value itself. Rather, it is the medium of exchange by which goods and services are acquired to satisfy an individual's wants and needs. Hence we can say that upon receiving $6.5 million cash at the end of three years, the owners will be as well off as they were at the outset if they can command the same kinds of goods and services with that cash in the same quantities as they could at the outset.

But suppose that prices generally rose during the three years from the time of the original investment to the time of the final withdrawal. That would mean that the owners generally could not purchase as many goods and services upon receiving their $6.5 million cash back at the end of three years as they could have purchased with the same amount at the time that they made their investment. If that is the case, then in the intervening three years conventional accounting net income did not faithfully represent to them the maximum amounts they could safely withdraw (receive as dividends) from the business and spend each year *and still preserve their initial investment economically intact.* Furthermore, one would also tend to question the extent to which conventional accounting net operating income characterizes "performance" in the sense of the enterprise's ability to generate cash (purchasing power) for distribution to owners over the long run.

Changing Replacement Costs. Technically, it must be assumed that an enterprise cannot exactly duplicate its past performance in the future. Too many variables in production processes cannot be controlled with absolute precision.

But if conditions exist that make it *unlikely* that the "performance" represented in the net operating income of one year (or several years) could ever be matched in subsequent years, then the relevance of net operating income as an index of long-run cash-generating ability would be subject to some doubt. Such is the case when the cost to replace a productive asset changes substantially before the end of the asset's useful life.

Suppose, for instance, that after the first three years had lapsed, the cost of new equipment capable of another three years of the same service as the old equipment has risen to $7 million from the $6 million paid at the beginning of year one. At the start of year four the enterprise, with its original money investment of $6.5 million intact, would not be able to replace the worn-out equipment without borrowing or additional investment from the owners. Thus, in the sense that the enterprise cannot continue to operate as before on its original capital, it is not as well off (as wealthy) as it was originally. In retrospect, then, net income did not turn out to be a faithful index of the amount of assets that could be withdrawn by (paid as dividends to) the owners in the first three years of operations and still preserve the enterprise's ability to continue its operations thereafter.

Furthermore, under the circumstances, net operating income for the first three years may not be a very representative index of the longer-run cash-generating ability of the enterprise. After all, if it replaces the equipment at $7 million and the equipment lasts only three years, as did the original equipment, the enterprise will have sacrificed $1 million more for the same productive ability as it had in the first three years of its life. Therefore, somehow the margin between its total revenue earned each year and its cost of merchandise sold must increase by at least $1 million in the following three years. Otherwise it will not do as well as the performance in its first three years of operations.

Price Changes and the Relevance of Conventional Accounting. Thus, for conventional accounting net income to be thought of as a clear and unambiguous performance measure and index of disposable wealth, economic conditions, particularly prices, must be unchanging. When prices are changing significantly, the relevance of conventional accounting is somewhat open to question. It should be noted, however, that there are suggested accounting techniques (models) that reflect changing prices as they take place. Although these alternative financial accounting models are rarely used except to provide supplemental information in present-day financial reporting, they are worthy of discussion, if only because price changes have become an increasingly significant economic phenomenon. Hence, several alternative models will be introduced, along with some of their apparent advantages and disadvantages, in Chapters 13-15.

Why Conventional Accounting?

In Chapter 3, when we introduced conventional accounting, we noted that it is the accounting model that is most evident in actual practice. In Chapters 3 and 4 and again in the first part of this chapter, we have developed conventional accounting with a view toward its potential decision relevance. In the immediately preceding discussion, however, we have introduced some limitations on the decision relevance of conventional accounting information induced by changing prices. In Chapters 13-15 we present other accounting models (systems) that produce potentially more decision-relevant information in times of changing prices. Perhaps it would be helpful, therefore, if we summarize here the other features of conventional accounting that make it so appealing in practice in spite of possible limitations on its decision relevance in times of changing prices.

Several of the relative advantages that many accountants attribute to conventional accounting can be summarized in the term *objectivity*. Accountants usually think of conventional accounting as being more objective than alternative models (other than the cash receipts and disbursements model). Typically, what they mean is that conventional accounting information is based on largely factual data, and that the original transaction values that are the basis of conventional accounting representations (statements) are relatively more verifiable than the valuations under alternative models.

The basic data used in conventional accounting are restricted to prices arrived at in the actual exchange transactions of the enterprise that have already taken place with outside, independent economic units, that is, the original transaction values from purchase and sales transactions. Hence, the data base is relatively factual (unlike the projections of future events, e.g., future cash flows required for management forecasts).

We acknowledged earlier that there is uncertainty in connection with asset and liability valuation and related revenue and expense recognition in conventional accounting. But, generally, any consistent overstatement or understatement of assets, liabilities, expense, or revenue will eventually be corrected as long as valuations are restricted to (unexpired) original transaction values. For instance, if an expense (say, depreciation) is understated in a given year, then the value of the related asset (say, equipment) is overstated (accumulated depreciation is insufficient). This means that in later years additional depreciation will be recognized equal to the deficiency in earlier years. Although compensating errors are not themselves desirable, the point is that within conventional accounting there are some limitations to errors (and manipulations), both as to amount and duration.

Furthermore, provided evidence of original transactions, such as sales slips and invoices, is not lost or destroyed, a skillful observer (usually a professional auditor) can *verify* on a sample basis that what the business enterprise represents on its financial statements is indeed a reasonable (fair) representation, within the conventional framework, of the status and activities of the enterprise. This verification process (called auditing) is such an important feature of present-day financial reporting by business enterprises to outside investors that it is discussed much more fully in Chapter 19. For now, it is sufficient to say that conventional accounting representations are considered to be relatively *amenable to verification,* which provides an additional deterrent (although not perfect protection, as we shall see later) against dishonesty and a safeguard against persistent error or personal bias.

SUMMARY

This chapter has been devoted to filling out the reader's understanding of conventional accounting income measurement, and especially the disposable wealth measurement aspects of conventional accounting net income. The discussion also covered a number of major qualifications as to conventional accounting's operational characteristics, such as implications of uncertainty and price changes. The discussion, however, is by no means complete. It would be impossible to cover all the details of conventional accounting in several volumes—to say nothing of several chapters! Instead, the discussion has been devoted only to significant aspects of the way that conventional accounting represents business enterprises and their activities *as a whole*. In the next two chapters we complete the broad overview of conventional accounting by first covering the third major financial statement prepared by most firms (the statement of changes in financial position) and then covering the financial accounting information system (including traditional bookkeeping). More specific aspects of conventional accounting are then discussed in Chapters 8–12.

Questions for Review and Discussion

5-1. Define:
   a. Paid-in capital
   b. Retained earnings
   c. Gains and losses
   d. Extraordinary gains and losses
   e. Net operating income (loss)
   f. Net income (loss)

5-2. Describe the Hicksian concept of disposable wealth. Of what relevance to parties external to the enterprise is the Hicksian concept?

5-3. Explain in your own words why conventional accounting net operating income conforms to the Hicksian concept of disposable wealth (in the absence of any extraordinary gains and losses).

5-4. The measurement of disposable wealth is potentially relevant to interested external parties besides owners who are concerned about dividends or withdrawals. Elaborate.

5-5. If an enterprise distributes cash dividends equal to net income each period from its inception, what minimum amount of recognized net assets will always be retained by the enterprise? Why?

5-6. What is the legal criterion for measuring disposable wealth? What is its significance? In general, how is the legal criterion accommodated within conventional accounting.

5-7. Why are extraordinary gains and losses excluded from the conventional accounting measure of performance?

5-8. List three reasons that an enterprise might have for not distributing dividends equal to disposable wealth.

5-9. What is *conservatism* in conventional accounting? What apparently motivates conservatism among accountants or managers?

5-10. One advantage of conventional accounting is its objectivity. Is it entirely objective? Explain.

5-11. Conventional accounting *assumes* that prices are static. True or false? Defend your position.

5-12. Suppose a company distributed cash dividends to owners equal to only one-half of its net income for a period. What are the implications of such a dividend policy for investors interested in the business? How would you describe the effect of such a policy on the business to someone who knows nothing about accounting (i.e., nothing about net income)?

5-13. In this chapter it was noted that conventional accounting is subject to uncertainty. What are some of the sources of uncertainty in conventional accounting? How is uncertainty dealt with in conventional accounting? If you could redesign conventional accounting to deal more effectively with uncertainty, how would you alter it?

5-14. Suppose that each year for the last several years Corporation X recognized a significant extraordinary loss in its income statement entitled "Loss on uncollectible customer accounts." What would you conclude about (a) the losses and (b) the management of the corporation?

5-15. The owner-manager of Small Business Limited is very pleased with the recent growth of his business and its prospects for future growth. Net income, he notes, is up 20 percent over last year. He therefore decides to withdraw 20 percent more than he did last year but is informed by his accountant that insufficient cash is available. "What is income for," he rages, "if not to tell you how much you can spend?" As his accountant, what would your answer be?

Exercises

5-1. **Identifying Changes in Owners' Equity and Income Measures.** For each of the following events, indicate its individual effect upon (a) the wealth (net assets) position, (b) the disposable wealth (net income) for the period, and (c) the performance of the company (net operating income) for the period
    a. The company pays off a bank loan.
    b. Wages for the period are paid by the company.
    c. One of the owners contributes cash to the company.
    d. The company makes cash sales.
    e. One of the owners uses company supplies for personal purposes.
    f. The *company* buys a small percentage of the outstanding stock of X Corporation.
    g. The company receives cash dividends on shares owned of X Corporation.
    h. Depreciation of equipment is recorded.
    i. Rent expense for the period is recorded.
    j. Owner contributes a motor vehicle to the corporation in exchange for additional shares.
    k. Advertising expense for the period is recorded—it is not yet paid.
    l. The *company* pays cash dividends.
    m. Three years' insurance is paid in advance.
    n. Sales on credit are made.
    o. Supplies are used by the company.

p. A motor vehicle owned by the company is sold for more than its unexpired cost.

q. A ship owned by the company is confiscated in a foreign port during a revolution.

5-2. Identifying Changes in Owners' Equity and Income Measures. Owners' equity is affected by each of the following transactions. Construct a table showing the ultimate effect of each transaction on retained earnings, paid-in capital, net income, and net operating income. (Note: (1) Many of the items will have an effect upon more than one of the measures, (2) the kind of business under consideration may be different from item to item, as indicated, and (3) it is assumed that the balances in paid-in capital and retained earnings are sufficient to absorb any appropriate decreases.)

Example:	Paid-in Capital	Retained Earnings	Net Income	Net Operating Income
Wages expense of $300	None	(300)	(300)	(300)

a. Sales revenue of $600.
b. Gain of $100 from sales of machinery (not purchased for resale).
c. Owners were paid dividends of $1,000.
d. Sales returns by customers of $80.
e. Additional new owners contributed $5,000 to business.
f. Uninsured loss from destruction of merchandise by arson ($200).
g. Depreciation expense of $1,000.
h. Newspaper company is forced to pay $5,000 damages in libel suit (not covered by insurance).
i. Partner signs over the title of his car (market value $3,000) to the business in exchange for a larger share in ownership.
j. Investors' club earns $500 in cash dividends.
k. Land speculation company earns $400 profit on sale of land.
l. Manufacturing company earns $1,000 profit on the condemnation of land for a freeway.
m. Partner is paid a $600 salary as the actual manager of the business.
n. A machine that had not been fully depreciated was unexpectedly determined to be completely worn out. It originally cost $5,000; depreciation to date is $4,000.

5-3. Cash and Disposable Wealth. Albany Rentals is a car rental firm which has been operating for several years. The owners have followed the practice of withdrawing cash equal to the net income of each period. The beginning of 1980 balances in the accounts of the business are as follows:

	(in thousands)		
Assets:		Liabilities and Owners' Equity:	
Cash	$ 1,000	Accounts payable	$ 2,000
Accounts receivable	2,500		
Gas and oil supplies	500		
Motor vehicles $16,000			
Accumulated		Owners' equity	15,000
depreciation (3,000)	13,000	Total liabilities and	
Total assets	$17,000	owners' equity	$17,000

During 1980 the following events were recorded:

(in thousands)	
Cash rentals earned	$4,000
Credit rentals earned	4,000
Purchases of gas and oil supplies (credit)	1,500
Rent paid for 1980	2,000
Depreciation expense for 1980	2,500
Supplies on hand at end of year	250
Repairs expense (all paid)	700
Payments on accounts payable	2,750
Receipts from accounts receivable	1,000

Required:

1. Record the information for 1980 on a financial position worksheet.

2. Produce an income statement for 1980.

3. Discuss whether the owners are able to follow their usual withdrawal policy. Explain your reasoning.

5-4. Uncertainty and Disposable Wealth Measurement. Max and several associates decide to go into business operating a charter bus service at tourist resorts. They commence the business on January 1, 1980, by placing $1 million in a bank account out of which the business purchases ten buses for $750,000. *They decide that each year they will withdraw all the disposable wealth* that the business earns. The buses are expected to have useful lives of five years, at the end of which Max and his associates expect to sell them for $15,000 each. Following are the other bus company transactions for 1980 and 1981:

	1980	1981
	(amounts in thousands)	
Cash fares	$1,200	$1,300
Charter fares (credit)	500	350
Insurance paid	150	70
Wages paid	750	700
Payments from customers	200	350
Gas and oil supplies purchased on credit	200	160
Payments to suppliers	50	310
Gas and oil on hand at year-end	40	-0-
Repairs and maintenance (all paid)	180	190
Insurance cost unexpired at year-end	50	-0-

All events for 1980 are recorded on the financial position worksheet in Exhibit 5-9. At the end of 1981 Max discovers to his horror that because a travel agency went bankrupt, the business will never collect $100,000 of the $300,000 that had been owing from 1980 and the debt must be considered a total loss. During 1981 one of the buses is totally destroyed in a civil disorder—a hazard not covered by the company's insurance.

Required:

1. Record all the facts as they took place in worksheet form for 1981. (Do not forget the depreciation of the bus.)

Exhibit 5-9

MAX'S BUS COMPANY

Financial Position Worksheet—1980
(amounts in thousands)

Description	Cash	Accounts Receivable	Prepaid Insurance	Supplies	Buses	Accumulated Depreciation	Accounts Payable	Owners' Equity
Balances, Jan. 1, 1980	1,000							1,000
Bus purchase	(750)				750			
Cash fares	1,200							1,200 (R)
Credit fares		500						500 (R)
Insurance	(150)		50					(100) (E)
Wages	(750)							(750) (E)
Customer payments	200	(200)						
Supplies				200			200	
Payments to suppliers	(50)						(50)	
Supplies used				(160)				(160) (E)
Repairs and maintenance	(180)							(180) (E)
Depreciation expense						(120)		(120) (E)
Withdrawal	(390)							(390) (W)
Balances, Dec. 31, 1980	130	300	50	40	750	(120)	150	1,000

2. Draw up an income statement for each of the two years.

3. In drawing up the income statement, did you show the losses on the customer's bad debt and from the destruction of the bus as extraordinary losses? Why or why not?

4. Assuming that the loss of the bus is considered an extraordinary loss, explain the implications in the long run for the company of 1981 withdrawals equal to (*a*) net operating income and (*b*) net income.

5-5. Extraordinary Gains and Losses: Following is an excerpt from the 1977 annual report of Millipore Corporation (an actual industrial company) showing comparative income statements for fiscal 1977 and 1976. Note that it follows fairly closely the format of Exhibit 5-5 (the only exception being that income from operations is arrived at in four steps instead of one).

Required:

1. Note the item entitled "Extraordinary credit from gain on sale of securities, net of related taxes," appearing in the fiscal 1976 column. Explain, in principle, why such an item should not be included in the calculation of income from operations.

2. Many businesses invest in marketable securities routinely so that cash generated by operations (or contributed by owners and creditors) does not remain idle while awaiting investment in such things as additions to inventories, property, and plant and equipment. Gains on sales of such securities are in the long run a routine, if not frequent, part of business activities. What characteristics did Millipore's investment in or sale of the securities have to have in order for the latter to be accorded extraordinary status in the 1976 income statement?

Income Statements	Year Ended December 31, 1977	Year Ended December 31, 1976
Net sales	$86,423,000	$68,015,000
Cost of sales	40,825,000	31,974,000
	45,598,000	36,041,000
Selling, general and administrative expenses	27,184,000	21,557,000
	18,414,000	14,484,000
Interest income	128,000	196,000
Interest expense	426,000	211,000
Income before federal and foreign income taxes	18,116,000	14,469,000
Federal and foreign income taxes	8,531,000	6,770,000
Income from operations	9,585,000	7,699,000
Extraordinary credit from gain on sale of securities, net of related taxes	—	1,166,000
Net income	$ 9,585,000	$ 8,865,000

5-6. Uncertainty, Gains and Losses, and Disposable Wealth. You and a fellow student, Jane Smith, pool your resources of $1,000 each in cash and enter the business of selling lecture notes on campus at the beginning of the autumn quarter, 1981. You intend to operate the business, Smith and Jones Enterprises, at least until the end of spring, 1982. Of the original investment, a minimum of $500 is required to meet each quarter's costs of supplies, insurance, wages, and so forth—while awaiting collection of revenues. The remaining $1,500 is used as a down payment to purchase a printing press at a total cost of $2,500 (the bank lends you $1,000—interest free). You expect that the press can be sold for $1,900 at the end of spring, 1982, or for $1,100 at the end of spring, 1983. You therefore depreciate the equipment at a rate of $200 per quarter. Your method of operation is simple—you and Smith collect the materials and print the lecture notes which you sell to three distributors. The distributors are given until the end of each quarter to pay Smith and Jones Enterprises.

At the commencement of business you and Smith have an argument. Smith considers that at the end of each quarter you and she should receive a cash dividend equal to the net income earned for the period. "It's disposable wealth, isn't it?" is her argument. You assert that "to be on the safe side" only 50 percent of the income should be withdrawn each quarter. You win.

At the end of the autumn quarter, things have gone well. You earned $800 profit and withdrew $200 each. The balances in the Smith and Jones Enterprises balance sheet were as follows:

SMITH AND JONES ENTERPRISES

Balance Sheet
As of the End of Autumn Quarter, 1981

Cash	$1,200	Accounts payable	$ 200
Supplies	100	Bank loan	1,000
Equipment	2,500	Total liabilities	$1,200
Accumulated depreciation	(200)	Owners' equity	2,400
Total assets	$3,600	Total	$3,600

In the next two quarters the following events occurred:

	Winter	Spring
Credit sales to distributors	$2,200	$1,800
Receipts from distributors	1,800	2,050
Wages paid	550	600
Advertising and insurance paid	50	100
Supplies purchased on credit	600	250
Repaid part of bank loan	500	500
Payments to accounts payable	700	350
Supplies on hand at end of winter	250	-0-

Additional information:

a. At the end of winter, one of the distributors, named Ripoff, owed $400. No action was taken as he promised to pay early in the spring quarter, which he did. During the winter $500 of the bank loan was repaid.

b. At the end of spring, Ripoff owed $150. The amount was written off as a bad debt, for a telegram was received from him saying that he was in Tahiti with a cocktail waitress from the Off Campus Tavern. Just at the end of spring quarter classes, vandals broke in and destroyed the printing press. The insurance company paid insurance proceeds of $1,150.

c. The policy that the cash dividend could not exceed 50 percent of net income was adhered to in both winter and spring.

d. A worksheet for winter and spring, 1982, appears in Exhibit 5-10.

Required:

1. Produce income statements for winter and for spring, 1982.

2. How did you classify the losses on bad debts and the printing press? Justify your treatment.

3. Assuming that the loss of the printing press is an extraordinary loss, explain the possible decision relevance of the net operating income and the net income figures for spring, 1982.

4. Explain the justification for not paying out all disposable wealth at the end of a period. What are the long-run financial implications of a 50 percent payout policy?

5. Explain (in terms of income recognized and owners' withdrawals) the difference between the original investment of Smith and Jones and the ending owners' equity as of the end of spring, 1982.

5-7. Detecting Misapplications of Conventional Accounting. The owner-president of the Gidgiegannup Electrical Contractors Company was elated, but at the same time concerned, by the financial results of his firm for the month of May. Knowing you to be a particularly astute student of accounting, he confides in you. "This business has lost money over the last few years. I was seriously considering going into another line of business, but look at the worksheet for May. It indicates our best month ever! One thing worries me though—at the end of April my accountant retired, and I replaced him with a new fellow. Now I don't know whether my previous accountant was dishonest or just making us look bad, or whether the new fellow has made mistakes favorable to us. Can you look into it?" He hands you the worksheet shown in Exhibit 5-11.

With typical determination you conduct a thorough investigation of the accounting records of the Gidgiegannup Electrical Contractors Company and discover the following:

a. That the equipment bought at the end of April 19X4 has a life of only five years, at the end of which it will have no salvage value.

b. That the prepaid insurance (paid on May 1) represented insurance for the period May 1, 19X4, to April 30, 19X5.

Exhibit 5-10

SMITH AND JONES ENTERPRISES

Financial Position Worksheet
Winter and Spring Quarters, 1982

Description	Cash	Accounts Receivable	Supplies	Equipment	Accumulated Depreciation	Accounts Payable	Bank Loan	Owners' Equity	
Opening Balances (beginning of winter)	1,200		100	2,500	(200)	200	1,000	2,400	
Credit sales		2,200						2,200	(R)
Receipts on account	1,800	(1,800)							
Wages	(550)							(550)	(E)
Advertising and insurance	(50)							(50)	(E)
Supplies purchased			600			600			
Payments to suppliers	(700)					(700)			
Supplies used			(450)					(450)	(E)
Bank repayment	(500)						(500)		
Depreciation					(200)			(200)	(E)
Withdrawal	(475)							(475)	(W)
Balances (beginning of spring)	725	400	250	2,500	(400)	100	500	2,875	
Credit sales		1,800						1,800	(R)
Receipts on account	2,050	(2,050)							
Wages	(600)							(600)	(E)
Advertising and insurance	(100)							(100)	(E)
Supplies purchased			250			250			
Bank repayment	(500)						(500)		
Payments to suppliers	(350)					(350)			
Supplies used			(500)					(500)	(E)
Depreciation					(200)			(200)	(E)
Bad debt loss		(150)						(150)	(L)
Loss of printing press	1,150			(2,500)	600			(750)	(L)
Balances (end of spring)	2,375	-0-	-0-	-0-	-0-	-0-	-0-	2,375	

Exhibit 5-11

GIDGIEGANNUP ELECTRICAL CONTRACTORS COMPANY

Financial Position Worksheet—May 19X4

Description	Cash	Accounts Receivable	Electrical Supplies	Prepaid Insurance	Prepaid Rent	Equipment	Accumulated Depreciation	Insurance Payable	Rent Payable	Wages Payable	Interest on Loan	Accounts Payable	Bank Loan	Owners' Equity
Opening Balances	6,000	2,000	500			6,000						5,000	3,000	6,500
Revenue earned		8,000												8,000 (R)
Receipts from customers	5,000	(5,000)												
Supplies purchased			1,000									1,000		
Payments to suppliers	(800)											(800)		
Wages paid	(1,600)													(1,600) (E)
Advertising paid	(100)													(100) (E)
Insurance paid	(600)			600										
Rent expense paid	(800)													(800) (E)
Supplies used			(700)											(700) (E)
Balances (end of May)	7,100	5,000	800	600		6,000						5,200	3,000	11,300

c. That the rent (which was paid on May 1) represented rent for the period May 1, 19X4, to June 30, 19X4.
d. That interest on the bank loan is 1½ percent per month, payable quarterly. The last quarterly payment was on April 30.
e. That advertising amounting to $150 had been billed by the local newspaper. Only $100 of that bill had been paid and duly recorded as an expense.
f. That the employees are paid at the end of the week following work performed and are thus owed wages for the last week of May amounting to $380. None of the wages paid this period related to work performed in previous periods.
g. That Fred Nurk, who owed the company $400, had skipped to Argentina.
h. That work had been completed and delivered to a customer at a price of $200 but had not been recorded in any way. No payment has been made by the customer.
i. That an electricity bill for $300 had been received at the end of May but was not reflected in the accounts.

Required:

1. Present an income statement for May 19X4 as it would have been had you not examined the records.

2. Starting with the May 31 balances as shown, make the necessary entries on a worksheet to record the facts that you have unearthed.

3. Draw up a revised income statement.

5-8. Conventional Accounting Transaction Interpretation. Following are a set of transactions and events for a hypothetical corporation for the year just ended. Interpret each according to the conventional accounting model and, in a table, (1) indicate the accounts or elements of the corporation's financial position that are affected by each item, giving the account name, amount, and direction of change (distinguish between paid-in capital and retained earnings), and (2) indicate the amount and direction of the effect of each item on net operating income and net income. (The first item is used as an example below.) If you feel you have to make any significant assumptions in order to interpret an item, show them as a footnote to your answer table.

a. The company had a combined beginning supplies inventory and purchases for the year with a total cost of $20,000. The supplies remaining at year-end originally cost $1,000.
b. Rent for the year amounted to $2,400. However, it had been paid in a two-year rent payment prior to the beginning of the year.
c. Equipment originally costing $20,000 and depreciated to date in the amount of $12,500 was lost due to a freak accident at the beginning of the year. Insurance proceeds were $9,000.
d Sales for cash amounted to $15,000. New credit sales equaled $75,000. Goods were delivered to customers who had advanced the full selling prices of $10,000 last year.

e. At the beginning of the period the *accumulated depreciation* on assets employed in the business was $225,000. At the end of the period it was $250,000.
f. New owners contributed $90,000 cash to the corporation.
g. Wage and salary payments made during the year equaled $55,000. However, wages of $5,000 were owed to employees at year-end for work already performed. No wages were owed at the beginning of the year.
h. Dividends of $20,000 were declared and paid to owners during the year.

Example:

	Income Measures Affected	
Accounts Affected	Net Operating Income	Net Income
a. Supplies inventory (19,000) Retained earnings (19,000)	(19,000)	(19,000)

5-9. **Financial Statement Relationships.** The statement of financial position for the Larson Electronics Corporation, which was based on the conventional accounting model, reflected the following information:

	12/31/X3	12/31/X4
Total assets	$5,200,000	$5,800,000
Total liabilities	1,200,000	1,000,000

During 19X4 the total revenue generated by normal business operations was $10 million. In addition, the company sold to the City (after condemnation) a parcel of land it had owned for several years at a gain of $200,000. The corporation declared and paid cash dividends to its shareholders amounting to $500,000 in 19X4.
1. What was the value of owners' equity on December 31, 19X4?
2. What was Larson's net income (disposable wealth) for 19X4?
3. What was Larson's net operating income (measure of performance) for 19X4?
4. What was the amount of the expenses associated with normal business operations recognized by Larson Electronics Corporation during 19X4?

5-10. **Calculating Gains and Losses.** In each of the following three different situations determine (*a*) the amount of gain or loss after tax effects and (b) whether the gain or loss is extraordinary or not. In every case assume that the applicable tax rate is 48 percent.

1. The Very Fashionable Corporation is a firm specializing in high-fashion apparel. During the year 19X3 the fashion market experienced very rapid changes in styles and consumer preferences which resulted in the disposal of discontinued styles and related accessories for $250,000 and $50,000, respectively. The total costs of these items were $300,000 and $80,000, respectively.
2. Winthrop Chemicals, Inc., manufactures chemicals for the drug industry. During the year 19X7 it was decided that some of Winthrop's storage equipment had become obsolete. The original cost of the equipment was $1.5 million. Accumulated depreciation as of the time of disposition of the equipment was $800,000. Market value at which the equipment was sold was $750,000.
3. A freak electrical storm occurred one night in the suburban area where one of the warehouses of Coolyter Grocery and Co. was located. The warehouse caught fire and burned to the ground. The building itself and the inventories stored in it were insured for a total of $2.53 million. The original cost of the building was $1.5 million with accumulated depreciation of $750,000. The inventories cost $1.2 million. After a thorough investigation the storm was determined to be a most improbable act of nature. Insurance will be received in the full amount stated on the policy.

5-11. **Statement of Retained Earnings.** Following is the statement of retained earnings from the 1977 annual report of Millipore Corporation. The letters *a, b,* and *c* have been substituted for certain intentionally omitted numbers. Otherwise the statement is almost identical in format to Exhibit 5-7.

Retained Earnings	*Year Ended December 31, 1977*	*Year Ended December 31, 1976*
Balance at beginning of year	$ (a)	$30,678,000
Net income	9,585,000	8,865,000
Deduct cash dividends declared (Note 1):		
1977—$.15 per share	1,247,000	—
1976—$.11 per share	—	(c)
Balance at end of year	$46,967,000	(b)

Required:

For letters *a, b,* and *c,* give the dollar amount that appeared in the Millipore Corporation statement.

5-12. Financial Statement Relationships. The statement of financial position for the GX Corporation, which was based on conventional accounting, reflected the following information:

	12/31/X1	12/31/X2
Total assets	$2,600,000	$2,900,000
Total liabilities	600,000	500,000

During 19X2 the total revenue generated by normal business operations was $5 million. In addition, a parcel of land the corporation had owned for several years was condemned by a local government for use as a park. The proceeds of the condemnation sale were sufficient to result in an after-tax gain of $100,000. The corporation declared and paid cash dividends to its shareholders amounting to $250,000 in 19X2. No additional shares of stock were sold during 19X2.

Required:

1. What was the amount of GX Corporation's owners' equity on December 31, 19X2?

2. What was GX's net income (disposable wealth) for 19X2?

3. What was GX's net operating income (measure of performance) for 19X2?

4. What was the amount of the expenses associated with normal business operations recognized by GX Corporation during 19X2?

5-13. Discontinued Operations and Extraordinary Gains and Losses. The comparative consolidated statements of earnings (income statements) from the annual report of Curtiss-Wright Corporation and Subsidiaries (actual companies) for the years ended December 31, 1970 and 1969, appear in Exhibit 5-12.

Required:

1. During 1970 it was decided to discontinue the operations of the corporation's East Paterson facility, Levon Properties Corp. and the Dorchem and Dortech Subsidiaries. Notice that Curtiss-Wright recognizes the operating losses from these subsidiaries on a separate line of its income statement, entitled "loss from discontinued operations." Explain, in principle, why such an item should be separated from the earnings from continuing operations reported by Curtiss-Wright.

2. The entry entitled "extraordinary items" is separated from continuing operations as well. However, these extraordinary items consisted of provisions for estimated costs and expenses resulting from

the discontinuance of the operations described in number 1 which were to be phased out completely in 1971. That is, they consist of *estimated* losses on sales of facilities, severance pay, or compensation to workers unemployed or relocated, etc. What rationale can you see for following the practice of recognizing such losses as (*a*) extraordinary and (*b*) before they are all actually incurred? Explain.

5-14. **Financial Statement Relationships.** Certain data from the 19X5 comparative statement of financial position for the YDC Corporation follow. The corporation uses the conventional accounting model.

	12/31/X4	12/31/X5
Total assets	$8,300,000	$9,200,000
Total liabilities	2,500,000	4,100,000

During 19X5 the total revenue generated by ordinary business operations was $15 million. In addition, the company sold a truck it had owned for

Exhibit 5-12

CURTISS-WRIGHT CORPORATION AND SUBSIDIARIES

Consolidated Statements of Earnings
For the Years Ended December 31, 1970 and 1969

	1970	1969
Revenues:		
Sales	$278,959,978	$277,076,412
Rentals and gain on sales of real estate and equipment	3,171,262	5,745,871
Interest, dividends and gain on sales of marketable securities	1,937,342	4,358,633
Fees, commissions and other income, net	4,310,130	1,204,456
	288,378,712	288,385,372
Costs and Expenses:		
Product and engineering	244,023,874	228,700,443
Selling and service	14,209,257	13,859,450
Administrative and general	20,488,442	23,087,246
Interest	3,251,414	3,093,061
Minority interest in net income (loss) from continuing operations of subsidiaries	923,498	(337,767)
	282,896,485	268,402,433
Earnings from continuing operations before federal and foreign income tax provisions	5,482,227	19,982,939
Provision for federal and foreign income taxes	2,100,000	7,000,000
Earnings from continuing operations	3,382,227	12,982,939
Loss from discontinued operations	(4,831,658)	(708,968)
Earnings (loss) before extraordinary items	(1,449,431)	12,273,971
Extraordinary items	(3,188,585)	—
Net Earnings (Loss)	$ (4,638,016)	$ 12,273,971

a few years at a gain of $6,000 net of tax. A most unusual flood during 19X5 resulted in enormous damage to a warehouse. A total loss of $2.5 million net of tax and insurance proceeds was incurred as a result. There was no new owners' capital contributed during 19X5 and no cash dividends were paid that year due to the flood loss.

Required:

1. Amount of YDC's owners' equity on December 31, 19X5?

2. Net income of YDC Corporation for 19X5?

3. Net operating income of YDC Corporation for 19X5?

4. Normal business expenses of YDC Corporation as recognized during 19X5?

5-15. Statement of Retained Earnings. Following is the statement of retained earnings from the 19X4 annual report of Super Retail Corporation. Figures are intentionally omitted at spaces marked *a, b, c,* and *d.*

Retained Earnings	Year Ended Dec. 31, 19X4	Year Ended Dec. 31, 19X3
Balance at beginning of year	$ (d)	$58,243,000
Net Income	(a)	(c)
Deduct cash dividends declared:		
19X4—$.23 per share	(b)	—
19X3—$.30 per share	—	2,700,000
Balance at end of year	$66,322,500	$63,043,250

Required:

Determine the dollar amounts represented by *a–d* which appeared in the above statement. (Note: The number of shares of stock outstanding was constant during the year 19X4.)

Resource Flows and Statements of Changes in Financial Position[1]

In earlier chapters we examined the broad concepts underlying the valuation of assets and liabilities and the measurement of income in conventional accounting, along with their presentations in statements of financial position (balance sheets) and results of operations (income statements). This chapter introduces the third major statement used in present-day financial reporting by business enterprises—the statement of changes in financial position.

As its modern title implies, this statement is rather sweeping in the scope of information that it is intended to provide. That is, the statement of changes in financial position is intended to show the flows of resources within the enterprise that together explain the transition from one financial position to the next *and, at the same time,* to associate these flows with their underlying causes among the activities of the enterprise. This breadth of scope makes the statement of changes in financial position relatively difficult to understand. For this reason the first part of the chapter focuses on the underlying linkage between the information conveyed in a statement of changes in financial position and the factors (activities) that influence the financial success of a business. We then discuss (1) how to assemble the information conveyed in such statements and (2) how to interpret the information presented.

---

[1] Certain passages of this chapter are adapted from W. Keith Henderson, Robert G. May, and Lawrence D. Schall, *Evaluating Business Ventures* (Portland, Oregon: United States National Bank of Oregon, 1980).

Income as a Measure of Resource Flows

The importance of income measures to decisions dealing with investments in, or distribution of economic benefits from, the enterprise has been emphasized in earlier chapters. We do not at this time suggest any lessening of this importance. Yet, while measures of income are useful for informed decisions of the types indicated, they may not adequately serve all other purposes as well. For example, in Chapter 5 we alluded to the possibility that sufficient cash may not be on hand to make distributions to the owners in an amount equal to net income. Similarly, we asserted that net operating income gives some clue to the long-run cash-generating ability of the firm. But exclusive reliance on this long-run indicator may cause the investor to overlook short-run deficiences in the actual flow of cash through the business.

Resource Flows: Income, Cash, and Working Capital

Example 6-1

The Dynamic Growth Company was formed at the beginning of 19X0 for the purpose of selling "do-it-yourself" wine-making kits. The formation of the company followed a countrywide spurt in demand for wine products, and business was very brisk and apparently quite profitable. Indeed, abbreviated income statements for 19X0–X1 (Exhibit 6-1) reflect rapidly growing profits. Yet the company became insolvent at the beginning of 19X2, that is, it did not have enough cash to pay its accounts payable when due.

How could such a situation develop in light of the very encouraging results reflected in the income statements? Is it perhaps that accounting measures of income are unreliable? Not necessarily. While income statements may on occasion be unreliable, that is not a complete answer. The business was in fact operating profitably. But net income measures the change in net assets for the period that resulted from the firm's operations, *giving equal weight to changes in assets and liabilities of all kinds.* Consequently, income statements alone do

Exhibit 6-1

DYNAMIC GROWTH COMPANY

Comparative Income Statements
For the Years 19X0 and 19X1

	19X0	19X1
Sales revenue	$200,000	$400,000
Expenses:		
Cost of sales	$100,000	$200,000
Operating expenses	50,000	76,500
	$150,000	$276,500
Net income	$ 50,000	$123,500

not reveal certain potentially relevant changes in the enterprise's "mix" of assets and liabilities.

Consider, for instance, the abbreviated statements of the financial position of Dynamic Growth Company at three points in its short life—as reflected in Exhibit 6-2. From these comparative statements of financial position, we can see that Dynamic Growth Company's good fortunes stimulated the owners to expand its capacity to operate. Warehouse and office facilities were apparently purchased, the stock of inventory was substantially increased to provide a better selection of products, and, as a consequence of expanding sales to a broader spectrum of customers, the amount of open (uncollected) accounts receivable increased. Assuming that the company continued to operate as it had in the past, this capacity to provide greater service would have been converted into additional profits, and the inflow of funds in the *long run* would have been substantial. But, unfortunately, the cash position of the firm at the end of 19X1 did become seriously low, leading in early 19X2 to the firm's inability to pay its accounts payable when due.

Example 6-1 demonstrates that there are several facets to a company's immediate history, not all of which are encompassed by the income statement. Whether viewed as a measure of enterprise performance or as an indicator of the amount that could be distributed without reducing wealth below the level of wealth at the beginning of the period, income is essentially a long-run concept. This point of view necessarily abstracts from many important short-run considerations. And, as was pointed out above, one of the important short-run considerations not revealed by the income measure is the change in the composition, or "mix," of the net assets of the enterprise.

At first glance, it would appear that comparative statements of financial position provide adequate information on changes in asset mix. In the example, the comparative statements of financial position at three points in time do reveal a continually deteriorating cash position. But, unfortunately, the changes in financial position communicated by the beginning and ending balance sheets reveal only the *cumulative effects* of all forces that tended to restructure the

Exhibit 6-2

DYNAMIC GROWTH COMPANY

Comparative Statements of Financial Position

	January 1, 19X0	*December 31, 19X0*	*December 31, 19X1*
Cash	$40,000	$ 20,000	$ 1,000
Accounts receivable	-0-	40,000	110,000
Inventory	-0-	50,000	150,000
Office and warehouse (net of accumulated depreciation)	-0-	-0-	112,500
Total assets	$40,000	$110,000	$373,500
Accounts payable	-0-	$ 20,000	$ 60,000
Mortgage payable	-0-	-0-	70,000
Total liabilities	-0-	$ 20,000	$130,000
Owners' equity	$40,000	$ 90,000	$243,500
Total liabilities and owners' equity	$40,000	$110,000	$373,500

composition of net assets during the period. While this information may indicate an imminent crisis at times, it does not convey the dynamics of the changes that took place during a period. Nor do comparative balance sheets alone provide as clear an indication of potentially serious financial situations (which may be avoided by appropriate planning) as when they are accompanied by a well-constructed statement of resource flows designed to reveal the decision-relevant aspects (causes) of changes in the levels of various categories within net assets. (Forecast statements of resource flows would provide still earlier warning. But for external use they are subject to the limitations discussed in Chapter 3.)

Causes of Changes in Financial Position

In order to grasp the potential decision-relevance of a statement of changes in financial position, one must understand how the activities of a business affect its financial position. For this purpose it is convenient to classify the activities that directly affect financial position into three broad categories—operations, investment activities, and financing activities.

Operations. Operations consist of all activities directly related to the regular production and delivery of products and services to customers.

Investment Activities. Investment activities consist of all activities related to the acquisition and disposition of assets such as plant, equipment, patents, and copyrights which provide the capacity over time to carry out the operations of the business.

Financing Activities. Financing activities are activities related to acquiring from (and repaying to) creditors and owners the funds necessary to acquire the resources required for the operations of the business.

Within operations we can differentiate two important subclasses of activities: (a) marketing activities, which relate to selecting the best product lines, product qualities, target sales volumes, prices, and promotional strategies, and (b) production activities, which relate to selecting the best methods of production for producing the desired quantity and quality of products. Together, these two classes of activities have two distinctly different effects on financial position. Marketing and production decisions have indirect effects on financial position in that they determine the desired levels of investment by the enterprise in assets of various types. For example, if a business must offer its customers credit in order to compete in a particular market, a certain "investment" in accounts receivable is required. Likewise, if the market in which the business competes is one in which customers expect to "buy off the shelf," then the firm must have a ready inventory of finished goods on hand at all times or sales will be lost due to "stockouts." At the same time, if a firm determines that the best way to produce its product is in a fully automated factory, this implies a higher level of investment in plant and equipment than if it selects a more "labor-intensive" production process. It should be observed that optimal operations plans cannot be made independent of investment and financing considerations. However, the methods of making and coordinating optimal business decisions are more properly the domain of disciplines such as marketing, microeconomics, and finance and therefore are beyond the scope of this text.

The more direct effects of operations on financial position are produced by the actual production of goods and services. Such activities involve the consumption of resources such as raw materials, labor, supplies, and plant and equipment. They also result in production of new products and services which when delivered to customers provide assets in a new form, cash or accounts receivable.

When the effects of operations, investment activities, and financing activities are put together in a sequence that links them logically to the management of a business, a definite pattern of impact on financial position emerges. First, marketing and production plans in conjunction with financing and investment considerations determine a desired level of investment in assets of various types. Funds in the form of cash (or other assets that can be readily converted to cash) to acquire the desired assets must either be on hand or be secured from new creditor or owner sources via financing activities. Such funds are then available for acquiring (investing in) the desired assets to support operations. Actual operations, in turn, produce cash flows from sales (collections of accounts receivable) to replace resources consumed in providing products and services and to compensate sources of invested funds.

All of this suggests that cash is the "eye of the needle." That is, it implies that all changes in cash are the result of either operating, investment, or financing activities *and* that the financial implications of all operating, investment, and financing activities are reflected in changes in cash in one period or another. The latter conclusion is not entirely true but is accurate enough for present purposes. We attend to the exceptions later.

The Concept of Working Capital

The pivotal role of cash suggests that by monitoring the changes in the cash account (for example, by means of a statement that appropriately reveals the changes in cash) decision makers gain considerable information about virtually all changes in financial position during a given period. Indeed this is the underlying rationale for the structure of all statements of changes in financial position. However, only a relatively small fraction of large industrial corporations in the United States focus on cash as the basis for "statements of changes . . . ." A much more frequently used basis is "working capital."

Working Capital. Working capital is the combined (or net amount of) current assets and current liabilities of the enterprise. It is measured by the difference between the sum of the values assigned to current assets and the sum of the values assigned to current liabilities.

Current Assets. Current assets include cash and those other assets whose benefits are expected to be realized (usually by conversion to cash) in one year or one operating cycle, whichever is longer. In addition to cash the current assets category typically includes accounts receivable, inventories, and soon-to-expire prepaid items (such as insurance premiums, rent, and taxes).

Current Liabilities. Current liabilities are those liabilities, usually incurred in connection with recurring operations, that will require liquidation (payment) in one year or one operating cycle, whichever is longer. Current liabilities typically include accounts payable, wages payable, taxes payable, and soon-to-be-paid installments on long-term liabilities.

The notion of an "operating cycle" is somewhat abstract. However, for purposes of defining current assets and current liabilities, the length of an operating cycle is usually thought of as the typical time lapse between the purchase of raw materials or merchandise and the cash collection from the sale of the merchandise or product produced with the raw materials.

Of course the definition of *working capital* based on the ideas of current assets and current liabilities suggests that the statement of financial position (balance sheet) is partitioned into broad categories related to the flows of resources through the business, that is, related to changes in financial position. For example, defining *current assets* as this term is defined above implies a second category of "noncurrent assets" including all assets whose conversion to cash will take more than one year (or one operating cycle if greater). Such assets, customarily called "fixed assets" or "long-lived assets," include land, buildings, machinery, patents, copyrights, and investments in affiliated companies.

Since the categories of current and fixed assets are defined with respect to the time that it typically takes to convert them into cash, they could just as aptly be labeled high-turnover and low-turnover assets, respectively. Also, note that current assets other than cash are usually related to the *short-run* operations of the enterprise. That is, they serve as buffers (leads and lags) between actual short-run operations and cash receipts and disbursements. Their levels are therefore directly influenced by the current volume of operations. Fixed or low-turnover assets, on the other hand, represent capacity to operate. Their levels fluctuate more intermittently and usually by more significant amounts (their costs per unit are typically rather large).

The above definition of *current liabilities* implies a second category, traditionally called *long-term liabilities,* which includes all liabilities due after one year (or one operating cycle, if longer). As with the current-asset and fixed-asset categories, some generalizations can be made with respect to the current and long-term liabilities distinctions. First, the basic definitions represent a "frequency-of-payment" perspective. Second, current debts (other than such items as long-term debt due within twelve months) are directly related to day-to-day operations of the business, whereas this is not the case for long-term debt. For instance, a current liability such as accounts payable serves as a buffer between the acquisition and use of high-turnover items (e.g., raw materials) and the actual cash payment for them. As a result, the levels of current liabilities are highly influenced by the volume of related operations—as are the levels of most current assets.

In Chapter 4 we defined *liabilities* as obligations of the business, and *owners' equity* as the residual interests or claims of owners. Another way to look at both debt (liabilities) and owners' equity is to view them as sources of the funds needed to acquire the desired assets of all types. From this point of view we look upon a statement of financial position (balance sheet) as representing cumulative sources of funds (debt and equity) and cumulative investments of funds (assets) at a point in time. Furthermore, the view emphasizes the common purpose of debt and equity—to supply the funds to support the investment in assets by the enterprise. The principal feature distinguishing one source of supporting funds from another is the terms of repayment: debt carries with it an actual or implied contractual schedule of principal and interest payments; while payments to suppliers of equity capital are discretionary at any particular point in time.

Exhibit 6-3 shows the typical relationship between the sums of the balances in the various balance sheet classifications described above. This visualization is useful in understanding and utilizing the concept of working capital and the relationships typically reflected in a statement of changes in financial position.

A noteworthy feature of Exhibit 6-3 is the implied dual definition of *working capital*. In the top half of the exhibit, working capital is shown to be the difference between current assets and current liabilities (the traditional accounting definition). At the same time, because working capital represents the "net investment" in current assets, (i.e., the investment in current assets net of the amount financed by current liabilities), it may also be defined as the amount that the long-term sources of funds must supply in excess of the investment in long-lived assets in order for the internal demand for assets in the enterprise to be aligned with (in balance with) the total supporting funds. This second definition is visually indicated in Exhibit 6-3 by the difference between the two lower blocks in the diagram.

Another noteworthy feature of Exhibit 6-3 is that the dual definition may also be seen symbolically in accounting equation form if we recognize the dis-

Exhibit 6-3

COMPONENTS OF A CLASSIFIED STATEMENT OF FINANCIAL POSITION

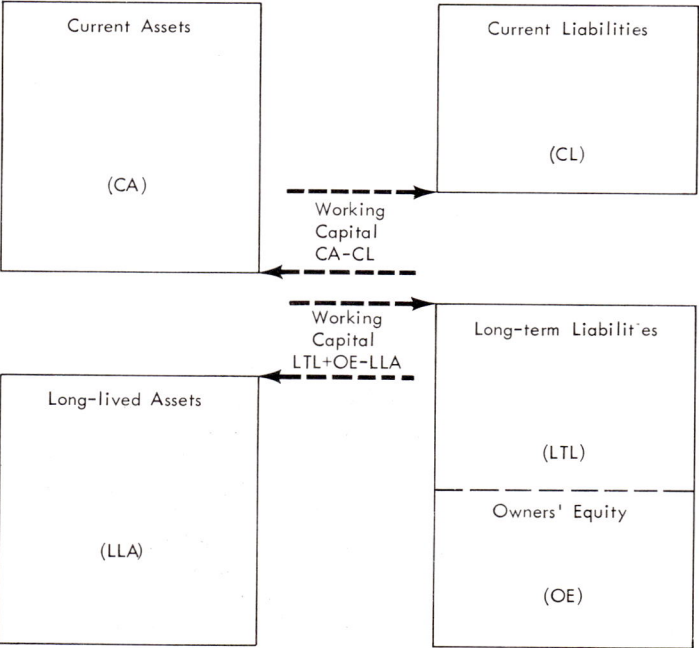

tinction between current assets (CA), long-lived assets (LLA), current liabilities (CL), and long-term liabilities (LTL) that are embedded in the definition of working capital and the use of classified balance sheets. The expanded equation in balance sheet form (balancing assets against liabilities and owners' equity) may be written:

$$A = L + OE \qquad (1)$$

$$CA + LLA = CL + LTL + OE \qquad (2)$$

If the terms are rearranged to isolate the working capital accounts on one side, equation (2) becomes

$$CA - CL = LTL + OE - LLA \qquad (3)$$

$$CA - CL = \text{Working capital} = LTL + OE - LLA \qquad (4)$$

Equation (4) is the dual definition expressed symbolically.

Statements of Changes in Financial Position—Working Capital Basis

Let us now summarize the points that have been introduced. Initially, we noted that whereas the income statement explains one important aspect of a firm's activities through time, namely the changes in net assets due to operations, it does not capture all relevant aspects of the transition from one net asset position to another. One important additional type of potentially relevant information is the change in net asset *mix* or the composition of financial position between points in time (e.g., between successive financial positions (balance sheets). Direct information on the changes in mix is, of course, available by comparing successive balance sheets. Yet such a comparison is not totally satisfactory because it does not identify how the changes in financial position came about. Were the underlying causes operating, investment, or financing activities of the firm? Thus the statement of changes in financial position has evolved specifically to show the effects on financial position of operating, investment, and financing activities.

Exhibit 6-4 contains a working-capital-based statement of changes in financial position for Dynamic Growth Company for the year ended December 31, 19X1. For convenient reference all events and transactions experienced by the company for that year are presented in the financial position worksheet shown in Exhibit 6-5.

Before discussing how a statement of changes in financial position is prepared from the information contained in the accounts of a company, several features of the statement in Exhibit 6-4 are worth noting. First, the statement is organized into two major sections—"sources of working capital" and "uses of working capital." This choice of labels is intended to emphasize the causes of changes in working capital as well as the amounts of the changes. Second, the format is such that all effects of operations on working capital are recognized together in a single section of the statement as one *net* source or use of working capital.

Exhibit 6-4

DYNAMIC GROWTH COMPANY

Statement of Changes in Financial Position
(Working Capital Basis)
For Year Ended December 31, 19X1

Sources of working capital:	
From operations:	
Net operating income	$123,500
Add: Depreciation expense	12,500
Net working capital provided by operations	$136,000
Other sources of working capital:	
Investment by owners	30,000
Proceeds of mortgage loan	75,000
Total sources of working capital	$241,000
Uses of working capital:	
Purchase of office-warehouse	$125,000
Payment on mortgage	5,000
Total uses of working capital	$130,000
Increase in working capital for 19X1	$111,000

Schedule of Changes in Working Capital Accounts

	December 31, 19X0	December 31, 19X1	Increase (Decrease)
Cash	$ 20,000	$ 1,000	$ (19,000)
Accounts receivable	40,000	110,000	70,000
Inventory	50,000	150,000	100,000
Current assets subtotal	$110,000	$261,000	$151,000
Accounts payable	$ 20,000	$ 60,000	$ 40,000
Working capital	$ 90,000	$201,000	$111,000

Third, working capital provided by operations is derived by adding depreciation expense to net operating income. This peculiarity arises out of the customary method of preparing a statement of changes, which is discussed fully in the next section. Fourth, financing and investment effects on working capital are *not* combined in separate categories. Rather, financing and investment activities are enumerated under the general headings entitled "other sources of working capital" or "uses of working capital," depending on whether their effects are to increase or decrease working capital, respectively. This may seem somewhat incongruous in that one of the objectives of a statement of changes in financial position is to depict changes in financial position according to the management activities that cause them, namely operations, investment activities, and financing activities. The best explanation is that by custom the effects of investment and financing activities are not separately summarized in statements of changes

Exhibit 6–5

DYNAMIC GROWTH COMPANY

Financial Position Worksheet
For Year Ended December 31, 19X1

Description	Current Assets			Long-Lived Assets (Office-Warehouse)		Current Liabilities	Long-Term Liabilities	Owners' Equity	
	Cash	Accounts Receivable	Inventory	Asset Cost	Accumulated Depreciation	Accounts Payable	Mortgage Payable	Capital Stock	Retained Earnings
Beginning Position	20,000	40,000	50,000	–0–	–0–	20,000	–0–	40,000	50,000
1. Additional investment by owners (new capital stock issued)	30,000							30,000	
2. Purchase of office-warehouse facilities for $125,000 ($50,000 cash and $75,000 mortgage)	(50,000)			125,000			75,000		
3. Purchase of inventory on account			300,000			300,000			
4. Sale of wine-making kits on account		400,000 (330,000)							400,000 (R)
5. Collections of accounts receivable	330,000	(260,000)							
6. Payments on accounts payable	(260,000)					(260,000)			
7. Payment of wages and salaries	(40,000)								(40,000) (E)
8. Payment of interest on mortgage	(6,000)								(6,000) (E)
9. Payment of miscellaneous expenses	(18,000)								(18,000) (E)
10. Payment of principal on mortgage	(5,000)						(5,000)		
11. Recognition of cost of wine-making kits sold			(200,000)						(200,000) (E)
12. Recognition of depreciation on office-warehouse facilities					(12,500)				(12,500) (E)
Ending Position	1,000	110,000	150,000	125,000	(12,500)	60,000	70,000	70,000	173,500

in financial position. However, very little harm is done in terms of the objectives of the statement, since there are relatively few different types of changes in financial position arising from investment and financing activities and the type of activity they represent is usually clearly evident, as the following list illustrates.

Possible nonoperating (investment/financing) *sources* of working capital:

1. Disposition of low-turnover, long-lived assets (investment)
2. Collections in the case of certain long-term notes or accounts receivable (financing)
3. Additions to long-term loans or long-term debt securities (financing)
4. Additional equity capital contributions or issues of stock (financing)

Possible nonoperating *uses* of working capital:

1. Acquisitions of low-turnover, long-lived assets (investment)
2. Repayments of long-term debt (financing)
3. Liquidations or retirements of equity interests (financing)
4. Payment of dividends or withdrawals of funds by proprietors or partners (financing)

One other point about Exhibit 6-4 should be mentioned. At the bottom of the statement of changes is an additional statement called "Schedule of Changes in Working Capital Accounts." This additional statement is a supplement to the statement of changes which enhances the potential decision-relevance of the statement. However, we will postpone discussion of this feature until later sections of this chapter.

Preparing Statements of Changes in Financial Position

The typical or customary approach to preparing a statement of changes in financial position (based on working capital) is by means of an analysis of the changes in non-working-capital (noncurrent) accounts. This approach is based on the dual definition of working capital introduced earlier and shown visually and symbolically in Exhibit 6-3 and equation (4), respectively.

By substituting into equation (4) the symbol Δ to represent changes in elements of financial position, the *change in* working capital for a period may be represented as in equation (5):

$$\Delta CA - \Delta CL = \text{Change in working capital} = \Delta LTL + \Delta OE - \Delta LLA \qquad (5)$$

Equation (5) shows that the change in working capital can be calculated by *either* the difference between (*a*) the sum of the changes in current assets and (*b*) the sum of the changes in current liabilities *or* the difference between

(a) the sum of the changes in long-term liabilities and owners' equity and (b) the sum of the changes in long-lived assets. The former relationship contains the information in the Schedule of Changes in Working Capital Accounts (refer again to the bottom part of Exhibit 6-4). The latter relationship (the differences in the changes in all noncurrent accounts) contains the information for preparation of a statement of changes in financial position (top of Exhibit 6-4). That is, the right-hand side of equation (5) suggests (a) that *increases in long-term liabilities or owners' equity* accounts and *decreases in long-lived asset* accounts *represent sources of working capital,* and (b) *decreases in long-term liabilities or owners' equity* accounts and *increases in long-lived asset* accounts *represent uses of working capital.*

This is intuitively correct when considering a change in noncurrent accounts such as an increase in long-lived assets due to, say, a purchase of equipment for cash. The expenditure of cash is a reduction in (use of) working capital (i.e., since cash is a current asset, an expenditure of cash reduces total current assets and thereby reduces working capital). Similarly, an increase in a long-term debt due to new borrowings of cash results in an increase in (source of) working capital. But the relationship between sources and uses of working capital and other changes in noncurrent account balances (e.g., an increase in accumulated depreciation) is not so obvious. Therefore, after illustrating the techniques for preparing a statement of changes in financial position from the changes in noncurrent account balances, we devote some attention to various less intuitive cases.

Deriving a statement of changes in financial position from changes in noncurrent account balances involves two steps:

Step 1: *Calculate* the differences between the beginning and ending balances in each of the firm's noncurrent accounts. At the same time, *examine* the individual changes in each account during the period to determine if there are significant categories of increases or decreases that may represent separate sources or uses of working capital. *Identify* each separate category of changes within the noncurrent accounts as either due to operations or due to other (investment/financing) causes. For these purposes various changes due to operations in the owners' equity account (for example, revenues and wages expense) are not considered separated sources and uses of working capital, since they are all due to operations and are collectively represented by net operating income.

Step 2: Arrange all noncurrent account changes derived in step 1 as sources or uses, with appropriate captions, in a statement of changes in financial position. For this purpose all changes in noncurrent account balances due to operations should be combined in one section showing operations as a single *net* source or use of working capital.

Example 6-2

Referring to the Dynamic Growth Company 19X1 financial position worksheet in Exhibit 6-5 and applying the two steps for preparing a statement of changes we get:

Step 1: The changes in noncurrent account balances that represent separate sources and uses of working capital are as follows:

Account	Increase (Decrease)	Cause
Office warehouse	$125,000	Investment
Accumulated depreciation	(12,500)*	Operations
Mortgage payable:		
Proceeds	75,000	Financing
Payments	(5,000)	Financing
Capital stock	70,000	Financing
Retained earnings—net operating income	123,500	Operations

*The change in accumulated depreciation for the period (depreciation expense) is treated here as a decrease in long-lived assets rather than as an increase in a contra-asset account.

Step 2: Appropriate labeling and arranging of the changes in noncurrent account balances results in the following 19X1 sources and uses of working capital for Dynamic Growth—the same sources and uses that appear in the statement of changes in financial position in Exhibit 6-4:

Sources of working capital:	
From operations:	
Net operating income	$123,500
Add: Depreciation expense	12,500
Net working capital provided by operations	$136,000
Other sources of working capital:	
Investment by owners	30,000
Proceeds of mortgage loan	75,000
Total sources	$241,000
Uses of working capital:	
Purchase of office-warehouse	$125,000
Payment on mortgage	5,000
Total uses	$130,000
Increase in working capital	$111,000

Notice that in applying step 1 to the Dynamic Growth Company example the mortgage payable account net change of $70,000 was split into separate positive and negative components, the loan proceeds of $75,000 and the loan payment of $5,000, respectively. In this case no other noncurrent accounts had significant separate increases and decreases that are recognized as separate sources and uses of working capital in a statement of changes. It should be noted, however, that many other such separate increases and decreases to other noncurrent accounts can occur and should be given separate recognition when they do. For example, if dividends had been paid, the overall change in retained earnings would be divided between (1) a positive (negative) component due to operations, corresponding to net operating income (loss), and (2) a negative component equal to payment of dividends, a financing-type use of working capital. Similarly, if depreciable assets are accounted for "net" of depreciation, then the overall account change might be composed of as many as three relevant components, an increase due to acquisitions and decreases due to dispositions and to the current period's depreciation expense.

In applying step 2, it is perhaps intuitively obvious how to classify changes in noncurrent accounts that are due to investment and financing activities and that involve direct expenditures or receipts of cash (or other working capital components). For example, Dynamic Growth's receipt of $30,000 cash in exchange for new ownership (stock) interests in the business is clearly due to a financing activity, and since it directly increased a positive component of working capital (cash), it clearly should be labeled as a source of working capital. However, as we mentioned earlier, other changes in noncurrent account balances are not as eminently classifiable within the format of the statement of changes in financial position. These less-tractable changes fall into two categories: (1) changes in noncurrent accounts that are offsetting components of investment and/or financing activities and therefore do not directly affect working capital, and (2) changes in noncurrent account balances that are associated with operations.

Recognizing Separate Sources and Uses Due to Single Transactions. The first category is illustrated by the increase in Dynamic Growth's office-warehouse account balance of $125,000 and the offsetting increase of $75,000 in the mortgage payable. These two changes in noncurrent accounts actually occurred as the result of a single transaction (transaction 2 in Exhibit 6-5). The transaction actually had only one effect on working capital; it decreased working capital (decreased cash) by $50,000. However, the $50,000 is the "net effect" on working capital of a compound event with both investment (purchase of the warehouse) and financing (securing the mortgage financing of the purchase) dimensions. If the statement of changes in financial position had as its only objective to show the increases and decreases in working capital, it would be sufficient to represent this event on a single line labeled "down payment on warehouse" under "uses of working capital." However, the objective of the statement is broader—i.e., the statement is intended also to reflect all financial implications of investment and financing (as well as operating) activities. To satisfy this objective the purchase of the office-warehouse is split into two components, even though the purchase for cash plus the mortgage note was probably executed in a single transaction. By treating the two noncurrent account changes separately, we impute to the transaction the receipt of cash (an increase in working capital) in the amount of $75,000 from the issuance of the mortgage note *as if* cash had actually been borrowed in advance. This appears in Exhibit 6-4 under "other sources of working capital."

Accordingly, the purchase of the productive facilities at a total price of $125,000 is treated *as if* it involved the payment of cash (a decrease in working capital) in the full amount. This is shown in Exhibit 6-4 as a use of working capital. Notice, however, that the net of these two imputed flows of working capital is equal to the amount actually expended ($50,000) in the single purchase transaction. Thus, by treating related financing investment changes in account balances separately, the statement of changes discloses the *full extent* of all investment and financing activities, independent of whether long-term financing is first secured and then productive capacity is acquired, or whether these two separate activities are combined in one transaction.

Working Capital Provided by Operations. The other area of difficulty in applying an analysis of changes in account balances to preparation of a statement of changes is the determination of working capital provided by operations. In Exhibit 6-4 and in Example 6-2, working capital provided by operations is determined by adding two noncurrent account changes for the year, namely net operating income and depreciation expense (the changes due to operations in retained earnings and long-lived assets, respectively). In order to understand this method of deriving working capital provided by operations, it is necessary first to understand all the ways in which operations affect the financial position of a company. Exhibit 6-6 illustrates the relationship between operations and financial position. It consists of the block diagram from Exhibit 6-3 to represent the four main segments of the classified balance sheet, along with a block inserted between the two sides of the balance sheet to represent operations (the income statement). The lines between blocks represent effects of day-to-day operations on the financial position of the enterprise. Those lines actually connecting the income statement block with the balance sheet elements (lines 3–7) represent the revenues and expenses recognized in connection with a given period's operations. Lines not intersecting the operations block (lines 1 and 2) are other flows that take place in connection with day-to-day operations (for example, the purchase of inventory or the payment of accounts payable) but are not recognized directly in the income statement.

The labels on each of the lines connecting the blocks in Exhibit 6-6 make the flows indicated largely self-explanatory. However, the reader is urged to study each label briefly, as we are about to use the diagram to bring out the important relationships between operations and financial position.

First, notice lines 1 and 2. They represent (1) acquisitions of current assets for current debt (e.g., purchasing inventory "on account"), and (2) liquidation of current debts by expenditures of current assets (e.g., expending cash to pay off accounts payable). Though these activities are very important components of operations, *they do not in themselves change the net working capital position* because they change current assets and current liabilities by equal amounts in the same direction. This means that any change in working capital due to a firm's operations results only from flows like those illustrated by lines 3–7 in Exhibit 6-6. Notice that these flows (lines 3–7) are the set of operating flows that receive recognition in the income statement. Therefore, by working through the income statement relationships, we ought to be able to understand and measure the change in working capital due to operations.

The income statement represents the definitional relationship: Revenues − Expenses = Net income (loss). Another way of stating this relationship is: Net income (loss) + Expenses = Revenues. This is shown by the top two blocks in the diagram in Exhibit 6-7. This diagram shows that the flows represented by lines 4–7 in Exhibit 6-6 together must equal the amount represented by line 3. Line 3 represents the revenues of the period which are increases in current assets, usually in the form of accounts receivable and cash. Revenue therefore equals the gross increase in working capital due to operations. At the same time, lines 4 and 5, which are the only other lines connecting income statement components to the current assets and current liabilities, represent drains on working capital which we refer to as "out-of-pocket" expenses (e.g., cost of goods sold which equals the gross decrease in inventories due to operations). The difference between the flow represented by line 3 and the flows represented by lines

Exhibit 6-6

RELATIONSHIP BETWEEN OPERATIONS AND FINANCIAL POSITION

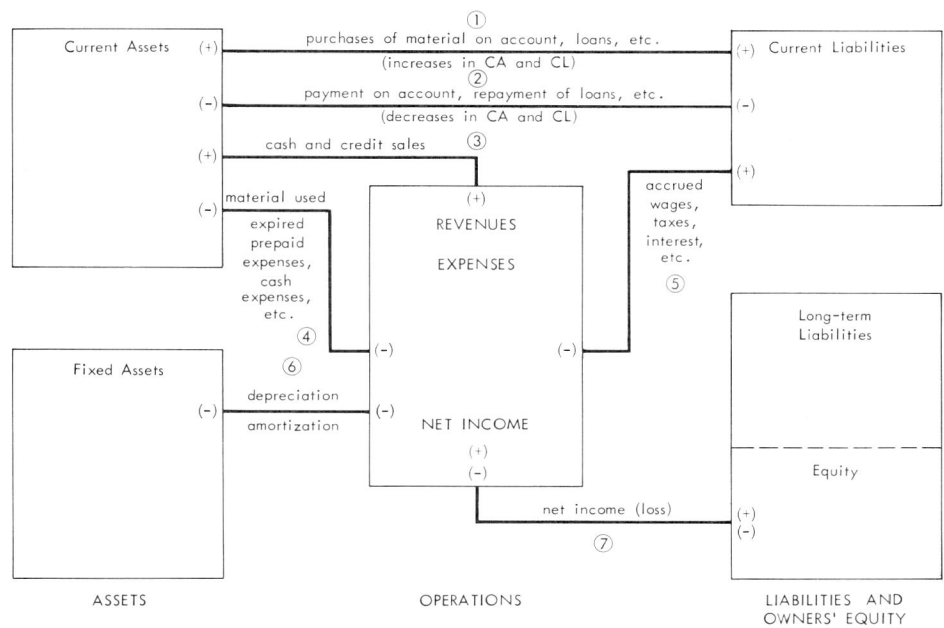

4 and 5, that is, *the excess of revenues over out-of-pocket expenses, represents the net increase in working capital attributable to operations.* This way of calculating working capital provided by operations, called the "direct" or transactions approach, is illustrated on the left side of Exhibit 6-8, using the Dynamic Growth Company data.

However, because of the identity relationship between (*a*) revenues and (*b*) *expenses plus income,* we know that the change in working capital due to operations is also equal to net income plus any *non*-out-of-pocket expenses deducted from revenues in determining net income. This is represented by the correspondence in Exhibit 6-7 between the bottom block and the net income plus non-out-of-pocket expense sections of the middle block. In Exhibit 6-6 this way of determining the net increase in working capital due to operations is represented by the flows depicted by lines 6 and 7. This way of calculating working capital provided by operations is illustrated on the right side of Exhibit 6-8.

Notice in Exhibit 6-8 that the only difference between the noncurrent account analysis approach and the direct (transaction analysis) approach is the format of the calculation of working capital provided by operations. The former starts with net income and "backs out" the non-out-of-pocket expense, depreciation; whereas the latter arrives at the same figure by deducting out-of-pocket expenses from revenue. Most authors argue that the direct approach is more informative. However, there are some reasons for learning the account analysis approach: (1) it is the method customarily used; (2) it is compatible

Exhibit 6-7

RELATIONSHIP BETWEEN THE INCOME STATEMENT AND WORKING CAPITAL PROVIDED BY OPERATIONS (p. 240)

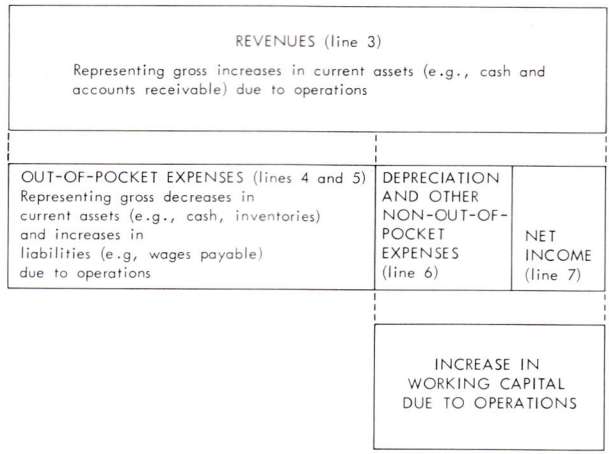

Exhibit 6-8

ALTERNATIVE METHODS OF CALCULATING WORKING CAPITAL PROVIDED BY OPERATIONS

(Dynamic Growth Company Data)

Direct (Transactions) Approach		*Changes in Noncurrent Account Balances Approach*	
Revenues	$400,000	Net operating income	$123,500
Less out-of-pocket expenses:		Add back non-out-of-	
Cost of goods sold	$200,000	pocket expenses:	
Wages and salaries expense	40,000	Depreciation	12,500
Interest expense	6,000	Working capital provided	
Miscellaneous	18,000	by operations	$136,000
Subtotal	$264,000		
Working capital provided			
by operations	$136,000		

with the usual approach to deriving all other sources and uses working capital, and (3) generally it takes up less space.

A word of caution about the account analysis approach is in order, however, because it can lead to the common misconception that depreciation *per se* is a source of working capital. This is not the case, of course. The use of capacity (long-lived assets) along with the incurrence of out-of-pocket costs produces products that generate revenues (increases in working capital). If there were no depreciation charges deducted for the use of capacity, *net operating income would equal* the difference between revenues and out-of-pocket expenses—that is, net operating income would equal *the increase* in *working capital* due to operations. Depreciation expense reduces net income relative to working capital provided by operations and is therefore added back to net income to arrive at the amount sought.

Another related word of caution is that depreciation is not the only non-out-of-pocket expense deducted in arriving at net income. It is the only one illustrated here for the sake of simplicity and because it is the most frequently encountered and the most widely understood. Other non-out-of-pocket expenses include the deferred portion of income tax expense (which is discussed in Chapter 12) and amortization of discounts on long-term debt included in interest expense (which is covered in Chapter 11). Such charges against income, if present, are also added back to net income to determine the increase in working capital due to operations. Similarly, there are some positive, but non-working-capital-related, components of the net income that are deducted from the net income figure to arrive at "working capital provided." Among them are amortization of premiums on long-term debt (Chapter 11) and undistributed earnings of affiliated companies (Chapter 12).

Summary of Statement Preparation Procedures. The account analysis approach to preparing a statement of changes begins with an examination of the changes in the noncurrent account balances. If the change in any given account is composed of both positive and negative components (for example, a positive change in retained earnings equal to net income and a negative change due to dividends paid), each component is evaluated separately. Each change in a noncurrent account is then determined to be a part of either the operating, investment, or financing activities of the firm. The statement of changes is prepared by appropriately arranging and labeling the noncurrent account changes. If a given change relates to operations (for example, the change in retained earnings equal to net operating income or the change in accumulated depreciation due to depreciation expense), it is combined with the operations-related changes in other noncurrent accounts to arrive at working capital provided by operations. Otherwise it is shown as an "other" source or as a separate use of working capital.

Interpretation of Statements of Changes. Now that we have illustrated the general format and method of constructing statements of changes in financial position, what about the information that can be derived from them? Consider the original motivation for the discussion of statements of changes. A business enterprise, Dynamic Growth Company, became insolvent (was unable to pay its obligations when due) but at the same time earned an impressive net income. We may now ask whether the statement of changes in financial position in Exhibit 6-4 gives us any insight into what happened. Taken by itself the statement of changes seemingly is a disappointment. For the statement of changes shows an increase in working capital (an excess of new sources for the period over uses) of $111,000. Thus, like the income statement, it appears to be conveying "good news" for a period in which the company was going broke. This is where the "schedule of changes in working capital accounts" (at the bottom of Exhibit 6-4) takes on importance. It shows the distribution of the overall or net change in working capital among the various current assets and current liabilities.

Taking the information in the statement of changes in financial position together with the schedule of changes in working capital accounts, one can readily construct a scenario explaining why Dynamic Growth Company went broke while making a profit.

Example 6-3

During 19X1 Dynamic Growth Company generated $136,000 in additional working capital from operations. This was augmented by new sources of working capital in the form of a $75,000 mortgage (used to finance a warehouse acquisition) and new equity capital of $30,000 from shareholders. A portion of the total of $241,000 of working capital provided by all sources was used for a new investment in a warehouse costing $125,000 (subject to the mortgage) and a principal payment of $5,000 on the mortgage, leaving a net increase in working capital of $111,000 for the year. This amount combined with an increase in financing of inventory purchases through accounts payable of $40,000 provided for an increase in the company's investment in current assets of $151,000. However, the growth in investment in accounts receivable due to increased sales and the growth in inventories in anticipation of further increases in sales together equaled $170,000. The difference of $19,000 was absorbed (financed) by a reduction in the cash balance of $19,000 to the $1,000 level at December 31, 19X1. This level was very low in relation to short-term obligations. Apparently new sales and the accounts receivable were not converted into cash at a fast enough rate early in 19X2 to cover the company's obligations.

This interpretation raises several new points. For example, it shows that although the statement of changes in financial position does not add a great deal of data to what is available from comparing the beginning and ending balance sheets, the data are arranged in a more informative pattern for revealing the short-run financial impact of a firm's activities. In addition, it not only provides information about the past but may be useful in making inferences about future prospects.

Example 6-4

Although Example 6-1 indicates that Dynamic Growth Company became insolvent early in 19X2, it does not say it was forced into *bankruptcy* (a legal proceeding in which creditors force the liquidation of a company and its assets are sold to satisfy the creditors' claims—with any residual proceeds going to the owners). The fact that the company appeared quite profitable in 19X0 and 19X1 along with the facts contained in the 19X1 statement of changes might be sufficient to convince the creditors to not press for bankruptcy proceedings. That is, the statement of changes along with the schedule of changes in working capital accounts indicates that the company is able to generate substantial net cash flows from operations. That it did not conserve enough of what was generated in 19X1 to make routine payments on its accounts payable was due to its ambitious growth plans, requiring additional investments in warehouse space, inventories, and accounts receivable. It was an apparent error of judgment that these new investments did not begin producing additional flows of working capital (and ultimately cash) soon enough. However, the fact that these investments are now made and may not need to be repeated in the near future, combined with the company's apparent robust profit opportunities (along with possible shareholder willingness to forgo dividends), could easily turn the situation around. Such a perception might convince present creditors to wait for payment or to refinance the company's obligations. It might also attract a long-term loan from a bank or additional paid-in capital from shareholders to carry the company over its (presumably) transitory cash shortage.

Cash-Based Statements of Changes

In our introduction to the considerations motivating the production of statements of changes in financial position, we referred to cash as "the eye of the needle" and the pivotal element of financial position. This point was reinforced in Example 6-3 in which we analyzed the information in the 19X1 working-capital-based statement of changes of Dynamic Growth Company. Recall that the analysis used the information in the statement of changes but combined that information with the schedule of changes in working capital accounts. Importantly, in the final steps, the analysis focused on the *cash inadequacy* that led to the condition of insolvency experienced by the company early in 19X2. Examples of this sort, along with the type of reasoning contained in the introductory discussion, have led many accountants (principally writers of articles and books) to express a preference for cash-based statements of changes. The authors of this text do not agree that cash-based statements are necessarily to be preferred. We believe that what can be achieved with cash-flow-based statements of changes can generally also be achieved with working-capital-based statements of changes used together with accompanying schedules of changes in working capital accounts (as Example 6-3 illustrates).

Realizing this basic equivalence is a key to understanding how to construct a statement of changes based on cash, once one has a grasp of how to construct the working-capital-based version. Given the change in working capital, it is easy to calculate the change in the cash account by *adding* to the change in working capital all increases in current liability accounts and all decreases in current asset accounts other than cash and then subtracting all decreases in current liabilities and all increases in noncash current assets. This can be demonstrated algebraically by starting with the following equation for the change in working capital (WC):

$$\Delta WC = \Delta CA - \Delta CL \tag{6}$$

Then by isolating the change in cash (ΔC) from the change in other, noncash current assets ($\Delta NCCA$),

$$\Delta WC = \Delta C + \Delta NCCA - \Delta CL \tag{7}$$

and solving for the change in cash, we get:

$$\Delta C = \Delta WC + \Delta CL - \Delta NCCA \tag{8}$$

This is illustrated in Exhibit 6-9 using the Dynamic Growth example.

Exhibit 6-9 points to the only usual difference between a statement of changes based on working capital and one based on cash. In the cash-based statement the changes in working capital accounts are used in calculating the sources and uses of cash, whereas in the working capital-based statement they are not needed, since they merely represent changes in the distribution of balances among the working capital accounts. Therefore to construct a statement of changes in financial position based on cash, accountants typically follow the

Exhibit 6-9

DYNAMIC GROWTH COMPANY

Calculation of the Change in the Cash Account
For Year Ended December 31, 19X1

Increase in working capital	$111,000
Add the increase in accounts payable	40,000
Subtotal	$151,000
Less:	
Increase in accounts receivable	(70,000)
Increase in inventory	(100,000)
Decrease in cash	$ (19,000)

same account-analysis technique as for a working capital statement, *but* the analysis is expanded to include the *noncash current accounts* as well as the various noncurrent accounts in a firm's financial position.

The result of the expanded analysis applied to the Dynamic Growth example is the statement of changes in financial position shown in Exhibit 6-10. Note that the analysis of and placement in the statement of changes of the increases and decreases in *noncurrent* accounts is the same as for the working capital analysis. What is different is the inclusion in the analysis of the increases and decreases in all of the noncash current (working capital) accounts.

Cash Provided by Operations. Notice the inclusion in Exhibit 6-10 of the changes in the noncash current accounts *under operations.* This deserves some explanation. The implied procedure for determining cash provided by operations is as follows:

1. Start with net operating income.

2. Add back such non-working-capital expenses as depreciation (and appropriately add or deduct other operations-related changes in noncurrent accounts) to get working capital provided by operations.

3. Add decreases and subtract increases in current assets other than cash—e.g., accounts receivable, inventory, and prepaid expenses.

4. Add increases and subtract decreases in current liabilities—e.g., accounts payable, wages payable.

The alternative to showing changes in noncash working capital accounts as adjustments to net operating income in arriving at cash provided by operations is to show each such change as a separate source or use of cash.

This is justified by reasoning that an increase (decrease) in a current liability is like borrowing (repaying) a loan and therefore may be thought of as a separate source (use) of cash. Similarly, current assets may be thought of as requiring (using) additional cash if they are increased, or as providing cash if they decrease (i.e., as if they are always bought and sold directly for cash). However, the authors feel that this type of treatment suggests an independence in managing the levels of current assets and liabilities that is usually not present in practice.

Exhibit 6-10

DYNAMIC GROWTH COMPANY

Statement of Changes in Financial Position
(Cash Basis)
For Year Ended December 31, 19X1

Sources of cash:	
From operations:	
Net operating income:	$123,500
Add: Depreciation expense	12,500
Working capital provided by operations	$136,000
Add: Increase in accounts payable	40,000
Deduct: Increase in accounts receivable	(70,000)
Deduct: Increase in inventory	(100,000)
Net cash flow from operations	$ 6,000
Other sources of cash:	
Investment by owners	30,000
Proceeds of mortgage loan	75,000
Total sources of cash	$111,000
Uses of cash:	
Purchase of office-warehouse facilities	$125,000
Payment on mortgage	5,000
Total uses of cash	$130,000
Net decrease in cash for 19X1	$ (19,000)

Certain noncash current accounts are relatively independent of operations and of other *current* elements of financial position—for example, marketable securities and current installments of long-term debt. Changes in such accounts may and should be treated as "other" sources and uses of cash. However, in order to receive additional financing through trade creditors (accounts payable), for instance, a firm must usually purchase more items. Purchases along with sales volume determine whether inventories rise or fall during a period, and sales volume determines whether accounts receivable tend to increase or decrease,

Exhibit 6-11

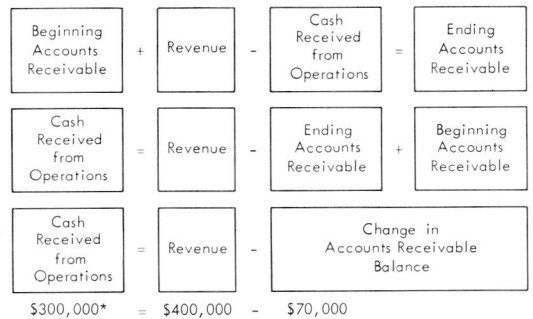

*See line 5 of Exhibit 6-5 for corroboration.

other things equal. Thus the authors tend to favor the view that operations-related noncash working capital assets and liabilities act as buffers between operations, as reflected in revenues and expenses and operating cash flows such as payments on accounts payable and receipts from accounts receivable. Exhibit 6-11 illustrates this idea for the relationship between revenues and cash receipts from operations (collections of accounts receivable) based on the Dynamic Growth example. The reader may find it a useful exercise to reconcile payments on accounts payable with cost of goods sold using the changes in inventories and accounts payable as reconciling items.

STATEMENTS OF CHANGES IN FINANCIAL POSITION—SOME ELABORATION

Treatment of Additional Accounts and Transactions

The number of accounts and transactions considered in our illustration in this chapter was intentionally small so that the complexity of the example data would not obscure the basic concepts we are introducing. Notwithstanding this limitation on the scope of the illustration, it does reveal the basic set of procedures and concepts required to prepare and interpret statements of changes. Little would be gained by going through a long enumeration of different types of accounts and special transactions, in terms of their special effects on the statement. We will, however, mention a few additional items that are commonly found in statements of changes to illustrate the application of the basic concepts to these particular items.

Dividends. We illustrated in our example a flow of cash from the owners to the business. This investment by owners was reflected in both statements of changes as a source of funds (cash or working capital) during the period. Obviously there could also be a flow of funds in the other direction, that is, the payment of dividends to owners, and indeed this is a use of funds commonly found in statements of changes. Resource flows to and from the owners of the business enterprise are not offset. New investments of capital are reflected in the statement as sources of funds; payments to the owners in the form of dividends are reflected as uses of funds.

Sale of Fixed Assets. Transactions involving the acquisition and use of long-lived assets have been covered in our illustration. We have seen that the acquisition of new productive capacity in the form of long-lived assets represents the use of resources during the period and is so reflected in the statements. On the other hand, the use of the facilities in operations, as reflected through the recognition of depreciation expense, does not affect cash or working capital *per se,* and thus it is added back to net operating income in calculating funds provided by operations. But how would we treat the disposition of a fixed asset? In measuring net income for the period, we calculate a gain or loss on the disposition of the asset as the difference between the proceeds of sale and the unexpired cost of the asset at the time of sale. For purposes of preparing a resource flow statement, however, the effect on cash (and working capital) is determined by the proceeds of sale; the amount of gain or loss calculated for income measurement purposes is generally not relevant. Therefore the resource flow statement will reflect as a source of resources during a period the total proceeds received on the disposition (sale) of any long-lived asset, and net operating income must be adjusted to exclude the effect of the gain or loss.

Status of Statements of Changes in Financial Position in Corporate Financial Reporting

Although the statement of changes in financial position has long been recognized as a source of potentially useful information for external decision makers, until recently its inclusion in the set of financial statements regularly presented to investors was at the option of management. However, current accounting policy requires that a statement of changes be presented along with the statement of financial position and the income statement.

The terminology employed in such statements has, in the past, varied widely among companies and among accountants. One term frequently used in the past for the statement itself is "funds statement," which is based upon the notion that the statement analyzes the flow of funds. Funds were interpreted as either cash, working capital, or some other resource base. However, current accounting policy recommends that the statement be titled "statement of changes in financial position." This recommendation is based, in part, upon the broad concept that is attributed to the statement, which requires that certain noncash or non-working-capital transactions (such as the acquisition of the warehouse in part for a mortgage debt by Dynamic Growth Company) have resource flows imputed to them.

Although the accounting policy-setting body (in this case the Accounting Principles Board of the American Institute of Certified Public Accountants) recommended the exclusive use of one title, it recognized the need for flexibility in form, content, and terminology of statements of changes in financial positions. Thus, one encounters in current practice statements of changes that vary in their appearance as well as in the resource base selected for analyzing the flows. But the substance of the statements is generally congruent with the basic principles developed in this chapter.

Questions for Review and Discussion

6-1. Define:
  a. Current assets
  b. Current liabilities
  c. Working capital

6-2. Explain briefly how a company earning a substantial annual income can become financially "embarrassed," that is, not be able to pay its obligations when due. Does this mean that income is really not a useful index of performance?

6-3. Several years ago the Accounting Principles Board of the American Institute of CPAs recommended the title "Statements of Changes in Financial Position." In what sense does a statement of changes in financial position disclose changes in financial position other than direct changes in the statement's basis (cash or working capital)?

6-4. Both cash and working capital are often chosen as the basis for statements of changes in financial position. What advantage(s) does each basis offer, if any?

6-5. Describe the steps that you would follow in preparing a statement of changes in financial position based on working capital. Describe how the procedures involved in preparing a statement based on cash differ from those described for a working-capital-based statement.

6-6. Describe the procedures and rationale for calculating working capital provided by operations, beginning with the net operating income figure. Repeat this requirement for cash provided by operations.

6-7. In recognizing sources and uses of working capital (or cash) other than from operations, resource flows are often imputed where no physical flow of resources (cash or working capital) actually took place. Explain why this is done.

6-8. An increase in merchandise inventory (usually considered a working capital account) is also an increase in working capital. However, "increase in merchandise" would never appear *as a source of working capital* on a statement of changes in financial position. Explain.

6-9. Working capital provided by operations is much more similar to net operating income than is cash provided by operations. Do you agree or disagree? Explain your position.

6-10. In the direct approach to deriving working capital provided by operations, depreciation expense is ignored. On the other hand, depreciation expense is explicitly used to derive working capital provided by operations using changes in noncurrent account balances. Is this a fundamental inconsistency? Why or why not?

6-11. What advantages, if any, are there to calculating cash or working capital provided by operations by starting with operating income rather than by reviewing the transactions of the enterprise for the period?

6-12. Working capital provided by operations would equal net operating income were it not for certain items entering into the calculation of net operating income. Name some typical items of this sort. Explain their treatment in deriving working capital provided by operations from the operating income figure.

6-13. In general, would you expect working capital provided by operations to tend to be greater than, equal to, or less than net operating income? Defend your position. Can you take the same kind of position with respect to the relative sizes of operating income and cash provided by operations?

6-14. In deriving cash provided by operations from the net operating income figure, changes in current assets and liabilities are added to, or subtracted from, operating income. Are such changes therefore sources or uses of cash *per se*? In what sense can such items be considered sources or uses of cash? Give examples and explain.

Exercises

6-1. Preparing a Statement of Changes in Financial Position. A worksheet describing the first year of operations of a new business is shown in Exhibit 6-12.

Required:

1. Prepare a 19X4 income statement.

2. Prepare a 19X4 working-capital-based statement of changes in financial position.

3. Prepare a 19X4 cash-based statement of changes in financial position.

6-2. Calculating Resource Flows from Operations. The following information was taken from the financial statements of Calendar Company for 19X1–X4.

	December 31, 19X1	*December 31, 19X2*	*December 31, 19X3*	*December 31, 19X4*
Cash	$ 5,000	$12,000	$14,000	$ 6,000
Accounts receivable	8,000	10,000	6,000	14,000
Inventory	12,000	9,000	12,000	16,000
Prepaid insurance	-0-	-0-	2,000	1,000
	$25,000	$31,000	$34,000	$37,000
Accounts payable	$ 5,000	$ 7,000	$12,000	$ 8,000
Accrued wages payable	-0-	-0-	3,000	2,000
	$ 5,000	$ 7,000	$15,000	$10,000
Working capital	$20,000	$24,000	$19,000	$27,000
Net income for year ending on indicated date	$10,000	$15,000	$18,000	$20,000
Depreciation expense for year ending on indicated date*	$ 3,000	$ 4,000	$ 4,000	$ 5,000

*Assume that depreciation is the only non-out-of-pocket expense.

Required:

For each of the years 19X2, 19X3, and 19X4, and for the three-year period ended December 31, 19X4, prepare a computation of the following:

1. Working capital provided by operations

2. Cash provided by operations

Exhibit 6-12
HOBIE'S BUS COMPANY

Financial Position Worksheet—19X4

Description	Cash	Bus	Accumulated Depreciation	Accounts Receivable	Supplies Inventory	Accounts Payable	Notes Payable	Owners' Equity
Balances, Dec. 31, 19X3	-0-	-0-	-0-	-0-	-0-	-0-	-0-	-0-
Initial investment by owners	6,000							6,000
Purchased bus for $2,500 cash and $5,000 note	(2,500)	7,500					5,000	
Cash fares	12,000							12,000 (R)
Credit fares				5,000				5,000 (R)
Payment of one-year insurance premium	(1,000)							(1,000) (E)
Wages paid	(7,500)							(7,500) (E)
Customer payments	2,000			(2,000)				
Supplies purchased					2,000	2,000		
Payments to suppliers	(500)					(500)		
Payment of principal and interest on note	(1,300)						(1,000)	(300) (E)
Supplies used					(1,600)			(1,600) (E)
Repairs and maintenance paid	(1,800)							(1,800) (E)
Depreciation expense			(1,200)					(1,200) (E)
Withdrawal	(3,600)							(3,600) (W)
Balances, Dec. 31, 19X4	1,800	7,500	(1,200)	3,000	400	1,500	4,000	6,000

210

6-3. Preparing Statements of Changes. Using the worksheet shown in Exhibit 6-13, satisfy the following requirements:
1. Prepare a working-capital-based statement of changes in financial position based on an analysis of changes in non-working capital accounts. Supplement this statement with a schedule of changes in working capital accounts.
2. Prepare a cash-based statement of changes in financial position for the period based on an analysis of changes in the noncash accounts.
3. Prepare schedules of (*a*) working capital and (*b*) cash provided by operations using the direct (transactions analysis) approach. Verbally contrast these schedules with the "operations" sections of the statements prepared in numbers 1 and 2.

6-4. Preparing Statements of Changes in Financial Position from Other Financial Statements. The financial statements for Underhill Corporation for 19X5 are as follows:

	December 31, 19X4	December 31, 19X5
Cash	$ 100,000	$ 200,000
Accounts receivable	350,000	600,000
Inventory	800,000	1,200,000
Land	750,000	1,000,000
Buildings and equipment	2,500,000	3,000,000
Accumulated depreciation—		
Buildings and equipment	(500,000)	(700,000)
	$4,000,000	$5,300,000
Accounts payable	$ 500,000	$ 800,000
Bonds payable	1,000,000	500,000
Owners' equity:		
Capital stock	1,000,000	2,000,000
Retained earnings	1,500,000	2,000,000
	$4,000,000	$5,300,000
Sales		$8,000,000
Expenses:		
Cost of sales	$4,800,000	
Depreciation expense	200,000	
Other operating expenses	2,300,000	7,300,000
Net income for 19X5		$ 700,000

Required:

From the information contained in these statements *and stating any assumptions that are necessary*, prepare the following:

1. A working-capital-based statement of changes in financial position
2. A cash-based statement of changes

Exhibit 6-13

BUENA VISTA ENTERPRISES

Financial Position Worksheet—19X4

Description	Cash	Accounts Receivable	Mer-chandise	Prepaid Rent	Equip-ment	Accumulated Depreciation Equipment	Accounts Payable	Wages Payable	Interest Payable	Mortgage Payable	Owners' Equity
Beginning Position	1,500	1,000	2,500	200	6,000	(1,500)	1,750	-0-	100	3,000	4,850
Cash sales	1,300										1,300 (R)
Purchased merchandise on credit			500				500				
Credit sales		3,500									3,500 (R)
Paid rent in advance	(100)			100							
Receipts from customers	2,500	(2,500)									
Payments to suppliers	(1,000)						(1,000)				
Purchased equipment	(500)				1,000					500	
Mortgage payment	(1,000)									(1,000)	
Paid wages	(700)										(700) (E)
Paid advertising	(300)										(300) (E)
Paid interest owing	(100)								(100)		
Purchased merchandise with cash	(200)		200								
Depreciation of equipment						(800)					(800) (E)
Merchandise used			(900)								(900) (E)
Rent expense for period				(150)							(150) (E)
Accrued wages								200			(200) (E)
Interest expense for period (not paid)									80		(80) (E)
Contribution by owner	2,000										2,000
Ending Position	3,400	2,000	2,300	150	7,000	(2,300)	1,250	200	80	2,500	8,520

6-5. Calculating Resource Flows from Operations. The financial statements of the Greenstone Company contained the following information for 19X4, 19X5, and 19X6:

	December 31, 19X6	December 31, 19X5	December 31, 19X4
Cash	$15,000	$20,000	$10,000
Accounts receivable	30,000	20,000	25,000
Inventory	40,000	35,000	30,000
	$85,000	$75,000	$65,000
Accounts payable	30,000	20,000	25,000
Working capital	$55,000	$55,000	$40,000
Net income for year	$45,000	$50,000	$40,000
Depreciation expense for year	$15,000	$12,000	$10,000

Required:

1. Prepare a schedule of working capital provided by operations for each of the years 19X5 and 19X6 and for the two-year period ended December 31, 19X6.

2. Prepare a schedule of cash provided by operations for the same periods as in number 1 above.

6-6. Resource Flow Concepts and Relationships. The consolidated statement of changes in financial position from the 1977 annual report of Millipore Corporation and its subsidiaries is shown in Exhibit 6-14. The statement is based on the working capital concept of financial resources. With reference to the statement, satisfy the requirements listed below.

Required:

1. Is depreciation a source of working capital? Explain why depreciation appears in the statement under the section headed "Sources of Working Capital."

2. From the information in the statement, estimate the amount of cash *provided by operations* experienced by Millipore in 1977. Show your work.

6-7. Account Analysis and Statements of Changes. Based on an analysis of the changes in the accounts in the financial position worksheet shown in Exhibit 6-15, satisfy the requirements listed below.

Required:

1. Prepare an income statement for the period.

2. Prepare a statement of cash receipts and disbursements (illustrated in Exhibit 3-3 on page 82).

Exhibit 6-14

MILLIPORE CORPORATION

Consolidated Statements of Changes in Financial Position

	Year Ended December 31, 1977	Year Ended December 31, 1976
Sources of Working Capital:		
Income from operations	$ 9,585,000	$ 7,699,000
Items not requiring working capital:		
Depreciation	2,214,000	1,866,000
Net deferred taxes on income	303,000	617,000
Working capital provided from operations	12,102,000	10,182,000
Extraordinary credit from sale of securities	—	1,166,000
Proceeds of sale of investment, net of income and related taxes thereon reported separately as extraordinary item above	—	204,000
Sale of common stock under stock option plans and Employees' Stock Purchase Plan	342,000	613,000
Other	13,000	79,000
	12,457,000	12,244,000
Applications of Working Capital:		
Purchase of property, plant and equipment, net	7,105,000	5,243,000
Cash dividends	1,247,000	914,000
	8,352,000	6,157,000
Increase in working capital	$ 4,105,000	$ 6,087,000
Changes in Working Capital:		
Increase (decrease) in current assets:		
Cash	$ 640,000	$ 740,000
Marketable securities	—	(4,639,000)
Accounts receivable	5,079,000	3,848,000
Inventories	3,127,000	6,455,000
Prepaid expenses and deposits	235,000	434,000
	9,081,000	6,838,000
Increase (decrease) in current liabilities:		
Notes payable	1,559,000	698,000
Accounts payable	502,000	731,000
Accrued expenses and other liabilities	1,246,000	294,000
Federal and foreign income taxes	1,669,000	(972,000)
	4,976,000	751,000
Increase in working capital	$ 4,105,000	$ 6,087,000

3. Prepare a cash-based statement of changes in financial position.

4. Prepare a working-capital-based statement of changes in financial position.

Exhibit 6-15

BAINBRIDGE DISTRIBUTING COMPANY, INCORPORATED

Financial Position Worksheet—19X4

Description	Cash	Accounts Receivable	Merchandise Inventory	Machinery and Equipment*	Buildings*	Land	Accounts Payable	Mortgage Notes Payable	Owners' Equity
Beginning Position	20,000	63,000	56,000	79,000	93,000	35,000	47,000	25,000	274,000
Purchase of inventory for sale			121,000				121,000		
Revenue from sales	26,000	265,000							291,000 (R)
Wages paid	(86,000)								(86,000) (E)
Collections of accounts receivable	256,000	(256,000)							
Payments of accounts payable	(136,000)						(136,000)		
Dividends paid	(10,000)								(10,000) (D)
Miscellaneous expenses (heat, light, taxes, etc.)	(29,000)								(29,000) (E)
Equipment purchased	(10,000)			30,000				20,000	
Equipment depreciation				(14,000)					(14,000) (E)
Buildings depreciation					(7,000)				(7,000) (E)
Advertising	(18,000)								(18,000) (E)
Cost of goods sold			(116,000)						(116,000) (E)
Paid principal and interest on mortgages	(6,500)							(5,000)	(1,500) (E)
Ending Position	6,500	72,000	61,000	95,000	86,000	35,000	32,000	40,000	283,500

*Balances are net of accumulated depreciation.

6-8. Preparing a Statement of Changes in Financial Position from Other Statements. Following is the financial position of the Herbert Medical Clinic at December 31, 19X3 and 19X4:

	December 31, 19X3	December 31, 19X4
Cash	$ 40,000	$ 45,000
Accounts receivable	80,000	70,000
Inventory	20,000	25,000
Equipment and furnishings	100,000	125,000
Accumulated depreciation—		
Equipment and furnishings	(40,000)	(55,000)
	$200,000	$210,000
Accounts payable	$ 15,000	$ 18,000
Accrued wages payable	5,000	2,000
8% notes payable, due 6/30/X8	50,000	-0-
Owners' equity:		
Capital stock	100,000	140,000
Retained earnings	30,000	50,000
	$200,000	$210,000

During 19X4 the clinic reported a net income of $110,000.

Required:

From the information contained in these statements, and stating any assumptions that are logical and necessary, prepare a *working-capital-based* statement of changes in financial position *and* the supporting schedule of changes in working capital elements for the year 19X4.

6-9. Resource Flows from Operations. The financial position of Teton Village Restaurant, Inc., at December 31, 19X7 and 19X8, is as follows:

	December 31, 19X7	December 31, 19X8
Cash	$ 4,000	$ 2,000
Inventory	8,000	7,000
Land	20,000	20,000
Building and equipment	40,000	50,000
Accumulated depreciation—		
Building and equipment	(12,000)	(15,000)
	$60,000	$64,000
Accounts payable	$ 6,000	$ 2,000
Mortgage payable	25,000	30,000
Owners' equity:		
Capital stock	20,000	25,000
Retained earnings	9,000	7,000
	$60,000	$64,000

During 19X8 Teton Village Restaurant, Inc., reported a net income of $12,000.

Required:

1. Prepare a schedule of the changes in working capital elements during 19X8 (*not a statement of changes in financial position*).

2. Prepare a computation of estimated working capital provided by operations for 19X8. (Make necessary assumptions explicit.)

3. Prepare a computation of estimated cash provided by operations for 19X8.

4. In addition to the cash provided by operations, indicate the nature *and* amount of—
   (a) *One* probable additional source of cash during 19X8
   (b) *One* probable additional use of cash during 19X8

6-10. Preparing Statements of Changes from Other Financial Statements and Supplemental Information. The financial statements for the Whitten Manufacturing Company are as follows (amounts in thousands):

	12/31/X7	12/31/X6
Current assets:		
Cash	$ 15	$ 20
Accounts receivable	30	25
Inventory	60	50
Prepaid expenses	5	10
	$110	$105
Property, plant, and equipment (net)	330	295
	$440	$400
Current liabilities:		
Accounts payable	$ 20	$ 25
Accrued expenses	15	10
Estimated income taxes payable	30	25
	$ 65	$ 60
Owners' equity:		
Capital stock	$240	$220
Retained earnings	135	120
	$375	$340
	$440	$400

Income Statement for 19X7

Net sales	$480
Cost of sales	330
Gross profit	$150
Operating expenses (including depreciation expense of 10)	75
Net income before taxes	$ 75
Provision for federal income taxes	35
Net income	$ 40

Required:

1. Compute the amount of dividends that were declared and paid during 19X7, the value of equipment purchased during 19X7, and the value at which capital stock was sold during 19X7.
2. Prepare a working-capital-based statement of changes in financial position.
3. Prepare a cash-based statement of changes in financial position.

6-11. Preparing a Statement of Changes in Financial Position. The financial position of Bulloch Wine and Spirits, Inc., at December 31, 19X3 and 19X4, follows:

	December 31, 19X3	December 31, 19X4
Cash	$ 25,000	$ 21,000
Accounts receivable	15,000	12,000
Inventory	40,000	50,000
Display equipment	25,000	40,000
Accumulated depreciation—		
Display equipment	(5,000)	(8,000)
Delivery truck		6,000
Accumulated depreciation—		
Delivery truck		(1,000)
	$100,000	$120,000
Accounts payable	$ 30,000	$ 25,000
10% notes payable, due 9/30/X7		10,000
Owners' equity:		
Capital stock	50,000	60,000
Retained earnings	20,000	25,000
	$100,000	$120,000

Required:

The corporation reported a net income of $25,000 for 19X4. During the year 19X4 no disposition of long-lived assets or retirements of capital stock took place. From the information presented and stating any assumptions that are logical and necessary, prepare a *cash-based statement* of changes in financial position.

6-12. Resource Flow Concepts and Relationships. Exhibit 6-16 shows the statement of changes in financial position from the 1976 annual report of United Brands Company and Subsidiary Companies.

Required:

1. The 1976 statement of changes in financial position is based on the working capital concept of "resources." Recast this statement based on

Exhibit 6-16

UNITED BRANDS COMPANY AND SUBSIDIARY COMPANIES

Consolidated Statement of Changes in Financial Position (in thousands)

	Year Ended December 31,	
	1976	1975
Working capital provided by:		
Operations		
Income before extraordinary income	$ 13,840	$ 10,068
Add: depreciation and other non-cash charges	40,864	45,254
Total provided by operations	54,704	55,322
Extraordinary income	2,500	700
Proceeds from long-term borrowings	6,600	738
Property, plant and equipment sold	15,511	14,056
Decrease in investments and long-term receivables	4,185	13,974
	83,500	84,790
Working capital applied to:		
Additions of property, plant and equipment	54,248	27,425
Retirement of long-term debt	33,644	43,208
Increase in other assets and deferred charges	3,336	—
Other—net	2,919	4,549
	94,147	75,182
Increase (decrease) in working capital	(10,647)	9,608
Working capital at beginning of year	220,582	210,974
Working capital at end of year	$209,935	$220,582
Increases (decreases) in working capital are as follows:*		
Cash	$ (17)	$ (67,426)
Certificates of deposit	(3,274)	29,877
Receivables	93	(7,122)
Inventories	(6,042)	1,977
Prepaid expenses	1,369	1,349
Notes payable	1,657	52,986
Accounts payable and accrued liabilities	(699)	7,199
Long-term debt due within one year	(3,715)	(2,152)
U.S. and foreign income taxes	(19)	(7,080)
	$(10,647)	$ 9,608

*Note that working capital is increased (decreased) as current liabilities are decreased (increased).

the "cash" concept of resources. Isolate the cash flow from operations in the recast statement.

2. Did the changes in "certificates of deposit" (similar to savings certificates) and "long-term debt due within one year" enter into your calculation of cash flow from operations? Explain why or why not.

3. "Extraordinary income" appears on the statement as a separate source of working capital. Why is this shown separately from the income figure used to calculate working capital provided by operations? Are there any other sources or uses of working capital to which extraordinary income relates?

Exhibit 6-17

ARMCO STEEL CORPORATION AND CONSOLIDATED SUBSIDIARIES

Statement of Changes in Consolidated Financial Position
For the years ended December 31, 1977 and 1976 (Dollars in thousands)

	1977	1976
Source of Funds		
Operations		
Income before cumulative effect of depreciation change	$119,832	$119,774
Add (deduct) items not involving cash in the period:		
Depreciation	110,958	93,115
Lease right amortization	14,819	15,003
Deferred income taxes	(51,917)	(26,583)
Equity in undistributed net income of Armco Financial Corporation and subsidiaries	(15,047)	(7,329)
Equity in undistributed net income of associated companies	(6,530)	(7,974)
Other—net	1,159	(728)
Total from operations	173,274	185,278
Increase in accounts payable and other accruals	96,983	2,263
Decrease (increase) in inventories	58,774	(74,628)
Decrease in investments	12,215	5,850
Proceeds from issuing long-term debt	5,294	108,381
Other—net	1,431	521
Total	347,971	227,665
Use of Funds		
Capital expenditures	146,387	271,963
Increase (decrease) in notes and accounts receivable	78,181	(36,729)
Dividends paid	60,454	57,331
Decrease (increase) in notes payable	32,569	(95,991)
Payments on long-term debt	19,513	26,123
Increase (decrease) in prepaid expenses and deferred charges	9,837	(636)
Payments on long-term lease obligations	6,506	6,838
Total	353,447	228,899
Decrease in Cash and Marketable Securities	(5,476)	(1,234)
Cash and Marketable Securities		
Beginning of year	42,487	43,721
End of year	$ 37,011	$ 42,487

6-13. Cash-based Statements of Changes. Exhibit 6-17 shows the statement of changes in financial position from the 1977 annual report of Armco Steel Corporation and Consolidated Subsidiaries. The statement's basis is cash plus marketable securities (which for practical purposes is the same as the cash basis).

Required:

1. Notice that in its statement Armco lists "increase in accounts payable and other accruals" and "decrease in inventories" as separate sources of "funds"; and it lists "increase in notes and accounts receivable"

and "decrease in notes payable" as separate uses. Discuss the rationale for treating such items as separate sources and uses. Describe and discuss the rationale for the alternate treatment.

2. Convert the 1977 statement as given to a statement of changes in financial position based on working capital and a separate schedule of changes in working capital accounts.

The Financial Accounting Information System | 7

All accounting processes and all accounting applications depend upon the availability of relevant data. Such data must reflect financial events and transactions affecting the unit to be accounted for and must be collected, analyzed, organized, summarized, and stored in some form of data-processing system. In a small organization these requirements are satisfied by a simple bookkeeping system operated by one or more clerks either manually or with the aid of bookkeeping machines. In the smallest organizations the system is usually manual and the data-processing and report preparation functions are performed by the owner-managers or by outside bookkeeping services. In larger, more complex, organizations the systems might be referred to as *financial information systems* and are usually based on computers and related peripheral equipment. Because the design and operation of an accounting system, whatever its level of complexity, are important aspects of accounting and management practice, the basic elements of such a system are examined briefly in this chapter.

We restrict our attention to a simplified manual accounting system for two reasons. First, one can easily generalize one's understanding of the basic elements of a simple accounting information system to a more complex, computer-based system without becoming involved in the technical characteristics of computer systems. Second, it is possible to draw upon the concepts and methodology developed in this simplified analysis to serve the purposes of other business and accounting courses. Occasionally, personal or business situations can be covered adequately on the basis of this simplified analysis alone.

The Financial Accounting Process (Cycle) as a System

When the financial position framework was introduced in Chapter 4, it was pointed out that a new financial position of the firm can be computed after analyzing the effects of each transaction. Indeed, by following such a procedure we illustrated that the fundamental equation—assets equal liabilities plus owners' equity—remained in balance at all times. A closer approximation of actual accounting data gathering and processing was then achieved through the introduction of the financial position worksheet. The device enabled us to defer the computation of each new financial position until the end of a chosen interval of time—whether a month, a quarter, or a year. The financial position worksheet is therefore a means of analyzing, organizing, and storing the transactions of the firm in a form that allows us to apply appropriate accounting principles and generate financial statements at periodic intervals. It is thus an accounting system, albeit a simple one.

What then are the limitations of the financial position worksheet as a practical accounting system, even for a small firm? One important limitation is the physical configuration of the worksheet. The average business, even a small one, has a larger variety of resources and obligations than we have used in our intentionally simplified examples. To use the worksheet format for a firm with, say, twenty-five different types of assets and liabilities, the accountant would be confronted with a "wall-to-wall" worksheet. Moreover, since most companies find it useful to record even summary transaction data at more frequent intervals than one accounting cycle, most businesses' financial position worksheets soon would stretch from "floor to ceiling" as well. To solve these problems the accounting system must be able to expand along both dimensions. That is, it must be able to accommodate both large numbers of accounts and large numbers of (often repetitive) transactions.

Another important limitation that relates to the physical configuration and the frequency with which summary transaction data are recorded is the ease with which the data may later be summarized in financial statements. A principal purpose of an actual financial accounting information system is to organize and summarize raw economic data into a form that makes the preparation of financial statements relatively convenient. However, for a firm with a fair number of summary transactions, it would be tedious to go back through the single owners' equity column of the financial position worksheet to determine the items and amounts that would be used in the construction of the income statement. One would essentially have to reanalyze every item included in this column and prepare independent summary totals for all similar items (e.g., the total of all salary and wage payments to be included under the single "salary and wage expense" classification in the income statement). It would be useful, therefore, if the system could be modified to perform this accumulation function as individual events are analyzed and recorded.

To avoid the above two limitations of the simple financial position worksheet mechanism, most businesses employ some variation of so-called general ledger bookkeeping. General ledger bookkeeping, which is described more fully in the next section, uses two interrelated recording devices, the general journal and the general ledger, in place of the financial position worksheet. It also employs a more elaborate set of procedures than the simplified accounting cycle described in Chapter 4.

One additional limitation of the simplified accounting approach (and general ledger bookkeeping, if taken by itself) should be noted. In the illustrations and examples in Chapter 4, and those used in the following section to illustrate general ledger bookkeeping, summary transaction data are taken as "given." This is not at all representative of a most important dimension of the financial accounting information system, namely, the "process" by which a business captures (originally records), stores, controls, and summarizes raw transaction data. This "process dimension" is discussed in the section following general ledger bookkeeping.

GENERAL LEDGER BOOKKEEPING

The General Journal

A general journal in an accounting system is a chronological record of transactions. Each entry in the general journal contains the date, the accounts affected, the dollar amounts of these effects, and occasionally an explanation of additional details of the transactions.

General journals used in accounting practice come in many different forms and designs. Most, however, use the special bookkeeping convention of expressing the effects of transactions and other events on a company's accounts in terms of "Debits" and "Credits." Exhibit 7-1 represents the traditional format of the general journal.

The first two columns of the general journal in Exhibit 7-1 are fairly self-descriptive. The first column contains the date of the transaction. The second column includes the accounts that are affected by the transaction, and an explanation of the nature of the transaction. After one achieves a certain degree of proficiency in analyzing transactions, explanations of the type shown in this example are generally unnecessary because the nature of the transaction is fairly obvious from the accounts affected. Thus, in practice, explanations are usually restricted to a more specific type of background information that recalls

Exhibit 7-1

AN ILLUSTRATIVE GENERAL JOURNAL IN TRADITIONAL BOOKKEEPING FORMAT

Date	Description	Dr	Cr
May 1	Owners' equity	1,200	
	Cash		1,200
	To record cash payment for monthly rent		
May 3	Merchandise inventory	10,000	
	Accounts payable		10,000
	To record purchase of merchandise on account		
May 4	Cash	2,500	
	Accounts receivable		2,500
	To record collection of accounts from customers		

the facts underlying a particular entry (e.g., the interest rate and the due date on a promissory note given to a lender in exchange for cash).

The last two columns of the general journal contain the dollar effects of the transaction on the accounts named in the second column. These increases and decreases could be represented algebraically as in the financial position worksheet but, instead, notational designations of "Debit" and "Credit" are used. These designations are typically abbreviated as "Dr" and "Cr." They have a Latin origin, since they evolved during the genesis of formal bookkeeping in medieval Italy. However, the Dr and Cr expressions no longer have any intrinsic language meaning—they are strictly arithmetic-type notations. Nevertheless, since they are not the kind of arithmetic (algebraic) notations we are used to, they require some explanation. Once one understands how "Debits" and "Credits" relate to the algebraic accounting relationships introduced earlier, they lose their mystery and become ready substitutes for more familiar notation (with a little practice).

Changes in accounts are changes in financial position and, therefore, can be expressed in terms of the accounting equation. Recall that based on the agreed-upon residual nature of the measurement of owners' equity, the following financial position relationship should always hold at any point in time:

$$A = L + OE \qquad (1)$$

But in order for relationship (1) to continue to hold as new transactions and events are recognized, the successive changes in financial position must also obey the relationship depicted in (2) below (where "Δ" denotes "the change in"):

$$\Delta A = \Delta L + \Delta OE \qquad (2)$$

This condition says that the change in assets (recognized in connection with a given event or transaction) must equal the recognized change (if any) in liabilities plus the recognized change (if any) in owners' equity.

Now if we simply expand condition (2) so that increases (Δ^+) in elements of financial position are distinguished from decreases (Δ^-), we get the more detailed expression (3) for condition (2):

$$[\Delta^+ A - \Delta^- A] = [\Delta^+ L - \Delta^- L] + [\Delta^+ OE - \Delta^- OE] \qquad (3)$$

Then by rearranging terms (so as to eliminate minus signs from the expression), we obtain the following:

$$\Delta^+ A + \Delta^- L + \Delta^- OE = \Delta^+ L + \Delta^+ OE + \Delta^- A \qquad (4)$$

$$\text{Debits} = \text{Credits} \qquad (5)$$

As expression (5) indicates, all left-hand elements in (4) are designated as debits, and all right-hand elements as credits. Therefore a *Dr* to an account signifies—

1. An increase if the account is an asset account, or
2. A decrease if the account is a liability or an owners' equity account.

In contrast, a *Cr* to an account signifies—

1. An increase if the account is a liability or an owners' equity account, or
2. A decrease if the account is an asset account.

The importance of expressions (4) and (5) is that together they indicate that *if in processing transactions the debits equal the credits,* condition (3) and, therefore, condition (1) is satisfied.

Before we illustrate the use of the Dr-Cr convention in recording transactions in the general journal, we might note some of its advantages and disadvantages. One advantage is that it simplifies notations because it eliminates negative numbers from the system and avoids some possible clerical errors (e.g., failure to put parentheses on numbers or to specify decreases). It also affords a numerical self-checking device, since the accounting equation implies that the sum of debits equals the sum of credits, and conversely. This self-checking property makes it easier to ensure that all the effects of transactions on financial position are in fact recorded.

The most serious disadvantage of the Dr-Cr convention is that it constitutes a rather special notational scheme which has to be learned and remembered before it can be applied.

Note from Exhibit 7-1 that (1) the defined equality in amount between debits and credits applies not only to the aggregate of all bookkeeping entries made during a period but to *each individual recorded transaction* as well; (2) by convention, the *Dr* portion of an entry precedes the *Cr* portion; (3) *Cr* portions of entries are customarily indented toward the right; and (4) left-hand amount columns are devoted to *Dr* portions of entries and right-hand amount columns to *Cr* portions. These procedures are universally used in the United States and therefore have some bookkeeping meaning in and of themselves.

Three unrelated sample transactions are included in the illustrative general journal (Exhibit 7-1). A brief review of these transactions follows:

Transaction 1. On May 1 the monthly rent of $1,200 was paid in cash (by check). The effect of this transaction is to decrease the asset account, cash, and to decrease the owners' equity account for rent expense. Accordingly, the affected accounts are identified in the second column, and the amount of the decreases in their balances are placed in the appropriate Dr-Cr columns. Cash is an asset, and thus its decrease is placed in the Cr column; the decrease in owners' equity is in the Dr column. If the reader is unclear as to why we make a debit entry for a decrease in owners' equity and a credit entry for a decrease in cash, it is a sign that equations (4) and (5) above should be reviewed once again (that is, compare their right-hand and left-hand sides). After the transaction is recorded, it is immediately apparent that the debits equal the credits. This is equivalent to observing that we have decreased total assets by $1,200 and also decreased the sum of liabilities and owners' equity by $1,200. Therefore the fundamental accounting equation remains in balance; total assets remain equal to the sum of liabilities and owners' equity.

Transaction 2. On May 3 inventory items were purchased at a cost of $10,000 and charged to an account payable with the supplier. The effect of this transaction is recorded by a debit to the asset account, merchandise inventory, and a credit to the liability, accounts payable. Again after this transaction is recorded, total debits equal total credits and the fundamental accounting equation remains in balance. Total assets increased by $10,000, and the sum of liabilities and owners' equity also increased by $10,000.

Transaction 3. In this last transaction in the illustration, $2,500 is collected from a customer, or customers, to whom the firm had previously sold merchandise on account. The effect of this transaction is to increase the firm's cash balance recorded by a debit to cash, and to decrease the total amount due from customers, recorded by a credit to accounts receivable. The transaction does not affect any liability or owners' equity accounts. Since the net effect of the transaction on total assets is zero, and similarly the total of liabilities and owners' equity is unchanged, the fundamental equation again remains in balance, and, of course, the debits still equal the credits.

The process of analyzing transactions and recording them in a general journal differs only in form, not substance, from the line-by-line analysis in the financial position worksheet. What advantage then does the general journal offer? The answer may already be apparent. We previously alluded to the size limitation imposed by the physical configuration of the financial position worksheet. As more and more accounts must be given recognition, the financial position worksheet becomes increasingly impractical as a data accumulation device.

However, the general journal has no such limitation. The physical dimensions of the general journal need not be varied, regardless of the number of accounts. The illustrated four-column format is sufficient because each account that is affected by a transaction is entered in the general journal at the time the transaction is recorded. All accounts whose balances are unaffected by a particular transaction are not needed to complete the recording of that transaction. The complete general journal for any period of time thus consists of a chronological series of entries (transactions) on as many pages as are required by the firm's volume of transactions.

Using the general journal, we have a manageable technique for recording all transactions. But how do we then periodically prepare a statement of financial position and an income statement from this chronological record of transactions? The answer is, We do not—financial statements are prepared from the record known as the general ledger.

The General Accounting Ledger

The general ledger is a collection of the accounts of the firm. Each account is normally placed on a separate page. After transactions have been recorded in the general journal, respective amounts are transferred (or posted) to the affected accounts in the general ledger. This posting process can be carried out immediately after each transaction is recorded in the general journal, or it may be done for a group of transactions at periodic intervals (e.g., weekly or monthly).

Exhibit 7-2 illustrates a form of general ledger account that is consistent with the general journal format we have used. Note that each account in the general ledger corresponds to a column in the financial position worksheet. The collection of all such accounts for a firm constitutes the firm's general ledger. In Exhibit 7-2, again by convention, Dr entries are posted on the *left* side of a general ledger account and Cr entries on the *right* side. This convention has become so deeply entrenched that the respective account sides are not even labeled "Dr" or "Cr." In fact, although the format shown in Exhibit 7-2 is representative of an actual traditional ledger account, accounting educators

Exhibit 7-2

AN ILLUSTRATIVE TRADITIONAL GENERAL LEDGER ACCOUNT FORMAT

Acctg. No. XXX		*Acct. Name: Cash*			*Year: 19XX*
Date (Entry #)	Reference	Amount	Date (Entry #)	Reference	Amount
April 30 May 4	Initial Bal. GJ-1	8,400 2,500	May 1	GJ-1	1,200
	Balance	9,700			

have for years used an even simpler representation known as the *T-account* for purposes of exposition. A T-account representation of the same information as that contained in Exhibit 7-2 is shown in Exhibit 7-3. Notice that all that is really needed is an account name and two columns, with convention specifying that the left column contains the debit entries and balances, and the right column the credit entries and balances.

The *balance* of any account is the difference between the sums of the amounts recorded on its two sides. Because of the way that debits and credits relate to assets, liabilities, and owners' equity, one would normally expect asset accounts to have debit balances, and liability and owners' equity accounts to have credit balances.

The cash account illustrated in Exhibits 7-2 and 7-3 is assumed to have a balance of $8,400 on April 30. This should correspond to the amount of cash the firm has on hand and in the bank on that date. Opposite and below this beginning balance, the cash receipts and cash disbursements transactions recorded in the general journal in Exhibit 7-1 are entered and a new balance is calculated. A new balance could be entered after each transaction is recorded, or it could be calculated only at convenient intervals (such as the end of a month). The effects of the transactions on the other accounts identified in each transaction entry in Exhibit 7-1 are transferred to the appropriate ledger accounts in a similar manner. The process of recording in the ledger accounts the amounts listed in journal entries is called *posting* (the journal entires) to the ledger. It is essential that all accounts debited or credited in each journal entry be posted with appropriate debit or credit amounts. Otherwise the general ledger accounts (which represent the elements of the financial position equation) will not be in balance (the debit balances will not equal the credit balances) even though the debits equal the credits in each journal entry.

The other columns of the account format in Exhibit 7-2 provide a means of indicating the date the transaction occurred, explanatory comments if any are desired, and the page of the general journal on which the particular transaction is recorded. The latter reference enables one to refer back to the details of the total transaction for any particular posting (increase or decrease) in an account.

Thus we see that the general journal and the general ledger taken together constitute an integrated system for recording and summarizing all the transactions of the firm. The general journal is a chronological record of the individual transactions, and the general ledger shows the effects of all transactions on the financial position—categorized by accounts. At any point in time at which all entries in the general journal have been posted to the general ledger, financial

Exhibit 7-3

AN ILLUSTRATIVE T-ACCOUNT

Dr   Cr

	Cash		
April 30	8,400	1,200	May 1
May 4	2,500		
Balance	9,700		

statements may be prepared using the balances indicated for each account in the general ledger.

This system is clearly more redundant than the financial position worksheet because each transaction is necessarily recorded twice. It is first recorded in the general journal, and then the components of the journal entry are recorded again in the general ledger. However, the system is a feasible one (whereas the financial position worksheet is not), and it also facilitates such management objectives as a degree of internal control. In Chapter 19 we note that a division of work functions (for example, recording in the general journal *and* recording in the general ledger) between two separate employees may yield certain protection against error and possibly against fraud or misuse of resources.

Use of Temporary (Period-Related) Accounts

We have not yet indicated how to resolve the other dimension-related limitation of the financial position worksheet, that is, the need to reanalyze and summarize each of the revenue and expense entries in the owners' equity account whenever one wishes to prepare an income statement. As the system has been explained to this point, the many different types of revenues and expenses for the period would be reflected by changes (credits and debits) to one owners' equity account. (We have ignored the distinction usually observed between paid-in capital and retained earnings. When the distinction *is* observed, revenues and expenses are, in effect, credits and debits to retained earnings.) *What we seek now is some means of summarizing the revenue and expense transactions into desired separate categories during the journal-ledger recording process.*

This objective is accomplished by introducing into the accounting system a new set of accounts for certain classes of revenue and expense items. These accounts are called *temporary accounts* (or nominal accounts). They are subdivisions of owners' equity (retained earnings) and maintain balances only for specified periods of time (usually one month or one year). At the end of the selected time interval, the net balance across all of the temporary accounts is transferred back (closed) in one entry to the owners' equity account.

Because the temporary accounts are subdivisions of owners' equity, initially we maintain "owners' equity" in parentheses along with the title of each such account that indicates the particular revenue or expense type it represents (although in actual practice, "owners' equity" does not explicitly appear in the titles of temporary accounts). For example, in the first sample transaction (May 1) in Exhibit 7-1, the payment of rent for the month was recognized as a debit to owners' equity. Using the temporary accounts, however, it would be recorded as a debit to the "rent expense (owners' equity)" account. Thus the following entry would be made in the general journal:

Date	Description	Dr	Cr
May 1	Rent expense (owners' equity) Cash	1,200	1,200

Since expenses are decreases in owners' equity, all expenses are debit entries. Revenue, on the other hand, increases owners' equity, and thus the temporary accounts for revenue items (e.g., sales) would normally have credit balances. The comprehensive example illustrated in Exhibits 7-4 through 7-8 shows the integrated use of temporary accounts within the general ledger bookkeeping system.

We want to reemphasize that the temporary accounts are merely *"change" components of the owners' equity account.* Selected categories of revenue and expense items are accumulated separately for a period of time rather than being recorded directly in the owners' equity (master) account. By expanding owners' equity with the temporary revenue and expense accounts in this manner, we have immediately available in the temporary account balances in the general ledger the summary information needed to prepare an income statement for the period. When the balances of the temporary accounts are transferred (closed) as net credits or debits to owners' equity for a given period, the accumulation of the amounts of expenses and revenues for that period terminates. Then we begin a new accumulation for the next period in new temporary accounts.

Illustration of General Ledger Bookkeeping

The general journal and the general ledger (including the set of temporary accounts, as well as the permanent accounts for assets, liabilities, and owners' equity) form the basis for a simple general ledger accounting system. Exhibits 7-5 and 7-6 present the system as it would appear after handling one month's transactions.

The data for this illustration are taken from the financial position worksheet for Fancy Flavors, Inc., in Chapter 4 which, for convenience, is reproduced as Exhibit 7-4. Although our choice of data demonstrates the congruence of the journal-ledger system with the financial position worksheet used earlier in the text, a comparative evaluation of the efficiency of the two systems from this illustration would be misleading. As pointed out earlier, the financial position worksheet breaks down as a viable system when the volume of transactions and/or the number of accounts increases. However, for ease of exposition, the illustration does not encompass either of these two conditions.

The general journal for Fancy Flavors is presented in Exhibit 7-5. To clarify unique elements of the accounting-processing function, the entries in the journal are divided into three categories: (1) entries to record transactions (external events) on page 1 of the general journal for August, (2) entries to give

FANCY FLAVORS, INC.

Financial Position Worksheet
(amounts in thousands)

Description	Cash	+	Accounts Receivable	+	Prepaid Rent	+	Ice Cream	+	Supplies	+	Equipment	+	Accumulated Depreciation	=	Accounts Payable and Accrued Liabilities	+	Bank Loan Payable	+	Owners' Equity
Prior Position	750																600		150
1. Purchase of equipment	(600)										600								
2. Prepayment of rent	(60)				60														
3. Purchase of supplies	(20)								20										
4. Purchase of ice cream							30								30				
5. Additional ice cream purchases							135								135				
6. Payments for ice cream purchased	(130)														(130)				
7. Additional supplies purchased									10						10				
8. Sales	400		50																450 (R)
9. Miscellaneous expenses paid	(10)																		(10) (E)
10. Payment of salaries and wages	(120)														30				(150) (E)
11. Cost of ice cream sold							(145)												(145) (E)
12. Cost of supplies used									(15)										(15) (E)
13. Recognition of expired rent					(20)														(20) (E)
14. Recognition of equipment depreciation													(10)						(10) (E)
15. Recognition of interest on loan															6				(6) (E)
16. Recognition of federal income tax obligation															24				(24) (E)
New Position	210	+	50	+	40	+	20	+	15	+	600	+	(10)	=	105	+	600	+	220

Exhibit 7-5

GENERAL JOURNAL FOR AUGUST 19XX

Date (Entry #)	Page 1 Description	Dr	Cr
	TRANSACTIONS		
(1)	Equipment	600,000	
	Cash		600,000
	To record purchases of equipment.		
(2)	Prepaid rent	60,000	
	Cash		60,000
	To record prepayment of three months' rent.		
(3)	Supplies inventory	20,000	
	Cash		20,000
	To record purchase of supplies.		
(4)	Ice cream inventory	30,000	
	Accounts payable		30,000
	To record purchase of ice cream on account.		
(5)	Ice cream inventory	135,000	
	Accounts payable		135,000
	To record additional purchases of ice cream on account.		
(6)	Accounts payable	130,000	
	Cash		130,000
	To record payment (partial) to the ice cream supplier.		
(7)	Supplies inventory	10,000	
	Accounts payable		10,000
	To record purchase of additional supplies on account.		
(8)	Cash	400,000	
	Accounts receivable	50,000	
	Sales (owners' equity)		450,000
	To record cash and credit sales.		
(9)	Miscellaneous expense (owners' equity)	10,000	
	Cash		10,000
	To record payment for miscellaneous services received during the month (e.g., cleaning services).		
(10)	Wages and salaries expense (owners' equity)	150,000	
	Cash		120,000
	Wages and accounts payable		30,000
	To record salaries and wages expense.		
	END-OF-PERIOD ADJUSTMENTS		
(11)	Cost of ice cream sold (owners' equity)	145,000	
	Ice cream inventory		145,000
	To adjust the ice cream inventory balance to the cost of ice cream on hand at the end of the month and recognize the cost of ice cream sold.		
(12)	Cost of supplies used (owners' equity)	15,000	
	Supplies inventory		15,000
	To adjust the supplies inventory balance to the cost of supplies on hand at the end of the month and recognize the cost of supplies used.		

Exhibit 7-5 (cont.)

Date (Entry #)	Page 2 Description	Dr	Cr
(13)	Rent expense (owners' equity)	20,000	
	Prepaid rent		20,000
	To recognize the portion of the rent prepayment that applies to the month of August as an expense.		
(14)	Depreciation expense (owners' equity)	10,000	
	Accumulated depreciation—equipment		10,000
	To recognize the depreciation of equipment applicable to August 19XX.		
(15)	Interest expense (owners' equity)	6,000	
	Accounts payable and accrued liabilities		6,000
	To accrue interest expense.		
(16)	Income tax expense (owners' equity)	24,000	
	Accounts payable and accrued liabilities		24,000
	To accrue income tax expense.		
	CLOSING ENTRY		
(17)	Sales (owners' equity)	450,000	
	Salaries and wages expense (owners' equity)		150,000
	Miscellaneous expense (owners' equity)		10,000
	Cost of ice cream sold (owners' equity)		145,000
	Cost of supplies used (owners' equity)		15,000
	Rent expense (owners' equity)		20,000
	Depreciation expense (owners' equity)		10,000
	Interest expense (owners' equity)		6,000
	Income tax expense (owners' equity)		24,000
	Owners' equity		70,000
	To close the temporary revenue and expense accounts to owners' equity.		

recognition to needed end-of-period adjustments (typically called adjusting entries) on pages 1 and 2, and (3) an entry to terminate (close) the temporary accounts to owners' equity (typically called a closing entry or entries), on page 2.

From the general journal in Exhibit 7-5, we proceed directly to an illustration of the corresponding general ledger in Exhibit 7-6. Explanations of the journal-ledger accounting system are given in the following section. Such explanations benefit from simultaneous references to all elements of the system.

In interpreting Exhibits 7-5 and 7-6, it is important to bear in mind that each entry and each balance is recognized according to the debit-credit convention. As noted earlier, debits and credits are used and interpreted properly only relative to the type of account involved. As a reminder the following table is offered:

Type of Account:	Increases are:	Decreases are:	Balances usually are:
Assets	Debits	Credits	Debits
Liabilities	Credits	Debits	Credits
Owners' equity	Credits	Debits	Credits
Revenues	Credits	Debits	Credits*
Expenses	Debits	Credits	Debits*

*Zero balances after closing entry.

Exhibit 7-6

GENERAL LEDGER

Cash

Date (Entry #)	Reference	Amount	Date (Entry #)	Reference	Amount
Aug. 1	Balance	750,000	(1)	GJ-1	600,000
			(2)	GJ-1	60,000
			(3)	GJ-1	20,000
(8)	GJ-1	400,000	(6)	GJ-1	130,000
			(9)	GJ-1	10,000
			(10)	GJ-1	120,000
Aug. 31	Balance	210,000			

Accounts Receivable

Date (Entry #)	Reference	Amount	Date (Entry #)	Reference	Amount
Aug. 1	Balance	-0-			
(8)	GJ-1	50,000			
Aug. 31	Balance	50,000			

Prepaid Rent

Date (Entry #)	Reference	Amount	Date (Entry #)	Reference	Amount
Aug. 1	Balance	-0-			
(2)	GJ-1	60,000	(13)	GJ-2	20,000
Aug. 31	Balance	40,000			

Ice Cream Inventory

Date (Entry #)	Reference	Amount	Date (Entry #)	Reference	Amount
Aug. 1	Balance	-0-			
(4)	GJ-1	30,000			
(5)	GJ-1	135,000	(11)	GJ-1	145,000
Aug. 31	Balance	20,000			

Supplies Inventory

Date (Entry #)	Reference	Amount	Date (Entry #)	Reference	Amount
Aug. 1	Balance	-0-			
(3)	GJ-1	20,000			
(7)	GJ-1	10,000	(12)	GJ-1	15,000
Aug. 31	Balance	15,000			

Equipment

Date (Entry #)	Reference	Amount	Date (Entry #)	Reference	Amount
Aug. 1	Balance	-0-			
(1)	GJ-1	600,000			
Aug. 31	Balance	600,000			

Exhibit 7-6 (cont.)

Accumulated Depreciation—Equipment

Date (Entry #)	Reference	Amount	Date (Entry #)	Reference	Amount
			Aug. 1 (14)	Balance GJ-2	-0- 10,000
			Aug. 31	Balance	10,000

Accounts Payable and Accrued Liabilities

Date (Entry #)	Reference	Amount	Date (Entry #)	Reference	Amount
(6)	GJ-1	130,000	Aug. 1 (4) (5) (7) (10) (15) (16)	Balance GJ-1 GJ-1 GJ-1 GJ-1 GJ-2 GJ-2	-0- 30,000 135,000 10,000 30,000 6,000 24,000
			Aug. 31	Balance	105,000

Bank Loan

Date (Entry #)	Reference	Amount	Date (Entry #)	Reference	Amount
			Aug. 1	Balance	600,000
			Aug. 31	Balance	600,000

Owners' Equity

Date (Entry #)	Reference	Amount	Date (Entry #)	Reference	Amount
			Aug. 1 (17)	Balance GJ-2	150,000 70,000
			Aug. 31	Balance	220,000

Sales (Owners' Equity)

Date (Entry #)	Reference	Amount	Date (Entry #)	Reference	Amount
(17)	GJ-2	450,000	Aug. 1 (8)	Balance GJ-1	-0- 450,000
			Aug. 31	Balance	-0-

Salary and Wages Expense (Owners' Equity)

Date (Entry #)	Reference	Amount	Date (Entry #)	Reference	Amount
Aug. 1 (10)	Balance GJ-1	-0- 150,000	(17)	GJ-2	150,000
Aug. 31	Balance	-0-			

Exhibit 7-6 (cont.)

Miscellaneous Expense (Owners' Equity)

Date (Entry #)	Reference	Amount	Date (Entry #)	Reference	Amount
Aug. 1 (9)	Balance GJ-1	-0- 10,000	(17)	GJ-2	10,000
Aug. 31	Balance	-0-			

Cost of Ice Cream Sold (Owners' Equity)

Date (Entry #)	Reference	Amount	Date (Entry #)	Reference	Amount
Aug. 1 (11)	Balance GJ-1	-0- 145,000	(17)	GJ-2	145,000
Aug. 31	Balance	-0-			

Cost of Supplies Used (Owners' Equity)

Date (Entry #)	Reference	Amount	Date (Entry #)	Reference	Amount
Aug. 1 (12)	Balance GJ-1	-0- 15,000	(17)	GJ-2	15,000
Aug. 31	Balance	-0-			

Rent Expense (Owners' Equity)

Date (Entry #)	Reference	Amount	Date (Entry #)	Reference	Amount
Aug. 1 (13)	Balance GJ-2	-0- 20,000	(17)	GJ-2	20,000
Aug. 31	Balance	-0-			

Depreciation Expense (Owners' Equity)

Date (Entry #)	Reference	Amount	Date (Entry #)	Reference	Amount
Aug. 1 (14)	Balance GJ-2	-0- 10,000	(17)	GJ-2	10,000
Aug. 31	Balance	-0-			

Interest Expense (Owners' Equity)

Date (Entry #)	Reference	Amount	Date (Entry #)	Reference	Amount
Aug. 1 (15)	Balance GJ-2	-0- 6,000	(17)	GJ-2	6,000
Aug. 31	Balance	-0-			

Exhibit 7-6 (cont.)

Income Tax Expense (Owners' Equity)

Date (Entry #)	Reference	Amount	Date (Entry #)	Reference	Amount
Aug. 1 (16)	Balance GJ-2	-0- 24,000	(17)	GJ-2	24,000
Aug. 31	Balance	-0-			

Recording and Posting Transactions

Each transaction journal entry (entries 1-10 in Exhibit 7-5) shows the financial effects of an exchange transaction between Fancy Flavors and an individual (e.g., an employee) or another business organization (e.g., the supplier of ice cream). As indicated before, recording these transactions in the general journal and then posting them to the general ledger produces results substantially equivalent to those produced in the financial position worksheet. For example, transaction (1) in the financial position worksheet (Exhibit 7-4) reflects a $600,000 purchase of equipment by decreasing cash $600,000 and increasing equipment $600,000. The same effect is achieved within the simple accounting system in Exhibits 7-5 and 7-6. The transaction is recorded in the general journal (Exhibit 7-5) wherein it is indicated that equipment is debited (increased) $600,000 and cash is credited (decreased) $600,000.

Following entry of the transaction in the general journal, it is transferred (posted) to the general ledger. Thus, referring to the general ledger in Exhibit 7-6, we note that the cash account reflects a credit of $600,000 (referenced back to entry number 1 on general journal page 1, GJ-1), and the equipment account contains a debit entry for $600,000 (similarly referenced). In like manner, the other nine transactions are recorded in the general journal and posted to the appropriate general ledger accounts with the same substantive effects as were achieved in the financial position worksheet.

As was pointed out in Chapter 4, we have in most of the entries aggregated the effects of a large number of individual exchanges. The entries shown are, in effect, summary transactions. For example, entry (8) records the total effect of all of the individual sales transactions during the month. While this degree of aggregation prior to recording in the general journal would be unlikely in most practical systems, it should be recognized that some prior summarization is not unusual. In the case of Fancy Flavors, for example, the accounting system might be designed to record in the general journal the total sales each week—this figure to be obtained from the cash register tapes for that period of time. We will say more about this aspect of the total accounting system in the next section.

Recognizing End-of-Period Adjustments

Merely recording transactions with outside parties in the manner indicated above does not complete the entire accounting cycle as described in Chapter 4. That is, we have not yet recorded all the changes in financial position that took place during the period. We need a set of entries (entries 11–16 in Exhibit 7-5) at the end of the accounting period to bring the balances in the accounts into agreement with the objectives of the conventional accounting model. This set of entries is referred to as *end-of-period adjustments,* or *adjusting entries.* Adjusting entries may be thought of as recognition of "internal events" in the business operations of the firm.

The end-of-period adjustments are of two basic types: (1) cost allocations and (2) accruals. The *cost allocation process* is one of examining balances of asset accounts at the end of the period (e.g., in our illustration, the prepaid rent account) and determining the portion that should be allocated as an expense to the period. The balance in the asset account may have been recorded in this or in some prior period. In either case, it is the result of an exchange transaction in which the firm acquired resources that were expected to be of benefit in the future. The decision as to how much of these resources (benefits) was consumed in the period is in many cases a product of specific accounting measurement rules, which are discussed in some detail in Chapters 8–12.

In the illustration, entries (11) and (12) both cause decreases in (credits to) the inventory accounts such that the remaining balances reflect the cost of items (or quantities) still on hand. At the same time, the decreases (credits) constitute recognition of the cost of items consumed (used or sold) as expenses of the period. For example, the ice cream inventory account had a debit balance of $165,000 after all transactions were recorded (see the general ledger, Exhibit 7-6). This balance reflects the cost of all ice cream purchased during the period. However, at the end of the period, the asset held is the ice cream still on hand from which the business can benefit (through sale) in the next period. The ice cream inventory account, therefore, needs to be adjusted to a balance that is equal to the cost of the ice cream still on hand. In the example, it is assumed that the cost of ice cream on hand is $20,000. The ice cream inventory account must therefore be credited (decreased) by $145,000, an amount that presumably reflects the cost of ice cream sold during the period. Thus adjusting entry (11) records the decrease to the inventory account, and the decrease (debit) to owners' equity through the temporary (expense) account, "cost of ice cream sold (owners' equity)."

The same reasoning is applied in entry (12), in which the cost of supplies on hand at the end of the period is assumed to be $15,000. It should be pointed out that estimates of the cost of inventory on hand at the end of the period for a business such as Fancy Flavors would be determined in practice by counting, measuring, or otherwise physically establishing the quantity on hand and then assigning the appropriate cost to this quantity. In larger businesses with more elaborate accounting systems, reasonable estimates of the inventory on hand can usually be made throughout a year without any physical survey. However, even these firms normally make a physical count of their inventory at least once each year. Accounting for inventories is discussed at some length in Chapter 10.

Entry (13) deducts (credits) the cost of renting the building space for August from (to) the asset, prepaid rent. The concurrent decrease (debit) is made to owners' equity via the account "rent expense (owners' equity)." The underlying transaction—entry (2)—recorded the prepayment of three months' rent. Thus, after recognizing the $20,000 rent expense for August, the $40,000 debit balance of the prepaid rent account at the end of the month reflects the cost of occupancy for September and October to which Fancy Flavors is still entitled.

Entry (14) allocates 1/60 of the cost of the equipment, which is assumed to have a five-year useful life, to depreciation expense for August. This amount is determined under the assumption that the services inherent in this equipment are realized equally during each month of its useful life. Other possible methods of recognizing depreciation are discussed in Chapter 10.

Accruals are end-of-period adjustments that give recognition to expenses incurred or revenues earned for which there have been no exchange transactions during the period. There are two accruals in the illustrative set of four adjusting entries, entries (15) and (16), and accrued wages payable are recognized among the transactions in entry (10) in the general journal. An adjusting entry to recognize an accrual is only necessary if it is not recognized in connection with the transactions of the period. Entry (15) recognizes the accrued but unpaid interest on the bank loan for the month, while entry (16) recognizes the income tax expense applicable to the difference between revenues and all other expenses of the month.

Preparing the Income Statement

After appropriate adjusting entries have been recorded in the general journal and the amounts posted to the general ledger, the financial statements for August can be prepared directly from the balances in the general ledger accounts. This process is analogous to using the balances on a financial position worksheet, with the new benefit that even though numerous transactions may have affected selected revenue and expense accounts, their effects will already be summarized (in the temporary accounts) for use in preparing the income statement.

The income statement in Exhibit 7-7 reflects the process of matching the efforts (expenses) and accomplishments (revenue) for the period as recorded in the various temporary accounts shown in Exhibit 7-6.

Exhibit 7-7

FANCY FLAVORS, INC.

Income Statement
For the Month of August 19XX

Sales		$450,000
Expenses:		
Salary and wages expense	$150,000	
Miscellaneous expense	10,000	
Cost of ice cream sold	145,000	
Cost of supplies used	15,000	
Rent expense	20,000	
Depreciation expense	10,000	
Interest expense	6,000	
Income tax expense	24,000	
Total expense		380,000
Net (operating) income		$ 70,000

Terminating (Closing) the Revenue and Expense Accounts

The revenue and expense accounts are, as we have stated before, temporary subdivisions of the owners' equity account. They are established merely to aggregate the effects of operations for the period into categories that facilitate the preparation of an income statement. At the end of the period, these accounts are terminated (closed) by transferring their balances to the owners' equity account. Thus the amount of owners' equity at the end of the period can be determined and the statement of financial position prepared.

Within Exhibits 7-5 and 7-6, the one revenue account, sales (owners' equity), accumulates the effects of operating transactions that increase owners' equity. Therefore the balance of the account, $450,000, is a credit balance. The entry to close this account, entry (17), records a debit to sales (owners' equity) so as to produce a zero balance in the sales account. In a similar manner, the other elements of entry (17), except the last, close the various expense accounts. The expense accounts summarize transactions or adjustments that decrease owners' equity. They therefore carry debit balances before closing and are closed to zero balances by credits.

The net effect of the recognized revenue and expenses of the period is an increase in owners' equity, corresponding to the net income for the period of $70,000. This is given recognition in the accounts by the credit to the owners' equity account indicated on the last line of entry (17). Had the net effect of the closing entry been a decrease in (debit to) owners' equity, it would imply that a net loss was incurred. After the closing entry (17) is recorded in the general journal and transferred (posted) to the general ledger accounts, all the temporary accounts have zero balances.

A special closing account, *revenue and expense summary,* is sometimes used so that individual revenue and expense accounts are first closed to the summary account with only the net effect of operations for the period (net income or loss) being transferred from the summary account to owners' equity. As its title implies, this account is merely a summarizing account. It always has a zero balance before and after the closing entries are made. Since its use is merely a procedural convenience, it is not illustrated in the example.

Preparing the Statement of Financial Position

In preparing the end-of-the-month statement of financial position, we use general ledger account balances *after* all appropriate adjusting and closing entries have been posted.

The statement of financial position in Exhibit 7-8 reflects the balances (unexpired costs in the cases of nonmonetary assets) of resources on hand and obligations due at the end of the month as indicated by the *balances in the permanent ledger accounts* shown in Exhibit 7-6. The balance of the owners' equity account shown in Exhibit 7-6 as of month-end equals the beginning balance plus the income (in some cases the loss) for the period. This is so because entry (17), the closing entry in this case, effectively adds (algebraically) the balances in all temporary accounts (revenue and expense accounts) to the beginning balance in the owners' equity account. The effect, again, is to add an amount equal to net income for the period to beginning owners' equity.

Exhibit 7-8

FANCY FLAVORS, INC.

Statement of Financial Position
As of August 31, 19XX

Assets:		
Cash		$210,000
Accounts receivable		50,000
Prepaid rent		40,000
Ice cream inventory		20,000
Supplies inventory		15,000
Equipment	$600,000	
Less: Accumulated depreciation	(10,000)	590,000
Total assets		$925,000
Liabilities and Owners' Equity:		
Wages and accounts payable		$105,000
Bank loan		600,000
Owners' equity		220,000
Total liabilities and owners' equity		$925,000

Preparation of the Statement of Changes in Financial Position

The preparation of a statement of changes in financial position proceeds in the same way as that described in Chapter 6 except that the changes (and components thereof) in the noncurrent, permanent account balances are derived from the various ledger accounts. Generally, credit changes to noncurrent accounts (e.g., an increase to a long-term liability account) represent sources of working capital, and debit changes (e.g., an increase in a long-lived asset account) represent uses. The only exception is that debit and credit changes in noncurrent accounts due to operations are considered together and are classified under sources or uses of working capital depending on whether they represent a *net* credit or debit, respectively. A statement of changes prepared from the changes in account balances of Fancy Flavors for August 19XX appears in Exhibit 7-9. Note that the assumed beginning position for purposes of preparing this statement is the position *before* the initial investment by the owners and the loan from the bank required to start the business (i.e., a hypothetical zero asset, liability, and owners' equity position).

Recap of the Process—The Accounting Cycle

The set of steps we have followed in the foregoing illustration is sometimes referred to as the *accounting cycle* because it is followed in the same sequence period after period. The accounting cycle was first introduced in Chapter 4 in connection with the financial position worksheet. To that earlier discussion we have now added some new terminology and have introduced some new processes uniquely related to general ledger bookkeeping. But the substance of the

Exhibit 7-9

FANCY FLAVORS, INC.

Statement of Changes in Financial Position
For the Month of August 19XX

Sources of working capital:	
Operations:	
Net income	$ 70,000
Add back depreciation	10,000
Total from operations	$ 80,000
Other sources:	
Investment by owners	150,000
Loan by bank	600,000
Total, all sources	$830,000
Uses of working capital:	
Purchase of equipment	600,000
Increase in working capital	$230,000

cycle discussed in Chapter 4 remains unchanged. To summarize, the essential steps of the accounting (general ledger bookkeeping) cycle are as follows:

1. Systematically collect data associated with transactions having a financial effect on the firm as they take place.

2. Record transactions (external events) with individuals or other business firms in the general journal, and transfer (post) the amounts recorded to the general ledger accounts.

3. Record and post end-of-period adjustments, giving recognition to the cost allocations and accruals necessary to reflect revenues and expenses of the period.

4. Prepare an income statement for the period.

5. Record and post closing entries to transfer the balances of the temporary accounts to owners' equity.

6. Prepare a statement of financial position as of the end of the period and a statement of changes in financial position for the period.

After the sequence of steps is completed for one period (in our case, a month), the cycle is resumed at step 1 at the start of the next period, and so on.

The major task of accumulating the financial data base for the firm is accomplished in steps 1 and 2 of the cycle. It is in this activity that the mass of individual transactions are identified and assimilated into the system. The "process" dimension of accounting mentioned earlier is principally concerned with this function. Steps 4, 5, and 6 are fairly mechanical, albeit necessary, operations. It is in step 3, however, that many of the major issues involving financial reporting under the conventional accounting model surface. The cost allocations and accruals that are necessary before financial statements can be prepared are largely the product of the measurement rules discussed in Chapters 8-12.

The Trial Balance and Financial Statement Worksheet

A very flexible and widely used tool in general ledger bookkeeping is the device known as the trial balance.

> **Trial Balance.** A trial balance is a listing in debit and credit format of all the *balances* in a company's general ledger accounts as of a given date. The balances may be as they appear in the general ledger accounts themselves (an *unadjusted* trial balance) or they may be as they would appear after tentative adjustments are made (an *adjusted* trial balance).

The most obvious advantage of the trial balance over the general ledger itself is that it lists all accounts and their balances on one or, at most, a few pages. Less obvious, but probably more important, a trial balance may be used for recording interim adjusting entries and avoiding closing entries altogether in the process of preparing financial statements at intervals less than one fiscal year (say, monthly or quarterly).

This can represent great convenience and savings of bookkeeping effort. That is, although our simple example does not bring it out, the process of "closing the books" (making periodic adjusting entries followed by closing the temporary accounts) can be tedious and costly. Moreover, certain kinds of adjusting entries can only be made with accuracy at annual intervals (examples are pension and profit-sharing expenses, accrual of the appropriate income tax expense, etc.). In such cases, if companies prefer to close the books only once per year and to restrict frequent adjusting entries in the general ledger, they may perform steps 3-6 of the accounting cycle described above by using an unadjusted trial balance in conjunction with a financial *statement* preparation worksheet.

A financial statement preparation worksheet is illustrated in Exhibit 7-10. In the two columns headed "Unadjusted Trial Balance" are the debit and credit balances *that would have appeared* in the general ledger accounts of Fancy Flavors after all the transactions for August had been recorded (entries 1-10) but *before any adjusting or closing entries*. The next two columns (headed "Adjustments") show the effects of the adjusting entries (11-16) for August on the respective account balances. The adjustments are numbered parenthetically as originally shown on pages 1 and 2 of the August general journal (Exhibit 7-5) so that the reader can refer to the journal to recall the nature of each adjustment and its explanation. The last two columns (headed "Adjusted Trial Balance") show the result of combining the unadjusted trial balance figures for the various accounts with any adjustments to the accounts that appear in the Adjustments columns.

With one exception, the figures in the "Adjusted Trial Balance" trace into the income statement (Exhibit 7-7) and the balance sheet (Exhibit 7-8) prepared earlier. The exception is that since the closing entry (17) is excluded from the worksheet procedure, the owners' equity figure in the adjusted trial balance is the beginning-of-period figure. To this figure must be added the net effect of closing the temporary accounts (that is, the net income or loss of the period) to arrive at the appropriate ending balance sheet amount. In this case $70,000 in net income is added to the beginning balance of $150,000 to get the appropriate ending balance of $220,000. This demonstrates very clearly that the financial statements in Exhibits 7-7 and 7-8 could have been prepared from

Exhibit 7-10

FANCY FLAVORS, INC.

Trial Balance and Financial Statement Worksheet
August 31, 19XX

Account Name	Unadjusted Trial Balance DR	Unadjusted Trial Balance CR	Adjustments DR	Adjustments CR	Adjusted Trial Balance DR	Adjusted Trial Balance CR
Cash	210,000				210,000	
Accounts receivable	50,000				50,000	
Prepaid rent	60,000			20,000(13)	40,000	
Ice cream inventory	165,000			145,000(11)	20,000	
Supplies inventory	30,000			15,000(12)	15,000	
Equipment	600,000				600,000	
Accumulated depreciation		-0-		10,000(14)		10,000
Accounts payable and accrued liabilities		75,000		30,000(15, 16)		105,000
Bank loan		600,000				600,000
Owners' equity		150,000				150,000
Sales (owners' equity)		450,000				450,000
Salary and wages expense (owners' equity)	150,000				150,000	
Miscellaneous expense (owners' equity)	10,000				10,000	
Cost of ice cream sold (owners' equity)	-0-		145,000(11)		145,000	
Cost of supplies used (owners' equity)	-0-		15,000(12)		15,000	
Rent expense (owners' equity)	-0-		20,000(13)		20,000	
Depreciation expense (owners' equity)	-0-		10,000(14)		10,000	
Interest expense (owners' equity)	-0-		6,000(15)		6,000	
Income tax expense (owners' equity)	-0-		24,000(16)		24,000	
Total	1,275,000	1,275,000	220,000	220,000	1,315,000	1,315,000

the worksheet in Exhibit 7-10 just as readily as by literally going through the full process of making adjusting and closing entries to the general ledger accounts themselves.

THE FINANCIAL ACCOUNTING DATA-PROCESSING SYSTEM

Accounting Data Gathering and Processing

In the introduction to this chapter we noted that although general ledger bookkeeping overcomes some of the limitations of the single financial position worksheet approach of Chapter 4, both of these systems for recording transactions data tend to be applied to summary data only. The source of such summary data is the process used by the business enterprise to record, store, control, and summarize data about individual transactions or events that should be ultimately reflected in the financial statements. Such processes are facilitated by systems, called data-processing systems, consisting of the following components:

1. *Source documents.* Source documents are used to record data about individual transactions and other events (within the business) as they take place. An example is a sales invoice that records a sale to a customer; the sales invoice contains details such as the customer's name, the customer's order number, the description and quantity of goods shipped, the prices of the goods shipped, the total amount paid or to be paid by the customer, the terms of the sale (cash or credit), and the date of shipment. Other examples of source documents are purchase orders, labor time cards, and suppliers' invoices.

2. *Subsidiary journals or registers.* Subsidiary journals or registers are records on which transaction data contained on source documents are entered in some kind of order (usually chronologically) and periodically summarized (daily, weekly or monthly) for purposes of recognition within the general ledger bookkeeping system. An example of a subsidiary journal is the sales journal, which is usually a multicolumn, multipage book (or computer printout) showing the details of successive sales transactions as originally recorded on sales invoices. In the typical sales journal there is one column in which the total amount of each sale is recorded, followed by a column to record cash received and a column to record additions to accounts receivable for credit sales. When these columns (and others such as "sales discounts" where applicable) are summed for a week or a month they provide the summary data for a *general journal* entry of the form:

Cash	XXXX	
Accounts Receivable	XXXX	
Sales revenue		XXXX
To record weekly/monthly sales		

Other examples of subsidiary journals or registers are the cash receipts and cash disbursements journals, the purchases journal, and the payroll register.

3. *Subsidiary ledger accounts.* Subsidiary ledger accounts are records of individual components of certain of a company's asset, liability, and owners' equity accounts. An example of a subsidiary ledger is the set of accounts receivable from individual customers. Customer A's account, for instance, would be debited for the total amount of invoices representing new shipments to Customer A and credited for cash receipts or returned goods from Customer A. One obvious nonfinancial accounting application of subsidiary ledger accounts is control and management of assets such as accounts receivable. Other examples of subsidiary ledgers are the inventory ledger (cards), the accounts payable ledger, and the shareholders' ledger (of corporations).

4. *Standardized procedures.* Procedures must be specified such that all transaction data are accurately recorded by the appropriate employee at the time the transaction takes place. The procedures must also give reasonable assurance that all valid (and only valid) transaction data are subsequently recorded and accurately summarized in the accounting records.

Exhibit 7-11 is a schematic representation of the relationships and flows of information within the overall financial accounting system, including the data-gathering and processing dimension as well as general ledger bookkeeping. Once the symbols are explained (a key is given in Exhibit 7-12) the schematic, or flowchart (as such displays are often called), is largely self-explanatory. However, we would like to make a few observations about Exhibit 7-11. For instance, the total surface of the schematic is separated by dashed lines into broad categories of activity or function. Dashes are used to convey the point that the separation of such functions is not or should not be very rigid within actual businesses. The flow begins at the upper left with the actual business operations that ultimately are to be reflected in financial statements. At their points of physical execution, transactions and other relevant events must be recorded by employees lest these events take place unnoticed by the formal accounting process.

Source documents appear on the boundary between the "business operations" and "accounting data gathering and processing" functions because they are as essential to the control of the operations of the business as they are to the accounting system. We will have more to say on this point later. Within the accounting system the data from source documents are recorded in subsidiary journals and posted to subsidiary ledger accounts. The source documents themselves are then filed for possible future reference in the event of error or for periodic tests (known as audits) of the correspondence between what appears in the company's financial statements and actual underlying transaction data.

At regular intervals the transaction data recorded in the subsidiary journals are summarized and the totals are entered into the general journal in journal entry format. From that point on the general ledger bookkeeping system takes over and functions as described in the preceding section of the chapter. As a final observation, however, note the dashed arrow in the flowchart, connecting

Exhibit 7-11

THE DATA FLOWS IN A FINANCIAL ACCOUNTING INFORMATION SYSTEM

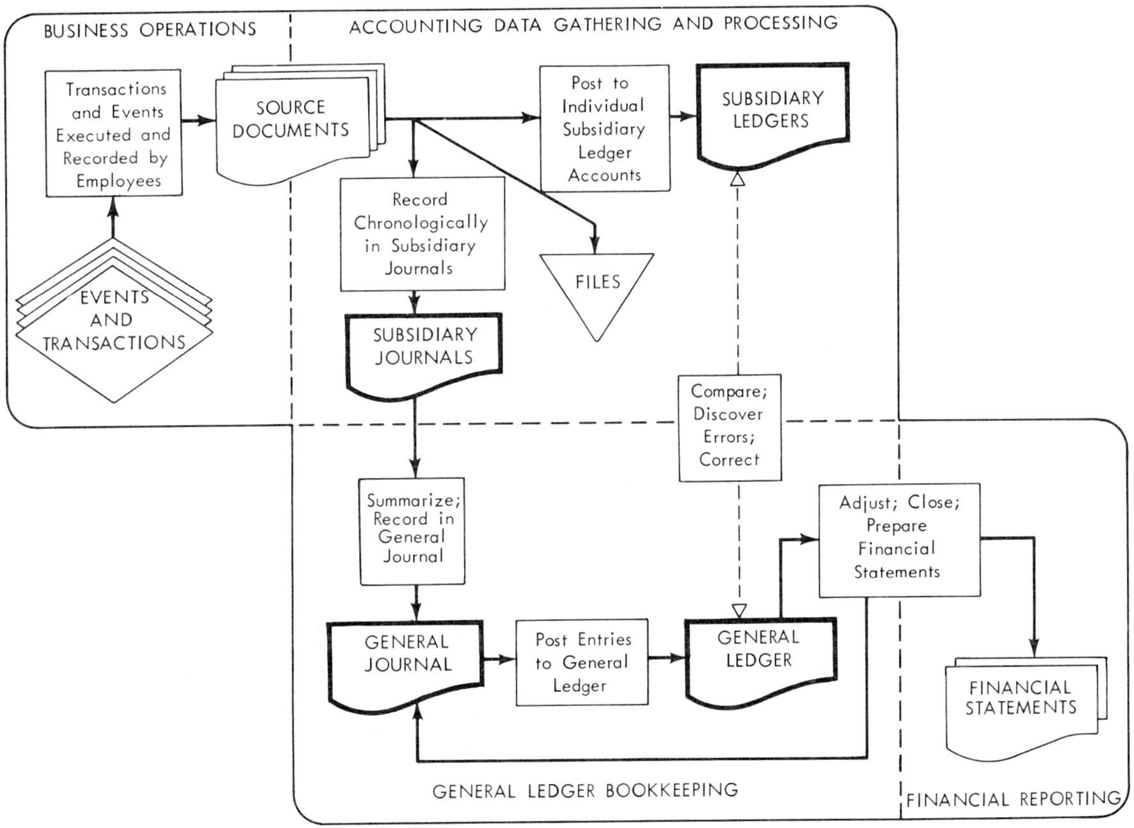

Exhibit 7-12

KEY TO FLOWCHART SYMBOLS

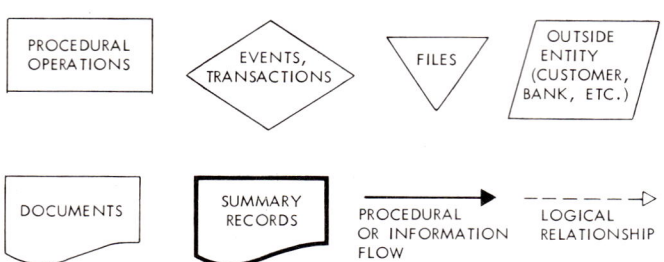

the general ledger and subsidiary ledgers. The same transaction data are (1) posted to individual subsidiary ledger accounts and (2) recorded in subsidiary journals, summarized, entered in the general journal, and posted to the general ledger. Therefore at any given date (if all transaction data have been fully recorded throughout the system), the sum of the balances in a given set of subsidiary ledger accounts (for example, the individual accounts receivable) should equal the balance in the corresponding general leadger account (accounts receivable). If it does not, an error is indicated. Therefore comparisons of subsidiary and general ledger balances represent important checks for accuracy within the system.

Accounting Subsystems and Related Operations

Along with understanding how accounting data gathering and processing relates to general ledger bookkeeping, it is also important to understand how data gathering and processing works within the structure of the business both to capture relevant information and to aid in the management and control of a company. All but the smallest companies find it convenient (efficient and effective) to divide their total financial accounting system into parts called subsystems. Moreover, there are certain natural divisions that center on sets of interrelated transactions and events that satisfy specific operational needs as well as accounting needs. Thus accounting subsystems and procedures tend to correspond to and are integrated with the operating subsystems and procedures of the business. A reasonable (perhaps typical) set of subsystems for moderate to large businesses that buy (or produce) products for sale to customers is as follows:

1. *The Sales and Collections Subsystem* is concerned with such things as filling customers' orders (or authorizing shipment); ensuring that only authorized sales are made (that is, to approved customers with ability to pay); accurately recording all valid sales (and only *valid* sales) and related accounts receivable; maintaining accurate customer accounts; collecting cash from customers and securely depositing it in the bank; and accurately recording all cash receipts and crediting the correct customer accounts.

2. *The Acquisitions and Payment Subsystem* is concerned with such things as placing orders for all authorized resource needs other than personnel; ensuring that acquisitions are received; accurately recording all valid liabilities arising from acquisitions; authorizing payment for *bona fide* (and only *bona fide*) acquisitions; remitting payments; and accurately debiting the appropriate liability accounts.

3. *The Payroll Subsystem* is integrated with both mainline operations and the personnel function and is concerned with such things as accurately recording labor costs in periods in which they are incurred; accurately calculating each employee's gross and net pay, payroll taxes, and fringe benefits; accurately assessing related employer payroll taxes, insurance premiums, pension contributions; properly recording all related liabilities (including wages payable); paying all such liabilities on a timely basis; and debiting the appropriate liability accounts when paid.

4. *The Inventory/Warehousing Subsystem* is concerned with such things as safeguarding the raw materials, work-in-process, and finished goods inventories; releasing materials for authorized uses within the company and appropriately deducting them from records of materials on hand; releasing finished goods for authorized deliveries (shipments) to customers and recording reductions in goods on hand; receiving, inspecting, and accurately recording purchases; periodically checking inventory records against physical counts of quantities on hand; periodically summarizing and recording costs of materials on hand (used), costs of work-in-process on hand (transferred to finished goods), and costs of finished goods on hand (sold).

5. *The Capital Acquisition and Repayment Subsystem* relates primarily to the long-term financing of the business and is concerned with such things as accurately recording capital contributed by owners and proceeds of borrowings from lenders; maintaining accurate shareholder records, dividends payable ledgers, bonds payable ledgers, etc.; accurately recording interest expense in the proper period; and timely payment of interest and principal on debts and dividends declared and payable (to the "owners of record").

From the accounting perspective, each of the above subsystems is made up of the four components mentioned earlier. That is, they all are made up of source documents, subsidiary journals, subsidiary ledgers, and sets of procedures tying the rest of the components together and integrating them with the operations of the business. In order to make such subsystem components work properly, one must be reasonably well acquainted with the discipline of *systems design*. However, the degree of sophistication required to actually design practical accounting systems is beyond the scope of this book. At the same time, some insight into the systems design dimension is helpful in understanding how the total financial accounting system works. To gain this insight we have provided an overview of the components and procedures in a fairly typical credit sales and collections subsystem in Exhibit 7-13.

The flowchart in Exhibit 7-13 is laid out in conventional fashion, with functional areas set out across the top, within-function activities flowing downward under the appropriate functional heading, and between-function flows of documents and procedures moving generally from left to right. Exhibit 7-13 uses the same symbols as those used in Exhibit 7-11 (explained in Exhibit 7-12) and is generally self-explanatory. For convenience and to prevent unnecessary crowding of the diagram, references to document files are omitted.

A careful study of Exhibit 7-13 will give the reader a general idea of how any accounting subsystem integrates with its related operations. An important thing to note in Exhibit 7-13 is how most source documents have operational (as well as accounting) functions and are originated by outside entities (for example, customers' orders) or operational employees (for example, bills of lading originated at shipment). Another important observation is how source documents (1) flow from operation to operation helping maintain or trigger proper procedures and (2) eventually flow into the sphere of the accounting function to serve as the basis for recording the transactions or other activities to which they relate.

An example is the flow of documents in the order-filling-billing-sales-recording sequence which the reader can trace starting in the left column of Exhibit 7-13. The customer order is either received by or written up in the sales department. It represents the customer's legal offer to buy. The order is transmitted to the credit department where it triggers an appropriate credit check. If the credit check is positive, the order is approved (the company is willing to make the sale). Approval is *noted on the order,* and the order is transmitted to the shipping department for which the approved sales order represents *authorization* to release or ship goods to the customer. The shipping department, in turn, prepares a bill of lading, one copy of which is shipped with the goods as a packing slip so that the customer will recognize the order when received. Other copies go to the billing department along with the approved sales order as evidence that the company has filled the order. For the billing department these documents indicate that the company has a *bona fide* claim against the customer for the price of the goods, and a multicopy sales invoice noting all the details of the sale is prepared. One copy of the invoice along with a second copy of the bill of lading is sent to the customer as notification of shipment and assertion of the claim to the account receivable. The other copies, along with the approved order and a copy of the bill of lading, go to the accounting and accounts receivable departments to stimulate (and provide documentation for) the recording of the sale and the related increase in the customer account. Once this recording of the basic transaction data takes place it is processed as described earlier, that is, it flows from the subsidiary records into the general ledger bookkeeping process.

Recap of the Financial Accounting Information System

In the first section of this chapter we developed the essentials of the general ledger bookkeeping system, the practical counterpart to the financial position worksheet. Although the effects of all transactions and events of a given period on financial position and net income cannot be represented visually as completely as with the worksheet tableau, general ledger bookkeeping can be used effectively in practical business applications where the numbers of accounts, transactions, and events are more than trivial.

Exhibit 7-13

OVERVIEW FLOWCHART OF A CREDIT SALES AND COLLECTIONS SUBSYSTEM

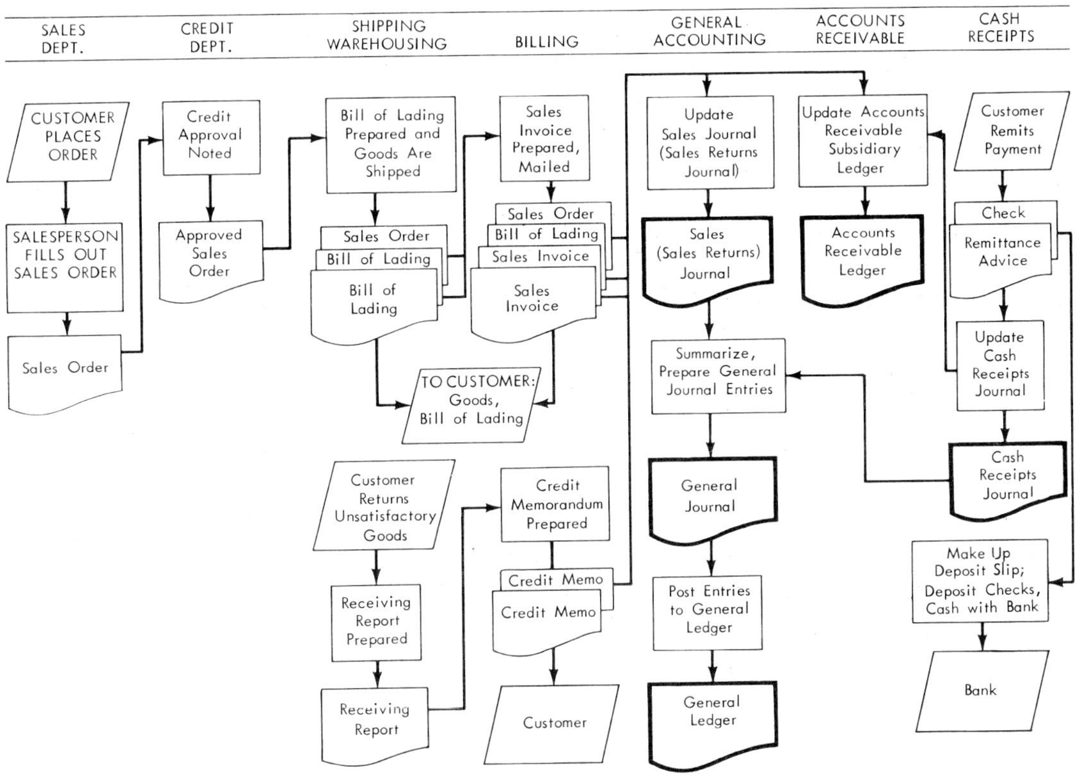

At the same time, general ledger bookeeping still operates only with summary transactions data in most applications. In order to understand the financial accounting system it is therefore necessary to understand accounting data gathering and processing which utilizes source documents, subsidiary journals, subsidiary ledgers, and coordinating procedures to capture store, control, summarize, and feed transaction data into the general ledger bookkeeping process.

For convenience, efficiency, and effectiveness the data-gathering and processing dimension is split up into subsystems along functional lines such as sales-collections, acquisitions-payments, and payroll. The kind of document flows and procedures described above for integrating the accounting sales and collection subsystem with the operational order-filling-through-collection sequence is repeated in all the other subsystems. We therefore need not describe all the subsystems in detail for the reader to gain sufficient insight for our purposes.

To complete the reader's awareness of the broader dimensions of the financial accounting system, we offer in Exhibit 7-14 a schematic design of the major subsystems mentioned earlier as they relate to the general ledger bookkeeping process. In the block depicting each subsystem are listed the documents and records that are typically employed within that subsystem. As in Exhibit 7-11, the solid lines represent the flow of summary transaction data from the subsidiary journals of each subsystem to the general journal. The dashed lines represent the logical (equality) relationship between the sum of subsidiary ledger balances and the balance in the related general ledger account balance.

Questions for Review and Discussion

7-1. Define:
   a. General journal
   b. General ledger
   c. Posting
   d. Temporary account
   e. Adjusting entry
   f. Closing entry
   g. Accruals
   h. Accounting cycle
   i. Dr-Cr convention
   j. Subsidiary journal
   k. Subsidiary ledger
   l. Source document
   m. Trial balance

7-2. State concisely the objectives of a financial accounting information system. How does such a system differ from other data-processing systems, for example, those relating to traffic tickets, university course grades, social security payments?

7-3. What three elements constitute a typical accounting journal entry?

7-4. List twenty general ledger account titles (including temporary accounts) that might be found in the accounting system of a large department store.

Exhibit 7-14

SCHEMATIC OF A FINANCIAL ACCOUNTING SYSTEM

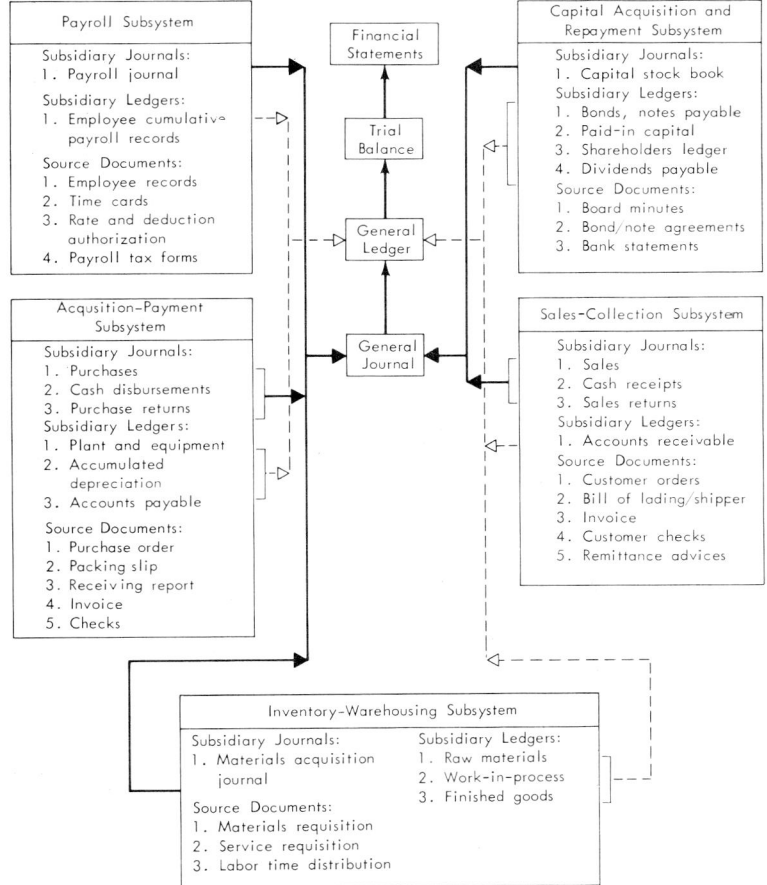

7-5. Distinguish between a permanent general ledger account and a temporary account.

7-6. Why are closing entries required? What accounts are normally affected by closing entries?

7-7. What distinguishes a subsidiary journal from the general journal?

7-8. List the advantages and disadvantages of the Dr-Cr convention of traditional bookkeeping.

7-9. Explain the reason behind the often quoted bookkeepers' maxim that debits must equal credits.

7-10. List the components of the accounting data processing system. What relationship does the data-gathering and processing system bear to general ledger bookkeeping?

7-11. Explain the role of source documents in accounting data gathering and processing. In business operations.

7-12. Distinguish between subsidiary ledgers and the general ledger. What relationship exists between these two types of accounting records?

7-13. Explain the advantages of the trial balance as a tool for preparing financial statements.

Exercises

7-1. **Making Journal Entries.** Refer to the external transactions listed in Exercise 4-11. Set up a general journal as illustrated in Exhibit 7-5 and record these transactions in journal entry fashion.

7-2. **Making Transaction and Adjusting Journal Entries.** Several transactions and events are described in Exercise 4-20. Set up a general journal as illustrated in Exhibit 7-5 and analyze and record the transactions described. Also make appropriate adjusting entries, distinguishing them from transaction entries.

7-3. **Dr-Cr Analysis.** Since the accounting equation has only three elements, there can be no more than nine possible *pairwise* changes of equation elements. For each of the following changes, specify a corresponding business event or transaction that could give rise to it:
1. Dr Asset = Cr Liability
2. Dr Asset = Cr Asset
3. Dr Asset = Cr Owners' equity
4. Dr Liability = Cr Asset
5. Dr Liability = Cr Liability
6. Dr Liability = Cr Owners' equity
7. Dr Owners' equity = Cr Asset
8. Dr Owners' equity = Cr Liability
9. Dr Owners' equity = Cr Owners' equity

7-4. **General Ledger Bookkeeping Cycle.** Refer to Exercise 4-8. Set up a general journal format like the one in Exhibit 7-5 and general ledger accounts in T-account format.

Required:

1. Record the listed transactions.

2. Make any necessary adjusting entries.

3. Post all entries to individual general ledger accounts. Use T-Account format.

4. Prepare an income statement for the Record Center for the month of July.

5. Prepare an entry to close the temporary accounts.

6. Prepare a balance sheet as of the end of July.

7-5. Account Analysis. The inventory account of Schilthorn Enterprises has a Dr balance of $32,000 at 12/31/X4. During the 19X4 accounting cycle, *a closing entry* was made debiting $142,000 to cost of goods sold (owners' equity). Inventory transactions during 19X4 included:
1. Purchases of $145,000 of inventory.
2. A Cr of $6,000 to the inventory account because some unacceptable items were returned to a supplier.
3. A Dr entry of $12,000 to the account because some inventories were discovered in a warehouse which had not been included in the 12/31/X3 inventory count.

Required:

Determine the 1/1/X4 beginning balance in the inventory account of Schilthorn Enterprises. Support your calculations.

7-6. Account Analysis and Closing Entry. The owners' equity account of Luft Corporation had credit balances of $830,000 on 1/1/X4 and of $785,000 on 12/31/X4 after closing entries had been made. Net sales revenue for the year 19X4 was $1.85 million and $25,000 in dividends was paid. Except for operating expenses and the foregoing events, no other items affected owners' equity during 19X4.

Required:

1. Calculate total operating expenses of Luft Corporation for 19X4.

2. On a Dr-Cr basis, make the appropriate closing entry as of 12/31/X4, using the information available to you. (*Hint:* Assume that only one temporary account was used to accumulate all expenses of the period.)

7-7. The General Ledger Bookkeeping Cycle. The financial statements of the NJW Art Shop at November 30, 19X4, follow:

NJW ART SHOP

Statement of Financial Position
As of November 30, 19X4

Cash	$ 4,200			
Accounts receivable	2,000	Accounts payable		$ 1,800
Merchandise inventory	4,000	Accrued salaries payable		200
Fixtures	3,500	Owners' equity:		
Accumulated depreciation—		Balance, January 1	$2,000	
Fixtures	(1,000)	Net income for		
Prepaid rent	300	eleven months	9,000	11,000
	$13,000			$13,000

NJW ART SHOP

Income Statement
For November 19X4 and Eleven Months Ended November 30, 19X4

	Month of November 19X4	Eleven Months Ended November 30, 19X4
Sales	$4,500	$51,000
Expenses:		
Cost of merchandise sold	$2,300	$26,000
Salaries expense	900	10,450
Rent expense	300	3,300
Advertising expense	150	1,700
Depreciation expense	50	550
	$3,700	$42,000
Net (operating) income	$ 800	$ 9,000

The NJW Art Shop engaged in the following transactions in December:

Dec. 2   Purchased frames (inventory) on account for $1,500.

Dec. 5   Paid salaries (including those accrued at the end of November) of $350.

Dec. 7   Paid $200 for a special Christmas advertising supplement put out by the local Junior Achievement.

Dec. 10 Collected $1,500 on account.

Dec. 15 Recorded sales for the first half of the month: cash sales, $4,000; credit sales, $1,000.

Dec. 15 Paid salaries of $500.

Dec. 17 Paid $2,200 to suppliers.

Dec. 18 Purchased art supplies (inventory) for $1,000 cash.

Dec. 24 Paid salaries of $800.

Dec. 28 Collected $1,200 on account.

Dec. 30 Paid $150 for advertising in the local newspaper for the month.

Dec. 31 Paid rent in advance for the first six months of 19X5, $1,800.

Dec. 31 Recorded sales for the last half of the month: cash sales, $5,000; credit sales, $800.

The information for the end-of-period adjustments follows:
   a. When the fixtures were purchased, it was estimated that they

would have a five-year life and a salvage value at the end of the five years of $500.
   b. The prepaid rent at the end of November was for the month of December.
   c. The cost of merchandise (frames and other art supplies) on hand at the end of December was $1,500.
   d. As of December 31, the total earned but unpaid wages amounted to $100.

Required:

1. Assuming the temporary (revenue and expense) accounts are only closed to owners' equity at the end of the calendar year, construct a general ledger (set of T-accounts) for NJW Art Shop with appropriate balances as of November 30, 19X4. (Note: The balance of the owners' equity account will be a credit of $2,000, since the temporary accounts have not yet been closed to it.)

2. Record the transactions for December in a general journal, and post them to the general ledger.

3. Record the end-of-period adjustments in the general journal, and post them to the general ledger.

4. Prepare an income statement for the month of December 19X4 and for the year ended December 31, 19X4.

5. Record a closing entry in the general journal, and post it to the general ledger.

6. Prepare a statement of financial position as of December 31, 19X4.

7-8. The General Ledger Bookkeeping Cycle. The financial statements of the Modern Sound Shop at November 30, 19X5, follow:

MODERN SOUND SHOP
Statement of Financial Position
As of November 30, 19X5

Cash		$ 12,000
Accounts receivable		5,000
Records and tapes		65,000
Furniture and fixtures		30,000
Accumulated depreciation—		
Furniture and fixtures		(6,000)
Prepaid rent		8,000
		$114,000
Accounts payable		$ 10,000
Accrued salaries payable		5,000
Owners' equity:		
Balance, January 1	$40,000	
Net income for		
eleven months	59,000	99,000
		$114,000

MODERN SOUND SHOP

Income Statement
For November 19X5 and Eleven Months Ended November 30, 19X5

	Month of November 19X5	*Eleven Months Ended November 30, 19X5*
Sales	$60,000	$720,000
Expenses:		
Cost of sales	$40,000	$480,000
Salaries expense	10,000	126,000
Rent expense	4,000	44,000
Advertising expense	1,000	8,250
Depreciation expense	250	2,750
	$55,250	$661,000
Net (operating) income	$ 4,750	$ 59,000

The modern Sound Shop engaged in the following transactions in December:

- Dec. 3   Paid $2,000 for advertising in the local paper for the month.
- Dec. 4   Received a special order of records and tapes for the Christmas season. The total cost was $32,000 (purchased on account).
- Dec. 5   Paid salaries accrued at the end of November. (The pay period is semimonthly; however, salaries are not paid until five days after the end of each pay period.)
- Dec. 12   Collected $4,500 on account.
- Dec. 15   Recorded sales for the first half of the month—cash sales, $40,000; credit sales, $2,000.
- Dec. 20   Paid salaries of $6,000 for the 12/1–12/15 pay period.
- Dec. 20   Paid $10,000 to suppliers.
- Dec. 21   Paid $1,000 for spot advertising over a local radio station.
- Dec. 31   Recorded sales for the last half of the month—cash sales, $44,000; credit sales, $4,000.

The information for the end-of-period adjustments follows.
  a. The cost of records and tapes on hand at 12/31/X5 was $36,000.
  b. Salaries for the 12/16–12/31 pay period totaled $6,500.
  c. The prepaid rent at the end of November was for December and January.
  d. The original estimated life of the furniture and fixtures was ten years; the salvage value was estimated to be zero.

Required:

1. Construct a general ledger (set of T-accounts) for the Modern Sound Shop with appropriate balances as of November 30, 19X5. Assume that the revenue and expense accounts are closed to owners' equity only at the end of the calendar year.

2. Record the transactions for December 19X5 in a general journal, and post them to the general ledger.

3. Record the end-of-period adjustments in the general journal, and post them to the general ledger.

4. Prepare an income statement for the month of December 19X5 and the year ended December 31, 19X5.

5. Record a closing entry in the general journal, and post it to the general ledger.

6. Prepare a statement of financial position as of December 31, 19X5.

7-9. **Making Adjusting Entries.** For each of the following *independent* situations, prepare a journal entry or entries to record appropriate end-of-period adjustments. Record all entries, using the Dr-Cr general journal format. Select descriptive account titles; however, it is not necessary to follow all temporary owners' equity accounts with the caption "Owners' Equity." Assume that December 31 is the end of the accounting period and that no previous adjustments have been made during the year unless otherwise specified.

1. The inventory on January 1 totaled $35,000. Purchases of inventory during the year totaled $200,000. The inventory on hand at December 31 totaled $25,000.

2. Rent was prepaid for four months on November 1. The total amount of the prepayment was $2,000. Rent payments for months prior to November have already been debited to the appropriate owners' equity temporary account.

3. Equipment costing $10,000 and having an estimated life of five years with $1,000 salvage value was purchased on January 1. The company uses the straight-line method for calculating depreciation.

4. The supplies inventory on January 1 totaled $4,000. Purchases of supplies during the year totaled $8,000. Calculations at year-end showed that $7,000 of supplies were consumed during the year.

5. A monthly magazine publisher received ten thousand annual subscriptions at $12 each, totaling $120,000 during the year. The liability account "subscription deposits" was credited upon receipt of the subscriptions; cash was debited. For five thousand of the subscriptions, eight issues were mailed during the year. For the remaining five thousand subscriptions, six issues were mailed.

6. On January 1 a company had wages payable of $10,000. During the year it paid employees $200,000. However, just before

year-end employees had earned $11,500 of wages as yet not paid.

7-10. Preparing Financial Statements from a Trial Balance. Exhibit 7-15 is the December 31, 19X8, *unadjusted* trial balance drawn up from the balances in the general ledger accounts of THW Corporation. All transactions for the year 19X8 and adjusting entries for the first three fiscal quarters had been recorded before drawing up the trial balance. THW Corporation follows the practice of making quarterly and year-end adjustments on a financial statement worksheet (see Exhibit 7-10) before actually making adjusting entries in the general journal and posting to the general ledger and (annually only) closing its temporary accounts. Its quarterly and annual financial statements are prepared from the worksheets.

Exhibit 7-15

THW CORPORATION

Unadjusted Trial Balance
December 31, 19X8

Account	Dr	Cr
Cash	400,000	
Accounts receivable	900,000	
Inventories	750,000	
Prepaid expenses	90,000	
Buildings and equipment	2,000,000	
Accumulated depreciation		700,000
Land	1,000,000	
Accounts payable		750,000
Interest payable		-0-
Wages payable		-0-
Taxes payable		-0-
Bank loan		1,500,000
Paid-in capital		1,000,000
Retained earnings (balance 12/31/X7)		275,000
Revenues		5,000,000
Cost of sales	1,400,000	
Wages and salaries expense	2,200,000	
Depreciation expense	300,000	
Interest expense	135,000	
Income tax expense	50,000	
	9,225,000	9,225,000

Information on which December 31, 19X8, adjusting entries are to be based is as follows:
1. A physical count and subsequent pricing (from purchase invoices) indicate that inventory costing $350,000 is actually on hand at December 31.
2. The December payroll (not yet included in expense), totaling $200,000, will not be paid until the end of the first week in January 19X9.

3. Depreciation expense is recognized at $400,000 *per year* on a straight-line basis. The first three quarters' depreciation has already been recognized.
4. Interest is payable at 12 percent *per year* in four installments, on the first days of January, April, July and October, on the bank loan of $1.5 million.
5. Income tax expense for the year as a whole is estimated to be $82,000. Three quarterly installments totalling $50,000 had been paid through December 31.

Required:

1. Prepare a trial balance and financial statement worksheet as of December 31, 19X8, for THW Corporation (see Exhibit 7-10) and enter the unadjusted balances given in Exhibit 7-15.
2. Make the necessary adjustments in "adjustment" columns and derive an adjusted trial balance.
3. Prepare an income statement for 19X8 and a statement of financial position as of December 31, 19X8, for THW Corporation.
4. Write the general journal entry that would properly close the temporary accounts of THW Corporation as of December 31, 19X8, assuming that *all* adjusting entries have already been posted to the general ledger accounts.

7-11. Preparing Financial Statements from a Trial Balance. The December 31, 19X6, unadjusted trial balance of Trigor Corporation is shown in Exhibit 7-16. It is drawn up from the corporation's general ledger account balances prior to adjusting entries. The corporation follows the practice of preparing year-to-date financial statements monthly using a trial balance and financial statement worksheet. After the financial statements are prepared each month, the adjustments in the worksheet are entered into the general journal and posted to the general ledger accounts. Therefore at the end of the year all that is required to prepare financial statements for the year are adjustments for December.

Information on which December adjustments are to be based is as follows:

1. A physical count (and pricing) of inventory showed that inventory costing $450,000 was actually on hand at December 31, 19X6.
2. Wages and salaries totaling $250,000 for the last two weeks of December would not be paid until January 19X7. They had not yet been recognized as expenses at December 31.
3. The unadjusted prepaid expenses balance consists of three months' rent ($300,000) and three months' insurance ($60,000), each paid on December 1 and due to expire on February 28, 19X7.
4. Depreciation on the equipment is recognized monthly on a straight-line basis and an assumed useful life of ten years and zero salvage value.
5. Interest expense on the bank loan is recognized at 1 percent per

month—with the next quarterly payment of $66,000 due on February 1, 19X7.

6. Income tax expense for December 19X6 is estimated to be $20,000.

Exhibit 7-16

TRIGOR CORPORATION

Unadjusted Trial Balance
December 31, 19X6

Account	Dr	Cr
Cash	450,000	
Accounts receivable	1,050,000	
Inventories	900,000	
Prepaid expenses	360,000	
Equipment	3,000,000	
Accumulated depreciation		575,000
Accounts payable		250,000
Wages and salaries payable		-0-
Interest payable		22,000
Taxes payable		32,000
Bank loan		2,200,000
Paid-in capital		1,000,000
Retained earnings		504,000
Revenue		9,500,000
Cost of goods sold	3,000,000	
Wages and salaries expense	3,300,000	
Rent expense	1,100,000	
Insurance expense	220,000	
Depreciation expense	275,000	
Interest expense	242,000	
Income tax expense	186,000	
	14,083,000	14,083,000

Required:

1. Prepare a combined trial balance and financial statement worksheet as of December 31, 19X6, for Trigor Corporation (see Exhibit 7-10) and enter the unadjusted balances from Exhibit 7-16.

2. Make the necessary adjustments on the worksheet and derive an adjusted trial balance.

3. Prepare an income statement for 19X6 and a December 31, 19X6, statement of financial position for Trigor.

4. Write journal entries to correspond to your adjustments in number 2.

5. Write a general journal entry to close Trigor's *adjusted* temporary accounts at December 31, 19X6.

CONVENTIONAL ACCOUNTING MEASUREMENT ISSUES

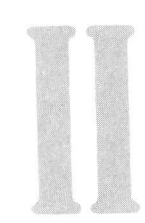

Revenue Recognition 8

Chapters 8 through 12 provide readers with additional exposure to the fundamentals of conventional accounting. We generally introduce this model as the basis of present-day financial accounting practices in Chapter 3. Chapter 4 elaborates the rudimentary ideas of conventional financial accounting and demonstrates the essentials of its most basic products—the statement of financial position and the income statement. Then, in Chapter 5, some additional aspects of conventional accounting income determination are developed and illustrated. Chapter 6 expands the framework to the analysis of enterprise resource flows and the related statement of changes in financial position. Chapter 7 describes the workings of the conventional financial accounting information system, which captures, classifies, and summarizes the data upon which the entire system is based. In this fashion the fundamental concepts, records, and outputs of financial accounting are brought into focus and readied for expansion and elaboration.

In the five chapters beginning with Chapter 8, we add enough "fine tuning" to operationalize the conventional financial accounting model for application to the great bulk of business situations found in the United States economy. Chapters 8 and 9 deal with concepts of revenue recognition and the accounting process needed to achieve such recognition. Similarly, Chapters 10 and 11 cover many of the considerations associated with the "expense side" of business income measurement. A number of selected special periodic income determination issues are addressed in Chapter 12.

As we begin the consideration of revenue we are reminded that a fundamental aim of financial accounting for business enterprises is the determination of periodic net income. At the end of Chapter 3 we indicate the importance of the way revenues and expenses are measured by stating that "net operating income is the arithmetic difference between recognized revenues and expenses."

To set the scene, the discussion of revenue and expense recognition starts with a review of the broad financial accounting concepts into which the entire business income measurement activity must fit. We also provide a synopsis of the relevant financial accounting policy formulation aspects.

REVIEW OF BASIC CONCEPTS

The Basic Premise: Information for Decision Making

Accounting is a field of knowledge that is concerned with *information* that is useful for a broad spectrum of decision making. The usefulness of information of various types, including accounting information, stems basically from the existence of scarce resources. In order to allocate these resources to achieve his goals, the decision maker (whether a business manager, a government official, or someone acting on his own behalf) seeks information that will enable him to understand and better predict the possible outcomes of various alternative courses of action (and the likelihood of their occurrence).

Accounting as an Information Specialization

The character of the information required for a particular decision is obviously a function of the type of decision problem confronting the decision maker. Where a group of decision makers with similar decision problems exists in society, information specialists tend to appear. Information specialists are individuals who devote their resources to producing (or providing others with the means to produce) decision-relevant information for others' use. Three conditions are necessary for specialization in information: (1) there must exist a class (or classes) of decision makers with common decision problems; (2) there must be identifiable kinds of decision-relevant information of value in solving these problems; and (3) one must become proficient in applying a specialized body of knowledge or expertise to produce efficiently and effectively the information relevant to the common class (or classes) of problems. Recognizing the way in which these conditions are satisfied for accounting as an information specialization serving decision makers external to the enterprise provides an important perspective on financial accounting.

Decision Problems Concerning the Business Enterprise

One way of identifying common classes of decision makers with common decision problems is to focus on particular types of organizational entities. Although accounting information has a role in decision problems revolving around many different types of organizations, as is pointed out in Chapter 1, we have chosen to place major emphasis in this book on the role of accounting in supplying information to several of the classes of decision makers concerned with the *business enterprise.*

A number of types of users of information about the business enterprise are identified in Chapter 1, including owners, creditors, suppliers, management, taxing authorities, employees, and customers. While each of these groups has special decision problems that benefit from accounting information, it is useful in the study of accounting to combine them into two groups, internal and external, according to how their individual decisions relate to the business enterprise. The emphasis of this book is on *accounting for the business enterprise for external parties.*

Classes of External Decisions. The decision interests of external users of information about the business enterprise can be divided into two important classes: (1) investment decisions and (2) decisions concerning the distribution of the current benefits from the operations of the enterprise.

Investment decisions involve selecting opportunities to exchange present resources (wealth) for rights to resources in the future (also wealth)—generally with the objective of maximizing wealth. The external parties who are concerned with business enterprises as investment alternatives (principally present and prospective owners and creditors) are called *investors.*

Decisions concerning the *distribution of the current benefits* from the operations of the enterprise focus on the ability of the firm to distribute money or other resources to parties with an interest in it, and the equity of the distributions that are made. Included in the class of interested parties are present owners, creditors, taxing authorities, and employees (particularly collective groups of employees).

Decision-Relevant Accounting Information

The kinds of decision-relevant information that accountants might provide are defined by the class of decision makers under consideration (external decision makers) and the classes of decision problems of interest to them. We introduced the net present value model in Chapter 2 as a means of describing the nature of investment decisions and as a simplified model for choosing among investment alternatives.

Financial Accounting Information for Investment Decisions. From the possession of goods and the use of services, individuals derive satisfactions that are multidimensional and unique to each individual. However, it is characteristic of investment decisions that the money equivalent of goods and services serves as a substitute for other forms of satisfactions. This follows from the role of money in a market economy as a general means of acquiring the goods and services one desires. Given this role of money, it follows that the information for investment decisions can be structured in terms of the *money flows* that are expected to result from various decision alternatives.

Because an amount of money possessed today is typically more valuable to the individual than possession of an equal amount of funds at some later date, it is necessary to develop a mechanism that takes into account timing differences in money flows. The present value model serves as the means of making such adjustments. Through the use of present value methodology, the decision maker (in a hypothetical world of certainty) can choose between two or more alternative courses of action involving cash flows that differ in amounts and timing.

However, in an uncertain world the valuation of alternate cash flows involves more than adjustments for their differential timing alone. Most individuals are not indifferent to different levels of risk (i.e., the potential that less-than-expected cash flows will actually be forthcoming from an investment opportunity). For the typical risk-averse individual a more risky alternative has less value per unit of *expected* cash flow than a less risky alternative. This principle can be incorporated into the simplified present value model by using certainty equivalents to represent uncertain future cash flows (which is one of several risk-adjustment techniques compatible with the simplified present value model).

While our earlier discussion of these *simplified* approaches to investment decisions is definitely only intended to brush the surface, it does permit us to infer that individuals faced with investment decisions are likely to be interested in the amount, timing, and riskiness of future cash flows.

Management-Provided Forecasts. Having established the probable investment decision relevance of the amount, timing, and risk associated with future cash flows, the next question is, What kind of (accounting) information should the management of a business enterprise provide to external investors? A first choice is management's own forecasts of future cash flows expected to be generated by the enterprise. This alternative has received more and more favorable support recently for several reasons. For instance, management usually prepares such forecasts for its own planning purposes. Furthermore, management is "closer" to the business than any external party and is thus in a better position to assess most internal factors (including its own plans) that have implications for future cash flows.

However, in spite of managements' probable comparative advantage in forecasting, and the urging of businesses by authorities (notably the Securities and Exchange Commission) to publish forecasts on a "safe harbor" basis, up to now such forecasts have rarely been made public. Reasons for the present dearth of management forecasts are (1) they might disclose strategic information to competitors, and (2) managements feel that they would be unduly exposed to accusations of intentional manipulation if their forecasts turn out to be substantially in error.

Alternate Information for Investment Decisions. Although management forecasts are not widely available at present, it is important to remember that the *investor's decision problem is unaltered* by the infeasibility of receiving ready-made forecasts from the enterprise. He must still arrive at forecasts if he wishes to base his decisions on present values (or some analogous measure of benefits) for each of his investment opportunities. To be decision relevant, accounting information must therefore contribute to an investor's ability to estimate the future cash flows that will be forthcoming from a given enterprise. On the other hand, lest they be infeasible for the same reasons that management-provided forecasts now are, alternate forms of information must be more grounded in fact (i.e., be less susceptible to management manipulation and bias).

Any largely factual representation of the enterprise that is supposed to give clues to future cash flows must of course be based on some assumed cause-and-effect relationship between what can be observed as fact today and what will materialize as cash flows tomorrow and in the more distant future. Financial accounting typically applies this notion by attempting to characterize the enterprise's long-run cash-generating ability as evidenced by its current period's *performance* (*operating income*).

Distribution-of-Benefits Decisions. The purpose of financial accounting information for distribution decisions is to facilitate the equitable distribution of residual benefits of the enterprise (which includes preservation of the wealth employed in the enterprise). In contrast to investment decisions, distribution decisions are not made by individuals strictly for their own benefit. They have to do with rights of different groups that have an interest in the enterprise.

However, all interests in the distribution of residual benefits of the enterprise have one thing in common: the determination or measurement of the amount of wealth of the enterprise that is actually residual or disposable at any point in time when a distribution of wealth is being considered. Generally, the criterion against which we measure disposability is the wealth at the beginning of the period, and from this (Hicksian) criterion we develop the second major type of accounting information for external decisions—the *measure of disposable wealth* (*net income*).

Risk-Evaluation-Related Decisions. Financial status (wealth position) is frequently evaluated by enterprise creditors and other outsiders with present or potential financial interests in the enterprise. These parties wish to judge the level of risk they face with respect to the ability of the enterprise to meet all of its financial obligations when due. The composition of *financial position* as of a given date (i.e., as reported in successive statements of financial position) and the nature and direction of *financial resource flows* (i.e., as reported in successive statements of changes in financial position) are important sources of information concerning an enterprise's ability to discharge its financial obligations. In combination, the individual financial accounting information "packages" appear to have effectively served the purposes of external enterprise decision makers.

FINANCIAL ACCOUNTING POLICY FORMULATION

In Chapters 2 and 3 we contrast and compare (1) the net present value model, (2) the strict cash-flow model, and (3) the conventional accounting model against the decision-relevant information wants of investors and other parties external to business enterprises. This line of thought is pursued further in Chapters 13 through 16, where still other financial accounting models are introduced, evaluated, and compared. The choice between alternative accounting models is most difficult. Different costs and different benefits attach to the various individuals and groups who both produce and use accounting information. Thus the choice between different accounting models is largely a matter of social choice. The whys and hows of this choice receive closer attention in Chapters 16 and 17.

Even in the absence of clear-cut agreement on an appropriate financial accounting model for use by business enterprises, it is important to recognize that, as a practical matter, operational financial accounting measurement issues must be resolved, irrespective of any disagreements over broader issues. Published research of business scholars, economists, and behavioral scientists has provided evidence that differential information typically leads to differential decision effects. This in turn can lead to differential wealth distributions among various individuals and groups operating in an economy. Therefore one finds continuous debate over the appropriate measurement rules to be employed at the operational level of conventional financial accounting. This debate is similar to the ongoing debate over the choice between alternative financial accounting models. Even highly trained and experienced professional accountants hold widely differing opinions concerning appropriate financial accounting models and relevant financial accounting measurement rules.

For example, the measurement of depreciation was illustrated from time to time in earlier chapters. In particular, the total cost (less expected salvage value) of a depreciable asset was allocated *equally* to each of the periods during which benefits are expected. It is often argued, however, that the benefits from a long-lived asset are not derived equally over the asset's life but that, instead, proportionately more value is obtained during the early years. Acceptance of such an argument implies that acquisition cost should be allocated to depreciation expense in larger amounts during the earlier periods. Some frequently used, nonconstant depreciation patterns are discussed and illustrated in Chapter 10.

Since there is no unanimity as to the most appropriate financial accounting model and measurement rules to be applied in practice, it is necessary to establish authoritative, acceptable financial accounting standards and rules by a process often referred to as *financial accounting policy formulation*. The financial accounting policies that evolve as a result of this process reflect not only accounting theory considerations but many economic, legal, political, and social influences past and present.

In the United States financial accounting policy is established by an independent body of rule makers functioning in the private sector (as opposed to legislative rule making in the public sector). The current policy-making body is known as the *Financial Accounting Standards Board* (FASB).[1] Corporate managements, CPAs, stock exchanges, governmental agencies, and courts of law all accept the standards now set by the FASB. Again, more is said about the FASB, its predecessors, and its mode of operations in Chapter 17, where capital market institutions are related specifically to financial reporting and the accounting policy formulation process.

The standards and interpretations adopted by the FASB are referred to with some frequency throughout the remainder of this book, but especially in this and the upcoming Chapters 9 through 12. Since we are concerned exclusively with the technical measurement aspects of the FASB standards and interpretations in the five chapters just mentioned, we feel that it is neither inconvenient

---

[1] The FASB succeeded the American Institute of Certified Public Accountants' (AICPA) *Accounting Principles Board* in 1973. In turn, in 1959 the *Accounting Principles Board* superseded the AICPA's *Committee on Accounting Procedure*, which was established in 1936. The earliest attempt at financial accounting policy making in the United States on any formal or institutional level occurred between 1933 and 1936 through the AICPA's *Special Committee on Development of Accounting Principles*.

nor illogical to postpone the discussion of the FASB and the broader aspects of financial accounting policy formulation until later. Of course, there is nothing to preclude reference to these later passages while the study of Chapters 8 through 12 is under way.

REVENUE—MEASUREMENT AND ASSOCIATION WITH PERIODS

The nature of business efforts and accomplishments is considered briefly in Chapter 3, which provides an overview of conventional financial accounting. Now we examine more carefully the properties of the two principal components (i.e., revenue and expenses) of conventional financial accounting income measurement. Specifically, we discuss and illustrate how these general concepts are applied to some important classes of transactions. Furthermore, we point out some conditions under which existing authoritative measurement rules ("generally accepted accounting principles") are modified in current corporate financial reporting. The revenue component of the "efforts and accomplishments" matching process is the first consideration. It is elaborated in the remainder of the present chapter and in Chapter 9.

The Objective of Revenue Recognition

Business activity generally takes place continuously over many time periods. The "real" economic accomplishment of an enterprise for any particular period of time, we postulate, is the total value that the enterprise has added to all resources (raw material, labor, buildings, etc.) that it controls, *by all of its productive efforts*. Measuring the total value added for each time period for which the enterprise reports (typically quarterly, and at least annually) is the objective or goal of the revenue recognition process. But if the total process of adding value is not started and completed within the period of time for which we wish to measure the accomplishments of the enterprise, the identification of the amount of "value added" during the period is subject to a variety of assumptions about future performance and market behavior. Therefore the measurement ideal is modified under conventional accounting by the adoption of a revenue realization principle (or convention).

The Realization Principle and Revenue

The realization principle is defined in Chapter 3 as follows:

> **The Realization Principle.** Accomplishment (revenue) should be recognized in the period when the prices to be received for products and services provided by the enterprise (1) become reasonably certain and (2) have been "earned" by the enterprise.

The realization principle posits two fundamental criteria for the *timing* of the recognition of revenue: (1) earning has taken place, and (2) the price to be received is relatively certain. The first of these criteria is largely motivated by the goal of seeking to measure the economic value added by an enterprise during a particular time interval. But the criterion is somewhat more flexible (and conceptually, therefore, less accurate). It suggests that revenue, or accomplishment, should not be recognized *before* earning has taken place, but there is no requirement that recognition track precisely with earning *as* it takes place. The compromise in the operational measurement rule from the conceptual ideal reflects the practical difficulties often encountered in attempting to identify, step by step, the creation of value. Indeed, as noted below, the most common application of the realization principle defers recognition of revenue until all, or substantially all, of the earning process has been completed.

The second criterion stems from the basic thrust of the conventional accounting model to provide objective, factually based measurements. If a high degree of uncertainty exists concerning the prices that will ultimately be received for a firm's goods or services, it is usually considered more desirable to defer recognition of revenue than to attempt to estimate these uncertain values. This position is also motivated, as is the conventional accounting model, by the desire to limit the susceptibility of the measurements to fraud and manipulation. For example, management is often rewarded, directly or indirectly, on the basis of the reported accomplishments of the enterprise. Hence one encounters managements who wish to report their accomplishments in the most favorable light. If a measurement concept is overly dependent upon uncertain estimates, the accounting results may be influenced by undesirable management motives. Accordingly, revenue recognition principles (as well as other conventional accounting measurement rules) are generally constructed so as to mitigate the possibility, or the appearance of the possibility, of this type of managerial action.

Under most circumstances in current financial reporting, the realization principle is satisfied by recognizing revenue at the *time of sale*. At this point in time, title to the goods or services usually passes to the buyer, and the seller has a legally enforceable claim in the amount of the price agreed upon in the sales transaction. Additionally, there is usually no major earning effort that takes place following the sale, and it is therefore appropriate to recognize the total accomplishment reflected in the selling price.

Thus, under the "point-of-sale" interpretation of the realization principle, revenue is or may be defined under conventional accounting as follows:

> **Revenue.** Generally, revenue is the sum of the selling prices (or fees) of all products sold and services provided to customers during the current period—whether or not the sales are cash sales or credit sales (credit sales are sales for which the customer promises to pay at a later time).

Although revenue for a period may differ (often substantially) from the total cash receipts from operations of the enterprise for the same period, recall that in the long run these two measurements will be roughly equal.

The point-of-sale interpretation of the realization principle is not, however, always the most appropriate interpretation. It represents one possible trade-off, or point of balance, between the two criteria specified by the realization principle—earning has taken place, and the price to be received is relatively certain. Other possible interpretations, or trade-offs, of these criteria range from, at one extreme, estimating accomplishment, or value created, as production progresses to the other extreme of deferring recognition of accomplishment until the cash price established by the sales transaction has been collected. We now examine some general types of business circumstances under which alternatives to the frequently used point-of-sale interpretation are considered more appropriate bases for recognizing enterprise accomplishment.

Firm Orders Prior to Delivery of Goods or Services

Although many retail businesses deliver merchandise to customers concurrent with their customers' expressions of desire to purchase the goods (for example, food stores), some retail firms and many other types of business enterprises receive *orders* for goods or services prior to their delivery. Sometimes the goods are in stock, and they are delivered shortly after the order is received. In many cases, however, a longer time period ensues between order and delivery. Products may have to be secured from suppliers, or perhaps even produced after the order is received. Services clearly cannot be stockpiled, and the resulting time delay in their delivery depends upon the scope of services requested and the degree of availability of the firm's staff. The important question here is whether this type of business arrangement justifies recognition of revenue at some time earlier than when the ordered goods or services are delivered to the customer. Two possible earlier time periods deserve consideration: (1) the date the order is received and (2) the period of time during which progress is achieved on the production of the ordered goods or services.

In considering first the possibility of recognizing at least some portion of the total price as revenue at the date the order is received, an argument can be made that the securing of orders is, in principle, an important part of the overall earning process (particularly in certain industries, such as magazine publishing). However, present accounting policy does not sanction recognition of revenue at such a time, primarily because of the practical difficulty in associating the total price with at least two distinct steps in the typical earning process: (1) securing the order and (2) producing and/or delivering the goods or services. Therefore, as a rule, no accounting recognition is given to the receipt of an order *unless* it is accompanied by an advance payment. Even when advance payment is received, the receipt of cash and the associated obligation to provide goods or services in the future are recognized—but no revenue is recognized.

Moving next to the second possible time period for earlier recognition of revenue—the period of time during which progress is achieved on the production of the ordered goods or services, we find here some situations in which revenue recognition is permitted under current accounting policy. It may be helpful to classify these conditions into three general categories: (1) production of unquestionably salable commodities like gold or silver, (2) production and delivery of separable units of a total order, and (3) production processes extending over an "extremely long" period of time where (usually because of the nature of the order) no partial deliveries can be made.

Production of Unquestionably Salable Commodities

It has long been recognized that certain commodities meet the conditions of the realization principle during their production or creation—namely (1) their prices are certain, and (2) the full amount of the certain price has been "earned" by the enterprise as soon as production is completed. In other words, the earning process involved is certain *and* measurable prior to delivery (i.e., sale) of the goods involved.

The possibility of recognizing revenue prior to the point of sale of a service or commodity has been established firmly in authoritative financial accounting measurement rules since 1947, at which time the applicable Accounting Research Bulletin (ARB) No. 29 was published by the AICPA. In the 1953 restatement of the bulletin, the following paragraph addresses the issue:

> It is generally recognized that income accrues only at the time of sale, and that gains may not be anticipated by reflecting assets at their current sales prices. For certain articles, however, exceptions are permissible. Inventories of gold and silver, when there is an effective government-controlled market at a fixed monetary value, are ordinarily reflected at selling prices. A similar treatment is not uncommon for inventories representing agricultural, mineral, and other products, units of which are interchangeable and have an immediate marketability at quoted prices and for which appropriate costs may be difficult to obtain. Where such inventories are stated at sales prices, they should of course be reduced by expenditures to be incurred in disposal, and the use of such basis should be fully disclosed in the financial statements.[2]

Although inventory measurement is the subject matter of Chapter 10, we recognize at this time that a direct interrelationship exists between inventory measurement (a financial position statement matter) and periodic net income determination (an income statement matter). As the above statement of principle implies, the only way in which one can recognize revenue (or income) at the time of production of unquestionably salable commodities is to assign them inventory account values equal to their applicable market prices.

Simplified journal entries necessary to accomplish production-related revenue recognition are best illustrated in three steps. First is the typical and very common recording of manufacturing costs:

```
1. Production expense                    XXXXX
      Wages and salaries payable                XXXXX
      Manufacturing materials and supplies      XXXXX
      Mining royalties payable                  XXXXX
      Other assets and liabilities              XXXXX
```

At the close of a bookkeeping period (typically a calendar month or quarter), the revenue recognition entry occurs in the form of an adjusting entry:

```
2. Inventory of gold bars                XXXXX
      Estimated shipping expense         XXXXX
      Production revenue earned                 XXXXX
```

---

[2] AICPA, *Accounting Research Bulletin No. 43* (Restatement and Revision of Accounting Research Bulletins), 1953, p. 34.

When a shipment of precious metal actually leaves company vaults in satisfaction of an accepted purchase order, a journal entry would show:

3. Accounts Receivable	XXXXX	
Inventory of gold bars		XXXXX
Cash (expenditure for shipping charges)		XXXXX

Production and Delivery of Separable Units

Example 8-1

> The Ja Magazine Company was recently formed to sell the new magazine *Ja*. The price of the magazine on the newsstand is $1 per copy. Additionally, individuals can subscribe to the magazine for one year for a price of $10. During the first month of operations, the company secured twelve thousand new annual subscriptions, accompanied by total advance payments of $120,000.

If the obtaining of orders were interpreted to satisfy the criteria for the recognition of revenue, the company would recognize $120,000 revenue in the first month of operation. But unless it can be argued that the order-getting process is the major part of the overall earning process, leaving only minor services yet to be performed, it would not be appropriate to recognize all the revenue at this point in time. The presumption of current accounting policy is that this argument cannot be made, and that further it is not possible to allocate the total price in a sufficiently objective way between the order-getting process and the production-delivery process. But although no revenue is recognized at this time, the *advance payment* must be given accounting recognition as an obligation of the firm either to provide future services or, failing to do so, to return the money. For the Ja Magazine Company, a liability entitled "advance payments on subscriptions" would be recorded.

The appropriate journal entry follows:

Cash	$120,000	
Advance payments on subscriptions		$120,000

Since performance of production and delivery on orders can be associated in this case with identifiable and separable units (i.e., individual magazines), the realization principle is presumed to be satisfied with each partial delivery, and a proportional amount of the total price is recognized as revenue. Thus, in the first month that magazines are produced and distributed, the company recognizes revenue of $10,000 (1/12 × $120,000). This is accomplished by reducing the liability, advance payments on subscriptions, by $10,000 and increasing revenue by a similar amount. In terms of a journal entry, Ja Magazine Company should record the following:

Advance payments on subscriptions	$10,000	
Subscription revenue earned		$10,000

This revenue recognition process continues each month until the company has provided the subscribers with their twelve copies of the magazine and earned the total revenue of $120,000. Presumably, the pattern of revenue produced by this process is a better indicator of the firm's periodic accomplishment than would be achieved by waiting until complete performance on the order before recognizing any revenue.

Prolonged Production Processes on Firm Orders

In many manufacturing circumstances, production occurs before a sale is made, and thus some earning occurs prior to the date of sale. However, in balancing the trade-off between the two realization principle criteria, the point-of-sale interpretation of the realization principle has the effect of deferring recognition of any value added during production until an enforceable claim against the customer has been created through the delivery of the product. This trade-off is not without merit for most types of business activity. But where the lead time between the start of production and final delivery extends over a relatively long period of time, particularly when two or more accounting periods are encompassed, the propriety of waiting for the completion and delivery of the product before recognizing accomplishment becomes more questionable. Indeed, in such instances we may elect to place more emphasis on the fact that revenue is being *earned* as the production process continues, and less emphasis on the fact that the ultimate profit on the project is somewhat uncertain. This exception is most often applied in the cases of long-term construction and research contracts where the ultimate price is specified in advance, and the customer is obligated under a contract to accept the product if it is satisfactorily completed.

Percentage-of-Completion Method Versus Completed Contract Method of Recognizing Revenue. In the case of long-term production (construction, research, etc.) contracts that extend over several accounting periods, there are two customary methods of recognizing revenue. One method, the *completed contract method,* recognizes revenue in accordance with the point-of-sale interpretation of the realization principle. That is, no revenue is recognized until the production is completed and accepted by the customer. All costs incurred in the production activity are accumulated and deferred (in a construction-in-process account) until delivery is made. At that time, the total sales price is recognized as revenue, and the accumulated costs of the resources sacrificed in production are recognized as an expense in accordance with the matching principle. By deferring the recognition of revenue until the period in which the project is completed, *the total accomplishment* (revenue and profit) is associated only with this period. No amount of accomplishment is attributed to prior periods, even though one or more of them may have been the locus of substantial productive activity on the project. Hence, if the long-term project(s) represents a significant part of the contracting firm's operations, the revenue recognition pattern produced by the completed contract method significantly distorts the performance (net income) reported by the firm over time.

The typical pattern of journal entries for completed-contract-method accounting begins with cost accumulations at the end of each accounting period during the time over which the contract runs:

1. Contract in process (asset)	XXXXX	
Materials and supplies inventory		XXXXX
Wages and salaries payable		XXXXX
Other assets and liabilities		XXXXX

At the time the contract is completed, revenue is recognized and related cost accumulation accounts are "closed out":

2. Accounts receivable—contract	XXXXX	
Contract revenue earned		XXXXX
Cost of contract completed (expense)	XXXXX	
Contract in process		XXXXX

Example 8-2

> The Clean Water Research Group of Ecology, Inc., made a proposal to an environmental protection agency of the federal government to study some new types of waste disposal units that could be economically installed and used on pleasure boats. This proposal was accepted by the agency, and a contract for $1.5 million was signed on January 1, 19X5. The research project was to extend over thirty-six months, and progress payments were to be made to the research group over the life of the contract on the basis of the number of hours of research time expended.
>
> The project supervisor estimated at the time the contract was received that the firm would incur costs on the project amounting to $1 million. The contract price is fixed and is not subject to renegotiation if cost overruns are incurred. Thus, at the outset of the project, the estimated profit is $500,000.
>
> Approximately six months after the receipt of this contract, which was a major source of revenue to the firm, Ecology decided to expand the amount of its capital. Therefore the management was vitally concerned with the basis on which the accomplishment on the contract would be measured and reported. If the total profit on the contract were not recognized until the completion of the project, the operating results of Ecology for the past year would probably not be adequate to attract new equity capital. But if some recognition could be given to the accomplishment that had been achieved on the project, the firm would have a better chance of marketing its new issue of stock.

An alternative to the completed contract method is the *percentage-of-completion method*. Under this method, a portion of the total projected accomplishment on a long-term project is assigned to each period that the company works on the project. The total measure of accomplishment that is allocated to the various periods is the estimated total profit on the project (selling price less estimated costs to be incurred), and the basis for the allocation is the estimated percentage of the total work required that has been achieved in the period. In estimating the percentage-of-completion that has been achieved in a period, many different approaches are found in current practice. Two common approaches used are (1) the ratio of costs incurred by the end of the period to the estimated total cost of the project at completion and (2) an independent expert's (generally an architect or engineer) estimate of the physical percentage-of-completion that has been achieved by the end of the period.

Referring back to Example 8-2, assume that the actual experience of Ecology, Inc., on the research project was as follows:

	19X5	19X6	19X7
Costs incurred	$400,000	$350,000	$275,000
Project supervisor's end-of-year estimate of costs *yet to be incurred* to complete the project	600,000	300,000	-0-

Using the ratio of costs incurred to estimated total costs as the basis for assessing achievement in a period, the accomplishment (profit) recognized each year under the percentage-of-completion method is reflected in Exhibit 8-1.

We note from Exhibit 8-1 that the amount of income to be assigned to each period is, under this method, a function of (1) the costs incurred during the period, (2) the revised estimate of costs yet to be incurred to complete the project, (3) the estimated income earned to date, and (4) the amount of income recognized in prior periods. In the first year (19X5), it is estimated that the percentage of the total work on the project that was achieved in that period was 40 percent, based on the ratio of costs incurred in that year ($400,000) to the end-of-year estimate of total costs on the project ($1,000,000 = $400,000 + $600,000). Based on the presently estimated total income of $500,000, $200,000 is recognized as income in 19X5. Respective journal entries recognize, first, all expense accumulations during 19X5:

1. Research contract expenses (19X5)	$400,000	
Various assets and liabilities		$400,000

Then the revenue earned on the "percentage-of-completion" basis is recognized:

2. Unbilled contracts in process	$600,000	
Contract revenue earned (19X5)		$600,000

Aside from appropriate revenue recognition for 19X5, progress payments (according to the text of Example 8-2) are to be made "on the basis of the number of hours of research time expended." In real-world situations, billable amounts are not necessarily the same as recognized revenue amounts.

Exhibit 8–1

APPLICATION OF PERCENTAGE-OF-COMPLETION METHOD TO CLEAN WATER RESEARCH GROUP PROJECT

	19X5	19X6	19X7
Contract price of project	$1,500,000	$1,500,000	$1,500,000
Less costs of project:			
Costs incurred to date	$400,000	$750,000	$1,025,000
Estimated costs to complete	600,000	300,000	-0-
	1,000,000	1,050,000	1,025,000
Total income on project (estimated at end of 19X5 and 19X6)	$ 500,000	$ 450,000	$ 475,000
Income to be recognized to date	$ 200,000*	$ 321,429†	$ 475,000
Cumulative income recognized in prior periods	-0-	200,000	321,429
Income to be recognized for year	$ 200,000	$ 121,429	$ 153,571

*($400,000/$1,000,000) × $500,000.
†($750,000/$1,050,000) × $450,000.

280   CHAPTER 8

For purposes of the present illustration, though, amounts billed equal those recognized as "contract revenue earned." The underlying journal entry therefore is as follows:

    3. Accounts receivable—partial contract billing $600,000
        Unbilled contracts in process $600,000

The difference between contract revenue earned and research contract expenses at 12/31/X5 is operating income of $200,000 for the year 19X5.

In 19X6 the same procedure is applied. But in this year, the sum of the costs incurred to date, and the revised (as of December 31, 19X6) estimate of costs to complete, produce a new estimate of total income from the project, $450,000. This new estimate of income is the basis for the allocation of projected accomplishment to past and future periods. The income to be recognized in 19X6, then, is the difference between income allocated to work done to date and the amount of income from the project already recognized in 19X5. Thus the income recognized in 19X6 reflects both the estimate of accomplishment in the period and the correction of amounts reported in prior periods that were based on a less current estimate of total income on the project.

Required journal entries are:

    1. Research contract expenses (19X6) $350,000
        Various assets and liabilities $350,000
    2. Unbilled contracts in process $471,429
        Contract revenue earned (19X6) $471,429
    3. Accounts receivable—partial contract billing $471,429
        Unbilled contracts in process $471,429

Comparing the effects of the foregoing journal entries with the arithmetic analysis shown in Exhibit 8-1, we note that total contract revenue earned to 12/31/X6 is $1,071,429. Total project costs incurred to the same point in time are $750,000. The difference is total operating income recognized on the contract for 19X5 and 19X6, namely $321,429 ($1,071,429 − $750,000 = $321,429) and is allocated $200,000 to 19X5 and $121,429 to 19X6.

In 19X7 the project is completed and the *total* income from it becomes known. Income recognized in 19X7 is merely the difference between the actual total income and the cumulative income recognized in the two prior years (see Exhibit 8-1 for details).

A long-term production project accounted for under the percentage-of-completion method is reflected as an asset in the statement of financial position while still in progress. At any point in time, the value assigned to the project is the sum of the costs incurred and the income recognized, less any progress billings to the customer provided for by the terms of the contract. In our example, *assuming no progress billings had been made,* the research project would be valued at $600,000 ($400,000 costs incurred plus $200,000 profit recognized) at the end of 19X5, and $1,071,429 ($750,000 cumulative costs incurred plus $321,429 cumulative profit recognized) at the end of 19X6.

Whenever the production period is significantly long and the customer's eventual payment is provided for in a contract, the percentage-of-completion method is applied in order to better associate the recognition of revenue (and income) with the period in which it is earned. Using the data of the illustration, we have the following contrast between the completed contract method and the percentage-of-completion method:

	Accomplishment (Income) Recognized under:	
	Percentage-of-Completion Method	Completed Contract Method
19X5	$200,000	-0-
19X6	121,429	-0-
19X7	153,571	475,000
	$475,000	$475,000

The percentage-of-completion method in this case clearly traces the productive activities of the firm better than does the completed contract method. But since the percentage-of-completion method introduces a much greater degree of uncertainty into the income measurement process, it should be used only when the estimates required can be made with an acceptable degree of accuracy. These estimates involve the price to be received when the project is completed, the costs to be incurred on the project, and periodic assessments of the percentage-of-completion that has been achieved. Where these estimates are believed to be reasonably dependable, current accounting policy expresses a preference for the use of the percentage-of-completion method. However, if the uncertainties associated with a long-term project are so great as to render the estimates of doubtful validity, the more conservative completed contract method should be used.

UNRESOLVED CONCEPTUAL ISSUES

Revenue recognition and the definition and application of the related realization principle have garnered significant attention since the very beginning of financial accounting. While there are many reasons for this condition, three stand out: (1) Whatever is recognized as revenue in a given period has a direct effect upon the amount of income reported for the same period; (2) given investor and creditor interest in forecasting future cash flows of the enterprise, revenue data are directly relevant to the information needs thus arising; and (3) growth rates and economic strength of companies are often indexed on the basis of revenue figures which attracts considerable management attention to applicable measurement, timing, and calculational procedures. It is little wonder, then, that the revenue recognition aspects of financial accounting are often the subjects of financial reporting controversies.

Point-of-Sale Timing of Recognition. Earlier in the chapter we observe that "under most circumstances in current financial reporting, the realization principle is satisfied by recognizing revenue at the *time of sale.*" While such timing is broadly consistent with the constraints and objectives of the conventional financial accounting model, it can be distortive whenever production of goods and services are roughly continuous while sales are seasonal or sporadic (e.g., manufacture and sale of lawnmowers) or whenever production is intermittent while sales are continuous (e.g., manufacture and sale of paint which is produced in large "batches"). In these circumstances, economic effort and accomplishment are improperly matched so long as revenue recognition is related to the timing of a sale without any recognition whatever of underlying production processes. Does the sale transaction *per se* "earn" revenue, or is revenue earned by the prior effort to ready goods or services for sale? Of course, we probably would not wish to recognize revenue on the basis of production alone—especially when the items produced simply pile up in warehouses possibly because they have limited or no salability.

In the preceding section of this chapter we present the generally accepted solution for coordinating (by means of the percentage-of-completion accounting method) incurrence of production costs and revenue recognition under fixed commitment, long-term construction contracts. In Chapter 15 we discuss at some length the pros and cons of revenue recognition proportionate to changes in market values of goods and services. Special business practices give rise to additional problems. For instance, the special problem of leasing is addressed in Chapter 12, where revenue recognition poses difficulties when an equipment manufacturer leases new equipment produced rather than selling it outright. Where is the "point of sale" here? Most accountants would agree that the timing of revenue recognition remains an unresolved issue for a number of business facts and circumstances.

Value Accretion and Appreciation. Quite a few economic commodities are subject to *accretion*—which simply means growth or enhancement of economic value during a period of time. For instance, timber on tree farms grows with the passage of time and is typically worth more at the end of an accounting period than at the beginning. Other examples are the aging of wine and alcoholic spirits where "natural causes" often produce value increments.

Appreciation produces similar results but without any physical changes. For example, corporate stocks or bonds may appreciate in value due to rises in respective market prices. Paintings in art collections sometimes appreciate, as do rare stamps and coins. Even though there is no physical change involved, economic value may grow through passage of time, changes in people's tastes and preferences, and the like.

While a few isolated instances are discussed in Chapter 15 in which a process of appreciation gives rise to a limited form of revenue recognition, strict application of the realization principle precludes the recognition of revenue on the basis of accretion and/or appreciation. The monetary amounts (i.e., prices) in any such economic value enhancements are typically not "reasonably certain" enough to warrant their inclusion among conventionally recognized revenue items. But accounting considerations should not obscure the fact that real changes in economic values take place.

Discovery and Donation of Economic Value. Still another misalignment between conventional accounting revenue recognition and economic facts occurs when valuable resources are *discovered* or when physical properties are *donated* with little or no directly related cost to the enterprise. In the former category are the discovery, for example, of mineral deposits or natural gas or oil reserves. The discoveries may involve additions to known reserves or new reserves altogether. Donations of physical properties like land and buildings may occur when a municipality, a state, or even a country is interested in attracting an enterprise to a particular geographic area and judges that an appropriate donation might help to accomplish such an objective. Has not the enterprise "accomplished" something when it makes a major natural resource discovery or receives a significant amount of donated physical property (or, for that matter, even an important tax concession)? If the answer is yes, then an appropriate revenue item should be recognized for the period in which the accomplishment occurred.

Typically, though, recognition of the full positive impact on the enterprise of events of the type described runs afoul of conventional accounting restrictions on two counts: (1) the realization principle proscribes recognition because the enterprise has not yet "earned" the discovered or donated resources, and (2) under the cost principle the value to be recognized, if any, is limited to the associable costs which may be zero (which, in turn, precludes any substantive recognition). In the present age of large-scale public concern over energy sources and new processes like ocean mining, the unresolved issue of revenue recognition related to resource discoveries is particularly bothersome and is receiving a great deal of attention from policy-making institutions such as the FASB and the SEC.

CURRENT REVENUE REPORTING PRACTICES

Exhibit 8-2 contains the top portion of the income statement taken from the *Westinghouse 1977 Annual Report.*

Reporting of revenue earned in published income statements is straightforward under current financial reporting practices. In the past various revenue adjustments like discounts and returns and allowances (see Chapter 9) were shown as subtractions from gross sales to arrive at a "net sales" figure. Today the caption "sales" simply means net revenue earned according to the realization principle.

Whenever something other than point-of-sale revenue recognition procedures is employed, companies furnish explanations thereof in statements of accounting policies selected by the company. Such statements typically appear as footnotes to financial reports and are required as a matter of financial accounting policy (*APB Opinion No. 22*).

Following is a footnote on revenue recognition as it appears in the 1977 annual report of Westinghouse Electric Corporation (same report as the one excerpted in Exhibit 8-2):

Revenue Recognition

Sales are recorded primarily as products are shipped.

The percentage of completion method of accounting is used only for nuclear steam supply system orders with durations generally in excess of five years and for certain construction projects where this method of accounting is consistent with industry practices. For other long-term contracts, sales are recognized as products are shipped.

Exhibit 8-2

WESTINGHOUSE ELECTRIC CORPORATION

Excerpt from Income Statement
(Amounts in thousands)

	Year Ended December 31	
	1977	*1976*
Income:		
Sales	$6,137,661	$6,145,152
Equity in income from non-consolidated subsidiaries and affiliated companies	34,001	21,050
Other income	128,019	88,089
	$6,229,681	$6,254,291

Reporting Business Segments. As companies have grown larger, particularly by expanding into new markets, aggregate totals for revenue and expense items have lost some information value because not all divisions and/or product segments of a company have the same "average" cash-flow-generating potential. It is therefore now a financial accounting policy in the United States to report a number of business operating statistics (including revenues) on a "business segments basis." Application of this policy really means nothing more than subdividing aggregate or "consolidated" revenue and expense figures into homogeneous line-of-business or geographic segments.

The U.S. Federal Trade Commission (FTC) as well as the FASB and the SEC require segmental financial reporting. The FTC is concerned with market domination in given lines of business and with fair competition in interstate commerce. It uses the *Standard Industrial Classification* of the Census Bureau to define reportable lines of business.

The FASB and the SEC accounting requirements leave the definition of lines of business to individual company managements. In general, business "segments" amounting to more than 10 percent of a company's business activities are to be reported separately.

When the underlying financial accounting policies were formulated, managements were concerned that segmental disclosures would reveal key information to competitors and would generally hamper innovative (i.e., unusual risk-taking) practices. Initial experience with segmental reporting appears to indicate that these fears were largely unfounded.

Exhibit 8-3 shows appropriate breakdowns provided by the Singer Company for nine different lines of business as well as four major geographic areas.

Expanded Historical-Cost-Based Revenue Recognition. Currently applicable corporate law in West Germany requires public companies to report as revenue not only net sales but increases in *costs of* inventories of semifinished and finished goods plus internally capitalized costs like self-construction of a machine tool or a building.

Note that this accounting practice is still in harmony with the cost principle, but it does broaden revenue recognition to include economic value increments resulting from enterprise cost expenditures. Exhibit 8-4 (p.288) is the English-

Exhibit 8-3

THE SINGER COMPANY AND CONSOLIDATED SUBSIDIARIES

The Company's business for purposes of reporting information pursuant to Statement of Financial Accounting Standards No. 14 adopted by the Company on January 1, 1977, is concentrated in three major product areas, segmented into nine lines of business. Information for 1976 is presented on a basis comparable with the current year.

		1977			
	Net Sales	Operating Income (Loss)	Assets	Depreciation and Amortization	Capital Expenditures
				(Amounts in Millions)	
Sewing Products:					
Consumer sewing machines and related products	$1,111.8	$ 94.5	$ 621.8	$27.5	$23.7
Industrial sewing machines and related products	123.0	(3.7)	116.4	1.6	.9
	1,234.8	90.8	738.2	29.1	24.6
Products Manufactured for the Consumer:					
Power tools and floor care	168.9	26.1	62.3	1.6	7.4
Furniture	141.6	17.7	65.2	3.6	2.6
Controls products	133.9	16.7	44.1	4.4	5.4
Air conditioning and heating equipment	101.6	1.7	47.8	1.4	.6
Meter products	63.5	7.4	29.5	1.1	1.4
	609.5	69.6	248.9	12.1	17.4
Products and Services for Government:					
Aerospace and marine systems	379.5	26.7	168.0	7.3	9.2
Education	61.0	6.1	19.6	1.8	.9
	440.5	32.8	187.6	9.1	10.1
Amounts applicable to product lines	2,284.8	193.2	1,174.7	50.3	52.1
Corporate (expenses), assets, depreciation and amortization, and capital expenditures	—	(19.5)	193.7	3.8	3.3
Discontinued operations	—	—	93.5	.8	—
Total	$2,284.8	$173.7	$1,461.9	$54.9	$55.4

Exhibit 8-3 Continued
THE SINGER COMPANY AND CONSOLIDATED SUBSIDIARIES

	United States	Canada and Europe	Latin America	Other International	Eliminations	Consolidated
				1977		
					(Amounts in Millions)	
Sales to unaffiliated customers	$1,306.3	$520.4	$190.4	$267.7	$ —	$2,284.8
Sales between geographic areas	43.2	63.8	8.7	2.2	(117.9)	—
Net sales	$1,349.5	$584.2	$199.1	$269.9	$(117.9)	$2,284.8
Operating income before general corporate expenses	$ 104.2	$ 20.7	$ 36.2	$ 32.1		$ 193.2
Less general corporate expenses						(19.5)
Operating income						$ 173.7
Operating assets	$ 567.3	$282.3	$141.2	$183.9		$1,174.7
Corporate assets						193.7
Discontinued assets						93.5
Total assets						$1,461.9
Net assets	$ 171.8	$112.8	$ 86.0	$ 86.8		$ 457.4

language income statement taken from the 1977 annual report of LINDE, a major West German refrigeration and machine tools company.

Questions for Review and Discussion

8-1. Define:
   a. The realization principle
   b. Revenue
   c. Percentage-of-completion method
   d. Accretion
   e. Segmental reporting

8-2. What is the objective of revenue recognition? Explain why this objective has been modified under conventional accounting through the adoption of the realization principle.

8-3. Describe the two criteria for revenue recognition imposed by the realization principle, and indicate when and why this principle is generally considered to be satisfied in current financial reporting.

8-4. Why is revenue generally not recognized on the date a firm order is received from a customer?

8-5. Describe the three general categories of business circumstances where revenue is recognized in relation to the progress that is achieved on the production of ordered goods or services. Indicate which criterion of the realization principle is given more weight in this modification than it is given in the balance struck under the strict point-of-sale interpretation.

8-6. When the percentage-of-completion method is used for recognizing revenue from a long-term production project, what amount is assigned to the project (inventory) on the statement of financial position?

8-7. Even though long-term construction contracts are typically negotiated for a fixed price, costs estimated to complete a given contract generally vary somewhat from period to period. Explain how the percentage-of-completion method accommodates varying contract completion cost estimates.

8-8. Write a two-paragraph explanation of the reason for relaxation of the realization principle in the case of revenue recognition accompanying the production of silver and gold.

8-9. Suppose you own a surfboard manufacturing shop in Honolulu. Over the years you have evolved a routine by which you manufacture surfboards on an assembly-line basis for six months and then close your operation for the following eighteen months while your surfboard inventory is sold. The same cycle repeats itself every two years. What are the shortcomings of the conventional revenue recognition procedure in this hypothetical circumstance? Would the financial reporting situation be improved if financial statements were prepared only every two years?

8-10. Write a short essay on the pros and cons of permitting large oil companies to recognize "discovery values" of oil reserves as revenues in their published income statements.

Exhibit 8-4

LINDE GROUP OF COMPANIES

Consolidated Profit and Loss Statement, 1977

	DM	DM	1976 Thousands DM
1. Sales	1,667,494,102		1,553,735
2. Addition to stock of finished goods and work in progress	153,711,966		114,745
	1,821,206,068		1,668,480
3. Internally utilized production	15,068,272		18,147
4. Total output	1,836,274,340		1,686,627
5. Raw materials, supplies, auxiliaries and goods purchased	835,995,591		788,371
6. Gross revenue		1,000,278,749	898,256
Other revenue			
7. Income from profit-sharing contracts	1,043,767		727
8. Income from investments in affiliated companies	5,288,089		2,178
9. Income from other financial investments	388,390		373
10. Other interest and similar income	35,845,657		23,977
11. Gain on sales of assets	4,619,863		5,039
12. Transfer from appropriations and accruals	1,259,727		1,703
13. Transfer from special items representing partial reserves	1,156,623		147
14. Sundry income	25,073,542		18,796
Including DM 1,748,202 extraordinary income			
		74,675,658	52,940
15. Total income (Items 6 to 14)		1,074,954,407	951,196
Expense			
16. Wages and salaries	511,855,745		464,632
17. Social service payments	72,625,283		65,739
18. Pensions and welfare fund	27,418,321		24,843
19. Depreciation on property, plant and equipment	67,937,347		62,842
20. Depreciation on investments	116,200		186
21. Depreciation on other current assets, including loss on disposals	9,687,991		8,653
22. Loss on disposal of property, plant and equipment	557,776		770
23. Interest and similar expense	34,484,911		34,256
24. Taxes			
a) Taxes on income, earnings and net worth 57,165,956			35,299
b) Other taxes 4,104,335			2,785
c) Equalization of Burdens Property Levy 11,135			103
(After withdrawal of DM 148,860 from debit item)			
	61,281,426		38,187
25. Transfer to special items representing partial reserves	11,107,520		2,854
26. Sundry expense	244,243,990		217,018
27. Total expense (Items 16 to 26)		1,041,316,510	919,980
28. Net profit		33,637,897	31,216
29. Profit brought forward		11,651	62
		33,649,548	31,278
30. Transfer from net profit to voluntary reserves		6,077,973	3,139
		27,571,575	28,139
31. Profit attributable to minority shareholders		4,532,445	4,231
32. Net consolidated profit		23,039,130	23,908

8-11. By reference to the Singer Company financial schedules appearing in Exhibit 8-3, identify the pros and cons of segmental financial reporting.

8-12. Would you advocate revenue reporting in the United States on the same basis as is now the custom in West Germany? Support your position carefully.

8-13. In a now classic court case involving the propriety of the reported income of Four Seasons Nursing Centers of America, Inc., one of the issues was the method used to determine the percentage-of-completion achieved by the company on the construction of nursing homes. Although the initial estimate of income under the percentage-of-completion method was based on architects' physical estimates of completion, the auditors tested these estimates by comparing costs incurred to total estimated costs and insisted that the percentage completion to date (and therefore income recognized) be reduced. Nevertheless, the auditors were criticized for having included approximately $2 million in costs incurred to date which, for the most part, consisted of the contract prices of special-order components and subcontract work done "off-site" toward completion of various nursing homes, but for which no deliveries had been made to the actual construction sites by year-end. Under what conditions, if any, do you believe that such off-site costs should be included in the calculation of percentage-of-completion achieved?

8-14. One of the booming industries in recent years is the franchising industry—partly, say some critics, because of the accounting methods employed. A franchise company has two principal sources of income: (1) sale of the initial franchise and related assets or services and (2) fees for continuing services based on the operations of the individual franchisees. A major accounting issue was how to deal with the initial franchise fee. For this fee, the franchisee is authorized to use rights (trademarks, trade names, patents, etc.) possessed by the franchisor, and to receive certain assistance in getting his operations started (e.g., assistance in site selection, assistance in construction, bookkeeping and advisory services, employee and management training, etc.). Typically, the franchisee makes a small down payment when the franchise agreement is signed, and he executes a note for the balance to be paid over a fairly long period of time (often at a favorable rate of interest). Based upon this general background, describe some alternative revenue recognition methods that might be used to account for the initial franchise fee, and indicate which method you would prefer. How would it affect your answer if large initial fees are required but continuing franchise fees are small in relation to future services?

Exercises

8-1. Motion picture rights are typically sold for television exhibition under a contract that covers a package of several films and permits one or more exhibitions of each film during specified license periods. A representative license agreement might include the following terms (adapted from *AICPA Industry Accounting Guide on Accounting for Motion*

Picture Films, Copyright © 1973 by the American Institute of Certified Public Accountants, Inc. and amended by *Statement of Position 79-4, 1979*):

Contract Execution Date—July 31, 19X3

Number of Films and Telecasts Permitted—4 films, 2 telecasts each

Fees, License Periods, and Print Delivery Dates:

Film	Total Fee	Stated License Periods		Print Delivery
		From	To*	
A	$ 800,000	10/1/X3	9/30/X5	9/1/X3
B	500,000	10/1/X3	9/30/X5	9/1/X3
C	375,000	9/1/X4	8/31/X6	12/1/X3
D	225,000	9/1/X5	8/31/X7	12/1/X4
	$1,900,000			

*The actual license periods expire at the earlier of (1) the second telecast or (2) the end of the stated license period.

Payment Schedule—$100,000 at contract execution date, $50,000 per month for 36 months commencing January 1, 19X4.

The AICPA committee studying this subject identified four methods in use for financial reporting of revenue from the licensing of films for television:

1. *Contract method:* Total revenue recognized on date the contract is executed.

2. *Billing method:* Revenue recognized as installment payments become due.

3. *Delivery method:* Revenue recognized at date the prints are delivered to licensee.

4. *Deferral or apportionment method:* Revenue spread evenly over the period of the license.

After deliberating the problem, the committee concluded that a licensing agreement should be considered as the sale of a right, and that revenue should be recognized "when a film may be shown for the first time under a licensing agreement" but not until all the following conditions have been satisfied:

1. The sales price for each film is known.

2. The cost of each film is known or reasonably determinable.

3. Collectibility of the full license fee is reasonably assured.
4. The film has been accepted by the licensee in accordance with the conditions of the license agreement.
5. The film is available; i.e., the right is deliverable by the licensor and exercisable by the licensee.

What amount of revenue would be recognized each year from 19X3 to 19X7 under each of the four methods in use at the time the committee studied the problem? Assuming that the first four of the five conditions promulgated by the committee are satisfied, what pattern of revenue would be recognized from 19X3 to 19X7 under this present accounting policy? Would you adjust the revenue computed under present accounting policy for the time value of money? Do you believe present policy is an improvement over the four methods the committee found in use in 1973?

8-2. **Completed Contract versus Percentage-of-Completion Revenue Recognition Methods.** Free Form Construction Company was awarded a contract in 19X3 by The Big University to build a new library. The contract price was $8 million, and Free Form expected to complete the job in 19X6. At the time construction began (early in 19X4), Free Form estimated that the total costs on the job would be $6 million.

During the construction period, the following financial data were compiled:

Date	Total Costs Incurred to Date	Estimated Additional Costs to Complete Project
12/31/X4	$1,500,000	$4,500,000
12/31/X5	3,900,000	2,600,000
12/31/X6	6,600,000	—0—

Required:

Determine the net income that would be reported for each of the three years and in total under (a) the completed contract method and (b) the percentage-of-completion method. Also, present appropriate journal entries for both accounting methods for 19X6.

8-3. **Timing of Revenue Recognition.** Prepare a schedule that shows (a) the time of likely revenue recognition, and (b) any special problems related to such recognition for each of the following types of business enterprises:
  a. Grocery store
  b. Broker securing motion picture rights for television networks from film studios
  c. Forest products company (growing and selling premium fir logs)
  d. Land developer building office parks and selling completed projects to groups of doctors, dentists, and lawyers

e. Computer software firm selling computer programs and computer time to small-business clients
f. Winery producing champagne typically aged three years
g. Travel agency
h. Full service bank with trust, mortgage, and international divisions
i. Engineering firm building hydroelectric power dams and bridges; typical contract completion time is three years
j. Art gallery
k. Private telephone company serving customers on an island chain of summer resort communities
l. Cattle ranch
m. Savings and loan association lending money for home mortgages
n. Leather shop producing custom order western saddles
o. Automobile-leasing company
p. College professor receiving royalties on textbook
q. CPA firm providing income tax advice to corporate client
r. Veterans' Administration Hospital
s. Gourmet restaurant
t. Municipal museum
u. Life insurance company
v. Ice follies road show
w. Toll Bridge Authority

8-4. Income from Long-Term Construction Contracts. Tower Construction Company builds high-rise office buildings in areas of the Midwest. The company is small, however, and only has one major project going at a time. It usually places bids for new contracts during the year of completion of the current contract. Then, by completion of the current contract, the company is immediately able to shift its labor force to the next job. Usually only a few months of overlap occur as the new project is being planned and the old one is being completed.

In 19X4 the company won the contract on the Life Insurance Building. The contract price of the building was $10 million. The construction of the building was to be started in July 19X4 and completed in June 19X6. The Life Insurance Company, the client, agreed in the contract to pay the Tower Construction Company on a limited percentage completion basis. Every six months a team of independent consulting engineers paid by Life would inspect the building and Tower's cost records to determine the percentage completion on the project. Life would then be billed by Tower for the percentage toward completion that occurred during the six-month period times the contract price, less 20 percent retainage to be due upon completion (to ensure Tower's interest in completing the building), and payment would be made within thirty days.

During the period July 1, 19X4, to June 30, 19X6, *the engineers* judged the project 15 percent complete by December 31, 19X4, 35 percent complete by June 30, 19X5, 65 percent complete by December 31, 19X5, and complete by June 30, 19X6. During that period of time, the following financial data were assembled by Tower's accountant:

Date	Costs Incurred to Date	Estimated Costs to Complete Project
12/31/X4	$2,125,000	$6,375,000
6/30/X5	3,825,000	4,675,000
12/31/X5	6,300,000	2,700,000
6/30/X6	9,100,000	-0-

In measuring income under the percentage-of-completion method, Tower Construction Company uses the cost data (costs incurred and estimated costs to complete the project) rather than the engineering estimates as an indicator of "percentage completion."

Required:

1. As of the end of each six-month period, determine the amounts called for below under (1) the completed contract method and (2) the percentage-of-completion method of accounting for long-term construction contracts:
    (a) Cash collected to date, assuming that Life paid each billing in the thirty days following the date of billing
    (b) Income for the six-month period
    (c) Balance in construction-in-process (or unbilled contracts in process) account

2. Appropriate journal entries for both accounting methods for 19X4 and 19X5

8-5. **Journalizing Revenue Transactions.** The West Gate Toll Bridge Authority has established the following rates for passenger automobile crossings: (1) 50¢ cash for cars with one or two occupants, (2) 15¢ cash for cars with three or more occupants, and (3) commuter ticket books costing $6 for a book containing twenty coupons.

Required:

Prepare journal entries for the following transactions:

1. Sale of 500-ticket books for cash

2. Appropriately authorized daily report from a toll booth showing cash collections of tolls of $875 plus 315 commuting coupons received

Enumerate whatever special problems you perceive in recognizing and reporting bridge toll revenues.

8-6. **Subscription Contracts.** The Sports Forecasting Company was formed in 19X1 to sell the sports newsletter "We-Pick-Em." The newsletter, which is published weekly from August through December, is sold by subscription only, and the subscription price for one year is $50.

The newsletter predicted the results of games correctly 80 percent of the time during 19X1–X2. Therefore the company expects an increase in subscriptions for 19X3. To take advantage of the current "seller's market," the company is offering a three-year subscription for $135. The entire amount must be paid before the customer is placed on the mailing list.

The company received total payment for the following number of subscriptions in 19X3–X4. (Subscriptions fell off in 19X4, since the newsletter was correct only 60 percent of the time in 19X3.)

	One-Year Subscriptions	Three-Year Subscriptions
19X3	5,000	3,000
19X4	4,000	1,000

Required:

Prepare a worksheet for 19X3–X4 that shows the effects of the above receipts in all the appropriate accounts, assuming that revenue is recognized in the year in which the service is provided. Assume that revenue is recognized at the end of each year. Ignore beginning balances. Also, prepare appropriate journal entries for 19X4.

8-7. **Financial Statement Effects of Subscriptions Received.** The Local Top Executive Newsletter was started on June 1, 19X7. Cash was received each month for *yearly* subscriptions to this monthly letter, the service to start at the beginning of the month following cash receipt. The following amounts of cash subscriptions were received from subscribers:

June (subscriptions to start July 1)	$5,400
July	6,000
August	4,100
September	4,800
October	7,500
November	6,400
December	4,500

All of the foregoing amounts were recorded in a current *revenue* account labeled "newsletter subscription revenue."

Required:

1. Appropriate adjusting journal entries as of December 31, 19X7

2. Identification of all applicable account titles and amounts in the December 31 statement of financial position and income statement

8-8. **Recognition of Discovery Values.** The Great Western Gold Mining Company has just completed a particularly significant year for the firm because, in the course of its regular mining operations, it discovered at midyear a large and rich vein of gold ore on its holdings. Independent consultants confirmed that the size, content, and purity of the gold in this vein means that it will eventually yield salable gold worth more than $75 million at the current government minimum purchase price of $75 an ounce.

As the executive assistant to the firm's management committee, you are aware that you could also sell gold at various retail markets in Europe at prices in excess of $200 per ounce. Management of the company believes that the value of this gold ore net of production costs should be included in its current annual reports to shareholders as a revenue item for the current year. Since the company has significant experience in gold mining, getting the metal out of the ore is a routine operating matter.

Required:

1. Does currently applicable financial accounting policy permit recognition of revenues from gold ore discoveries? Be specific in supporting your answer.
2. Assume that authoritative conventional financial accounting rules permit revenue recognition of gold ore discoveries. How would the current discovery appear in this year's financial statements of the Great Western Gold Mining Company?
3. State whatever you deem to be the most appropriate financial accounting rule in relation to discovery of independently proven reserves of gold ore and defend the position taken.

8-9. **Accounting for Rental Revenues.** Video-X Company has developed a videotape library that is continually being updated and further developed. These tapes can be used in connection with several hundred integrated training courses. Video-X Company rents access to the tape library for a minimum annual fee, plus additional charges for usage above the level covered by the minimum fee.

The basic accounting policy question faced by the company's financial vice-president is whether the contracts constitute completed sales and thus permit the recognition of revenue at the dates of the contracts.

After careful study and deliberation the vice-president proposes that 50 percent of the "economic contribution" (defined as total contract revenues less commissions and estimated royalties and servicing costs, all discounted at appropriate interest rates) be recognized at the date a contract is signed and that the remaining 50 percent be recognized on a straight-line basis over the life of the contract. His principal reasons for proposing this accounting treatment are:

1. The AICPA *Motion Picture Films Guide* applies to the Video-X Company (see Exercise 8-1 above).
2. All uncertainties with respect to collection of revenues and determination of related costs (as contemplated in the *Motion Picture Films Guide*) have been substantially removed.

Required:

1. As you understand the facts presented, does the *AICPA Industry Accounting Guide on Accounting for Motion Picture Films* apply?

2. Assume you are the independent CPA of the Video-X Company and are asked to review this particular accounting proposal. State whether you will or will not accept it and give appropriate reasons.

3. Irrespective of existing authoritative financial accounting rules and policies, take a position on how Video-X Company's revenues should be accounted for in the interest of external investment decision makers. Defend your answer.

8-10. Timing of Revenue Recognition for Professional Services. On October 1, 19X8, Dr. John Collins, a dentist specializing in orthodontia, initiated teeth positioning treatment and bite correction on Kent Mueller. After previous examination and consultation with Kent's parents, Dr. Collins had estimated that the corrective treatment would take approximately twenty months. Kent's parents have agreed to pay $400 in cash at the time treatment is initiated and then make twenty-four monthly payments of $35 each. Dr. Collins has agreed to provide as many treatment sessions and as much mechanical equipment as is needed for the desired corrections. His expected revenue flow from the Muellers is roughly proportionate to the volume of professional services he expects to provide.

Required:

1. How would Dr. Collins recognize revenue from his contract with the Muellers under the realization principle?

2. Assume that you are a banker and that Dr. Collins has applied for a substantial loan to move his offices and purchase additional equipment. Would you treat the value of the contract with the Mueller family for credit evaluation purposes the same as it is interpreted under generally accepted accounting principles? What additional information would be helpful to you as a banker evaluating an appropriate loan limit for Dr. Collins?

3. Enumerate three other economic fact situations in which similar revenue recognition problems occur.

8-11. When Is a Sale Not a Sale? In October 19X3 Miller Distribution Company sold one-half of a parcel of undeveloped land to Jones Pipe Company, an unaffiliated company. Miller had owned the land for a number of years and had always planned on developing it someday. At the time of the sale, Jones was said to be considering a plan to build and sell condominium units on the parcel of land it acquired from Miller.

The portion of the land that Miller sold to Jones had a book value of $750,000; Jones paid $1,250,000 in cash.

In January 19X4 the two companies announced a new joint venture agreement. Each partner put in its parcel of land as its contribution of capital. The partnership plans to retain an independent general contractor to build a condominium complex on the two contiguous parcels of land.

Miller management is confident that the partnership will be able to obtain construction financing. Also, it is sure that once construction begins, permanent financing will be available. The partners agree to share equally any profits or losses from the condominium operation.

Required:

1. Under generally accepted accounting principles, what amount of revenue would the Miller Distribution Company recognize from the October 19X3 sale transaction?
2. Would your answer be different if the joint venture had been formed in October 19X3 prior to the sale of the land and by virtue of a total land contribution on behalf of the Miller Distribution Company and a $1,250,000 cash contribution from the Jones Pipe Company?
3. To what extent should subsequent events influence or change prior accounting decisions? Defend your reasoning.

8-12. Analysis of Segmented Financial Information. Exhibit 8-5 shows business segment disclosures made by Westinghouse Electric Corporation in its 1977 annual report (the same report as the one utilized for purposes of Exhibit 8-2).

Required:

1. For the year 1977 calculate for each of Westinghouse's four major lines of business:
    (a) Operating profit to total revenue ratios
    (b) Operating profit to identifiable asset ratios
2. Calculate the same ratios for Westinghouse Electric Corporation as a whole for 1977 and interpret the results.

Exhibit 8-5
WESTINGHOUSE ELECTRIC CORPORATION

Westinghouse Financial Information by Segments
(Amounts in thousands)

Earnings Information for the Year Ended December 31:	1977	1976	1975	1974	1973
Sales to unaffiliated customers:					
Power Systems	$2,254,238	$2,052,537	$1,983,103	$1,803,389	$1,623,259
Industry Products	2,256,737	2,083,846	1,939,249	2,010,849	1,635,344
Public Systems	1,404,971	1,315,826	1,297,842	1,405,672	1,387,732
Broadcasting	175,821	172,350	145,816	138,354	123,075
Other	45,894	520,593	496,737	440,249	331,713
	$6,137,661	$6,145,152	$5,862,747	$5,798,513	$5,101,123
Intersegment sales:					
Power Systems	$ 109,436	$ 100,659	$ 91,863	$ 94,361	$ 75,140
Industry Products	60,292	54,237	56,870	123,139	68,175
Public Systems	10,692	10,250	18,794	23,508	9,142
Other	29,151	25,718	32,491	17,351	57,176
	$ 209,571	$ 190,864	$ 200,018	$ 258,359	$ 209,633
Total revenue:					
Power Systems	$2,363,674	$2,153,196	$2,074,966	$1,897,750	$1,698,399
Industry Products	2,317,029	2,138,083	1,996,119	2,133,988	1,703,519
Public Systems	1,415,663	1,326,076	1,316,636	1,429,180	1,396,874
Broadcasting	175,821	172,350	145,816	138,354	123,075
Other	75,045	546,311	529,228	457,600	388,889
	6,347,232	6,336,016	6,062,765	6,056,872	5,310,756
Eliminations	(209,571)	(190,864)	(200,018)	(258,359)	(209,633)
	$6,137,661	$6,145,152	$5,862,747	$5,798,513	$5,101,123

Exhibit 8-5 (cont.)
WESTINGHOUSE ELECTRIC CORPORATION

Earnings Information for the Year Ended December 31:	1977	1976	1975	1974	1973
Operating profit:					
Power Systems	$ 113,700	$ 113,095	$ 67,443	$ 43,739	$ 143,839
Industry Products	220,591	198,865	193,782	186,029	166,371
Public Systems	68,853	49,298	59,837	66,554	62,456
Broadcasting	52,444	52,000	41,705	39,626	38,733
Other	(15,313)	6,522	(4,525)	5,731	(11,773)
Adjustments and eliminations	(10,744)	(13,518)	5,747	(3,618)	(4,688)
	429,531	406,262	363,989	338,061	394,938
Equity in income (loss) from non-consolidated subsidiaries and affiliated companies	34,001	21,050	(4,513)	(32,285)	3,341
Other income	128,019	88,089	70,374	71,890	63,567
General corporate expenses	(118,517)	(101,849)	(78,514)	(60,237)	(60,566)
Interest expense	(46,107)	(52,347)	(76,425)	(111,261)	(69,317)
Income before taxes	$ 426,927	$ 361,205	$ 274,911	$ 206,168	$ 331,963

Asset Information at December 31:	1977	1976	1975	1974	1973
Identifiable assets:					
Power Systems	$2,034,111	$1,741,644	$1,652,565	$1,651,332	$1,542,014
Industry Products	1,101,559	998,810	970,790	1,002,317	923,045
Public Systems	662,809	696,345	731,198	759,716	886,554
Broadcasting	103,845	99,909	103,773	88,890	96,858
Other	95,529	509,315	526,969	520,180	323,655
Adjustments and eliminations	(76,131)	(67,486)	(58,489)	(60,433)	(43,813)
	3,921,722	3,978,537	3,926,806	3,962,002	3,728,313
Investments	559,342	386,505	289,188	226,209	183,575
Corporate assets	1,046,564	953,300	650,292	625,407	696,799
	$5,527,628	$5,318,342	$4,866,286	$4,813,618	$4,608,687

Revenue Recognition Refinements

9

Chapter 9 complements the preceding chapter. It extends the concepts and basic applications of revenue recognition to a number of special cases and issues. Throughout the study of the material in this chapter three basic propositions must be kept in mind: (1) long-term cash-flow forecasting, as mentioned many times before, is a central concern of investors in corporate securities and therefore the representation of cash-generating ability is also a central concern of financial reporting to third parties; (2) the basic revenue recognition framework developed in Chapter 8 applies to all the topics raised in the present chapter; and (3) the direct relationship between revenue recognition procedures and business income determination is at the core of many recent, as well as pending, financial accounting policy decisions.

Chapter 9 endeavors to increase the reader's understanding of the *measurement* issues surrounding revenue recognition policies and procedures. Chapter 8, we recall, focuses mainly on the allocation of recognized revenues to individual accounting periods and the various "sufficient" conditions for accounting recognition of revenue at different points in the production-sale-collection sequence. We now consider some further issues in revenue recognition.

RECOGNIZING UNCERTAINTY OF COLLECTION

Upon completion of a sale transaction, the seller either receives cash or has a legally enforceable claim against the buyer. However, a legally enforceable claim is not a guarantee that payment will be received. Whether short term or long term, all receivables (claims against customers) have a common characteristic—there is some uncertainty about their ultimate collectibility. When the uncertainty is judged to be low, or reasonably measurable, the criterion of certainty of price to be received is considered to be sufficiently satisfied to warrant recognition of the earning that has taken place at the date of sale. Normally there is concurrent recognition of the estimated losses that will be sustained from accounts that, in retrospect, turn out to be uncollectible. However, when the degree of uncertainty regarding the ultimate collection of cash is high (most frequently when the collection period extends over a long period of time), recognition of revenue is sometimes deferred beyond the point of sale. We first cover the procedures for handling the estimated losses from bad accounts when revenue is recognized at date of sale, and then some alternative ways of deferring revenue recognition beyond the point of sale under conditions of high uncertainty.

General Uncertainty Adaptation—Estimating Bad Debts

When a customer is unable to pay his account, we call the loss suffered by the business a *bad debt loss*. Obviously, one way of handling these losses would be to recognize them as an expense of the period in which it is determined that the account in uncollectible. But is this treatment consistent with the matching principle? Generally it is not. Because of the desire to exhaust all legal remedies in attempting to collect such accounts, recognition of bad accounts often occurs in periods subsequent to the period of sale. Yet the matching principle clearly calls for recognition of the bad debt in the same period that the sale giving rise to the account is recognized as revenue. The reason is that in most instances the extension of credit and the concomitant acceptance of the risk that some accounts will ultimately prove to be uncollectible are costs directly related to the generation of the revenue recognized. Indeed, some view the cost of bad accounts as one form of sales promotion expense.

How can this association between *future* bad accounts and related *current* sales revenues be accomplished? Firms generally do not make specific credit sales that they expect to prove uncollectible. But they do have historical evidence of their experience with bad accounts, and using this experience base they can *estimate* the amount of bad debts that they expect to suffer ultimately from the current period's sales. This estimate then provides the measure of the bad debt expense to be assigned to the current period. Alternatively, the estimated bad debts may be disclosed as a direct reduction from the gross amount of sales in the period to reflect the estimated "net" amount of cash that will ultimately be realized from those sales. Both of these alternatives deal only with classification *within* the income statement. Whether treated as an expense or as a reduction of revenue, the estimated bad debts method associates or matches the anticipated amount of uncollectible accounts with the related revenue.

The recognition of estimated bad debts also involves an adjustment to accounts receivable. The balance of accounts receivable is reduced from the sum of the amounts due from the individual customers to the net amount estimated to be ultimately realizable from the group of claims against customers arising out of current sales. Since the firm does not know which particular accounts will prove to be bad, the adjustment to accounts receivable is normally made using a contra-asset account similar to the accumulated depreciation account. This valuation account is typically designated "allowance for doubtful accounts." Each time that *estimated* bad debts are recognized as an expense, the negative balance of the account increases.

The typical journal entry is as follows:

Bad debts expense	XXXX	
Allowance for doubtful accounts		XXXX

Note that the expense account is an income statement account; the allowance account appears in the financial position statement as a contra account to accounts receivable—typically a current asset.

When an individual account included in accounts receivable is determined to be bad, the balance of the uncollectible account is deducted from both accounts receivable and allowance for doubtful accounts, with no resulting change in the net amount estimated to be collectible.

The journal entry involved is as follows:

Allowance for doubtful accounts	XXXX	
Accounts receivable		XXXX

Exhibit 9-1 demonstrates the concomitant financial position effect.

Exhibit 9-1

	Beginning Position	Write-off ($2,000 actual account)	Ending Position
Accounts receivable	$75,000	($2,000)	$73,000
Allowance for doubtful accounts	(5,000)	2,000	(3,000)
Net accounts receivable	$70,000	-0-	$70,000

The only way that actual experienced losses will influence the net receivable value reported on the financial statement is if an end-of-period review suggests that such losses were substantially different than originally estimated, and that therefore an additional (essentially retroactive) adjustment to expense and the valuation account is required. Because of a tendency toward conservatism in setting asset values, this adjustment is triggered more quickly by experiencing greater losses than were predicted; when the converse situation is encountered (fewer losses than predicted), the allowance may remain unadjusted longer until there is more evidence that the loss rate has actually changed.

Example 9-1

Easy Sales Company makes many of its sales to customers on credit. The treasurer's staff screens the credit application of each new customer before delivery of the first order. If the customer is judged credit-worthy, the goods are delivered and the customer is billed by mail. If the customer is judged not credit-worthy, the goods are delivered COD. As a result of this policy, only about 2 percent of total credit sales turn out in the long run to be uncollectible.

Sales and collection data for Easy Sales for 19X3 and 19X4 are as follows:

Year	Sales Cash	Sales Credit	Collections of Accounts Receivable	Accounts Determined to Be Uncollectible
19X3	$50,000	$300,000	$245,000	$5,000
19X4	40,000	360,000	370,000	9,000

The company adheres to a practice of offsetting the *estimated* uncollectible portion of new accounts receivable against its recognized sales revenue each year for income measurement purposes. At the end of each year (as well as points in between), all unpaid customer balances are reviewed for their estimated collectibility. If the balance in the "allowance" account is deemed inadequate to absorb the estimated uncollectible accounts receivable, an additional adjustment is made.

On January 1, 19X3, the balances of accounts receivable and allowance for doubtful accounts were $40,000 and $1,500, respectively. At the end of 19X3, the review of open accounts indicated that the end-of-year allowance was adequate to absorb the estimated uncollectible accounts. But at the end of 19X4, it was believed that the balance of the allowance was about $3,000 lower than the estimated uncollectible portion of ending accounts receivable. The cause of the inadequacy was the totally unexpected bankruptcy of a customer who owed the company $3,000 at the beginning of the year.

The facts given in Example 9-1 are analyzed in the partial financial position worksheet in Exhibit 9-2. The partial worksheet includes complete data for only two accounts—accounts receivable and allowance for doubtful accounts, because these accounts are central to our examination of the treatment of estimated and actual bad debts. Columns are provided for two other accounts (cash and owners' equity), without beginning and ending balances, to permit disclosure of the *effects* of the relevant transactions.

The estimated bad debts related to a particular year's *credit* sales are shown in the second line of the worksheet for each year as a reduction of owners' equity and an increase in the absolute value of the negative balance in the allowance account. Each estimate is 2 percent of credit sales for the year. The effect of the first two lines, therefore, is to recognize (1) the "net" revenue of the period and (2) the value of assets received as a result of current sales *at the "expected value" of customers' promises to pay*. The expected value of the assets to be received is, of course, represented by the combined balances in "accounts receivable" *and* "allowance for doubtful accounts." The expected

Exhibit 9-2

EASY SALES COMPANY

Partial Financial Position Worksheet—Treatment of Bad Debts

Description	Effect upon Cash	Accounts Receivable	Allowance for Doubtful Accounts	Effect upon Owners' Equity
19X3				
Beginning Balances	—	40,000	(1,500)	—
1. Sales	50,000	300,000		350,000 (R)
2. Estimated bad debts expense			(6,000)	(6,000) (E)
3. Write-off of bad accounts		(5,000)	5,000	
4. Collections on account	245,000	(245,000)		
Ending (Beginning) Balances	—	90,000	(2,500)	—
19X4				
1. Sales	40,000	360,000		400,000 (R)
2. Estimated bad debts expense			(7,200)	(7,200) (E)
3. Write-off of bad accounts		(9,000)	9,000	
4. Collections on account	370,000	(370,000)		
5. Adjustment to allowance for doubtful accounts			(3,000)	(3,000) (E)
Ending Balances	—	71,000	(3,700)	—

value of current revenue is represented by the *net* increase in owners' equity corresponding to the nominal amounts of the new accounts receivable of the period *less* the associated bad debts expense. The third item on the worksheet in each year reveals how the recognition of actual bad accounts is handled (compare these entries with the debit-credit pro forma journal entries presented earlier in this chapter).

At the end of each year, the balance of the allowance for doubtful accounts is evaluated to see if it represents an adequate estimate of accounts that the firm then believes will prove to be uncollectible in the future. The credit manager or treasurer generally makes this decision after reviewing the status of each unpaid account at the end of the year. In the example, the allowance is considered adequate at the end of 19X3; but at the end of 19X4, the review of the accounts suggested that the balance of the allowance for doubtful accounts was understated by $3,000. That is, the net amount estimated to be collectible from the open accounts at the end of 19X4 is believed to be $3,000 less than the *net* recorded accounts receivable (accounts receivable less allowance for doubtful accounts). Therefore an additional adjustment of $3,000 is required (line 5 of the 19X4 worksheet section). This adjustment further reduces 19X4 net revenue and increases the balance of the allowance for doubtful accounts (thus reducing the net accounts receivable).

Such an adjustment might be considered to be an "extraordinary" loss item, requiring special recognition in the income statement for the period. Indeed, if the estimating procedure has been fairly accurate in the past and this adjustment is largely related to the one unexpected event, there is considerable merit in this position. However, while this type of adjustment may be given special disclosure (a separate line) in the income statement, it may not be handled as an extraordinary item (i.e., it must be recognized as a deduction in arriving at *net operating income*) under currently prevailing authoritative standards for financial reporting. The reason for this restriction is that such adjustments to the "allowance" may be caused jointly by (1) unexpected events or conditions and (2) management's estimation errors. Thus management might make its performance look better currently by purposely underestimating bad debts expense and later recognizing the estimation error (bias) as an extraordinary loss. The fact that such adjustments are not permitted to be treated as extraordinary items means that they will inevitably show up as part of future periods' performance (operating income), which presumably reduces the incentive for manipulation.

We are now in a position to structure journal entries relating to bad debts recognition and write-offs for the Easy Sales Company for 19X4:

Bad debts expense	7,200	
Allowance for doubtful accounts		7,200
(Line 2 of Exhibit 9-2)		
Allowance for doubtful accounts	9,000	
Accounts receivable		9,000
(Line 3 of Exhibit 9-2)		
Bad debts expense	3,000	
Allowance for doubtful accounts		3,000
(Line 5 of Exhibit 9-2)		

Parenthetically we note that bad debts allowances may be calculated in a number of different ways arithmetically. Generally accepted accounting principles (as well as federal income tax regulations) stipulate only that appropriate calculations be (1) systematic, (2) related to actual bad debts experience, and (3) consistent from period to period. In our example we used a percentage of the period's credit sales as the bad debts estimator. Some firms employ a percentage of total receivables outstanding at year-end as the appropriate coefficient. Still other firms prepare elaborate "aging schedules" which classify all of their receivables according to the length of period for which they have remained unpaid. Then, on the basis of such classifications, they assign uncollectibility ratios to different age groups of accounts receivable. Some enterprises employ combinations of the foregoing methods. The important point for all of them, though, remains the goal of appropriate matching in the income statement and an appropriate statement of collectibility (net realizable value) of the underlying receivables in the statement of financial position.

Adaptation to High Uncertainty—Deferral of Revenue Recognition

The bad debts estimation procedure is applicable to all situations involving credit sales, regardless of the period of time over which the accounts are to be collected. Use of this method permits timely recognition of revenue when sales take place, with an allowance for the normal uncertainty associated with the extension of credit. However, there are instances, such as in the case of *some* long-term installment contracts, where the uncertainty is so great that the bad debt modification of measured accomplishment does not adequately deal with the problem. Because of the high degree of uncertainty, the point-of-sale basis for recognizing revenue may be abandoned in favor of a revenue recognition basis that is tied directly to the collection of cash. The most frequently used cash-collection-based method is known as the *installment sales method*.[1]

Installment Sales Method.

Example 9-2

> The Funtier Land Company has been organized to develop and sell lots in West Texas. The company's objective is to create a retirement community paralleling some of those already developed in Arizona and Florida. While the owners of the company believe that the climatic conditions are suited to this type of development, they realize that many potential customers may have reservations about the viability of the project. Under these circumstances it will be difficult to sell the lots on a cash basis, or even on credit if the terms of sale provide for full payment to be made within a fairly short time. Yet some lots must be sold and building initiated if this potential customer apprehension is to be alleviated. Therefore the developers decide initially to offer the lots for sale for $99 down, and $400 at the end of each year for the next five years. If a customer fails to make a payment on his contract within a sixty-day grace period after each annual due date, title to the land reverts to the developer.

Under conditions such as those described in Example 9-2, it is difficult to determine at the time of sale the amount of cash that will ultimately be realized from any single customer. Previous experience on projects of this type and risk indicates that many customers will default, often early in the life of the contract, and therefore the unadjusted total value of sales transactions of a period may be a poor indicator of accomplishment for that period of time. If a reasonable estimate of the potential losses from the installment contracts can be made, the total revenue can be recognized in the period of sale and the estimated bad debt expense matched against it. Note that the estimate of losses on bad accounts must take into account the estimated market value (perhaps the *cash* value) of the land that reverts to the developer upon default of a contract. However, the management of Funtier may decide that it is not possible to make a reasonably dependable estimate of the number of land contract accounts that will default or prove to be "bad." Therefore it might elect to recognize the

---

[1] Note that the installment sales *method* is not the only way to account for so-called installment sales contracts. The point-of-sale method may also be employed. Point-of-sale revenue recognition of installment sales contracts is illustrated later in this chapter.

profit from the transaction in some relationship to actual collections of cash using the installment sales method.

If the cost of each lot to Funtier Land Company was $1,099, the total profit to be recognized when the cash is ultimately collected will be $1,000 ($2,099 − $1,099). Under the installment sales method of recognizing accomplishment, the profit to be recognized in any period is determined by multiplying the $1,000 total potential profit by the ratio of cash collections in that period to the total cash to be collected over the life of the contract. This method is illustrated in Exhibit 9-3.

Exhibit 9-3

REVENUE RECOGNITION PATTERN FOR FUNTIER LAND COMPANY UNDER INSTALLMENT SALES METHOD

Year	Cash Collection	Ratio of Cash Collected to Selling Price	Profit Recognized
1	$ 499	$499/$2,099 = 24%	$ 240 (24% × $1,000)
2	400	400/ 2,099 = 19	190 (19 × 1,000)
3	400	400/ 2,099 = 19	190 (19 × 1,000)
4	400	400/ 2,099 = 19	190 (19 × 1,000)
5	400	400/ 2,099 = 19	190 (19 × 1,000)
	$2,099	100%	$1,000

At the point of sale (1) the account containing the cost of the item sold is reduced by that cost (in this case $1,099), (2) the cash account is increased by the amount of the down payment ($99), (3) the account "installment contracts receivable" is increased by the amount of the installments (in this case $2,000), (4) a *negative balance* contra-asset account, "deferred income on installment contracts" is set up equal to the portion of the estimated income on the yet-to-be-collected installments (in this case $950), and (5) owners' equity is increased via a temporary account by just the portion of total estimated income applicable to the down payment (in this case $50). This procedure is illustrated by the following journal entry (line numbers follow the preceding explanations):

(2) Cash	99	
(3) Installment contracts receivable	2,000	
(1) Lot inventory (West Texas)		1,099
(4) Deferred income on installment contracts		950
(5) Realized income on installment contracts (owners' equity)		50

Thereafter, as each installment is received: (1) cash is increased and installment contracts receivable is decreased by the amount of the installment ($400 per year), and (2) the negative balance of the deferred income on installments is reduced and owners' equity is increased by the portion of the total income applicable to the installment ($190 for each installment). Again, the respective journal entries are as follows:

(1) Cash $400
    Installment contracts receivable $400

and

(2) Deferred income on installment contracts   190
    Realized income on installment contracts (owners' equity)   190

Cost Recovery Method. An even more conservative response than the installment sales method to a high degree of uncertainty is to defer recognition of income altogether until the cost of the product sold has been fully recovered. Thus, in the example, no income would be recognized until cash of $1,099, equal to the cost of the land, had been collected. After the total cost had been recovered, all subsequent collections would be recognized as income. This very conservative approach, which represents an extreme form of the trade-off between the two realization criteria (in favor of certainty of price), has few supporters, however, and would probably be encountered only rarely in current financial reporting. On the other hand, the installment sales method of recognizing revenue is applied in current financial reporting by some companies, and by many more in the recognition of taxable income for types of business transactions qualifying for such treatment under provisions of the federal income tax code (because it results in a deferral of tax payments).

PROVISION OF JOINT PRODUCTS (GOODS AND FUTURE SERVICES) FOR A SINGLE PRICE

In many instances a single sales price includes goods that are delivered at the date of sale and the promise to provide future services. The additional services yet to be performed by the seller, which may be of many different types, often include the provision of financing services, the warranty of products for a specified period of time, and franchising services to franchisees. Whatever the type of service, it is inappropriate to recognize the total sales price as revenue of the current period, because the company has not satisfied the *earning* criterion of the realization principle with respect to the future services. Rather, the single price must be broken down into the amounts of compensation received for each of the two distinct products sold to the customer, and revenue then recognized as earned. The portion of the price allocated to the goods that are delivered at the date of sale may be recognized in that period in accordance with the point-of-sale interpretation of the realization principle. The portion of the price allocated to future services will be recognized as revenue concurrently with the delivery of these services. This procedure is illustrated below for three types of future services specifically mentioned—financing services, warranties, and franchising.

Providing Credit as well as a Product to the Customer

When we initially considered the simple investment decision model in Chapter 2, we recognized that dollars received at different points in time are of differing values to a recipient because of his time preference for money. The present value principles developed in that analysis are equally valid for the enterprise because it has a time preference rate based upon the opportunities it has to invest dollars on hand. Conceptually, therefore, all contractual obligations of customers to pay agreed-upon prices for delivered goods or services at some future time should be discounted at the time of sale to determine the cash equivalent value of the credit sale. This cash equivalent (present value) of the future amount to be paid by the customer is the best measure of the accomplishment reflected by the delivery of goods. The remaining portion of the total contract price which will eventually be collected represents compensation for a second service—financing the purchase for the customer. Since this compensation has not been earned at the date of sale, it should not be recognized at that time. Rather, the "financing revenue" is recognized over the period of time that the loan is outstanding in accordance with the present value techniques developed in Chapter 2.

We note at the outset that in many instances the period of time between the date of sale and the collection of cash is of such short duration that application of the present value methodology would not produce a material change or difference in the measurement of accomplishment and the related valuation of accounts receivable. But when the length of the collection period is substantial, the difference between the present value and the total amounts due from customers may be important, or material, to the statement user. If it is, the present value technique can be applied to allocate the total price between the goods and the financing service.

Example 9-3

> Referring back to Example 9-2, the Funtier Land Company offered lots for sale for $99 down and $400 at the end of each year for five years. Under these circumstances the total price of $2,099 represents compensation for two services: conveying land and providing financing. To measure the values attributable to each of these two different services, we must calculate the present value of the sales contract. Assuming Funtier has an opportunity rate of 10 percent, *and ignoring the question of the degree of uncertainty existing as to the ultimate collectibility of the contracts,* we can measure the present value of a contract as illustrated in Exhibit 9-4.

The calculation of the present value of the sales contract in Exhibit 9-4 implies that the Funtier Land Company would be willing to accept $1,614 today in lieu of the contract provision of $99 down and $400 per year for five years. Thus the measure of accomplishment to be associated with the sale of the land is more properly stated at $1,614 than at the total contract price of $2,099. The difference of $485 ($2,099 - $1,614) is the amount of revenue that will be earned from providing a financing service over the five-year life of the contract.

The amount of revenue to be recognized each period from the financing

Exhibit 9-4

CALCULATION OF PRESENT VALUE OF A FUNTIER LAND COMPANY SALES CONTRACT

Year	Cash Flow	$PV_{(n, 0.10)}$	Present Value of Cash Flows
0	$ 99	1.0	$ 99
1	400	0.909	364
2	400	0.826	330
3	400	0.751	300
4	400	0.683	273
5	400	0.621	248
	$2,099		$1,614

operation is, as mentioned above, based upon the present value principles outlined in Chapter 2. At the start of the first period, the receivable from a customer would amount to $1,515—the $1,614 present value (or cash equivalent value) of the contract less the $99 down payment. Then, in the first year, the firm earns (imputed) interest income of 10 percent on the $1,515 balance, or approximately $152. Since $400 is collected at the end of each period, the balance of the receivable at the end of the first year would be calculated as follows:

Accounts receivable, start of year 1	$1,515
Imputed interest income (10% × $1,515) at end of first year	152
	$1,667
Collection of first $400 installment at end of first year	400
Accounts receivable, end of year 1	$1,267

Continuing in this fashion, the firm will recognize an increase in the balance of the receivable (and a concurrent increase in owners' equity) due to the imputed interest income on the accounts receivable balance as it stood at the start of each year. Then the balance of the receivable will be reduced each time a $400 cash collection is received. At the end of the life of the contract, the balance of the receivable will be reduced to zero. The pattern of revenue from the financing service and the related value assigned to the receivable is summarized in Exhibit 9-5.

Assuming that the installment sales method of revenue (and gross profit) recognition *is not used* for purposes of Example 9-3, the following journal entries are required at the beginning of year one:

Cash	99	
Installment contracts receivable	1,515	
Revenue from lot sales		1,614

Exhibit 9-5

PATTERN OF REVENUE RECOGNITION AND RELATED VALUATION OF RECEIVABLES FOR FUNTIER LAND COMPANY'S FINANCING OPERATIONS (ONE SALES CONTRACT)

	Year				
	1	2	3	4	5
Accounts receivable balance, start of year	$1,515	$1,267	$ 994	$694	$364
Imputed interest income (10% of beginning balance) as of end of year	152	127	100	70	36
	$1,667	$1,394	$1,094	$764	$400
Collection of $400 installment payment at end of year	400	400	400	400	400
Accounts receivable balance, end of year	$1,267	$ 994	$ 694	$364	$-0-

and

Cost of lots sold	1,099	
Lot inventory (West Texas)		1,099

(Note that "Revenue from Lot Sales" is the lead-off income statement caption in this case, whereas "Realized Income on Installment Contracts" is the corresponding caption when the installment sales method is used.)

The following journal entries recognize the interest earned and the payment received at the end of year one:

Installment contracts receivable	152	
Interest income realized		152

and

Cash	400	
Installment contracts receivable		400

These two entries are then repeated each year—with the "interest income realized" amounts different each year as the balance of the receivable declines (see the second line of Exhibit 9-5).

At the end of year five, there is a final journal entry:

Cash	400	
Installment contracts receivable		364
Interest income realized		36

It is important to note the overall modification in the measurement of revenue that results from recognizing the provision of two separate services instead of merely recognizing revenue in the amount of the face value of the contracts when a sale is made. If the total contract price of $2,099 is associated solely with the sale of the land, revenue of $2,099 would be recognized in the year the contract is signed and no accomplishment would be reflected over the remaining life of the contract. However, when it is recognized that two distinct services are sold or provided, and the present value methodology is used to measure the compensation received for each of them, a smaller amount of revenue (the cash equivalent value of the contract) is associated with the sale of land and recognized in the year of sale, and the remainder of the contract price is recognized as interest income over the five-year period. These comparative revenue recognition patterns are shown in Exhibit 9-6.

Note that column 2 in Exhibit 9-6 reflects the "installment sales method" of revenue recognition, column 3 reflects the strict point-of-sale recognition method, and the final column the "sale with financing method" utilizing imputed interest calculations.

The total revenue recognized under all three methods is equal over the five-year period—$2,099. And, as we have previously noted, total revenue recognized under the conventional accounting model will in the long run be equal to total cash receipts. But the principal objective in moving from a cash basis to the concept of revenue embodied in the conventional accounting model was to reflect the accomplishment of each period. To this end, the recognition of the time value of money to measure what Funtier has earned each period from each of the two services it provides is clearly preferable. Although generally recognized to be conceptually superior, recognition of the time value of money in measuring accomplishment was not often used in practice until recently. However, the emergence of businesses like land development companies, with sale terms similar to those outlined in the example, made obvious the need for some type of modification. Current accounting policy for financial reporting requires that the present value technique be applied whenever the difference between the present value and the total amount of a receivable is material. The example illustrates a situation where the present value model is used as the valuation base for one enterprise resource (accounts receivable), with the related modification in the recognition of revenue.

Exhibit 9-6

COMPARATIVE REVENUE PATTERNS FOR FUNTIER LAND COMPANY'S TOTAL OPERATIONS (ONE SALES CONTRACT)

Year	Collections	Revenue (Sales) Assigned Solely to Sale of Land	Revenue from Land Sale and Financing Operation		
			Sales	Interest Income	Total
1	$ 499	$2,099	$1,614	$152	$1,766
2	400	-0-	-0-	127	127
3	400	-0-	-0-	100	100
4	400	-0-	-0-	70	70
5	400	-0-	-0-	36	36
	$2,099	$2,099	$1,614	$485	$2,099

One final comment about Example 9-3 may be in order to avoid a possible misleading impression. The hypothetical sales contracts of the Funtier Land Company contain no explicit interest rates or charges. However, the concepts proposed and the approach developed are equally valid even when an interest rate is explicitly stated in a sales contract. For example, the contract might have specified interest payments at 4 percent on the unpaid balance, even though the seller's opportunity rate is 10 percent. In this case it would still be appropriate to calculate the present value of the future cash flows (including the cash interest payments to be received) *at the seller's opportunity rate* in arriving at the measure of accomplishment to be reported from the sale of land and the balance of accounts receivable at the start of the period. The present value of the contract will simply be less (greater) than the face amount of the contract if the opportunity rate is greater (less) than the arbitrary contract rate. Of course, if the interest rate included in a contract is equal to (or approximates) the firm's opportunity rate, the present value will be equal to (or will approximate) the face value and no allocation is required. Under these conditions, the cash interest payments will properly reflect the compensation earned from the financing operations.

Providing Warranty Services as well as a Product to the Customer

When merchandise is sold with a warranty or service guarantee, the total selling price is again composed of two elements: (1) a price for the product itself and (2) a price for the warranty on the product. Under the realization principle, the amount of the selling price that is attributable to the product itself has been earned and should be recognized in the period of sale. However, the portion of the selling price that represents compensation to the seller (or manufacturer) for the guarantee he provides has not yet been earned. As in the case of the provision of financing services, this portion of the total sales proceeds should be deferred and recognized in some fashion over the life of the warranty.

Example 9-4

The Modern TV Company sells 21-inch color television sets at a price of $495. This includes a warranty on all parts and labor for a two-year period.

In establishing the selling price, the company assumed that the average cost per customer of servicing defective units would be approximately $45 in the first year of the warranty and $80 in the second year of the warranty. Since it wishes to earn a 20 percent return on its cost on this type of activity, it marked up the product $150 (120 percent $\times$ $125) to cover the warranty. Therefore it would be willing to sell the TV unit without a service warranty at a price of $345.

Based upon these factors, it is appropriate to recognize revenue at the time of sale in the amount of $345 per unit. The additional $150 that is received at the time of sale is payment for undelivered services, and it is deferred to future periods for recognition as it is earned throughout the warranty period.

Assuming a credit sale based on the facts of Example 9-4, the following revenue recognition journal entry is made at the point of sale:

Accounts receivable	495	
Sales revenue		345
Warranty service liability		125
Deferred income on future warranty services		25

During the first year after the sale, warranty service expenses turned out to be $45 as estimated. This prompts the following type of journal entry:

Warranty service liability	45	
Cash (or other assets or liabilities)		45

and, at the end of the year:

Deferred income on future warranty services (45/125 of $25)	9	
Realized income on warranty services		9

The recognition of revenue as described in Example 9-4 is the preferable way to handle warranty and service contracts that are attached to the sale of merchandise. Application of the method depends upon the ability to separate the total price of the product into the portion applicable to the product itself and the portion applicable to the warranty. A less preferable method of handling this type of sale is to recognize all the revenue in the period of sale, and to accrue the expenses estimated to be incurred in the future under the warranty. Based on the facts stated above, the Modern TV Company would recognize $495 revenue in the period of sale for each unit sold, and additionally accrue a warranty expense (and the related liability for future services) of $125 per unit in the same period. Although this accrual method does not assign the revenue for the warranty to the periods of time in which it is presumably earned, it does adhere to the matching principle by associating the expenses incurred or estimated to be incurred with the related revenue. The method is, therefore, superior to merely recognizing the total selling prices of the TV sets as revenue in the period they are sold, without giving any recognition in that period to the expenses that will be incurred as a result of the guarantee given to the customer—as might result if one merely applied the point-of-sale criterion to this type of sale without considering the future service yet to be rendered.

Similarly, in all types of cases involving goods *and future services* sold as a package for a single price, the critical question revolves around when the enterprise *earns* the revenue from each of the product and service components. Except in cases involving insuperable measurement problems or an immaterial level of future services, all sales that involve the provision of goods *and future services* for a single price should be separated into their component parts and the realization principle applied to each component individually.

Providing Franchising Services as well as Various Products to the Customer

Franchising has become a significant economic activity throughout the Western world. Fast-food operations, car and equipment rental agencies, computer service bureaus, and hotels and motels, plus many other economic products and services, are currently made available to customers through franchising operations.

Franchising typically occurs when the holder of a patent or the owner of a unique process, service, or product becomes a franchisor—a person willing to make the brand name, process, system, and so forth, available to others in exchange for the payment of certain fees. Normally an initial fee is required when a franchise contract is signed; later period payments come about through the continued use of the franchise by the franchisee plus purchase of franchise-related items from the franchisor. Items later purchased might include foods, menus, and restaurant furniture for a franchise restaurant; or office layouts, office equipment, paper forms, and computer programs for a computer services operation. In a certain sense the franchising situation is the inverse of the warranty case discussed in the preceding section. Even though initial contract payments are often large, the franchisor delivers relatively little product at the time the franchising operation begins. On the other hand, in the warranty case, the primary product is delivered to start with, and generally less significant future service flows are not necessarily related to or connected with additional product deliveries.

Example 9-5

> The Photo Lab franchise was set up to distribute unexposed films for amateur photographer use and to provide "lightning speed" photo developing services. Since little physical space is required for the Photo Lab sales operation (supplies are reordered biweekly from central warehouses, and developing is done in central processing laboratories serviced by convenient air-freight connections), franchise holders typically occupy small (and often otherwise unusable) counter spaces in shopping malls or drive-up booths in parking lots and the like.
>
> The typical franchise contract requires a $12,000 initial payment for which the Photo Lab organization will suitably paint and equip the interior of a small shopping center location or install a drive-up parking lot sales booth. Space rentals, utility costs, taxes and insurance, and so forth, are the responsibility of the franchisee.
>
> Photo Labs operate with a fixed price schedule for all customer services. Costs to individual franchisees of both supplies and processing are at a discount of 25 percent from the published prices. In turn, the franchisee is obligated to pay the Photo Lab organization 10 percent of all gross receipts. For this 10 percent fee the central organization supplies money credit, regular bookkeeping services, occasional advertising in local news media, training of sales personnel, and occasional management consulting as required or needed by franchise holders.

The revenue recognition problem for the hypothetical situation sketched in Example 9-5 is, of course, complex. The initial contract payment from a new franchisee to the central organization no doubt exceeds the value of the product delivered (interior furnishings of a small sales outlet). Therefore a part of the initial $12,000 payment should be deferred over the length of the respective franchise contract, since the "earning" process required by the realization principle has occurred only partially.

Provision of supplies and film-developing services later on at an agreed-upon price between the franchisor and the franchisees causes no particular revenue recognition complication. The prices charged to the franchisees are revenue amounts to the franchisor. If the Photo Lab organization can purchase supplies or develop films at costs less than those charged to the franchise holders, it obviously earns income at each biweekly point of sale for supplies, and each delivery of processed films.

However, an additional complication arises from the assessment of the periodic franchise fee because the services provided in exchange for this fee are likely to occur in uneven amounts from year to year. Advertising and bookkeeping services probably vary little, whereas sales training and consulting services may vary greatly. Of course a part of the annual franchise fee also relates to the continuing use of the franchise. As a practical matter, therefore, the annual franchise fee is recognizable revenue of the Photo Lab organization in the period assessed, provided the franchising contract continues.

In summary, the initial contract amount of $12,000 presents the biggest revenue recognition problem. This problem is confounded when a new franchisee does not have enough cash to pay the entire amount outright and borrows from the franchisor against personal notes payable. Then the financing services procedures discussed earlier in this section come into play in addition to the allocation procedure for the initial $12,000.

Based on the facts presented in Example 9-5 and the subsequent discussion related to the example, the following revenue recognition procedures are likely to be appropriate for the Photo Lab franchising operation (from the viewpoint of the franchisor):

Event	Revenue Recognition Method
1. Receipt of initial $12,000 franchise fee	1. (a) Recognize as revenue when contract is signed that portion which represents costs plus a reasonable markup on such costs to establish franchisee at the chosen business location (b) Allocate remainder in equal amounts to periods covered by the initial contract (contract renewal or extension options may be ignored for this purpose)
2. Receipt of payments for supplies delivered and films developed	2. Point-of-sale revenue recognition
3. Receipt of annual management fees from franchisees	3. Recognition as realized revenue at end of each year to which fee applies
4. Payments received under financing contracts with franchisees	4. Present value revenue method (i.e., the implicit rate of interest times the financing contract balance outstanding yields the amount of realized interest income recognized each period)

Since franchising contracts are not standardized, accounting for them cannot be standardized either. It is therefore imperative that readers of financial statements consider the applicable notes to financial statements which typically describe special measurement procedures employed in cases of franchising. The matter of notes to and explanations of financial statements is discussed further in Chapter 18.

DISCOUNTS AND ALLOWANCES

Our discussion of specific revenue measurement and recognition issues would be incomplete without some attention to two more topics, namely (1) price and payment discounts and (2) merchandise returns and allowances and/or forgiven billings.

Price Discounts (also known as Trade Discounts)

In some industries it is common practice to have a set of standard prices, together with a series of discounts granted to customers based on the volume of products they order. Sometimes these price discounts are stated in terms of a single percentage reduction from the list price, say 10 percent. The cash price would then be 90 percent of the stated list price. At other times the price discounts are stated as a *series* of percentage discounts from the list price, say 20/10/5. When a series of discounts is offered, the first discount is applied against the list price, and then succeeding discounts are applied sequentially to the price established after taking into account the previous discount.

Example 9-6

The Globe Steel Company sells a wide range of steel products. It maintains a standard set of list prices for these products, together with a series of price discounts based on the volume each customer orders. In one instance the Globe Steel Company sold 1,000 units of a particular product to a customer at a price of $20 per unit with price discounts of 20/10/10. The actual cash selling price to the customer is computed as follows:

List price (1,000 units @ $20)	$20,000
Less: 20% price discount	−4,000
	$16,000
Less: 10% price discount	−1,600
	$14,400
Less: 10% price discount	−1,440
	$12,960

In this instance the selling price of the goods is not the list price of $20,000, but rather the $12,960 price the customer is committed to pay. Therefore revenue from this transaction is recognized by the seller in the amount of $12,960.

In general, where price discounts are made available to customers, revenue is recognized for each sale in the amount of the *net cash price* to the customer after price discounts are deducted. The price discounts are not expenses; rather, they are means of adjusting the set of list prices to prevailing or "competitive" cash prices. Readers are reminded that the older terminology of "trade discounts" is still found frequently in accounting textbooks, handbooks, and periodical literature.

Prompt Payment Discounts (also known as Cash Discounts)

In addition to price discounts, sellers often grant a small prompt payment discount, or reduction in the amount that the customer has to pay, if payment is received within a fairly short time. A buyer often has thirty days or more to settle his account without penalty, and the prompt payment discount represents an inducement to the buyer to make payment at an earlier date. This inducement is offered by the seller because of a principle mentioned several times earlier—money has a time value. Hence the seller prefers to receive the amount due to him from the sale as soon as possible. The discount provision may also reduce the risk of bad debt losses, to the extent it induces payment of amounts due.

The terms of credit sales where prompt payment discounts are available are normally stated in the following form: terms 2/10, net/30. This means that under these specific terms the customer is entitled to a 2 percent discount if he pays his account in ten days, but if he does not elect to take this discount he must pay the balance in thirty days. If these terms were applied to a sale for $1,000 on July 1, the customer would have the option of settling his account for $980 if he made payment within the ten-day period following the sale, or by July 11; if the customer did not make payment in time to receive the cash discount, he would then have to make full payment ($1,000) by July 31.

Two different treatments of prompt payment discounts are found in accounting practice. Under the older method, the seller would recognize the discount, *when taken by the buyer,* as an expense or negative revenue item of that period. The seller in the above example would report revenue of $1,000 and would then deduct the $20 "cash" discount taken. The $20 deduction would either be offset against revenue to determine net revenue or be reported as "cash discounts expense." When this method of treating prompt payment discounts is used, the preferred treatment is to report the discounts taken as an offset to revenue.

A weakness in the treatment described is that it does not recognize revenue at the cash equivalent price *when the customer fails to take the discount.* If the customer in the above example fails to take the discount, the sales revenue would be recognized in the amount of $1,000. However, the cash equivalent price of the sales transaction was $980—the amount at which the merchandise could have been purchased with a cash payment at date of sale or anytime during the next ten days. In response to this weakness, an alternative method of treating "cash" discounts is to record the revenue *and* the accounts receivable at the cash equivalent price at the date of sale—in the example, $980. Then, if the discount is taken, no further adjustments are required. However, if the customer fails to take the discount, the seller receives $1,000 and the accounts receivable is stated at $980. The $20 difference is reflected by the seller in his income statement as income from discounts allowed but not taken by the buyer—revenue from the short-term credit or financing service the seller has provided.

The problem of reporting prompt payment discounts, whether taken or not, exists for the buyer as well as the seller. The two alternatives described above for the seller are equally applicable to the buyer. Under the first alternative, the buyer records his purchases of merchandise and the related accounts payable at their invoice price and then deducts all "cash" discounts that he takes from the cost of merchandise. The second alternative calls for all purchases of inventory and the related accounts payable to be recorded at the cash equivalent price, whether the discount is taken or not. If an available discount is not taken, it is reported under this second method as an expense (discounts lost) of the period in which it was lost.

Under traditional types of discount terms, it is generally highly desirable that a business not lose any discounts available to it. This observation stems from the high effective rate of interest that is usually implicitly imbedded in the discount terms. For example, with terms of 2/10, net/30, the seller is offering a 2 percent reduction in the amount owed to him if the buyer makes payment twenty days earlier than the final due date. That is, he can pay within ten days and still take the discount, but if he does not, he must pay the full amount within the next twenty days or his account becomes delinquent and subject to contractual or statutory interest charges. Assuming that the buyer is planning to make payment within the thirty-day credit period, failure to make the payment within ten days and take the discount means that he is merely deferring payment for up to twenty days. Given the 2 percent discount terms, this amounts to an effective *annual* interest rate on the use of money for these twenty days of 36 percent (360 days ÷ 20 days × 2 percent). Therefore, in most instances, the business would be much better off economically by borrowing money at normal bank rates rather than losing available prompt payment discounts on its trade accounts.

Merchandise Returns and Allowances

Many business enterprises, especially retail stores, give customers the privilege of returning merchandise recently purchased and either left unopened in original packages or found defective, mislabeled, or otherwise different from its displayed appearance. When the merchandise is returned unopened, it is typically returned to the seller's inventory and later sold to another customer. This type of activity is fairly common with items purchased as gifts for others—e.g., Christmas or birthday gifts.

When a resalable merchandise item is returned, the usual bookkeeping entries are as shown below and at the top of page 320.

Sales returns	XXXX	
Accounts receivable (or cash)		XXXX

Merchandise inventory	XXXX	
Cost of merchandise sold		XXXX

The foregoing entries in effect "reverse" the entries that accompanied the original sale. The only difference is that "sales revenue" was not debited (i.e., reduced). Instead a separate account, "sales returns," is used so that management accumulates a record of the amount of sales that were returned or exchanged. At the end of the period, though, the account "sales returns" is netted against the total in the sales revenue account and thus has the appropriate effect on the calculation of the net sales figure that appears in the income statement. Published income statements almost never show returns or other sales revenue adjustments separately. These adjustments are typically not significant enough in size to warrant separate attention in published financial statements.

Allowances on items sold usually result from defective or otherwise unusable merchandise. Here the item cannot be returned to the regular inventory and is either sent out for repair, returned to the manufacturer, or, when both of these alternatives are unavailable or too costly, simply sold at a discount or destroyed. Allowances thus represent reductions in effective revenue for a period without any corresponding inventory changes. Among industrial suppliers, allowances are typically recognized when the seller sends a "credit memo." Such a memorandum signifies that the seller has "credited" the account receivable from the buyer for the amount of the allowance (i.e., the dollar amount shown on the "credit memo").

The appropriate journal entry is of the form:

Sales allowances	XXXX	
Accounts receivable (or cash)		XXXX

In some firms merchandise returns as well as sales allowances are recorded in a single temporary account called "sales returns and allowances" because the number of transactions of this type is expected to be small.

Forgiven Billings

Professional people such as architects, CPAs, dentists, doctors, and lawyers often recognize revenue only on an "eventual ability to pay" basis. That is, they render some services on a public interest basis for which they expect no payment at all and some services to persons who are simply unable to pay normal professional rates. In such cases it does not make sense to record revenue at regular billing rates only to have such recognition reversed again as "allowances" at a later date.

In certain situations, of course, bills rendered are adjusted or forgiven altogether. This happens when a client is very unhappy about the quality of service received or when, in the light of subsequent events (e.g., zoning law changes, bankruptcy, or professional liability), it seems inappropriate to collect for the particular service rendered.

In unusual cases retail stores or restaurants also forgive an existing billing, but when this happens in other than a personal service situation, it is usually considered a sales allowance.

The key point to be made here is that forgiven billings require no bookkeeping entries or adjustments when revenue is recognized on a cash basis only. Where the accrual basis is employed, forgiven billings are treated just like sales returns or allowances.

SUMMARY

Our principal purpose in the foregoing discussion has been to outline and illustrate the general types of situations that justify an exception to our normal point-of-sale basis of revenue recognition under the conventional accounting model. Yet, how different do the conditions have to be in order to drop the point-of-sale criterion? It should be relatively clear that the circumstances described in our examples are not totally different from the typical conditions surrounding most sales transactions. All credit sales involve a lag in cash collection, and most business activities involve some production or service before or after the point of sale (or both). Circumstances that justify departure from the point-of-sale criterion are therefore a matter of the degree of disparity from "normal" conditions. Thus, in the application of the point-of-sale criterion, as well as the modifications we review, it should be apparent that there is need for both conventions (or practical guidelines) and professional judgment in determining whether a particular business circumstance falls within the range of acceptability for application of the point-of-sale criterion or whether it calls for one of the acceptable modifications.

Questions for Review and Discussion

9-1. Define:
   a. Bad debts
   b. Installment sales method
   c. Cost recovery method
   d. Warranty services
   e. Franchising
   f. Future service transactions
   g. Price discounts
   h. Prompt payment discounts
   i. Merchandise returns and allowances
   j. Sale with financing method

9-2. There is some uncertainty about the ultimate collectibility of all receivables, but the accounting treatment varies depending upon the degree of uncertainty. Describe in general terms the two alternative approaches to uncertainty, and indicate which, if either, of the two criteria of the realization principle is given more weight under each approach than it is given in the balance struck under the strict point-of-sale interpretation.

9-3. Why are bad debts that may be incurred in future periods estimated and reflected as expenses of the current period rather than merely reflected as expenses of the period in which they are determined uncollectible?

9-4. What effect does the write-off of a bad account receivable have on the net value of accounts receivable and expense of the current period?

9-5. In published financial statements should estimated bad debt losses be reported as reductions from sales revenue or as a separate expense item? What difference does it make, if any, how bad debt losses are reported in financial statements?

9-6. Arithmetically, there are at least four different ways of estimating future bad debt losses. Which of these four methods do you think yields the most acceptable results. Give the reasons for your conclusion.

9-7. When a single sales price includes goods that are delivered at date of sale and the promise to provide future services, describe in general terms the modification that is made to the point-of-sale interpretation of the realization principle (assuming both components are material and measurable). Indicate which criterion of the realization principle is given more weight in this modification than it is given in the balance struck under the strict point-of-sale interpretation.

9-8. Not every installment sales (i.e., long-term payments) *contract* is accounted for by the installment sales *method* of revenue recognition. Why? Describe a business situation where point-of-sale revenue recognition is appropriate for an installment sales contract.

9-9. On July 1, 19X4, Local Speculation Company sold a parcel of land it had acquired ten years ago at a cost of $500,000 to Giant Manufacturing Company for $1.8 million. Local received a non-interest-bearing note due July 1, 19X7, in payment. Assuming 12 percent is the appropriate time preference rate for Local, indicate how Local would record the sale transaction on July 1, 19X4. Also, prepare a schedule of revenue that Local would recognize for each year from 19X4 through 19X7, and calculate the value at which the note receivable would be carried in the statement of financial position at the end of 19X4, 19X5, and 19X6.

9-10. The installment sales method of accounting for highly risky installment accounts receivable is described in the body of the chapter. An alternative to that method is one in which (1) the present value method is used to value the accounts receivable, with an appropriately high discount rate which recognizes the high opportunity cost for such risky credit granting, and (2) a substantial allowance for bad debts. Contrast the pattern of income recognition and asset valuation under this alternative with the installment sales method. Make up an example to illustrate your explanations. Which method do you prefer? Defend your position.

9-11. Existing financial accounting policies require that the present value method be employed in financial statement reporting of certain receivables. Why are some accounts receivable stated at actual transaction values and others at present values? Is revenue recognition affected by the choice between these two measurement methods?

9-12. Why is it so difficult, in an economic sense, to account for future services like warranties provided at a single price jointly with physical products? What are the key accounting problems encountered in recognizing both revenues and expenses related to warranty services?

9-13. Financing, warranty, and franchising activities are all identified in the text as future service elements encountered in some business operations and posing special revenue recognition challenges. Identify three critical dimensions on which these three types of future services (a) differ from each other and (b) are similar or alike. Be specific.

9-14. When prompt payment discounts are offered, both the seller and the buyer have the option of recording the transaction either at the gross amount (i.e., before any discount is taken) or at the cash equivalent (i.e., net) amount. Is the same transaction recording procedure appropriate for both seller and buyer? Which of the two methods do you recommend and why?

9-15. For each of the following events (a) describe, in a sentence or two, the economic effects involved, and (b) write a representative accounting journal entry or entries to record it.
1. Merchandise sold on credit by a department store is returned in resalable condition.
2. A piece of furniture is returned to a furniture store after it is damaged by a customer opening the packing crate at home. The store refunds the full cash purchase price and plans to resell the item at a coming sale at 50 percent of its usual price.
3. A box of stereo equipment was mislabeled and returned by a customer to the high-fi store where it was purchased and from there it was returned to the manufacturer. Full-price credit is allowed in each instance. Take the point of view of the store only.
4. The owner of a real estate development withholds 5 percent of the total construction contract price billed by the contractor because the completed project did not meet contract specifications in several important details. Take the contractor's point of view—assume the billing is forgiven.
5. Center City Hospital does all of its accounting on the accrual basis. It decides to forgo billing two foreign students who required and received emergency treatment after being involved in an automobile accident.
6. Dr. Justinius Davidson keeps all of his records on a cash basis. He treats some intestinal disorders of a number of elementary

school students who are spending two weeks at a nearby forest camp away from their inner-city homes. The camp's health insurance policy pays for one-third of the doctor's fees—and he decides not to bill the children's families for the remaining two-thirds.

Exercises

9-1. Bad Debts Adjustments. In the recent past, Columbine Corporation has annually debited bad debts expense and credited allowance for doubtful accounts at 1.5 percent of credit sales for the year. Pertinent data are as follows:

	19X5	19X6	19X7
(1) Sales on account	$300,000	$350,000	$320,000
(2) Cash collections on these sales:			
In 19X5	$200,000	—	—
In 19X6	80,000	$300,000	—
In 19X7	14,000	45,000	$260,000
(3) Amounts written off as uncollectible:			
In 19X5	500	—	—
In 19X6	4,800	600	—
In 19X7	700	4,400	300
	$300,000	$350,000	
(4) Accounts receivable balance, December 31, 19X7			59,700
			$320,000

As indicated above, all balances due from customers arising from sales of 19X5 and 19X6 have, by December 31, 19X7, either been collected or written off. The bookkeeper has made no entries or adjustments beyond those necessary to reflect the sales, the collections from customers, the annual addition to allowance for doubtful accounts, and the write-off of individual accounts against the allowance.

Required:

Assume that all beginning balances at January 1, 19X5, were zero.

1. Prepare T-accounts that show the effects of the foregoing transactions as the bookkeeper would have recorded them in the records of the Columbine Corporation.

2. In journal entry form, present whatever adjusting entry or entries you deem necessary as of December 31, 19X7. State any assumptions you make to accomplish this requirement.

3. Suppose that on January 15, 19X8, after appropriate adjustments as of December 31, 19X7, a recovery of $1,000 cash is made on an

account receivable that was recorded in 19X5 and written off as worthless in 19X6. Present an appropriate journal entry to record the recovery as of January 15, 19X8.

9-2. Write-off and Recovery of an Account. During 19X9 Clyde Hill Wholesalers experienced the following chain of events:

1. On January 15 Redmond Suppliers, a customer whose overdue account for $2,900 was included in accounts receivable at December 31, 19X8, offered a sixty-day note in settlement of the account. The face value includes interest for the overdue period. The note, with a face value of $3,000, is non-interest-bearing. It was accepted on the terms offered.
2. The note from Redmond Suppliers was sold to (discounted at) King County State Bank at a discount of 2 percent on January 20, 19X9. The proceeds from this discounting were added to Clyde Hill Wholesalers' checking account with the bank.
3. Redmond Suppliers failed to pay the note at maturity. Accordingly, the amount of the note was charged to (i.e., subtracted from) the checking account of Clyde Hill Wholesalers at the note's face value—$3,000.
4. On July 1, 19X9, Clyde Hill Wholesalers wrote off the note as worthless. At this time it had determined, through a small-claims court process, that the note was in fact uncollectible.
5. Two years later, on January 15, 19Y1, Redmond Suppliers paid off the previously defaulted note with compound interest at 10 percent for the intervening two-year period.

Required:

1. Prepare journal entries to record all the foregoing events on the books and records of Clyde Hill Wholesalers.
2. Discuss the revenue recognition implications arising from the chain of events as described.
3. Why would Redmond Suppliers wish to satisfy an obligation that had been "written off" two years earlier? Were there any special recording problems on the part of Clyde Hill Wholesalers when restitution on the defaulted note was made in 19Y1?

9-3. Recognition of Bad Debts. The Buy Now–Pay Later Department Store makes approximately one-half of its sales to customers on credit. The customer obtains credit by completing an application for a credit card. After the information on the application is checked by the credit department and the credit manager approves the application, the customer is issued a credit card which he must present when he purchases merchandise on credit.

The store sends a "balance forward" statement (showing beginning balance due, new purchases, payments, and ending balance due) to each customer with a nonzero ending balance at the end of each month. Payment is due when the customer receives the statement. An account becomes past due if the total balance due is not received before the next month's statements are prepared. A list is maintained of accounts with a balance past due for more than ninety days so that no further credit sales to those accounts will be made.

A study of collections on credit sales for 19X0-X4 indicated that approximately 1 percent of credit sales proved to be uncollectible. Also, a study of account balances at year-end showed that differing percentages of year-end balances were ultimately uncollectible, depending on the age of the account. The percentages were as follows:

Current accounts	½%
Accounts past due— 1-30 days	1%
Accounts past due—31-60 days	5%
Accounts past due—61-90 days	20%
Accounts past due—over 90 days	30%

The store follows the practice of matching the estimated uncollectible portion of credit sales against recognized sales revenue (i.e., an "allowance for doubtful accounts" is used). Whenever a customer account is determined to be uncollectible, the balance of that account is "written off" against the balance of the allowance account. Also, at year-end the store applies the appropriate percentages (by age category) to customer balances to determine if the balance in the allowance account is sufficient to cover estimated losses in the year-end customer receivable balance. If not, an additional adjustment is made.

The store used the percentages developed in the 19X0-X4 study for its accounting adjustments in 19X5-X6. Sales and collection data for 19X5-X6 follow:

Year	Cash Sales	Credit Sales	Collections on Account	Accounts Determined to be Uncollectible
19X5	$800,000	$ 800,000	$774,000	$ 6,000
19X6	800,000	1,000,000	889,000	11,000

The "age distribution" of customer accounts at year-end for 19X5-X6 follows:

Year	Total A/R Balance	Current Accounts	1-30 Past Due	31-60 Past Due	61-90 Past Due	Over 90
19X5	$140,000	$120,000	$10,000	$ 6,000	$ 2,000	$ 2,000
19X6	240,000	180,000	20,000	20,000	10,000	10,000

Account balances at the end of 19X4 were as follows:

Accounts receivable	$120,000
Allowance for doubtful accounts	(4,000)

Required:

1. Prepare a financial position worksheet that shows the effects of the above sales, collections, and bad debts experience for 19X5–X6. Provide columns for Effect on Cash, Accounts Receivable, Allowance for Doubtful Accounts, and Effect on Owners' Equity.

2. What are the implications of the analysis of the customer balances at the end of 19X6?

9-4. Installment Sales Method. On June 30, 19X4, Wilson Corporation sold a parcel of land adjacent to its main plant to Deakin the Developer for $4 million. Wilson received 10 percent down, and a three-year, 12 percent (per annum) note for the balance. The terms of the note provide that each three months Deakin is to pay $300,000 principal, plus interest on the unpaid balance. The land cost Wilson Corporation $1.2 million five years ago.

The officers of Wilson Corporation are not sure that Deakin will be able to meet his payment obligations on the note. However, they completed the deal because they believed that the price agreed upon was a very favorable one to them; $400,000 was received as a down payment. If Deakin defaults, title to the land reverts to Wilson.

Because of the uncertainty regarding the collectibility of the note, this transaction is recorded using the installment sales method of recognizing revenue.

Required:

Assuming that Deakin the Developer makes all payments as they come due, prepare a schedule showing the income that would be recognized by Wilson Corporation (on this transaction) each year from 19X4 to 19X7.

9-5. Journal Entries for Installment Sales Transactions. Office Music Systems, Inc., started business on January 1, 19X1. It sells high-quality stereo music systems to businesses and professional firms. If requested to do so, it will also install stereo music systems in new office buildings. The stereo systems and components it carries are sold on regular thirty-day open accounts or twenty-four-month installment contracts. Business activities for 19X1 can be summarized as follows:

30-day regular sales	$620,000
Installment sales	740,000
Installation revenues (all cash)	120,000

Continued on page 328

Cost of 30-day open account sales	380,000
Cost of installment sales	370,000
Cost of installation services	140,000
General administrative, sales, and operating expenses	200,000
19X1 collections on 30-day open account sales	550,000
Collections on installment sales	260,000

Required:

Prepare journal entries to record all transactions enumerated above. Assume that the installment sales method of recognizing revenue is employed to account for all sales made on the installment basis. (For expense-recording entries, assume that resources used are represented by "various asset and liability accounts.")

9-6. Joint Sale of Product and Installment Financing Services. The Reliable Equipment Company buys construction equipment from heavy-equipment manufacturers and in turn sells the equipment to small to medium-sized construction contractors. The contractors buy from Reliable rather than from the equipment manufacturer because Reliable sells equipment on the installment basis. All of the company's sales are made on an installment basis involving 20 percent down and the remainder in two equal annual installments.

The earnings of the company are composed of (1) trading profits from the sale of equipment and (2) the interest on installment sales contracts. The explicit rate is stated to be 12 percent in the sales contracts (explicitly stated because of the Truth-in-Lending Act). Sales prices are set so that if the required payments are discounted at 12 percent, the present value is equal to the list price the customer would have to pay if he bought directly from the manufacturer. Reliable makes a trading profit because it only pays 90 percent of the list price (due to volume discounts).

The company began operations at the start of 19X3. Following are the total contract sales prices of the equipment sold each year for 19X3–X5:

Year	Contract Sales Price
19X3	$1,000,000
19X4	1,600,000
19X5	2,000,000

Required:

1. Compute the cost to Reliable of the equipment sold for each of the three years. Assume that all purchases and sales occur at the *first* of the year and that installment payments are made at the end of the year.
2. Prepare all necessary journal entries for 19X3–X5 to reflect sales, costs, and collection experience, assuming the sale-with-financing method of recognizing income. Be sure to recognize the effects of the time value of money.

9-7. Joint Services and Normal Uncertainty Combined. Computer Sales Company buys and sells small standardized computer systems. All of the company's sales are made on an installment plan involving one-third down, and the remainder in two equal annual installments.

Computer Sales Company's long-run earnings are composed of two major components: (1) trading profits from the sale of the computers and (2) the implicit interest on the installment sales contracts that the customer signs. No explicit interest charge is included in the installment sales contracts. But the company has designed the contract so that when the required payments are discounted at 10 percent, the present value is approximately equal to the market value of the computers in a cash sale. The 10 percent interest rate also approximates the market rate of interest on installment loans of equal risk (considering the contract terms, the class of clientele, etc.).

Computer Sales Company started operations at the beginning of 19X4. Since that time, it has had the following sales and collection experience:

		Collections	
Year	Sales	Down Payments	Installment Payments
19X4	$ 600,000	$200,000	—0—
19X5	900,000	300,000	$200,000
19X6	1,200,000	400,000	500,000

The costs of the computers sold each of these three years were:

19X4	$480,000
19X5	720,000
19X6	960,000

Required:

1. Record, in T-account form, all the effects of the above sales and collection experience according to the sale-with-financing method of recognizing income from installment sales, taking into account the time value of money. For convenience assume—
   (a) That all sales are made and all collections received at the end of each year.
   (b) That the cost of computers sold is paid in cash by Computer Sales to the manufacturers at the time it sells the systems to its own customers (the manufacturer then delivers direct to Computer Sales' customers).
   (c) The company began business in 19X4 with $1.6 million cash and $1.6 million owners' equity.
   (d) The company experiences no other expenses or revenues except as described above.

2. Suppose now that Computer Sales Company recognized income under the strict point-of-sale method, taking into account expected bad debts but ignoring the time value of money.

The industry experience has been that approximately 5 percent of the total value of the accounts receivable *at the time of sale* proves to be uncollectible. During the past years, the actual collection experience of the company was as follows:

	Collections		Amounts Determined to Be Uncollectible	
Year	Down Payments	Installment Payments	From 19X4 Sales	From 19X5 Sales
19X4	$200,000	-0-	-0-	-0-
19X5	300,000	$192,000	$16,000	-0-
19X6	400,000	467,000	5,000	$40,000

Using the income recognition method indicated above (i.e., point of sale with recognition of estimated bad debts), record in worksheet form the effects of the sales, expenses, and revised collection experience for Computer Sales Company.

3. Suppose now that Computer Sales Company recognized income under the sale-with-financing method, taking into account *both* time value of money and expected bad debts. Under this income recognition method, prepare all necessary journal entries to record the effects of Computer Sales Company's transactions for the *first two years only*.

9-8. Warranty Contracts. The Waterfall Appliance Company assembles washing machines and dryers (the components are purchased from other manufacturers) and retails the appliances through its own appliance stores. To maintain a competitive position, the company offers a two-year warranty (the industry average) on parts and labor. The appliance store provides a repair service for warranty and general repairs. The repair service is considered to be a revenue-producing function.

Price-cost data for washers and dryers are as follows: (the data apply to 19X2, 19X3, and 19X4):

	Washers	Dryers
Unit sales price	$225	$150
Unit total cost (includes components and labor)	110	90
Average unit cost of warranty service in the first year of warranty	10	5
Average unit cost of warranty service in the second year of warranty	30	5

Sales data for 19X3 and 19X4 are as follows:

Year	Washers Units	Washers Dollars	Dryers Units	Dryers Dollars
19X3	1,000	$225,000	800	$120,000
19X4	1,200	270,000	1,000	150,000

Required:

1. (a) Calculate the markup percentage (on cost including average unit warranty cost) for both appliances.
   (b) Assuming that the percentages calculated above are appropriate for determining (1) revenue from sales and (2) revenue from warranty repairs, what portion of the selling price (for each appliance) should be recognized in the year of sale?

2. Prepare appropriate journal entries that show the effects of the above sales and costs (for 19X3–X4), using the preferred method of deferring revenue from warranty sales until it is earned. You may assume the following:
   (a) Beginning balances are irrelevant and may be ignored.
   (b) All purchases, sales, and wages are for cash.
   (c) In a given year, the company produces only the units that it expects to sell (i.e., no year-end inventories).
   (d) If a part is required for a warranty repair, the part is purchased for cash when the repair is made.
   (e) All claims for first-year warranty service for units sold in 19X3 are made in 19X4, and so forth.

3. Calculate the expected effects of 19X5–X6 warranty repair transactions (as a result of 19X3–X4 sales and ignoring other 19X5–X6 transactions). What are the balances of the "warranty service liability" and "deferred income on future warranty services" accounts at the end of 19X6 (as a result of 19X3–X4 sales)?

4. (a) Prepare a schedule showing revenue and net income for 19X3 and 19X4 for the following alternative revenue-expense recognition methods:
   (1) Defer warranty service income until earned
   (2) Recognize total selling price as revenue in period of sale, and accrue expected future warranty expenses
   (b) Under what set(s) of circumstances might each of the above alternatives be appropriate?

9-9. Effect of Price and Prompt Payment Discounts on Revenue Recognition. The Swivel Equipment Company sells office equipment. The company maintains a catalog which contains standard list prices, product descriptions, and sales terms. Sales terms include allowance of price discounts (depending upon dollar volume of an order) and prompt payment discounts (for payment of an invoice within ten days).

Some transactions of the company during July and August are as follows:

    a. Sold equipment having a list price of $200 to the Handy Office Supplies store. No price discount was allowed, but prompt payment discount terms were 2/10, net/30.

    b. Sold equipment having a list price of $15,000 to the Globe Steel Company. A price discount of 20/10 was allowed, and prompt payment discount terms were 1/10, net/30.

    c. Sold equipment having a list price of $6,000 to the Downtown Office Equipment Company. A price discount of 20 percent was allowed, and prompt payment discount terms were 1/10, net/30.

    d. Received payment from Handy Office Supplies after ten days. The store had deducted the prompt payment discount, even though it was not entitled to do so.

    e. Received payment from the Globe Steel Company. All allowable discounts had been deducted.

    f. Received full payment from the Downtown Office Equipment Company after ten days. The company had not deducted the prompt payment discount.

Required:

1. (a) What revenue would be recognized from sales for transactions *a-c,* assuming that prompt payment discounts are recognized at the time of sale?
   (b) What additional revenue would be recognized at a later time, if any?

2. (a) What revenue would be recognized from sales for transactions *a–c,* assuming that prompt payment discounts, if any, are recognized when payment is received?
   (b) What revenue offsets would be recognized at a later time, if any?

3. Prepare a table contrasting sales revenue, discounts taken, discounts allowed but not taken, and total net revenue for the two alternative methods of recognizing prompt payment discounts.

9-10. Alternative Methods of Recording Transaction Discounts in Journal Entry Form. Refer to transactions *a* through *f* described in Exercise 9-9.

Required:

Divide some blank 8½-X-11-inch working paper into two columns. Prepare journal entries for each of the six transactions described by showing, side by side:

1. The method of recognizing discounts at the time of sale

2. The method of recognizing discounts when payments are received

(*Hint:* You should have two sets of journal entries, one for each transaction.)

9-11. Journal Entries for Sales Discount and Return Transactions. Elegant Office Interiors, Inc., sold a set of office furniture and equipment to Coast Menu Company on September 3. The sales price is $2,500 with terms 2/10, n/60. On September 4 the furniture is delivered to Coast Menu Company. Four days later, on September 8, an invoice totaling $125, terms n/30, is received by Coast Menu Company from Custom Transport Service for delivery of the merchandise.

Immediately on receipt of the furniture, on September 4, the office manager of Coast Menu Company notified Elegant Office Interiors, Inc., that one executive chair costing $250 contained flaws that rendered it worthless. The next day, Office Interiors issued a credit memo covering the worthless chair and asked that it be returned at company expense. The freight on this merchandise return was $25, paid by Coast Menu Company on September 10. Coast Menu Company paid the balance due (net of the $25 freight) on September 12 to Elegant Office Interiors, Inc.

Required:

1. Prepare journal entries on the books of Elegant Office Interiors, Inc., to record each of the foregoing events, assuming that revenue is recorded net of allowable discounts.

2. Repeat the journal entry made to record the invoice payment from Coast Menu Company to Elegant Office Interiors, Inc., under the assumption that payment is not made until October 30 and thus without taking the available prompt payments discount.

9-12. The Case of the Disappearing Income. This case concerns franchising, which is, in its simplest terms, an arrangement to distribute and sell goods or services within a specified area or at a given location. Involved are a franchisor who originates an idea for a product or service with the attendant trade name, packaging, and promotion and then grants to a franchisee the right to market at retail. The franchisor generally offers consultation and management advice for opening a product or service outlet and training and controlling its management. The franchisee usually agrees to pay a fee for the franchise as well as to purchase certain supplies from the franchisor.

In most cases a franchisor will collect only a down payment when a franchise is granted, and the balance of the franchise fee becomes payable in future years. Accounting problems have arisen because franchisors have reported the entire franchise fee as income at the time of the grant, even though the down payment is inconsequentially small and the probability of collection highly uncertain.

Accounting problems related to franchising operations may be illuminated by considering an actual example. Of interest are the consolidated statements of income of Career Academy, Inc., and Subsidiaries for the year ended December 31, 1968, as reported in the 1968 annual report of the company and again reported in the 1969 report of the company.

On January 30, 1970, Career Academy announced a major change in accounting for its franchising operations. This change is described in a note to the 1969 statement and is also reproduced here.

Required:

1. Identify the accounting conventions that supported the amount recorded for 1968 sales of directorships as shown in the income statement from the 1968 annual report of Career Accademy, Inc. (See page 336.)

2. Which accounting conventions support the alternative figure given for 1968 sales of directorships in the 1969 annual report? (See below.)

3. Identify three major balance sheet accounts affected by Career Academy's 1970 change in accounting methods.

4. Where, in the published financial statements, would one find the 1968 income that disappeared for purposes of the 1969 annual report?

CAREER ACADEMY, INC. AND SUBSIDIARIES

Consolidated Statements of Income
For the Years Ended December 31, 1969 and 1968

	1969	*1968*
Revenues:		
Income from students	$16,541,501	$12,613,757
Income from directorships	1,907,300	789,516
	$18,448,801	$13,403,273
Costs and Expenses:		
Instruction	$ 2,816,990	$ 2,445,820
Selling, general and administrative	10,762,006	8,033,536
Provision for doubtful accounts and student contract terminations	696,781	602,000
	$14,275,777	$11,081,356
Operating income	$ 4,173,024	$ 2,321,917
Other Income (Expense):		
Interest expense	$ (270,206)	$ (189,490)
Other income, net	301,228	211,075
	$ 31,022	$ 21,585
Income before provision for income taxes	$ 4,204,046	$ 2,343,502
Federal and State Income Taxes:		
Current	$ 300,000	$ 260,000
Deferred	1,928,000	982,000
	$ 2,228,000	$ 1,242,000
Net income	$ 1,976,046	$ 1,101,502
Earnings Per Common and Common Equivalent Share	$.43	$.25

NOTE TO 1969 STATEMENTS

Accounting Methods Change

On January 30, 1970, Career Academy announced a retroactive change in the accounting methods used to determine income from the sale of Directorships. The following is a comprehensive explanation of this change and its effect on past and future income.

Reasons for the Change

Late in 1969 and early in 1970 a number of publications, including the *Wall Street Journal* and the *Journal of Accountancy* carried articles that discussed the accounting methods used by firms deriving a significant portion of their income from the sale of franchises. These articles suggested that the liberal attitude toward recognizing all income at the time of sale should possibly be replaced by more conservative methods. We reaffirmed, with the concurrence of our auditors, the validity of our accounting methods and that our system avoided the problem areas being pointed out in the articles.

Nevertheless, a high degree of speculation and uncertainty arose during the third and fourth weeks in January, 1970, within the financial community as to whether we would change our methods and how our income might be affected by a change. This speculation involved a number of different earnings projections, based on various accounting methods. The result was a seriously confused and uncertain condition that demanded clarification on our part.

Since we felt our existing accounting methods, and certain alternative methods were equally acceptable, we decided to adopt a more conservative method in order to end the uncertainty and speculation. Our auditors, Arthur Andersen & Co., concurred with our decision.

Accordingly, the new accounting method was retroactively instituted for 1969 and prior years.

The Substance of the Change

Our former accounting method provided that all income from a sale of a Directorship was recognized at the time a contract was signed. Under the new method, we will recognize income from the sale of Directorships on the basis of several performance criteria—the principal one being the number of students enrolled by the Directorship organization each year.

An amount equal to approximately 15% of the sale price is recorded as income over a period of one to two years. The remaining revenues will be recognized over an estimated 5 to 7 years period on the basis of the number of students enrolled by the Directorship each year.

Certain costs, directly associated with the establishment of Directorship organizations, will be amortized against income on the same basis.

The Effects of the Change

Since this change in accounting methods was a retroactive one, it not only affects the present and future years, but also all prior years. The major effect of the change involves the deferral of Directorship revenue. You will find this change reflected in our December 31, 1969, balance sheet under the heading "Unearned Directorship Revenue." The indicated net deferral as of that date is $8,258,982, of which $1,049,329 is estimated to be realized within one year.

It should also be pointed out that there is a reserve of $2,070,000 for possible losses on Installment Notes Receivable from Directorships.

In 1969, the change in accounting methods resulted in a reduction of net income from 85¢ per share to 43¢ per share. In addition, the Notes to Financial Statements in this report contain references to and further explanations of the new accounting method.

CAREER ACADEMY, INC. AND SUBSIDIARIES

Consolidated Statements of Income
For the Years Ended December 31, 1968 and 1967

	1968	1967
Revenues:		
Income from students	$11,921,474	$6,786,881
Sales of directorships	5,327,002	2,627,076
	$17,248,476	$9,413,957
Costs and Expenses:		
Instruction cost	$ 2,245,820	$1,430,422
Selling, general and administrative expenses	7,711,147	4,405,027
Provision for doubtful accounts, student contract terminations and estimated losses on installment notes receivable	1,522,000	828,790
	$11,478,967	$6,664,239
Operating income	$ 5,769,509	$2,749,718
Other Income (Expense):		
Interest expense	$ (189,489)	$ (107,875)
Other income, net	193,070	49,146
	$ 3,581	$ (58,729)
Income before provision for income taxes	$ 5,773,090	$2,690,989
Federal and State Income Taxes:		
Current	$ 260,000	$ 290,000
Deferred	2,800,000	1,004,400
	$ 3,060,000	$1,294,400
Net income for the year	$ 2,713,090	$1,396,589
Earnings per share	$.60	$.32

Expense Recognition and Related Asset Valuation Issues

10

In the preceding two chapters we examine the revenue recognition patterns, and the related set of criteria governing their use, that are found in present-day financial reporting. In that discussion, we rely on the general notions (principles) of matching and cost measurement when it is necessary to consider expenses together with revenue (as, for example, in the discussion of the installment sales method). Moreover, the development of the fundamental ideas of the conventional accounting model in Chapters 3 through 5 largely deals with these important expense-recognition principles in broad, conceptual terms. But certain additional problems associated with the measurement of expenses recur frequently in practice and cannot be resolved by simple recourse to broad statements of the principles. In response, a set of acceptable measurement rules has evolved (or been promulgated) in accounting practice. In many cases particular expense measurement problems are sufficiently difficult to resolve that single approaches cannot achieve unanimous or even widespread support. Thus we observe that there is often more than one "acceptable" method to solve a given measurement problem. In this and the next chapter we examine some of the more common expense measurement problems and the alternative ways they can be treated.

EXPENSE MEASUREMENT AND ASSOCIATION WITH REVENUE (PERIODS)

The Objective of Expense Recognition in Review

To achieve the hoped-for cause-and-effect association between measured effort and measured accomplishment, measurement of conventional accounting expense for a period generally is conditioned upon revenue recognized for the period, as reflected in the definition of expense introduced in Chapter 3:

> **Expense.** Insofar as possible, total expense for a period includes the costs of all resources that were sacrificed to produce the revenue recognized in the current period.

This concept of expense is the combination of two fundamental measurement principles of conventional accounting—the matching principle and the cost principle. The matching principle provides the key to the *timing* of expense recognition, and the cost principle establishes the amount, or value, at which the expense is *measured*. Together, the matching and cost principles answer the questions *when* and *how much* with respect to expense recognition. But these general concepts require some elaboration if one is to understand the way they are applied in an operational context.

Elaboration of the Matching Principle

Most expenditures are made for the purpose of generating future service potentials, or sources of future benefits to the firm. The basic objective embodied in the matching principle is to find satisfactory bases of association—hopefully, causal relationships—for linking efforts (expenses) with related benefits (revenue).

> **Matching Principle.** Insofar as possible, the total sacrifices made in all periods to produce and sell a particular product or service are recognized as expense in the period in which the revenue from the same product or service is recognized.

To be strictly applied, the matching principle requires that virtually every sacrifice of any resource in a given period (1) be specifically identified with a particular product or service, (2) have its original price (cost) to the enterprise accumulated with the costs of all other sacrifices made to produce that product or service, and (3) be recognized as an expense in the period in which the particular product or service is sold or provided. But this scrupulous matching of resource sacrifices with products or services is often difficult or impossible to achieve. Furthermore, in many instances, identification of the desired relationships is very *costly* to achieve. Therefore, as was pointed out in Chapter 3, a rough dichotomy is usually followed in recognizing expenses for a given period.

If a resource sacrifice has been made in a particular accounting period, an accountant will consider the way in which the resource was used. If consumption of the resource can be identified or associated (at a reasonable cost) with a specific product or service, or batch of products or services, its original cost to the enterprise is accumulated in an asset account such as inventory or construction in process (that is, "attached" to the product or service) until the period in which the specific products or services are sold. In that period (when the related revenue is recognized), these accumulated resource costs logically attaching to the products or services are recognized as expenses. Because of their nature, these expenses are often referred to as *product expenses.*

But if a resource is consumed during a period and consumption bears no discernible relation to the production of any *particular* present or future product(s) or service(s), that is, it cannot be identified with a unit of present or future revenue, the cost is recognized as an expense in the period in which the resource is consumed or sacrificed. Such costs, like salaries of a firm's executives, are called *period expenses.*

Thus we do not attempt to contrive a causal relationship, or network, between all enterprise expenditures and related revenues. In the absence of a clearly discernible relationship, however, it is generally desirable that the accountant be able to establish some systematic basis for matching expenditures against revenue, or at least periods of time presumably benefiting from the expenditures, in order to achieve the hoped-for association between effort and accomplishment. In most instances the "systematic matching" of the conventional accounting model is grounded in the assumption that we are able to identify, in a general sense, *patterns of benefits* to be derived from the use of a resource.

Example 10-1

> When a firm acquires a long-lived asset, say an office building with an expected life of forty years, we are usually unable to identify specific units of revenue generated from the use of the resource. Clearly, we would not want to recognize the total expenditure made to purchase the asset as an expense of the period in which it was acquired. Therefore we might elect to spread the cost of the building equally over its estimated useful life (as depreciation expense), under the assumption that the benefits from the use of the resource will be received uniformly (or approximately so) over the same period. If we made a different assumption about the pattern of benefits to be received, we might recognize a correspondingly different pattern of expenses.

But even this systematic, albeit somewhat arbitrary, matching is not always possible to achieve in practice. For example, advertising expenditures often reflect efforts that contribute to more than one product for more than one time period. Such costs, referred to as *joint costs,* are not unusual. They include many, if not all, of the administrative costs of a business, and frequently a large bulk of the marketing costs. For expenditures of this type, the notion of a period cost, in its most extreme form, is often applied. The entire expenditure is "matched" against the period in which the expenditure is made, as there is virtually no discernible basis for systematically matching it against more than one period (as there is in the case of the depreciation of long-lived assets). One justification for this treatment of such period costs is that by their very nature they usually tend to be relatively uniform from one period to the next. Even if there were some pattern of benefits to be derived that could be identified with a large enough expenditure of effort, it is assumed that the amount of expense recognized in each period would not be substantially different from the actual expenditure made. Where this assumption is not valid, as is sometimes the case, expedience is then the only justification for recognizing an entire expenditure as expense of the period in which it takes place.

Elaboration of the Cost Principle

Once we have determined as best we can the resources that have been used in the production of the recognized revenue of a period, either by direct association with products or services sold or through a more indirect method, we then seek to *measure* the sacrifice associated with the resources' use. This measurement process is based upon the cost principle.

> **Cost Principle.** The measure of sacrifice associated with the acquisition and subsequent use of any resource is the price paid for the resource, that is, its cost in the exchange or exchanges in which it was acquired.

Cost, as the term is used in accounting, refers to values (generally expressed as prices) established in *external transactions* involving the exchange of resources between entities. While the matching principle, not the transaction, controls the timing of expense recognition, the prices established by transactions provide the data base for ultimate expense recognition. In some instances the occurrence of a transaction is coincident with the recognition of expense (for example, in the payment of wages). But in many instances a transaction involves the acquisition of resources (assets) that will be used to produce revenue in the future. In the period of time elapsing between the acquisition and the utilization of assets, the transaction price (cost) is the basis for the value assigned to the asset in the accounts of the business. Thus, in conventional accounting, one way to interpret the values associated with assets that will be consumed in the production of future revenue is to view them as future expenses measured in terms of original transaction values or *unexpired costs.* Similarly, all expenses can be regarded as *expired costs.*

Original Transaction Value. What are the "original transaction values" that are established in exchange transactions? In Chapter 4 this central notion of conventional accounting valuation was defined under the limiting condition that cash or other monetary items were involved in the transaction:

> **Original Transaction Value.** The original transaction value of an asset or a liability is the value established in the exchange(s) in which the asset was acquired or the liability incurred. Usually such exchange values are determined by the amounts of monetary items given, promised, received, or to be received, depending on the circumstances.

Although this definition is adequate for identifying the original transaction value in most exchange transactions, it must be expanded somewhat to cover all types of transactions.

The measure of the original transaction value, or cost, of acquiring assets is generally established by applying one of the following criteria, *in order of priority:*

1. Cash or other monetary consideration given (provided no nonmonetary consideration is given)
2. Cash or other monetary consideration paid (if any), plus the current exchange value of any *nonmonetary consideration given*
3. Current exchange value of monetary (if any) and nonmonetary consideration received
4. Cash or other monetary consideration paid (if any), plus the unexpired cost of nonmonetary consideration given

For any of the four criteria, it is assumed that the time value of money will be taken into account, when significant, in valuing monetary consideration given or received.

Example 10-2

The Roark Computer Service Company operates a computer service facility that processes information for businesses that do not have their own computers. At the present time, the company has a HAL 1975 Computer. The company has made a study of its future computer needs and has decided to trade in the computer on the larger HAL 2001 Computer.

The new computer, the HAL 2001, with a list price of $850,000, is acquired in exchange for the HAL 1975 plus a cash payment of $500,000. The estimated current market value of the HAL 1975 at the present time is $325,000. The original cost of the HAL 1975 is $500,000. Accumulated depreciation to date is $240,000.

Applying criteria 2-4 of the above set to the facts of this case (criterion 1 is inapplicable), we arrive at the following alternative transaction values (costs):

  I. Criterion 2: $500,000 + $325,000 = $825,000
 II. Criterion 3: $850,000
III. Criterion 4: $500,000 + $260,000 = $760,000

The following journal entries would serve to record the exchange in which the HAL 2001 is acquired under the respective valuation criteria:[1]

---

[1] Recall that the journal entry for recording the acquisition of an asset strictly for cash was illustrated in Chapter 7. Its general form is as follows:

```
Asset account        XXXX
    Cash                     XXXX
```

I.	Computer equipment	825,000	
	Accumulated depreciation—computer equipment	240,000	
	Computer equipment		500,000
	Cash		500,000
	Gain on trade-in of computer equipment		65,000
II.	Computer equipment	850,000	
	Accumulated depreciation—computer equipment	240,000	
	Computer equipment		500,000
	Cash		500,000
	Gain on trade-in of computer equipment		90,000
III.	Computer equipment	760,000	
	Accumulated depreciation—computer equipment	240,000	
	Computer equipment		500,000
	Cash		500,000

Notice that in each of the journal entries the debit of $240,000 to accumulated depreciation and the credit of $500,000 to computer equipment together remove the unexpired cost ($260,000) of the HAL 1975 from the company's accounts. The difference between the cost established for the HAL 2001 and the cash paid determines the imputed proceeds of the trade-in. The imputed proceeds minus the unexpired cost equals the gain (if any).

Choice of the appropriate criterion in Example 10-2 depends both upon the order of priority of the criteria noted above and upon the *relative reliability* of the estimated current exchange values. In arriving at valuation alternative I, the estimated current exchange value of the HAL 1975 is used in conjunction with the cash payment of $500,000 to arrive at a transaction value (cost) of $825,000. For valuation alternative II, the estimated current exchange value of the new HAL 2001 (which for this example is the list price) is used to establish a transaction value (cost) of $850,000. Choice between these two alternative values (costs) will depend upon the facts of the particular case. In some instances, because of the wide prevalence of discounts, list prices are not good estimates of the current exchange value of an asset. If the accountant has no reason to believe that the estimated current exchange value of the consideration given (the $325,000 estimated market value of the HAL 1975) is biased, he would opt for criterion 2 in establishing the transaction value (cost) of the new HAL 2001. However, if the accountant believes that the estimated market value of the HAL 1975 is lacking in objectivity and reasonableness, he might elect to use the list price ($850,000) of the new computer as the measure of the transaction value in accordance with criterion 3—particularly if he believes that this list price is a relatively good measure of the exchange value of the asset acquired. If both of these estimated market values are suspect as to their objectivity and/or validity, the accountant would reluctantly apply criterion 4 (the last in order of priority) to arrive at a transaction value of $760,000—the cash paid ($500,000) plus the unexpired cost ($260,000) of the asset given in the exchange (the old HAL 1975 computer). This last method implicitly assigns proceeds of $260,000 to the disposition of the old computer and thus results in no gain or loss on the disposition. It should be noted that this "no profit or loss" method is often applied for federal income tax purposes in so-called nontaxable exchanges.

When cash and other monetary items are the only consideration given to acquire a nonmonetary asset, the original transaction value (cost) is uniquely determined under conventional accounting measurement rules. In all other cases, however, the accountant must exercise judgment in his determination of the cost of the new nonmonetary asset acquired. When this judgment has been exercised and a market value (or, in rare cases, an unexpired cost) is used as the value of one of the nonmonetary assets exchanged in the transaction, the cost thus determined is thereafter treated in the same manner as if the transaction had been solely for cash.

Inclusiveness. We have illustrated above that identification of the cost of acquiring a nonmonetary asset is a more complex measurement problem than it appears at first glance. Yet there is still an additional dimension to the problem. The cost of an asset, as the term is used in accounting, is a more inclusive concept than merely the price of the item. It includes all outlays to acquire and transform the asset for ultimate use or sale. The total cost of a nonmonetary asset would include, in addition to its purchase price, any outlays required to transport and/or install the asset. Additionally, if an asset is transformed in a manufacturing process into a different physical form, the cost of the transformed asset and all the other outlays involved in the manufacturing process "attach" to the output of the production process. The sum of these attached costs then constitute the cost of the "new" asset.

Example 10-3

Returning to the facts of Example 10-2, let us now assume that the Roark Computer Service Company determined that the cost of its new HAL 2001 computer was $825,000, in accordance with criterion 2—cash ($500,000) plus the current exchange value ($325,000) of the HAL 1975 that was traded in for the new computer. But in addition to this outlay, the Roark Computer Service Company also paid $5,000 to transport the new computer from the manufacturer's place of business to the Roark operating facilities and incurred a $1,000 cost to install the computer. Given these facts, the total cost of the new computer is $831,000 ($825,000 + $5,000 + $1,000), and the following journal entry would record the acquisition:

Computer equipment	831,000	
Accumulated depreciation—computer equipment	240,000	
Computer equipment		500,000
Cash		506,000
Gain on trade-in of computer equipment		65,000

If Roark Computer Service Company has been required to make any outlays for the removal of the old computer that was traded in, that is, if additional cash had to be expended for this purpose, the additional expenditure generally would not be treated as an additional cost of the new computer. Rather it would normally be incorporated into the calculation of the gain or loss on the disposal of the old computer. In this case the disposal of the old computer resulted in a gain of $65,000 (imputed proceeds of $325,000 less the unexpired cost of $260,000).

Just as the cost of a purchased item should include all costs of acquiring the item and putting it in service, the cost of finished products resulting from a manufacturing process is the sum of all the outlays (costs) made to acquire the raw material inputs and the outlays made to transform these resources for ultimate sale. When the finished product is sold, and the revenue is recognized, the cost would then be recognized as an expense (cost of sale) of that period.

Example 10-4

Walker Art Wholesalers, Inc., assembles oil paintings for distribution in large shopping centers. Its "manufacturing" effort involves the acquisition of oil paintings from one source, the acquisition of frames from another source, and the assembly of the canvases and frames for distribution at several local shopping centers. In a particular case, assume that a canvas was acquired at a cost of $16, and the frame that was used on this canvas was purchased for $12. These two separate transaction values provide the basis for the valuation of the items in the two types of inventory—canvas inventory and frame inventory—before they are used in the assembly process. The estimated labor cost to assemble a finished painting is $3 per painting. Thus, when this particular painting has been assembled, or "manufactured," the cost of the new finished goods inventory (framed oil paintings) is $31 ($16 + $12 + $3). The transaction values (costs) of the raw material inputs from the two different inventories, plus the $3 outlay for the labor required to assemble the final product, *attach* to the third type of inventory item (framed oil paintings) to generate a new cost, or imputed transaction value, of $31.

Duality of Asset and Liability Valuation and Related Expense Recognition

We have noted several times previously that there is a valuation linkage between the statement of financial position and the income statement. If a value is assigned to the ending balance of an asset or a liability in accordance with conventional accounting valuation principles, the related expense measure is merely a derivative calculation. Conversely, if an expense is measured independently, the related asset or liability value is inescapably altered by this expense measurement process. The two related values—expense and asset or liability value—are not independent calculations under the conventional accounting model.

The interdependency, or duality of valuation, follows from our retention of an original transaction data base for assigning values. For the case of asset valuation and the related expense recognition, the duality principle is expressed by the following basic relationship:

Ending asset value = Beginning asset value + Acquisitions − Expenses

or

Beginning asset value + Acquisitions = Expenses + Ending asset value

For any given accounting period, the beginning asset value was established at the end of the prior period. The new acquisitions of the period are a matter of record, that is, the result of observable business transactions. Under the conventional accounting model, the sum of these two values establishes an upper limit on the amount of expense that can be recognized in the period from the use of these assets. Indeed, *over the life of the business, the total expense recognized will be equal to the total expenditures made to acquire resources minus any salvage value.* But, in the interim, the fundamental problem is to determine how to allocate, or split, the pool of costs associated with resources acquired and available for use between expense of the period and asset value at the end of the period. Once a decision is made on the expense, the ending value of the asset is produced as a residual calculation, and vice versa.

Example 10-5

> Audio Dealers, Inc., had an inventory of high-fidelity equipment at the start of the year valued at $10,000. During the year, the company purchased merchandise in the amount of $80,000. Thus the total value (cost) of inventory available for sale during the period amounts to $90,000. Now if Audio Dealers determines that the value (cost) of its ending inventory is $20,000, the related expense (cost of sales) for the period is but a derivative calculation—$70,000. The duality relationship for this case is schematically depicted in Exhibit 10-1.

The same principles apply to the valuation of liabilities and related expenses.

While the basic duality relationship is a simple concept, it is at the same time important to keep in mind as we explore the alternative patterns of expense recognition and asset and liability valuation for specific classes of assets and liabilities.

Exhibit 10-1

SCHEMATIC OF THE DUALITY PRINCIPLE FOR ASSET AND EXPENSE VALUATION

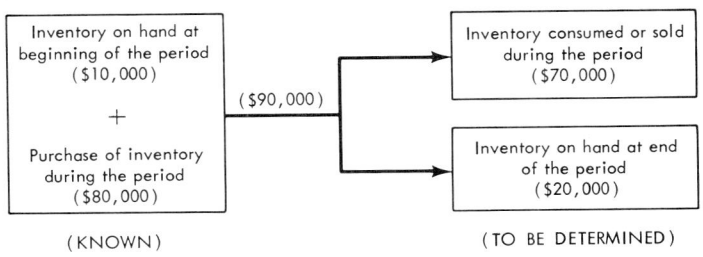

INVENTORY VALUATION AND RELATED EXPENSE RECOGNITION

In the earlier discussions of the adjustments (internal transactions) that are made at the end of each accounting period to recognize the cost of inventory sold during the period as an expense, we have assumed that we know either the cost of the inventory on hand at the end of the period or the cost of the inventory sold or used. However, the way in which these values are determined is an important accounting issue, involving many physical and clerical tasks and some important valuation assumptions. We will now explore the inventory valuation problem in greater detail, with particular emphasis on the alternative assumptions from which the accountant may choose in arriving at these measures.

The Physical Quantity Problem

Typically, the first problem in the process of assigning values to inventory "on hand" at the end of the period (and cost of sales for the period) is to determine the physical quantities applicable to these two categories. That is, we must allocate the total quantity of inventory available for sale during the period (the sum of inventory on hand at the start of the period and the purchases of inventory during the period) between

(1) the quantities on hand at the end of the period and
(2) the quantities that were used or sold during the period.

This allocation problem can be resolved mathematically by independently determining either of these two variables, and then inferring the measure of the other variable based on the total number of units to be allocated—the duality principle in operation for units as well as values.

To independently determine the quantity of units consumed or sold during the period, the firm may choose to maintain some type of record system that is continuously updated throughout the period. On the other hand, the quantity of units on hand at the end of the period can be determined by means of a physical count of the inventory. If the records and the physical counts are equally accurate, both of the methods should produce the same measures of the quantities of inventory consumed and on hand. However, in most business enterprises, either a physical count of inventory is employed in lieu of maintaining the detailed records of usage or such a count is made periodically to verify the accuracy of the records that are maintained.

Example 10-6

Wholesale Steel Co. is a steel service center that buys rolled sheet steel and steel bars in large quantities and sells smaller quantities to its customers. Wholesale Steel keeps perpetual (continuously adjusted) inventory ledger cards on each major item stocked and each year-end reconciles the physical quantity balances on the cards to actual counts of the quantities of each item on hand. For 19X1 the beginning inventory quantity of #2006 cold-rolled steel bar was 451 linear meters. The company's inventory and purchase records show that 6,000 meters were purchased during the period, and the #2006 inventory card shows a year-end balance of 389 meters. However, at year-end employees counted 349 meters of #2006 actually on hand. The end-of-year physical balance on the inventory card was adjusted downward to 349 meters and a total of 6,102 meters of #2006 were presumed to have been sold during 19X1.

The Assignment of Cost Problem

Having determined the quantity of units of inventory allocable to the two key variables—units on hand and units sold or consumed—the next task is to associate cost data (prices paid) with the quantities. The assignment is accomplished by electing one of several alternative pricing, or costing, assumptions.

In illustrating the alternative methods of arriving at ending inventory values and the complementary cost-of-goods-sold figures, it is helpful to introduce the step-by-step procedures that have evolved over many years in general ledger bookkeeping. Until now we have always used a single permanent inventory account to handle directly the recording of beginning and ending inventory balances, all purchases, and the recognition of cost of goods sold. The only temporary account we have used in connection with inventory is the expense account, cost of goods sold. In practice, however, at least one other temporary account is used. It is called the purchases account and is used to record all additions to inventory during a given accounting period. Like all other temporary accounts it starts and ends each accounting period with a zero balance. To illustrate the role of the purchases account in the methods of recognizing beginning and ending inventory balances and the cost of goods sold for the period, *and* to serve as a basis for illustrating the various valuation methods discussed below, we use Example 10-7.

Example 10-7

Aesthetic Arts Limited is an art gallery of impeccable reputation. One of its most successful lines of business consists of buying up copies, signed by the artists, of multiple-copy, limited edition art objects. At the present time it holds in inventory 150 copies of a 200-copy signed, limited edition print of a painting by a famous painter. Thirty copies were acquired eight years ago at a price of $200 each. A second block of 80 copies was purchased three years ago at $550 each. Aesthetic Arts therefore began the current year with an inventory of 110 prints having a cost of $50,000. This year 40 more copies were purchased at $1,000 each, including shipping, packaging, and insurance costs. This gave Aesthetic Arts the near "corner" on the market for the prints that was desired, and it launched an advertising campaign offering 100 of the prints to the public at $1,500 each. All 100 were sold.

In accordance with customary bookkeeping practice, Aesthetic Arts recorded the current year's purchases of the prints with the following journal entry:

Purchases	40,000	
Accounts Payable		40,000

(Note: Some companies use other temporary accounts to record shipping, packing, and insurance-in-transit costs separate from the actual purchase cost which is recorded as above. However, we do not add this extra detail because the balances in such accounts at year-end are accorded the same treatment as the balance in purchases illustrated below.)

At the end of the year Aesthetic Arts made the following two customary journal entries:

    1. Cost of goods sold   50,000
         Inventory   50,000
    2. Cost of goods sold   40,000
         Purchases   40,000

In effect, year-end entries 1 and 2 above zero out the balances in the inventory and purchases accounts and transfer their balances to the cost of goods sold account. The balance at this stage in cost of goods sold is actually the *cost of goods available for sale* for the period ($90,000). The purchases account, being a temporary account, is now properly closed for the period. However, the inventory account should not be left with a zero balance (unless no inventory is on hand), and the cost of goods sold account should not be left with a balance equal to cost of goods available. A final journal entry in the year-end sequence takes care of this problem. It is illustrated as entry 3:

    3. Inventory   XXXX
        Cost of goods sold   XXXX

In principle, entry 3 backs out of the cost of goods sold account an amount equal to the cost of the ending inventory and establishes this amount as the balance (previously zero) in the inventory account. What remains is therefore the cost of goods actually sold during the period rather than the cost of goods available. The specific amounts are omitted from entry 3 because they are dependent on the "costing" method selected. Four alternatives are discussed below, giving four different versions of entry 3.

Specific Identification. The intuitively obvious method of assigning costs to the quantities of inventory on hand or consumed is to identify the specific costs of each particular item consumed and/or on hand. Unfortunately, this method is *feasible* only under certain limited conditions. That is, the inventory items must be (1) uniquely identifiable and (2) of sufficient value to justify, for business as well as accounting reasons, maintaining the detailed records necessary to know the status of each separate inventory item.

Example 10-8

It is unlikely that a business that purchases, stores, and sells large quantities of wheat could identify the separate purchases (probably at varying prices) of wheat in its ending inventory because of the fungibility (interchangeability) of this type of inventory item. Therefore, in such a circumstance, it would be impossible to use the specific identification method to, say, identify with each bushel sold the price actually paid for the grain contained in it. On the other hand, for a business such as a jewelry shop, the individual inventory items are often uniquely identifiable. And because of the high value per item, the jewelry shop may maintain the necessary detailed records to aid in such activities as setting or negotiating selling prices or in providing evidence required in the event insurance claims might have to be filed. If this is the case, the specific identification method of assigning costs to units sold and on hand is feasible.

In addition to the two constraints on the feasibility of the specific identification costing method, it is also subject to another practical limitation. We note in Chapter 9 that one of the major considerations in the evaluation of alternative revenue methods is the degree to which any particular method is susceptible to fraud or manipulation. We are equally concerned about this potential problem for expense recognition alternatives. And if a business elects to use the specific identification method of inventory costing, it is possible to "manage" reported income for the period by selecting the specific unit that the business chooses to sell based upon the relative costs of the items. This potentiality is present primarily when the inventory items are (1) uniquely identifiable in physical terms, (2) interchangeable in economic terms (of equal value), and (3) substantially different in terms of their acquisition costs.

Example 10-9

Aesthetic Arts in Example 10-7 has sold 100 of its 150 copies of the limited edition print. The specific identification method of inventory valuation is feasible here because each print can be identified by its serial number and a specific cost associated with it. Yet, in terms of their economic value, the prints are interchangeable. If the specific identification method is elected, Aesthetic Arts can affect the amount of income that will be recognized in the period by its choice of specific prints to be sold. Thus the management of Aesthetic Arts can increase its income for the period by including in the prints to be sold all the prints with a cost of $200 per print. If, on the other hand, the management were satisfied with the income that would be reported for the period and did not wish to increase it significantly with this transaction, it might elect to retain in its inventory all of the prints with a cost of $200 per print, and to sell all of the prints with a cost of $1,000 per print.

For the latter alternative the inventory would consist of 30 prints (at $200) and 20 prints (at $550) and journal entry 3 would be:

3. Inventory	17,000	
Cost of goods sold		17,000

This leaves cost of goods sold at $73,000 (40 prints at $1,000 plus 60 prints at $550).

Average Cost Method. An appealing alternative to the specific identification method is to use some form of average cost. We can calculate a weighted average cost per item of inventory by adding the cost of the inventory on hand at the beginning of the period to the cost of inventory purchased during the period, and then dividing by the total number of units of inventory available for sale. The single weighted average cost calculated in this manner is then assigned both to the units of inventory sold during the period and to the units on hand at the end of the period.

Example 10-10

Using the data for Aesthetic Arts in Example 10-7, we would apply the average cost method (assuming 100 copies were sold) as follows:

Inventory, beginning of period		
30 copies @ $200	$ 6,000	
80 copies @ $550	44,000	$50,000
Purchases during period (40 copies @ $1,000)		40,000
Total cost of inventory available for sale		$90,000

Weighted average cost per copy = $90,000/150
= $600 per copy

Total cost of inventory available for sale allocated:		
To cost of goods sold (100 copies @ $600)		$60,000
To ending inventory (50 copies @ $600)		30,000
		$90,000

Journal entry 3 under this method would be:

3. Inventory	30,000	
Cost of goods sold		30,000

Therefore, using the average cost method, Aesthetic Arts would recognize the following from the sale of 100 copies:

Sales (100 @ $1,500)	$150,000
Cost of goods sold	60,000
Gross income on sale	$ 90,000

The average cost method of inventory valuation is generally easy to apply in practice. To use it, we need only know the total cost and total units of inventory on hand at the start of the period and acquisitions of inventory during the period—data that are generally available from the accounting system. Additionally, the method is not highly susceptible to manipulation, and it produces fairly reasonable cost allocations between inventory and cost of sales. There are, however, two other costing methods that are frequently encountered in current financial reporting. These are now examined.

First-in, First-out (Fifo) Method. In contrast to the specific identification method, which attempts to identify the costs associated with specific physical inventory flows, there is a class of costing assumptions that relies upon *assumed* flows of costs through the business enterprise. One of these methods, the Fifo method, assumes that the earliest inventory items purchased are the first inventory items sold—in measuring cost of goods sold, the first unit in is assumed to be the first unit out. This assumption about cost flows is in many instances justified by normal business practices. That is, the physical flow of inventory in and out of an enterprise coincides in many types of business with this assumed cost flow. This follows from the normal business objective of trying to maintain an orderly flow of its product so that it does not have old merchandise on hand.

Example 10-11

Again using the data of Example 10-7, Aesthetic Arts had the following inventory acquisitions:

	Units	Unit Cost	Total
First purchase	30	$ 200	$ 6,000
Second purchase	80	550	44,000
Third purchase	40	1,000	40,000
	150		$90,000

Using these data, and the fact that 100 units (copies) were sold, we can assign values to either cost of goods sold or ending inventory in the following manner:

	Units	Unit Cost	Total
Cost of goods sold:	30	$ 200	$ 6,000
	70	550	38,500
	100		$44,500
Ending inventory:	40	$1,000	$40,000
	10	550	5,500
	50		$45,500

Thus the total cost of inventory available for sale is fully allocated between cost of goods sold and inventory. Journal entry 3 accomplishes this allocation as follows:

3. Inventory 45,500
    Cost of goods sold 45,500

In applying the first-in, first-out method to establish the value of the ending inventory, the unit cost of the latest purchase is assigned to the number of units in that purchase or in the ending inventory, whichever is smaller. If there are still more units in the ending inventory to be valued (as there are in Example 10-11), the unit cost from the next latest purchase is applied in a similar manner. We continue in this fashion until all the units in the ending inventory have been assigned costs. If we wish to assign a value to cost of sales rather than to the ending inventory, the same procedure is followed except that we begin with the unit cost associated with the first purchase (which is assumed to be sold first). Of course, once either one of the values (inventory or cost of goods sold) has been established, the other can be determined by using the duality principle illustrated earlier.

Last-in, First-out (Lifo) Method. An alternative costing method which is also predicated upon an assumption about the flow of costs is the last-in, first-out (Lifo) method of inventory costing. Under this method, it is assumed that items sold come from the latest acquisitions, or at least that the cost flows associated with the items sold are based upon the latest costs incurred. This method has fewer analogies in terms of physical flows of inventory units, but there are business situations where it is encountered. For example, the classic illustration of a Lifo flow of physical units is an inventory of coal, where each new acquisition is placed on top of the coal pile. In this case the quantities used are, in the main, drawn from the latest units acquired. However, the method does not derive its principal appeal from an assumed physical analogy, but rather from the fact that it generally matches prices paid most recently for goods with current revenue.

Example 10-12

Using the Lifo method of inventory valuation for Aesthetic Arts' prints, we arrive at the following allocation of costs:

	Units	Unit Cost	Total
Cost of goods sold:	40	$1,000	$40,000
	60	550	33,000
	100		$73,000
Ending inventory:	30	$ 200	$ 6,000
	20	550	11,000
	50		$17,000

Thus, under the Lifo cost flow assumption, the $90,000 total cost of inventory available for sale is again totally allocated between cost of goods sold and inventory on hand at the end of the period. But the amounts allocated to the two variables are significantly different from the allocations that were made under the Fifo method. Under this alternative, journal entry 3 would be:

3. Inventory	17,000	
Cost of goods sold		17,000

Summary of Costing Methods. To recap the inventory costing methods that we have examined, Exhibit 10-2 reflects the allocation of costs under each of these methods. The hypothetical data for Aesthetic Arts illustrate the potential disparity in the allocation of "costs" between cost of goods sold and inventory, depending upon the cost or pricing method that is adopted. In most practical applications, the disparity would not be as great as in this example, but the different inventory costing methods would nonetheless produce different values for the two variables, and thus different profit measures for the period. But where the units of inventory available for sale (beginning inventory plus purchases during the period) do involve substantial differences in unit costs, the potential for variations such as those illustrated here does exist.

Exhibit 10-2

AESTHETIC ARTS LIMITED

Comparative Summary of
Alternative Costing Methods

Costing Method	Cost of Goods Sold	Inventory, End of Period
Specific identification	Depends on actual physical flows	Depends on actual physical flows
Average cost	$60,000	$30,000
First-in, first-out (Fifo)	$44,500	$45,500
Last-in, first-out (Lifo)	$73,000	$17,000

In this brief summary of inventory costing methods, we have implicitly assumed that the allocation of costs will be made at the end of the period. If the inventory is valued in this manner, that is, based upon the number of units on hand at the end of the period and the inferred number of units sold during the period, we refer to the approach as the *periodic method* of inventory valuation. An alternative approach is to assess the cost of sales and new inventory position throughout the period as sales are made. When this technique is used, we refer to it as the *perpetual method* of inventory valuation. The two approaches are illustrated in comparative form in Appendix A of this chapter.

**Departures from Cost Basis
for Valuing Inventories**

Although inventories are normally valued at cost under the conventional accounting model, there are some exceptions to this general valuation rule. Some exceptions were noted in Chapter 8 in discussing revenue recognition. One is the special case in which inventory is valued at realizable value at the completion of the production process. Another is the case of construction-work-in-progress inventories valued at cost plus profit in proportion to percentage completion. Two other important exceptions that involve write-downs rather than write-ups of inventory are the general "lower of cost or market" test and the valuation of obsolete or damaged merchandise.

Lower of Cost or Market Rule. Inventory valuation in conventional accounting begins with an assessment of the cost of the inventory using one of the alternative costing methods discussed above. As a matter of general practice, the cost-based value (using individual inventory items, or categories of inventory, or the total inventory) is then compared with the current replacement cost ("market" in the terminology of inventory valuation) of the inventory. If cost exceeds market, the inventory is valued at the lower replacement cost amount. If market is in excess of the cost value, the inventory is valued at cost. This valuation approach is widely used for valuing inventories in current financial reporting and is referred to as *lower of cost or market* valuation.

Lower of cost or market valuation reflects an inherent conservative bias in the conventional accounting model. An implicit assumption of the method is that a drop in the replacement cost of inventory portends a drop in future selling prices, and based on this assumed market reaction, the conservative conclusion under conventional accounting is that the potential loss should be recognized as soon as possible. Note that the converse position is seldom found under conventional accounting valuation procedures; that is, *potential* gains are not given early recognition since they have not yet been realized. As a consequence of valuing inventory at the lower of cost or market, the inventory values in the statement of financial position are also conservatively oriented. For statement users who may rely specifically on resource values for their actions (e.g., extending short-term credit), this conservatism is probably a desirable attribute of conventional accounting statements. Whether the method distorts, to some degree, the performance measure produced under conventional accounting is, however, an equally important issue to the broad class of statement users looking primarily to the firm's long-run cash-generating ability as a basis for their investment decisions. Some distortion of the performance index does seem to exist, particularly in the direction of reporting lower net income in the current period so that a more "normal" income can be reported when the goods are sold in the succeeding period.

Market is generally defined for this inventory valuation purpose as current replacement cost. But there are instances where another value may be used. In particular, the lower of cost or market test specifies that market (current replacement cost) shall not exceed net realizable value (that is, expected selling price less costs expected in connection with disposition). Nor should it be less than net realizable value reduced by a normal profit margin. If current replacement cost does exceed net realizable value, then the net realizable value becomes the "market" amount to be compared against cost. Here the reasoning is that inventory should never be valued at an amount in excess of what can be recovered upon sale. Similarly, if current replacement cost is below net realizable value less a normal profit margin, the higher figure is used because inventory need not be written down below an amount that will, upon sale, allow a normal profit when matched against revenue. Both of these tests are used in arriving at a value for "market." After this value for "market" is determined, it then is compared against cost, and the lower of the two values is used.

Obsolete or Damaged Merchandise. When inventory items have suffered damage or obsolescence, the original costs of the items can no longer be presumed to bear any significant relationship to potential benefits (revenue). Under these circumstances, cost is abandoned as a valuation base, and the items are generally valued at their net realizable value.

Estimating Inventories from Aggregate Data

In certain situations we would like to estimate the value of inventory on hand at the end of the period without a detailed record of physical quantities on hand and/or detailed cost data for these items. For example, if a firm sustains a substantial loss to its inventory through a natural disaster, it will of course want to estimate the amount of this loss for insurance purposes. In the absence of detailed perpetual inventory records, the firm's only recourse will be to attempt to develop an estimate based on the information it does have available. Additionally, a firm may wish to test the reasonableness of the inventory value determined through the physical inventory process through the use of aggregate data. Both of these types of problems, as well as others that may arise, can be resolved by using the gross profit method of estimating inventory, which is described in Appendix B of this chapter.

Treatment of Manufacturing Costs

All of the discussion to this point has focused on companies that purchase inventory for resale in the same form. There are, however, additional measurement problems in the valuation of the inventories of a manufacturing firm.

A manufacturing firm has, in general, three basic classes of inventory:

1. Raw material inventory
2. Work-in-process inventory
3. Finished goods inventory

These categories correspond to the major forms in which the manufacturing firm holds inventory, that is, units not yet placed into the production process (raw material), partially completed units at some stage in the production process (work in process), and completed units held prior to shipment to customers (finished goods).

How do we assign costs to these various classes of inventory? Exhibit 10-3 depicts the basic inventory relationships for the three classes of inventory. We note first that no new problem is presented by the need to assign values to raw material inventories. The inventory valuation principles described previously are sufficient to value raw material inventories. Valuation of the work-in-process and finished goods inventories is, however, a more involved process. These inventories often result from the combination of several resources and the application of large amounts of labor and capital. The valuation principle we rely on for this type of measurement problem is the "costs attach" assumption.

The "costs attach" notion, which we allude to briefly in our earlier discussion of the cost principle, assumes that the costs of inputs (material, labor, or capital) introduced into production attach to the units of production as they flow through the production process. Applying this principle to the valuation of manufacturing inventories, the cost of units in process is the sum of the costs incurred to bring the units to their present stage of completion. These costs include the cost of raw materials consumed, the cost of labor employed directly in the manufacture of the products, and a pro rata share of the general overhead costs of the factory. Thus two major additional problems involved in this measurement process are the determination of the completion status of

Exhibit 10-3

INVENTORY RELATIONSHIPS IN A MANUFACTURING FIRM

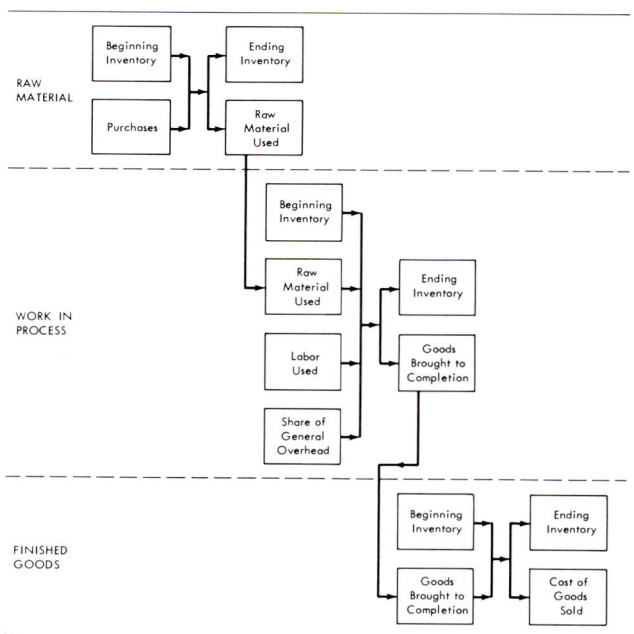

the work in process and the identification of the costs incurred to bring units to that stage of production.

The finished goods inventory is the inventory of units that have moved completely through the production process and are on hand waiting shipment to wholesalers, dealers, or other retail customers. Valuation of this inventory class draws on the same principles that are used to value work-in-process inventories. Indeed the measurement problem is somewhat easier because the stage of completion is not a factor to be determined.

Effect of Inventory Errors on Reported Income

Because the determination of the actual quantity of goods on hand is a difficult task, particularly for a firm with a large and diversified inventory, we should consider what the effect of an error in this process (or, for that matter, the subsequent assignment of costs) will be on the reported income of the firm. In assessing the impact of a possible error in inventory valuation on reported income, we return to the basic duality relationship for asset (inventory) valuation and expense (cost of sales) measurement:

Cost of sales = Beginning inventory + Purchases − Ending inventory

From this relationship, we readily observe that if the value of the ending inventory of a period is overstated, the cost of sales for the period will be understated. Conversely, if the ending inventory value is understated, the cost of sales for the period will be overstated.

Note, however, that any error in inventory valuation is then carried forward into the next period, because the beginning inventory of one period is merely the ending inventory of the prior period. Returning to the basic relationship, if the ending inventory of the current period is overstated, the cost of sales will be understated for the period, and therefore net income will be overstated. But in the succeeding period, the beginning inventory will be overstated, and thus cost of sales for the succeeding period will also be overstated, and net income will be understated. The overstatement and the understatement of net income in the two periods are of identical amounts. Therefore, over two periods, inventory errors are offsetting (self-correcting) with respect to reported net income.

The existence of this two-period, self-correction feature should not be construed to mean that the effect of an inventory error is unimportant. Our concern in formulating an index of long-run cash-generating ability (operating income) is with achieving the best matching that we can of efforts and accomplishments of each period. If an inventory error (either overstatement or understatement) develops, operating income will be in error for both periods. To the extent that these errors distort the trend of earnings, as they may well do, the decision relevance of the information may be substantially reduced. Additionally, an error in the ending inventory valuation is also reflected in the statement of financial position at the end of the period.

LONG-LIVED ASSETS (TANGIBLE AND INTANGIBLE): VALUATION AND RELATED EXPENSE RECOGNITION

A second major class of assets that creates important problems of valuation and related expense recognition is the so-called long-lived assets class. The major differences between long-lived assets and inventories are that the long-lived assets are acquired for *use* rather than sale, and the benefits to be derived from the long-lived assets generally extend over a much longer period of time than for inventories.

Long-lived assets are divided into two categories: tangible and intangible. The long-lived tangible assets class includes items such as buildings and machinery and equipment, and vehicles such as delivery trucks, as well as any natural resources that the firm holds, such as land and mineral rights. On the other hand, the long-lived intangible assets class, as the term is used in accounting, consists principally of rights acquired under law which do not themselves have physical substance, such as patents, copyrights, franchises, and trademarks. Because certain other assets (such as accounts receivable) also lack "physical substance," we should note that the basic test for inclusion within the intangible category is to a certain extent a matter of convention, rather than precise definitional stipulation.

The major problems in accounting for long-lived assets may be classified as follows:

1. Valuation at date of acquisition
2. Determination of the appropriate treatment of expenditures made over the life of the asset to maintain and/or improve it
3. Measurement of benefits that have been consumed in the production of revenue
4. Recognition of gain or loss on the disposal of the assets

Each of these classes of accounting problems will be considered in turn.

Valuation of Long-lived Assets at Acquisition

In conventional accounting, long-lived assets are valued at acquisition on the basis of the outlays made to acquire them. This problem is considered at the beginning of this chapter in the discussion of the cost principle. Indeed, in Example 10-2 describing the acquisition of a new computer by the Roark Computer Service Company, we address the problem of the valuation of long-lived assets at date of acquisition. We need only reiterate that this valuation is based upon the application of the criteria for the determination of cost and should be construed broadly to include all expenditures made to acquire the asset and install it in position for use.

Expenditures to Maintain and/or Improve Long-lived Assets

After an asset has been acquired, additional expenditures will often be made over the life of the asset to maintain or improve its operating capability. If these expenditures do not add to, or increase, the potential benefits that can be derived from the asset, but merely maintain the asset's operating efficiency, the expenditures are generally regarded as normal repairs and maintenance and are reported as expenses of the period in which the outlays are made. On the other hand, some expenditures are made to increase the level of benefits that may be derived from the long-lived asset. Expenditures of this type are added to the unexpired cost of the asset and are then matched against revenue in future periods as the additional benefits are derived.

In many practical situations, the distinction between an expenditure that improves the asset and one that merely maintains it in proper operating order is fuzzy. In these situations, judgment must be exercised by the accountant in order to properly classify the expenditure. In making this judgment, the significance (materiality) of the expenditure is often an important consideration. If the expenditure is judged to be relatively immaterial, it will normally be treated as an expense of the period, even though it may in fact be a minor improvement. However, if the potential impact of the expenditure is material, the accountant must assess more carefully the effect of the expenditure on the services to be derived from the asset in future periods.

Measurement of Benefits Derived from Long-lived Assets

Use of long-lived assets represents a consumption of the benefits, or service potentials, inherent in the asset. Presumably, this use of resources contributes to the production of revenue of the period. In accordance with the matching principle, we wish to reflect as an expense of the current period the cost of these inherent benefits or service potentials that were consumed. Because of the indivisibility of long-lived assets, however, it is often difficult to ascertain precisely the benefits derived in a particular period.

In general, two different approaches to this problem are available. One approach is based upon the *output* of the asset. Where benefits potentially available from an asset can be expressed in terms of a maximum potential output, the total cost of the asset may under the output method be allocated to periods based upon the output produced in a period.

Example 10-13

> The Jones Company acquired a machine that is expected to have a potential output of 25,000 units of the product produced on it over its life. The cost of the machine is $50,000, and Jones does not anticipate that there will be any salvage value at the end of the machine's useful life. Applying the output measure of expense assessment, we recognize as an expense of the period a cost of $2 ($50,000/25,000) for each unit produced on

the machine. Therefore, if the company produced 4,000 units of product on this machine during the current period, the depreciation expense for the period would be $8,000 (4,000 × $2).

Where we can determine fairly accurately an identifiable output from a long-lived asset and also estimate the total potential output over its life, the output method produces a satisfactory matching of effort and accomplishment.

Obviously, however, we are not able to identify the specific output from a number of different types of long-lived assets—for example, an office building. In these cases we must turn to an assessment of the service potentials consumed from the use of the asset based upon the passage of time. Such recourse to a time-based calculation is admittedly a pragmatic compromise of the matching objective. However, there are tangible assets (such as buildings) whose service potential is primarily influenced by the passage of time (forces of weather, etc.), and for which unused capacity in one period is not necessarily usable in future periods. In these cases the time-based method of determining expense is a sensible approach to matching.

Generally, where time is used as the primary basis for determining the services derived from the use of an asset, and thus the related expense measure, we must—

1. Estimate the useful life of the asset.
2. Estimate the residual value of the asset at the end of its useful lfie.
3. Select a method of depreciation.

We have, in our previous discussions of the depreciation of long-lived assets, selected a depreciation method that allocates an equal portion of the depreciable cost (cost less estimated salvage value) of the asset to each period of time in its useful life. This method is called the *straight-line* method of depreciation.

There are, however, other methods or patterns of allocating the cost to be depreciated to the various periods over the useful life of a long-lived asset. Frequently, these methods produce larger measures of expense in the early years of the asset's life, and correspondingly smaller expense measurements in the later years. Two of these "accelerated expense recognition" methods which are often encountered in current practice are the sum-of-years-digits method and the declining-balance method.

Sum-of-years-digits Depreciation Method. The sum-of-years-digits method is one of the depreciation methods that produces larger measures of depreciation expense in the early years in the life of the asset than in the later years. This pattern of depreciation expense results from applying decreasing depreciation rates to the depreciable cost (cost less the estimated salvage value).

Example 10-14

The Longhorn Manufacturing Company was formed on January 1, 19X5, to manufacture various types of gift items with Longhorn emblems embossed on them. Immediately after the company was formed, embossing machinery was purchased at a cost of $16,000. It was estimated that the machinery would have a life of five years and that the residual, or salvage, value of the machinery at the end of that period of time would be $1,000. The amount of depreciation recognized under the sum-of-years-digits method is reflected in Exhibit 10-4.

The depreciation rate to be used under this method is determined by first summing the digits from 1 to n, where n is the number of years of useful life that the asset is expected to be productive. In Example 10-14, the asset has an expected useful life of five years, and the sum of the digits from one to five is fifteen $(1 + 2 + 3 + 4 + 5 = 15)$.[2] This sum is placed in the denominator in determining the depreciation rate. The numerator of the depreciation rate changes each year, starting with the largest number in the sum (i.e., 5), and decreasing by one each year until in the last year the numerator is 1. Therefore the depreciation rate for the first year is 5/15, and when this rate is applied to the depreciable cost (cost less estimated salvage value) of $15,000, we obtain depreciation expense of $5,000. In the second year, the numerator of the depreciation rate is reduced by one to 4, and the rate is 4/15. Applying this rate again to the depreciable cost of $15,000, the depreciation expense for the year is $4,000. This modification of the depreciation rate continues until the last year, when the depreciation rate is 1/15. At the end of the five-year life of the asset, the asset is valued (cost less accumulated depreciation) at $1,000—the amount of the estimated salvage value.

Exhibit 10-4

ILLUSTRATION OF SUM-OF-YEARS-DIGITS DEPRECIATION METHOD

Year	Asset Value, Beginning of Year	Depreciation Rate	Depreciation Expense	Asset Value, End of Year
1	$16,000	5/15	5/15 × $15,000 = $ 5,000	$11,000
2	11,000	4/15	4/15 × 15,000 = 4,000	7,000
3	7,000	3/15	3/15 × 15,000 = 3,000	4,000
4	4,000	2/15	2/15 × 15,000 = 2,000	2,000
5	2,000	1/15	1/15 × 15,000 = 1,000	1,000
		1.00	$15,000	

Sum-of-years-digits = 1 + 2 + 3 + 4 + 5
= 15

Declining-balance Depreciation Method. Under the declining-balance depreciation method, which also is a method that assigns larger amounts of depreciation to the earlier years, a fixed percentage is applied to the *balance of the asset* (cost less accumulated depreciation) at the start of each year to determine depreciation expense for that year. Two common percentages that are used (particularly due to their acceptability for tax purposes) are 150 percent of the straight-line rate and 200 percent of the straight-line rate. For the data of Example 10-14, the straight-line depreciation rate, given a five-year life,

---

[2] For larger numbers of years it is very handy to know that the sum of the years digits is always equal to $n (n + 1) \div 2$, where n is the number of years. For example, for $n = 5$ the formula is $5 (6) \div 2 = 15$.

is 20 percent. That is, we allocate 20 percent of the depreciable cost of the asset to each year if we adopt the straight-line depreciation method. Therefore, using a 150 percent declining-balance depreciation method, the rate would be 30 percent (20 percent × 150 percent); and under the 200 percent, or double-declining-balance depreciation method, the depreciation rate is 40 percent (20 percent × 200 percent). Obviously the double-declining-balance depreciation method assigns a larger portion of the cost of the long-lived asset to the early periods than will the 150 percent declining-balance method.

After the depreciation rate has been determined, the depreciation for the year under the declining-balance method is determined by multiplying this rate by the asset net value at the beginning of each year. When this method is applied, no estimate of salvage value is used in the calculation. *However, the total amount of depreciation expense recognized over the life of the asset cannot exceed the difference between cost and salvage value, that is, the unexpired cost of the asset is not reduced below its salvage value.* Application of the double-declining-balance depreciation method to the facts of Example 10-14 is illustrated in Exhibit 10-5.

Exhibit 10-5

ILLUSTRATION OF DOUBLE-DECLINING-BALANCE DEPRECIATION METHOD

Year	Asset Value, Beginning of Year	Depreciation Rate	Depreciation Expense			Asset Value, End of Year
1	$16,000	40%	$16,000 × 40%	=	$ 6,400	$9,600
2	9,600	40	$ 9,600 × 40	=	3,840	5,760
3	5,760	40	5,760 × 40	=	2,304	3,456
4	3,456	40	3,456 × 40	=	1,382	2,074
5	2,074	40	2,074 × 40	=	830	1,244
					$14,756	

To briefly review the procedures followed in Exhibit 10-5, we note that in the first year depreciation expense is calculated by multiplying the double-declining-balance depreciation rate (40 percent) by the original cost of the asset ($16,000), or $6,400 depreciation expense. The so-called book value (unexpired cost) of the asset at the end of the year, then, is the original cost of the asset ($16,000) less the accumulated depreciation ($6,400), or $9,600. This value at the end of year one is also the asset value at the beginning of year two, and it is the base for the calculation of depreciation expense in the second year. We therefore multiply the 40 percent rate by the $9,600 book value of the asset at the beginning of the second year to compute the $3,840 depreciation expense for the second year. Continuing in this fashion, at the end of year five we have an ending asset value of $1,244 (which appropriately is not less than the estimated salvage value of $1,000), and total depreciation expense for the five-year period amounts to $14,756. In general, the total depreciation expense recognized under the declining-balance depreciation method will not equal the total depreciable cost (which is the amount allocated under the straight-line and sum-of-years-digits methods), although the difference will normally be fairly small. One way of handling the difference is to simply follow the method described above until the last year in the life of the asset. In that year depreciation expense can simply be recognized as the difference between beginning book value and expected salvage value. For Example 10-14 this would lead to year-five depreciation expense of $1,074 and total five-year depreciation of $15,000, as with the other methods. This is illustrated in the last column of Exhibit 10-6.

Exhibit 10-6

COMPARISON OF DEPRECIATION EXPENSE DETERMINED UNDER ALTERNATIVE DEPRECIATION METHODS

Year	Straight-Line	Sum-of-Years-Digits	Double-Declining-Balance
1	$ 3,000	$ 5,000	$ 6,400
2	3,000	4,000	3,840
3	3,000	3,000	2,304
4	3,000	2,000	1,382
5	3,000	1,000	1,074*
	$15,000	$15,000	$15,000

*Note that year five depreciation has been "plugged" under this method to ensure that the asset is "fully depreciated" by the end of year five.

Discussion of Alternative Depreciation Patterns

The different amounts of depreciation expense that would be recognized each year for the data of Example 10-14 under the alternative depreciation methods we have considered are summarized in Exhibit 10-6. As noted earlier, the straight-line method allocates the depreciable cost equally over the asset's life, while the two "accelerated" methods allocate larger amounts to the early years of the asset's life. Although there exist additional alternative depreciation methods, these three methods are probably selected most frequently in current practice.

The introduction of different methods of determining each period's depreciation expense (that is, allocating depreciable cost to the periods in the life of the asset) does not alter the form of the end-of-period adjusting journal entry used to record depreciation expense. All are of the form illustrated in Chapter 7, that is:

    Depreciation expense   XXXX
        Accumulated depreciation   XXXX

Selection of different methods merely results in different amounts in each entry during the life of the asset.

The disparity of the amounts allocated to the different periods raises the question of what factors the accountant considers in choosing a depreciation method. Recall that our initial premise is that we are trying to derive a measure of effort, as reflected in the consumption of services from the long-lived asset, to match against the related revenue generated in the period. When we are selecting from depreciation methods that are related to the passage of time, however, it is difficult to apply the matching principle to uniquely identifiable revenue increments. The rationale for the selection of a particular time-based depreciation method must necessarily be related to *general* revenue and/or cost considerations. One basis that is often used to decide between alternative time-based depreciation methods is the pattern of related costs associated with the long-lived asset. A business enterprise expects some normal pattern of expenditures for repairs and maintenance over the life of a long-lived asset. If the expectation is that these costs will increase as time passes, we may conclude that a larger portion of the services inherent in the asset are consumed in the early years of its life, and thus a depreciation method should be selected that allocates a larger amount of the depreciable cost to the early years. Or the same conclusion may be reached by arguing that if repairs and maintenance expenditures are increasing over time, a combination of this expense pattern with a decreasing depreciation expense will result in a fairly uniform pattern of total expense (depreciation expense plus repairs and maintenance expense) recognized each period over the life of the asset—a condition that may be reasonably consistent with the pattern of benefits the firm expects to derive from the use of the asset.

Alternatively, the decision on the depreciation method to be selected may be based upon the expectation as to revenue patterns. For example, if the revenue to be derived from the asset is expected to remain fairly uniform over the life of the asset without any significant change in other related expenses, this may add credence to the use of the straight-line depreciation method (provided related expenses are also constant). On the other hand, if there is an expectation of decreasing productivity over the life of the asset, this might suggest that a larger percentage of services would be consumed in the early years of the asset's life, and thus one of the two methods that produce decreasing depreciation expense over time should be adopted.

Finally, the choice of the depreciation method is sometimes influenced by a desire to report the same depreciation expense for financial reporting purposes as is reported for income tax purposes. Present income tax law allows a company to select any of the three methods we have illustrated. In many circumstances, business enterprises opt for a depreciation method that allocates a larger portion of the expense to the early periods of the asset's life, in order to reduce their taxable income and therefore their tax liability in the early years. While the *total* income tax over the life of the asset is unaffected by the choice of any particular depreciation method (assuming no tax rate changes occur), the time preference for money concept clearly supports any action (including choice of a depreciation method) that results in the deferral of cash expenditures the firm must make. Thus, *although the income tax law does not require that the same amounts be reported for tax and financial reporting purposes, many companies may wish to do so for record-keeping convenience.* (In Chapter 12 we discuss the problems presented when a company *does not* choose the same methods for tax purposes and financial reporting purposes.)

Land and Natural Resources

Our discussion of the measurement of benefits received from long-lived assets and related expense recognition has to this point concentrated on fabricated, or constructed, physical assets, such as buildings or machinery. Certain other types of long-lived tangible assets, however, have a finite reservoir of service potentials. As these benefits are consumed over time by a business enterprise, the cost of the asset must be matched against revenue in the same manner as described above.

Natural resources that are exploited by a company, such as mineral deposits or stands of timber, are examples of this class of nonconstructed assets. In many cases the "production or output method" of recognizing the expense of consuming such resources is used. The first step is to estimate the total quantity of the resource available (e.g., number of tons of iron ore). Dividing the total cost of the asset by this estimate of total units available, we obtain a cost per unit. Then as the resources are extracted or otherwise consumed, the expense to be recognized is calculated by multiplying the cost per unit by the number of units consumed. Where it is impossible to estimate the total quantity of resources available, the measure of expense may have to be determined using a time-based exploitation pattern.

Although the recognition of the expense associated with the use of natural resources is similar to depreciation expense, a difference in terminology should be noted. The allocation of the cost of constructed, or fabricated, assets to time periods is labeled depreciation expense. The allocation of the cost of natural resources to time periods is referred to as *depletion expense.*

Land that is acquired by a company for use as a site for its manufacturing, marketing, or administrative operations represents a special case. We assume generally that the value of land for "site purposes" is unaffected by the passage of time or the intensity of use. That is, the service potential of land as a site remains unchanged over time. Accordingly, none of the cost of land used for site purposes needs to be allocated to periods or otherwise matched against revenue, and under conventional accounting, this asset (site land) will continue to be valued at its original cost, with no accumulated depletion. However, land held because of the natural resources it contains (including, for example, agricultural land) will be valued at original cost less accumulated depletion.

Unique Properties and Characteristics of Intangibles

Intangible assets include such resources as patents, copyrights, trademarks, franchises, and goodwill. These are real, often extremely valuable, assets, notwithstanding their lack of physical substance. The treatment of intangible assets is not in principle substantially unlike that accorded long-lived tangible assets. Intangibles are originally valued at the cost incurred to acquire them, and this cost is then allocated to expense over the expected useful life of the asset. In many cases the life of the intangible is reasonably well defined by the legal right that the company holds (for example, the seventeen-year life of a patent).

Example 10-15

> Meyer Tobacco Company, Limited, manufactures pipes. The pipes have a special finish, due largely to the unique finishing process used by the company. A newly registered patent on this process was acquired from the inventor several years ago at a cost of $51,000. The patent is legally binding for seventeen years.
>
> The patent is given recognition as a long-lived intangible asset in Meyer's statement of financial position. At the date of acquisition, the value of the asset would be $51,000. The company would then allocate a portion of its cost to expense each year. Typically, an equal amount is assigned to each year. If the useful life of the patent were expected to be equal to its legal life, $3,000 ($51,000/17) would be recognized as expense of each year, reflecting the estimate of the cost of the services derived from the patent during the period.

In other cases, however, the estimated useful life of an intangible is not apparent from legal or other criteria, and a more arbitrary judgment must be made.

Example 10-16

> Jack Hinrichs purchased the Ford distributorship in Dime Box, Texas, from the estate of the former owner for $225,000. The business had been very successful during the past fifteen years and enjoyed an extremely high reputation in the community. Assuming that the tangible assets of the firm had current market values amounting to only $150,000, it may be inferred that Jack paid $75,000 for the intangible properties of the distributorship—often referred to as "goodwill" in financial statements.
>
> The goodwill, like the patent in Example 10-15, is initially valued at its original cost ($75,000) in the statement of financial position. Allocation of the cost to expense is a more difficult problem, because the future periods benefiting from the firm's present reputation are somewhat indeterminate, and indeed subject to change. Thus we may have to resort to some arbitrary number of years. (Under current official accounting standards, the $75,000 cost would be recognized as an expense over a period of time not to exceed forty years.)

Where expenditures are made to develop intangible assets (for example, research and development programs), difficult measurement problems are created. The central questions are, (1) Does an intangible asset exist? and, if so, (2) What is its value? Until recently, some companies elected to recognize their expenditures for research and development not as expenses of the period in which the expenditure took place but as intangible assets (or, in some cases, as assetlike elements of financial position labeled *deferred costs*). These assets' costs were then allocated to expense in future periods—often on an arbitrary basis (this type of expense is often labeled *amortization* in financial statements). Where this practice was followed, the statement user had to be wary of the possible intentional or unintentional overstatement of the firm's assets, that is, the recognition of the expenditures as assets when in fact assets did not exist or the values (in terms of future benefits) of the intangible assets were not sufficiently large to warrant recognition at the amount of the expenditure. For one particularly impressive example see Exercise 10-16 at the end of the chapter. Because of many observed tendencies on the part of management to capitalize research and development expenditures under questionable circumstances, accounting standards were modified by the FASB in 1974 to require recognition of these expenditures as expenses of the current period. This policy is obviously conservatively biased in the measurement of net operating income of the current period. *By eliminating all management discretion,* the policy also results in the understatement of a firm's assets (and future expenses) when intangibles have actually been created by a research and development program.

Disposal of Long-lived Assets

At the time a long-lived asset is disposed of, which may be at the end of its previously estimated useful life or at some other earlier or later time, the gain or loss on the disposition is recognized. This gain or loss can easily be measured by comparing the book value of the asset (original cost less accumulated depreciation) with the sales proceeds. If there are additional expenses incurred to dispose of the asset, these expenses will also be deducted in the computation of the gain or loss from disposal of the asset. In years past, gains and losses on disposition of long-lived assets were treated as "extraordinary" items in the income statement. However, as was pointed out in Chapter 5, while such gains and losses may not occur in every period, they are not genuinely extraordinary. Hence accounting standards concerning gains and losses were recently changed, and now one will normally find the gain or loss on the disposal of long-lived assets as a component of net operating income (i.e., it is *not* treated as an extraordinary item). The elimination of management discretion in determining whether such gains are extraordinary is, in part, a response to the notion that gains or losses on disposal of long-lived assets are jointly a function of (1) market conditions (which determine the price received) *and* (2) *postacquisition management decisions* concerning depreciation of the assets (which determine the unexpired cost of the asset at the time of disposition). By forcing the inclusion of such gains and losses in operating income, that is, "performance," in the period of disposition, accounting policy makers have presumably removed some of the incentive that management might have had to understate depreciation on such assets during their use (and thus overstate net operating income) with the underdepreciation showing up later as part of an extraordinary loss (and thus excluded from operating income) in the period of disposition.

Where the disposal of a long-lived asset is in the form of a trade-in to acquire a new asset of the same kind, there is an alternative method of accounting for the transaction which involves valuing the new asset at the sum of the cash payment plus the unexpired cost of the asset traded in. This alternative results in *no gain or loss* being recognized on the disposition of the old asset. Because of its acceptability under the income tax law, this alternative receives considerable support and is illustrated along with approaches leading to recognition of gains (losses) on trade-ins in Example 10-2 (the example concerned with the cost of a new computer).

In Chapter 5 we noted that when gains or losses of corporations on disposition of assets are subject to the federal or state corporate income taxes, the related gains and losses are recognized on a net of tax basis. This treatment and illustrative journal entries for dispositions of assets for cash or other monetary assets are presented in Example 10-17. Journal entries for dispositions in connection with trade-ins (in which cases there usually are no *taxable* gains or losses) were illustrated earlier in connection with Example 10-2.

Example 10-17

Z Corporation disposed of a piece of equipment with an original cost of $50,000 and accumulated depreciation up to the time of disposition of $30,000. Journal entries appear below corresponding to cash or other monetary proceeds of (a) $25,000 and (b) $15,000. A tax rate of 45 percent and sufficient tax liability from other taxable income to absorb the tax benefits of a loss on disposition are assumed.

(a)	Cash (or other monetary assets)	25,000	
	Accumulated depreciation	30,000	
	Equipment		50,000
	Income taxes payable		2,300
	Gain on disposition		2,700
(b)	Cash (or other monetary assets)	15,000	
	Accumulated depreciation	30,000	
	Income taxes payable	2,300	
	Loss on disposition	2,700	
	Equipment		50,000

APPENDIX A: INVENTORY VALUATION—
PERIODIC VERSUS PERPETUAL ASSESSMENT OF COSTS

In our discussion in the chapter of the pricing, or costing, methods that are available for the accountant to choose from, we assumed implicitly that the allocation of costs would be made at the end of the period. If this is the way in which the inventory is valued, that is, based upon the number of units on hand at the end of the period and the inferred number of units sold during the period, we refer to it as the *periodic method* of inventory valuation. An alternative approach is to assess the cost of goods sold throughout the period as sales are made. When this technique is used, we refer to it as the *perpetual method* of inventory valuation. These two methods will produce different valuations for inventory and cost of goods sold only if there are purchases and sales that are intermingled throughout the period, *and* only under certain of the costing methods. In particular, the specific identification and the Fifo methods produce identical results under both the periodic and the perpetual techniques. However, the average cost and the Lifo methods of inventory valuation produce different valuations depending upon whether one uses the periodic or the perpetual technique of inventory valuation. These observations are illustrated in Exhibit 10-7.

In Exhibit 10-7 we see that the Fifo method is unaffected by the application of the periodic or the perpetual techniques. Both techniques assign a value of $4,200 to the ending inventory and a value of $5,800 to cost of goods sold.

However, the Lifo and the average cost method produce different results under these two techniques. In the average cost method, the reason for the different result is that the average cost per unit of inventory is changed each time a new purchase is made. If units sold are assigned costs at the time they are sold, as they are under the perpetual method of inventory valuation, the average cost is a function of the aggregate costs of units on hand *at that time*. Where the periodic method is applied, however, the average cost per unit is determined on the basis of *all acquisitions* during the period, and thus one weighted average cost is applied uniformly to all units sold and all units remaining in the inventory. In the Lifo method, the difference arises when some of the older acquisitions of stocks of goods are sold before new acquisitions are made. Under the perpetual method, some of these older costs will be assigned to cost of goods sold, and thus they cannot be later assigned to the ending inventory. Applying the periodic method, however, inventory on hand at the end of the period is based first upon units on hand at the start of the period and then upon the earliest acquisitions during the period—notwithstanding the fact that some of these units may have been sold before the acquisitions to replace them had been made.

Exhibit 10-7

PERIODIC VERSUS PERPETUAL INVENTORY VALUATION

BASIC DATA:	Units	Unit Cost	Total Cost
Jan. 1—Inventory on hand	100	$10	$ 1,000
3—Sale	(100)		
5—Purchase	500	12	6,000
10—Sale	(300)		
18—Purchase	200	15	3,000
25—Sale	(100)		
On hand, end of period	300	Cost of goods available	$10,000

FIFO:

Periodic Method				Perpetual Method			
Units	Unit Cost	Total		Units	Unit Cost	Inventory	Cost of Goods Sold
Inventory on hand:							
200	$15	$ 3,000	Jan. 1	100	$10	$1,000	
100	12	1,200	3	(100)	10	(1,000)	$1,000
300		$ 4,200		-0-		-0-	
			5	500	12	6,000	
				500	12	6,000	
Cost of goods sold:							
100	$10	$ 1,000	10	(300)	12	(3,600)	3,600
400	12	4,800		200	12	2,400	
500		$ 5,800	18	200	15	3,000	
				400		5,400	
Total cost allocated		$10,000	25	(100)	12	(1,200)	1,200
				300		$4,200	$5,800

Exhibit 10-7 (cont.)

LIFO:

Periodic Method				Perpetual Method			
Units	Unit Cost	Total		Units	Unit Cost	Inventory	Cost of Goods Sold
Inventory on hand:							
100	$10	$ 1,000	Jan. 1	100	$10	$1,000	
200	12	2,400	3	(100)	10	(1,000)	$1,000
300		$ 3,400		-0-		-0-	
			5	500	12	6,000	
				500	12	6,000	
Cost of goods sold:							
200	$15	$ 3,000	10	(300)	12	(3,600)	3,600
300	12	3,600		200	12	2,400	
500		$ 6,600	18	200	15	3,000	
				400		5,400	
Total cost allocated		$10,000	25	(100)	15	(1,500)	1,500
				300		$3,900	$6,100

AVERAGE COST:

Periodic Method				Perpetual Method			
	Units	Cost		Units	Cost of Inventory	Average Unit Cost	Cost of Goods Sold
Inventory, beginning of period	100	$ 1,000	Jan. 1	100	$1,000	$10	
Purchases	700	9,000	3	(100)	(1,000)	10	$1,000
	800	$10,000		-0-	-0-		
Average cost/item			5	500	6,000		
= $10,000/800 = $12.50				500	6,000	12	
			10	(300)	(3,600)	12	3,600
Allocated to:				200	2,400	12	
Cost of goods sold			18	200	3,000		
(500 @ $12.50)		$ 6,250					
Inventory				400	5,400	13.50	
(300 @ $12.50)		3,750	25	(100)	(1,350)	13.50	1,350
Total cost allocated		$10,000		300	$4,050	13.50	$5,950

APPENDIX B: GROSS PROFIT METHOD OF ESTIMATING INVENTORY

A common method of estimating the value of inventory on hand by using aggregate data is the gross profit method. Assuming that the firm has a record of the aggregate purchases and sales for the period of time between the date the last set of financial statements was prepared and the date on which it wishes to estimate the value of the inventory, this method requires only that the firm have, or be able to estimate, the gross profit percentage—ratio of gross profit (sales − cost of sales = gross profit) to sales—that it has earned on sales of the period.

The variables we are dealing with in this measurement problem are clearly highlighted by again recalling the basic asset-expense duality relationship:

$$\text{Ending inventory} = \text{Beginning inventory} + \text{Purchases of inventory} - \text{Cost of sales (to be estimated)}$$

The accounting records of the firm will reflect the inventory at the beginning of the period, based upon the physical inventory count at the end of the prior period. Additionally, these records would also generally provide the total cost of purchases made during the period. Therefore, to estimate the ending inventory, we need only estimate the cost of sales from the beginning of the period to the point in time at which we wish to estimate the ending inventory on hand (e.g., the end of the period, or the time of a natural disaster).

Can the cost of sales be reasonably estimated from the information generally available in the accounting records? The answer to this question is frequently yes! The firm may calculate from its prior income statements the gross profit percentage that it has been earning on sales. The conditions for using the gross profit percentage in immediately preceding periods are either that it is fairly representative of the percentage during the current period, or that we can otherwise estimate what the effects of current period pricing and cost changes have been on the gross profit percentage. If one of these two conditions is met, we can apply the gross profit percentage to the recorded sales for the period to determine the estimated gross profit earned on these sales. Then, we can estimate cost of sales as follows:

$$\text{Estimated cost of sales} = \text{Sales} - \text{Estimated gross profit}$$

With this estimate of cost of sales in hand, we have value measures for the three variables needed to estimate the value of the ending inventory.

Example 10-18

> The Craig Outdoors Company is engaged in the retail sales of sporting goods items. On August 7 of the current year, Craig suffered a fire which completely destroyed its stock of inventory. It did not maintain perpetual inventory records and thus had available only the financial statements of prior periods, and accounting records providing aggregate data on transactions engaged in during the current year.
>
> The data available from the accounting records indicated that the inventory at the start of the period was valued at $20,000, purchases during the current period amounted to $60,000, and sales for the current period amounted to $75,000. Craig has earned a gross profit percentage over the last few years of approximately 40 percent, and its pricing policies (markups based on cost) were consistent in the current period with what they had been in prior periods. Therefore the president of the company agreed that 40 percent was a reasonable estimate of the gross profit percentage earned during the current period before the fire.

Based on this information, we can estimate the value of inventory on hand at the time of the fire as follows:

Cost of goods available for sale:		
Beginning inventory		$20,000
Purchases		60,000
Cost of goods available for sale		$80,000
Estimated cost of sales:		
Sales	$75,000	
Estimated gross profit (.40 × $75,000)	30,000	
Estimated cost of sales		$45,000
Estimated ending inventory		$35,000

Thus, using this method of estimating ending inventory, Craig has a reasonable basis for filing a claim with its insurance company for the loss sustained in the fire.

Questions for Review and Discussion

10-1. Define or briefly explain the following terms:
  a. Expense
  b. Matching principle
  c. Gain (loss)
  d. Cost principle
  e. Original transaction value
  f. Market (in "lower of cost or market")
  g. Gross profit and gross profit percentage (see Appendix B)
  h. Tangible and intangible assets
  i. Depreciation, depletion, and amortization expenses

10-2. Distinguish between product expenses and period expenses. Why is the distinction necessary?

10-3. What are the criteria to be applied (in order of preference) in determining the original transaction value, or cost, of acquiring nonmonetary assets?

10-4. The cost of an asset, as the term is used in accounting, is a more inclusive concept than merely the price of the item. Explain what is encompassed in cost.

10-5. Express in equation form the duality of asset valuation and the related expense recognition.

10-6. Explain briefly the major inventory costing methods used in conventional accounting.

10-7. Identify the major exceptions to valuing inventory at cost in conventional accounting. What is the justification for each exception?

10-8. Since the effect of an inventory valuation error is normally "offsetting" in a succeeding time period, why should one be concerned about this type of error?

10-9. Identify the major problems in accounting for long-lived assets.

10-10. What factors should one consider when choosing a depreciation method?

10-11. In applying the "lower of cost or market" rule for valuing inventories, "market" typically refers to the current replacement cost of the inventory. What value would you choose for "replacement cost" if a series of prices was quoted, depending on the size of the order?

10-12. Many firms account for their operations on a calendar year basis; however, some adopt what is called a "natural business year." The natural business year for a firm is usually defined as a year ending on a date when operations (and usually inventory) have reached the lowest point in their annual cycle. For example, retail department stores often choose a fiscal year for accounting for their operations that ends on February 28—presumably their natural business year. How might the choice of a natural business year reduce the potential for the significant differences in net income that may result solely from firms' arbitrary choices of different (but acceptable) inventory methods?

10-13. Ozzo Corporation adopted the Lifo method for valuing its inventory of flour used in making its special brand of spaghetti when the company was formed in 1947. Since that time, the quantity of flour normally maintained in inventory has increased only slightly because the owners decided not to expand the volume of their operations in order to maintain the quality of their product. The price of flour has increased an average of 5 percent per year since 1947. At the end of previous fiscal years, the number of tons of flour on hand has usually been within 10 percent of the normal inventory level. However, during the last few months of 1980, the corporation encountered substantial difficulties in purchasing flour, and at the end of the year, its inventory had been depleted to approximately 20 percent of its normal level. What effect would this temporary inventory reduction have on net income for 1980? Would the effect be the same if the company used Fifo? If the inventory stockout is regarded as a temporary, abnormal phenomenon, do you believe that some modification of the Lifo method might be justified? If so, what modification might be suitable?

10-14. Each year Chivas Walker purchases 100 cases of scotch whiskey. He stores the whiskey for eight years and then sells the aged product. In preparing his financial statements, Chivas asks you if it would be appropriate to include the interest costs he has incurred on money borrowed to finance his inventories of aging whiskey as an addition to the purchase cost of the inventory rather than as an expense of the period in which paid. How would you respond (giving specific attention to the cost and matching principles of the conventional accounting model)? Would your answer change if Chivas provided the financing from invested rather than borrowed funds?

10-15. An investor purchases a motel in Florida for $550,000. The motel is situated on land that has been leased for ten years. At the end of the ten-year period, ownership of all structures thereon reverts to the owner of the land (there is no option for renewal of the lease).
   (a) What factors would you consider in deciding how to recognize the purchase price of the motel as an expense over the life of the venture?
   (b) If the average occupancy rate was 80 percent from November to May, and 40 percent from June to October, would this affect your measurement of expense for annual income statements? For monthly income statements? How?

Exercises

10-1. Comparative Inventory Valuations. Pryor Data Terminals compiled the following data on one of its principal products, the Datapoint 6000, for the month of August:

Date Purchased	Units	Price/Unit	Cost
Beginning inventory	20	$400	$ 8,000
8/5	40	375	15,000
8/13	50	340	17,000
8/25	40	350	14,000

At the end of August, a physical inventory count indicated that Pryor had 50 units of the Datapoint 6000 on hand.

Required:

1. Write a summary journal entry to record the new Datapoint 6000 acquisitions of the month in the purchases account.

2. Calculate the value of the ending inventory and the cost of sales for August under each of the three inventory costing methods:
   (a) Fifo
   (b) Lifo
   (c) Weighted average

3. Write adjusting journal entries to establish the appropriate month-end balances in the inventory and cost of goods sold accounts under the three costing methods listed in number 2. Assume that temporary accounts are closed monthly. Do not repeat entries that are the same under all of the alternatives.

10-2. Comparative Inventory Valuations. Jones Electronics Wholesalers, Inc., has compiled the following data on one of its principal products, the XT-100, for the month of May:

Date Purchased	Units	Price/Unit	Cost
Beginning inventory	100	$5.00	$ 500
5/3	600	4.50	2,700
5/16	800	5.50	4,400
5/25	500	6.00	3,000

At the end of May, a physical inventory indicated that Jones had 400 units of the XT-100 on hand.

Required:

1. Calculate the value of the ending inventory and the cost of sales for May under each of the three costing methods:
   (a) Fifo
   (b) Lifo
   (c) Weighted average
2. Write all the journal entries, beginning with recording May purchases, required to ultimately establish the appropriate month-end balances in the inventory and cost of goods sold accounts. Assume that the company closes temporary accounts (e.g., purchases) monthly and that it uses the Fifo inventory costing method.

10-3. Inventory Valuation and Reported Income. The following item appeared in the *Wall Street Journal*, May 2, 1974. (Reprinted with the permission of The Wall Street Journal, © Dow Jones & Company, Inc., 1974.)

> When it reported first quarter profits last week, Mobil [Oil Corporation] cited inventory gains from foreign oil as a factor in the 66% increase in overall earnings from a year earlier. Other international oil companies also had major inventory profits in the first quarter as a result of the sharp increases in prices of foreign oil posted by the producing governments at the beginning of the year.
>
> But unlike some of the other internationals, Mobil utilizes what it calls an average cost inventory accounting in its foreign operations. Income is charged with an average of current cost and historic cost. In the first quarter, Mobil said, if it had charged foreign income with current costs only, its earnings would have been lower by about $90 million.

Assume that what is meant by *current cost* in the above quotation means recent prices paid, whereas *historic cost* means prices paid earlier in the year or prices included in beginning inventory cost. Also, *inventory gains* as used here means the margins between recently increased purchase prices and relatively low costs established in past exchange transactions.

Required:

1. What inventory valuation method did Mobil apparently use for inventory and cost of sales?

2. In selecting an inventory valuation method, Mobil might also have chosen Fifo or Lifo. Indicate whether the "inventory profit" would probably have been *higher* or *lower* than $90 million if these methods had been used:
   (a) Fifo
   (b) Lifo

10-4. Comparative Depreciation and Asset Disposition. On January 1, 19X4, Demkon Corporation acquired a new machine for producing its product at a cost of $175,000. The machine is expected to have a useful life of five years, and a salvage value at the end of the five years of $25,000.

Required:

1. Calculate the depreciation expense for *19X5* (the second year) under each of the three depreciation methods:
   (a) Straight-line
   (b) Sum-of-years-digits
   (c) Double-declining-balance

2. Suppose that Demkon had actually used the straight-line method and on 12/31/X6 sold the machine for $95,000. Write the journal entry to record the sale. Assume a tax rate of 46 percent.

10-5. Asset Acquisition and Comparative Depreciation Methods. The Cruse Company acquired a new machine on January 1, 19X5, for $125,000 cash plus the trade-in of an old machine having an original cost of $150,000, accumulated depreciation to date of $90,000, and a market value of $95,000. Costs of installation totaled $5,000, all paid in cash. The company estimates that the new machine will have a useful life of six years, and a salvage value at the end of six years of $15,000.

Required:

1. Write the appropriate journal entry to record the acquisition of the new machine. Ignore income taxes.

2. Calculate the annual depreciation expense for 19X5 through 19Y0 under the following alternative depreciation methods:
   (a) Straight-line
   (b) Sum-of-years-digits
   (c) Double-declining-balance

3. Assuming that Cruse Company had revenue of $800,000 and expenses (exclusive of depreciation expense) of $600,000 for each of the next six years, determine the net income that Cruse would report in the first and the sixth year under each of the three alternative depreciation methods. Assume the machine was sold for $15,000 at the end of the sixth year.

10-6. Inventory Valuation: Physical Flows and Cost Flows. The Stanley Steel Company is a metals service center. The company buys metal sheets, bars, rolls, and so forth, in large quantities from the producers and sells in smaller quantities to local manufacturers. One of the company's most popular items is 24-by-$\frac{1}{8}$-inch rolled sheet steel that it buys in 200-foot rolls and then cuts (to order) for customers in smaller lengths.

During February 19X3 the company had the following amounts of this particular rolled sheet steel available:

Date Received	Number of Rolls Purchased	Price per Roll	Total Price
Beginning inventory	10	$100	$1,000
2/7/X3	20	110	2,200
2/15/X3	12	112	1,344
2/24/X3	10	116	1,160
	52		$5,704

The company uses the periodic inventory method for establishing the levels of inventory and number of rolls of steel sold. At the end of February, a count showed that 15½ rolls of the 24-by-⅛-inch steel were on hand.

Required:

1. Determine the value of the ending inventory and the cost of sales for February with respect to the 24-by-⅛-inch steel based on each of the following cost flow alternatives:
   (a) Fifo
   (b) Lifo
   (c) Weighted average

2. Suppose that the company had kept perpetual inventory records as illustrated in Appendix A of this chapter. Indicate for each of the cost-flow assumptions whether the cost of sales and inventory amounts under the perpetual inventory valuation would have been greater than, equal to, or less than the amounts recognized under the periodic method. Support your conclusion logically. You may assume that sales took place relatively evenly over the whole month. (Note: Because specific sales data are not provided, it is not possible to make actual calculations of the perpetual inventory valuations.)

10-7. Inventory Valuation: Physical Flows and Cost Flows (Perpetual Method). Refer to the data presented in Exercise 10-6. Assume that the sales of rolled sheet steel (in terms of 200-foot rolls) were made throughout February as follows:

Sale Date	Number of Rolls
2/4/X3	5
2/12/X3	15
2/22/X3	8
2/27/X3	8½
	36½

Required:

Determine the value of the ending inventory and the cost of sales in February for each of the cost-flow alternatives below. Assume that the company uses the *perpetual* inventory method.
(a) Fifo
(b) Lifo
(c) Weighted average

(Note: Use of a schedule such as the following may be helpful in developing your answers.)

Date	Purchases			Sales			Balance		
	Quantity	Unit Cost	Total Cost	Quantity	Unit Cost	Total Cost	Quantity	Unit Cost	Total Cost

10-8. Effect of Inventory Errors on Reported Income. For each of the seven independent situations below, determine the effect of the error(s) on reported net income, ending asset balance, ending liability balance, and ending owners' equity for both 19X3 and 19X4. Enter your answers into a table with headings as shown below. Use +'s to indicate overstatements, –'s to indicate understatements, and 0's to indicate no effect. Assume that the periodic inventory method is used for determining inventory quantities at year-end. The answers for Situation 1 have been filled in as an example. (Note: In determining the effect of an error on net income, you must first determine its effect on cost of sales.)

Situation	19X3				19X4			
	Net Income	Assets	Liabilities	Owners' Equity	Net Income	Assets	Liabilities	Owners' Equity
1	+	+	0	+	–	0	0	0
2								
etc.								

Situations:

1. The inventory items on shelf 15-D were counted twice during the 19X3 year-end physical inventory count.

2. An invoice for goods received in 19X3 (and included in the physical count on 12/31/X3) was not received and recorded until 19X4.

3. An invoice received in 19X3 was recorded as a purchase in 19X3. The goods were not received until 19X4 and were not included in the 12/31/X3 inventory.

4. Same as Situation 3 above, except that the cost of the goods was added to the 12/31/X3 inventory figure.

5. The items in inventory area 114 were not counted during the 19X3 year-end physical inventory.

6. Goods received on 12/30/X3 were placed in the receiving area and were not included in the physical inventory. The purchase was not recorded in the books until 19X4.

7. Due to clerical multiplication errors, the cost of the 12/31/X3 inventory was overstated.

10-9. Effects of Inventory Valuation on Financial Statements. Exhibit 10-8 shows the statements of financial position from the 1977 annual report of Sears, Roebuck and Co. and consolidated subsidiaries. The statement covers the fiscal years ended January 31, 1978 (fiscal 1977) and January 31, 1977 (fiscal 1976). Note 6 to Sears's financial statements indicates that Sears uses the Lifo method of inventory valuation (costing). The note also indicates the differences between current cost and Lifo for inventory balances on 1/31/77 and 1/31/78:

> 6. *Inventories*
> The company employs the last-in, first-out (LIFO) method of inventory valuation for substantially all domestic inventories. If the inventory were valued at its approximate current cost, it would have been $187,000,000 and $88,000,000 higher than reported at January 31, 1978 and January 31, 1977.

Required:

1. Assuming that year-end current cost figures approximate Fifo inventory values, estimate what the beginning and ending inventory balances for the fiscal year ended 1/31/78 would have been if Sears had used FIFO rather than LIFO. (Note that the amounts shown in the statement are in thousands.)

2. Estimate the effect on cost of goods sold (i.e., would it have been greater or less and by how much?) for the year ending 1/31/78 if Sears had used Fifo instead of Lifo. (*Hint:* Recall that beginning inventory is added to purchases and ending inventory is subtracted from the result to get cost of goods sold. Total purchases for a year is the same regardless of what inventory valuation method is used.)

Exhibit 10-8

SEARS, ROEBUCK AND CO. AND CONSOLIDATED SUBSIDIARIES

Statements of Financial Position
($ in thousands)

	January 31	
	1978	1977
Assets		
Current Assets		
Cash	$ 237,382	$ 223,112
Receivables	6,671,402	5,672,270
Inventories (note 6)	2,626,070	2,215,141
Prepaid advertising and other charges	106,821	90,445
Total Current Assets	9,641,675	8,200,968
Investments		
Allstate Insurance Company (cost $62,156 and $62,072)	1,735,382	1,433,945
Other investments and advances	822,788	695,368
	2,558,170	2,129,313
Property, Plant and Equipment	2,534,841	2,487,790
Deferred Charges	11,561	8,935
Total Assets	$14,746,247	$12,827,006
Liabilities		
Current Liabilities		
Short-term borrowings		
Commercial paper	$ 2,586,051	$ 1,940,578
Banks	404,936	305,869
Agreements with bank trust departments	717,958	655,046
Current maturity of long-term debt	30,473	54,969
Accounts payable and accrued expenses	1,124,713	990,762
Unearned maintenance agreement income	276,969	242,143
Deferred income taxes	917,645	855,893
Total Current Liabilities	6,058,745	5,045,260
Deferred Income Taxes	173,139	154,959
Long-Term Debt	1,990,295	1,706,099
Total Liabilities	$ 8,222,179	$ 6,906,318
Shareholders' Equity	$ 6,524,068	$ 5,920,688

10-10. Estimation of Inventories—Gross Profit Method. The Handyman Company sells general hardware items at retail. The company uses the periodic inventory method to determine inventory quantities on hand at year-end. Interim inventory counts are not made. However, the company's accountant is responsible for preparing interim financial statements for each month throughout the year. Since a figure for cost of inventory on hand is required for each month, the accountant uses the gross profit method to estimate the interim inventory cost figures.

During 19X3, total retail sales were $1 million and total cost of sales was $700,000. The cost of the 12/31/73 inventory was $150,000. The company's pricing policy for 19X4 is substantially the same as its 19X3 pricing policy.

For January and February 19X4, total retail sales and purchases were as follows:

	Sales	Purchases
January	$ 70,000	$60,000
February	110,000	50,000

Required:

1. What is the gross profit percentage to be used in estimating 19X4 month-end inventories? (Note: See Appendix B for related text.)

2. Determine estimated ending inventory figures and estimated cost-of-sales figures for January and February.

10-11. Valuation of Assets at Time of Acquisition. The Acme Leasing Company leases passenger cars on a two-year basis. At the end of the lease period, the customer has the options of purchasing the car at a price specified in the original lease contract or returning the car to Acme. Cars returned to Acme are traded in on new cars. If necessary, Acme purchases new cars for cash to compensate for cars purchased by customers.

For 19X3, the following data apply:

Number of leases expiring	20
Number of cars purchased by customers	10
Number of cars returned to Acme (and traded in on new cars)	10
Number of new cars purchased by Acme	20
List price of new cars purchased	$4,800
Trade-in allowance (on list price) per car received by Acme on cars traded in	$2,000
Total cash price per car for cars purchased for cash by Acme	$4,700
Average wholesale price per car for cars returned by customers	$1,900
Average retail price per car for cars returned by customers	$2,300
Lease contract selling price	$2,200
Original cost of cars returned to Acme by customers	$4,400

Acme depreciates the total price of cars over an estimated five-year life (sum-of-years-digits method), even though Acme never owns the cars for more than two years.

Required:

1. What value should be recorded for the ten cars purchased for cash only? Write the journal entry to record their acquisition. Assume that the value of the ten cars purchased for cash is independent of the value of the cars acquired by trade-in.

2. Identify several alternative approaches that might be used in determining the value of the ten cars acquired by trade-in, and determine the total value that would be assigned to the ten cars for each alternative. Write the journal entry to record the transaction for each alternative.

3. Comment briefly on the propriety (or relative desirability) of each of the alternative approaches you developed in number 2 above.

10-12. Valuation of Copyright. The Expensive Hardback Press published a book that luckily turned out to be a best-seller. Because of short-term cash considerations, the author and the Expensive Hardback Press sold the copyright rights to the Cheap Paperback Company for a lump sum of $130,000.

The copyright has twenty-six years remaining out of its twenty-eight-year life and can be renewed for an additional twenty-eight years. However, the Cheap Paperback Company expects to make sales of the book only during the next five years, after which the book will probably be out of print.

Required:

1. What is the expected useful life of the copyright acquired by the Cheap Paperback Company? Why?

2. What portion of the initial valuation of the copyright should be recognized as expense each year of the copyright's useful life?

10-13. Comparative Depreciation Methods. The Skyline Construction Company purchased new construction equipment at the beginning of 19X4 for $300,000. The company estimated that the useful life of the equipment would be ten years and that the net salvage value would be $25,000.

Required:

1. Prepare a depreciation schedule indicating (a) the annual depreciation expense and (b) the net asset valuation at the beginning of the year for each year of the estimated ten-year life under the following alternative depreciation methods:
   (a) Straight-line
   (b) Double-declining-balance
   (c) Sum-of-years-digits

2. Assume that the equipment is sold at the end of the eighth year for $50,000. Write a separate journal entry recognizing the disposition, assuming each of the above depreciation methods has been used. Ignore taxes.

3. Assume that the equipment is traded in on new equipment at the end

of the sixth year. The net cash paid for the new equipment is $200,000. If no gain or loss is to be recorded, what initial value should be assigned to the new equipment for each alternative depreciation method?

10-14. Treatment of Repairs and Maintenance. In December 1980 the Burp Beer Company purchased a secondhand portable conveyor line for use in loading beer trucks from various inventory areas. The conveyor line was composed of four independent sections, with each section having its own electric motor. The original (new) price of the conveyor line was $6,000, but the company paid only $4,000. At the time of purchase, the company estimated the salvage value to be $800 and the remaining useful life to be four years.

During 1981 the company performed only routine maintenance on the conveyor line, at a total cost of $200.

In 1982 two motors "burned up" due to overloading and had to be replaced. The cost of the motors was $600. Other maintenance expenditures in 1982 totaled $300. Also, in December 1982 the company purchased an additional section of conveyor line to serve as a backup if another section broke down and to increase the length of the conveyor line. The acquisition cost of the additional section was $1,200, and the estimated increase in salvage value was $400.

During 1983 repairs and maintenance totaled $900 because of recurrent breakdowns. As a result, in December the company stopped using the conveyor line and reverted to manual loading of the beer trucks. The conveyor line was put up for sale, but it was not sold until April 30, 1984, for a cash price of $1,500.

Assume that depreciation is calculated on a straight-line basis.

Required:

1. What valuation should be assigned to the conveyor line at the date of acquisition?

2. How should the acquisition of the additional section of conveyor line in 1982 be treated—i.e., is it an expense? Why?

3. How much depreciation should be recorded in 1984? Why?

4. Prepare a schedule showing the expense in total and by categories (depreciation expense and repairs and maintenance expense) associated with the conveyor line for each year of its life.

5. Calculate the gain or loss incurred in 1984 when the conveyor line was sold.

10-15. Calculation of Depletion. In 19X3 the Black Gold Company acquired an option to purchase a five-year lease on a block of acreage. The option included the right to perform seismographic surveys on the land. A survey was performed and indicated the presence of strata with oil-producing potential. Therefore the company exercised its option to acquire the lease (for 19X3–X7).

A well was drilled during 19X3, and oil was found. The total recoverable barrels were estimated to be 100,000. Production was scheduled to begin in 19X4.

At the end of 19X3, the total of the expenditures made in 19X3 subject to depletion (option price, survey costs, and cost of lease) was $20,000. The total expenditures made in 19X3 subject to depreciation (tangible well costs) amounted to $30,000. The company planned to depreciate the depreciable costs over the remaining life of the lease. The salvage value of depreciable equipment was estimated to be $2,000.

Production figures for 19X4–X7 are as follows:

Year	Barrels of Oil Produced and Sold
19X4	15,000
19X5	25,000
19X6	40,000
19X7	30,000
Total	110,000

Operations were discontinued at the end of 19X7, and the lease was not renewed. The company received $2,000 for the salvageable wellhead equipment and pipe.

Required:

Prepare a schedule showing cost depletion and depreciation for each year of the well's life. Assume that the company did not change its estimate of recoverable barrels until 19X7.

10-16. Development and Start-up Costs. The accounting treatment of the costs of development and/or start-up of a major new program is a controversial issue. Late in 1974, the FASB modified accounting policy to require companies to recognize these costs as expenses of the period in which the expenditures are made—a conservative treatment that may not produce a very satisfactory matching of costs and related revenue. Prior to this time, however, the costs could be capitalized as assets and matched against (potential) revenues from the project in future periods. The hazard under this previously acceptable alternative is that the assets and net income of the early periods would be overstated if the project were not ultimately successful. This hazard was strikingly revealed in a report on the fortunes of Lockheed Aircraft Corporation (*Wall Street Journal,* June 3, 1974):

> A huge write-down of its financially troubled L1011 "TriStar" commercial aircraft program, probably totaling at least $600 million, is the key element in a complex plan for a far-reaching financial restructuring of Lockheed Aircraft Corp., sources close to Lockheed said.
>
> . . .
>
> Some Lockheed critics have long contended the company was engaging in "fantasy accounting" in its handling of the books for the L1011 program and doubtless will

say, in the wake of one of the biggest writeoffs in American corporate history, that the company and its auditors should have "bitten the bullet" some time ago. The auditing firm . . . has regularly qualified its opinions of the extensively footnoted Lockheed financial statements because of uncertainties over "realization of the L1011 inventories" and the maintenance of financing arrangements.

At the end of 1973, Lockheed was carrying $1.16 billion of its total assets of $1.85 billion (and current assets of $1.56 billion) in the form of net inventories in the TriStar program. This unrecovered TriStar investment comprises the plane's development costs, initial tooling and other nonrecurring costs and production costs, less payments for planes delivered to date and customer advances on future deliveries.

Lockheed said in its latest annual report that it expected to recover this inventory through the anticipated sale of 300 TriStars, though it cautioned this could take into the early 1980s and was subject to certain variables and uncertainties. Although it had delivered 56 TriStars through 1973, Lockheed said it didn't expect to reach the point at which current production costs of each plane will be less than the sales price of planes then being delivered until mid-1974. It said the inventory at the end of 1974 would be only slightly less than a year earlier and eventual recovery of about $900 million of gross inventory depended on firm orders beyond the 129 in hand at year-end 1973.

A write-down of the L1011 inventories of about $600 million without a new cash infusion wouldn't drop Lockheed into a negative working-capital position but also wouldn't leave much room between current assets, which would drop to less than $1 billion based on the year-end $1.56 billion figure, and current liabilities, which stood at $718 million at year-end. It would, apparently, wipe out the company's retained earnings, which totaled $192.8 million at year-end.

Lockheed hasn't recorded any loss (or profit) on its L1011 deliveries to date, posting those delivered at the full sales price ($730 million in 1973 and $302 million in 1972). It has charged to income slightly over $300 million to date in general administrative expenses, however. The current sales price of an L1011 is about $20 million.

Currently, Lockheed has firm orders, including those already delivered, for 135 TriStars and second buys, or options, for 67 more, or a total of 202. Airline industry sources say, however, that prospects for substantial additional orders in the next few years are almost nonexistent and, except for a few instances, airlines holding the L1011 options aren't likely to convert options to firm orders during 1974.

. . . .

Lockheed posted 1973 net income of $16.8 million, or $1.48 a share. This result includes an operating profit on programs other than the TriStar and new ship construction of $165.8 million and a loss of $69.7 million from general and administrative costs on the TriStar program. Sales of $2.76 billion included the $730 million from TriStars, on which zero profit or loss was recorded, as noted earlier.[3]

---

[3] *Wall Street Journal*, June 3, 1974. Reprinted with the permission of the Wall Street Journal, © Dow Jones & Company, Inc., 1974.

Required:

1. In capitalizing the development and start-up costs of its TriStar program, do you believe that Lockheed was engaging in "fantasy accounting" as alleged by some of its critics? Would your answer have been different at the outset of the program than it is now with the benefit of hindsight?

2. Assuming it is appropriate to capitalize development and start-up costs (and many companies formerly did so):
   (a) Do you believe that the investment in the TriStar program was properly classified as a current asset—that is, inventory? Why might a corporation wish to reflect development and start-up costs as a current asset rather than some noncurrent asset such as "other assets"?
   (b) What justification might be offered for the policy of capitalizing the "net" production costs (the excess of current production costs over the sales proceeds from this production) of early production (at a minimum, at least the first 60–70 planes based on Lockheed's statement that "it didn't expect to reach the point at which current production costs of each plane will be less than the sales price of planes then being delivered until mid-1974")?
   (c) In view of the policy of capitalization adopted by Lockheed in (b) above, why do you suppose that it did not elect to capitalize the general administrative costs (presumably related to the program) rather than recognizing them as expenses of the period in which incurred?
   (d) After capitalizing the plane's development costs, initial tooling, and other nonrecurring costs, what system of matching these costs against future revenues was adopted by Lockheed? Do you believe this results in a proper matching of these costs with related revenue?

3. What do you suppose was the basis for the proposed $600 million write-down of an inventory carried at a "cost" of $1.16 billion (i.e., why was the proposed write-down not some larger or smaller amount)?

4. While a major program is still in the development stage, do you believe that an auditor's qualification (or caveat) that the fairness of the financial statement presentation depends upon the "ability to realize capitalized development costs" is adequate for external investors? If not, what alternative financial data and/or auditor actions would you suggest?

Expense Recognition and Related Equity Valuation Issues

11

In Chapter 10 we examine the expense recognition patterns associated with the two major classes of nonmonetary resources under conventional accounting, and the related valuation of these resources in the statement of financial position. We now turn to the valuation of liabilities and owners' equity—the claims against the assets of the business enterprise.

LIABILITIES

Basic Characteristics of Liabilities

Liabilities are obligations of the firm to external parties (individuals or other organizations) other than the owners of the firm. In general, liabilities are characterized by the following two attributes:

1. A future cash payment is required to discharge the obligation.
2. There is a time element—the time between the date the obligation is created and the date on which payment is made—that influences, implicitly or explicitly, the amount of the future cash payment(s).

On certain occasions, liabilities are discharged by some means other than a cash payment, such as the liability arising from advance payments by customers, which is discharged through the provision of products or services. The time element is, however, always present, even though it may be a very short period of time.

Obligations may be created either by acquiring resources with a provision for deferred payment (e.g., ordinary credit purchases of merchandise) or by borrowing money from some credit-granting individual or institution. The Appendix to this chapter offers a good summary of business borrowing and various types of obligations that can be created. In the cases of all liabilities, however, there is an input (implicitly in the case of credit purchases) of funds into the business from an outside source. Since these funds are by definition from an individual or institution other than the owners of the business, they may be characterized as "non-owner-provided factors of production." Like all factors of production, it is presumed that the firm can utilize this particular factor of production in a profitable manner—that is, that the output from the use of the factor of production will exceed its cost.

But what is the cost associated with the use of funds? As in the case of the costs of assets used in a business, the *lifetime* cost of funds associated with a particular liability is relatively easy to measure. The *total cost* that the firm will incur from using funds supplied by a particular creditor may be determined as follows from the data captured by the conventional financial accounting system:

$$\text{Total cost of funds} = \text{Sum of payments} - \text{Proceeds of liability}$$

In this fundamental relationship, the *sum of payments* includes all payments labeled as interest plus the repayment of the face amount, or principal, of the obligation at its maturity date. The *proceeds of liability* refers to the value of the resources (money or other resources) received at the date that the liability was created. Since time elapses between the acquisition of the money and the ultimate repayment, and because it is presumed that all individuals and institutions have a time preference for money, the value of the resources acquired (either cash or other resources) should be equal to the present value of the future payments that the enterprise is committed to make.

Example 11-1

In order to finance a required growth in its current assets, the treasurer of High Turnover Company signed a note payable to Local Bank. The note calls for payment of $10,000 one year from the date of signature. The bank's required interest charge is 12 percent per year, but the note does not call for separate interest payments. Hence the proceeds of the loan were $8,928.57, the present value of $10,000 to be received (paid) in one year at 12 percent. The total cost of funds from this source over the whole duration of the loan is $1,071.43—the difference between the total proceeds, $8,928.57, and the total payments, $10,000. Not surprisingly, the $1,071.43 is equal to 12 percent, the bank's required rate, on the $8,928.57 of funds provided.

In some instances the period of time between the acquisition of resources and the ultimate repayment is very short. In such instances (principally those in which inventories of materials or supplies are purchased on credit) the cost of funds may not be explicitly recognized—for example, by simply recognizing the cost of the item(s) acquired at an amount equal to the full payment. Nonetheless, the cost exists, even though it may be ignored for financial accounting purposes because it is not material. In other instances the period of time between the acquisition of resources or money and the ultimate repayment is quite long. In these instances an explicit charge for the use of the funds is normally provided for in the contract or promissory note representing the liability. This additional charge is normally expressed as a rate of interest on the balance due.

In spite of the relative ease with which the lifetime cost of funds can be calculated for a given liability, two problems are encountered in dealing with liabilities and the cost of funds provided by creditors in *periodic* accounting:

1. How do we allocate the total cost of using the money over the life span of a liability to appropriate periods of time within that life span?

2. How do we determine, at any point in time, the magnitude of the undischarged liability?

A Simple Expenditure Approach to Accounting for Liabilities

An intuitive way to deal with the measurement problems associated with liabilities is to use a simple expenditure approach. Under this approach, all payments to creditors or lending institutions that are labeled "interest" according to the terms of the note or other debt instrument are recognized as costs of using money, and these costs are assigned to the period of time in which they are paid (or accrued). The final payment to discharge the face amount of the obligation is, under this approach, not regarded as a cost of money.

Example 11-2

> On January 1, 19X4, Janco Corporation borrowed $10,000 from the First National Bank of Frankfort to acquire new equipment for an expansion program. The money was borrowed at an interest rate of 8 percent, and interest payments were to be made at the end of each year. The promissory note that the company signed with the bank indicated that the face amount of the liability is to be repaid on December 31, 19X8. Treatment of the required payments, and the related accounting measurements, under the simple expenditure approach are illustrated in Exhibit 11-1.

Journal entries to record the above bank loan and related cost of funds (interest expense) over the life of the liability according to the expenditure approach are as follows:

Initial Entry
1/1/X4

Cash	10,000	
Loan payable—bank		10,000

Annual Entries
12/31/X4, X5, X6, X7

Interest expense	800	
Cash		800

Final Entry
12/31/X8

Interest expense	800	
Loan payable—bank	10,000	
Cash		10,800

As Exhibit 11-1 illustrates, the simple expenditure approach produces a measure of the cost of funds that is consistent with the basic relationship:

Cost = Sum of payments − Proceeds of liability

      = $14,000 − $10,000

      = $4,000

Moreover, the allocation of this total interest cost to periods of time ($800 per year) is an intuitively reasonable expression of the sacrifice made by the firm in order to use the funds, because there is a constant amount of creditor funds in use and constant interest expense each period. We should note, however, that if the promissory note signed by Janco had stipulated that the "interest payments" were to be made on the first day of each year (beginning January 1, 19X5, rather than December 31, 19X4), the matching principle would require

Exhibit 11-1

JANCO CORPORATION

Simple Expenditure Approach to Accounting for Bank Loan

Date	Cash Receipts	Cash Payments during Year	Interest Expense for Year	Accounting Carrying Value* of Liability
1/1/X4	$10,000			$10,000
12/31/X4		$ 800	$ 800	10,000
12/31/X5		800	800	10,000
12/31/X6		800	800	10,000
12/31/X7		800	800	10,000
12/31/X8		10,800	800	-0-
Totals	$10,000	$14,000	$4,000	

*The term *carrying value* of a liability is a common term used by accountants as a synonym for the more descriptive but awkward label *undischarged original transaction value.*

an accrual of interest expense at the end of each year and recognition of a liability for accrued interest payable. The following annual journal entries would then be used:

12/31

Interest expense 800
  Accrued interest payable   800

1/1

Accrued interest payable 800
  Cash   800

This recognition of accrued obligations does not substantially modify the basic orientation of the expenditure approach. The recognition of interest expense for a period is still based on expenditures—paid or accrued during the period.

Finally, in this case the expenditure approach produces a valuation of the liability at the end of each period ($10,000) that generally reflects the liquidation value of the firm's economic obligation at that point in time. That is, if Janco had decided to repay its liability earlier than required, say on December 31, 19X6, a $10,000 payment should (in the absence of any prepayment penalty provisions in the promissory note) fully discharge its obligation to the First National Bank of Frankfort.

While the expenditure approach produces intuitively reasonable measures of periodic interest expense and the related liability under the simple set of circumstances described in Example 11-2, transactions giving rise to the creation of a liability typically involve certain complications which tend to invalidate the method. For example, the promissory notes issued by many enterprises, particularly large corporations, are often in the form of bonds with a stated face amount and interest rate. A corporation might issue a series of bonds with a face value (principal) of $1,000 per bond and a stated interest rate of 8 percent. This means that the holder of each bond will receive $80 ($1,000 × .08) per year in interest, and $1,000 repayment of principal at the maturity date of the bond. If, however, the prevailing market rate of interest for bonds of equal risk is greater (less) than the 8 percent rate stated on the bond, the market will adjust the actual interest cost to the borrower by paying or conveying less (more) than $1,000 for each bond. If the amount paid for the bond is more than the face amount, we refer to the difference as a *premium*. If it is less than the face amount of the bond, we call it a *discount*.

Example 11-3

Holland Corporation decided to issue on January 1, 19X4, 100 five-year bonds with a stated interest rate of 8 percent and a face value per bond of $1,000. The appropriate documents were prepared and the bonds were offered for sale. At the time the bonds were offered to potential buyers, the prevailing interest rate was higher than 8 percent, and the buyers compensated for the difference between the market rate and the nominal interest rate (8 percent) on the face of the bonds by paying only $950 per bond. Therefore, ignoring the costs associated with marketing the bonds, Holland Corporation received $95,000 for bonds with a face value of $100,000, and it had the additional obligation of making $8,000 cash interest payments each year (interest payments are based on the face amount, not the proceeds received). If this transaction is handled under the expenditure approach, we obtain the results illustrated in Exhibit 11-2.

The measure of the cost associated with the use of the borrowed funds in Exhibit 11-2 is again consistent with the basic relationship:

$$\text{Cost} = \text{Sum of payments} - \text{Proceeds of liability}$$
$$= \$140,000 - \$95,000$$
$$= \$45,000$$

Exhibit 11-2

HOLLAND CORPORATION

Simple Expenditure Approach to Accounting for Bond Issue

Date	Cash Receipts	Cash Payments during Year	Interest Expense for Year	Accounting Carrying Value of Liability
1/1/X4	$95,000			$95,000
12/31/X4		$ 8,000	$ 8,000	95,000
12/31/X5		8,000	8,000	95,000
12/31/X6		8,000	8,000	95,000
12/31/X7		8,000	8,000	95,000
12/31/X8		108,000	13,000	-0-
Totals	$95,000	$140,000	$45,000	

Journal entries that record the amounts recognized according to the above approach are as follows:

Initial
1/1/X4

Cash	95,000	
Bonds payable		95,000

	Annual 12/31/X4, X5, X6, X7	
Interest expense	8,000	
Cash		8,000

	Final 12/31/X8	
Interest expense	13,000	
Bonds payable	95,000	
Cash		108,000

However, the carrying value of the liability at the end of each period preceding the year of repayment (i.e., $95,000) is generally a poor measure of the firm's obligation. Thus the existence of premiums or discounts on the original issue of corporate bonds stimulates the need for a more refined approach to the valuation of liabilities and measurement of the related expense. Moreover, we question whether the total cost of funds of $45,000 has been properly allocated to each of the years in the five-year period that the bonds are outstanding. Specifically, should the last year bear an interest cost significantly higher than the costs recognized in each of the preceding four years merely because it is at this point in time that the difference between the $100,000 face amount of the bonds and the $95,000 original cash receipts is recognized in the form of a cash expenditure? The answer is that this allocation is not justified given the facts about the loan and the economic logic that applies generally to loans. After all, the $5,000 discount is a reduction in proceeds of the bond issue to compensate the lenders (bondholders) for the fact that the 8 percent interest rate paid on the face amounts of the bonds is not an adequate interest rate to warrant loaning the company the full face amount. By loaning less than face value the bondholders earn an effective interest rate *over the life of the bonds* that is greater than 8 percent. We must therefore devise some means of taking the $5,000 original discount into account *over the life of the bonds* as we assess the interest cost of each period. This is discussed in the next section.

The problems illustrated above that are brought about by the existence of an issue premium or discount are not the only problems associated with the expenditure approach. Another characteristic of some types of obligations also makes the expenditures approach unreasonable. Certain types of obligations call for periodic installment payments consisting of both principal and interest. Under such conditions we cannot assess the cost of the borrowed funds in terms of the expenditure of funds during the period. We clearly must separate that portion of each payment that represents reduction of the principal from the portion of the payment that is made for the use of money. When installment payments, or other forms of reduction of principal over the life of a liability (such as serial bonds), are combined with the existence of premiums or discounts, the weakness of the expenditure approach becomes even more evident. Therefore we now turn to a more refined method of dealing with the accounting problems associated with liabilities.

The Effective Interest Approach to Accounting for Liabilities

In developing the effective interest approach to accounting for liabilities, we maintain the basic relationship referred to several times above relative to the *total cost* of the use of the borrowed funds over the life of the liability:

Total cost = Sum of payments − Proceeds of liability

But the objective now is to develop a better method of measuring the portion of this cost that is identifiable with any particular period of time. Such cost allocations may not be, and probably will not be, equal to the payments that are made in the same time period.

Finding the Effective Rate. When a liability with fixed terms (for example, a bond or a note payable) is issued at a discount or a premium, the effective interest rate that the lender receives over the life of the liability can be determined based on the present value methodology developed in Chapter 2.

Effective Interest Rate. The effective interest rate of a liability at the time it is issued is that interest rate at which the present value of the principal and interest payments to be made over the life of the liability exactly equals the proceeds to the borrower.

What the above definition says is that to find the effective interest rate in any given situation, one must try different interest rates (r's) until the following relationship is satisfied:

$$\text{Proceeds} = \frac{\text{First payment}}{(1 + r)} + \frac{\text{Second payment}}{(1 + r)^2} + \ldots$$

Unfortunately, in most cases there is no way to shortcut the "trial-and-error" method for finding the right interest rate. However, the following steps can make the search process more efficient:[1]

1. If the liability is issued at a discount (premium), start the search at an interest rate above (below) the stated rate (that is, above the rate that specifies the interest payments as a percentage of face value).
2. After selecting a trial interest rate, calculate the total present value of all payments (principal and interest).
3. Compare the present value computed in step 2 with the proceeds of the liability. If the present value and proceeds are *approximately equal,*

---

[1] Larger firms generally have stored computer ("library") programs to conduct such a search.

stop—the rate selected *is* the effective rate. If the present value of the payments is greater (smaller) than the proceeds, select a greater (smaller) trial rate and repeat steps 2 and 3. When on successive trials you come up with one present value that is higher (lower) than the proceeds, followed by another that is lower (higher), it is time to reduce the amount by which you increase or decrease the interest rate after each trial.

Example 11-4

Holland Corporation's bonds described in Example 11-3 were issued at a discount, presenting the following implicit interest problem (to be solved for *r*):

$$\$95{,}000 = \frac{\$8{,}000}{(1+r)} + \frac{\$8{,}000}{(1+r)^2} + \frac{\$8{,}000}{(1+r)^3} + \frac{\$8{,}000}{(1+r)^4} + \frac{\$108{,}000}{(1+r)^5}$$

The discount implies that the trial rate should be greater than the 8 percent rate of interest payments (on face value). Selecting 10 percent somewhat arbitrarily, the search process proceeds as follows:

Trial 1 (at 10 percent):[2]

$$PV = \frac{\$8{,}000}{1.10} + \frac{\$8{,}000}{1.10^2} + \frac{\$8{,}000}{1.10^3} + \frac{\$8{,}000}{1.10^4} + \frac{\$108{,}000}{1.10^5}$$

$PV = \$8{,}000(.909) + \$8{,}000(.826) + \$8{,}000(.751) + \$8{,}000(.683) + \$108{,}000(.621)$

$PV = \$92{,}420$

Since the present value of the payments at 10 percent is less than the proceeds, 10 percent is higher than the actual effective rate.

Trial 2 (at 9 percent):

$$PV = \$96{,}112$$

At 9 percent the present value ($96,112) is greater than the proceeds, suggesting that the trial rate should be increased. However, we know that the rate should not be increased by a full percent because that would take us back to 10 percent. We choose to proceed in increments first of 0.5 percent, then 0.1 percent. The remaining trials produced present values as follows:

Trial 3 (at 9.5 percent):[3]

$$PV = \$94{,}240$$

(Less than proceeds; reduce trial rate.)

---

[2] Recall that for whole (integer) interest rates Table 2-1 gives present value factors corresponding to $1/(1+r)^n$ for various rates and numbers of periods.

[3] For fractional interest rates, it is more accurate to calculate present value factors than to interpolate between factors for various whole interest rates given in Table 2-1.

Trial 4 (at 9.4 percent):

$$PV = \$94,610$$

(Less than proceeds, reduce trial rate.)

Trial 5 (at 9.3 percent):

$$PV = \$94,982$$

(Approximately equal to proceeds; *stop.*)

Measuring Interest Expense and Valuing Liabilities. Having demonstrated how to find the implicit interest rate to be earned by the creditors over the life of a liability, we can now deduce the implicit interest expense that the debtor ought to recognize. As we show below, the appropriate recognition of interest expense simultaneously influences the valuation of the liability. Let us review the reasoning by way of an additional example.

Example 11-5

The Escola Company issued on January 1, 19X4, five-year bonds with a total face value of $50,000 and a stated interest rate of 8 percent. Based upon the market determination of the value of the bonds at the prevailing interest rate, Escola Company received $46,210. Therefore it had a discount on the issuance of the bonds of $3,790 ($50,000 − $46,210). Using the trial-and-error method described above, the effective interest rate is determined to be 10 percent.

For the buyers of the bonds in Example 11-5, the ownership of the bonds is the equivalent (in terms of the aggregate benefits to be received over five years) of having $46,210 cash invested at 10 percent, since $46,210 is the present value at 10 percent of the set of payments to be received. We therefore conclude that the bondholders' effective interest earned and Escola Company's interest expense for the year 19X4 must be 10 percent of $46,210, or $4,621. However, the first interest payment on 12/31/X4 is only $4,000 according to the terms of the bonds (that is, 8 percent times the face amount of $50,000). This discrepancy is of no consequence to the bondholders because their 10 percent rate of earning is based on the total set of payments, not the payment in any one year. In effect the difference between the interest earned by the bondholders ($4,621) and the interest paid ($4,000) is like an additional loan of $621 to Escola Company at the end of 19X4. It should therefore be added to the $46,210 original proceeds to get a new liability value of $46,831.

Another way of arriving at the same conclusion is to recognize that the liability of $46,210 earned interest for the bondholders and therefore caused Escola Company to incur expense of $4,621. If no payment was called for at the end of 19X4 (there are bonds, called "balloon payment" bonds, on which all payment is postponed until the end of the term of the bond), the $4,621 would be added to the original liability of $46,210 to get a balance of $50,831. However, since a $4,000 payment was made, the balance is reduced as of 12/31/X4 to $46,831.

Exhibit 11-3

ESCOLA COMPANY

Present Value of Bonds at 12/31/X4

Date	Interest	Remaining Payments Repayment of Principal	Total	Present Value Factor (10% rate)*	Present Value
12/31/X5	$ 4,000		$ 4,000	0.90909	$ 3,636
12/31/X6	4,000		4,000	0.82645	3,306
12/31/X7	4,000		4,000	0.75113	3,004
12/31/X8	4,000	$50,000	54,000	0.68301	36,883
Totals	$16,000	$50,000	$66,000		$46,830*

*Note that more accurate present value factors are used here than the decimal factors appearing in Table 2-1. This reduces rounding error when working with large numbers (in this case the result is a rounding error of $1 rather than $5).

A very important feature of this reasoning is that $46,831 is equal to the present value as of 12/31/X4 of the remaining payments from the bonds at the original 10 percent effective rate. This is shown in Exhibit 11-3. Therefore, in effect, the remainder of the bond contract is equivalent to a new loan of $46,831 at 10 percent interest as of 12/31/X4. The interest expense for 19X5 should be 10 percent of this new balance of $46,831, or $4,683. If no payment were made on 12/31/X5, this full amount would be added to the liability, giving a balance of $51,514. Subtracting the actual 12/31/X5 payment of $4,000 gives an actual balance of $47,514, which, incidentally, is the present value at 10 percent of the remaining payments as of 12/31/X5.

We may now summarize the analysis by noting the basic relationship that we rely upon above between the value of a liability and the flows between parties to the borrowing transaction:

Ending value of liability = Beginning value of liability + Additional proceeds + Interest expense − Cash payments

This relationship holds at any point in time. Therefore, at the date on which the liability is created, the value of the liability is established by the value of the proceeds received in the exchange transaction. In the first period, three types of events can change the initial value of the liability:

1. Additional proceeds can be derived from additional borrowing (of which there is none in Example 11-5).
2. Interest expense is incurred.
3. Payments are made for interest and/or principal.

The values for additional proceeds (if any) and payments can be determined from the respective exchange transactions. We therefore have concentrated on how to measure the proper amount of interest expense for the period.

The critical element in the calculation of interest expense is the rate of interest that was established in the market or by the lending institution at the time the liability was created. The rate the lenders wish to impose on the borrowing company is important because it is applied to the series of payments that they will receive from the company (interest payments and repayment of principal) to arrive at the present value of the liability. This present value of the liability is the amount that the lenders are willing to pay for the bonds or other obligations of the enterprise. By accepting this price, the borrowing corporation accepts an interest cost based upon the lenders' effective rate.

Thus the borrower calculates the interest expense for a period in the following manner:

Interest expense =
Effective rate of interest implicit in establishing the original value of the liability × Recognized value of the liability at the beginning of the period

For Example 11-5, the effective rate of interest is 10 percent, and thus we can restate the above relationship as follows:

Interest expense = 10 percent × Recognized value of bonds at start of period

And the recognized, or carrying, value of the bonds at the end of the period can now be determined from the general relationship between the value of a liability and the flows between parties to the transaction (ignoring here additional proceeds):

Ending value of liability = Beginning value of liability + Interest expense − Cash payments

These relationships are applied to the data of Example 11-5 in Exhibit 11-4.

Exhibit 11-4

ESCOLA COMPANY

Calculation of Interest Expense and
Carrying Value of Liability

Year Ended	Proceeds	(1) Carrying Value of Liability, Start of Year	(2) Interest Expense for Year— 10% × (1)	(3) Cash Payment, End of Year	Carrying Value of Liability, End of Year— (1) + (2) − (3)
12/31/X4	$46,210	$46,210	$ 4,621	$ 4,000	$46,831
12/31/X5		46,831	4,683	4,000	47,514
12/31/X6		47,514	4,751	4,000	48,265
12/31/X7		48,265	4,826	4,000	49,091
12/31/X8		49,091	4,909	54,000	-0-
Totals	$46,210		$23,790	$70,000	

Note: Check on total interest expense:

Total cost (interest expense) = Sum of cash payments − Proceeds of loan

= $70,000 − $46,210

= $23,790

Using this effective interest approach, the total interest expense recognized over the period of time the obligations are outstanding is equal to the excess of cash payments over the proceeds received in the loan, as the earlier transaction-based reasoning requires. Additionally, this expense is allocated to the periods of time presumably benefiting from the "effective amount of funds on loan" using the rate of interest (10 percent) established *implicitly* in the transaction in which the liability was originally created. Although the market rate of interest for liabilities of equal risk and stated terms may vary over time, the original loan transaction established the effective rate of interest, and the total interest cost, that Escola Company (in this case) must pay over the life of the bonds that were issued.

The journal entries required to accomplish recognition of interest expense and the related liability value under the effective interest method, applied to the facts of Example 11-5 as analyzed in Exhibit 11-4, are as follows:

1/1/X4

Cash	46,210	
Bonds payable		46,210

12/31/X4

Interest expense	4,621	
Bonds payable		4,621
(Liability balance is now $50,831)		

Bonds payable	4,000	
Cash		4,000
(Liability balance is now $46,831)		

An alternate method of accomplishing in a single (compound) entry what is accomplished above in two is as follows:

Interest expense	4,621	
Bonds payable		621
Cash		4,000

Because compound entries are more efficient, we carry through using this particular journal entry method:

12/31/X5

Interest expense	4,683	
Bonds payable		683
Cash		4,000
(Liability balance is now $47,514)		

12/31/X6

Interest expense	4,751	
Bonds payable		751
Cash		4,000
(Liability balance is now $48,265)		

12/31/X7

Interest expense	4,826	
Bonds payable		826
Cash		4,000
(Liability balance is now $49,091)		

12/31/X8

Interest expense	4,909	
Bonds payable		909
Cash		4,000
(Liability value is now $50,000)		

Bonds payable	50,000	
Cash		50,000

Note that we have separated the recognition of the final year's interest expense and interest payment from the retirement of the bonds to show how the carrying value of the liability finally equals face value just before retirement of the debt. Thus no unusual interest expense is recognized in the final period (as under the expenditure approach) just because the bonds were originally issued at a discount and later retired at face value. The discount together with the annual interest payments equals the total cost of funds incurred over the life of the liability. Under the effective interest method, the discount portion of the total cost of funds is automatically allocated to the periods in the life of the liability. As an exercise, the reader may wish to show that in the above example the discount at issue equals the sum of the increments to the liability recognized over the years as part of the annual recognition of interest expense.

Valuing the Liability. In conventional accounting, the original transaction-based effective interest rate is used for all subsequent valuations of the liability and expense allocations, notwithstanding subsequent variability in market rates of interest. As a consequence of the effective interest method of expense measurement, the recognized value of the liability at any point in time reflects the present value of the remaining cash payments to be made, *at the 10 percent "original transaction" rate of interest.* If the market rate of interest also remains at 10 percent, the carrying value of the liability will equal the value at which the bonds can be traded in the market (sold by holders or redeemed by Escola). But if the prevailing market rate of interest is not equal to 10 percent, the market value of the bonds will not be the same as the value recognized under the conventional accounting model. This relationship between the conventional accounting measure of the liability and the market value of the liability is illustrated in Exhibit 11-5 for the example data as of December 31, 19X6 (after the cash interest payments on that date). From Exhibit

Exhibit 11-5

ESCOLA COMPANY

Comparison of Present Values of Bonds
at December 31, 19X6, at *Assumed* 10% and 12%
Market Rates of Interest Prevailing on That Date

A. *Assumed* market rate of interest = 10%

Date	Remaining Cash Flows			Present Value Factor (10% rate)	Present Value
	Payment of Interest	Repayment of Principal	Total		
12/31/X7	$4,000		$ 4,000	0.90909	$ 3,636
12/31/X8	4,000	$50,000	54,000	0.82645	44,628
Totals	$8,000	$50,000	$58,000		$48,264

B. *Assumed* market rate of interest = 12%

Date	Remaining Cash Flows			Present Value Factor (12% rate)	Present Value
	Payment of Interest	Repayment of Principal	Total		
12/31/X7	$4,000		$ 4,000	0.89286	$ 3,571
12/31/X8	4,000	$50,000	54,000	0.79719	43,048
Totals	$8,000	$50,000	$58,000		$46,619

Note: The carrying value of the bonds on December 31, 19X6, under conventional accounting (from Exhibit 11-4) is $48,265. The difference between this carrying value and the present value of the remaining payments at 10 percent in *A* above is due to the rounding error present even in five-place present value factors. Conceptually, the two values are equal.

11-4 we observe that the conventional accounting measure of the liability on December 31, 19X6, is $48,265. This value is not changed by fluctuations in the market rate of interest. However, as is illustrated by Exhibit 11-5, the market value of the bonds is dependent upon the market rate of interest *at that time.*

Valuation of a liability using the prevailing market rate of interest would be consistent with the objectives of the *current market-value model,* which is discussed in Chapter 15, because this value would reflect the amount of cash necessary to liquidate the obligation. The conventional accounting model, on the other hand, relies on original transaction values, and accordingly changes in the market rate of interest are not recognized under this model.

Installment Liabilities

As was mentioned earlier, the terms of many liabilities, especially long-term bank loans and long-term leases (which are discussed in Chapter 12), call for regular payments that include both principal and interest. Valuing such liabilities and recognizing interest expenses connected with them presents no particular problem under the effective interest rate method. One simply applies the basic relationship introduced earlier.

Example 11-6

On December 15, 19X2, Poorhouse Inc. applied for a five-year term loan from Regional Bank. The bank agreed to a loan (a note payable) calling for annual (year-end) payments of $200,000 per year for five years. The bank's required (effective) rate was 12 percent and it remitted cash of $720,955 to Poorhouse on January 1, 19X3. The journal entry to record the loan is as follows:

1/1/19X3

Cash	720,955	
Note payable—bank		720,955

The following journal entries would be used to record the first year's interest expense (at 12 percent of the beginning balance) and cash payment:

12/31/X3

Interest expense	86,515	
Note payable—bank		86,515
Note payable—bank	200,000	
Cash		200,000

Following is a T-account general ledger representation of the liability for the full five years. Notice that each year interest expense is recognized at 12 percent of the beginning unpaid balance of the liability and the cash payments reduce the new principal-plus-interest balance.

		Notes Payable—Bank		
Payment	12/31/X3	200,000	720,955 1/1/X3	Proceeds
			86,515 12/31/X3	Expense
Payment	12/31/X4	200,000	607,470 12/31/X3	Balance
			72,896 12/31/X4	Expense
Payment	12/31/X5	200,000	480,366 12/31/X4	Balance
			57,644 12/31/X5	Expense
Payment	12/31/X6	200,000	338,010 12/31/X5	Balance
			40,561 12/31/X6	Expense
Payment	12/31/X7	200,000	178,571 12/31/X6	Balance
			21,429 12/31/X7	Expense
			–0– 12/31/X7	Balance

Retirement of Debt before Maturity

At the maturity date of a debt instrument, the carrying value of the liability is equal to the face amount of the debt. Thus, when repayment of the principal is made, there is no change in owners' equity (i.e., cash and the liability are decreased by the same amount). However, at other points in time prior to maturity, the carrying value of the liability will generally not be equal to either the face value or the current market value of the debt. Therefore, if the corporation elects to retire, or extinguish, debt prior to its maturity, either by exercising a "call" provision or by purchasing the debt securities in the open market, a difference will probably exist between the repurchase price and the carrying value of the liability. If the repurchase price is less than (exceeds) the carrying value of the liability, owners' equity will be increased (decreased). Under current accounting policy, this change in owners' equity is recognized as an extraordinary gain (or loss) in the period in which the debt is retired.

Disclosure of Liabilities

The balances in various liability accounts will of course appear opposite appropriate captions in the statement of financial position. It is also appropriate, particularly for long-term liabilities, to disclose the terms of the liabilities, such as the rates at which interest is paid on face amounts, the dates that interest and principal (or combined installment) payments are due, and so forth. If a company has relatively few, uncomplicated liabilities, such facts can be given parenthetically in the statement of financial position itself. Otherwise a lump-sum amount can be shown opposite the caption of each major category of liabilities in the statement of financial position with details disclosed in notes to the financial statements. An example of such a note is given in Exhibit 11-6.

Exhibit 11-6

NOTE TO THE COMBINED FINANCIAL STATEMENTS OF ALLIS-CHALMERS CREDIT, FINANCIAL, AND LEASING SERVICES CORPORATIONS

Long-term debt Long-term debt consists of the following:

	December 31 1977	1976
	(thousands of dollars)	
Term Notes to Insurance Companies:		
Senior notes—8.55% Due in 1979	$ 25,000	$ 25,000
$4\frac{7}{8}$% Due $720,000 annually, maturing in 1983	23,520	24,240
$5\frac{1}{4}$% Due $600,000 annually, maturing in 1985	20,800	21,400
$6\frac{3}{8}$% Due $720,000 annually, maturing in 1987	26,400	27,120
$10\frac{7}{8}$% Due $2,000,000 annually, starting in 1981, maturing in 1990	20,000	20,000
$9\frac{3}{4}$% Due $2,000,000 annually, starting in 1982, maturing in 1991	20,000	20,000
$8\frac{1}{2}$% Due $1,000,000 annually, starting in 1978, maturing in 1992	20,000	20,000
$8\frac{3}{4}$% Due $1,470,588 annually, starting in 1981, maturing in 1997	25,000	—
Sub-total	180,720	157,760
Senior subordinated notes—$5\frac{1}{4}$% Due $280,000 annually, maturing in 1983	7,480	7,760
$5\frac{1}{2}$% Due $280,000 annually, maturing in 1985	8,040	8,320
$6\frac{3}{4}$% Due $280,000 annually, maturing in 1987	8,600	8,880
$11\frac{5}{8}$% Due $1,000,000 annually, starting in 1981, maturing in 1990	10,000	10,000
$10\frac{3}{8}$% Due $1,000,000 annually, starting in 1982, maturing in 1991	10,000	10,000
$9\frac{1}{8}$% Due $800,000 annually, starting in 1978, maturing in 1992	16,000	16,000
$9\frac{1}{8}$% Due $1,176,470 annually, starting in 1981, maturing in 1997	20,000	—
Sub-total	80,120	60,960
Term Notes to Banks:		
7.8% Due $3,750,000 quarterly, starting in 1979, maturing in 1981	30,000	—
Commercial paper supported by non-cancelable credit agreements maturing in 1981	20,000	—
Total long-term debt	$310,840	$218,720

OWNERS' EQUITY

In much of the discussion in earlier chapters we treat owners' equity as a *single residual calculation*—the difference between the independently valued assets and liabilities of the enterprise. A growing number of accountants are supporting the notion that this single measure of owners' equity embodies most, if not all, of the decision-relevant information that can be provided about the equity of owners under conventional accounting. However, accountants have traditionally reported owners' equity for corporations by using a classification scheme that seeks to reflect the different *sources* of owners' equity. Because this classification scheme is encountered in most contemporary corporate financial reports, it is summarized below. Additionally, several important classes of transactions between the corporation and its shareholders are briefly reviewed.

The General Distinction between Earned and Contributed Capital

Corporations would not exist legally were it not for permissive legislation on the part of state governments, allowing for the chartering of corporations. One of the desirable attributes of the corporate form of business is the limitation of the liability (potential losses) of the owners of the corporation to the amount of their current interest in the corporation. To protect other parties, however, the state laws governing corporations often restrict dividends paid to owners, so that the original capital contributed to the corporation by owners remains intact (in the form of recognized net assets) to satisfy the rightful claims of other parties. That is, dividends may only be distributed to the extent that net assets exceed the money capital or equivalent contributed by owners to the enterprise in exchange for shares of stock. Thus, in response to the presumed decision relevance of this general legal notion for dividend-distribution decisions, the owners' equity component of financial position is usually split into two basic categories: (1) paid-in capital and (2) retained earnings.

> **Paid-in Capital.** Paid-in capital is that part of total owners' equity equal to the amount of money or other capital contributed by owners to the enterprise in exchange for ownership interests.
>
> **Retained Earnings.** Retained earnings is that part of owners' equity equal to the cumulative excess of net income over dividend distributions to owners since the inception of the business.

Classifications of Paid-in Capital

Paid-in capital is further subdivided into additional groups or categories. One distinction is based on the type of ownership interest—the various classes of stock issued by the corporation. Another distinction evolves from the specification of "legal values" for shares of stock. We now consider each of these in turn.

Classes of Stock. Each share of stock of a corporation conveys certain rights to owners of the share. In general, owners of shares of *common stock* have the following rights:

1. Right to vote for members of the board of directors and, subject to applicable state laws, to vote on certain types of major corporation decisions (for example, merging with another corporation).

2. Right to purchase their pro rata share of any new stock issue so as to maintain the same proportionate interest in the corporation—called the preemptive right. (Many corporations have recently eliminated this right from their charters.)

3. Right to share proportionally in dividends declared by the corporation.

4. Right to share proportionally in the net assets of the firm if the corporation is liquidated.

On some occasions a corporation will issue other classes of stock which are explicitly given preference over common stock on certain of these rights, but which may also forfeit one or more of the rights. One such general class of stock is commonly referred to as *preferred stock.* Typically, if preferred stock with a dividend (liquidation) preference is outstanding, then no dividend (distribution of assets in the event of liquidation) may be paid to common-stock holders *unless* the preferred-stock holders also receive their (specified) payment. On the other hand, preferred-share holders may be paid their specified payments and *no* payment *need be made* to common-share holders. Preferred stock, however, does not usually carry voting rights.

Example 11-7

Hinrichs Corporation has two classes of stock outstanding: 1,000 shares of preferred stock, which are entitled to an annual dividend of $5 per share, and 5,000 shares of common stock. Under these circumstances, no dividends can be paid to the common-share holders in any year unless the holders of the preferred stock also receive a total dividend distribution that year of $5,000 (1,000 × $5).

Another important characteristic of preferred stock is whether the dividend preference is cumulative or noncumulative. If the dividend preference is *cumulative,* any annual dividends of prior periods that the preferred-share holders were entitled to receive (if declared by the board of directors) but were not paid must be "made up" in order for any dividend distribution to be made to common-share holders. If the preferred stock is entitled only to its annual dividend and forfeits any right to past dividends not declared and paid, it is referred to as *noncumulative* preferred stock.

Example 11-8

Referring to the facts of Example 11-7, assume that Hinrichs Corporation had paid dividends to both classes of shareholders each year since the preferred stock was issued. But in 19X4 a tight cash position resulting from a significant expansion of its plant capacity caused the directors to pass the dividends for that year. In 19X5 the cash position improves and the directors decide to resume dividend payments.

If the preferred stock is cumulative, a dividend distribution of $10,000 ($5,000 dividends *in arrears*—not paid—from 19X4, and the current $5,000 dividend) must be paid to the preferred-share holders in order for any dividends to be paid to the common-share holders. If the preferred stock is noncumulative, only the $5,000 current dividend need be paid to preferred-share holders in order to make a distribution to the common-share holders.

If the preferred-share holders are paid the dividend they are entitled to, the directors may distribute whatever amount they wish to the common-share holders (subject to applicable state laws).

Obviously the cumulative provision is an important right, and most issues of preferred stock currently outstanding carry this right.

Another important preference, or special right, that has recently been attached to many issues of preferred stock is a *conversion* right. Preferred stock with this right entitles the holder, at his option, to convert each share of preferred stock into a specified number of shares of common stock. Thus, *convertible preferred stock* provides the preferred stock virtue of greater assurance of a dependable annual dividend, combined with the potential common-stock virtue (through conversion) of sharing in the future success (large profits) of the company.

"Legal Values" for Stock. In conformity with the objective of providing a specified capital buffer to protect the legal claims of nonowners against the corporation, the states have traditionally (at one time exclusively) provided for the specification of a value for each share of stock. This value is referred to as the *par value* of the stock. Shares of stock that carry par values are called *par-value stock*.

Par-value stock generally cannot be issued for consideration (value) less than this stated amount. In those states that permit the issuance of par-value stock at less than par value, the purchaser (shareholder) generally assumes an obligation to creditors and other legal claimants for the difference between the par value and the amount paid, if at some future time the net assets of the corporation are insufficient to satisfy all nonowner claims. This special *contingent* liability, the amount of which is fixed by the share-purchase transaction between the corporation and the shareholder, *overrides the general limitation of the shareholder's liability* (which limits the liability to loss of the shareholder's interest in the corporation).

Many states now permit the issuance of no-par stock—that is, stock without a specified par value. While no-par stock appears at first glance to compromise the notion of providing a capital buffer for nonowner interests, in reality it does not. Since the par value of stock can in most instances be of any amount, ranging down for example to $1 or less per share, the effective buffer provided by par-value stock is often negligible. The actual security for creditors is provided by the actual asset values and related earning power possessed by the corporation—not an arbitrary amount of capital specified by law. The use of no-par stock merely recognizes this fact.

In many instances, state law authorizes the board of directors to place a *stated value* on no-par stock. When this option is exercised, there is little practical difference from an accounting point of view between no-par stock with a stated value and par-value stock—although there may be some minor legal differences.

The par value or stated value of shares of stock is the basis for an additional accounting classification in the owners' equity section of the statement of financial position. The total proceeds from the sale of shares of stock are divided into two categories of paid-in capital: (1) the amount of the par (or stated) value of stock issued and (2) the excess of the paid-in proceeds over the par (or stated) value of stock issued. The legal significance of the division depends upon the state in which the corporation is chartered.

Example 11-9

Corporation Y issues 10,000 shares of $5 par-value stock to new shareholders in exchange for $170,000. The journal entry to record the transaction shows the split of the new paid-in capital between the two categories:

Cash	170,000	
Common stock—par value		50,000
Paid-in capital in excess of		
par value on common stock		120,000

When preferred stock is issued with a par value, the dividend preference is usually stated in terms of a percentage of this par value. If the preferred stock does not carry a par value, the dividend preference is expressed in terms of a dollar amount per share.

Example 11-10

Corporation X issued 8 percent, $100 par-value preferred stock. Corporation Y issued no-par preferred stock with a dividend preference of $8 per share. Both issues of preferred stock will pay the same dividend—$8 per share. Any difference in price that investors would pay for these two stocks would therefore be solely related to the relative degrees of risk they associate with the two companies.

Dividends on Stock

The return that investors receive on their investment in a corporation is composed of two parts: (1) cash dividends and (2) changes in the market price of the stock. The market price of the stock is affected by many factors, including reinvestment of earnings and changes in the expectations of investors. Fluctuations in the market price of the stock, while of major importance to each individual shareholder, do not affect the net assets *of the corporation,* and thus they do not affect the valuation of owners' equity. Cash dividends, on the other hand, reduce the net assets of the corporation, and they must therefore be given accounting recognition.

Cash Dividends. Cash dividends (whether on preferred or common stock) must be formally authorized by the board of directors of a corporation. Three dates are important for cash dividends. Cash dividends are declared at some point in time (*declaration date*), payable to stockholders of record as of a second (future) date (*date of record*), and actually to be paid on a third (latest) date (*payment date*).

Example 11-11

> The board of directors of Boston Corporation declared a cash dividend of $1.20 per share on November 28, 19X4 (declaration date). The dividend is payable to shareholders registered as legal owners of the shares as of December 6, 19X4 (record date), and it will be paid on December 14, 19X4 (payment date).

At the date of declaration, the total dividend to be paid becomes a binding liability on the corporation. Therefore, on this date, the retained earnings of the corporation (a component of the total owners' equity) is reduced and a liability, dividends payable, recognized. Payment of the dividend at the later payment date then results in a decrease in cash and a decrease in dividends payable.

Example 11-12

> Suppose that the Boston Corporation of Example 11-11 had 1.34 million shares of common stock outstanding on November 28, 19X4, and there were no increases or decreases due to new issues or retirements through December 19X4. The following journal entries would be used to record its 19X4 dividend:

11/28/X4

Retained earnings	1,608,000	
Dividends payable		1,608,000
To record dividend declaration		

12/14/X4

Dividends payable	1,608,000	
Cash		1,608,000
To record payment of dividends		

Stock Dividends. At times a corporation declares a dividend on a class of stock (usually common stock) payable in shares of the same stock. This type of dividend is called a *stock dividend.*

Many accountants and other financial experts acknowledge that a stock dividend does not by itself represent income to the shareholder. Although each shareholder has more shares of stock after the stock dividend, his proportionate interest in the corporation is unchanged. Furthermore, with more shares of the corporation outstanding, one would expect the market price of the stock to adjust downward proportionately. Under these circumstances the only accounting recognition that ought to be given to a stock dividend would be to reflect the increased "legal capital" (additional shares times the par or stated value) and to reduce the balance in retained earnings by the same amount.

Example 11-13

Wright Corporation has 10,000 shares of $1 par-value common stock outstanding. The board of directors of Wright Corporation decides not to pay a cash dividend on these shares, but it does authorize a 10 percent stock dividend. This action means that Wright Corporation will issue 1,000 new shares of $1 par-value common stock, and each shareholder will receive 1 new share for each 10 shares he now owns.

The following journal entry would be used to recognize the change in Wright Corporation's paid-in capital:

Retained earnings	1,000	
Common stock—par value		1,000

However, following many stock dividends, the market price does not appear to adjust downward proportionately, and the shareholders are in a real sense "better off." Because of this seeming paradox (which many attribute to the expectations that dividends per share will remain the same, making each share worth as much as before), some accountants have proposed a different treatment for recognizing stock dividends—a treatment that is currently supported by financial accounting policy (unless it is reasonable to assume that the price of a share will adjust for the additional shares outstanding). They contend that the value of the stock dividend should be measured by the number of shares issued times the current fair market value per share of the shares outstanding. Retained earnings should therefore be decreased (debited) by this amount. The corresponding credit is to paid-in capital and is allocated between "legal capital" (in an amount equal to the par or stated value of the new shares issued) and "paid-in capital in excess of par value of stock issued" (the remaining amount).

One rationale supporting this treatment is that when a corporation substitutes a stock dividend for a cash dividend, it is analogous to having the corporation pay out cash dividends and then having the owners reinvest the proceeds in new shares of the corporation's stock (ignoring personal income taxes). This is what the accounting for stock dividends simulates. Under current accounting policy, this second treatment (valuing stock dividends at the fair market value of the shares) is used when the stock dividend is 25 percent or less. Presumably, a stock dividend larger than 25 percent does not justify the assumption that the market price will not adjust proportionately to reflect the new number of shares outstanding. For stock dividends of more than 25 percent, the method described above and illustrated in Example 11-13 is applicable.

Example 11-14

Referring back to Example 11-13, suppose that the market value of Wright Corporation's $1 par-value stock is $15 at the time of the stock dividend. Also assume that the corporation's retained earnings balance exceeds the total market value of the shares issued as a stock dividend. The journal entry to record the stock dividend according to the market-value method is as follows:

Retained earnings	15,000	
Common stock—par value		1,000
Paid-in capital in excess of par value of common stock		14,000

From Example 11-14 it is clear that a stock dividend has the effect of "capitalizing" some portion of the firm's retained earnings. The amount to be capitalized (added to paid-in capital) depends of course upon the size of the stock dividend and the market value per share at the time. The practical significance of this capitalization action is to reduce the total amount of retained earnings and thereby reduce the maximum amount that the board of directors could declare in the future as a cash dividend to shareholders. However, the specific amount of the reduction in potentially declarable dividends depends upon the statutory provisions of the state in which the corporation is chartered.

Stock Splits

Stock dividends have the effect of increasing the number of shares outstanding. An alternative method of achieving this objective, without the "capitalization of retained earnings" that accompanies a stock dividend, is the *stock split*. In a stock split, the old shares of stock are called in by the corporation, and new (generally more) shares of stock with a different par value (generally proportionately less than the old par value) are issued to the shareholders. The total amount of legal capital is maintained unchanged by a stock split. Therefore the par value of the new shares must be adjusted in accordance with the number of new shares that the board of directors wishes to issue.

Example 11-15

Archer Corporation has 100,000 shares of $10 par-value stock outstanding. The board of directors wishes to double the number of shares outstanding in order to reduce the market price *per share* (presumably making the company's stock more easily purchased by the average investor), but it does not want to capitalize retained earnings (as would be necessary if a stock dividend were declared). Therefore the board declares a two-for-one stock split. As a consequence of this action, each shareholder will receive 2 new shares of $5 par-value stock of Archer Corporation for each old share of $10 par-value stock held.

Before the stock split illustrated in Example 11-15, the total legal capital of Archer Corporation was $1 million (100,000 shares with a par value of $10 per share). After the split, Archer's legal capital still remains at $1 million (200,000 shares with a par value of $5 per share). Because the legal capital is unchanged (as are all other elements of owners' equity), no accounting recognition is required for a stock split—that is, the financial position of the firm has not changed. Therefore no journal entry or entries are required to record a stock split.

Treasury Stock

From time to time, corporations decide to repurchase some of their outstanding shares of stock in the open market or directly from shareholders. This action is taken for a number of reasons, including the need for shares to be issued to executives under stock option plans or perhaps because management believes the stock is undervalued in the market. If the stock is not legally retired or canceled following reacquisition, but rather is held by the corporation for possible reissue in the future, the stock is called *treasury stock*.

In accounting for treasury stock, the first question that must be dealt with relates to the nature of the treasury stock. Is it an asset or is it a reduction of owners' equity? Although some arguments can be developed in support of treating treasury stock as an asset (for example, it can be resold in the marketplace for cash like any other security), the settled position under present-day reporting practice is to treat treasury stock as a reduction of owners' equity. Several minor variations on this treatment are available. A common method of reporting treasury stock, however, is to show the total cost of the reacquired shares as an "unallocated deduction" from total owners' equity before considering treasury stock. Whatever other variation may be employed, the effect on *total* owners' equity will be the same—the amount of total owners' equity prior to reacquisition of the shares is reduced by the total *cost* of the treasury shares.

If the treasury shares are subsequently sold, any difference between the proceeds of sale and the cost of the treasury stock is generally reflected in paid-in capital. Irrespective of any specific alternative selected to account for this "sale" transaction, *no* income or loss is recognized because the sale of treasury shares is not considered substantively different from merely issuing the same number of previously unissued shares of the corporation's stock.

Stock Options

A popular form of executive compensation used by corporations in recent years is the stock option. A *stock option* is a legal instrument permitting the holder to acquire a specified number of shares of stock of the issuing corporation at a specified price. The options are typically valid for a limited period of time (usually up to five years), and they generally are not transferable. Among the reasons for the use of stock options as a form of compensation are potential tax benefits to the executive (although current tax rules tightly restrict this benefit) and the linking of the executive's compensation to the fortunes of the company.

The important accounting issues related to the existence of a stock option plan are (1) the need for disclosure of the potential number of new shares of stock that may be issued if options are granted and exercised (so that present shareholders are apprised of how their *proportionate* shares may change if the options are exercised), and (2) to the extent that a *measurable* amount of compensation (to the executives) accompanies the issuance of the stock options, the compensation should be recognized as an expense of the period, or periods, benefiting.

The disclosure issue is handled by adding supplementary information to the financial statements which reflects the general provisions of the stock option plan, the number of options granted and exercised during the period, and the number of options outstanding at the end of the period.

Measuring compensation associated with the issuance of stock options is a more controversial issue. Although it is generally conceded that granting options conveys something of value to the recipient (as part of a compensation package), determination of that value is not an easy task. Since the options are generally not transferable, no market price can be used to assess this value. Accordingly, some other basis for measuring the value of the options must be found. For "simple" stock option plans not involving a variable number of shares or a variable option price depending upon future conditions (for which more complex measurement rules are prescribed), current accounting policy calls for measurement of the value of the compensation as the amount of the difference between the price that the holder must pay for the shares if he exercises the options and the fair market value of the stock *on the date the options are granted*.

Example 11-16

> Continental Corporation issues stock options on December 31, 19X6, to its senior executives, which, if exercised, will allow them to purchase 10,000 shares of the company's $5 par-value stock at $30 per share. On this date, the fair market value of Continental's stock is $40 per share. Accordingly, the amount of compensation imputed to the issuance of the options is $100,000—10,000 shares at $10 per share ($40 – $30). The date on which the options may first be exercised is December 31, 19X8. By this date each senior executive will also have fulfilled all duties for which the options are to compensate.

Other milestone dates over the life of a stock option that have been proposed as more appropriate than the date of grant for the comparison of fair market value and exercise price in measuring the compensation that has been granted include (1) the date on which the grantee has satisfied all conditions necessary to be entitled to exercise the option, (2) the date on which the grantee may first exercise the option, and (3) the date on which the option is exercised. All of these potential comparison dates (including the date of grant) are, however, only alternative approaches to the fundamental measurement objective—measuring the value of the benefit at the time of its award, and none of the approaches are considered completely suitable as a general measurement methodology. Therefore, as more research is completed on this problem, a new and different measurement technique may evolve.

The compensation cost, however measured, is then recognized as an expense of the period, or periods, in which the employee performs the services for which the options were granted. Since options are generally assumed to be issued for future rather than past services, the cost will generally be recognized as an expense of several periods in the future.

Example 11-17

Using the data of Example 11-16, at the date of grant an asset (deferred compensation expense) is recognized in the amount of $100,000, and since payment will be made (if the options are exercised) through the issuance of stock, paid-in capital is also increased by the same amount. Thereafter the company recognizes a portion of the total deferred expense as compensation expense in each of the two years 19X7 and 19X8 during which the executives are earning the right to exercise the options. The original journal entry recording the grant of the options and the subsequent two year-end adjusting entries are as follows (assuming an equal annual allocation):

12/31/X6

Deferred compensation expense	100,000	
Paid-in capital—stock options		100,000

12/31/X7

Executive compensation expense	50,000	
Deferred compensation expense		50,000

12/31/X8

Executive compensation expense	50,000	
Deferred compensation expense		50,000

Assuming that on January 1, 19X9, all the options were exercised, the following journal entry would be used to record the exercise of the stock options:

1/1/X9

Cash	300,000	
Paid-in capital—stock options	100,000	
Common stock—par value		50,000
Paid-in capital in excess of par value of common stock		350,000

SUMMARY

We have briefly summarized some of the major components of owners' equity that appear in the financial reports of many publicly held corporations. An illustrative owners' equity section of the statement of financial position is shown in Exhibit 11-7.

Exhibit 11-7
ILLUSTRATIVE OWNERS' EQUITY SECTION OF A CORPORATE STATEMENT OF FINANCIAL POSITION

Shareholders' Equity			
Capital stock:			
Preferred stock:			
6% cumulative, convertible, $100 par value; 100,000 shares authorized, 50,000 shares issued	$5,000,000		
Paid-in capital in excess of par value of stock	300,000	$5,300,000	
Common stock:			
Common stock, without par value, stated at $5 per share; shares authorized and issued—100,000	500,000		
Paid-in capital in excess of stated value of stock	8,300,000	8,800,000	
Total contributed capital			$14,100,000
Retained earnings			9,200,000
			$23,300,000
Less—Treasury stock, at cost:			
Preferred—1,100 shares		91,000	
Common—1,455 shares		369,000	460,000
Total shareholders' equity			$22,840,000

As we noted at the outset of this section, the classification scheme used in the owners' equity section is intended to report the *sources* of the owners' equity of the corporation. Whether this classification, which in large part originated in old state corporation codes, has any substantive decision relevance is open to question. A case can certainly be made for reporting information that is relevant for dividend distribution decisions. But, in reality, when the legality of possible dividends becomes a major issue, it is doubtful that the general classification scheme used in present reports provides useful and accurate information, because legal, rather than accounting, considerations usually prevail.

Additionally, several important classes of transactions between the corporation and its shareholders (or potential shareholders in the case of stock options) have been briefly reviewed. While the specific treatment of the transactions within the conventional owners' equity classification system may not be highly significant, the expense or income recognition issues flowing from certain types of transactions (e.g., issuance of stock options and sale of treasury shares) are important questions.

APPENDIX

The material in this Appendix is a capsule (as opposed to complete) summary of business borrowing. It consists of the two broad topics of "business borrowing" and "borrowing method," followed by a number of definitions and descriptions of specific methods and instruments for borrowing. All of the following material is either quoted directly or paraphrased from Donald W. Moffat, *Concise Desk Book of Business Finance* (Prentice-Hall, 1975).

BORROWING

The nature and mechanics of business borrowing methods are influenced by the purpose for which the loan is intended, the size of the business, the form of business organization, and the type of business (whether wholesale, retail, manufacturing, industrial, etc.).

Purpose of the Loan. Borrowed capital is sought to meet the financial requirements that cannot be covered by ownership capital. The purposes may range from the short term need to finance an immediate purchase requiring a loan for, say 90 days, to the acquisition of fixed assets like plant and machinery that might entail borrowing for a relatively long term. Hence, borrowing may be for short or long-term needs. The possible sources of funds may vary with the term for which the funds are needed.

When money is borrowed for the purchase of merchandise that is to be resold (commercial, self-liquidating loan), the term for which the loan is made is usually the time it is expected to take to resell the goods. But when money is borrowed for the purchase of land, the construction of a building, or for acquiring any other capital goods, the term of the loan is likely to be long enough to give the borrower time to repay the loan out of the earnings of the ... [business].

Size of the Business. There are numerous sources of funds for business borrowing. Some are available to all firms regardless of size, others can be tapped by large businesses only. For example, small business firms may borrow from their local banks, from the small business administration, etc., while large firms may borrow from these sources and by floating bond issues.

Form of Business Organization. For all practical purposes, corporations, proprietorships, and partnerships have access to the same sources of funds except, of course, that only corporations borrow by selling bonds. New, small, individually owned businesses or partnerships can sometimes secure bank loans more easily than small corporations because of the *limited liability* of the stockholders of a corporation. However, as a practical matter, incorporating a small business does not provide the owners with an escape from liability for loans made by the business because lenders will not make a loan to such a business without a cosigner, and it is usually the owners (now stockholders) who cosign.

Type of Business. Many industries have developed methods of financing that are peculiar to their own trades. Factoring (see "Accounts Receivable Financing"), as a source of funds, started in the textile industry and its use has spread to producers of shoes, radio tubes, and many other fields. Few banks will finance exporters except on warehouse receipts. In *bottomry* a ship is pledged as security for a loan and is a unique situation because the creditor is without a security interest if the ship is lost. Small service businesses with proportionately small investments in equipment have to rely heavily on the personal credit type of loan.

Sources of Short-term Borrowing

Temporary . . . needs [for funds] are ordinarily met by short-term borrowing from any of the following sources:

(1) commercial banks
(2) industrial banks
(3) small-loan companies
(4) factors
(5) commercial finance companies
(6) commercial paper houses
(7) suppliers, equipment manufacturers, and wholesalers
(8) the Small Business Administration
(9) Federal Reserve Banks
(10) FHA
(11) community development groups.

Sources of Long-Term Borrowing

A business that must borrow for permanent capital needs can receive long-term loans from the following sources: (1) commercial banks, (2) insurance companies and institutional investors, and (3) the public sale of bond issues through investment bankers.

1. *Commercial banks.* Long-term capital requirements can be met by a *term loan,* usually of two to ten years. Term loans are used principally to finance fixed capital expenditures. Ordinarily the banks are willing to make these loans only when the owners can show a substantial investment in the business. The loan agreement usually provides for amortization [payment in installments] of the loan and it may include restrictions on such items as borrowing, working capital ratios [see Chapter 18 for discussion of ratios], and pledging of assets. The term loan in practice is not usually made to smaller businesses.

2. *Insurance companies and institutional investors.* These groups (endowment funds, colleges, life and fire insurance companies, etc.) are constantly seeking investment outlets. Although their lending is confined to large businesses for the most part, some of the insurance companies make loans on commercial and industrial properties to the smaller firms. Their rates are approximately the same as bank interest rates.

3. *Public sale of bond issues through investment brokers.* The principal function of investment bankers is to purchase an entire issue of securities from a corporation and market them to the public. Since the cost of floating issues under $250,000 is prohibitive, this method of financing is almost closed to the smaller firm.

BORROWING METHODS

Borrowing, in the meaning ordinarily ascribed to the term . . . , may be secured or unsecured. If a corporation, by reason of its excellent financial standing, can obtain a loan without furnishing any security, or by the simple expedient of executing a note as evidence of the obligation, the borrowing is unsecured. In loans to individuals, this is a common way of raising funds, for the lender is willing to rely upon the personal obligation and integrity of the borrower. In the case of corporations, however, it is only the rare lender of small sums who will risk a loan to a corporation without some additional assurance of repayment.

The most common methods employed by a corporation to raise money are:

1. By *mortgage* of specific corporate property, both real and personal.
2. By *pledge* of personal property.
3. By issuance of bonds, secured by a mortgage or pledge of corporate property, or unsecured.
4. By issuance of short-term *notes,* secured or unsecured.

The corporation may offer as security for repayment of its debt a mortgage covering:

1. Real property owned by the corporation.
2. Personal property owned by the corporation.
3. All the property owned by the corporation at the time of execution of the mortgage and to be acquired by it in the future.

A mortgage may be given to secure future advances. In that event, the mortgage becomes operative when the advances are actually made. The property, in the meantime and until the lien accrues, may become subject to the claims of creditors.

Accounts Receivable Financing

Obtaining . . . funds by (1) borrowing with accounts receivable as collateral, or (2) selling accounts receivable outright (factoring).

Borrowing on Accounts Receivable. The commercial banks and commercial finance companies . . . are the principal sources of accounts receivable loans. Such financing is carried out through a formal agreement called the *underlying agreement* or *working plan,* which is a continuing arrangement for loans against open accounts. This agreement specifies what percentage of the value of pledged accounts receivable will be advanced by the lender (usually from 75 per cent to 85 per cent); sets forth the rights and liabilities of the parties and the overall conditions by which each assignment will operate.

. . . .

Selling Accounts Receivable Outright—factoring. In certain lines of business, principally textiles, factoring companies are used to convert accounts receivable into cash. A continuing agreement is made between the seller of the merchandise and the factoring company under which the factor contracts to buy all the accounts receivable as they arise out of sales by the seller. The factor assumes all the risks and has no recourse if the accounts receivable prove uncollectible. The factor, therefore, passes upon the credit standing of the customer to whom the goods are sold. Most factors operate on a notification basis. In fact, the invoice for the goods is sent to the factor who mails it to the customer. The invoice shows that payment is to be made to the factoring company.

The factor is paid a fee of 1 or 2 percent each month on the face amount of all accounts bought. This charge is for assuming the credit risk. In addition, the factor charges [an additional] . . . rate . . . per year for cash advanced to the seller, and the charge is deducted from the payment for the accounts.

Corporate Bonds

Corporate bonds are written promises . . . to pay a specified sum of money at a fixed time in the future, usually more than ten years after the promises are made, with interest at a fixed rate, payable at specified interest dates. All bonds, whether specifically secured or not, are, in effect, long-term promissory notes, but they differ from ordinary notes in that they are more formal and their provisions are more complex. Unsecured bonds are called *debentures*.

There are three parties or groups involved in every bond issue: the debtor corporation, the bondholder, and the trustee. Because of the fact that bonds change hands so frequently, and because of the difficulties of making separate contracts with a large number of individual creditors, the basic contract, called the *trust indenture* or *deed of trust,* is made out between the corporation and the trustee (usually a trust company). The bond instrument itself merely contains a promise to pay a specific amount of the total debt with interest, and gives a summary of the main terms of the borrowing. The bondholder must look to the indenture for the full details of the issue. A corporate bond is usually one of a number of similar bonds, all of which are covered by the trust indenture. Bonds are generally issued in denominations of $1,000.

. . . .

Distinction Between Stocks and Bonds. The basic difference between corporate stock and a corporate bond is that the former evidences proprietorship, while the latter evidences a debt. Thus a bondholder is a creditor of the corporation while a stockholder is an owner.

Types of Bonds. Corporate bond issues may be secured or unsecured. A secured bond does not necessarily have greater investment merit than an unsecured bond because the grade of the bond depends more upon the earnings of the issuer than upon the security pledged to protect it. Generally, if earnings are adequate, interest is paid and the question of security never arises. Security is merely a device for giving the bondholder a somewhat stronger position in case of financial failure and it becomes important only in case the issuer is unable to meet the interest and other obligations under the bond. Specific pledges of security are important principally in that they determine the relative strength of the positions of the several classes of security holders in the bargaining that takes place when the corporation is reorganized after financial failure.

Corporations may use the ordinary real estate mortgage as security to finance the acquisition of a specific building or other pieces of real property. Or the security it offers may take the form of a general mortgage on all property owned or later acquired by the debtor. Most large corporate bond issues are usually secured by the latter method.

. . . .

All bonds—secured or unsecured—may have the following features:

1. *Redemption provisions.* Most indentures created in recent years give the company the right to call in bonds issued under them before maturity. The call feature, also known as the redemption feature, enables the corporation to pay off the bonds before maturity, if the company can afford to do so, or to refund the bonds by issuing other securities, less costly to the corporation, in their place.

2. *Conversion provisions.* A convertible bond is one that gives the security holder the right to exchange his bonds for some other security, usually preferred stock or common stock of the corporation, on a fixed basis described in the indenture. The conversion privilege adds a . . . [capital gain] interest to bonds and is given to make them more attractive and salable. The conversion privilege is found more frequently in debentures than in secured bonds.

3. *Sinking fund provisions.* A sinking fund bond is one that imposes upon the corporation the obligation to set aside a certain sum . . . periodically for the purpose of reducing or retiring the bonded indebtedness. Since the fund is usually turned over to the trustee to be invested in the "same issue," it is not actually a fund, but a partial extinction of the debt.

Inventory Financing

Inventory financing includes (1) . . . obtaining needed capital for a business by borrowing money with inventory used as collateral . . . and, (2) . . . financing the purchase of inventories . . . , e.g., purchasing inventory on account.

Mortgage

A mortgage is . . . a deed . . . given to secure the performance of some act upon the part of the mortgagor (borrower), usually his repayment of a loan made by the mortgagee (lender) at the time of execution and delivery of the mortgage. Thus, in the usual transaction, the mortgagor borrows money from the mortgagee and gives as security a deed of property. This deed provides that it shall be null and void if at the time appointed the mortgagor repays the loan.

Note

A note is . . . written promise to pay unconditionally a definite sum of money on demand or at some specified time in the future. It is signed by the maker—the person who promises to pay. The person to whom the note is payable is the payee. If payable to a particular person's order or to bearer, the note is negotiable; [that is,] the title may be transferred by endorsement and delivery. When in possession of the payee or a *holder in due course,* it is a *note receivable;* with reference to the maker, it is a *note payable.*

Series Bonds

Series bonds are . . . authorized to be issued in series under limited and *open-end mortgages.* Series bonds should not be confused with *serial bonds.* Serial bonds have a common date of issuance but varying dates of maturity. Series bonds have different dates of issuance but are all issued under the same *mortgage.*

Short-Term Loans

Short-term loans are . . . made for a period of a year or less, usually at a fixed rate of interest and evidenced by a *note, acceptance,* or some other instrument. It may be secured by collateral or may be given on the note of the borrower without collateral if the credit rating of the borrower is strong enough.

Term Loan

A term loan is . . . a bank loan, usually with a maturity of not less than two and not more than ten years, repayable in installments. Term loans are made to finance expansion, to refinance corporate mortgages or mortgage bonds, to retire preferred stock, to make permanent additions to . . . [current assets] , and for other purposes.

Most term loan agreements contain provisions to make certain that the character of the business will not change. The provisions may relate to maintenance of working capital position, maintenance of property in good condition, keeping a required amount of insurance in force, and rendering financial statements at fixed intervals (usually monthly or quarterly, more rarely semiannually). Similarly, restrictive conditions are often included. These include prohibitions against other borrowing, merger or consolidation with any other business, sale of assets other than in the usual course of business, pledge of assets, payment of excessive dividends, payment of management bonuses, too rapid expansion, and extension of credit other than in the usual course of business. Few term loans are supported by agreements requiring all of the obligations and restrictions mentioned.

Questions for Review and Discussion

11-1. Define:
  a. Liability
  b. Bond premium and discount
  c. Face value of a bond
  d. Maturity date of a bond
  e. Stated rate of interest
  f. Effective rate of interest

g. Common and preferred stock
h. Cumulative and noncumulative preferred stock
i. Convertible preferred stock
j. Par value
k. Stated value (on no-par stock)
l. Stock dividend
m. Stock split
n. Treasury stock
o. Stock option

11-2. What two attributes are generally common to all liabilities?

11-3. In what ways are liabilities typically created? How are liabilities typically discharged?

11-4. The total cost that a firm will incur from using non-owner-provided money capital may be measured using two total amounts from a transaction-based accounting system. State this fundamental relationship.

11-5. What two measurement problems are associated with liabilities?

11-6. State the basic relationship that exists between the value of a liability at the end of an accounting period and the flows between parties to the borrowing transaction.

11-7. Explain how to calculate the effective rate of interest of a liability at the time it is incurred (issued).

11-8. How is interest expense calculated, using the effective interest approach?

11-9. Explain the difference between the value that is assigned to a liability under the conventional accounting model and the value that would be calculated using current market-value.

11-10. Enumerate the three dates that are important for cash dividends. How do you think the market price of a publicly traded stock would react at each of these dates?

11-11. Explain the two alternative ways of accounting for a stock dividend, and indicate the circumstances when each is appropriate under current accounting policy.

11-12. Explain the similarities and differences (including the accounting treatment) between a stock dividend and a stock split.

11-13. Explain the relationship between (1) the stated and effective rates of interest and (2) the face amount of bonds and the proceeds that will be received when the bonds are issued.

11-14. The financial statements in the 1972 annual report of the Times Mirror Company included the following information on the company's stock option plans:

> The executive stock option plans adopted prior to 1971 are qualified plans and provide that options may be granted to key executive employees to purchase shares

of the Company's Common Stock at a price at least equal to the fair market value of the stock at date of grant. The 1971 Executive Stock Option Plan (a non-qualified plan) provides that options may be granted to key executive employees to purchase shares of the Company's Common Stock at a price at least equal to 75 percent of the fair market value at the date of grant. In general, the options under all plans are not exercisable until one year after date of grant and thereafter are exercisable in whole or in increments over a period not to exceed five years, dependent upon the terms of each option.

Accounting entries are made only when options are exercised under the qualified plans. At the time options are granted under the 1971 Plan, the difference between the market price and the option price is . . . [added] to the additional paid-in capital account. That amount is deferred and is charged to operations over the period from the date of grant until the option becomes exercisable. Operations were charged $191,133 and $178,914 in 1972 and 1971 for such grants. At December 31, 1972, $33,694 was deferred and will be charged to operations in subsequent years. At the time the options are exercised under the plans, the cash proceeds are . . . [added] to the common stock and additional paid-in capital accounts.

Why do you suppose accounting entries are made only when options are exercised under the "qualified" plans? Under current accounting policy, is there any compensation expense associated with "qualified" plans? Why or why not? Does the treatment of the measured compensation on the "non-qualified" plans seem reasonable? Why or why not?

11-15. The following news story appeared in the *Wall Street Journal* in May 1973:

. . . [the] senior vice president of giant Gulf Oil Corp. doesn't like what he calls "glib criticism."

And when the criticism is directed at Gulf's repurchase in March of 13 million of its own common shares—for which it paid a whopping $338 million—he gets downright annoyed.

"It was a good decision then," he insists, "and we still feel that way now. We didn't borrow any funds for the purchase, our debt is low and we have tremendous borrowing power."

It's a cogent argument. A company has what it considers excess cash lying around, its capital spending requirements have been amply taken care of—what better way to use the money than by purchasing its own stock? The case becomes even stronger when, as in Gulf's case, the stock is selling at a relatively low multiple of earnings and has a relatively high dividend yield. Not only will a large repurchase of shares save the company money in dividends it no longer has to pay out, but shrinkage of the total number of shares outstanding will drive up earnings a few cents a share and might, the theory goes, increase investors' confidence in the company, perhaps driving up the price of its shares.

"Purchase of our own shares appears to be an attractive outlet for surplus funds at this time," is the way . . . [the senior vice president] put it when the March buyback was completed.

Trouble is, the decision has cost Gulf a bundle, on paper at least. Since March, the price of a share of Gulf stock has tumbled from $25.375 to $23.125. That means the company has sustained a paper loss of around $30 million on its own shares.

And, predictably, the criticism is coming. Gulf isn't the only target (though its size and the size of its buy-back make it, in the words of one critic, "symbolically . . . the kickoff player"). A small but growing number of analysts and economists are beginning to question the logic behind moves by hundreds of companies recently to buy back their own stock at a record clip.

They're suggesting . . . that "buying back shares for reasons other than standard treasury requirements doesn't accomplish any really worthwhile corporate objective, and there may be more risks in it than management is willing to recognize."[4]

How would the "paper loss of around $30 million" on the treasury shares be recognized under the conventional accounting model? What would be the difference if the treasury shares were resold for $23.125? How does the Gulf situation differ from the early retirement of debt on which income or loss is recognized? Do you think that retirement of long-term debt and reacquisition of common shares should be treated differently in measuring income? Do you see any potential conflicts of interest in a management decision to reacquire its own stock?

11-16. You are walking along a high-suspension bridge in Queen City enjoying the view when you spot a well-dressed, middle-aged man poised on the railing, apparently about to jump to his death. You yell "Stop!" He hesitates, giving you a chance to move closer and ask him why he wants to "end it all." In a sobbing voice the despondent man explains that he is the president of a medium-size corporation and just this afternoon he was informed by the chief accountant that the head bookkeeper ran off to Argentina with all the company's stockholders' equities. As president he had conscientiously insured all of the company's assets but had never thought of providing for this kind of loss. He is sure that the stockholders would sue him for everything he has. Without his XX-7 sports car, life is not worth living. With those few words he turns away to jump. Is there anything you can say about his problem that might make him change his mind?

Exercises

11-1. Calculation of Interest Expense and Liability Value. Gammon Corporation issued on January 1, 19X4, five-year bonds with a total face value of $10,000 and a stated interest rate of 10 percent. Cash interest payments to holders of the bonds are to be made annually on December 31. The market rate of interest at the date of issue was 12 percent. Based upon the market determination of the value of the bonds at the prevailing interest rate of 12 percent, Gammon Corporation received $9,275 for the bonds.

---

[4] *Wall Street Journal,* May 22, 1973. Reprinted with the permission of The Wall Street Journal, © Dow Jones & Company, Inc., 1973.

Required:

1. Using the effective interest method of accounting for liabilities, calculate the interest expense for 19X5 and the carrying value of the bonds (the amount at which they will be valued in the financial statements) at December 31, 19X5. (Note that calculations are for the *second year* the bonds are outstanding.)

2. Write the journal entry or entries to record the 19X5 interest expense.

11-2. Journal Entry Treatment of Bond Liability. Bonds with a face value of $100,000 were issued on January 1, 19X6, for $92,420. The stated interest rate is 8 percent, and the effective rate of interest at issue is 10 percent. The interest is payable each year on December 31.

Required:

1. Calculate the following values for 19X6 and 19X7:
   (a) Cash interest payment for the year
   (b) Interest expense for the year
   (c) Carrying value of the liability at the end of the year

2. Set up a T-account for bonds payable. Prepare journal entries to record (*a*) issue of the bonds and (*b*) interest paid and interest expense for 19X6 and 19X7. Post the changes in the bonds payable account due to each of these journal entries and clearly label the balance in the account as of December 31, 19X6 and 19X7.

11-3. Value and Interest Expense—Installment Debt. On March 31, 19X0, LOFLO Corporation officers sign a note payable to HIFLO Bank. The note calls for three annual payments to the bank of $1.5 million on March 31, *the end of* LOFLO's *fiscal year*. The rate of interest charged by the bank on the loan is 11 percent. The bank paid LOFLO the proceeds of the loan on April 1, 19X0.

Required:

1. Determine the proceeds of the note and make a journal entry recording the proceeds and the liability.

2. Set up a notes payable T-account and record the note payable at April 1, 19X0.

3. Present journal entries recording the 19X1 interest expense and payment on the note and post the related changes in the liability to the T-account.

4. Trace the remaining history of the note payable by making the remaining annual entries in the T-account (no journal entries required).

11-4. Gain or Loss on Early Retirement of Debt. Refer to the facts in Exercise 11-3. Suppose that on April 1, 19X1, LOFLO Corporation's management wants to reduce its total debt. The note payable to HIFLO Bank contains a clause permitting early retirement of the note at any time for 101 percent of the present value of the remaining payments based on the original 11 percent effective interest rate.

Required:

1. Calculate the loss that LOFLO would experience if it retired the note on April 1, 19X1.

2. Assuming management proceeded with the early retirement, write a journal entry to record the transaction.

11-5. Cash Dividends, Stock Dividends, and Stock Splits. The owners' equity section of Miller Corporation's statement of financial position on December 31, 19X7, follows:

Common stock:		
$10 par value stock;		
500,000 shares authorized,		
100,000 shares issued	$1,000,000	
Amount received in excess		
of par value of stock	1,500,000	$2,500,000
Retained earnings		4,500,000
Total shareholders' equity		$7,000,000

Required:

Determine the balances of each of the components of Miller Corporation's owners' equity at the end of 19X8 and 19X9, taking into account the following events:

(a) On March 15, 19X8, Miller Corporation paid a cash dividend of $10 per share.

(b) On September 15, 19X8, Miller Corporation paid a 50 percent stock dividend. The fair market value of Miller Corporation's stock on this date was $150 per share.

(c) Net income for 19X8 was $1.6 million.

(d) On March 15, 19X9, Miller Corporation paid a cash dividend of $8 per share.

(e) On June 30, 19X9, Miller Corporation paid a 20 percent stock dividend. The fair market value of Miller Corporation's stock on this date was $100 per share.

(f) On December 15, 19X9 Miller Corporation split its stock four for one.

(g) Net income for 19X9 was $2 million.

11-6. Interest Measurement and Liability Valuation. On January 1, 19X3, the Acme Manufacturing Company issued five-year bonds with a face value of $100,000 and a stated interest rate of 10 percent. On that date the market rate of interest was 9 percent, and the bonds were sold at a price equal to the present value of future payments discounted at 9 percent. Interest is payable on December 31 of each year.

Required:

1. Prepare a schedule to support the calculation of the amount that Acme received on January 1, 19X3. Write the journal entry to record the issue of the bonds.
2. Set up a bonds payable T-account and post the account to record the issue of the bonds. Calculate the annual interest expense and the carrying value of the liability at the end of each year over the life of the bonds. Prepare journal entries for annual interest payments and interest expense and for the final payment on the bonds, and post the changes in the liability to the T-account. Calculate the balance in the account and label it for each December 31.

11-7. Interest and Liability Valuation. Bonds with a face value of $50,000 were issued by a company on January 1, 19X1. The stated interest rate was 7 percent. However, the bonds sold for $46,269. Interest is paid annually on December 31. The bonds mature on December 31, 19X3 (three years after issue).

Required:

1. Determine the effective rate of interest at issuance of the bonds.
2. Prepare journal entries to recognize the issuance of the bonds, the annual interest expense, and annual cash payments for each year over the life of the bonds and the retirement of the bonds.
3. Set up a T-account for the bonds payable and record the effects of the above entries, noting the balance at each year-end.

11-8. Calculation of Selling Price of Bonds—Present Value Method. A company plans to sell $100,000 worth of bonds immediately. The stated interest rate of the bonds is 8 percent, and the bonds will mature in four years. Interest will be paid annually.

Required:

1. Calculate the selling price of the bonds, using the present value method for each of the following market (effective) rates of interest:
   (a) 6 percent
   (b) 8 percent
   (c) 10 percent
2. What is the relationship (greater than, equal to, or less than) between the market rate of interest and the stated rate of interest for each of the following situations?
   (a) Bonds are sold at a discount.
   (b) Bonds are sold at a premium.
   (c) Bonds are sold for face value.

11-9. Effective Interest Rates and Liability Valuation. On July 1, 19X2, Paymore Corporation sold 1,000 negotiable notes payable, each promising four annual payments of $300 beginning June 30, 19X3. The notes were sold to a major insurance company for $911,205.

Required:

1. Determine the effective rate of interest (to the nearest whole percent) on the notes.

2. Suppose that a particular pension fund had also been interested in buying the notes but had submitted a late bid. If the pension fund had offered an effective interest cost (rate) of 11 percent, would it have been willing to pay more or less for the notes than the insurance company? Explain your reasoning.

11-10. Interest Measurement and Liability Valuation. On December 31, 19X3, a company issued six-year bonds with a face value of $50,000. The stated interest rate was 9 percent; interest is payable on December 31 of each year. The market rate of interest was 10 percent, and the bonds were sold at a price equal to the present value of future payments discounted at the market rate of interest.

Required:

1. Calculate the selling price of the bonds.

2. Calculate the annual interest expense and carrying value of the liability at the end of each year over the life of the bonds.

11-11. Cash Dividends on Preferred and Common Stock. The Acorn Company was incorporated in 19X6. The company was authorized to issue 100,000 shares of $10 par-value common stock and 10,000 shares of 8 percent, *cumulative* preferred stock (par value $100).

In December 19X6 the company sold 10,000 shares of the common stock at a price of $15 per share and 1,000 shares of the preferred stock at par. Operations began in January 19X7.

Net income for 19X7, 19X8, and 19X9 was $30,000, $2,000, and $40,000, respectively.

The board of directors adopted the general dividend policy of paying out 50 percent of the net income for the year in dividends on December 31. This policy was followed in 19X7 and 19X9, but because of the low earnings in 19X8, dividends were not paid in that year.

Required:

1. Prepare a schedule that shows the following for each year of the three-year period:
   (a) Net income
   (b) Total dividends paid on preferred stock
   (c) Total dividends paid on common stock
   (d) Dividends paid per common share
   (e) Total owners' equity

2. Prepare the owners' equity section of the statement of financial position as of December 31, 19X9.

11-12. Owners' Equity—Statement Presentation. Prepare the owners' equity section of the statement of financial position as of December 31 from the following information:

Retained earnings at beginning of year	$1,209,000
Number of 8%, cumulative, $100 par-value preferred shares authorized	100,000
Premium on bonds payable at issue	$27,000
Total proceeds received from original issue of 100,000 common shares	$4,000,000
Net income for the year	$600,000
6% bonds payable, due at end of 19X0	$500,000
Number of no-par common shares authorized	1,000,000
Dividends in arrears at the beginning of the year	$100,000
Cost of treasury stock (1,000 common shares)	$35/share
Number of preferred shares issued (all at par)	20,000
Total amount of dividends on common shares declared on December 31 ($1/share)	$99,000
Stated value of no-par stock	$10/share

11-13. Retiring Debt before Maturity. Debtor Corporation issued 20-year bonds with an aggregate par value of $10 million on January 1, 19X1. The bonds pay 9 percent interest, or $900,000 each year on December 31. At the time the bonds were issued the market rate for bonds of equal risk was above 9 percent. That is, the proceeds from issuing the bonds were only $9.15 million, giving an effective interest rate of 10 percent.

By December 19X4 the market rate of interest was about 7 percent on bonds of equivalent risk to Debtor Corporation's bonds. A provision in the original bond indenture agreement provided that at any time after January 1, 19X4, but before maturity, the original bonds could be retired at 105 percent of par value. Management of Debtor Corporation is considering retiring the original bonds on January 1, 19X5, and reissuing on the same date $10 million in bonds paying 7 percent, or $700,000 annually (on December 31). The administrative costs of the retirement of the old bonds are expected to be about $300,000.

The management of Debtor Corporation has asked you to provide it with advice on this matter.

Required:

1. Assuming that Debtor Corporation can earn an average 12 percent return on assets employed in the business, should management retire the bonds? Support your position with appropriate calculations.

2. At what amount will the present bonds be recognized on the corporation's December 31, 19X4, balance sheet? How much expense will be recognized with respect to long-term debt in 19X4?

3. Assuming that the corporation *does not* retire and reissue the bonds, how much expense will be recognized with respect to the long-term debt in 19X5 and 19X6?

430 CHAPTER 11

4. Assuming that the corporation *does* retire the old bonds and reissue new ones on January 1, 19X5, what total effect on income (interest expense and gain or loss, if any) with respect to long-term debt will be recognized in 19X4, 19X5, and 19X6? Assume (*a*) that the new bonds are issued for net proceeds (after costs of issuing) equal to the par value of $10 million, and (*b*) that the cost of retiring the old bonds was $300,000, as expected. Is the contrast between this pattern of expense and the expense amounts called for in numbers 2 and 3 consistent with your answer to number 1?

11-14. Recognizing Changes in Owners' Equity. Below is the stockholders' equity section of the consolidated balance sheet presented in the 1977 annual report of Consolidated Freightways, Inc., and Subsidiaries. However, the 1977 balances in the stockholders' equity accounts have been removed. Following the statement segment is some additional information.

	1977	1976
Shareholders' Equity		
Preferred stock, no par value		
Authorized 5,000,000 shares; none issued	—	—
Common stock, $.625 par value		
Authorized 30,000,000 shares; issued 12,952,891		
and 12,815,916 shares, respectively	—	$ 8,010,000
Capital surplus [paid-in in excess of par]	—	44,647,000
Retained earnings ($99,022,000 available for dividends)	—	143,412,000
		$196,069,000
Less cost of reacquired common stock (455,144 shares)	—	2,875,000
Total shareholders' equity	?	$193,194,000

Additional information about 1977:
  a. Stock options were exercised during 1977 resulting in purchase by executives of 34,200 common shares for a total of $596,000. Assume that no previous paid-in capital had been recognized with respect to the options.
  b. Convertible notes payable in the amount of $1,843,000 were converted (exchanged for) 102,775 shares of common stock.
  c. Net income of $52,500,000 was recognized.
  d. Cash dividends of $10,836,000 were paid.

Required:

Based on the 1976 balances and the additional information, determine the end-of-1977 stockholders' equity account balances (to nearest $1,000).

11-15. Recognition of Stock Options and Compensation. On November 1, 19X2, Highflier Corporation put into effect a stock option for its executives. On December 31, 19X2, options for 40,000 shares of the company's $2 par-value common stock were granted to its executives. The options may be executed any time after December 31, 19X4, at a per-share purchase price of $25. The market value per share on December 31, 19X2, is $31. The board of directors intends the spread between the exercise price and the market value at date of grant to be additional compensation to the executives over the two-year eligibility period. All of the options are exercised during 19X5.

Required:

1. Calculate the total executive compensation expense to be recognized in connection with the options.

2. Prepare journal entries to record the granting of the options and the expense allocated to 19X3 and 19X4.

3. Make the journal entry to record the exercise of the option.

11-16. Recognizing Cash Dividends. On October 15, 19X3, Big Payout Company's board of directors declared a dividend of $1.10 per share for 19X3. The dividend is payable to stockholders of record on November 30, 19X3, and will be paid on December 15, 19X3. On November 30, 19X3, 453,000 shares were outstanding.

Required:

1. Write journal entries to record the declaration and payment of the dividend.

2. All other things being equal, what would probably happen to the price per share of the company's stock after November 30 relative to the price before that date? Explain your answer.

11-17. Cash Dividends, Stock Splits, and Stock Dividends. Following is the stockholders' equity section of the December 31, 19X7, statement of financial position of Wiltsie Corporation:

Common stock:		
$2 par-value stock:		
1,000,000 shares authorized		
547,000 shares issued	$1,094,000	
Paid-in capital in excess of par value	6,206,000	$ 7,300,000
Retained earnings		4,700,000
Total shareholders' equity		$12,000,000

Required:

1. Write journal entries (where applicable) to record each of the following events occurring during 19X8:
   (a) On April 1 Wiltsie declared a cash dividend of $1.30 per share which it paid on June 1 to stockholders of record on May 15.

(b) On July 1 the company split its stock two for one and reduced the par value to $1.
(c) On September 1 the company issued a 10 percent stock dividend. On that date the market value of the stock was $21 per share.
(d) Net income for the year was $1,310,000. (Assume that all individual expense and revenue accounts already have been closed to a single temporary account entitled "revenue and expense summary," whose balance equals net income.)
(e) On December 31 the company purchased 14,000 of its own previously issued shares "for the treasury" at $24 per share.

2. Based on the above events, prepare the stockholders' equity section of Wiltsie Corporation's 19X8 statement of financial position.

11-18. Effects of Changes in Owners' Equity. Exhibit 11-8 contains the statement of shareholders' equity from the 1977 annual report of Crown Zellerbach and Subsidiaries. Based on the information in the statement, satisfy the following requirements.

Required:

1. Approximately how many shares of common and preferred stock were outstanding in 1976 and 1977 on the dates of record for dividends?
2. Based on the information in the statement concerning retirements of preferred stock:
    (a) What is the par value per share of preferred stock (approximately)? Note that dollar amounts in the statement are in thousands.
    (b) At what average price per share was preferred stock retired in 1976? In 1977? (Note: no gain or loss is recognized on preferred-stock transactions. Differences between retirement price and par value are debited or credited to "other capital"—which in this case represents paid-in capital in excess of par value on both preferred and common stock).
    (c) What was the amount of proceeds (ignoring past compensation recognized) per share from exercise of stock options in 1976? In 1977?

11-19. Effective Interest and Liability Values. Exhibit 11-9 contains Note E accompanying the financial statements in the 1977 annual report of PACCAR, Inc., and Consolidated Subsidiaries. Based on the information in the note, satisfy the following requirements:

Required:

1. Based on the balances in long-term debt given in the table and the additional information given in Note E, what was the approximate average effective interest rate on all of PACCAR's long-term debt during 1977? (*Hint:* Recall how interest expense is calculated under the effective rate method.)
2. Given the beginning and ending balances of the mortgage notes payable in the table and the annual payment in the third paragraph below the table, how much apparent interest expense was recognized during 1977?

Exhibit 11-8

CROWN ZELLERBACH AND SUBSIDIARIES

Statement of Shareholders' Equity
(in thousands of dollars, except per share data)

	Cumulative Preferred Stock	Common Stock	Other Capital	Income Retained in the Business
Balances, January 1, 1976	$15,299	$124,822	$64,855	$576,655
Proceeds from sale of 38,000 common shares under option plans	—	190	888	—
Issuance of common shares by a subsidiary	—	—	(119)	—
Retirement of 6,223 shares of preferred stock	(622)	—	248	—
Net income	—	—	—	97,629
Cash dividends declared:				
On $4.20 cumulative preferred stock	—	—	—	(637)
On common stock, $1.80 per share	—	—	—	(44,703)
Other, net	—	43	66	426
Balances, December 31, 1976	14,677	125,055	65,938	629,370
Proceeds from sale of 29,200 common shares under option plans	—	146	678	—
Issuance of common shares by a subsidiary	—	—	(222)	—
Retirement of 14,167 shares of preferred stock	(1,417)	—	492	—
Net income	—	—	—	109,152
Cash dividends declared:				
On $4.20 cumulative preferred stock	—	—	—	(603)
On common stock, $1.85 per share	—	—	—	(46,312)
Other, net	—	—	58	—
Balances, December 31, 1977	$13,260	$125,201	$66,944	$691,607

433

3. What is the apparent effective interest rate on the mortgage notes assuming (*a*) that the annual payment was made at the beginning of the year, or (*b*) that the annual payment was made at the end of the year?

Exhibit 11-9

NOTE TO 1977 FINANCIAL STATEMENTS OF PACCAR, INC., AND CONSOLIDATED SUBSIDIARIES

Note E—Long-Term Debt

Long-term debt includes the following:

	December 31	
	1977	1976
	Thousands of Dollars	
8.10% Sinking Fund Debentures due 1966	$13,500	$14,250
Notes payable to banks by foreign subsidiaries	3,701	5,897
Mortgage notes payable	3,271	3,384
Other	510	1,110
Less installments classified as current liability	(1,074)	(1,604)
	$19,908	$23,037

The indenture for the 8.10% Sinking Fund Debentures requires that the Company shall provide for the retirement of $750,000 principal amount of debentures on March 1 in each of the years 1978 to 1995, inclusive, through a sinking fund. The 1978 retirement has already been made. Among other covenants, the indenture limits payments for cash dividends and redemption of capital stock to the sum of (a) consolidated net earnings (as defined) of the Company after December 31, 1970, (b) proceeds from sale of shares of the Company's capital stock, plus (c) $10,000,000. Under provisions of this agreement, $188,232,000 of retained earnings are available for cash dividends at December 31, 1977.

Notes payable to banks bear interest based on the banks' prime rates. The principal repayments are due evenly during the next five years.

The mortgage notes are principally comprised of a 6.875% note in the remaining amount of $3,234,000 which is payable in installments totaling $331,000 annually, including interest. The Company's headquarters building is mortgaged as collateral for this note.

The principal amounts due in each of the five years commencing January 1, 1978 are $1,074,000, $1,832,000, $1,772,000, $1,671,000, and $1,474,000, respectively.

Interest expense applicable to long-term debt was $2,054,000 in 1977 and $2,213,000 in 1976.

Valuation and Income: Some Further Issues | 12

The preceding four chapters focus on broadening the reader's awareness of actual situations with which an accounting model or policy must effectively deal. They concentrate on applying the principles of conventional accounting to the acknowledged varieties of situations within broad classes of transactions or elements of financial position; for example, in Chapters 8 and 9 the realization principle is applied to situations involving widely varying lags between productive activity and sale and between sale and cash collection. In this chapter still another alteration in the focus of discussion is employed to further broaden the reader's awareness of the present-day corporate reporting environment. We consider several significant and/or generally controversial issues concerning corporate financial statements: (1) accounting for income taxes, (2) accounting for long-term noncancelable leases, and (3) accounting for related companies.

Although these few additional issues are not the only significant issues not covered earlier, in two important respects they give excellent representation to the issues that have confronted policy makers in recent years. First, they are among the issues affecting the largest number of publicly owned companies. Second, they are among the most widely studied and debated—and in some cases the most difficult to resolve—of recent corporate reporting problems.

ACCOUNTING FOR INCOME TAXES

Accountants generally agree that income taxes are genuine expenses of doing business for any enterprise whose income is subject to tax. But income tax expense is incurred or levied in a way that is unique among all the expenses incurred by business enterprises. As a result, there is some ambiguity as to how income tax expense ought to be matched against revenues (i.e., in what periods and in what amounts).

Income Tax Assessments: Some Basics

In the United States the federal income tax is levied on taxable income *as defined by the Internal Revenue Code.*

At this writing, the corporate income tax rate structure (which has been changed several times in recent years) is as follows:

Rate	*Taxable Income*
17%	First $25,000
20	$25,000–$50,000
30	$50,000–$75,000
40	$75,000–$100,000
46	Over $100,000

Conventional Accounting Basis. Taxable income, as defined by the Internal Revenue Code, is largely based on conventional accounting principles. As a general rule, taxable income is based on the difference between revenue realized and the original cost of resources used to produce the revenue of the period. However, certain kinds of revenue (e.g., a portion of the dividends received by a corporation due to investment in the common stock of another corporation) and certain kinds of expenses (e.g., "excessive" business entertainment expenses) are not included in taxable income as a matter of national tax policy (but *not* because they are not genuine items of revenue and expense in an accounting sense).

Thus, with the exception of certain kinds of revenue and expense that are systematically (and permanently) excluded from the calculation of taxable income, taxable income tends to be approximately equal to before-tax conventional accounting income *over the whole life of the enterprise.* However, the emphasis on the "whole-life" equality of taxable income and before-tax conventional accounting income is important. Differences in measurement rules selected for accounting and tax assessment purposes mean that in any given period, taxable income will probably differ from before-tax accounting income—often by a substantial amount.

Differences in Measurement Rules and Timing. Although both before-tax conventional accounting income and taxable income are based on the same general principles (i.e., realization, matching, and original transaction cost valuation), they both allow some latitude in selection of the measurement rules used to implement those principles in a given situation. Furthermore, with few exceptions an enterprise need not select the same measurement rule for tax accounting purposes that is selected for financial accounting purposes. Exhibit 12-1 shows some of the alternative measurement rules possible under the Internal Revenue Code. Chapters 8-11 have already acquainted the reader with the various alternatives that may be employed in conventional financial accounting.

Exhibit 12-1

SELECTED CATEGORIES OF ALTERNATIVE MEASUREMENT RULES PERMISSIBLE UNDER THE INTERNAL REVENUE CODE

Revenue Recognition	
Installment sales method	
Recognition in period of sale	

Inventory (Cost of Sales) Valuation	*Depreciation Expense*
Specific identification	Straight-line
Fifo	Sum-of-years-digits
Lifo*	Declining-balance

*Lifo is an exception to the general rule that different measurement rules may be selected for tax and financial accounting purposes. Only those enterprises that adopt Lifo for financial accounting purposes may use Lifo for determining their taxable income.

Except in those cases where the Internal Revenue Code does not allow a measurement rule that is permissible under conventional accounting, *there is no reason why taxable income must necessarily be different from before-tax conventional accounting income* (allowing for the items permanently excluded from taxable income). Indeed, if the same measurement rules are adopted for both purposes, the numbers will be the same (again, allowing for permanently excluded items in the tax calculations). However, as a general rule, the measurement rules selected for financial accounting and tax purposes will not necessarily be the same. The reason is that two different purposes motivate their selection. For financial accounting purposes, the selection of measurement rules is dominated by the intent to best represent the financial status and activities of the enterprise within the framework of conventional accounting. For tax purposes, wherever a choice is available, the objective in selecting a measurement rule is to optimize the financial effects (the amount and timing) of the taxes that the enterprise will have to pay.

Example 12-1

Vending Machine Company owns and operates a large number of vending machines. The company buys a completely new supply of machines every three years from the manufacturer, who allows 40 percent of the original cost of three-year-old machines as a trade-in allowance on new machines. The company purchased its first set of machines in

19X1 for $1 million. All of its sales are for cash, and all expenses incurred other than depreciation are cash expenditures at the time incurred (for both tax purposes and accounting purposes). The supplies in the company's vending machines are the property of the suppliers, who bill the company only for the supplies sold. The company's sales for *each* of its first three years of operations were $1 million for both financial accounting and tax purposes. Expenses other than depreciation for both purposes were $600,000 each year. However, the company determined its depreciation on a straight-line basis for financial accounting purposes and on a sum-of-years-digits basis for tax purposes. Thus the company's before-tax financial accounting income and taxable income for 19X1–X3 were as shown in Exhibit 12-2.

Exhibit 12-2
VENDING MACHINE COMPANY

Comparative Income Statements
19X1–19X3

Before-Tax Financial Accounting Income

	19X1	19X2	19X3	Total
Revenues	$1,000,000	$1,000,000	$1,000,000	$3,000,000
Less expenses:				
Depreciation	200,000	200,000	200,000	600,000
Other expense	600,000	600,000	600,000	1,800,000
Before-tax income	$ 200,000	$ 200,000	$ 200,000	$ 600,000

Taxable Income

	19X1	19X2	19X3	Total
Revenues	$1,000,000	$1,000,000	$1,000,000	$3,000,000
Less expenses:				
Depreciation	300,000	200,000	100,000	600,000
Other expense	600,000	600,000	600,000	1,800,000
Taxable income	$ 100,000	$ 200,000	$ 300,000	$ 600,000

Two Sets of Books? Several aspects of Exhibit 12-2 are worth noting. For one thing, the before-tax financial accounting income and the taxable income calculations agree *in total* for the three years. This will usually be the case except for (allowing for) items permanently excluded from the tax calculations. The two income calculations differ only in the amounts of expense (depreciation) and income recognized *in the individual years*.

Another important observation is that Exhibit 12-2 illustrates the phenomenon of having "two sets of books" for the same set of facts. Although this phenomenon is often thought of by laypersons as being "shady" or dishonest, there is nothing illegal, immoral, or unethical in having separate records for financial and tax purposes—as long as all the revenue and expenses recognized under the Internal Revenue Code are accounted for according to permissible measurement rules in the enterprise's tax calculations.

In fact, the management of an enterprise has an obligation to act in its shareholders' interests. With respect to income taxes, this generally means payment of no more taxes than necessary and no sooner than necessary.

Example 12-2

In the case of Vending Machine Company, management had a choice between using straight-line or sum-of-years-digits depreciation for tax purposes. Tax calculations under the two methods (assuming a tax rate of 46 percent) are shown in Exhibit 12-3. Notice that the sum of the three-year tax bill is the same under each alternative. However, under the S-Y-D depreciation alternative, less tax is paid initially and more is paid later. Because money has a time value, such postponement is in the interest of the enterprise and therefore its owners.

Income Taxes and Matching

As noted above, selection of the best measurement rules for financial accounting and tax purposes, respectively, often means that before-tax financial accounting income will differ from taxable income. Although there is nothing morally wrong with this divergence (and, indeed, it may be the only way to serve the interests to which management is responsible), it creates a certain ambiguity as to how income tax expense ought to be recognized.

Exhibit 12-3

VENDING MACHINE COMPANY

Comparative Income Tax Calculations

	19X1	19X2	19X3
S-L Depreciation:			
Taxable income (see before-tax financial accounting income in Exhibit 12–2)	$200,000	$200,000	$200,000
Income tax at 46% of taxable income	92,000	92,000	92,000
S-Y-D Depreciation:			
Taxable income (from Exhibit 12–2)	$100,000	$200,000	$300,000
Income tax at 46%	46,000	92,000	138,000

Income Taxes as Period Costs. Some accountants argue that income taxes are assessed and payable according to the taxable income of a given period (as defined by the set of permissible measurement rules adopted by the enterprise). As such they are inherently period costs. Under this interpretation, the income tax expense recognized in a given period is equal to the amount of tax calculated on the taxable income of that period (though it may be paid in part after the start of the next period). However, many accountants object in principle to the effect on after-tax accounting income of this interpretation. To illustrate, Exhibit 12-4 shows the after-tax financial accounting net income for Vending Machine Company based on the facts originally given in Example

12-1 and assuming that income tax expense equals income taxes paid or payable for the year based on sum-of-years-digits depreciation.

Exhibit 12-4

VENDING MACHINE COMPANY

After-Tax Income
19X1-19X3

	19X1	19X2	19X3
Before-tax accounting income (based on S-L depreciation)	$200,000	$200,000	$200,000
Income tax expense (based on S-Y-D depreciation)	46,000	92,000	138,000
After-tax accounting income	$154,000	$108,000	$ 62,000

Income Taxes Matched Against Related Revenue and Expense. Critics of the period-cost interpretation of income taxes are uneasy with the disparity in the pattern between before-tax and after-tax income that can occur under the period-cost approach illustrated by Exhibit 12-4. They argue that income taxes are a function of the revenues and expenses of the enterprise. Income tax expense should therefore be recognized (for financial accounting purposes) in the period in which the revenues and expenses giving rise to the taxes are recognized for financial accounting purposes. *The timing of recognition of those same revenues and expenses for tax purposes is relevant only insofar as it determines when income taxes actually become payable.* Implementation of the matching of income tax expense with the related revenues and expenses requires a (minor) complication in accounting for the enterprise called "interperiod tax allocation."

Interperiod Tax Allocation Illustrated. Perhaps the most straightforward approach to introducing the reader to interperiod income tax allocation is by means of an illustration. We take this approach, using the example below. However, we restrict ourselves to the one method (the deferral method) for tax allocation that is supported by the authority of the APB (whose opinions prevail until the FASB supersedes them). There are other methods, but a discussion of their advantages and disadvantages relative to the deferred method is best left to more advanced texts.

Example 12-3

In earlier examples and exhibits we noted that for Vending Machine Company, before-tax income based on straight-line depreciation was $200,000 in 19X1, 19X2, and 19X3 (Exhibit 12-2). Also, the assumed income tax rate was 46 percent (Example 12-2). This implies that to be matched properly with related revenue and expense of the period, the company's income tax expense should be $92,000 in each of the years (i.e., 46 percent of $200,000). On the other hand, we noted that with taxable income based on sum-of-years-digits depreciation, the actual assessed taxes (taxes payable) for the three years were $46,000, $92,000, and $138,000, respectively. The T-accounts in Exhibit 12-5

Exhibit 12-5
VENDING MACHINE COMPANY

General Ledger Accounts
19X1, 19X2, and 19X3
(amounts in thousands)

ASSETS

Cash

19X1			
Sales	1,000	600	Expenses
		46	Tax payment (2)
19X2			
Beginning balance	400	600	Expenses
Sales	1,000	92	Tax payment (4)
19X3			
Beginning balance	754	600	Expenses
Sales	1,000		
	1,062		

Vending Machines

19X1			
Beginning balance	1,000		
19X2			
Beginning balance	1,000		
19X3			
Beginning balance	1,000		
	1,000		

Accumulated Depreciation

		19X1
	200	Depreciation expense
		19X2
	200	Beginning balance
	200	Depreciation expense
		19X3
	400	Beginning balance
	200	Depreciation expense
	600	

LIABILITIES AND OWNERS' EQUITY

Taxes Payable

			19X1
		46	Tax payable (1)
			19X1
(2) Payment	46	46	Beginning balance
		92	Tax payable (3)
			19X3
(4) Payment	92	92	Beginning balance
		138	Tax payable (5)
		138	

Deferred Income Tax Liability

			19X1
		46	Deferred tax (1)
			19X2
		46	Beginning balance
			19X3
(5) Tax expense	46	46	Beginning balance
	-0-		

Owners' Equity

			19X1
		1,000	Beginning balance
		1,000	Sales
Expenses	600		
Depreciation expense	200		
(1) Tax expense	92		
			19X2
		1,108	Beginning balance
		1,000	Sales
Expenses	600		
Depreciation expense	200		
(3) Tax expense	92		
			19X3
		1,216	Beginning balance
		1,000	Sales
Expenses	600		
Depreciation expense	200		
(5) Tax expense	92		
		1,324	

show how we handle the seemingly divergent schedule of taxes payable and the desired schedule of income tax expense in a consistent manner for all three years. The entries are based on the additional assumptions that (1) the company started 19X1 with $1 million of vending machines as the only assets, and (2) each year's taxes payable are paid at the beginning of the following year. (In actual practice, taxes payable would be estimated and paid quarterly.) Also, for simplicity, we do not use temporary accounts for revenues and expenses but rather make direct entries to "owners' equity." Notice that several entries to the accounts in Exhibit 12-5 are the same in each year because the underlying facts are identical. The journal entries corresponding to these repetitive items are as follows:

Cash	1,000,000	
Owners' equity		1,000,000
(To record revenue from sales)		

Owners' equity	600,000	
Cash		600,000
(To record out-of-pocket expenses)		

Owners' equity	200,000	
Accumulated depreciation		200,000
(To record depreciation expense)		

The nonrepetitive entries for the three years all involve the recognition of income tax expense or the payment of the related (but not identical) tax liabilities. The postings of these entries to the T-accounts are numbered to correspond to the following numbered journal entries:

19X1

(1) Owners' equity (income tax expense)	92,000	
Taxes payable		46,000
Deferred income tax liability		46,000
To record 19X1 income tax expense		

19X2

(2) Taxes payable	46,000	
Cash		46,000
To record payment of 19X1 income tax		

19X2

(3) Owners' equity (income tax expense)   92,000
       Taxes payable   92,000
          To record 19X2 income tax expense

19X3

(4) Taxes payable   92,000
       Cash   92,000
          To record payment of 19X2 income tax

(5) Owners' equity (income tax expense)   92,000
     Deferred income tax liability   46,000
       Taxes payable   138,000
          To record 19X3 income tax expense

The key feature of the deferral method of recognizing income tax expense as illustrated above and in Exhibit 12-5 is the use of the account "deferred income tax liability." It is used to coordinate the desired level of income tax expense determined by the level of before-tax *accounting* income with the level of currently payable taxes determined by *taxable* income. For instance, in 19X1, with $200,000 before-tax income, the income tax expense recognized is $92,000. However, the then-current tax liability is only $46,000 because the S-Y-D depreciation used to calculate taxable income is $100,000 greater than the S-L depreciation used for before-tax accounting income in that year. But it is known that in some future period (in this case 19X3) the relationship will reverse because the lifetime depreciation of the assets (and hence, lifetime income) must be equal under the two depreciation methods. Thus the difference between the income tax expense recognized in 19X1 and the tax that must be paid for 19X1 *will presumably be paid in some future period* (in this case 19X3). For 19X1 the debit to owners' equity of $92,000 for income tax expense is therefore offset by a credit to the current liability "taxes payable" of $46,000 and a credit of $46,000 to the "deferred income tax liability" (see journal entry (1) above).

In 19X2 the before-tax accounting income and taxable income are equal by coincidence, meaning no further deferral is necessary in that year. The recognition of income tax expense by a debit of $92,000 to the owners' equity account is offset by an equal credit to taxes (currently) payable (see entry (3)). In 19X3, when the reversal in the relationship between accounting and tax depreciation takes place, the $138,000 taxes payable exceeds the appropriate expense of $92,000 by precisely the $46,000 that was deferred in 19X1. Thus in recognizing the 19X3 current tax liability and expense, the deferral is reversed (see entry (5)).

As a result of the strong stand taken by the APB favoring income tax allocation according to the deferral method, the method is widely adopted in practice. A reader of financial statements will frequently see deferred tax liabilities in published financial statements. Furthermore, the treatment of income tax expense will often resemble the treatment shown in Exhibit 12-6 based on the Vending Machine Company example.

Exhibit 12-6

VENDING MACHINE COMPANY

After-Tax Income Calculations
For the Years 19X1, 19X2, and 19X3

	19X1	19X2	19X3
Before-tax income	$200,000	$200,000	$200,000
Less income tax expense:			
Currently payable	46,000	92,000	138,000
Increase (decrease) in deferred tax liability	46,000	-0-	(46,000)
Income tax expense	$ 92,000	$ 92,000	$ 92,000
After-tax income	$108,000	$108,000	$108,000

ACCOUNTING FOR LONG-TERM NONCANCELABLE LEASES

A business enterprise requiring certain long-lived assets for its operations can usually acquire and finance their acquisition in a number of different ways. One way is to rent available assets on a period-by-period basis. A great advantage of such short-term rental arrangements is that at any one time the enterprise only has to pay for a fraction of the service potential of an essentially large, indivisible resource. A major disadvantage is the possible lack of availability of suitable assets or the abrupt withdrawal by the owner of assets currently in use. Furthermore, assets rented on a short-term basis may have a higher cost due to the owner's risk that the renter may also abruptly discontinue renting.

Another way to acquire resources, of course, is by outright purchase. Through ownership, the enterprise assures itself of an ample and relatively more certain supply. But ownership of long-lived assets also requires the commitment of considerably more of the enterprise's money capital or greater risk to owners due to financing the purchase through additional debt. Ownership also carries with it the additional risk that the economic life (usefulness) of the assets may end abruptly due to obsolescence, malfunction, or excessive maintenance costs.

In between the extremes of acquiring long-lived assets by outright purchase and acquiring their use on a strictly period-by-period basis is a spectrum of arrangements that we will refer to as long-term noncancelable leases. A long-term noncancelable lease is a contract between a lessor (owner) who agrees to provide use of the assets for a specified number of periods and a lessee (renter) who agrees to pay a specified schedule of rent payments in exchange. To the lessor a long-term noncancelable lease represents insurance against lack of demand; to the lessee it is insurance against lack of supply. This is so because neither party can unilaterally fail to perform without being held liable for damages to the other. On the other hand, a long-term noncancelable lease is usually an *executory contract,* meaning that although neither party is free to withdraw, if one party does fail to perform its contractual obligation, the other party need not continue to perform as agreed.

Most accountants would concur, in principle at least, as to the recognition to be given to the various expenses, revenues, assets, and liabilities involved in an outright purchase or in short-term rental of assets by one entity from another. Such arrangements for acquiring and using long-lived assets have not usually presented controversial problems to accounting policy makers. Long-term noncancelable leases, on the other hand, present a perplexing problem due to uncertainty (and resultant disagreement) about their nature—particularly relative to other means of acquiring the services of long-lived assets. Those who see long-term noncancelable leases as more similar to outright purchases (sales) of assets advocate one kind of accounting treatment. And those who see long-term noncancelable lease agreements as more similar to period-by-period rental of assets advocate another kind of treatment.

The Capitalization-Financing (Purchase-Sale) Treatment of Leases

The Lessee. In a sense, a long-term noncancelable lease may be likened to the purchase of an asset by the lessee (the asset being *the rights* to a number of periods of service). The seller (lessor) extends credit to the buyer, with the purchased asset as security (meaning, if the buyer defaults on the payments, the seller may repossess the asset and resell or rerent it to satisfy the uncollected balance of the original lease agreement). In cases where the above analogy applies, the long-term noncancelable lease agreements should be recognized by the lessee as liabilities in a manner consistent with other long-term debt. As described in Chapter 11, this involves recognizing the present value of the contractual lease payments as a liability at the time the lease agreement is entered upon. It also involves recognizing at the same time the related asset received in exchange for that liability, that is, the rights to use the leased assets for the full term of the lease—also at the discounted present value of the lease payments. Thereafter, the expense to the lessee of using the leasehold assets is recognized in the form of amortization (depreciation) of the initial asset value over the term of the lease. In addition, but independent of the actual consumption of the inherent service potential of the leased assets, interest expense is recognized each period on the present value of the remaining lease payments. Accountants commonly refer to this total treatment of leases by the lessee under the single term *capitalization* because it requires that the lease payments be discounted or "capitalized" in order to value the lease liability and related asset initially.

The Lessor. If a particular lease is judged essentially an installment sale, it should be recognized by the lessor as such, that is, in the manner described in Chapter 9. This means that in the period that the lease agreement is consummated, the present value of the lease payments is recognized as revenue, and the unexpired cost (adjusted for any expected salvage or residual market value at the end of the lease term) of the leased asset is recognized as expense (cost of sales). In implementing such recognition of revenue and expense at the consummation of the lease, the lessor recognizes a new asset, "lease payments receivable," valued at the present value of the lease payments, in place of the cost of the leased assets that is expensed (cost of sales). During the term of the lease, the "lease receivable" balance is reduced in each accounting period by any payments received from the lessee and increased by interest on the present value of the remaining payments, the interest being recognized as additional (financing-type) income from the lease in that period. This method of handling the financial effects of the lease by the lessor is referred to as the *financing method* because it follows from the conclusion that the lessor has in effect sold the assets to the lessee and "financed" the purchase for the lessee by extending long-term credit.

The Capitalization-financing Treatment Illustrated. Since the capitalization approach for the lessee and the financing approach for the lessor are basically the same approach, they can be illustrated by a single example.

Example 12-4

Slammer Stamping Company has just entered into a six-year lease agreement with Elipse Equipment Company. According to the lease agreement, Elipse will provide Slammer for a six-year period with certain heavy equipment that Elipse manufactures. Slammer in turn has agreed to payments of $300,000 at the end of each of the six years. Neither party may cancel or fail to perform any of the terms of the lease without the consent of the other. The retail price of the rights to use of the equipment acquired by Slammer is $1,233,422. Based on this price, the effective interest rate (the rate at which the present value of the set of lease payments approximates the value received) is 12 percent, which is also equal to the market rate of interest for secured loans of risk equal to the lease agreement.

Assuming that Slammer recognized the lease rights as an asset and the lease obligation as a liability at the time of signing the lease, and assuming that the company felt that straight-line amortization (depreciation) of the asset was appropriate, all of the financial accounting effects of capitalizing the lease agreement over its six-year life may be summarized as in Exhibit 12-7.

The journal entries to record in Slammer's accounts (*a*) the acquisition of the equipment, (*b*) the first year's amortization, (*c*) the first year's interest expense, and (*d*) the first year's lease payment are as follows:

(a)	Leased equipment	1,233,422	
	Long-term lease liability		1,233,422
(b)	Amortization expense	205,570	
	Leased equipment		205,570
(c)	Interest expense	148,011	
	Long-term lease liability		148,011
(d)	Long-term lease liability	300,000	
	Cash		300,000

Looking at Exhibit 12-7, several important relationships are worth noting. First, the initial value of both the liability and the asset recognized, $1,233,422,

Exhibit 12-7
SLAMMER STAMPING COMPANY   Lease-Related Asset, Liability, and Expense—Capitalization Treatment

	Asset and Related Expense		Liability and Related Expense				Total Expense
Year	Amortization Expense	Year-end Balance	Beginning Liability Balance	Add 12% Interest Expense	Less Lease Payment	Year-end Liability Balance	Amortization plus Interest
Lease signed		$1,233,422				$1,233,422	
1	$ 205,570	1,027,852	$1,233,422	$148,011	$ 300,000	$1,081,433	$ 353,581
2	205,570	822,282	1,081,433	129,772	300,000	911,205	335,342
3	205,570	616,712	911,205	109,344	300,000	720,549	314,914
4	205,570	411,142	720,549	86,466	300,000	507,015	292,036
5	205,571	205,571	507,015	60,842	300,000	267,857	266,413
6	205,571	–0–	267,857	32,143	300,000	–0–	237,714
	$1,233,422			$566,578	$1,800,000		$1,800,000

is equal to the discounted value of the lease payments at the effective interest rate of 12 percent. Thereafter the asset value is adjusted downward by the amount of amortization expense recognized each year—just as would happen with any long-lived intangible asset with a specific life expectancy (see Chapter 10). Likewise, the balance of the liability is increased by the amount of interest expense recognized each year and is reduced by the amount of the annual payment—just as would happen with any long-term liability (see Chapter 11).

Second, during the term of the lease while

1. substantial assets are in use in the business, and
2. Slammer Stamping is under a substantial obligation to Elipse Equipment, these conditions are represented in the financial position (balance sheet) of the company as an asset and a liability, respectively.

Furthermore, they appear in magnitudes approximating those that would appear if Slammer had acquired the same rights by purchase and financed the purchase with a secured loan involving an identical schedule of payments.

Third, the sum of the amortization plus interest expense recognized over the six-year term (see the last column of Exhibit 12-7) equals the total of the lease payments (see the Less Lease Payment column). Therefore the capitalization method may be thought of as one way to allocate the total cost of leasing the equipment to the various periods in the life of the lease. As is customary in financial accounting, the portion of this total cost that is related to the use of the resource in operations (amortization) is separated from the portion that is related to financing the acquisition of the resource (interest).

Example 12-5

Now assume also that the lease is judged to be an installment sale (in effect) from the point of view of Elipse. Suppose further that Elipse's cost to manufacture the leased assets had been $1 million and Elipse expects zero recoverable (salvage) value after six years. The equipment was recognized at the $1 million cost in Elipse's financial position at the time the lease agreement was consummated. Elipse now recognizes a lease receivable from Slammer equal to the discounted value of the lease payments, $1,233,422, and includes that amount in its revenue immediately. At the same time the cost of the leased assets, $1 million, is expensed, and the assets themselves no longer appear in the company's financial position. The difference between the present value of the lease payments and the cost of the leased assets, $233,422, is recognized in full as income in the period of inception of the lease. In addition, interest income will be recognized each year. For convenience, it may be assumed that Elipse recognizes the same balance of lease receivable and interest income that Slammer recognizes as its liability balance and interest expense, respectively. Thus, from the Interest Expense column of Exhibit 12-7 we see that Elipse has interest income of $148,011 in year one, $129,772 in year two, and so forth. A schedule showing the lease receivable balance, interest income, and so forth, that are recognized by Elipse according to the financing method appears in Exhibit 12-8.

The following journal entries recognize (a) the delivery (sale) of the right to the equipment to Slammer, (b) the cost of the equipment as an expense associated with the sale, (c) the first year's interest income on the lease receivable, and (d) the first year's payment from Slammer:

Exhibit 12-8

ELIPSE EQUIPMENT COMPANY

Lease-Related Asset and Income
Financing Treatment

Year	Beginning Receivable Balance	Add 12% Interest Income	Less Lease Payment	Year-end Receivable Balance
1	$1,233,422	$148,011	$ 300,000	$1,081,433
2	1,081,433	129,772	300,000	911,205
3	911,205	109,344	300,000	720,549
4	720,549	86,466	300,000	507,015
5	507,015	60,842	300,000	267,857
6	267,857	32,143	300,000	-0-
Total		$566,578	$1,800,000	
Income recognized at time lease is signed		233,422		
Total income		$800,000		

(a)	Lease payments receivable	1,233,422	
	Revenue		1,233,422
(b)	Cost of equipment sold (under lease)	1,000,000	
	Manufactured equipment		1,000,000
(c)	Lease payments receivable	148,011	
	Interest income		148,011
(d)	Cash	300,000	
	Lease payments receivable		300,000

Exhibit 12-8 makes several important points in connection with the financing treatment of leases by the lessor. First, the financing method for the lessor is analogous to the capitalization treatment for the lessee.

Second, under the financing method the treatment of the lease is the same as the sale-with-financing method for dealing with any long-term installment sales contract. That is, initially a receivable is recognized at the present value of the set of payments to be received in the future. Thereafter the receivable is increased by the amount of interest income recognized in each period (at the original effective rate) and reduced by payments received.

Third, the total income from the lease recognized over its entire term is equal to the sum of the income recognized in the period of inception plus all the interest on the lease receivable recognized period by period. In the above example, this total is equal to $233,422, income recognized at the time the lease is signed, plus $566,578, the sum of the Interest Income column of Exhibit 12-8. The sum of these two amounts, $800,000, is also equal to the difference between the sum of the six lease payments, $1.8 million, and the cost of manufacturing the equipment, $1 million. The financing method is therefore one means of allocating this total income (difference) to the periods in the total life of the lease.

The Short-Term Rental or "Operating" Treatment of Leases

Most accountants would agree that when a lease *is* in substance an installment sale for a lessor or an installment purchase for a lessee, the financing-capitalization treatment is appropriate. If the lease is not in substance a sale (purchase), the appropriate accounting method is called the "operating method" (traditionally, the term has been applied only to the lessor, but we will use it for both). Under the operating method, the rent paid by the lessee is recognized as expense by the lessee and revenue by the lessor in the period for which it covers occupancy or use of the assets by the lessee according to the rental agreement. The leased assets continue to be recognized in the financial position of the lessor at their unexpired cost, reduced each period by the depreciation charges that are matched against the recognized rental revenue. No assets (except perhaps some prepaid rent) or liabilities are recognized in connection with the lease by the lessee.

Example 12-6

Suppose that the Slammer-Elipse lease was judged not to be a sale (purchase). Suppose further that it was considered appropriate for Elipse to depreciate the leased assets on a sum-of-years-digits basis over the six-year term of the lease and that no salvage value was expected. The schedule of rent expense for Slammer and the schedules of (1) the declining unexpired leased asset balance, (2) the depreciation expense, (3) the rental revenue, and (4) the rental income that would be recognized by Elipse over the term of the lease, according to the operating method, appear in Exhibit 12-9.

Unlike the capitalization-financing method, the operating method does not call for any recognition of the signing of the lease or delivery of the equipment in the accounts of either the lessor or the lessee. Instead the lessee, Slammer, merely recognizes each annual rent payment as rent expense for the year:

Rent expense	300,000	
Cash		300,000

Elipse correspondingly recognizes lease revenue in the amount of the payment received each year and matches the related depreciation expense on the equipment against the lease revenue. For the first year of the lease the entries are as follows:

Cash	300,000	
Lease revenue		300,000
Depreciation expense	285,714	
Accumulated depreciation		285,714

Exhibit 12-9

THE SLAMMER STAMPING-ELIPSE EQUIPMENT LEASE—OPERATING METHOD

Slammer Stamping (Lessee)		Elipse Equipment (Lessor)			
Year	Rent Expense	Year-end Balance Leased Assets	S-Y-D Depreciation	Rental Revenue	Rental Income
Lease signed		$1,000,000			
1	$ 300,000	714,286	$ 285,714	$ 300,000	$ 14,286
2	300,000	476,190	238,096	300,000	61,904
3	300,000	285,714	190,476	300,000	109,524
4	300,000	142,857	142,857	300,000	157,143
5	300,000	47,619	95,238	300,000	204,762
6	300,000	-0-	47,619	300,000	252,381
Total	$1,800,000		$1,000,000	$1,800,000	$800,000

Two important observations about the contrast between the schedules in Exhibit 12-9 and those appearing in Exhibits 12-7 and 12-8 should be noted. First, the total income recognized by the lessor (Elipse) over the term of the lease is the same under both the financing and the operating treatment. But the timing and nature of the amounts recognized in each period differ. This illustrates the notion that the financing and operating methods are two alternative ways of allocating total income from the lease to the various periods in the life of the lease. Second, the nature and the amount of the lease-related asset recognized under the two methods differ. Under the financing method, the leased assets are considered to have been exchanged by the lessor for another asset, "lease payments receivable," in a *bona fide* exchange transaction.

In the case of the lessee (Slammer) the schedule of rent expense (paid) is all that is necessary under the operating method, whereas the capitalization method required the recognition of the leasehold asset and related amortization expense along with the lease liability and related interest expense. Again it is important to recognize that the sum of the periodic amortization and interest expenses recognized by the lessee under the capitalization treatment is equal to the sum of the periodic rent expense that would be recognized under the operating method, illustrating that the two methods represent alternative ways to allocate life-time cost to the periods in the life of the lease.

Accounting for Leases: Positions and Controversies

For the sake of the illustration above, we have simply assumed that it was appropriate to apply either the capitalization-financing method or the operating method to a given situation. However, the two alternative accounting methods (when applied to a given situation) can produce substantially different revenue, expense, asset, and liability recognition period by period for both the lessor and the lessee. This naturally poses the question, Which of the two methods is better? Unfortunately, opinions differ. Until recently a view that we characterize as the "situational" view has predominated practice. However, accounting for leases by both lessors and lessees has often been under fire in recent years from virtually all quarters which have a substantial interest in financial reporting practice.

The Situational Point of View. The situational point of view is oriented toward deciding which treatment ought to be accorded a given lease based on the facts in the individual case. The selection of method depends both on the terms of the lease and whether the choice of accounting method is being made for a lessor or a lessee. (The treatment of a given lease can differ for the lessor and the lessee under the situational point of view.)

Sale or "No Sale." Since the choice of the financing method or operating method on the part of the lessor determines whether or not revenue will be recognized immediately or postponed to the periods of collection of the lease payments, *the appropriate criterion is the realization principle.* Applying the situational point of view means that if the lease payments can be considered "realized" at the inception of a given lease, the financing method is appropriate. If the lease payments cannot be considered "realized" at the outset, the operating method is appropriate.

Basically, the same conditions are necessary for realization in the case of leases as in the case of any other transaction. The agreed-to payments (1) must be reasonably certain with respect to ultimate collection, and (2) further efforts (costs) required to "earn" the payments must be relatively minor and must be reasonably predictable at the inception of the lease. The second condition will not ordinarily hold for lease agreements under which the lessor agrees to cover highly uncertain future costs (i.e., unspecified as to amount) associated with the leased assets, such as maintenance costs. The first condition will not ordinarily hold for lease agreements under which the lessor continues to bear most of the risk of ownership of the leased assets, for example, if the lessor agrees to guarantee that the assets will not become obsolete during the term of the lease.

In the past critics of accounting practices of lessors generally have not taken exception to the situational point of view in principle. Instead they point out that too frequently lessors interpreted their situations with unwarranted optimism, with the result that many lease agreements were treated as "sales" which did not seem to warrant such treatment when subjected to close scrutiny. Understandably, then, recent pronouncements of accounting policy makers (the FASB) have been very detailed and explicit as to the terms and characteristics of lease agreements that do and do not qualify them for treatment as sale transactions.

The Situational Point of View Applied to Lessees. The situational view is the view represented by the past authoritative pronouncements emanating from the accounting profession on accounting for long-term leases by lessees. For instance, the Accounting Principles Board expressed the view that long-term noncancelable leases do not constitute liabilities (or assets) *per se.* If circumstances indicate that a given lease *is in substance an installment purchase* of assets, capitalization is warranted. Otherwise, no long-term liability or related asset is recognized in connection with the lease. Instead, the basic condition of any significant lease agreement, including information about the required future payments, is to be disclosed in a footnote to the financial statements. Rent payments (the only effects of such leases that actually appear in the financial statements themselves) are recognized as expenses in the periods for which they cover occupancy according to the lease.

Naturally, the question of when a lease is "in substance a purchase" is open to judgment. Since judgments can and do differ about the same sets of facts, the FASB has set forth certain arbitrary criteria, any one of which, if met by a given lease, requires that the lease be accounted for as a "capital lease" (in our terms, a lease that is in substance a purchase). All such leases must be accorded capitalization treatment as described above. An example of the FASB's criteria is the presence in the lease of "a bargain purchase option." Presumably, such a criterion implies that payments required in the lease agreement tend to buy more rights than just the service of the leased assets period by period during the initial term of the lease and therefore warrant capitalization and recognition as an asset from the inception of the lease.

Critics of the situational point of view for lessee accounting typically disagree that such arbitrary conditions are necessary in order for capitalization of leases by lessees to be warranted. They argue that under a long-term noncancelable lease, the lessee is obligated to a greater extent than in a short-term rental arrangement, since upon failure to pay the contractual rent payment (as opposed to not renewing a short-term rental arrangement) the lessee would not only give up the use of the leased assets but also be liable for damages (possibly up to or exceeding the unpaid rent). It is in this respect that all long-term noncancelable leases are similar to long-term liabilities incurred to finance the purchase of assets. Hence the accountants who take this view conclude that all long-term noncancelable leases should be treated in a manner consistent with other long-term liabilities (i.e., capitalized).

Not surprisingly, defenders of the situational view do not share the view expressed above that *any noncancelable lease* that specifies a contractual set of payments over a number of future periods ought to be treated by the lessee as a long-term liability. Many focus on the executory nature of the lease contract in differentiating leases from long-term debt, that is, if the lessor ever fails to provide assets in usable condition during the term of the lease, the lessee is not obligated to pay. Others focus on the fact that many leases require that the *lessor* continue to incur most of the risks as well as the ultimate rights of ownership of the assets; for example, the lessor often is required to maintain the assets and pay the taxes, and, of course, the owner may retain the right (or obligation) to sell or otherwise dispose of the asset when the lease term expires. It is felt that such reservation of the rights and risks of ownership on the part of the lessor argues against recognition of the assets as assets of the lessee. Still others focus on the notion that portions of scheduled lease payments are not for use of the leased assets themselves but are often really reimbursements to the lessor for services rendered period by period, such as the payment of taxes and utilities, and the handling of maintenance. To the extent that a purchaser of equivalent assets would not recognize such future routine expenditures as assets and liabilities at the time of purchase, it is argued that they should not become recognized as assets and liabilities at the inception of a long-term lease.

ACCOUNTING FOR INVESTMENTS IN CORPORATE STOCK

When examining a set of recent financial statements of any significant public corporation, one usually finds a reference to marketable corporate stock of one or more consolidated or unconsolidated subsidiaries. Thus a thorough treatment of present-day accounting reporting issues, even at the introductory level, must include some discussion of accounting for enterprises that are related through intercorporate investments (stock ownership).

Degrees of Intercorporate Investment

The degree of investment in (ownership of) one corporation by another can range from zero to 100 percent. At either extreme there is not much doubt as to the relationship between the corporation owning stock (the investor corporation) and the corporation whose stock is owned (the investee corporation).

Investments in Marketable Shares. When a corporation buys only a relatively small percentage of the outstanding common stock of one or more other corporations, it is usually for temporary investment purposes—that is, to make the best use of surplus cash available at that time (possibly for several years) until it is needed for acquisition of assets related to the corporation's primary earning activity. For such purposes it is usually unsound policy to invest in more than a small percentage ownership in any one company. Furthermore, it is usually wise to invest only in shares of large companies whose shares are traded on major securities exchanges, so that the shares can be sold with little difficulty when funds are needed for other purposes. Thus no special or extraordinary relationship necessarily develops between the corporation owning shares and the corporation whose shares are owned, when the percentage owned is quite small.

Such investments in the marketable securities of other corporations are given the same general treatment in practice by accountants as are investments in government securities and corporate bonds. However, there are some complications induced by the fact that there is no guarantee of a specific amount of proceeds from sale of common stocks (as there is for redemption values of bonds). As a result of this lack of guaranteed proceeds, portfolios (one or more shares) of stock of other corporations are valued at their aggregate acquisition cost unless their aggregate market value is lower. In the latter case the portfolio is valued at market value, and an unrealized loss is recognized. If the portfolio is a noncurrent asset (i.e., expected to be held for more than one year), this difference between cost and *a lower* market value (or the change in this difference from year to year) is recognized in a special debit-balanced, permanent owners' equity account called "net unrealized gain on noncurrent marketable securities." This account then shows up on the balance sheet as part of the owners' equity section whenever aggregate market value is less than cost of the portfolio. If the marketable securities are current assets (held for resale within the next year), any change in the difference between market value and cost is a gain or loss of the current period and is recognized as such in the income statement.

In any case, dividends are recognized as income at the time they are "declared" by the corporations whose shares are owned (i.e., when they are legally "receivable" and therefore realized). When the shares are ultimately sold, the difference between their original cost (carrying value if the shares are current assets) and the proceeds of sale is recognized as a gain or a loss.

Example 12-7

During 19X3 Acme Corporation invested in a portfolio of marketable equity securities (common stocks) with a total cost of $1.4 million. Although Acme intended to occasionally add to or sell off some of the securities acquired, in general the intent was to maintain the portfolio for several years. Dividends received during 19X3 amounted to $110,000, and by December 31, 19X3, the aggregate market value of the portfolio (contrasted to aggregate cost) was as follows:

Stock of Company	Aggregate Cost	Aggregate Market Value	Net Unrealized Gain (Loss)
A	$ 600,000	$ 570,000	($30,000)
B	400,000	410,000	10,000
C	400,000	400,000	
Portfolio totals	$1,400,000	$1,380,000	($20,000)

The following general journal entries would be used to account for Acme's marketable securities transactions for 19X3 (ignoring taxes):

Marketable securities	1,400,000	
Cash		1,400,000
To record acquisition		

Cash	110,000	
Dividend income		110,000
To record dividends received		

Unrealized loss—noncurrent marketable securities	20,000	
Marketable securities*		20,000
To record unrealized loss		

*For simplicity we have ignored the practice preferred by the FASB of recording the difference between market value and cost in a contra-asset (allowance) account.

In the 19X3 balance sheet the accounts related to the marketable securities are disclosed as follows:

Asset:
Marketable securities, carried at market value
 (which is lower than cost) at 12/31/X3 $1,380,000

Owners' equity:
Unrealized loss—noncurrent
 marketable securities   ($20,000)

During 19X4 Acme sold half of its holdings of "A" Company shares for $290,000 and received $80,000 in dividends. At year-end the cost and market value of the portfolio were as follows:

Stock of Company	Aggregate Cost	Aggregate Market Value
A	$ 300,000	$ 280,000
B	400,000	480,000
C	400,000	400,000
Portfolio totals	$1,100,000	$1,160,000

Therefore the following journal entries are required for 19X4 (ignoring taxes):

Cash	290,000	
Loss on sale of marketable securities	10,000	
Unrealized loss—noncurrent marketable securities		15,000
Marketable securities		285,000
To record sale of marketable securities		

Marketable securities	5,000	
Unrealized loss—noncurrent marketable securities		5,000
To revalue marketable securities at cost		

Note that, as the above table of values and journal entries imply, marketable securities will appear on the end-of-19X4 balance sheet at their $1.1 million *aggregate cost* (which is less than aggregate market value at 12/31/X4). Since market value exceeds cost in the aggregate, the "unrealized loss—noncurrent marketable securities" account would have a zero balance and thus would not show up on the balance sheet at 12/31/X4.

The above treatment—called the *lower of cost or market method*—contrasts sharply with the alternative of recognizing *all changes* in market values of marketable securities (and related gains and losses) from one reporting date to the next. We illustrate the contrast between these alternatives in Chapter 15. Although the official sanction of accounting policy-making authorities (the FASB) has favored the lower of cost or market value method, the question of possible recognition of market values comes up from time to time as proponents of market-value recognition rekindle the controversy. It should be noted, too, that when marketable securities are shown in the balance sheet at cost (market value), the FASB requires corporations to report, as supplemental information, the aggregate market values (aggregate costs) of securities held, either parenthetically on their balance sheets or in footnotes to their financial statements.

One Hundred Percent Intercorporate Ownership. When one corporation owns 100 percent of the outstanding stock of another corporation, the "owned" corporation is hardly a separate entity except in a narrow legal sense. Exceptions to this commonsense rule, however, are those cases in which the "owned" corporation is set up (or acquired) and maintained as a separate legal entity because its activities are distinctly different from the owner company and perhaps require a separate identity to be pursued. Examples are insurance, finance, and banking subsidiaries of industrial corporations. On the other hand, where the owner and 100 percent-owned corporations are not economically or legally incompatible (merely legally separate), they are viewed by accountants as one economic entity. In such cases financial statements showing the combined financial position and results of operations of the several related corporations (known as *consolidated financial statements*) are considered essential in order to satisfy the purposes for which published financial statements are intended. (Consolidated financial statements are discussed later in this section.)

Three Recognized Gradations in Intercorporate Ownership and Control. We have now established that a case of minimal ownership interest in one corporation by another merely calls for recognition of the investment by the latter as an asset (usually called "marketable securities") valued at its cost or market, whichever is lower, with recognition of dividend income as realized. We have also established that if one corporation is 100 percent-owned by another, the financial position and results of operations of the owned corporation should be combined with those of the owner corporation into a single set of financial statements unless there is significant economic or legal reason for not combining them. The question is how to account for the many degrees of ownership in between the extremes.

As one would expect, cases close to the extremes of near-zero and near-100 percent ownership are generally agreed to be best handled as described above for the extremes. Naturally, though, the farther ownership departs from either zero or 100 percent, the less agreement there will be as to the appropriateness of treatment of the investment as just another investment in securities, or treatment of the companies involved as a single accounting entity, respectively.

As a result, certain "reasonable, but arbitrary," ownership-percentage cutoffs have been prescribed by accounting policy-making authorities, along with the appropriate treatment of cases falling between the cutoffs. The ownership percentage cutoffs that have been deemed significant are 20 percent and 50 percent.

Ownership of less than 20 percent of the stock of a corporation is considered insufficient to justify any special treatment beyond recognition of the investment as an investment in the marketable securities of the other corporation. If, on the other hand, one corporation owns more than 20 percent of the ownership shares of another corporation, there is assumed to be a relationship in which the investor corporation exerts a significant influence on the investee corporation. When one corporation exerts such a significant ownership influence on another, it is considered appropriate to account for its investment according to the *equity method* (to be described later in this section), which differs significantly from the cost or market method. If the degree of ownership extends beyond 50 percent and therefore to majority status, not only is there a significant relationship, it is usually considered to be that of "parent and subsidiary." In such cases consolidation of financial statements is usually considered warranted (except where reason dictates that the entities should not be combined, as mentioned above).

The 20 percent cutoff which determines whether a given investment is deemed to be a "significantly influential" investment in an investee corporation is arbitrary, of course. But it is clear that as a given ownership interest in any corporation increases from negligible to successively larger percentages, the given owner (whether an individual or another corporation) at some percentage becomes more than an ordinary shareholder. For instance, since the individual owner can vote its (their) shares in a block, it (they) may be able to ensure the election of one or more selected individuals to the board of directors. The percentage at which a given owner becomes "influential" varies from case to case with such conditions as the number of other shareholders and the size of their respective shareholdings. Thus an established, reasonable (though arbitrary) cutoff like the 20 percent cutoff is useful in the sense that it overcomes the necessity of an in-depth case-by-case analysis of the very nebulous notion of "influence" over the corporation whose shares are owned. As a practical matter, the 20 percent cutoff probably embraces few actual cases in which no substantial influence is present but excludes some (perhaps only a few) cases in which ownership is less than 20 percent but where a substantial degree of influence is nevertheless present.

The 50 percent cutoff is less arbitrary—or so it seems intuitively. Since it is already above the first cutoff, a greater than 50 percent ownership interest carries with it the presumption of extraordinary influence. But, since greater than 50 percent ownership also constitutes a majority interest, it means that the influence actually extends to *de jure* control of the investee by the investor corporation. This means that the two corporations may be operated (except for organizational and legal convenience) as one entity and should be recognized as such by accountants. Of course, many corporations can be controlled *de facto* with less than 50 percent ownership. In the absence of the legal reinforcement that comes with majority ownership, however, accountants are reluctant to recognize such investee corporations as "one" with the parent. One troublesome question arises when the financial statements of an investee corporation that is more than 50 percent owned, but not "wholly" owned, are consolidated with the investor corporation's statements. The question is what to do about the interests of the minority shareholders. As will be illustrated in later discussion, that problem is solved by recognition of "minority interests" in the consolidated financial statements themselves.

Accounting for Investments in Other Corporations

In the discussion above we have noted that accountants recognize three distinct classes of intercorporate relationship that result from investment by one corporation in the shares of another. The three classes of relationship dictate three levels of accounting recognition, as summarized in Exhibit 12-10.

Exhibit 12-10
INTERCORPORATE OWNERSHIP AND ACCOUNTING TREATMENTS

Degree of Ownership	Accounting Treatment
0%– 20%	Lower of Cost or Market Method
20%– 50%	Equity Method
50%–100%	Equity Method plus Consolidation (except where consolidation is unreasonable)

The basic features of the first level of recognition have been covered earlier. The other two levels are covered in the remainder of this section.

Accounting for 20 Percent to 50 Percent Ownership Interests. We noted earlier that when the ownership interest in one corporation is greater than 20 percent but does not exceed 50 percent, an accounting treatment is accorded the investment that departs significantly from the lower of cost or market method (for accounting for marketable securities). Specifically, the accounting treatment of 20 percent to 50 percent ownership interests consists of the following:

1. At the time of acquisition, the investment in the stock of the investee corporation is valued at the cost to the investor corporation of acquiring the shares.
2. Thereafter the value of the investment is altered periodically in the following ways:
    a. Each period, the investment account is increased by an amount equal to the investor's percentage (of ownership) interest in the recognized net income of the investee. The increase in the investment account is considered income to the investor, that is, reflected by an increase in owners' equity (retained earnings) equal to the increase in the investment account. Losses are given opposite treatment.
    b. Concurrently, the investment account and owners' equity (retained

earnings) are reduced through amortization of any excess of (1) the cost of the stock of the investee over (2) the investor's share in the net assets of the investee at the time of acquisition. This reduction of the investment account is considered an expense of the investor associated with its share in the earnings of the investee.

c. As dividends are declared by the investee and therefore become legally receivable (or actually received) by the investor, the investment account is reduced by the amount of the dividends while the dividend receivable (or cash) account is increased concurrently.

The contrast between the above method, called the *equity method,* and the lower of cost or market method is readily apparent. Under the latter, items 2*a* and 2*b* are ignored altogether. Income is recognized by the investor corporation only to the extent that dividends become legally receivable (or received) from the investee corporation (item 2*c*). To make the above features of the equity method clearer, it is helpful to apply them to an example.

Example 12-8

On January 1, 19X1, Investor Company purchased 40 percent of the ownership shares of Investee Company from Investee's then-present shareholders for $2.5 million. The purchase is recorded by the following journal entry:

Investment in Investee Co.	2,500,000	
Cash		2,500,000

Immediately after the investment by Investor, the balance sheets of the two companies appeared as shown in Exhibit 12-11. The 19X1 income statement and December 31, 19X1, balance sheet for Investee Company appear in Exhibit 12-12. (Note that all amounts shown in the exhibits are in thousands of dollars.) Notice that the only effect of the initial investment that is evident in any of the statements is the recognition of the investment account (at cost) on Investor Company's January 1, 19X1, balance sheet. No effect appears in the balance sheets of Investee Company because Investor Company purchased its interest from former shareholders, that is, the transaction took place between parties outside Investee Company. If Investor Company had acquired its interest by purchasing new shares issued by Investee, there would have been an infusion of assets and an increase in paid-in capital beyond the levels previously recognized by Investee Company. However, in either case the 19X1 income statement of Investee Company would be as shown in Exhibit 12-12 (since the distribution of ownership interests in a company is extraneous to the determination of its income).

Exhibit 12-12 indicates that Investee Company's net income for 19X1 is $1,250,000. Since Investor Company owns 40 percent of Investee Company's stock, it is presumed that its equitable interest in the company is increased by 40 percent of any advance in the net assets of the company (e.g., net income) from sources other than contributions by other owners. This reasoning calls

Exhibit 12-11

INVESTOR COMPANY

Balance Sheet
As of January 1, 19X1
(amounts in thousands)

Assets:		Liabilities and Owners' Equity:	
Cash	$ 4,000	Accounts payable	$ 1,200
Accounts receivable	500		
Inventory	2,500		
Net plant and equipment	7,200		
Investment in stock of		Paid-in capital	10,000
Investee Co.	2,500	Retained earnings	5,500
Total	$16,700	Total	$16,700

INVESTEE COMPANY

Balance Sheet
As of January 1, 19X1
(amounts in thousands)

Assets:		Liabilities and Owners' Equity:	
Cash	$ 100	Accounts payable	$ 200
Accounts receivable	100	Bonds payable	1,000
Inventory	1,200	Paid-in capital	4,000
Net plant and equipment	4,800	Retained earnings	1,000
Total	$ 6,200	Total	$ 6,200

for the following entry to recognize Investor Company's "equity" in the earnings of Investee Company:

| Investment in Investee Co. | 500,000 | |
| Equity in income of Investee Co. | | 500,000 |

In this entry an increase in the investment asset is offset by an equal increase in retained earnings (via the temporary account, "Equity in income of Investee Co."). This is a manifestation of the central theme of the equity method, that is, that an investor company recognizes, as income, its equitable share of any earnings recognized by its investee companies.

It is apparent from Exhibits 12-11 and 12-12 that Investee Company declared and paid $500,000 in total dividends during 19X1 (its income was $1,250,000 for 19X1, but retained earnings went up by a net amount of only $750,000 for the year). Rather than being income to Investor Company, its share of the total dividends, $200,000, merely represents the severance and

Exhibit 12-12

INVESTEE COMPANY

Income Statement
For 19X1
(amounts in thousands)

Revenue (all from sales)		$5,500
Less expenses:		
Cost of sales	$3,100	
Interest	50	
Depreciation	600	
Other expense	500	4,250
Net income		$1,250

INVESTEE COMPANY

Balance Sheet
As of December 31, 19X1
(amounts in thousands)

Assets:		Liabilities and Owners' Equity:	
Cash	$1,450	Accounts payable	$ 300
Accounts receivable	300	Bonds payable	1,000
Inventory	1,100	Paid-in capital	4,000
Net plant and equipment	4,200	Retained earnings	1,750*
Total	$7,050	Total	$7,050

*Retained earnings were increased by income of $1,250,000 and reduced by dividends of $500,000 during 19X1.

transfer of cash from Investee to Investor Company. Thus we want to recognize a $200,000 increase in Investor Company's cash and a concurrent decrease in its investment in Investee Company, reflecting Investor's equitable share of the total decrease in Investee's cash (i.e., 40 percent of $500,000). This is accomplished with the following journal entry:

Cash	200,000	
Investment in Investee Co.		200,000

Aside from the rather straightforward recognition of an investor company's equity in the earnings and dividends of its investees, the equity method implies one complication that frequently occurs in practice. When Investor Company acquired 40 percent of the ownership shares of Investee Company on January 1, it paid $2.5 million. That amount is $500,000 more than 40 percent of Investee's recognized net assets of $5 million at January 1, 19X1 (paid-in capital of $4 million plus retained earnings of $1 million—see Exhibit 12-11). In essence, what this means is that Investor Company paid more than 40 percent of the unexpired cost of the net assets of Investee Company in order to obtain the rights to a 40 percent equitable share in the benefits to be generated by those assets. This is not surprising, since the unexpired costs of assets are not purported to represent their value (in generating future benefits) to an outside investor. However, in representing *the income to Investor Company resulting from its equitable interest in the revenue of Investee Company,* it is not sufficient to recognize as expense only the original cost of the assets of Investee Company consumed in producing its revenues (the expense recognized by Investee). Some recognition should also be given to the additional cost incurred by Investor Company to acquire (produce for Investor Company) its equitable interest in the revenues of Investee.

To recognize this additional cost, Investor Company would make an entry of the following form:

Amortization expense	50,000	
Investment in Investee Co.		50,000

With this entry Investor Company will have reduced its investment account and retained earnings (via amortization expense) by one-tenth ($50,000) of the original excess of the cost of the investment over 40 percent of the net asset value of Investee Company at the time of acquisition. Thus we have "matched" a portion of that excess against the related benefits (Investor Company's share of Investee's earnings) realized in 19X1. Our use of one-tenth, implying a ten-year total expiration period, was selected for illustrative purposes only. In practice the period selected for amortization of the differential cost would depend on the individual circumstances (but in no case may it exceed forty years, according to present accounting policy).

With the above recognition of amortization of Investor Company's excess of cost over equity at time of acquisition, all aspects of the investment that affect Investor Company's December 31, 19X1, financial position and its 19X1 income have been recognized. The December 31, 19X1, balance in the "Investment in Investee Co." account is $2,750,000 (cost of $2,500,000 plus equity in earnings of $500,000 less dividends received of $200,000 less amortization of $50,000). Assuming that in its own right Investor Company earned revenues of $15,500,000 and incurred cost of sales, depreciation expense, and other expense of $9,500,000, $900,000, and $2,100,000, respectively, its 19X1 income statement appears in Exhibit 12-13. Notice that Investor's interest in Investee's earnings and the additional amortization are recognized in the income statement, but the dividends received are not.

As a final note about the equity method, it should be added that there has been some disagreement in the past as to whether unconsolidated investees (or even consolidated investees) should be accounted for in the investor company's (separate) financial position according to the equity method or the straight cost method. Arguments can be made for both positions. However, the APB strongly

Exhibit 12-13

INVESTOR COMPANY

Income Statement
For 19X1
(amounts in thousands)

Revenue		$15,500
Less expenses:		
Cost of sales	$9,500	
Depreciation	900	
Other expense	2,100	12,500
Investor Co. operating income		$ 3,000
Income from Investee Co.:		
Equity in income of Investee Co.	$ 500	
Less amortization of excess of cost of investment over net assets of Investee Co. at acquisition	(50)	450
Net income		$ 3,450

favored the equity method for cases in which the investor influences the operating and financial policies (including dividend distribution policy) of the investees—which is the presumption, according to the APB, when ownership exceeds the 20 percent cutoff. The APB's successor, the FASB, has not chosen to disagree with the prior position of the APB on this issue.

Accounting for Greater than 50 Percent Ownership Interests. Accounting for more than 50 percent ownership interests in investee companies (usually called *subsidiaries* if more than 50 percent owned) is an extended version of the accounting treatment prescribed for investments in the 20 percent to 50 percent range. The reason is that separate financial statements are often prepared for the subsidiary (investee) and parent (investor) corporations as well as consolidated financial statements for the combined entities. Primary among the reasons for separate financial statements is that creditor and other interests (including minority shareowners of the subsidiaries) do not usually transcend the separate, individual legal entities.

According to present accounting policy, the *statements of the parent corporation* are prepared according to the equity method whether or not the subsidiary or subsidiaries are to be consolidated. The only difference, then, in accounting for consolidated subsidiaries versus unconsolidated investee companies (including certain subsidiaries) is the eventual consolidation of the separate statements. Again, an example will serve to bring out the similarities and the important difference between the two treatments.

Example 12-9

Reconsider the Investor Company–Investee Company example introduced above (Example 12-8). Let us take two companies identical to Investor and Investee Company on January 1, 19X1, and name them Parent Company and Subsidiary Company, respectively. Suppose that Parent and Subsidiary continued to be identical to Investor and Investee Companies *except that* on January 1, 19X1, Parent Company did two things differently than Investor Company. First, suppose that it acquired 80 percent (instead of 40 percent) of the outstanding ownership interest in Subsidiary Company for $5 million (instead of $2.5 million). (Note that the $5 million exceeds 80 percent of the net assets of Subsidiary as of January 1, 19X1, by $1 million; i.e., all of the figures relating to Parent Company's stock ownership of Subsidiary are doubled relative to Investor Company's ownership of Investee.) Second, suppose that Parent also acquired all of the outstanding bonds of Subsidiary Company from the former bondholders at their face value of $1 million (the bonds require interest to be paid annually at 5 percent of face value). All other facts remain as assumed in the earlier example. The effects of these facts on the financial position of Parent Company as of January 1, 19X1, are depicted in Exhibit 12-14.

Exhibit 12-14

PARENT COMPANY

Balance Sheet
As of January 1, 19X1
(amounts in thousands)

Assets:		Liabilities and Owners' Equity:	
Cash	$ 500	Accounts payable	$ 1,200
Accounts receivable	500		
Inventory	2,500		
Net plant and equipment	7,200		
Investment in Investee Co.			
Bonds	1,000	Paid-in capital	10,000
Stock	5,000	Retained earnings	5,500
Total	$16,700	Total	$16,700

The 19X1 income statement for Parent Company under the revised set of facts is shown in Exhibit 12-15.

Notice that down to the "Parent Co. operating income" figure of $3 million, Exhibit 12-15 is identical to the income statement illustrating the earlier example of 40 percent stock ownership (Exhibit 12-13). The only differences are the $50,000 interest income received on the investment in Subsidiary Company bonds, the doubling of Parent Company's equity in Subsidiary's earnings, and the amount of additional cost amortization—in accordance with the new assumption of 80 percent ownership. Incidentally, it should also be noted that the assumed increase in the ownership share in Subsidiary Company owned by Parent Company has no effect whatever on Subsidiary's separate financial statements for 19X1. They would be identical to Investee Company's statements illustrated in Exhibits 12-11 and 12-12.

Parent Company's investment account balances at the end of 19X1 (consistent with the above facts) are $1 million for the bonds of Subsidiary Company and $5.5 million for the stock ($5 million cost, plus $1 million equity in earnings, less $400,000 in dividends and $100,000 amortization).

Consolidation of Financial Statements. Having given due consideration to the recognition of the effects of investments in consolidated subsidiaries in the *separate* financial statements of the parent, our attention now turns to the

Exhibit 12-15

PARENT COMPANY

Income Statement
For 19X1
(amounts in thousands)

Revenue		$15,500
Less expenses:		
Cost of sales	$9,500	
Depreciation	900	
Other expense	2,100	12,500
Parent Co. operating income		$ 3,000
Income from Subsidiary Co.		
Interest received	$ 50	
Equity in earnings of Subsidiary Co.	1,000	
Less amortization of excess of cost of investment over net assets of Subsidiary Co. at acquisition	(100)	950
Net income		$ 3,950

consolidation of parent and subsidiary statements. Essentially, the process of consolidating balance sheets consists of adding together the balance sheets of the parent and subsidiary companies after (1) substituting the subsidiary's balance sheet for the parent's investment account (allowing for recognition of minority interests), and (2) making certain eliminations. The eliminations are necessitated by the need to avoid double counting of assets, liabilities, expenses, and revenues within the corporate group when combining statements. To see why double counting is a potential problem, consider the following example:

Example 12-10

Suppose that a group of owners founded Holding Company with a $100,000 combined contribution of cash in exchange for 100 percent of the authorized common stock of the company. Suppose further that Holding Company engaged in no activities of its own, but rather invested its full $100,000 cash endowment in all of the shares of another newly formed company, Held Company. Immediately thereafter, each company has $100,000 in assets (cash in the case of Held Company; an investment in Held Company's stock in the case of Holding Company) and $100,000 in owners' equity. Does that mean that in combination the two companies command $200,000 in total assets? Certainly not! Holding Company is a mere legal shell through which the single set of owners controls the single set of assets (equal to $100,000) which is legally owned by Held Company.

The extremity of the above example makes quite obvious the motivation for making certain eliminations in the process of consolidating the financial statements of parent corporations and subsidiaries that are more than 50 percent owned. Our preceding example, however, provides a more realistic setting for illustrating the consolidation process. We proceed by first illustrating the combined status (consolidated balance sheet) of Parent and Subsidiary Companies immediately after Parent Company acquired all of the bonds and 80 percent of the stock of Subsidiary Company on January 1, 19X1. We then consolidate the balance sheets as of December 31, 19X1, and the income statements for the year 19X1.

Consolidated Balance Sheet at Acquisition. Exhibit 12-16 depicts the consolidation of the Janaury 1, 19X1, balance sheets (in adjusted trial balance format) of Parent and Subsidiary Companies. In the data columns, note that the first two sets of columns contain the separate balance sheets of the two companies. (The amounts are traceable back to the balance sheet in Exhibit 12-14 for Parent Company and back to the balance sheet in Exhibit 12-11 for Investee Company.) The most significant feature of Exhibit 12-16 is the third set of columns. It contains sets of related debit and credit adjustments to the combined figures of the first two columns.

The third column is necessary to avoid the kind of double counting of assets and ownership interests pointed out in Example 12-10 and to reclassify certain amounts that should be captioned differently in the consolidated balance sheet than in the related companies' separate balance sheets.

The first elimination of double counting, the debit and credit labeled (1) in the third set of columns, is intuitively very easy to understand. Since the purpose of the consolidation is to look at the parent and subsidiary as one entity (controlled by Parent Company's shareholders), it is nonsense to portray as assets and liabilities the bonds of Subsidiary Company owned by Parent Company. The combined, single entity cannot "owe" itself. Thus the $1 million in bonds is eliminated from the assets of Parent Company by the credit to the "Investment in Subsidiary Co. Bonds" labeled (1); and the liability "Bonds of Subsidiary Co." is eliminated by the similarly labeled debit.

The other entry in the third set of columns, whose components are labeled (2a), (2b), etc., is more complex—yet taken in parts it can be understood at the intuitive level as well. First we wish to draw an analogy to entry (1). That is, just as a single entity cannot owe itself money, it also cannot "own itself." We therefore eliminate the asset representing Parent Company's ownership of Subsidiary stock. This is accomplished by a credit to this account equal to its full balance of $5 million—the entry labeled (2a). At the same time, a portion of the total balance in this account *is not* represented by recognized claims by Parent Company to the net assets of Subsidiary Company as represented by the latter's paid-in capital and retained earnings. The reason is that Parent Company paid $1 million more for Subsidiary's stock than its 40 percent share in Subsidiary's *recognized* net assets. Thus in entry (2b) we reclassify the $1 million by debiting the new asset account entitled "Excess of investment cost over equity acquired in net assets of Subsidiary Co." (which does not exist on the separate balance sheets). The combined effect of entries (2a) and (2b) is to eliminate from consolidated assets only Parent's equity in the net assets of Subsidiary, that is, $4 million.

To complete the second entry we first recognize that just as Subsidiary's bonds *owed to Parent Company* had to be eliminated in entry (1), Subsidiary's paid-in capital and retained earnings—to the extent that they represent Parent's equity in Subsidiary Company—must also be eliminated. Entries (2c) and (2d) actually eliminate *all* of Subsidiary Company's paid-in capital and retained earnings by debiting the respective accounts in amounts equal to their full balances. However, this overelimination is offset by entry (2e), which credits the new account "minority interest" in the amount of $1 million. This amount

Exhibit 12-16

PARENT COMPANY–SUBSIDIARY COMPANY

Consolidation of Balance Sheets
As of January 1, 19X1
(amounts in thousands)

Accounts:	Parent Company Dr	Parent Company Cr	Subsidiary Company Dr	Subsidiary Company Cr	Eliminations and Reclassifications Dr	Eliminations and Reclassifications Cr	Consolidated Dr	Consolidated Cr
Assets:								
Cash	500		100				600	
Accounts receivable	500		100				600	
Inventory	2,500		1,200				3,700	
Net plant and equipment	7,200		4,800				12,000	
Investment in Subsidiary Co.:								
Bonds	1,000					1,000 (1)		
Stock	5,000					5,000 (2a)		
Excess of investment cost over equity acquired in net assets of Subsidiary Co.					(2b) 1,000		1,000	
Total assets	16,700		6,200				17,900	
Liabilities and Owners' Equity:								
Accounts payable		1,200		200				1,400
Bonds of Subsidiary Co.				1,000	(1) 1,000			
Paid-in capital:								
Parent Co.		10,000						10,000
Subsidiary Co.				4,000	(2c) 4,000			
Retained earnings:								
Parent Co.		5,500						5,500
Subsidiary Co.				1,000	(2d) 1,000			
Minority interest						1,000 (2e)		1,000
Total liabilities and owners' equity		16,700		6,200				17,900
Total eliminations and reclassifications					7,000	7,000		

468

represents Subsidiary's minority shareholders' 20 percent interest in its combined paid-in capital (0.20 × $4,000,000 = $800,000) and retained earnings (0.20 × $1,000,000 = $200,000). Thus the combined effect of entries (2c), (2d), and (2e) is to eliminate Parent Company's 80 percent interest in Subsidiary's combined paid-in capital (0.80 × $4,000,000 = $3,200,000) and retained earnings (0.80 × $1,000,000 = $800,000). The combined amount is $4 million, which equals the net amount of Parent's investment eliminated in entries (2a) and (2b).

After all appropriate eliminations have been recognized in the elimination and reclassification columns, the first three sets of columns are summed across to arrive at the balances in the consolidated balance sheet columns for the combined entity. Those amounts appear in the Consolidated columns of Exhibit 12-16. Note that (a) the consolidated total assets figure is less than the sum of the asset totals from the separate balance sheets due, of course, to the elimination entries, (b) the same is true of the total liabilities and owners' equity, and (c) the sum of the debit eliminations and reclassifications equals the sum of the credits.

Consolidation of Balance Sheets and Income Statements Subsequent to Acquisition. Consolidation of balance sheets subsequent to the date of acquisition does not differ in principle from consolidation at acquisition. Hence Exhibit 12-17, which shows the consolidation of balance sheets for Parent and Subsidiary companies as of December 31, 19X1, needs no great elaboration. In fact, the same eliminations and reclassifications are made, with only the amounts differing appropriately. We might note, however, that the Parent Company equity in the net assets of Subsidiary Company, which is eliminated by entries (2a) and (2b), is now $4.6 million, an increase of $600,000 over the beginning-of-the-year figure of $4 million. This is due to recognition in the course of the year of (a) Parent's equity in the earnings of Subsidiary (80 percent of $1.25 million, or $1 million), (b) less dividends received of $400,000. Notice too that the unamortized excess of Parent's investment cost over its equity in the net assets of Subsidiary, which is reclassified in column four, is $100,000 less than at the beginning of the year ($900,000 instead of $1 million) due to amortization of $100,000 during the year.

Since a year has passed from the date of acquisition and the companies have therefore operated for a period *as related companies,* it is necessary also to consolidate their income statements for 19X1. Again the process is one of summing the amounts in the separate statements after some appropriate eliminations and adjustments. The process is illustrated for the 19X1 income statements of Parent and Subsidiary companies in Exhibit 12-18. Notice that, as in the consolidation of balance sheets, we first array the separate income statements of Parent and Subsidiary companies, in the first two columns. We do not use the debit-credit format for the income statement consolidation because the debits do not equal the credits in income statements as they do in balance sheets. Therefore, nothing is gained from the debit-credit regimen.

Column one of Exhibit 12-18 is simply the separate 19X1 income statement of Parent Company—traceable item for item back to Exhibit 12-15. Looking at column two we observe that (a) the top portion consists of the 19X1 income statement of Subsidiary Company (traceable item for item to the identical Investee Company statement in Exhibit 12-12), and (b) the lower portion of

Exhibit 12-17

PARENT COMPANY–SUBSIDIARY COMPANY

Consolidation of Balance Sheets
As of December 31, 19X1
(amounts in thousands)

Accounts:	Parent Company		Subsidiary Company		Eliminations and Reclassifications		Consolidated	
	Dr	Cr	Dr	Cr	Dr	Cr	Dr	Cr
Assets:								
Cash	4,850		1,450				6,300	
Accounts receivable	750		300				1,050	
Inventory	2,000		1,100				3,100	
Net plant and equipment	6,300		4,200				10,500	
Investment in Subsidiary Co.:								
Bonds	1,000					1,000 (1)		
Stock	5,500					5,500 (2a)		
Unamortized excess of investment cost over interest in net assets of Subsidiary Co.					(2b) 900		900	
Total assets	20,400		7,050				21,850	
Liabilities and Owners' Equity:								
Accounts payable		950		300				1,250
Bonds of Subsidiary Co.				1,000	(1) 1,000			
Paid-in capital:								
Parent Co.		10,000						10,000
Subsidiary Co.				4,000	(2c) 4,000			
Retained earnings:								
Parent Co.		9,450						9,450
Subsidiary Co.				1,750	(2d) 1,750			
Minority interest						1,150 (2e)		1,150
Total liabilities and owners' equity		20,400		7,050				21,850
Total eliminations and reclassifications					7,650	7,650		

the column consists of some adjustments that are necessary to eliminate double counting and overstatement in arriving at consolidated net income.

The first adjustment, labeled "(1)," eliminates double counting. Since all of Subsidiary's revenue and expenses are brought into the consolidated statements through its separate statement (the top portion of column two), Parent's equity in Subsidiary's earnings appearing in Parent Company's separate statement (column one) is redundant. Hence the elimination labeled "(1)" offsets and eliminates the redundancy.

Then, too, it must be recognized that the earning ability of the combined entities would be overstated by simply aggregating the separate income statements of the companies (after elimination of Parent's equity in Subsidiary's earnings), without giving recognition to the minority shareholders' interest in the separate earnings of Subsidiary Company. Thus we have inserted in the second column a $250,000 reduction (item 2) representing a segregation from the combined income attributable to the interests of Parent's shareholders of the 20 percent minority interest in the 19X1 earnings of Subsidiary.

Turning now to the third column, the first elimination entry rids the consolidated statement of some additional double counting. Since the Parent Company statement shows $50,000 interest income and the Subsidiary Company statement shows the same $50,000 as an interest expense, the two amounts are eliminated. Taken as a whole, the combined entities did not pay

Exhibit 12-18

PARENT COMPANY-SUBSIDIARY COMPANY

Consolidation of Income Statements
For 19X1
(amounts in thousands)

Description	Parent Company	Subsidiary Company	Eliminations and Reclassifications	Consolidated
Revenue	$15,500	$5,500		$21,000
Less expenses:				
Cost of sales	$ 9,500	$3,100		$12,600
Interest		50	$ (50) (1)	
Depreciation (and amortization)	900	600	100 (2)	1,600
Other expense	2,100	500		2,600
Total expense	$12,500	$4,250	$ 50	$16,800
Operating income	$ 3,000	$1,250	$ (50)	$ 4,200
Income from Subsidiary Co.:				
Interest	50		(50) (1)	
Equity in earnings	1,000	(1,000) (1)		
Less amortization of excess of cost of investment over interest in net assets of subsidiary	(100)		100 (2)	
Less minority interest in subsidiary net income		(250) (2)		(250)
Net income	$ 3,950	-0-	-0-	$ 3,950

or receive interest to or from any other entity. Furthermore, the total income is not changed by the offsetting reductions of income and expense.

The second entry in column three is really just a reclassification. The $100,000 *amortization* of Parent's excess of cost over its interest in Subsidiary's net assets should *not* be eliminated from the consolidated income statement for the same reason that the unamortized portion of the "excess" is not eliminated from the consolidated balance sheet. However, with the elimination of Parent's equity in Subsidiary's earnings (the first elimination in column two), the amortization is best lumped together (or classified with) the depreciation and amortization of other assets of the combined companies. This is accomplished by the adjustments labeled "(2)" in column three.

With all appropriate eliminations, reclassifications, and adjustments, the consolidated income statement results from summing across the first three columns of Exhibit 12-18. An important feature of the consolidated net income figure arrived at in this way ($3,950,000) is that *it equals the separate net income figure arrived at earlier for Parent Company under the equity method* (see Exhibit 12-15).

This will always be the case, assuming that consistent measurement rules are used for both the consolidation eliminations and the application of the equity method to separate accounting for the parent company. Furthermore, it makes intuitive sense. Under the equity method the income of the parent is combined with *only* its equitable share of subsidiary earnings. In consolidated statements an attempt is made to portray the earnings of all assets under the control of the parent company shareholders (the same ownership group in both cases) by combining the net income of parent and subsidiaries (eliminating double counting) *and then* deducting from the total the equitable interests in subsidiary earnings *not attributable* to the parent shareholder group (the minority interests). The final figure ought to be the same in either situation.

Elimination of Intercompany Profits. It should be pointed out that we have not been able to illustrate all types of possible intercompany eliminations in this simple example. One particularly significant omission from the example is intercorporate profits in inventories. When one company sells goods to a related company at a markup, but the related company has not sold those goods to an outside entity by the end of the period, the gross profit on the goods will not have been *realized* (through sale to an outside entity) by the companies as a single entity. Such unrealized profits must be eliminated from the cost of the inventory (on the balance sheet of the buyer) and owners' equity and income for the period (of the related seller) in consolidating the companies' financial statements.

The Purchase versus Pooling Controversy

We should not leave the total topic of accounting for related companies without brief mention of one of the most heated recent controversies in financial reporting practice. The controversy centers on the application of the "pooling-of-interests" method of accounting for parent companies and subsidiaries whose stock is acquired from former shareholders by issuing stock of the parent company in exchange—rather than with cash or other consideration.

The controversy arises because such stock-for-stock transactions can be interpreted two different ways. One way is that if the parent company's stock was readily marketable, the transaction may be considered to be a purchase in substance. That is, it is presumed that the parent company could have issued the stock for cash and then traded the cash to the former shareholders of the subsidiary for their stockholdings. Under this interpretation, a stock-for-stock acquisition is accounted for as described above for a cash purchase of subsidiary stock (i.e., under the equity method with consolidation of subsidiaries more than 50 percent owned)—with the "investment in subsidiary stock" valued at the *market value* of the parent stock issued in exchange for it. An important thing to note is that any excess of the value of the stock issued over the equity in the net assets of the acquired subsidiary is amortized or matched against the parent's equity in the postacquisition earnings of the subsidiary (or the combined earnings in the case of consolidation).

The other interpretation of a stock-for-stock acquisition is that it represents a mere coming together (i.e., a pooling) of the interests of (1) the original parent corporation shareholders and (2) the shareholders who give up their shares in the subsidiary to become shareholders of the parent corporation and bring with them in exchange control over the subsidiary. The pooling-of-interests method of accounting implements this reasoning. The investment is assigned a value equal to the equity acquired by the parent in the subsidiary's net assets. Thus even though the acquisition price exceeds the value of the acquired equity, no additional amortization expense need be offset against the postacquisition combined income of the parent and subsidiary—meaning that recognized combined income will be higher subsequent to acquisition than under the "purchase" interpretation.

It is this latter feature that critics of the pooling-of-interest interpretation feel has led to widespread abuses of the method—particularly during the so-called merger movement of the 1960s. They (the critics) assert that the pooling philosophy really only applies to those cases where the new combined ownership group of the parent is composed of two former ownership groups who both retain substantial influence over the combined entity. However, the critics hasten to point out that pooling accounting has been used for many very small subsidiaries that have been literally swallowed by giant parent companies. There is no pooling of interests in such cases, since the parent corporation buys out the *controlling* interest that the shareholders of the subsidiary once had, and their new ownership interest in the parent represents an infinitesimal rather than an influential interest. But, in pooling-of-interests accounting for the combined entities, no recognition is given to the value of the parent's stock given up to acquire control of the subsidiary and its (the subsidiary's) future earning power. As indicated above, this means that higher combined income may be recognized (no additional amortization) subsequent to acquisition (which, of course, makes parent company management look better) than if the acquisition is recognized as an effective purchase.

The increasing frequency of such abuses and the ensuing public criticism of pooling accounting as a possible encouragement for managements to pursue otherwise undesirable acquisitions led to action by the APB. The action came in the form of an opinion clearly prescribing the conditions that must be satisfied by a stock-for-stock acquisition to be considered a genuine pooling of interests for accounting purposes. All acquisitions not meeting the conditions are to be treated as purchase acquisitions. It should be noted that if many of the "pooling" acquisitions of the sixties had been consummated after the effective date of the opinion, they would probably not be considered poolings of interests under the guidelines of the opinion.

Questions for Review and Discussion

12-1. Define or describe:
   a. Before-tax accounting income
   b. Taxable income
   c. Long-term noncancelable lease
   d. Executory contract
   e. Subsidiary company
   f. Consolidated financial statements

12-2. Explain why income taxes present problems in asset and liability valuation and expense recognition.

12-3. In what ways are conventional financial accounting and taxable income calculations similar? In what ways do they differ?

12-4. It is basically deceptive and immoral for a company (or an individual) to keep two sets of books, one for financial accounting purposes and one for tax purposes. Do you agree or disagree? Defend your position.

12-5. Explain the nature of the account "deferred tax liability" that appears on many corporate balance sheets year after year.

12-6. In what sense (if any) may a long-term noncancelable lease be considered equivalent to long-term debt? In what sense (if any) do they differ?

12-7. Describe the two kinds of accounting treatment that may be used by lessors and lessees for valuing the assets and liabilities and recognizing the expenses and revenues associated with leases.

12-8. Under the financing-capitalization method of accounting for leases, what assets, liabilities, expenses, and revenues (if any) are recognized by (*a*) lessors and (*b*) lessees?

12-9. Under the operating method of accounting for leases, what assets, liabilities, expenses, and revenues are recognized by (*a*) lessors and (*b*) lessees?

12-10. Describe the situational approach to selecting accounting methods for the treatment of leases by lessors and lessees.

12-11. According to accounting policy makers, there are three significant gradations in degree of ownership of one corporation by another for purposes of accounting for the investor corporation's investment. Describe the gradations and the reasoning behind the distinction drawn between them. Name the accounting treatment accorded each.

12-12. Describe the lower of cost or market method of accounting for an investment by one corporation in the stock of another. Include such things as (1) how the investment is originally valued, (2) what increases and decreases are recognized, and (3) what is recognized as income periodically.

12-13. Describe the equity method of accounting for intercorporate investments. Include in the description the items listed in 12-12 above.

12-14. Explain in words what is involved (in principle) in consolidating the financial statements of parent and subsidiary companies.

12-15. Discuss the reasoning behind offsetting (as an expense) a portion of the excess of cost to an investor company over its equity in net assets of an investee company against the investor company's equitable share in the earnings subsequent to acquisition of the investee.

Exercises

12-1. **Selecting Tax Accounting Measurement Rules and Interperiod Tax Allocation.** Computer Services Company began business on January 1, 19X1. Its balance sheet on that date follows:

COMPUTER SERVICES COMPANY

Balance Sheet
As of January 1, 19X1

Assets:		Liabilities and Owners' Equity:	
Cash	$ 100,000	Accounts payable	$ 50,000
Supplies inventory	50,000	Long-term debt	1,000,000
Computer equipment	2,000,000	Owners' equity	1,100,000
	$2,150,000		$2,150,000

The company is in the business of supplying small businesses with computer assistance for their inventory control, payroll accounting systems, and so forth. The computer equipment on the balance sheet is new. It is expected to be traded in four years later. The manufacturer has agreed to take it back at $400,000 cash or trade-in allowance at that time.

With the exception of depreciation on the computer equipment, the company recognizes all revenues and expenses on the same basis for financial accounting and tax purposes. The company has selected straight-line depreciation for financial accounting purposes but has not yet selected a method for tax purposes. Its options for tax purposes are straight-line, sum-of-years-digits, and declining balance at double the straight-line rate.

Required:

1. Assuming that (1) the company has an after-tax opportunity rate of 8 percent, (2) taxes will be paid at the end of the year for which they are assessed, and (3) the tax rate is 40 percent, which depreciation method should be used for tax purposes? Defend your choice. (*Hint:* Consider the differential effects of the methods on the tax bill in each year, assuming all other things are constant and that there is sufficient revenue that taxable income will be positive in every year regardless of the method selected.)

2. Assuming that the sum-of-years-digits method is selected for tax purposes, give the year-end balance, if any, in the deferred tax liability account for each of the years 19X1–X4. Assume that the tax rate is 40 percent.

12-2. Some Tax Allocation Inferences from Partial Information. An excerpt from the income statement of Taxpayer Corporation follows:

Before-tax income		$150,000
Income tax expense:		
Taxes currently paid or payable	$100,000	
Decrease in deferred tax liability	(25,000)	75,000
After-tax income		$ 75,000

Which of the following conditions could definitely be true of Taxpayer Corporation based on the statement excerpt? Which are not necessarily true but might be true? *Assume that the tax rate is 50 percent.* Explain your answers.

    a. Taxpayer Corporation uses straight-line depreciation for tax purposes.
    b. Taxpayer Corporation's taxable income is less than or equal to $150,000.
    c. Taxpayer Corporation uses S-L depreciation for accounting purposes and S-Y-D depreciation for tax purposes, and its depreciable assets are generally all past the midpoint in their useful lives.
    d. Same as *c,* only S-L depreciation is used for tax purposes and S-Y-D for accounting purposes.
    e. Taxpayer Corporation's taxable income is greater than $150,000.
    f. Taxpayer Corporation uses S-L depreciation for tax purposes and double-declining-balance depreciation for accounting purposes.

12-3. Some Tax Allocation Inferences from Income Statement Data. Following is the statement of earnings from the 1977 annual report of Evans Products Company and Consolidated Subsidiaries. In the summary of accounting policies included in the annual report as an integral part of the financial statements, the company noted that it recognizes deferred taxes on earnings to provide for the tax effect of timing differences between components of financial accounting income and taxable income—primarily arising from use of accelerated depreciation methods for tax purposes (straight-line for financial reporting purposes).

Required:

1. Based on what you observe in Evans's 1977 statement of earnings, approximately in what stage of their useful lives were Evans's fixed assets (on the average) during 1976 and 1977?

EVANS PRODUCTS COMPANY AND CONSOLIDATED SUBSIDIARIES

Statement of Earnings
Years Ended December 31
(amounts in thousands)

	1977	1976
Revenues		
Sales	$919,123	$779,586
Other income	5,430	4,903
Gain on sale of assets	1,007	3,500
Earnings before taxes of unconsolidated subsidiaries	15,632	16,712
	941,192	804,701
Costs and expenses		
Costs of operations	775,248	670,579
Selling and administrative	63,841	53,648
Depreciation and amortization	14,339	13,495
Interest	16,108	17,851
Estimated losses of discontinued facilities	2,000	5,250
	871,536	760,823
Earnings before Taxes and Extraordinary Items	69,656	43,878
Taxes on Earnings		
Current	18,600	12,700
Deferred	10,200	4,150
	28,800	16,850
Earnings before Extraordinary Items	40,856	27,028
Extraordinary Items, Net of Tax	1,334	3,697
Net Earnings	$ 42,190	$ 30,725

2. Estimate the amount of depreciation and amortization expense recognized for tax purposes in 1977 by Evans. (Assume that depreciation and amortization expense accounted for virtually the total difference between financial accounting and taxable income and that "costs of operations" contained no depreciation costs.) For this purpose assume a tax rate of 48 percent.

3. Within the concepts and principles of the conventional accounting model, what justification (if any) is there for interperiod allocation (deferral in this case) of income tax expense?

12-4. **Effects of Income Tax Allocation.** Because of differences in timing of recognition of certain items of expense, Longhorn Corporation reported the following for 19X1–X3:

	19X1	19X2	19X3
Taxable income per tax return	$30,000	$55,000	$65,000
Financial accounting net income before taxes	50,000	50,000	50,000

Assuming that the company's income is taxed at a 40 percent rate and that interperiod tax allocation is applied, answer the following questions for each of the three years:
1. What is the income tax payable for the year?
2. What is the income tax expense for the year?
3. What is the net income for the year?
4. What is the *balance* of the deferred tax liability account at the end of each year, assuming a zero balance at the beginning of 19X1?

12-5. Inferring Effects of Alternative Methods from Deferred Taxes. Below is an excerpt from Note 8 to the financial statements in the 1977 Annual Report of Sears, Roebuck and Co. and Consolidated Subsidiaries. The report covers the fiscal years ended Janaury 31, 1978 (fiscal 1977), and January 31, 1977 (fiscal 1976). Based on the information contained in the note, satisfy the following requirements:

Required:

1. Note 8 gives information about Sears's Consolidated Income Tax Expense. In Note 8 the company indicates that $96 million of deferred income tax expense for the year ended 1/31/78 was due to installment sales. In general, what does this imply about the relationship between taxable income and pretax accounting income attributable to installment sales? Explain. What methods of accounting for installment sales probably being used for (*a*) accounting purposes and (*b*) tax purposes?

2. Based on the information in Note 8 and supplemental information from Note 13 (not shown) to the effect that depreciation expense for the year ended 1/31/78 for financial reporting purposes was $196,014,000, estimate the depreciation recognized for tax purposes for the year ended 1/31/78. Assume a tax rate of 48 percent.

8. Income taxes

Federal and state income taxes on current operations include:

(*In Millions*)	Year Ended January 31	
	1978	1977
Current portion	$262	$341
Investment tax credit (flow-through method)	(16)	(13)
Deferred tax expense—		
Current		
Installment sales	96	93
Receivable reserves	6	(8)
Maintenance agreement income	(8)	(11)
Supplemental pension costs		9
Other	(9)	(4)
Long-term		
Depreciation	21	28
Other	4	
Total Deferred	110	107
Financial statement income tax provisions	$356	$435

12-6. **Effects of Income Tax Allocation.** Because of differences in timing of recognition of certain items of income, Finegan Corporation reported the following for the fiscal years 19X4 through 19X6:

	19X4	19X5	19X6
Taxable income per tax return	$90,000	$45,000	$30,000
Financial accounting net income before taxes	40,000	65,000	60,000

Assuming that the company's taxable income is taxed at 40 percent, answer the questions following for each of the three years:
1. What is the income tax payable for the year?
2. What is the income tax expense for the year?
3. What is the net income for the year?
4. What is the *balance* of the deferred tax liability account at the end of each year? (Assume that the balance is zero at the beginning of 19X4.)

12-7. **Accounting for a Lease by the Lessor.** Central Property Company purchased a building for $100,000 on January 1, 19X0. The building was immediately leased to a highly credit-worthy former customer for twenty years at $12,265 per year, payable January 1 of each year. The company expects that the building will have a zero salvage value at the end of the lease period. The company is trying to decide whether to use the financing method or the operating method to account for the lease. The interest rate implicit in the lease payments is 8 percent. The present value of the lease payments is therefore approximately $130,000. If the company uses the operating method, it will use straight-line depreciation on the building.

Required:

1. How much income will be recognized in connection with the lease under each of the two methods of accounting—
   (a) For 19X0?
   (b) Over the whole duration of the lease?
   Discuss any significant differences and similarities in the amounts.
2. What assets and liabilities (if any) will be recognized by Central in connection with the lease under each of the two accounting methods—
   (a) Immediately after the inception of the lease?
   (b) At December 31, 19X0?
   (c) At January 2, 19X1?
3. What considerations should enter into the selection of an accounting method for the lease?

12-8. **Accounting for a Lease by the Lessee.** Assume the same facts as in Exercise 12-7.

Required:

1. How much of each type of expense will be recognized by a lessee under the operating and financing methods—
   (a) In 19X0?
   (b) Over the life of the lease?

2. What assets and liabilities will be recognized, if any, under each of the two methods—
   (a) Immediately after inception of the lease?
   (b) At December 31, 19X0?
   (c) At January 2, 19X1?

3. Which method should be used by the lessee? Defend your position.

12-9. Lessor and Lessee Accounting for the same Lease. At the beginning of 19X5 Shipping Company leased a large warehouse on Pier 67 in Port City from the owner of the warehouse, Storage Company. The lease agreement extends for five years and calls for payments as follows:

Initial Payment	Payment at the Beginning of:			
	19X6	19X7	19X8	19X9
$100,000	$50,000	$50,000	$30,000	$30,000

Storage Company would have accepted a lump-sum payment of $225,000 at the outset for the same five-year occupancy. The lease payments therefore include a 12 percent effective interest charge.

Shipping Company accounted for the lease over its duration according to the capitalization method, using straight-line amortization of the leasehold asset. Storage Company, on the other hand, has accounted for the lease according to the operating method. The unexpired cost at the time the lease was signed was $150,000. The warehouse was then expected to be demolished at the end of the five years. Its salvage value was expected to equal the cost of demolition and removal. Storage Company depreciated the warehouse on a sum-of-years-digits basis.

Required:

1. Prepare a schedule showing the annual expense to Shipping Company recognized in connection with the use and financing of the warehouse, along with the year-end balances in the related asset and liability accounts, for the years 19X5–X9. (Note: The leased asset and the lease liability will not start out equal in this case because of the initial payment of $100,000.)

2. Prepare a schedule for Storage Company of the lease-related revenue and expense recognized and contribution to net income, along with the year-end asset balances, for 19X5–X9.

3. At the 19X6 annual meetings of both Shipping Company and Storage Company, a representative of the Stockholders Protection Association accused both companies' managements and auditors of fraud and deception. In support of his charge he pointed out that both companies recognized the warehouse facility as an asset. Since it was impossible for the same building to belong to both companies, the companies were obviously misleading their stockholders. Can you defend the practices of the two companies? What explanations of the situation, if any, can you give that might counter the criticism?

12-10. Financial Statement Presentation of Leases. Following is a note to the financial statements presented in the 1977 annual report of UAL, Inc. (United Airlines) and Consolidated Subsidiaries. Referring to the information in this note, satisfy the requirements at the end of this exercise.

Lease Obligations

United currently leases 86 of its aircraft. The majority of these leases have terms of 15 years and expiration dates ranging from 1978 through 1988. Under the terms of leases for 30 of the aircraft, United has the right of first refusal to purchase the aircraft for fair market value at the end of the lease term. Majority-owned subsidiaries of Western International operate eight hotels (one of which is subleased to another hotel operator) under leases expiring from 1982 through 2007. Other leases include airport passenger terminal space, aircraft hangars and related maintenance facilities, cargo terminals, flight kitchens, other equipment and automobiles. In addition to minimum fixed rentals, certain hotel rentals are contingent based on a percentage of operating profits and revenues.

Certain leases arising subsequent to December 31, 1976 are considered to be capital leases as defined in Statement of Financial Accounting Standards No. 13, "Accounting for Leases" ("SFAS No. 13") and have been capitalized. The amount of such capitalized leases at December 31, 1977, included in other property and equipment, was $2,631,000, less $46,000 accumulated amortization. Lease amortization is included in depreciation expense.

Future minimum lease payments as of December 31, 1977 under capital leases and under noncancelable operating leases having initial or remaining lease terms of more than one year are shown below:

(In Thousands)	Capital Leases	Operating Leases
Payable during:		
1978	$2,056	$ 120,895
1979	126	113,185
1980	126	109,819
1981	126	100,775
1982	126	91,660
After 1982	629	747,489
Total minimum lease payments	3,189	$1,283,823
Estimated executory costs and profit	(37)	

continued

Net minimum lease payments	3,152	
Imputed interest (at rates of 8½% to 8¾%)	(567)	
Present value of net minimum lease payments	$2,585	n/a

The present value of net minimum capital lease payments is presented in the December 31, 1977 statement of consolidated financial position as current portion of long-term debt ($568,000) and long-term debt ($2,017,000).

Certain leases arising prior to January 1, 1977, presently considered to be operating leases, will be retroactively classified and accounted for as capital leases at a future date in 1978, under early application provisions of SFAS No. 13. Accordingly, UAL's consolidated financial statements for prior periods will be restated at that time. If such leases had been accounted for as capital leases in prior years, leased property under capital leases, less accumulated amortization, would have been greater by approximately $392,760,000 at December 31, 1977 and $443,513,000 at December 31, 1976 (including $281,678,000 and $327,401,000, respectively, of flight equipment); obligations under capital leases would have been greater by approximately $478,048,000 and $525,745,000 at those dates; and net earnings would have been decreased by approximately $3,176,000 ($.13 per share) in 1977 and $5,844,000 ($.23 per share) in 1976. Rental expense for all operating leases was as follows:

(In Thousands)	1977	1976
Minimum rentals	$138,661	$137,694
Contingent rentals	5,435	3,491
Sublease rentals	(2,892)	(2,715)
	$141,204	$138,470

There were no additional contingent rentals pertaining to capital leases.

Required:

1. Based on the information in the note, what is the amount included on the balance sheet of UAL, Inc., as of December 31, 1977, for assets leased under "capital" leases (i.e., leases that are in effect installment purchases)? What is the total balance of the related lease liability? If these two amounts differ, explain in words how such a difference could come about.

2. Assuming that the total balance in the lease liability account at December 31, 1977, is $2,585,000, write the journal entries to record the changes in this liability expected during 1978. Ignore the distinction between the current and long-term portion of the liability. Assume a weighted average interest rate of 8.6 percent. Also, assume that no new capital leases are added and that payments are made at the beginning of the year.

3. The note reports that certain leases accounted for as operating leases in 1977 will have to be accounted for retroactively as capital leases in 1978 (due to the new FASB standard regarding such leases). If these leases *had been capitalized in 1977,* what would the balances have been as of December 31, 1977, in (*a*) the company's leased assets and (*b*) lease liabilities? What would have been the effect of capitalizing these additional leases in 1977 on 1977 net income? In words, what accounts for this income effect?

12-11. Financial Statement Presentation of Leases. Following is Note 3 to the financial statements in the 1977 annual report of Sears, Roebuck and Co. and Consolidated Subsidiaries.

3. Change in accounting

In 1977, the company and its consolidated subsidiaries modified their method of accounting for leasing transactions as prescribed by Statement No. 13 of the Financial Accounting Standards Board. The new accounting rules require the capitalization of any lease that transfers substantially all of the benefits and risks of ownership to the lessee. The financial statements for 1976 and prior years have been restated for this change as follows:

(In Thousands)	Net Income— Year 1976	Retained Income— Years through 1975
As previously reported	$694,516	$4,833,182
Effect of capitalizing leases	(394)	(15,842)
As restated	$694,122	$4,817,340

Capital leases are amortized over the term of the respective leases. Lease amortization is included in depreciation expense.

Note 3 explains a change in accounting method whereby Sears, for the first time during the year ended 1/31/78, capitalized certain of its long-term noncancelable leases.

Required:

1. Based on the information given, what was the effect on retained earnings as of 1/31/77 (end of fiscal 1976) of capitalizing these leases? Show your work.

2. Explain in words the source or sources of the effect on retained earnings of the change in method of accounting for leases.

3. Based on your answer to number 1, an assumed tax rate of 48 percent, and the additional information that the capitalized lease obligation balance was $142,587,000 on 1/31/77, estimate the amount of the unamortized cost of the leased occupancy rights included in Sears's assets *as of 1/31/77.* (See note on page 484.)

(NOTE: The lease obligations are included in long-term debt and the lease rights are included in property, plant, and equipment on the statements of financial position. *Hint:* The effect of capitalization of the leases as of 1/31/77 [fiscal 1976 year-end] on retained earnings is equal to the difference between the capitalized asset and liability values on that date *times* one minus the tax rate.)

12-12. Marketable Equity Securities. In 19X5 Big Industrial Company (BIC) began to accumulate surplus cash that was not needed until its next major plant expansion, planned for 19X9. The company therefore began investing in marketable equity securities to utilize the funds effectively in the meantime. Its transactions and year-end portfolios for 19X5, 19X6, and 19X7 were as follows:

19X5—Purchased securities costing $1,800,000. Dividends were received in the amount of $90,000. Year-end portfolio:

Company	Cost	Market Value
X	$ 800,000	$900,000
Y	1,000,000	870,000

19X6—Sold half of X holdings for $500,000. Purchased shares of Z for $1,500,000. Dividends of $130,000 were received. Year-end portfolio:

Company	Cost	Market Value
X	$ 400,000	$ 450,000
Y	1,000,000	950,000
Z	1,500,000	1,550,000

19X7—Sold all Y holdings for $950,000. Purchased additional X shares for $1,200,000. Dividends of $50,000 were received. Year-end portfolio:

Company	Cost	Market Value
X	$1,600,000	$1,630,000
Z	1,500,000	1,420,000

Required:

Prepare the appropriate journal entries to record all of BIC's 19X5, 19X6, and 19X7 transactions related to marketable securities and to recognize the appropriate year-end aggregate value in the marketable securities account. Ignore taxes.

12-13. Some Inferences Based on Partial Consolidation Information. Following are some excerpts from the December 31, 19X3, balance sheets of Big and Small Corporations plus some supplemental information. Based on these items, answer the questions that appear after them.

Assets of Big Corporation:	
Cash	$ 1,500,000
Accounts receivable	2,500,000
Inventory	3,500,000
Net plant and equipment	4,500,000
Investment in Small Corporation:	
Loans	1,500,000
75% stock ownership	3,500,000
Total assets	$17,000,000
Liabilities and Owners' Equity	
of Small Corporation:	
Accounts payable	$ 500,000
Loans from parent company	1,500,000
Paid-in capital	3,000,000
Retained earnings	1,000,000
Total liabilities and owners' equity	$ 6,000,000

Supplemental information:

a. None of the inventory on hand at December 31, 19X3, of either company had been purchased from the other company.

b. Of the total December 31, 19X3, accounts payable of Big Corporation (not shown), $100,000 was owed to Small Corporation.

Required:

1. What amount should appear in the consolidated financial statements to represent the minority interests? Support your answer.

2. Will any amount show up on the consolidated financial statements opposite the caption "Unamortized excess of cost of investment over equity in net assets of subsidiary"? If so, what amount? Support your answer.

3. What will be the total amount of consolidated assets as of December 31, 19X3?

12-14. Income Statement Consolidation. Following are the separate 19X3 income statements of Giant Sales and its subsidiary (70 percent owned), Pee Wee Products, along with some supplemental information. Prepare a consolidated income statement for 19X3.

GIANT SALES COMPANY

Income Statement
For 19X3

Revenue		$35,000,000
Less expenses:		
Cost of sales	$20,000,000	
Interest expense	400,000	
Wages and salaries	10,000,000	
Depreciation expenses	1,000,000	
Other expense	500,000	31,900,000
Operating income		$ 3,100,000
Income from subsidiary:		
Interest	$ 100,000	
Equity in earnings	700,000	
Amortization of excess of cost over equity in net assets	(50,000)	750,000
Net income		$ 3,850,000

PEE WEE PRODUCTS COMPANY

Income Statement
For 19X3

Revenue		$10,900,000
Less expenses:		
Cost of sales	$5,380,000	
Interest expense	120,000	
Wages and salaries	3,700,000	
Depreciation expense	500,000	
Other expense	200,000	9,900,000
Net income		$ 1,000,000

Supplemental information:

During the year, Pee Wee sold $1 million worth of its products to Giant. Giant in turn sold all the goods purchased from Pee Wee. At year-end Pee Wee had been paid by Giant for all past purchases, and none of Pee Wee's products remained in Giant's inventory.

12-15. Effects of Alternate Methods of Accounting for Intercorporate Investments. Following is a supplemental table included in the notes to Corning Glass Works' financial statements for the fiscal year ended January 2, 1972 (fiscal 1971). Corning accounted for its unconsolidated associated companies (unconsolidated subsidiaries) according to the cost method (market value, in the aggregate, was apparently much higher). Corning owned 50 percent interests in both Pittsburgh Corning and Dow Corning and a 27.3 percent interest in Owens-Corning Fiberglas.

    1. What other alternative is *now* required for accounting for these three associated companies?

2. What total income before taxes from the associates would Corning have recognized for fiscal 1971 under (a) the cost method (the method used) and (b) the alternative method? Show your calculations where appropriate.

Investments in associated companies not consolidated

	Pittsburgh Corning Corporation and Dow Corning Corporation	Owens-Corning Fiberglas Corporation	Foreign Associated Companies	Total
Year ended January 2, 1972				
Investment	$11,244,563	$ 2,282,155	$ 6,629,354	$ 20,156,072
Equity in Net Assets	$55,417,500	$74,395,238	$14,385,028	$144,197,766
Dividends received	$ 4,375,000	$ 3,023,443	$ 803,269	$ 8,201,712
Equity in Undistributed Income for the year	$ 674,120	$ 3,857,379	$ 559,173	$ 5,090,672
Year ended January 3, 1971				
Investment	$11,244,563	$ 2,302,691	$ 6,741,911	$ 20,289,165
Equity in Net Assets	$53,333,110	$71,012,475	$15,298,752	$139,644,337
Dividends received	$ 4,500,000	$ 2,897,090	$ 898,532	$ 8,295,622
Equity in Undistributed Income for the year	$ 3,279,132	$ 2,807,343	$ 1,057,056	$ 7,143,531

The aggregate quoted market of Owens-Corning Fiberglas Corporation shares was approximately $209,496,000 in excess of the investment at the end of 1971 and $173,659,000 in excess of the investment at the end of 1970.

12-16. Equity Method Accounting. On January 1, 19X3, Ranger, Inc., purchased 8,000 shares of San Juan, Inc., common stock on the open market for $180,000. The shareholders' equity accounts of San Juan, Inc., as of January 1, 19X3, were: common stock ($10 par), $100,000; retained earnings, $50,000.

In reviewing the assets of San Juan in order to determine the source of the excess of Ranger's cost over the equity acquired in San Juan's net assets, it was determined that $20,000 is applicable to a building with five years of remaining life. (Such "assignable" differences are amortized over the lives of the related assets.) The remainder of the differential could not be identified with any *specific* tangible or intangible asset, and Ranger elects to amortize it over the maximum period of time permissible under current accounting policy (i.e., forty years).

For the year 19X3, the following information on operations and dividends is available:

	Ranger	San Juan
Net income	$15,000*	$15,000
Dividends paid	5,000	8,000

*Not including any effects of subsidiary operations or dividends for 19X3.

Ranger uses the *equity method* of accounting for its investment in San Juan.

1. What was the balance of Ranger's investment in San Juan account at December 31, 19X3?
2. What income did Ranger report for 19X3?

12-17. Consolidation of Financial Statements. Following are the 19X4 balance sheets and income statements (before consolidation) of Super Sales, Inc., and its 80 percent-owned subsidiary, Tiny Toys, Inc., along with certain supplemental information. (Super Sales' financial statements are not published separately, but Tiny Toys' statements are.)

Required:

1. Prepare a consolidated sheet as of December 31, 19X4.
2. Prepare a consolidated income statement for 19X4.
3. What was the balance in Super Sales' investment (account) in Tiny Toys at December 31, 19X3? (The equity method is used by Super Sales.)

Supplemental information:

a. Super Sales purchased its share of Tiny Toys on January 1, 19X3, at which time it was decided that the excess of its cost over its equity in the net assets of Tiny Toys should be amortized over the maximum period allowed under accounting policy (forty years).

b. Tiny Toys paid total dividends to its stockholders of $500,000 in 19X4.

c. During 19X4 Tiny Toys sold toys to Super Sales at a markup of 50 percent. The toys cost Tiny Toys $4 million. None of those toys were still in Super's inventory at December 31, 19X4. However, as of December 31, 19X4, Super Sales still owed Tiny Toys $1 million on its past toy purchases.

SUPER SALES, INC.

Balance Sheet
As of December 31, 19X4

Assets:		Liabilities and Stockholders' Equity:	
Cash	$ 5,000,000	Accounts payable	$ 3,000,000
Accounts receivable	4,000,000	Wages payable	1,000,000
Inventory	5,000,000	Taxes payable	1,000,000
Prepaid expenses	1,000,000		
Property, plant, and equipment (net)	18,200,000	Paid-in capital	25,000,000
Investment in Tiny Toys, Inc.	11,800,000	Retained earnings	15,000,000
	$45,000,000		$45,000,000

SUPER SALES, INC.

Income Statement
For the Year Ended December 31, 19X4

Revenue		$20,000,000
Less expenses:		
Cost of sales	$12,000,000	
Depreciation and amortization	3,000,000	
Other expense (including taxes)	3,000,000	18,000,000
Income from Super Sales' operations		$ 2,000,000
Add equity in earnings of Tiny Toys less amortization		
of excess of cost over equity in net assets		700,000
Net income		$ 2,700,000

TINY TOYS, INC.

Balance Sheet
As of December 31, 19X4

Assets:		Liabilities and Stockholders' Equity:	
Cash	$ 500,000	Accounts payable	$ 2,000,000
Accounts receivable	2,000,000	Wages payable	750,000
Inventory	2,000,000	Taxes payable	250,000
Prepaid expenses	500,000		
Property, plant, and		Paid-in capital	8,000,000
equipment (net)	8,000,000	Retained earnings	2,000,000
	$13,000,000		$13,000,000

TINY TOYS, INC.

Income Statement
For the Year Ended December 31, 19X4

Revenue		$10,000,000
Less expenses:		
Cost of sales	$6,000,000	
Depreciation	1,000,000	
Other expense (including taxes)	2,000,000	9,000,000
Net income		$ 1,000,000

12-18. **Equity Accounting in Financial Statements.** The financial statements and the notes thereto appearing in the 1976 Ashland Oil annual report included the following items pertaining to Ashland's unconsolidated subsidiaries and affiliates.

Excerpt from the income statement:

	Year ended September 30	
	1976	1975
	(Thousands of dollars)	
Income		
Sales and operating revenues*	$4,348,169	$3,881,736
Equity income—Note C	13,796	16,224
Interest and other income	38,083	38,619
	4,400,048	3,936,579

Excerpt from the statement of changes in financial position:

	Year ended September 30	
	1976	1975
	(Thousands of dollars)	
Working capital was provided from		
Operations:		
Net income	$135,983	$119,367
Add expenses not requiring outlay of working capital in the current year:	106,528	92,320
Depreciation, depletion and amortization	17,466	5,962
Write-off or amortization of exploration costs and undeveloped leases	29,420	35,880
	289,397	253,529
Less equity income (net of dividends)—Note C	11,309	13,166
Working capital provided from operations	278,088	240,363

Note C—Unconsolidated subsidiaries and affiliates
Ashland's investments in unconsolidated subsidiaries and affiliates, which are accounted for on the equity method, consist principally of a 48.9% interest in Arch Mineral Corporation, a coal company, and various interests in chemical and petroleum companies. Following is a condensed summary of combined financial data of such companies for 1976 and 1975 [see page 491].

Required:

1. Based on the information in Note C, reconcile the 1976 "equity income" figure in the income statement and the 1976 "less equity income" item in the statement of changes in financial position. Show the details of the reconciling items by category of affiliated companies. Ashland uses the equity method to account for affiliates and unconsolidated subsidiaries.

2. Since Ashland's investment account includes the amounts of advances (loans) to affiliates as well as the investment in affiliates, it can increase due to additional loans and decrease due to payments on loans from affiliates as well as from the usual investment-related

Excerpt from the notes to the financial statements:

	Domestic				Foreign	
	Arch Mineral Corporation (48.9% owned)		Others (20% to 50% owned)		Subsidiaries and affiliates (various interests)	
	1976	1975*	1976	1975	1976	1975
	(Thousands of dollars)					
Total assets	$154,744	$119,484	$46,854	$47,896	$217,258	$168,235
Total liabilities	98,843	85,007	23,413	29,636	166,322	113,427
Net assets	$ 55,901	$ 34,477	$23,441	$18,260	$ 50,936	$ 54,808
Revenues	$133,469	$125,053	$31,038	$28,780	$235,387	$224,924
Net income	21,423	27,040	7,664	6,125	6,628	7,400
Ashland's investment including accumulated equity income and advances	43,300‡	32,729	7,339	6,357	30,858	33,966
Ashland's share of net income (loss)	11,033††	13,842††	3,027	1,183	(264)	1,199
Dividends received	—	—	1,836	1,549	651	1,509

*Restated.
†Includes $1,517,000 tax benefit from loss carry-forward.
‡In addition, Ashland received royalty income of $4,527,000 in 1976 and $4,434,000 in 1975.

sources. From the information available, and assuming Ashland did not invest in any additional common stock of affiliates during 1976, estimate the net increase or decrease in loans to affiliates during 1976. Indicate whether the change was an increase or a decrease and show your work. Note the balance in Ashland's "investment" accounting at September 30, 1975 and 1976, was $73,052,000 and $81,497,000, respectively.

3. Describe in words what the balance in Ashland's investments in and advances to unconsolidated subsidiaries and affiliates represents as of any given balance sheet date. That is, describe its components.

ALTERNATIVE FINANCIAL ACCOUNTING MODELS

Alternative Financial Accounting Models: Modifications for General Price-Level Changes

13

In Chapter 5 we observe that in times of changing prices, the conventional accounting model loses some of its intuitive appeal as a means of measuring enterprise performance and disposable wealth. The purpose of this and the next two chapters is to introduce three alternative financial accounting models that are now under serious consideration by the accounting profession and the business community in response to an increasingly inflationary environment.

The implications of changing prices can be assessed at two levels. First, there is general inflation or deflation. Inflation or deflation refers to the general drift upward or downward in prices, the exchange rates at which money is traded for all goods and services. Second, the prices of some goods or services rise (rise more rapidly) or fall (fall more rapidly) *relative* to the prices of other goods and services whether or not prices are generally rising or falling. This chapter approaches the problem of changing prices at the former (general) level; the next two chapters approach the problem at the latter (specific) level.

The Relevance of Changes in General Purchasing Power

What we are about to describe in this chapter is the basic technical methodology and the underlying rationale for adapting conventional accounting to the phenomenon of general inflation or deflation. The result of the adaptation is a modified conventional accounting model that includes measures of performance and disposable wealth *that have the same characteristics in times of generally changing prices that conventional accounting measures have in times of static prices.* Before proceeding, however, some attention to our motivation is in order.

Generally, the prices of all goods and services do not rise and fall together. Some rise or fall faster than others; and the prices of some goods may actually move in the opposite direction to the general inflationary trend. Furthermore, all economic units—businesses as well as individuals—tend to have unique spending patterns. As a result, inflation or deflation will have a different impact on each economic unit depending on the relative price changes of the goods and services it prefers. But if inflation or deflation has a unique impact on each business and individual, why attempt to modify conventional accounting on the basis of the general trend in prices? The answer lies in the rationale for using money values as a *common unit* of expression under any circumstances (i.e., static prices or not).

Since the prices of some goods and services go down while others go up (or they change at different rates), it is certainly true that some people will derive relatively more or less *satisfaction* from money than others as prices change. However, the satisfaction we get from spending is not a basis on which we can defend using money as a common unit of expression in the first place—even in times of perfectly stable prices. The mere fact that individuals' tastes and preferences change over time means that satisfaction from spending will change *even though no prices change.* The basis for using money as a unit of measure is its meaning as an index or unit of command over quantities (and varieties) of goods and services. The power of money generally to command goods and services is a function of the quantities of the various goods and services available and the prices of those goods and services. When prices generally go up or down, that power changes proportionately for everyone, quite apart from individual tastes and preferences. That is, in exercising individual purchasing preferences at any point in time, each individual sacrifices or forgoes just what everyone else forgoes in alternative goods and services for every dollar spent on a particular item.

When prices generally rise or fall, it alters the *sacrifice* of alternate goods and services embodied in spending any given dollar on any given item. This is why the original transaction costs employed (recognized) in conventional accounting gradually become less relevant over time when prices generally rise or fall. An amount of dollars actually spent in the past to acquire a resource ceases to represent currently the *original* sacrifice of alternate goods and services to possess that particular resource. *In adjusting original transaction values for changes in general purchasing power, the purpose is to express the original sacrifice in terms of the number of current (or recent) dollars that, if spent today, would mean the forgoing of the same alternate real goods and services.*

With this rationale established, we proceed by (1) describing briefly some tools for recognizing and adjusting for changes in purchasing power, (2) developing an easily calculated measure of disposable wealth that takes into account generally rising or falling prices, and (3) showing finally that this measure of disposable wealth is composed of two parts, each of which measures an aspect of enterprise performance in times of changing prices.

Price-Level Indexes and Comparative Purchasing Power in Constant Dollars

We have heretofore referred to changes in purchasing power without describing how such changes are measured, or even how purchasing power itself is measured. As a rule, purchasing power and purchasing power changes are characterized by means of price-level indexes.

Price-Level Index. A price-level index is a numerical score representing the cost of a particular bundle of goods and services as of one point in time (some year) *relative to* the cost of the same bundle of goods and services at some reference point in time (usually called a "base" year).

The hypothetical bundle of goods is usually constructed so as to contain typical or representative proportions of the goods and services purchased by a class of economic units whose purchasing power is of interest, such as households, businesses, unmarried college students, or all economic units in the economy.

Constructing Index Numbers. Suppose that the typical or average bundle of goods for some particular class of economic units has the costs shown in the second column of Exhibit 13-1 in the years 1975-1980—the total costs being derived by (1) determining how much of each product or service was included in the typical bundle, (2) multiplying each product's quantity by its price, and (3) totaling the amounts calculated in (2).

Exhibit 13-1
COST OF GOODS
AND PRICE-LEVEL INDEX

Year	Cost	Index Value
1975	$1,980	90
1976	1,870	85
1977	2,090	95
1978	2,200	100
1979	2,420	110
1980	2,310	105

As is the usual custom, let us choose one year, say 1978, as the base year and set its index value to 100 (we could use any convenient number and still gain the manipulative advantages of an index). We are saying that $2,200 on the money scale is equivalent to 100 on *our* price-level index scale. Using proportions, we can then work out index values for all the other years relative to the base year. For instance, to get an index value for 1979 we need only pose the question, $2,420 is to $2,200 as *what* index value is to 100? Letting *i* represent the unknown value, the answer can be worked out as follows:

$$\frac{\$2,420}{\$2,200} = \frac{i}{100}$$

$$i = \frac{2,420}{2,200} \times 100$$

$$i = 110$$

Posing similar questions for the other years fills out the price-level index column of Exhibit 13-1.

Using Price-Level Index Numbers. Now we can conveniently make some statements about the purchasing power of the hypothetical class of economic units of interest. For instance, we can say that in 1980 it took $105, on the average, for that class of economic units to buy what it could buy in 1978 for $100. In other words, prices for this group had risen on the average to 1.05 of what they were in 1978 (105/100). Or in still other words, a dollar in 1980 was worth only 95.24 percent of what it was worth to this group in 1978, on the average (i.e., it would buy only 100/105 as many goods and services).

Similar comparisons can be made for other years—and we are not restricted to comparisons between the base year and nonbase years. For instance, since 1977 has an index value of 95 and 1976 has a value of 85, we know that prices for the group rose 11.76 percent on the average between 1976 and 1977, i.e., 1977 prices were 95/85, or 1.1176 of 1976 prices on the average.

Finally, and most important for our purposes, if we have a set of price-level index values and the price paid for a particular good purchased in a particular year, we can translate the price paid into an equivalent money sacrifice in the dollars of any other year. For instance, if an item purchased by our hypothetical group cost $240 in 1978 (when the index was 100), we can say that it would have required $264 to make the same sacrifice of alternate goods and services in 1979 (when the index was 110), that is, $240 × (110/100) = $264. This type of translation is a fundamental element of the techniques introduced in later sections of the chapter.

Selecting an Appropriate Index

Before leaving the topic of price-level indexes and their applications, an additional point relevant to the purpose of this financial accounting model should be made. The purpose of general price-level adjustments is to preserve, in times of generally changing prices, the meaning that the original transaction values employed in conventional accounting have in times of static prices. Accordingly, the model, which might appropriately be labeled a general price-level adjusted conventional accounting model, retains the price paid in exchange transactions as a point of departure and adjusts for the change in the size (purchasing power) of the unit of measure (the dollar) used to express those values.

To accomplish this purpose, the price-level index used to characterize general purchasing power should possess certain properties. It should be broadly based—including quantities and prices of as many of the available goods and services in the economy as possible. In addition, it should include correction factors for changes in the quality of the goods and services available. Changes in quality are a major confounding force in attempts to characterize changes in the size of the dollar (general purchasing power) over time. If prices generally rise so that a dollar purchases less on the average, the sacrifice in quantity of goods and services forgone in spending a dollar goes down. However, if products improve in quality, the sacrifice of real economic service of those products forgone does not go down in proportion to the quantity reduction. So some qualitative correction is certainly in order if a price-level index is to express changes in general purchasing power accurately in an economy characterized by rapidly changing technology.

Although it is almost impossible to prepare an ideal price-level index for the U.S. economy, several reasonably good indexes are provided by certain government agencies. The Gross National Product Implicit Price Deflator produced by the U.S. Department of Commerce is broadly based. But some authors find it objectionable because it is not corrected for changes in quality of goods and services. On the other hand, the Bureau of Labor Statistics' Consumer Price Index is widely accepted as a measure of general price levels and is not as greatly affected by changes in quality of products as some indexes. However, it is not our purpose to go into great detail about the suitability of various available indexes.

Conventional Accounting in Times of Generally Changing Prices

To review briefly the problems encountered in conventional accounting in times of inflation or deflation and to suggest the means to their solution, let us consider an extremely simple example. Example 13-1 is easily followed through to a complete solution. Yet it can be used to illustrate the basic concepts and much of the necessary technical skill involved in adjusting conventional accounting for changes in the general level of prices.

Example 13-1

> Our hypothetical case will be the Trading Corporation founded by Mr. Speculator a year ago to buy and sell various products on a strictly cash basis. Mr. Speculator started Trading Corporation with an investment of $8,000 of his own money plus $2,000 borrowed from a friend at 5 percent interest per year. The friend agreed that the interest was to be accrued continuously in each year but need not be paid each year. Rather, it could be added to the loan balance, accumulated, and paid at the end of the five-year loan period.
>
> At the beginning of the year Trading Corporation made several large purchases of surplus commodities and retail products at going-out-of-business auctions, spending $9,000 of its cash. No other purchases were made during the year. Instead, the goods purchased at the beginning of the year were gradually sold off throughout the year until only $900 of the original inventory remained at year-end. Total cash sales amounted to $12,000 during the year.
>
> The conventional accounting treatment of these facts is presented, for convenience, in a

financial worksheet format in Exhibit 13-2. The last line of the worksheet has, however, been changed from "Ending Position" to "Preliminary Balances." This label implies that something remains to be recognized. That is indeed the case. Mr. Speculator has not made his annual withdrawal of cash from the business. The purpose of arriving at what we have labeled Preliminary Balances is to give Mr. Speculator an idea of what ending financial position would be if no withdrawal were made. The "preliminary balance" numbers in each element of financial position are calculated as if they were the amounts in the enterprise's ending position.

Exhibit 13-2

TRADING CORPORATION

Financial Position Worksheet
For the Year 19X1

Description	Cash	Inventory	Loan	Owner's Equity
Beginning Position	10,000		2,000	8,000
Purchases	(9,000)	9,000		
Sales (throughout year)	12,000			12,000 (R)
Cost of sales		(8,100)		(8,100) (E)
Interest			100	(100) (E)
Preliminary Balances	13,000	900	2,100	11,800

Exhibit 13-2 points up a dilemma faced by Mr. Speculator. He wants to determine how much of the end-of-year cash he should withdraw from Trading Corporation for his personal use in the coming year. Mr. Speculator owns several small businesses that have generally provided him with a good living. But to ensure that this continues, he has always tried to restrict his withdrawals to amounts that do not impair his original investment in each business. That policy has been easy to follow in recent years. Prices generally have not changed (hypothetically, of course), and the yearly conventional accounting net income from each business has served as a reasonably satisfactory index of how much he could withdraw. But this year is different. Severe inflation has set in, so that the general price-level index went from 100 at the beginning of the year to 121 at the end, averaging 110 during the year.

As Exhibit 13-2 reflects, conventional accounting net operating income for Trading Corporation for its first year of operations is $3,800 ($12,000 sales revenue less $8,200 total expense). If Mr. Speculator withdraws cash in an amount equal to net operating income of $3,800, as he has done in past years with his other businesses, the effect on Trading Corporation's financial position is illustrated in Exhibit 13-3, which picks up where Exhibit 13-2 leaves off.

A withdrawal of $3,800 in cash would leave net assets of $9,200 cash plus inventory with an original cost of $900 less a liability of $2,100, a total equal in number of dollars to Mr. Speculator's original investment of $8,000. But Mr. Speculator's original investment of $8,000 was made when the price-level index was at 100. By the end of the year, with the price-level index at 121, it would take 121/100 × $8,000, or $9,680, to represent the same amount of general

Exhibit 13-3

TRADING CORPORATION

Financial Position Worksheet
As of the End of 19X1

Description	Cash	Inventory	Loan	Owner's Equity
Preliminary Balances	13,000	900	2,100	11,800
Withdrawal	(3,800)			(3,800) (W)
Ending (Beginning) Position	9,200	900	2,100	8,000

purchasing power as $8,000 represented at the beginning of the year. Thus, to withdraw $3,800 would be to shrink the asset base of the business below its original purchasing power. Conventional accounting net income therefore does not serve at least one of its purposes—that of a reliable index of disposable wealth—in times of rising prices.

Disposable Wealth in Times of Generally Changing Prices

Now suppose Mr. Speculator wanted to withdraw only as much cash as would not impair the original purchasing power invested in Trading Corporation. How would he determine that amount? A first impulse might be to look to the conventional accounting preliminary balances shown on the worksheet and observe that before any year-end withdrawal there would be $13,000 cash plus inventory with an original cost of $900 less a liability of $2,100—a total of $11,800 of net assets possessed by the business. A hasty conclusion would then be that Mr. Speculator could withdraw cash equal to the difference between the net assets possessed prior to the withdrawal, $11,800, and the end-of-year dollar equivalent of his original $8,000 investment, or $9,680. Although it is perhaps intuitively appealing, this conclusion is logically inconsistent.

The $9,680 is the amount of end-of-year dollars equivalent in purchasing power to $8,000 at the beginning of the year, whereas the $11,800 is a mixture of dollars of different purchasing power. That is, the $11,800 is the sum of $13,000 year-end cash and $900 original cost of inventory in *beginning-of-year dollars* less the year-end liability balance of $2,100. We simply cannot subtract $9,680 *end-of-year dollars* from this mixed sum of $11,800 and get meaningful results. First, some adjustment has to be made in order to measure Trading Corporation's preliminary ending position on the same basis as the $9,680 criterion amount, that is, end-of-year dollars. In making this adjustment, we encounter an important application of the difference noted in Chapter 4 between monetary and nonmonetary assets and liabilities.

Adjusting Ending Balances in Accounts. Recall that by definition monetary assets (including cash) and monetary liabilities are rights to receive and obligations to pay fixed amounts of dollars at specified times. Although the purchasing power of a dollar may change over time, such specific amounts do not change. Monetary assets and liabilities, valued at their specified or nominal amounts, are always stated in current dollars. Hence, adjustment for changes in purchasing power of year-end balances of monetary assets or liabilities is neither necessary nor appropriate. In the case of Trading Corporation, then, no adjustment is made to either the preliminary ending cash balance of $13,000 or the ending loan balance of $2,100.

However, the same is not true of nonmonetary items, which, in the case of Trading Corporation, includes only the inventory with an original cost of $900. Each of those 900 beginning-of-year dollars originally spent on the items in the ending inventory represents a purchasing power sacrifice different from a one-dollar sacrifice at the end of the year. In fact, we know that in order to have given up as much purchasing power at the end of the year as was given up at the beginning of the year for those items, it would take 121/100 × $900 = $1,089. To state the entire ending position of Trading Corporation in year-end dollars, it is necessary to adjust the original cost of the inventory upward from $900 to $1,089.

Although such an adjustment satisfies the purpose of measuring all assets of Trading Corporation in terms of year-end dollars, it raises some questions as well. First, how can we arbitrarily alter the amount of an asset held by the enterprise as of a point in time? Second, what does it mean when we increase the dollars of Trading Corporation's ending inventory from $900 to $1,089? Has the enterprise gained something?

The answer to both questions is that we have not altered the inventory element of financial position by making our adjustment. Rather, the whole process is like dealing with a foreign currency. By the time we get to the end of the year—the point in time at which we wish to calculate disposable wealth—beginning-of-the-year dollars are no longer the dollars we deal in. Because of inflation, we deal in a new currency—no matter that we call it by the same name, dollars.

Now suppose that all the purchases at the beginning of the year had been conducted in a foreign currency, but at the end of the year Trading Corporation switched to dollars. Would it alter financial position to restate in terms of the new currency the costs of the nonmonetary assets purchased with the old currency? No, it would just be stating the same facts in terms of the new currency. Essentially that is what we do when we state the original purchasing power *cost* of Trading Corporation's ending inventory in end-of-year dollars. Furthermore, since the end-of-year assets of the enterprise are unaltered by the conversion to a new currency, no change in the wealth of the enterprise (gain or loss) occurs. The larger "adjusted" inventory of $1,089 is simply the same wealth item (inventory) valued at the same value, the original purchasing power given in exchange for it. But, inasmuch as prices have generally risen during the year, it requires more dollars (each of lesser purchasing power) than at the time of the purchase *to represent the sacrifice made in the original transaction.*

Calculating Disposable Wealth—Summary. Now, in summary, we can conclude that (1) prior to any withdrawal by Mr. Speculator, Trading Corporation has net assets expressed in end-of-year dollars of $11,989 ($13,000 in cash plus ending inventory having an original purchasing power cost in *end-of-year dollars* of $1,089 less a liability of $2,100), (2) it is necessary to have only $9,680 of net assets in end-of-year dollars to have an end-of-year purchasing power equivalent of the original $8,000 invested in the business, and (3) therefore, $2,309 of cash ($11,989 − $9,680) can be withdrawn from the business at year-end without reducing the recognized purchasing power of the recognized net assets (owner's equity) below the level at the beginning of the year.

The latter conclusion is just what Mr. Speculator wants to know. He can withdraw $2,309 from Trading Corporation at the end of its first year of operations without impairing the purchasing power that he originally invested in the business. Furthermore, the steps required to arrive at this amount are straightforward and few in number, even for the most complicated business enterprise. The steps are listed below and illustrated with reference to Trading Corporation in Exhibit 13-4.

1. The end-of-year balances of all nonmonetary elements of financial position are adjusted to their equivalent purchasing power in end-of-year dollars. (In the example the $900 original cost of the ending inventory was adjusted to end-of-year dollars of equivalent purchasing power, $1,089—lines 7 and 8 of Exhibit 13-4.)

2. The net (or sum) of all monetary and adjusted nonmonetary assets and liabilities is calculated to get a price-level-adjusted end-of-period net asset figure. (In the example, we added the end-of-year cash balance of $13,000 to the adjusted ending inventory figure of $1,089 and subtracted the liability balance of $2,100 to get the adjusted net asset figure of $11,989—line 8 of Exhibit 13-4.)

3. The end-of-year dollar equivalents must be calculated for the net assets (assets minus liabilities) *at the beginning of the period*. (In the example there were net assets of $8,000 at the beginning of the year; the end-of-year dollar equivalent of the $8,000 was $9,680—line 9 of Exhibit 13-4.)

4. Subtract the amount described in number 3 above from the adjusted net asset figure in number 2 to get the amount, if any, of withdrawable

Exhibit 13-4

TRADING CORPORATION

Price-Level-Adjusted Net Income
(Disposable Wealth)
For the Year 19X1

Description	Cash	Inventory	Loan	Owner's Equity
1. Beginning Position	10,000		2,000	8,000
2. Purchases	(9,000)	9,000		
3. Sales	12,000			12,000 (R)
4. Cost of sales		(8,100)		(8,100) (E)
5. Interest			100	(100) (E)
6. Preliminary balances	13,000	900	2,100	11,800
7. Adjustment factor		121/100		
8. Price-level-adjusted balances	13,000 +	1,089 −	2,100 =	$11,989
9. P-L-A beginning net assets (owner's equity) $8,000 × 121/100			=	9,680
10. P-L-A net income (disposable wealth)				$ 2,309

assets, i.e., disposable wealth. *We will call this amount price-level-adjusted net income.* (In the example, we subtracted $9,680 from $11,989 to get $2,309—lines 8, 9, and 10 of Exhibit 13-4.)

The effect of a cash withdrawal of $2,309 on Trading Corporation's ending financial position is illustrated in Exhibits 13-5 and 13-6. Notice particularly that (1) the financial position worksheet in Exhibit 13-5 starts with the price-level-adjusted preliminary balances from Exhibit 13-4 (line 8), and (2) the after-withdrawal owner's equity equals the criterion amount of $9,680 in both Exhibits 13-5 and 13-6.

As a final observation, the reader should be aware that the method of calculating disposable wealth worked out in this section is a direct application of the Hicksian definition of income (disposable wealth) discussed in Chapters 2 and 5. That definition states that disposable wealth is the amount of wealth that an economic unit can dispose of during a period without leaving itself worse off at the end of the period than at the beginning. Direct application of the definition therefore implies that beginning and ending wealth (net assets) are measured (allowing for owner investments and withdrawals) and that the difference between the two figures is disposable wealth for the period. That is precisely what the technique described in this section does—with the additional refinement that both beginning and ending net assets are measured in terms of the same

Exhibit 13-5

TRADING CORPORATION

Financial Position Worksheet
19X1

Description	*Cash*	*Inventory*	*Loan*	*Owner's Equity*
P-L-A preliminary balances	13,000	1,089	2,100	11,989
Withdrawal	(2,309)			(2,309) (W)
Ending Position	10,691	1,089	2,100	9,680

Exhibit 13-6

TRADING CORPORATION

Balance Sheet
As of the End of 19X1

Assets:		Liabilities and Owner's Equity:	
Cash	$10,691	Loan	$ 2,100
Inventory	1,089	Owner's equity	9,680
Total assets	$11,780	Total liabilities and owner's equity	$11,780

units—end-of-year dollars. Where owner investments and/or withdrawals are present during the period, they too must be price-level adjusted to end-of-year dollars before they are incorporated into the calculation of net income.

Thus we can say with confidence that regardless of the complexity of the business, we can find the amount of disposable wealth in times of rising or falling prices that, if distributed by the business, will leave its initial purchasing power intact. This amount (price-level-adjusted net income) thus serves as a reliable index of disposable wealth in times of changing prices in the same sense that conventional accounting net income serves that purpose in times of stable prices.

Price-Level Changes and Performance Measurement

It should be recalled, however, that in times of stable prices, conventional accounting income measures have another desirable property as well as measuring disposable wealth. Net operating income measures the performance of the enterprise. That is, net operating income characterizes the enterprise's recognized current ability to produce products whose values to customers (revenues) exceed the costs of resources sacrificed to produce them (expenses). And to the extent that current performance is sustainable, or a measure of the business's continuing capability, net income presumably can provide owner-investors and creditors with valuable information about the future cash-generating ability of the enterprise.

Therefore, even though we now have a way of determining a reliable index of disposable wealth in times of changing prices, we ought to go further and ask the question, Is there also a way of characterizing performance in times of changing prices, comparable to conventional accounting net income in times of stable prices? The answer is yes. But it will take some additional analysis of our example to see that this is so.

Conventional Accounting Performance Measurement and Changing Prices. One place to start in arriving at a performance measure in times of changing prices is the logic of conventional accounting performance measurement. The appeal of conventional accounting net income as a performance measure is the matching principle—according to which revenues are offset by *causally related* expenses to get the index of performance, net operating income. So as a first step we might ask, Does conventional accounting net operating income have the same appeal as a performance measure in times of changing prices that it has when prices are stable? If not, why not?

The answer to the first question is no. The reason is apparent when we analyze the conventional accounting net operating income for Trading Corporation's first year, shown in Exhibit 13-7.

Why is the $3,800 conventional accounting net operating income figure unsuitable as a performance measure under the hypothetical circumstances of our example? We noted above that it was unacceptable to add the $13,000 preliminary end-of-year cash balance to the $900 beginning-of-year cost of the ending inventory. Each dollar included in one of the figures represents a different amount of purchasing power than each dollar in the other figure. Hence to add

Exhibit 13-7

TRADING CORPORATION

Income Statement
For the Year 19X1

Sales revenue		$12,000
Less expenses:		
Cost of sales	$8,100	
Interest	100	8,200
Net operating income		$ 3,800

them gives a result that is meaningless in conveying total purchasing power. Similarly, the revenue figure of $12,000, the expense (cost of sales) figure of $8,100, and the interest expense figure of $100 in Exhibit 13-7 *do not* represent total accomplishments and total sacrifices in equal-sized purchasing-power units, that is, on the same measurement scale.

Price-Level-Adjusted Operating Income. The $8,100 originally paid for the goods sold was sacrificed at the beginning of the year when the price level was at 100, whereas the $12,000 received from customers was received throughout the year as the price-level index averaged 110. By year-end, when all the interest had been accrued, the index had reached 121. Thus, as a result of price-level changes, none of the unadjusted amounts convey the purchasing power given or received at the times of the original transactions. Because the meaning of one dollar continued to change throughout the year, original numbers of dollars exchanged lost their ability to convey the significance of the original economic events. But the situation is not without remedy. Just as we adjusted the 900 original dollars paid for the ending inventory to 1,089 equivalent end-of-year dollars in an earlier section, we can adjust conventional accounting revenues and expenses of the period to their end-of-year dollar equivalents. The appropriate translations appear in Exhibit 13-8.

Exhibit 13-8

TRADING CORPORATION

Statement of Price-Level-Adjusted Operating Income
For the Year 19X1

	Original Transaction Value	Adjustment Factor	Price-Level-Adjusted Value
Sales revenue	$12,000	121/110	$13,200
Less expenses:			
Cost of sales	8,100	121/100	$ 9,801
Interest expense	100	121/110	110
Total expense			$ 9,911
Price-level-adjusted operating income			$ 3,289

The reasoning behind the translations in Exhibit 13-8 is basically the same as that used earlier. Since the price level averaged 110 as sales revenues were received throughout the year and since the price level had reached 121 by year-end, we can conclude that on the average for every $110 received from customers during the year, Trading Corporation would have had to receive $121 at year-end to receive the same amount of purchasing power. Hence the 13,200 end-of-year dollars, that is, $12,000 × (121/110) shown in the Price-Level-Adjusted Value column, equals the *purchasing power equivalent of the 12,000 actual revenue dollars received* during the year shown in the Original Transaction Value column. The item in the Adjustment Factor column, 121/110, is the ratio of end-of-year dollars to average-of-year dollars of equivalent purchasing power. It is used to get the adjusted figure from the actual dollar total. Note again that the purpose of the adjustments is not to alter the original transaction value basis, but rather to express all revenues and expense amounts in equal-sized units, namely, end-of-year dollars.

Perhaps it is also best recognized at this point that the above method for price-level adjusting total revenue is purely an expedient method. A more precise way for price-level adjusting an aggregate of many individual exchange prices, like total revenue for a period, is to first adjust the price received (or paid) in each individual transaction, according to the price level at the time that the individual exchanges took place. Then the individually adjusted prices can be summed to arrive at an adjusted aggregate. However, such a method involves considerably more effort than the use of the average index method employed above. Furthermore, provided the set of sales or other individual transactions is fairly evenly distributed over the period, relatively little difference in the results of applying the two methods is to be expected. In practice, the selection of a method would involve a trade-off between precision and clerical cost and effort. But since nothing is gained by greater precision for purely expositional purposes, we will continue to use the more convenient average index method in the present discussion.

The reasoning underlying the adjustment of expenses (cost of sales and interest) is similar to that for revenues. Since the cost of the goods sold to customers during the period was expended at the beginning of the year when the price-level index was 100, we know that it would take 121 end-of-year dollars for every $100 actually spent to represent the original purchasing power sacrificed. Thus the cost of sales in end-of-year dollars is $9,801 (121/100 × $8,100). Since the interest was accrued continuously over the period with the offsetting credit to Loan Payable—a monetary liability, it is adjusted like the revenue.

When we subtract the $9,911 adjusted total expense from the $13,200 adjusted sales revenues we get $3,289, the amount labeled *price-level-adjusted operating income* in Exhibit 13-8.

Price-Level-Adjusted Operating Income. Price-level-adjusted operating income equals price-level-adjusted revenue minus price-level-adjusted expense for the period.

Notice that the amount is different from (in this case, less than) the $3,800 net income calculated earlier using conventional accounting. This, of course, is a result of the adjustments to take account of changes in purchasing power in measuring revenue and expense—but it is only a result of the adjustments. With respect to matching revenues and expenses based on original transaction values, the price-level-adjusted calculation agrees with the unadjusted version. One might expect then that price-level-adjusted operating income would have *all* of the characteristics in times of changing prices that conventional accounting net operating income has in times of stable prices. But the $3,289 price-level-adjusted operating income calculated above hardly agrees with the amount of disposable wealth of $2,309 calculated in Exhibit 13-4—which brings us to the final major issue in our discussion of performance measurement in times of changing prices.

Relationship between Performance and Disposable Wealth in Times of Changing Prices

In Chapter 5 we noted that in the absence of gains and losses, conventional accounting net operating income served the dual role of both a performance index and a disposable wealth index. The duality was entirely sensible. After all, disposable wealth is the advance in net assets of the enterprise over and above what it would take to simply retain its initial position. But in the long run one would expect such advances (apart from extraordinary gains and losses) to result from the productive efforts, that is, performance, of the enterprise. Indeed the question can be asked, What is performance if it is not the generation of disposable wealth? So, in the normal course of events, we would think that a good measure of "performance" should also be a good measure of disposable wealth as well—barring extraordinary events.

Of what interest is the duality notion to our discussion of price-level-adjusted operating income? Price-level-adjusted operating income is analogous to conventional accounting net operating income in the aspect of "performance" that it measures, that is, it characterizes the enterprise's efficiency and effectiveness in producing products or services. But price-level-adjusted operating income does not, by itself, measure disposable wealth (even in the absence of extraordinary gains and losses). This suggests that perhaps in times of changing prices there is an additional aspect of wealth change (and possibly of performance change) besides the enterprise's active efforts to produce products and services. And there is! In times of rising or falling prices there is a real, though subtle, *additional* source of increases and decreases in enterprise wealth—quite apart from the so-called productive activity engaged in by the enterprise. Interestingly, we will see that the distinction between monetary and nonmonetary assets again becomes important in explaining this "additional source" of wealth.

Monetary Assets and Liabilities in Times of Changing Prices. If you have ever heard the expression "Go in debt and let inflation bail you out," you have some idea of what happens to debtors and creditors as prices rise. A liability usually specifies that a particular number of dollars be paid by the debtor to the creditor at specific future times. If prices rise between the time the debt is incurred and the time it is paid off, the debtor benefits by paying back less in purchasing power than agreed to at the time the debt was incurred—and vice versa if prices fall. Conversely, the creditor gets back less purchasing power than bargained for during a period of rising prices and more when prices are falling. True, the debtor may pay and the creditor may receive compensating interest payments. But then the interest paid may not all be disposable if the creditor wishes to maintain his purchasing power intact. Furthermore, most individuals and businesses find it necessary to hold cash in hand (or in "checking" accounts) where it earns no compensatory interest, simply to facilitate the payment of debts when due and to acquire assets directly for cash when necessary. Holders of cash balances are affected in the same way as creditors in times of rising and falling prices. If a business holds a specific, fixed amount of dollars as prices rise, it is losing purchasing power. The longer it waits, the fewer goods and services it will be able to command with the given amount of dollars—and vice versa when prices are falling.

Perhaps these basic facts about the effects of inflation or deflation are already familiar to the reader. What may not be so familiar is that virtually every business holds some monetary or fixed-dollar assets (typically including at least some cash and accounts receivable), and at least some monetary liabilities as well. Depending on the balance between monetary assets and liabilities, the enterprise will have the advantage (or disadvantage) of being either a "net" debtor or a "net" creditor in times of changing prices.

Monetary Gains and Losses. Why are we interested in the net debtor-creditor characteristics of the firm? Because the *monetary gains and losses* experienced by the enterprise are the additional explanatory factors linking price-level-adjusted operating income to disposable wealth in times of inflation or deflation.

> **Monetary Gains and Losses.** Monetary gains (losses) are increases (decreases) in purchasing power that result from holding monetary assets and/or carrying monetary liabilities during a period of changing prices.

Calculating Monetary Gains and Losses. To see the relationship between (1) net monetary gain or loss, (2) price-level-adjusted operating income, and (3) price-level-adjusted net income (disposable wealth), reconsider the Trading Corporation example. Trading Corporation had only two monetary items, cash and a loan. The presence of only two such items greatly simplifies our exposition of the relationship. And rather than losing from the simplicity, the discussion will benefit. Although we will only deal directly with a single monetary asset (cash), a single liability (the loan), and a period of rising prices, our reasoning and techniques apply with only minor modification to any business situation in times of falling as well as rising prices.

Example 13-2

> Recall Trading Corporation's cash position and the changes that took place in that position during its first year of operations (see Exhibit 13-2). The company began operations when the price-level index was at 100 with $10,000 of cash. It immediately expended $9,000 of its cash for inventory while the price-level index was still at 100. Then, throughout the year, it received a total of $12,000 from sales to customers as the price-level index went from 100 to 121, averaging 110. The company ended the period with $13,000 actual cash on hand. Since the company held cash, a monetary asset, as prices rose during the year it was losing purchasing power. The only question is, How much purchasing power did it lose as a result of its cash holdings? To answer this question we have to pose several other questions.

Suppose that Trading Corporation had done nothing more than hold its original $10,000 throughout the year, neither spending any of it nor receiving any additional cash. It would have lost purchasing power. It would still only have $10,000 at year-end, but prices generally rose, that is, the index went from 100 to 121. One way of assessing the loss of purchasing power is to ask the question, How much cash would Trading Corporation have to have at the end of the year to have as much purchasing power then as it had at the beginning of the year with $10,000? The answer is that it would take 121/100 × $10,000 or $12,100 at year-end, *to have no loss in purchasing power*. So, if Trading Corporation had done nothing more than hold its $10,000, it would have lost purchasing power equivalent to 2,100 end-of-year dollars—the difference between the no-loss amount of $12,100 and the amount it would actually have possessed, $10,000.

But Trading Corporation did not just hold its $10,000 in cash. For one thing, it spent $9,000 of its original cash on inventory at the start of the year when the index was still at 100. Assuming for the sake of argument that the corporation had *no* cash receipts, the expenditure on inventory would have reduced the actual cash balance by $9,000 to $1,000. In addition, since the purchasing power of the $9,000 of cash was actually utilized when the index was at 100, the no-loss, end-of-year cash requirement is reduced by 121/100 × $9,000, or $10,890. So the expenditure of $9,000 (of the original $10,000) at the beginning of the year means that the corporation would not need $12,100 at year-end, but rather $12,100 – $10,890, or $1,210. The net amount of $1,210, of course, equals the $1,000 balance remaining after the inventory purchase times the factor 121/100.

Now we can take account of the effect of the gradual cash receipts of $12,000 from sales during the year. The receipts from sales increased the actual balance of cash from $1,000, right after the inventory expenditure, to $13,000 by year-end, the corporation would have to have 121/110 × $12,000, or rising, they increase the no-loss end-of-year cash requirements. Since the price level averaged 110 as the $12,000 was gradually received, but had reached 121 by year-end, the corporation would have to have 121/110 · $12,000, or $13,200, included in its end-of-year cash to not have lost purchasing power from holding the additional $12,000 of cash receipts. Adding this to the no-loss requirement of $1,210 for the $1,000 balance (after the expenditure) gives a total no-loss requirement of $14,410.

We now have the information required to assess the total loss of purchasing power experienced by Trading Corporation from holding cash during a year of rising prices. Since it would take a total year-end cash balance of $14,410 to experience no loss from holding cash, and Trading Corporation only had an actual balance of $13,000, its monetary loss from holding cash for the year was $1,410. The steps in arriving at this conclusion are summarized in Exhibit 13-9.

The similar reasoning that applies to monetary liabilities is illustrated in Exhibit 13-10 with respect to the loan made to Trading Corporation by a friend of the owner. At the beginning of 19X1 when the price-level index was at 100, the friend loaned $2,000 to the corporation, none of which was paid back during the year. In addition, $100 in interest became due during 19X1, but rather than being paid, that amount was added to the balance of the loan (with the agreement of the lender) to be subject to future interest. As Exhibit 13-10 shows, the end-of-period dollar equivalent of the loan plus the interest equals more than the actual year-end balance of the loan. Thus Trading Corporation experienced a monetary gain during 19X1 with respect to the loan.

Exhibit 13-9

TRADING CORPORATION

Monetary Loss from Holding Cash
For the Year 19X1

	Cash Account	Adjusting Factor	Price-Level-Adjusted Amounts
Beginning balance	$10,000	121/100	$12,100
Inventory purchase	(9,000)	121/100	(10,890)
Sales revenue	12,000	121/110	13,200
Ending balance	$13,000		$14,410
Less actual balance			13,000
Monetary loss			$ 1,410

Exhibit 13-10

TRADING CORPORATION

Monetary Gain from Loan
For the Year 19X1

	Loan Account	Adjusting Factor	Price-Level-Adjusted Amounts
Beginning balance	$2,000	121/100	$2,420
Interest	100	121/110	110
Ending balance	$2,100		$2,530
Less actual balance			2,100
Monetary gain			$ 430

Calculation of Monetary Gains and Losses—Summary. Although the logic underlying the calculation of monetary gains and losses is somewhat abstract and perhaps difficult to understand, Exhibits 13-9 and 13-10 illustrate that such calculations can nevertheless be reduced to just five simple steps for any monetary element of financial position:

1. Array the beginning balance and all increases and decreases in the monetary item in tabular form and calculate the ending position (or balance).
2. Translate the beginning balance and all increases and decreases to the number of end-of-year dollars of equivalent purchasing power.
3. Using the price-level-adjusted figures, calculate the price-level-adjusted ending balance in the same way the actual balance was calculated.

4. Find the difference between the actual ending balance and the price-level-adjusted (no-monetary-gain-or-loss) ending balance.

5. Interpret the difference.

With the exception of step 5, the process is illustrated by Exhibits 13-9 and 13-10. Since step 5 is the only nonmechanical step remaining after we have systematized the process, we now briefly consider this interpretation step.

Interpreting Monetary Gains and Losses. Interpretation of the difference between the actual and the price-level-adjusted ending balance for a monetary item depends on two things: (1) the direction of the difference and (2) whether the monetary item is an asset or a liability. If, for instance, the monetary item is an asset and the price-level-adjusted balance is greater than the actual balance (this happens when prices rise), it means that the enterprise actually *has less* of that asset at the end of the period than would be required to *not* have a loss of purchasing power. Thus the difference constitutes a monetary loss. On the other hand, if the actual ending balance of a monetary asset is greater than the price-level-adjusted balance (this happens when prices fall), the difference is interpreted as a gain.

Converse reasoning applies to monetary liabilities. The price-level-adjusted balance of a monetary liability is the amount that the enterprise would have to owe its creditor(s) to owe the same purchasing power as it received at the time it incurred the debt. Hence if the actual balance is *less* (as it would be if prices have risen), the enterprise will have gained—will owe less purchasing power than originally promised. The opposite is true if the actual balance of the liability is more than the price-level-adjusted balance (prices have fallen), that is, a monetary loss has been sustained.

Price-Level-Adjusted Net Income. Recall now that when we earlier calculated Trading Corporation's price-level-adjusted operating income for 19X1, we knew that we had not finished the task of measuring total performance in a manner consistent with measured disposable wealth in times of changing prices. After all, price-level-adjusted operating income was $3,289—considerably more than the $2,309 we had already determined would lead to nonexcessive withdrawals. The discrepancy between these two figures indicated that there must have been some identifiable loss in purchasing power that resulted from some source other than the productive activity of the year.

As we have since shown, there was indeed a monetary loss of $1,410 and a monetary gain of $430 experienced by Trading Corporation in 19X1. Together they make up a *net* monetary loss of $980. With this net monetary loss, we can now reconcile the $3,289 price-level-adjusted operating income with the $2,309 disposable wealth figure that we earlier labeled *price-level-adjusted net income.*

Price-Level-Adjusted Net Income. Price-level-adjusted net income is composed of price-level-adjusted operating income plus or minus the net monetary gain or loss experienced by the enterprise.

The identity relationship implied by this definition is illustrated with the Trading Corporation example in Exhibit 13-11.

Exhibit 13-11

TRADING CORPORATION

Statement of Price-Level-Adjusted Net Income
For the Year 19X1

		Year-end Dollars
Sales revenue		$13,200
Less expenses:		
Cost of sales	$9,801	
Interest	110	9,911
P-L-A operating income		$ 3,289
Less net monetary loss:		
Monetary gain from loan	$ 430	
Monetary loss from cash	(1,410)	(980)
P-L-A net income		$ 2,309

Notice that the price-level-adjusted net income is identical in amount to the $2,309 determined earlier to be the amount of disposable wealth produced during the year. It is in fact the same number, simply calculated in a different, perhaps more meaningful, way. Thus we not only have a reliable measure of disposable wealth (price-level-adjusted net income), we have it broken down by source. Price-level-adjusted operating income (in this case $3,289) is the advance in wealth (net assets), measured in end-of-year dollars, recognized in connection with the productive activities of the enterprise. It would all be disposable wealth were it not for the net monetary loss (in this case $980) due to the effect of inflation on the purchasing power of the enterprise's holdings of monetary items.

Unlike our Trading Corporation example, in actual practice even relatively small businesses are likely to have several monetary assets and liabilities. To arrive at the net monetary gain or loss directly in such cases involves the two-step process illustrated above, consisting of (1) determining the monetary gain or loss from each monetary asset or liability and (2) determining the net monetary gain or loss by finding the difference between the sum of the individual monetary gains and the sum of the individual monetary losses.

Clearly, the direct approach to finding the net monetary gain or loss could involve extensive calculations in the case of large businesses. But fortunately the direct approach can be avoided by taking advantage of the identity relationship:

P-L-A net income = P-L-A operating income ± Net monetary gain (loss)

By calculating any two of the three amounts indicated in a given case, the identity can be solved for the third. Thus direct calculation can be avoided for whichever of the three figures would be most burdensome to calculate directly.

Price-Level-Adjusted Income Measurement—Interpretation

Considerable effort has been devoted in this chapter to developing techniques to compensate for general price-level changes in arriving at measures of performance and disposable wealth in times of changing prices. The effort led first to a description of an easily calculated measure of disposable wealth. We called that disposable wealth measure *price-level-adjusted net income.* Then, in seeking to satisfy the intuitive idea that the disposable wealth produced by the enterprise ought to be the result of identifiable types of performance, we determined that price-level-adjusted net income could be broken down into two parts. One of these parts, *price-level-adjusted operating income,* clearly relates in concept to the conventional accounting measure of performance. It agrees item for item (all revenues and expenses) with conventional accounting net operating income, but with each item now adjusted to its original purchasing power equivalent in end-of-period dollars. The other part of total disposable wealth for a period is the subtle (but real) change in purchasing power experienced by the enterprise from holding monetary assets and having monetary liabilities in times of changing prices. When we add the *net monetary gain* or subtract the *net monetary loss* experienced by the enterprise to its price-level-adjusted operating income, we get price-level-adjusted net income—the amount of disposable wealth generated by the enterprise for the period.

At this point a final question of interpretation remains. Is price-level-adjusted net income or net operating income an index (in times of changing prices) of long-run ability to produce products with values in excess of the costs of resources used to produce them—at least in the same sense that conventional accounting net income constitutes such an index in times of static prices? The answer is generally no. Conventional accounting operating income has a high degree of intuitive appeal as a performance measure *under static prices* for a good reason. If in a future period the enterprise provides the same quantity and quality of products to customers as in the current period, using the same quantity and quality input resources with the same efficiency, it will have the *same operating income* (assuming no price changes). This will generally not be true of price-level-adjusted income measures in times of generally rising or falling prices *unless* the prices charged for products and the prices paid for input resources by the enterprise have *changed in proportion* to the general trend in prices. If this condition is not met, then adjustments for changes in the prices of the *specific* products sold and resources used by the enterprise are necessary to replicate in times of changing prices the properties of conventional accounting operating income (under static conditions). Such adjustments are the subject of Chapter 14.

Assuming, however, that the prices received and paid by the enterprise do change in approximate proportion to the general trend, the appropriateness of the price-level-adjusted income values as measures of performance is still subject to some further qualification. Whether price-level-adjusted operating income or net income best characterizes "performance" depends on the kind of inflation experienced during the accounting period. If the economy experienced a short-lived, once-and-for-all burst of inflation during the accounting period, there is some question about the long-run performance relevance of the net income measure, since it incorporates net monetary gains and losses. Although net monetary gains or losses do indeed represent current period gains or losses in purchasing power, the forces that give rise to them are not forces that originate within the firm. If the forces of inflation or deflation that contributed to the current period's monetary gains or losses are known to have ceased, the enterprise will not experience continued monetary gains or losses. Under such circumstances, price-level-adjusted *operating income,* rather than price-level-adjusted net income, is the current period's manifestation of the enterprise's ongoing productive ability.

In the case of ongoing inflation or deflation, monetary gains and losses become an ongoing part of an enterprise's economic activities. The measure of efficient management, even in times of stable prices, is the excess of the value of products and services that it can produce over costs of resources consumed, with a given level of investment in both nonmonetary *and monetary* assets. But in times of ongoing inflation or deflation, another dimension is added to the management of a business enterprise—that being to regulate or manage its mix of monetary items in such a way as to accomplish its production objectives with a minimum monetary loss or maximum monetary gain. Thus, in times of ongoing inflation or deflation, price-level-adjusted net income, which includes monetary gains and losses, is a better index of long-run productive ability of the enterprise than is price-level-adjusted operating income.

Some Additional Measurement Issues

The highly simplified example we used as the basis for our discussion of modifying the conventional accounting model for general price-level adjustments allowed us to focus on most of the basic issues involved. But some additional measurement issues are commonly encountered in preparing and/or using general price-level adjusted financial statements, and these are briefly covered below.

Long-Lived Assets. The general principles applied in price-level adjusting long-lived assets, and the related depreciation expense, are the same as those illustrated for inventory and cost of sales. But because the collection of long-lived assets typically includes assets purchased over many prior years, the computational process is more burdensome and requires the exercise of some care in the identification of appropriate adjustment factors.

In general, the process involves, first, identification of an appropriate general price-level index with each asset, and then calculation of the price-level adjusted asset cost, accumulated depreciation, and annual depreciation expense for each separately identified asset. One concession to expediency that is often followed is the assignment of a single, representative general price-level index to all acquisitions of a single year—typically the average price index for the year. This simplification should not of course be applied when most or all of the acquisitions were concentrated at the beginning or the end of a year and the within-year change in the general price-level index was substantial.

Example 13-3

On December 31, 19X4, Capital Products Company decided to modify its conventional financial statements by making general price-level adjustments. Upon examining the subsidiary records supporting the plant and equipment account, you find the following information:

Asset	Purchased*	General Price-Level Index	Original Cost	Estimated Life	Annual Depreciation Expense	Accumulated Depreciation, 12/31/X4
A	19X1	100	$30,000	10 years	$ 3,000	$12,000
B	19X2	120	20,000	5	4,000	12,000
C	19X2	120	16,000	10	1,600	4,800
D	19X3	125	30,000	6	5,000	10,000
			$96,000		$13,600	$38,800

*To simplify "first-year" depreciation calculations, it is assumed that all assets were purchased on January 1 of the indicated year.

No new assets were purchased in 19X4. The general price-level index at December 31, 19X4, is 150.

In making the general price-level adjustment at December 31, 19X4, we first adjust the cost of each of the individual long-lived assets as follows:

Asset	Original Cost	Adjustment Factor	General Price-Level-Adjusted Value
A	$30,000	150/100	$ 45,000
B	20,000	150/120	25,000
C	16,000	150/120	20,000
D	30,000	150/125	36,000
	$96,000		$126,000

Thus the aggregate original transaction value of the plant and equipment, measured in end-of-19X4 dollars, is $126,000. But since each asset has a different estimated life and/or applicable price index, adjusted accumulated depreciation and adjusted depreciation expense must also be calculated on an individual-asset basis. This calculation is illustrated as follows (all values expressed in end-of-19X4 dollars):

Asset	General Price-Level-Adjusted Asset Value	Estimated Life	General Price-Level-Adjusted Annual Depreciation Expense	Elapsed Service Life, 12/31/X4	General Price-Level-Adjusted Accumulated Depreciation, 12/31/X4
A	$ 45,000	10 years	$ 4,500	4 years	$18,000
B	25,000	5	5,000	3	15,000
C	20,000	10	2,000	3	6,000
D	36,000	6	6,000	2	12,000
	$126,000		$17,500		$51,000

Thus the original transaction value of the plant and equipment, measured in end-of-19X4 dollars, is determined to be:

Asset cost	$126,000
Less: Accumulated depreciation	51,000
	$ 75,000

For purposes of calculating general price-level-adjusted net income, we determine the difference between owners' equity at the beginning and the end of the period, both measured in end-of-year dollars. In determining the ending owners' equity in end-of-19X4 dollars in this example, the value of the plant and equipment would be the $75,000 determined in the above calculations. Note that beginning owners' equity would also have to be restated in end-of-19X4 dollars. In this example the asset cost would be unchanged because we assumed no purchases during 19X4, but the accumulated depreciation would have to be recalculated on the basis of one less year elapsed service life. Of course, other assets and liabilities on hand at the beginning of the year would also have to be individually restated in end-of-19X4 dollars in determining the restated beginning owners' equity. In the comprehensive example in the chapter, the beginning owners' equity was restated with but a single calculation only because we assumed that the business began operations on that date. The only other circumstance where such a simple adjustment technique would be justified is when all the beginning values are expressed in beginning-of-the-year dollars.

The depreciation expense that would be recognized in the general price-level-adjusted income statement for this example would be $17,500, the sum of the general price-level-adjusted annual depreciation measures for the four assets. A common misconception in connection with the adjustment of depreciation expense is that the original transaction values should be adjusted using the average price index for the period, since the depreciation measures the consumption of resources *over the period*. It is true that the resources are most often consumed over the period, but the conventional accounting measure of depreciation expense is based upon the original transaction value expressed in the dollars of the date the asset was acquired. It is the dollar measure of asset value that must be restated into end-of-period dollars, and it then follows that the depreciation expense based upon this adjusted asset value will reflect an adjustment of dollars from prior periods, not the average dollars of the current period. When an average index for the period is properly applied in the adjustment process, it is because the underlying original transaction values reflect the fairly uniform receipt or expenditure of dollars of the current period.

A final observation suggested by our consideration of long-lived assets is that inflation or deflation during recent periods need not be particularly large to produce a significant adjustment in original transaction values for a company that has a large investment in long-lived assets that was made many years prior to the current period. The overall effects of general price-level adjustment in such circumstances may be largely localized in the measures of long-lived asset value and depreciation expense, but nonetheless the effect on net income and the value of total assets may be significant.

Choice of "Common" Dollars. In our examples we have always restated original transaction values into end-of-the-current-period dollars. Yet we know from our discussion of indexes that values may be restated in the dollars of *any* period. Why have we made this choice, and is it what we would expect to find in practice? The choice in our examples was originally motivated by the desire to develop a measure of disposable wealth for the period that would indicate the cash dividend that could be paid at the end of the period and still leave the firm as well off as it was at the beginning of the period. Since the cash dividend was to be paid in end-of-period dollars, it was logical to develop a measure of disposable wealth in the same dollars. But companies in practice are confronted with this same decision, and thus use of end-of-period dollars as our common unit of measure seems justified on practical grounds as well. There is another practical reason for choosing end-of-period dollars. At the time that the financial statements are prepared and distributed, individuals are engaging in economic transactions based upon the dollars then in circulation, and thus there is a presumed tendency on their part to think in terms of the values that these particular dollars possess. To restate the financial statements into common dollars of some "base" period would force a mental adjustment on the part of users that most accounting theorists and practitioners believe would reduce the informational value of the statements. Thus, when and if the general price-level-adjusted model is applied, it is highly probable that the dollars at the end of the current period will be chosen as the basic unit of measurement.

Restating Prior Years' Financial Statements. The financial statements of a firm are typically presented in comparative fashion—i.e., the financial statements (or summaries thereof) of prior years are presented along with the current year's statements. Some of the reasons for this custom are discussed in Chapter 18. But of concern to us at this point is the adjustment procedure that would be applied to prior years' statements under the general price-level-adjusted conventional accounting model. Since the statements of the current year are measured in terms of end-of-the-current-period dollars, meaningful comparisons with prior years are possible only if they too are measured in the same dollars. Therefore the financial statements of the prior years must be restated into current dollars. Assuming that the firm has been applying general price-level adjustments for some period of time, all the values in each of the prior years will be measured in common dollars—i.e., dollars at the end of each of the years. But unless there has been no intervening inflation or deflation, these dollars will be noncomparable. Thus each value in each financial statement of a particular year will be adjusted into dollars at the end of the current period by multiplying it by a common adjustment factor, namely, the ratio whose numerator is the index of current dollars and whose denominator is the index of end-of-period dollars of the year being adjusted. Referring back to Example 13-1, the statement of financial position for Trading Corporation at the end of 19X1 (Exhibit 13-6) is measured in end-of-19X1 dollars, or "121" dollars. If this statement were included with a set of financial statements prepared in, say, 19X2 when the end-of-period index was 135, the adjustment factor to "roll forward" the 19X1 statements would be 135/121, and this factor would be applied to each value in the 19X1 statement of financial position. The same adjustment factor would also be applied to each value in any of the other 19X1 financial statements that were included with the 19X2 statements.

Estimating the Net Monetary Gain or Loss. Should one be interested in estimating the amount of the net monetary gain or loss for a firm without having access to the detailed record of transactions for the year, a good approximation of the actual value can be obtained if it is reasonable to assume that the change in the net monetary position (monetary assets minus monetary liabilities) occurred uniformly over the year. In this case the net monetary gain or loss is estimated as the sum of two components: (1) the gain or loss on the beginning net monetary position, and (2) the gain or loss on the change in the net monetary position. These components are calculated as follows:

1. *Gain or loss on the beginning net monetary position.* This is calculated by multiplying the net monetary position at the beginning of the year by the ratio of the ending and beginning price indexes, and then subtracting the balance of the beginning net monetary position. This procedure is equivalent to multiplying the beginning net monetary position by the rate of inflation for the year. Assuming that prices increased during the year, this value would be a monetary loss if the firm had a net monetary asset position, and a monetary gain if the firm had a net monetary liability position.

2. *Gain or loss on the change in the net monetary position.* This component is calculated by multiplying the change (increase or decrease) in net monetary position over the year by the ratio of the ending and average price indexes, and then subtracting the amount of the change. This procedure is equivalent to multiplying the change in net monetary position by the rate of inflation from average dollars to ending dollars. Assuming again increasing prices during the year, if the change is toward a net monetary asset position (increase in an existing net monetary asset position at the beginning of the year, or reduction in the amount of a net monetary liability position at the start of the year), the change component is interpreted as a monetary loss; if the change is toward a net monetary liability position, the calculated value is interpreted as a gain.

A careful comparison of this approximation technique with the detailed computational procedure illustrated for Trading Corporation in Exhibits 13-9 and

13-10 reveals that the two are equivalent *if* all increases and decreases in the monetary accounts occur at the average dollar index for the period. Thus the accuracy of the approximation will depend upon the extent to which the actual changes in monetary assets and liabilities conform to the assumption of uniform change over the year.

Example 13-4

Assume that the following balances were extracted from a firm's statement of financial position at December 31, 19X1:

	1/1/X1	*12/31/X1*
Monetary assets	$ 180,000	$ 200,000
Monetary liabilities	(730,000)	(700,000)
Net monetary asset (liability) position	$(550,000)	$(500,000)

Additionally, the following general price-level indexes were ascertained:

1/1/XI	200
Average for 19X1	210
12/31/X1	224

With this information, the net monetary gain or loss for 19X1 can be estimated as follows:

	Net Monetary Loss (Gain)
Monetary gain on beginning net monetary liability position (224/200 × $550,000) − $550,000	$ (66,000)
Monetary loss on change for 19X1 (224/210 × $50,000) − $50,000	3,333
Net monetary gain for 19X1	$ (62,667)

Present Status of General Price-Level Accounting

Financial reporting on a price-level-adjusted basis has been required for many years in several high-inflation countries in South America and the Far East. But accounting practitioners in the United States (and other highly industrialized countries) historically showed little interest in any type of departure from the conventional accounting model. This attitude has changed over the past ten to fifteen years as the pace of inflation has quickened. In 1969 the Accounting Principles Board (the U.S. accounting policy-making body in the private sector before the formation of the Financial Accounting Standards Board)[1] issued a statement (APB Statement No. 3) recommending the presentation of general price-level-adjusted data as supplementary information in annual reports to shareholders. This recommendation received little response from companies, but in the early 1970s the accounting policy-making bodies in the United States, the United Kingdom, Australia, and Canada all released exposure drafts of proposed standards that would have made the general price-level-adjusted conventional accounting model mandatory (at least as supplementary information). In the United States the Financial Accounting Standards Board sponsored a major field test of the proposed standard in an attempt to identify any problems prior to the anticipated implementation of the standard in 1976. But before this and the other proposed standards were officially adopted, a series of events occurred that caused reconsideration of the appropriateness of this course of action. In essence, all the policy-making bodies reconsidered (or were asked by governmental agencies to reconsider) the alternative of using *current prices* rather than price-level-adjusted original transaction values.

Various forms of current price accounting have recently been implemented, but the basic choice between alternative valuation models is still in the experimental stage in the United States. The SEC in 1976 instituted a policy requiring the larger companies under its jurisdiction to file certain current price data as supplementary information;[2] and in late 1978 the FASB proposed a new reporting requirement, again applicable only to larger companies, that called for supplementary information on either a current price or a general price-level-adjusted (constant dollars) basis.[3] Furthermore, for companies adopting the current price alternative, certain general price-level-adjusted information must also be supplied. These reporting requirements, both of which are characterized by the policy-making units as being experimental in nature at this time, are discussed in more detail in Chapter 14.

While the debate over this fundamental accounting issue was in progress, some companies made voluntary disclosures of certain general price-level-adjusted information to their shareholders. An example of this type of voluntary disclosure from Shell Oil Company's 1976 annual report is presented in Exhibit 13-12. Although the format of this disclosure differs somewhat from what is required (under the "constant dollars" option) in the FASB proposal, the substance of the disclosure is similar.

---

[1] For a more complete discussion of the accounting policy-making process in the United States, see Chapter 17.

[2] Securities and Exchange Commission, "Notice of Adoption of Amendments of Regulation S-X Requiring Disclosure of Certain Replacement Cost Data," *Accounting Series Release No. 190*, March 23, 1976.

[3] Financial Accounting Standards Board, "Financial Reporting and Changing Prices," *Proposed Statement of Financial Accounting Standards,* December 28, 1978.

Exhibit 13-12

SHELL OIL COMPANY

1976 Annual Report

	Historical Dollars	Dollars of Current Purchasing Power*			
(Millions of dollars except per share amounts)	1976	1976	1975	1974	1973	1972
Summary Statement of Income						
Revenues	$9,309	$9,495	$8,885	$9,042	$6,375	$5,593
Cost and expenses:						
Depreciation, depletion, etc.	639	833	781	735	704	658
Income and operating taxes	780	796	763	563	332	298
Interest and discount amortization on indebtedness	79	80	77	71	79	81
Other costs and expenses	7,105	7,263	6,857	7,099	4,973	4,344
Income before purchasing power gain or loss on monetary items	706	523	407	574	287	212
Purchasing power gain (loss) on:						
Long-term debt	—	65	72	131	93	41
Other monetary items	—	5	(17)	(5)	(5)	3
Net income	$ 706	$ 593	$ 462	$ 700	$ 375	$ 256
Summary Balance Sheet						
Current assets	$2,465	$2,615	$2,738	$2,429	$2,195	$2,163
Investments and long-term receivables	244	277	130	146	124	119
Property, plant and equipment (net)	5,082	6,650	6,154	5,782	5,513	5,532
Deferred charges	45	51	54	48	69	76
Current liabilities	1,653	1,653	1,616	1,430	1,233	1,251
Long-term debt	1,175	1,175	1,269	1,097	1,257	1,382
Deferred credits—federal income taxes	417	417	388	360	382	395
Shareholders' equity	$4,591	$6,348	$5,803	$5,518	$5,029	$4,862
Per Share Data†						
Net income	$10.11	$ 8.50	$ 6.82	$10.39	$ 5.57	$ 3.80
Cash dividends paid	$ 2.80	$ 2.85	$ 2.80	$ 2.88	$ 3.10	$ 3.27
Ratios						
Net income to shareholders' equity	18.0%	10.2%	8.4%	13.9%	7.7%	5.3%
Net income to total capital	14.6%	9.0%	7.6%	11.7%	6.6%	5.0%
Net income to revenues	7.6%	6.2%	5.2%	7.7%	5.9%	4.6%
Dividends paid to net income	27.6%	33.5%	41.1%	27.7%	55.7%	86.1%
Long-term debt to total capital	20.4%	15.6%	17.9%	16.6%	20.0%	22.1%

*Based on purchasing power of the dollar at December 31, 1976.
†Per weighted average shares outstanding each year.

Exhibit 13-12 (cont.)

SUPPLEMENTARY PRICE LEVEL ADJUSTED FINANCIAL INFORMATION

Although the rate of inflation has moderated, it continues to erode the purchasing power of the dollar and distort traditional measurements of income and wealth. During the five years covered by this report the purchasing power of the dollar declined 29 percent. In the last thirty years it has been reduced to less than one third of its former purchasing power. Financial statements prepared under generally accepted accounting principles report the actual number of dollars received or expended without regard to changes in the purchasing power of the currency. Investments made over extended periods of time are added together as though the dollars involved were common units of measurement. Amortization of these prior periods costs is deducted from current period revenues in calculations of net income. Since the purchasing power of the dollar has changed materially, this change must be considered for a proper assessment of economic results.

Individual business enterprises are affected differently by inflation. Holders of monetary assets, such as cash or receivables, lose purchasing power during inflationary periods since these assets will purchase fewer goods and services in time. Conversely, holders of liabilities benefit during such periods because less purchasing power will be required to satisfy their obligations. Rates of return and other financial ratios are also influenced greatly by the ages of the investments and subsequent changes in the purchasing power of the dollar.

In the accompanying price level adjusted financial statements all historical dollar amounts have been restated to a common unit of measurement, i.e., the December 1976 dollar. For example, a capital asset acquired in 1966 for $1 is restated to $1.78 in terms of 1976 dollars for each year shown and depreciation is similarly restated. Each year is therefore expressed on a comparable basis which provides a better measure of economic progress.

Profitability ratios for Shell are substantially lower when both income and investments are stated in common units of measurement. Some of the profits reported for 1976 and prior years are therefore not a true economic gain, but merely the result of erosions in the purchasing power of the dollar. One of the principal factors is depreciation, depletion and amortization. When the historical cost of assets is restated in equivalent current dollars, the 1976 depreciation provision increased 30 percent or $194 million. Other meaningful comparisons are the indicated purchasing power gain on long-term debt relative to the interest and discount amortization on this indebtedness. Also, a high proportion of income is absorbed by taxes. Because of inflation, effective tax rates are significantly greater than the rates enacted by legislative bodies.

Explanatory Note

The accompanying supplementary price level adjusted financial information, expressed in terms of December 31, 1976 dollars, is based on the historical dollar financial information. Both the supplementary and historical financial information presented here should be read in conjunction with the notes and other financial statement information in this Annual Report. The supplementary

Exhibit 13-12 (cont.)

> price level information reflects adjustments only for changes that have occurred in the general purchasing power of the dollar as measured by the Gross National Product Implicit Price Deflator. The amounts shown, therefore, do not purport to represent appraised value, replacement cost, or any other measure of the current value of assets.
>
> The Accounting Principles Board Statement No. 3 and a proposal issued by the Financial Accounting Standards Board which give general guidance for the preparation of price level financial statements, treat deferred income taxes as non-monetary items. But for purposes of Shell's general price level restatement, such balances were classified as monetary items because Shell believes that when reversals of such tax differences take place, they give rise immediately to taxable income and to additional taxes payable in current dollars at that time. Had Shell followed the non-monetary treatment for deferred income taxes, restated net income would have been reduced by approximately 4 percent or less and restated shareholders' equity would have been reduced by about 2 percent or less in each of the last five years.

Questions for Review and Discussion

13.1. Define:
    a. Price-level index
    b. Price-level-adjusted net income
    c. Price-level-adjusted operating income
    d. Monetary gain (loss)
    e. *Net* monetary gain (loss)

13-2. Given that all economic units have unique preferences for different kinds of goods and services, how can we justify adjusting original transaction values for changes in the general purchasing power of the dollar?

13-3. Briefly explain how a price-level index is constructed. In what way does technological change enter into the construction and use of a general price-level index?

13-4. Suppose you have been asked to construct a price-level index for the U.S. consumer:
    a. How would you go about constructing such an index?
    b. What characteristics would you like it to have?
    c. Would you use the same index for the Northwest Computer Manufacturing Company? Explain.

13-5. For purposes of general price-level adjustments of financial statements, what properties should the price-level index selected possess?

13-6. Price-level-adjusted net income measurement is an example of an application of the Hicksian definition of income. Do you agree or disagree? Explain your position.

13-7. In preparing a general price-level-adjusted income statement, the revenue recorded under the conventional accounting model should be adjusted for the change in the general level of prices between the date of sale and the end of the period. True or false? Defend your position.

13-8. Explain why debtors gain and creditors lose in times of general inflation.

13-9. a. How do we distinguish monetary assets (liabilities) from nonmonetary assets (liabilities)?
b. Classify each of the following as to whether it is a monetary or a nonmonetary item. Explain, in each case, why you chose the classification you did.

>Cash
>Merchandise inventory
>Marketable securities
>Note payable
>Obligation to deliver goods in the future
>Accounts receivable
>Goods purchased but not yet paid for
>A note payable secured by a mortgage
>U.S. government bonds held by the firm
>Taxes owed to the federal government
>A parcel of land owned

13-10. Assuming that the prices paid and received by the enterprise change in approximate proportion to the general trend, which price-level-adjusted income measure is the most appropriate measure of enterprise performance? Explain.

13-11. When prices generally increase, owners of monetary assets lose while owners of nonmonetary assets gain. True or false? Defend your position.

13-12. When prices generally rise, conventional accounting operating income is clearly irrelevant as a measure of enterprise performance in the long-run cash-generating-ability sense. Do you agree or disagree? Defend your position.

13-13. In measuring price-level-adjusted net income, the monetary assets and liabilities at the beginning of the year are adjusted (or restated) in determining the adjusted beginning owners' equity, whereas in the calculation of ending owners' equity, monetary assets and liabilities are valued at their nominal amounts. Is this an inconsistency? Explain your position.

13-14. Price-level-adjusted operating income has all of the properties in times of changing prices that conventional accounting operating income has when prices are static. Do you agree or disagree? Defend your position.

13-15. Barden Corporation, a manufacturer with large investments in plant and equipment, began operations in 1948. The company's history has been one of expansion in sales, production, and physical facilities. Recently some concern has been expressed that the conventional financial statements do not provide sufficient information for decisions by investors. After consideration of proposals for various types of supplementary financial statements to be included in the 1980 annual report, management has decided to present a balance sheet as of December 31, 1980, and a statement of income and retained earnings for 1980, both restated for changes in the general price level.

a. On what basis can it be contended that Barden's conventional statements should be restated for changes in the general price level?

b. Distinguish between financial statements restated for general price-level changes and current-value financial statements.

c. Distinguish between monetary and nonmonetary assets and liabilities, as the terms are used in general price-level accounting. Give examples of each.

d. Indicate the major similarities and differences between the proposed supplementary statements and the corresponding conventional statements.

e. Assuming that in the future Barden will want to present comparative supplementary statements, can the 1980 supplementary statements be presented in 1981 without adjustment? Explain.

(AICPA adapted)

Exercises

13-1. Present Value and the Price Level. Mrs. Ann Smith, in looking forward to retirement, invested $10,000 on January 1, 1970, in U.S. government bonds. The bonds paid interest at a rate of 10 percent per year, compounded, with repayment of principal and interest on January 1, 1980. In effect, she postponed consumption in 1970 in favor of consumption during her retirement. At the time she invested, her time preference rate between current and future consumption was 10 percent and she expected no inflation. However, during the 1970 to 1980 time period, the price level moved from a beginning level of 100 to a 1980 level of 140.

Required:

1. In retrospect (i.e., on January 1, 1980), how do you suppose Mrs. Smith felt about her investment? Explain.

2. If she had anticipated the inflation, what is the maximum amount she would have paid for the investment in 1970?

13-2. Present Value and the Price Level. Mr. Al Johnson is considering purchase of a bond with a face value of $5,000 which is to be repaid in six years. It has a coupon interest rate of 6 percent. He realizes that the price level has been rising at an average rate of 3 percent per year during the last two years and expects inflation to continue at that rate for the life of the bond.

Required:

1. How might Mr. Johnson recognize this in considering the investment?

2. What is the maximum amount he would be willing to pay for this bond under these circumstances if his time preference rate is 4 percent for cash flows of constant purchasing power?

13-3. Computation of Price-Level Indexes. Suppose the U.S. Bureau of Labor Statistics had been buying what it considered to be a representative "basket" of consumer goods over the last six years with year-end costs as follows:

1974	$2,400
1975	2,700
1976	2,500
1977	3,000
1978	3,300
1979	3,200

Required:

Construct a price-level index based on these figures, using 1977 as the base year. What is the rate of inflation (deflation) in each of the years?

13-4. Computation of Monetary Gains (Losses). The Ace Novelty Company has experienced the following changes in its accounts receivable during the past year:

Beginning balance	$ 23,000
Sales on account January through March	46,000
Sales on account April through June	41,000
Sales on account July through September	33,000
Sales on account October through December	52,000
Payments received (uniformly during year)	160,000

The beginning price-level index was at 100. Average quarterly indexes were 105, 110, 115, and 120, respectively, with an ending price-level index of 125. The average index during the year was 112.5. Compute the monetary gain (loss) from accounts receivable during the year. Is it a gain or a loss? Why?

13-5. Monetary Gains (Losses)—Annual versus Quarterly Data. Suppose you had only the following information concerning the changes in accounts receivable for the Ace Novelty Company during the past year:

Beginning balance	$ 23,000
Sales on account	172,000
Payments received on account	160,000

The beginning price-level index was 100. During the year, the price-level index averaged 112.5 and was at a level of 125 at year-end.

Required:

1. Assuming sales and payments on account occurred uniformly during the year, what is the monetary gain (loss) on accounts receivable?

2. Compare this with your answer in Exercise 13-4 above. Explain the differences.

13-6. Calculating General Price-Level-Adjusted Values. Calculate the specified values for each of the following independent cases.

Case 1. The conventional accounting balance sheet of the Root Company showed the original cost of depreciable assets as $5 million at December 31, 1979, and $6 million at December 31, 1980. These assets are being depreciated on a straight-line basis over a ten-year period with no salvage value. Acquisitions of $1 million were made on January 1, 1980. A full year's depreciation was taken in the year of acquisition.

Root Company presents general price-level financial statements as supplemental information to its conventional accounting financial statements. The December 31, 1979, depreciable assets balance (before accumulated depreciation), restated to reflect December 31, 1980, purchasing power, was $5.8 million. What amount of depreciation expense should be shown in the general price-level income statement for 1980 if the general price-level index was 100 at December 31, 1979, and 110 at December 31, 1980?

Case 2. The Chalk Company reported sales of $2 million in 1979 and $3 million in 1980 made evenly throughout each year. The general price-level index during 1978 remained constant at 100, and at the end of 1979 and 1980 it was 102 and 104, respectively. What approximate amount should Chalk report as sales for 1980, restated for general price-level changes?

Case 3. On January 2, 1980, the Mannix Corporation mortgaged one of its properties as collateral for a $1 million, 9 percent, five-year loan. During 1980 the general price level increased evenly, resulting in a 5 percent rise for the year. In preparing a balance sheet expressing financial position in terms of the general price level at the end of 1980, at what amount should Mannix report its mortgage note payable? What was the amount of the monetary gain or loss that Mannix realized on the outstanding note in 1980 (assuming the interest was paid in 1980)?

(AICPA adapted)

13-7. Price-Level-Adjusted Operating Income. The accountant for the Northern Equipment Corporation, a small manufacturer of camping equipment, has just completed recording all the adjustments for 1980 and has prepared the following trial balance as of December 31, 1980 (conventional accounting basis):

Cash	$ 52,600	
Accounts receivable	30,000	
Inventory (12/31/80)	90,000	
Equipment	36,000	
Accumulated depreciation—Equipment		$ 12,000
Buildings	52,000	
Accumulated depreciation—Buildings		20,000
Land	17,000	
Accounts payable		30,000
Notes payable		28,000
Owners' equity (1/1/80)		167,000
Sales		316,000

Wages and salaries	90,000	
Heat, light, etc.	4,000	
Miscellaneous expenses	12,000	
Interest expense	1,400	
Cost of sales	180,000	
Depreciation of equipment	4,000	
Depreciation of building	4,000	
	$573,000	$573,000

The accountant has noted that the firm has experienced serious inflation for the first time during 1980 and is concerned about its impact on operating performance.

In anticipation of making general price-level adjustments to these conventional accounting data, the accountant develops the following information:

    a. Price-level indexes for the year were:

January 1, 1980	87
December 31, 1980	100
Average index during 1980	91

    b. The beginning inventory (with an original transaction value of $70,000), equipment, and buildings were all acquired when the general price-level index was 87. All of the beginning inventory has been consumed during 1980, and its cost is included in cost of sales. Purchases of inventory during 1980 (amounting to $200,000) are assumed to all have been made at the average price-level index for the year.

    c. Sales were made uniformly over the year, and all expenses other than depreciation and cost of sales were incurred uniformly over the year.

    d. No dividends were paid by Northern during 1980, nor were there any additional investments by owners.

Required:

1. Compute conventional accounting net income for the year.
2. Compute price-level-adjusted operating income for the year. (Carry calculation of adjustment factors to two decimals only.)
3. How are the two income numbers you have computed conceptually different?

13-8. Estimating Net Monetary Gain or Loss. Given that Northern Equipment Corporation in Exercise 13-7 had a net monetary *asset* position at January 1, 1980, of $16,000, estimate the net monetary gain or loss that the company experienced during 1980.

CHAPTER 13

13-9. Estimating Net Monetary Gain or Loss. The following balances were extracted from the financial statements of Fellingham Enterprises at December 31, 1980:

	1/1/80	12/31/80
Monetary assets	$ 225,000	$ 250,000
Monetary liabilities	(825,000)	(950,000)
Net monetary asset (liability) position	$(600,000)	$(700,000)

The following general price-level indexes applied to the year:

January 1, 1980	230
Average for 1980	240
December 31, 1980	253

Required:

Assuming that the change in the net monetary position occurred uniformly over 1980, estimate the net monetary gain or loss for Fellingham Enterprises during 1980 as a result of the change in the general purchasing power of the dollar.

13-10. Estimating Net Monetary Gain or Loss. The following balances were taken from the financial statements of Lasater Company at December 31, 1980:

	1/1/80	12/31/80
Monetary assets	$325,000	$300,000
Monetary liabilities	(125,000)	(150,000)
Net monetary asset (liability) position	$200,000	$150,000

The following general price-level indexes applied to the year:

January 1, 1980	250
Average for 1980	260
December 31, 1980	270

Required:

Assuming that the change in the net monetary position occurred uniformly over 1980, estimate the net monetary gain or loss for Lasater Company during 1980 as a result of the change in the general purchasing power of the dollar.

13-11. Price-Level-Adjusted Net Income. The Rainbow Distributing Company acts as a wholesaler of various leisure-time products, including boats, swimming gear, ski equipment, and all-terrain vehicles. As part of its operations, it performs final assembly of much of the equipment from component parts. Thus its principal assets are the land, buildings, and some machinery required in its assembly lines. It also carries a large inventory from which it satisfies the seasonal demands of its customers. The financial position worksheet shown in Exhibit 13-13 reflects the company's operations for 1980 on the basis of the conventional accounting model.

Required:

1. Calculate conventional accounting net income for the year.
2. Prices during the current year have risen from a January 1 level of 200 to a year-end level of 220, averaging 210 during the year. All of the nonmonetary assets on hand at the beginning of the year were acquired when the price-level index was 200, and all of the transactions during the year can be assumed to have occurred uniformly over the year. The ending inventory is assumed to consist of units purchased at the average price-level index. Based upon this information, calculate price-level-adjusted net income for the year.
3. Discuss briefly the reasons for the difference between the income computed in number 1 and that computed in number 2.
4. If management pays dividends equal to price-level-adjusted net income, can it be sure that it will retain enough capital in the firm to always be able to repurchase its operating resources as required and continue to carry on the business? Explain.

13-12. Price-Level-Adjusted Operating Income. The conventional accounting income statement of the Fullmer Sales Company for the year ending December 31, 1980 is shown on page 532.

Prior to 1980, prices had been stable at a price level of 75. However, during 1980 the economy experienced rapid inflation. By the end of 1980 the price-level index was at 90. The average index during the year was 82. Merchandise sold was purchased uniformly throughout the year, and wages and commissions were paid as earned, also uniformly throughout the year. Interest was accrued continuously. No new equipment purchases were made during the year.

Required:

1. What is price-level-adjusted operating income for 1980? (Carry calculation of adjustment factors to only two decimals.)

Exhibit 13-13

RAINBOW DISTRIBUTING COMPANY

Financial Position Worksheet

Description	Cash	Accounts Receivable	Inventory	Machinery and Equipment*	Buildings*	Land	Accounts Payable	Notes Payable	Owners' Equity
Beginning Position	20,000	63,000	56,000	79,000	93,000	35,000	47,000	25,000	274,000
Purchase of inventory for sale			121,000				121,000		
Revenue from sales	26,000	265,000							291,000 (R)
Wages paid	(86,000)								(86,000) (E)
Collections of accounts receivable	256,000	(256,000)							
Payments of accounts payable	(136,000)						(136,000)		
Miscellaneous expenses (heat, light, taxes, etc.)	(29,000)								(29,000) (E)
Equipment depreciation				(14,000)					(14,000) (E)
Buildings depreciation					(7,000)				(7,000) (E)
Advertising	(18,000)								(18,000) (E)
Cost of goods sold			(116,000)						(116,000) (E)
Paid interest on note payable	(1,500)								(1,500) (E)
Ending Position	**31,500**	**72,000**	**61,000**	**65,000**	**86,000**	**35,000**	**32,000**	**25,000**	**293,500**

*Balances are net of accumulated depreciation.

FULLMER SALES COMPANY

Income Statement
For the Year Ending December 31, 1980

Revenue from sales		$1,750,000
Less expenses:		
Cost of goods sold	$1,400,000	
Wages and sales commissions	175,000	
Interest expense	22,000	
Equipment depreciation	43,000	
Total expenses		1,640,000
Net income		$ 110,000

2. In what way does price-level-adjusted operating income differ conceptually from conventional accounting operating income? Is the price-level-adjusted figure a better measure of performance? Explain.

13-13. Disposable Wealth with Price-Level Movements. The University Student Services Company had the following financial position as of January 1, 1980.

UNIVERSITY STUDENT SERVICES COMPANY

Balance Sheet
As of January 1, 1980

Assets:			Liabilities and Owners' Equity:	
Cash		$ 900	Note payable	$2,000
Inventory		3,500		
Office equipment	$2,500		Owners' equity	4,400
Less accumulated				
depreciation	500	2,000	Total liabilities and	
Total assets		$6,400	owners' equity	$6,400

During 1980, its second year of operation, the company entered into the following transactions:
    a. Sold merchandise for a total of $14,000.
    b. Purchased additional merchandise for $8,200.
    c. All of the beginning inventory was sold.
    d. $2,800 worth of the merchandise purchased remained at year-end.
    e. Paid wages to employees totaling $3,000.
    f. Recorded depreciation on office equipment for the year totaling $500.
    g. Made an annual payment on the note payable totaling $500, of which $100 was interest charges.

All merchandise was sold uniformly throughout the year for cash. Likewise, purchases occurred throughout the year and were paid for with cash. Wages were paid as earned.

Required:

1. Record the above in a financial position worksheet.
2. The company is operated as a student cooperative, with all profits distributed to students at the end of each year. During 1980 the price level, after remaining stable for several years, has moved from a January 1 level of 240 to a December 31 level of 264, averaging 251 during the year. The members of the cooperative suspect that the inflation has had an impact on the amount they should distribute to students. They have come to you for help.
    (a) Compute their price-level-adjusted net income for 1980. (Carry calculation of adjustment factors to only two decimals.)
    (b) Is the answer in (a) the amount you would recommend distributing in 1980? Why or why not?

13-14. Adjusting Long-Lived Assets. On December 31, 19X5, Newman Company decided to modify its conventional financial statements by making general price-level adjustments. The plant and equipment for the firm consists of the following individual assets:

Asset	Purchased	General Price-Level Index	Estimated Life (in years)	Original Cost
A	1/1/X1	120	10	$ 90,000
B	1/1/X2	125	20	150,000
C	1/1/X3	175	8	140,000
				$380,000

No other long-lived assets were purchased subsequent to January 1, 19X3. The general price-level index at December 31, 19X4, was 190; and at December 31, 19X5, it is 200.

Required:

1. Calculate the general price-level-adjusted values at December 31, 19X5, for plant and equipment and accumulated depreciation, and depreciation expense for 19X5—all in December 31, 19X5, dollars.
2. Assuming that at the beginning and end of 19X5 Newman Company's only other asset was cash (1/1 balance—$50,000; 12/31 balance—$110,000), that there were no liabilities at either date, and that the owners made no investments or withdrawals during 19X5, calculate general price-level-adjusted net income for 19X5 (in December 31, 19X5, dollars).

13-15. Adjusting Long-Lived Assets. The following schedule lists the general price-level index at the end of each of the five indicated years:

1976	100
1977	110
1978	115
1979	120
1980	140

These indexes should be used in solving each of the following independent cases.

Case 1. In December 1979 Merle Corporation purchased land for $300,000. The land was held until December 1980, when it was sold for $400,000. The general price-level statement of income for the year ended December 31, 1980, should include how much gain or loss on this sale?

Case 2. On January 1, 1977, the Silver Company purchased equipment for $300,000. The equipment was being depreciated over an estimated life of ten years using the straight-line method, with no estimated salvage. On December 31, 1980, the equipment was sold for $200,000. The general price-level statement of income prepared for the year ended December 31, 1980, should include how much gain or loss from this sale?

Case 3. An analysis of the Gallant Corporation's machinery and equipment account as of December 31, 1980, follows:

Machinery and Equipment	
Acquired in December 1977	$400,000
Acquired in December 1979	100,000
Balance	$500,000

Accumulated Depreciation	
On equipment acquired in December 1977	$160,000
On equipment acquired in December 1979	20,000
Balance	$180,000

A general price-level balance sheet prepared as of December 31, 1980, would show machinery and equipment, and the related accumulated depreciation, at what amounts?

(AICPA adapted)

13-16. **Relationship between Price-Level-Adjusted Net Income, Operating Income, and Net Monetary Gain or Loss.** The Regina Stamping Company has been in business for three years. Its operations and other changes in financial position during year three are reflected in the conventional accounting worksheet shown in Exhibit 13-14. For both of the first two years of operations, the general price-level index remained steady at 200. But during year three, the index went from 200 to 242, averaging 220 for the year as a whole.

Required:

1. Determine price-level-adjusted *net* income for the period. The steel was all purchased (line 1) at the beginning of the year, whereas all other external transactions were made at intervals throughout the year. Show your computations.

2. Determine price-level-adjusted *operating income.* Show your computations.

3. Calculate the monetary gains and losses from each monetary asset and liability and the *net* monetary gain or loss for the period. Be sure to note whether it is a net gain or a net loss amount.

Exhibit 13-14

REGINA STAMPING COMPANY

Financial Position Worksheet—Year Three

Description	Cash	Accounts Receivable	Sheet Steel	Net Equipment	Accounts Payable	Owners' Equity
Beginning Position	3,000	3,000	6,000	20,000	2,000	30,000
1. Purchased steel			16,000		16,000	
2. Rent and wages paid	(11,000)					(11,000) (E)
3. Sales		43,000				43,000 (R)
4. Payments on account	(15,000)				(15,000)	
5. Receipts on account	41,000	(41,000)				
6. Steel used			(17,000)			(17,000) (E)
7. Equipment depreciation				(2,000)		(2,000) (E)
Preliminary Balances	18,000	5,000	5,000	18,000	3,000	43,000

13-17. Price-Level-Adjusted Financial Statements. Ms. Barbara Smith, a stockholder in the Midwestern Packing Company, has just received the firm's annual report for 1980. Introductory comments to the financial statements included in the report explain that the company has provided two sets of financial statements for the year. One set has been prepared using conventional accounting. The other set has been adjusted for the inflation that has occurred during the year. The company explains that it has elected to include both sets of statements due to the inflation in the current year, which occurred for the first time in the company's history. It notes that it feels that the 10 percent inflation experienced during the year has had a significant impact, and it believes that the price-level-adjusted statements will provide significant additional information to the investor. Ms. Smith does not understand the difference between the statements and has come to you for an explanation. She presents you with the following.

MIDWESTERN PACKING COMPANY

Conventional Accounting Balance Sheet
As of December 31, 1980

Assets:			Liabilities:	
Cash		$ 50,000	Accounts payable	$ 64,000
Accounts receivable		170,000	Notes payable	17,000
Inventory		83,000	Mortgage on building	52,000
Equipment	$120,000		Total liabilities	$133,000
Less accumulated depreciation	44,000	76,000		
Buildings	$ 96,000		Owners' equity	350,000
Less accumulated depreciation	24,000	72,000	Total liabilities and owners' equity	
Land		32,000		
Total assets		$483,000		$483,000

MIDWESTERN PACKING COMPANY

Conventional Accounting Income Statement
For the Period Ending December 31, 1980

Revenue from sales		$680,000
Less expenses:		
Cost of goods sold	$479,500	
Wages and salaries	90,000	
Heat, light, etc.	15,000	
Property taxes	5,000	
Interest expense	4,500	
Equipment depreciation	12,000	
Building depreciation	4,000	
Total expenses		610,000
Net income		$ 70,000

MIDWESTERN PACKING COMPANY

Price-Level-Adjusted Balance Sheet
As of December 31, 1980

Assets:			Liabilities and Owners' Equity:	
Cash		$ 50,000	Liabilities:	
Accounts receivable		170,000	Accounts payable	$ 64,000
Inventory		87,150	Notes payable	17,000
Equipment	$132,000		Mortgage on building	52,000
Less accumulated depreciation	48,400	83,600	Total liabilities	$133,000
Buildings	$105,600			
Less accumulated depreciation	26,400	79,200	Owners' equity	372,150
Land		35,200	Total liabilities and owners' equity	
Total assets		$505,150		$505,150

MIDWESTERN PACKING COMPANY

Price-Level-Adjusted Income Statement
For the Period Ending December 31, 1980

Revenue from sales		$714,000
Less expenses:		
Cost of goods sold	$503,475	
Wages and salaries	94,500	
Heat, light, etc.	15,750	
Property taxes	5,250	
Interest expense	4,725	
Equipment depreciation	13,200	
Buildings depreciation	4,400	
Total P-L-A expenses		641,300
Price-level-adjusted operating income		$ 72,700
Less monetary loss		8,550
Price-level-adjusted net income		$ 64,150

In addition, the annual report provides the following information:
- a. Although prices in general were up a total of 10 percent for the year, prices were up an average of 5 percent during the year.
- b. The company began the year with no inventory and made inventory purchases uniformly throughout the year.
- c. No new buildings or equipment were acquired during the year.
- d. Taxes and interest are accrued throughout the year.
- e. Wages and salaries, as well as heat, light, etc., were paid as incurred uniformly throughout the year. Sales revenue and collections of accounts receivable similarly occurred uniformly during the year.
- f. There were no dividends paid or additional investments by owners during the year.

Required:

1. Reconcile the differences, that is, show the calculations involved in computing the price-level-adjusted statements. (Note: For convenience, calculate adjustment factors to only two decimal places.)

2. Explain the meaning of the monetary gains (losses) that you compute.

13-18. Relationship between Price-Level-Adjusted Income Measures. The conventional accounting income statement of Planetary Gears Corporation for 19X3 follows. The revenues earned during the year, the wages paid, and the miscellaneous expenses all resulted from transactions taking place throughout the year. The rent was all prepaid at the end of the prior year. The steel used was purchased in part ($300,000) prior to the beginning of the year and in part ($500,000) at regular intervals throughout the year. However, it was used at a fairly even rate during the year. Interest was accrued continuously. No equipment was purchased during the year. During 19X3 the price-level index rose from 120 to 135, averaging 125 for the

PLANETARY GEARS CORPORATION

Results of Operations (in thousands of dollars)
For the Year Ended December 31, 19X3

Revenues		$3,000
Less expenses:		
Steel used	$ 800	
Rent	30	
Wages	1,000	
Depreciation	500	
Interest	70	
Miscellaneous	100	2,500
Net operating income		$ 500

year as a whole. All beginning balances in nonmonetary assets had been previously adjusted to beginning-of-year dollars.

Required:

1. Determine price-level-adjusted operating income. (For convenience round adjustment factors to two decimals.)

2. Assume that price-level-adjusted net income was $400,000. Was there a net monetary gain or a net monetary loss for the period? What amount?

3. Assuming that the company started 19X3 with equal amounts of monetary assets and liabilities, what does your answer to number 2 imply about the mix of monetary assets and liabilities during the year? Explain your answer.

13-19. Relationship between Price-Level-Adjusted Income Measures. The Walker Book Company has been in business for two years. Its operations and other changes in financial position during year two are reflected in the conventional accounting worksheet shown in Exhibit 13-15. For the first year of operations, the general price-level index remained steady at 90. But during year two the index went from 90 to 120, averaging 100 for the year as a whole.

The purchase of new books (line 1) was made at the beginning of the year (when the general price-level index was still 90), whereas all other external transactions were made at intervals throughout the year.

Required:

1. Determine price-level-adjusted *net* income for the period. Show your computations.

2. Determine price-level-adjusted *operating income*. Show your computations.

3. From your answers in numbers 1 and 2, calculate the net monetary gain or loss for the period. Be sure to note whether it is a net gain or a net loss amount.

Exhibit 13-15

WALKER BOOK COMPANY

Financial Position Worksheet—Year Two

Description	Cash	Accounts Receivable	Book Inventory	Fixtures	Accumulated Depreciation— Fixtures	Accounts Payable	Owners' Equity
Beginning Position	6,000	3,000	12,000	9,000	(900)	3,000	26,100
1. Purchased books			18,000			18,000	
2. Rent and wages paid	(10,000)						(10,000) (E)
3. Sales		50,000					50,000 (R)
4. Payments on account	(15,000)					(15,000)	
5. Receipts on account	45,000	(45,000)					
6. Cost of books sold			(24,000)				(24,000) (E)
7. Depreciation of fixtures					(900)		(900) (E)
Preliminary Balances	26,000	8,000	6,000	9,000	(1,800)	6,000	41,200

13-20. Price-Level Changes and Disposable Wealth. The president of the Mideastern Transportation Company has become concerned about the impact of inflation on the financial position of his company. He has presented you with the worksheet shown in Exhibit 13-16 in which beginning balances have been restated for all prior changes in purchasing power. Recorded transactions occurred uniformly throughout the year.

In addition, the president has told you that the beginning-of-year price level was 120, the end-of-year price level is 132, and the average level during the year was 126.

Required:

1. Based on the information he has supplied, what is the price-level-adjusted change in owners' equity for the year? (Calculation of adjustment factors required to two-decimal accuracy only.)

2. Can the president pay out this amount as a dividend to stockholders and rest assured that the firm is retaining enough resources to replace assets as they wear out? Explain.

3. The president is also interested in the impact of inflation on operating performance. Compute both conventional accounting operating income and price-level-adjusted operating income for the year.

13-21. Calculating Price-Level-Adjusted Income Measures. On January 1, 19X1, Jones Company was incorporated by the owner, J.J. Jones, with his investment of $95,000 and a bank loan of $75,000 at an interest rate of 10 percent. On the same date, all but $5,000 of the available cash was invested in inventory and the building.

Exhibit 13-16

THE MIDEASTERN TRANSPORTATION COMPANY

Financial Position Worksheet

Description	Cash	Accounts Receivable	Trucks	Accumulated Depreciation— Trucks	Buildings	Accumulated Depreciation— Buildings	Land	Notes Payable	Owners' Equity
Beginning Position*	16,000	8,000	24,000	(12,000)	52,000	(16,000)	40,000	7,000	105,000
Revenue from sales	42,000	14,000							56,000 (R)
Payment on accounts receivable	12,000	(12,000)							
Miscellaneous expense	(16,000)								(16,000) (E)
Wages	(24,000)								(24,000) (E)
Truck depreciation				(4,000)					(4,000) (E)
Building depreciation						(2,000)			(2,000) (E)
Ending Position	30,000	10,000	24,000	(16,000)	52,000	(18,000)	40,000	7,000	115,000

*All balances stated in beginning-of-year dollars (index of 120).

A trial balance for Jones Company at December 31, 19X1, follows:

Cash	$ 15,000	
Accounts receivable	40,000	
Inventory (12/31)	25,000	
Building	100,000	
Accumulated depreciation—Building		$ 5,000
Notes payable		75,000
Owners' equity (1/1)		85,000
Sales		90,000
Cost of sales	40,000	
Wages and salaries	20,000	
Interest expense	7,500	
Depreciation on building	5,000	
Miscellaneous expense	2,500	
	$255,000	$255,000

Additional information:

a. Price-level indexes for 19X1: Beginning of the year—100; end of the year—115; average during the year—110.
b. Mr. Jones received a cash dividend of $20,000 from the company when the general price-level index stood at 105, and later in the year had to make an additional cash investment of $10,000 in the company when the general price-level index was 110.
c. Sales and collections of accounts receivable occurred evenly over the year. Also, all expenses other than cost of sales and depreciation expense were incurred evenly over the year.
d. After the initial inventory purchase on January 1, no additional purchases of inventory were made during the year.

Required:

1. Determine conventional accounting net income for the year.
2. Determine price-level-adjusted net income for the year.
3. Determine price-level-adjusted net operating income for the year.
4. Determine the net monetary gain or loss for the year.

Alternative Financial Accounting Models: Current Entry Prices (Replacement Costs)

In the preceding chapter the characteristics and implications of modifying conventional accounting to recognize changes in the general price level are examined. We also observe that this modified accounting model differs from conventional accounting only in that it adjusts the dollar amounts used to represent original transaction values for changes in the purchasing power of the dollar. The purpose of the adjustments, however, is to capture with a new number the *original* value (in purchasing power) given or received in a past transaction.

In this and the next chapter we consider two additional financial accounting models that represent genuine departures, *in principle*, from the original transaction value concept and thus the conventional accounting model. Both models are implemented using current exchange prices. One uses *current entry prices* and is often referred to as the *replacement cost model;* the other model uses *current exit prices* and is alternatively labeled the *market-value model.* Both models are motivated by a desire to achieve a more relevant representation of enterprise status and activities in times of changing prices than either the conventional model or the general price-level-adjusted conventional model produces.

Since both of these new models use a form of current price, we first consider the general notion of current exchange prices. After establishing the necessary distinctions between the prices used in the two models, we examine the essential elements of the current entry price, or replacement cost, model in the remainder of this chapter and the current exit price, or market-value, model in Chapter 15.

Current Exchange Prices

An *exchange price* is the amount of cash (or equivalent) paid, received, or promised *in exchange* for some right or possession.

Current Exchange Price. As the term implies, current exchange prices are prices that are being paid or received in exchange for particular rights or possessions at the present time.

Current exchange prices are therefore of obvious significance for all economic units. They reflect current conditions of supply and demand in the markets in which individuals and business enterprises buy resources for use in production and sell resulting products and services. Thus, current exchange prices provide information to individuals and enterprises as to their exchange options. As mentioned above, current exchange prices may also be used for valuation purposes to reflect desired concepts of enterprise wealth and income.

Entry and Exit Prices. A distinction between current exchange prices (which will become significant in our later discussion) has to do with which side of the exchange transaction the economic unit is on.

Current Entry Price (Replacement Cost). When taking the point of view of the buyer of a product or service, we usually refer to the current exchange price as the *entry* or *input* price. The terms *entry* and *input* express the notion that the exchange price is the amount required to "enter" the item into the control of the buyer. Among accountants, the current entry price of a resource is usually referred to as its current *replacement cost.*

Current Exit Price (Market Value). The obvious counterpart terminology, when we take the point of view of the seller, is *exit* or *output* price, expressing the notion that for the seller the exchange price is the amount received as one of his products or services is given up. Among accountants, the current exit price of a resource is usually referred to as its current *market value.*

Although this distinction between entry and exit prices may seem trivial at first glance, in many cases it can be significant. Often the current exit and entry prices of a given asset are different when we take the point of view of the same economic unit buying and selling that asset.

Example 14-1

Take the position of a used-car dealer with respect to the purchase or sale of a particular used-car model. The current entry price for the dealer is likely to be the local wholesale price for the particular model, whereas the dealer's current exit price is probably the local retail price of the same model. There may be several hundred dollars difference between the two prices.

Now consider the individual interested in buying or selling the same used car model. Unless the individual has time to locate another individual buying or selling the used-car model that he wishes to sell or purchase (respectively), he will have to go to a dealer. Thus the dealer's current exit price is the individual's current entry price, and vice versa. For both the individual and the dealer, there is a difference between the current entry price and the current exit price of the given used-car model (although the relationship between the two amounts is reversed).

Even when we are considering both sides of the same exchange, the entry price for the buyer may differ from the exit price of the seller, and both may differ from what we will call the nominal selling price in the exchange.

Example 14-2

> Suppose that a homeowner puts his house up for sale. A buyer comes along and makes the homeowner an offer of $60,000 for the house. The homeowner accepts. The nominal selling price is $60,000. But the buyer will actually pay more than $60,000 and the seller will receive less because of certain additional costs of the transaction. The most obvious additional cost of the transaction is usually a sales or excise tax levied against either the buyer or the seller according to the law of the state in which the sale takes place. Other transaction costs in this case include the real estate commission (seller), the title search and insurance (buyer and/or seller), and the cost of securing a mortgage (buyer usually; seller in some instances).

Now that we have some idea as to what is meant by current exchange prices, we are ready to apply them to the problem of accounting for the business enterprise, beginning with the current entry price (replacement cost) model.

Money (Financial) vs. Physical Capital

To establish the motivation for using the current replacement costs of resources, we start by contrasting the basic concept of the enterprise underlying conventional accounting with the enterprise concept that is often proposed as a reason for the recognition of replacement costs. We refer to the two concepts as the *money,* or *financial, capital* and the *physical capital* points of view, respectively, and note that these are referred to as alternative *capital maintenance* criteria for the disposable wealth measure.

The Money Capital Point of View. When we introduced conventional accounting performance measurement in Chapter 3, we alluded to an operating sequence or cycle as the backbone of our model of the enterprise. For present purposes, we can paraphrase the stages in that sequence as follows: (1) the enterprise starts with invested cash, (2) it converts the cash into physical factors of production, (3) it commits its factors to production of products and services, (4) it provides the products and services to customers, and (5) it thereby converts them back into cash. Thus we can think of the business enterprise as a *reservoir of cash* which is continuously converted into productive resources and back into cash of greater quantity. This is the basic philosophy or concept of the enterprise that is implicit in the use of conventional accounting net income as a performance measure and as a measure of disposable wealth. In performance measurement, the measure of the sacrifice or effort expended in using a resource in production is the money committed to acquire it for use. The measure of accomplishment is the money received or to be received for products or services provided. In disposable wealth measurement, the essential thing in preserving the economic essence of the enterprise is the preservation of assets equal to its cash or money endowment. This may be referred to as the money capital point of view of the enterprise.

As we illustrated in Chapter 5 in our discussion of the disposable wealth concept, if the enterprise continues to distribute cash to owners equal to net income period after period, it will continue to retain net assets (owners' equity) equal to the initial money capital contributed by the owners. Furthermore, if and when an enterprise that follows such a policy finally ceases to operate (assuming no losses on final disposition of its assets), it will end its life with cash equal to the original investment of the owners.

When original transaction values are modified for changes in the general price level, this money capital point of view is altered only to the extent that it refers to the general *purchasing power* of the original dollar investment of the owners, rather than merely the *number* of dollars invested. Hence, as we have noted before, general price-level adjustments of original transaction values do not substantially alter the fundamental concepts of the conventional accounting model.

The Physical Capital Point of View. However, there are ways of viewing the business enterprise under which preservation of its original cash (or purchasing power) endowment is not the really essential factor in preserving its economic essence. One such view is the physical capital point of view. The physical capital approach does not view the business enterprise as a reservoir of cash that is converted into productive resources and then back into cash via the sale of products or services. Rather, it takes the point of view that enterprises are formed and continue to operate in a market economy for purposes of providing specific products and services efficiently. And they are able to stay in business only so long as they maintain at least a long-run capability to provide some product or service that is valued more highly by customers than its resource costs.

The essence of the enterprise that must be preserved, therefore, is not an arbitrary amount of cash, but a more abstract "capability to produce." More specifically, the enterprise is viewed as (1) a *reservoir of physical resources,* (2) which, when combined efficiently, are capable of providing products and services of value, (3) which in turn can be sold to customers, (4) producing infusions of cash into the enterprise, (5) to be used to replace the productive capacity of resources used up in providing the products and services.

Thus the relevant test of effort in measuring the ongoing cash-generating capability of the enterprise (performance) is the cost to replace resources used up in the production of revenues earned. And the relevant test for preserving the economic muscle of an enterprise at a particular point in time is whether or not it has the capability to replace its productive resources (or the services they perform) as they are consumed. Of course, as long as economic conditions remain static (prices do not change), the amount of original money capital contributed to the enterprise continues to be adequate to replace any resources purchased and used in the business as they wear out. Thus, under static conditions, original money capital would be equivalent to the original physical capital requirement. (Similarly, if *all prices* in the economy change by the *same percentage* over a period of time, ability to replace the assets employed in the business can be maintained so long as the original purchasing power of the money capital invested in the business is maintained—by using price-level-adjusted net income as the measure of disposable wealth.) A problem arises, though, when the prices of the productive resources of a particular enterprise rise disproportionately relative to all other prices in the economy.

This problem (arising from the desire to maintain the firm's physical capital) is illustrated by considering a wholesale operation in a highly simplified business environment—simplified to focus attention on the environmental variables and accounting measurements that are the source of dispute between the two alternative ways of viewing the firm.

Example 14-3

Houston Wholesalers, Inc., was incorporated on January 1, 19X1, with an initial cash endowment of $5 million. The purpose of the corporation is to purchase crude oil from a variety of wildcatters and resell it to small local refineries. Both the buying and the selling markets are highly competitive, and thus Houston Wholesalers pays a market-determined price when purchasing the crude oil, and sells at a market-determined price to the refineries. The selling price of the crude oil is normally 150 percent of the current purchase price.

On January 1, 19X1, the purchase price of crude oil was $5.00 per barrel, and the company purchased 1 million barrels. During 19X1 the replacement cost of the oil remained at $5.00, and thus Houston Wholesalers was able to sell all of the January 1 purchase at $7.50 per barrel. Ignoring all operating expenses other than the purchase cost of the crude oil, the 19X1 income statement prepared for Houston Wholesalers in accordance with the conventional accounting model is shown in Exhibit 14-1. Assuming that the owners of Houston Wholesalers, Inc., wish to distribute all of the firm's disposable wealth at the end of the year as a cash dividend, $2.5 million is distributed, leaving the firm with a cash balance (and owners' equity) of $5 million—the amount of the original cash endowment.

On January 1, 19X2, Houston Wholesalers purchased another 1 million barrels of crude oil at $5.00 per barrel. Then, before any of this purchase was resold, the replacement cost of the crude oil jumped to $10.00 per barrel, and the market selling price increased to $15.00 (150 percent of the current cost of $10.00).

The conventional accounting income statement for 19X2 (Exhibit 14-1) reveals income of $10 million for the year. The large increase over the preceding year is due to the purchase of the crude oil at the *old* price and subsequent sale of the oil at the *new* price; in a sense, there is a "one-shot" windfall reflected in the current year's income. And this windfall is the source of the difference in views referred to above. If all the net income, as measured under the conventional accounting model, is distributed in the form of a cash

Exhibit 14-1

HOUSTON WHOLESALERS, INC.

Income Statements
(Basis: *Conventional Accounting Model*)

	(000 omitted)		
	19X1	*19X2*	*19X3*
Sales	$7,500	$15,000	$7,500
Cost of sales	5,000	5,000	5,000
Net income	$2,500	$10,000	$2,500
Number of barrels purchased and sold	1,000	1,000	500

dividend, the firm will be left with $5 million cash (and owners' equity) as in the preceding year. The original money endowment will be maintained. But at the current replacement cost of $10 per barrel, the firm will not have sufficient resources (cash in this case) to acquire 1 million barrels of crude oil with which to operate in 19X3. Hence the operating capability, or physical capital, of the firm will have to be cut back unless a smaller dividend is paid or new financing is obtained.

The income statement for 19X3 in Exhibit 14-1 reflects the consequences of paying a $10 million cash dividend at the end of 19X2 (equal to conventional accounting net income) and then cutting back the level of operations rather than seeking new financing.

Viewing the enterprise as a reservoir of physical resources (rather than cash), a measure of disposable wealth (such as the one calculated above) that implies a cutback in the level of resources from their beginning-of-year level is clearly inadequate. And the inadequacy stems from the adherence to the original transaction value of the resources consumed during the year.

To correct this alleged deficiency, the replacement cost model values consumed resources at the amount that would be required to replace the asset—i.e., the expenditure required to put the firm back into the same position (in terms of physical resources) that it was in immediately before it consumed the resource. The difference between the replacement cost of the resources consumed and their original transaction value is classified as a *realized holding gain (loss)*. Two major components of the replacement cost model income statement are now defined as follows:

Replacement-Cost-Based Current Operating Income. Replacement-cost-based current operating income equals revenue, measured in terms of prices actually received from sales, minus related expenses, measured in terms of the current replacement costs of the resources actually consumed in producing the revenue of the period. The "current" replacement costs are the current entry prices of the resources *on the date that they are consumed*.

Realized Holding Gains.[1] A realized holding gain is measured by the difference between the current replacement cost and the original transaction value of resources consumed in the production of revenue. The realized holding gain (loss) is an indication of the benefit (or detriment) accruing to the firm as a consequence of actually purchasing a resource at a price lower (or higher) than its replacement cost on the date the resource is consumed. When the replacement cost at the date of consumption exceeds the original transaction value, a holding gain results; if it is lower, there is a holding loss.

From the above definitions, we observe that the algebraic sum of replacement-cost-based current operating income and realized holding gains simply equals conventional accounting net income. The reason is that realized holding gains are measured by the difference between original transaction values and replacement costs of resources used to produce current revenue and thus "add back"

---

[1] Holding gains (losses) are sometimes referred to as "cost savings," in recognition of the way in which the benefit (or detriment) is realized. We have elected to use the term *holding gain (loss)* because it is more commonly encountered in discussions of current accounting practice.

as a separate income component the incremental amounts (over original transaction values) that were deducted in arriving at replacement-cost-based current operating income. Replacement-cost-based *net income* will be defined after we have introduced some additional concepts. But *for our present purposes.* it is the algebraic sum of replacement-cost-based current operating income and realized holding gains.

With these definitions in hand, we can return to the situation described in Example 14-3 to see what changes would result from applying the replacement cost model. The income statements for the three years on a replacement cost basis are reflected in Exhibit 14-2. Notice first that for 19X2, the year of the cost increase, replacement-cost-based current operating income of $5 million plus realized holding gains of $5 million equals 19X2 conventional accounting net income of $10 million (See Exhibit 14-1). However, the replacement-cost-based current operating income serves, in this simplified example, as a measure of the firm's disposable wealth, as well as an indication of the firm's long-run cash-generating ability. The realized holding gain in 19X2 is regarded as a nondistributable, and possibly nonrepeatable, addition to owners' equity. More will be said about this interpretation later. But accepting it for purposes of this example, the cash dividends for the three years are $2.5 million, $5 million, and $5 million, respectively, and sufficient resources (cash) remain after each dividend to purchase 1 million barrels of crude oil at the start of each year. Thus, from the physical capital perspective, the disposable wealth measure (i.e., replacement-cost-based current operating income) achieves its objective of indicating the maximum dividend that can be paid without impinging upon the firm's beginning-of-year level of "well-offness."

Although we wish to introduce some additional concepts before considering the properties of the replacement cost numbers as measures of disposable wealth, this example does suggest several observations at this point. First, the validity of the alternative ways of viewing the essence of the business enterprise may be assessed differently by different parties having an interest in the fortunes of the firm. Investors may well be content to have a disposable wealth measure that merely seeks to maintain the original cash (or purchasing power) endowment of the firm. If the specific prices confronting the firm rise, maintenance of the same level of operations requires either a smaller cash dividend

Exhibit 14-2

HOUSTON WHOLESALERS, INC.

Income Statements
(Basis: *Replacement Cost Model*)

	(000 omitted)		
	19X1	19X2	19X3
Sales	$7,500	$15,000	$15,000
Cost of sales	5,000	10,000	10,000
Replacement-cost-based current operating income	$2,500	$ 5,000	$ 5,000
Realized holding gains	-0-	5,000	-0-
Replacement-cost-based net income	$2,500	$10,000	$ 5,000
Number of barrels purchased and sold	1,000	1,000	1,000

than indicated by the conventional accounting model or additional financing. But the investor may wish to make that decision himself after receiving the cash dividend, rather than being confronted with an accounting measure of disposable wealth that implicitly makes the decision for him. Referring back to Exhibit 14-1, the 19X3 income was based upon a distribution of the "windfall" gain, or realized holding gain, at the end of 19X2, and subsequent curtailment of the level of operations. Notwithstanding this fact, the dollar level of operations in 19X3 is identical to that in 19X1, and both are based upon a *dollar* investment of $5 million. The investor can then independently decide whether he wishes to reinvest the "windfall" gain in the firm, or the industry, or perhaps reallocate his investment to a different industry. Or he may wish to consume rather than invest this amount. On the other hand, management may have a strong vested interest in maintaining (if not increasing) the level of activity. If this is the case, management may well opt for the replacement cost measure of disposable wealth that provides an arguable basis against distributing or taxing the realized holding gain.

Second, it is implicitly assumed in the calculation of disposable wealth in Example 14-3 *under the physical capital maintenance criterion* that *all* of the additional investment that is required due to increasing prices should come from the equity shareholders. Although in the example it appears that all the capital was previously contributed by the shareholders, this does not imply that they would not consider long-term credit to finance additional investments. Actually, the physical capital view of disposable wealth generally ignores the existence of outstanding long-term loans which might be increased along with equity capital in order to compensate for rising prices. One could then argue that realized holding gains are "nondistributable" only up to the percentage that current equity financing bears to total financing. Yet this too ignores the possibility of a deliberate management and/or investor decision to change the financing mix because of the problem of rising prices.

Third, the validity of the physical capital point of view depends upon the firm's *actually* maintaining or increasing its level of operations. When physical operating capability is maintained or increased, the realized holding gains may be regarded as a nondistributable type of "capital adjustment" because this amount has been "reinvested" in the resource replacements. But should the firm subsequently liquidate its operations, thereby ceasing to require any level of physical resources, the focal point and support for the physical capital view disappears and the accumulated holding gains can properly be viewed as distributable and taxable additions to the money capital of the firm (although purchasing power adjustments could still be supported for tax purposes).

Finally, a general price-level-adjusted measure of disposable wealth would adequately deal with the problem from a physical capital point of view *only if* the percentage change in the general level of prices is equal to the percentage change in the specific price of the resource the firm is acquiring—crude oil in our example. Such an equivalence is unlikely in most time periods. And since we are concerned here with those situations where the specific price changes are not proportionate to the changes in the general level of prices, we cannot rely upon the general price-level-adjusted measure of disposable wealth to achieve maintenance of physical capital.

Valuing Assets and Liabilities

Our analysis of the replacement cost model is now extended to consider the valuation principles applied to assets and liabilities at the end of a period, and the effects of these valuations on the income statement.

The general rule for valuing assets is to assign a value in an amount equal to the price that would have to be paid at the present time in order to acquire an equivalent asset. For liabilities, a value is assigned in an amount equal to the proceeds that would be received at the present time if a debt with equivalent payment requirements were incurred. Although there are some minor exceptions, these general rules essentially imply that *monetary* assets and liabilities be valued at the present value of their respective future cash flows, using the *current rate of interest* to calculate the present value.

Nonmonetary assets constitute the resource class that is most strikingly affected by the adoption of the replacement cost model. Consider the two most frequently encountered types of nonmonetary assets—inventory and plant and equipment. The *inventory* on hand at the end of the period is valued at the price that would have to be paid to acquire the resources, purchased in quantities that are normal for the business. *Plant and equipment* (including land) are valued at the price that must be paid at the present time to acquire a similar asset. Since land generally is not subject to depreciation, the full replacement cost of the land is reflected in the statement of financial position. However, for assets that are subject to depreciation, the amount in the statement of financial position should reflect the replacement cost of an asset *in similar condition*. If the replacement price is obtained from the used-asset market, then no further adjustment is necessary. However, in many cases the replacement price data will come from the market for new assets. In such cases the replacement cost (new) must be adjusted for the number of years of service life that have elapsed through a recognition of accumulated depreciation on the replacement cost (new). The net value—replacement cost (new) less accumulated depreciation—presumably measures the current replacement cost of the asset *in its present condition*.

Example 14-4

On January 1, 19X1, Abney Company acquired a new machine that cost $3,000 and had an expected service life of three years and no salvage value. At the end of the year, the replacement cost (new) for the machine was $4,500. The following values would be assigned to the asset in the statement of financial position at December 31, 19X1, under the conventional accounting model and the replacement cost model:

	Conventional Accounting Model	Replacement Cost Model
Asset cost	$ 3,000	$ 4,500
Less: Accumulated depreciation	1,000	1,500
Asset, net of depreciation	$ 2,000	$ 3,000

In both models, the asset is valued at the purchase price (new), although that price is a historical price under the conventional accounting model and a current price under the replacement cost model. The accumulated depreciation reflects the passage of one year since acquisition, calculated on the basis of the cost assigned to the asset. Hence the machine would be valued at $2,000 under the conventional accounting model and $3,000 under the replacement cost model.

Before leaving the subject of valuing long-lived assets (plant and equipment) under the replacement cost model, we must recognize that in practice it may sometimes be difficult to associate a specific replacement cost with a specific asset. One major reason for this difficulty is that changing technology and changing forces of supply and demand may greatly alter the forms and service characteristics of resources available to the enterprise. It may be physically impossible to replace a specific asset with an identical asset at any price. If this is the case, no current replacement costs (new) for such assets will be observable. And if no secondhand market for the asset exists, it may be necessary to estimate the current replacement cost of the asset on hand by some method other than direct pricing. One possibility is to select a specific price index for a class of resources encompassing the asset in question (e.g., a price index for machine tools) and adjust the original transaction value in the same way that we adjust for general price-level changes. Another approach is to estimate the current replacement cost of assets or services that will provide roughly *equivalent production or service potential* as do the assets employed in the business in their present form. Indeed, some accountants believe that this latter approach is conceptually superior to approaches that seek to determine the replacement cost of an identical asset. They argue that a firm that wishes to maintain its physical operating capability is not interested in replacing resources in kind, but rather in replacing equivalent productive capacity. As improvements in technology are achieved, the firm will probably replace its present assets with technologically superior assets, and it is the replacement cost of equivalent productive capacity from the improved assets that is the relevant measure.

Example 14-5

Axle Forging Company owns an XR-1 stamping machine purchased ten years ago for $100,000. Its capacity of 3,000 stampings per hour is still adequate for the company's needs, but it will have to be replaced in another two years. Unfortunately, the XR-1 model is no longer being produced. Virtually all available substitutes are faster and much more expensive. The nearest thing to an XR-1 available at present is another manufacturer's XX-4. It has a capacity of 4,000 stampings per hour and costs $200,000. After some thought, company management decided that if the XR-1 were presently worn out, it would be replaced by an XX-4. The current replacement cost of the XR-1 is therefore $150,000 ($200,000/4,000 × 3,000). However, management has concluded that if the price of an XX-4 rises to as much as $250,000 in the next two years, it will not replace the XR-1. Instead, it will buy stampings from an outside supplier. In this case the replacement cost of the asset would be calculated using the cost of obtaining the required number of stampings from the outside supplier.

In extreme cases the increasing replacement costs of productive resources may mean that the enterprise will in the future actually change its line of business and will therefore cease to have need for the type of service provided by the assets now owned. In these cases the replacement costs of such assets may be no more useful in arriving at relevant measures of enterprise performance and disposable wealth than are long outdated original transaction values.

Unrealized Holding Gains and Replacement-Cost-Based Net Income

To highlight the basic idea, our initial replacement cost example had no assets other than cash in the firm's beginning and ending financial positions. We were therefore able to define *replacement-cost net income* (the amount that equals the difference between beginning and ending owners' equity) as replacement cost current operating income plus realized holding gains. When there are no noncash assets or any liabilities, these are the only components of replacement cost net income. However, valuation of the noncash assets and the liabilities of the firm at the end of each period at their then-current entry prices introduces yet another holding gain, which is classified as unrealized until the firm consumes the resources.

> **Unrealized Holding Gains.** An unrealized holding gain is measured by the difference between the current (end-of-period) replacement cost and the original transaction value of assets and liabilities on hand at the end of the period. The unrealized holding gain (loss) is an indication of a potential benefit (or detriment) that accrues to the firm when the resource is consumed.

For reasons of simplicity in this introduction to the replacement cost model, we will restrict our attention to unrealized holding gains on the nonmonetary, productive assets of the firm (inventory and plant and equipment). But the reader should be aware that unrealized holding gains can be generated on all of the assets and liabilities whenever their end-of-period replacement costs differ from original transaction values.

With this definition of unrealized holding gains, we can define replacement-cost-based net income.

> **Replacement-Cost-Based Net Income.** Replacement-cost-based net income is equal to the algebraic sum of replacement-cost-based current operating income, realized holding gains, and the *change* in unrealized holding gains over the period.

When the beginning and ending assets and liabilities of the firm are valued at current replacement costs on the respective balance sheet dates, the above definition of replacement-cost-based net income in terms of its components is equivalent to our familiar definitional form for all net income measures:

> **Replacement-Cost-Based Net Income.** Replacement-cost-based net income is equal to replacement-cost-based ending owners' equity (adjusted for additional contributions and dividends) minus replacement-cost-based beginning owners' equity.

554 CHAPTER 14

In view of this inclusiveness, we note that replacement-cost-based net income must encompass all of the holding gains (realized or unrealized) that were generated *during the period* from changes in the replacement costs of assets (and liabilities). Recall, however, that when an asset is consumed during the period, the *realized* holding gain is measured by the *full* difference between the replacement cost and the original transaction value of the resource. To the extent that all or a portion of this holding gain was recognized in a prior period as an *unrealized* holding gain, the full *realized* holding gain overstates the holding gain generated solely in the current period. It is for this reason that measurement of replacement-cost-based net income in terms of its three components includes *only the change in unrealized holding gains* for the period.

Example 14-6

Assume that an analysis of a company's inventory records for 19X2 disclosed the following:

	Units	Original Transaction Value/Unit	Replacement Cost/Unit
Inventory, 1/1/X2	200	$ 10	$ 13
Purchases during 19X2	400	14	—
	600		
Consumed during 19X2:			
From beginning inventory	200	$ 10	$ 15
From purchases made in 19X2	300	14	15
	500		
Inventory, 12/31/X2	100	14	16
	600		

The unit replacement costs for the units in inventory at 1/1/X2 and 12/31/X2 are the prices prevailing at the end of 19X1 and 19X2, respectively. The unit replacement costs for the units consumed during 19X2 are the prices prevailing at the dates the resources were consumed.

With the information provided, we can calculate the amount of *total* holding gains generated during 19X2 as follows:

Additional holding gains generated in
19X2 on units in beginning inventory
200 × ($15 − $13) $ 400

(Note: As of 1/1/X2, the unrealized
holding gain of $13 − $10 had already
been recognized.)

Holding gains generated on units
purchased and sold during 19X2
300 × ($15 − $14)   300

> Holding gains generated, but not yet
> realized, during 19X2 on units
> purchased during the year but still
> remaining in the ending inventory
> 100 × ($16 - $14)   200
>
> Total holding gains generated in 19X2 $ 900

Because we assumed that replacement costs were always higher than the related original transaction values (or beginning of year replacement costs), all of the holding gains (losses) are gains.

Now let us look at how the holding gain components of the definition of replacement-cost-based net income will generate the same *net* figure for 19X2 holding gains. The components are:

> Realized holding gains in 19X2:
> 200 × ($15 - $10) $ 1,000
> 300 × ($15 - $14)   300
> $ 1,300
>
> Unrealized holding gains at:
> 1/1/X2   200 × ($13 - $10) $ 600
> 12/31/X2 100 × ($16 - $14)   200
> Change in unrealized holding gains $ (400)
>
> Net holding gains in 19X2—Realized
> holding gains plus change in
> unrealized holding gains $ 900

It is clear from these data that the change in unrealized holding gains has two effects when added to the realized holding gains: (1) It effectively deducts the unrealized holding gains at the beginning of the period from the realized holding gains (because they were recognized as income in the prior period); and (2) it adds the unrealized holding gains at the end of the period.

The example illustrates that all the *unrealized* holding gains at the end of the current period (in this case, $200) may well have been generated in the current period, but the amount of *unrealized* holding gains at the beginning of the period ($600)—which was recognized in replacement-cost-based net income in the prior period—may be included in the *realized* holding gains of the period. Thus, the *change in the unrealized holding gains*—which may be positive or negative—effectively adjusts for this potential double-counting. Indeed, *if the change in unrealized holding gains is combined directly with the measure of realized holding gains* for the period, we have a direct measure of *new* holding gains generated during the period.

In the examples that follow, we do *not* net the two holding gain components for two reasons. First, as was previously noted, the sum of the replacement-cost-based current operating income and the realized holding gains is equal to conventional accounting net income for the period, and disclosure of this amount in the income statement provides a useful point of reference. Second, some accountants believe that use of current replacement costs to segregate conventional accounting net income into (1) the portion attributable to the difference between selling price and replacement cost at the time of sale (current operating income), and (2) the portion arising from earlier purchases at prices lower than replacement cost at time of sale (realized holding gains) may be useful disclosure, but they are not prepared to recognize income (in the form of holding gains) in a period prior to realization through sale. Hence, for these accountants, realized and unrealized holding gains are not comparable measures that can be combined in the income statement of the current period. Indeed, they probably would not include the change in *unrealized* holding gains anywhere in the income statement. Since accounting thought has not coalesced on this issue, we refrain from combining the two measures of holding gains but do reflect both in the income statement. In this manner, the statement user may act upon whatever income concept he believes appropriate.

The Replacement Cost Model Applied

Having completed the introduction of the set of general concepts and valuation principles that together compose the replacement cost model, we now illustrate the model by considering some representative events that might be experienced by a hypothetical service firm during the first two years of its life.

Example 14-7

Panozzo Labs, Inc. was incorporated on January 1, 19X1 in the state of Illinois for the purpose of providing laboratory analyses for physicians. For the year 19X1, the transactions of the firm and the relevant replacement costs are as follows:

1. On January 1, 19X1, Leo and Donald Panozzo, the founders of the firm, contributed cash of $10 million in exchange for all the capital stock of the new firm.
2. On January 2, 19X1, the firm purchased laboratory equipment for $8 million cash. The equipment had an estimated service life of ten years and no salvage value.
3. During the year, the firm purchased inventory (supplies) of $3.6 million on account.
4. Revenue for the year, all in cash, amounted to $6 million.
5. The firm made cash payments for various types of operating expenses of $1 million.
6. Payments on account to trade creditors amounted to $2.6 million.
7. Cost of sales for the year were:

On original transaction value basis	$3 million
On replacement cost basis	$3.4 million

8. Depreciation expense for the year on the basis of original transaction value was $800,000, and on a replacement cost basis was $950,000.
9. The replacement cost of ending inventory was $700,000.
10. The replacement cost (new) of the laboratory equipment at the end of 19X1 was $9.5 million.

11. A cash dividend of $650,000, equal to the replacement-cost-based current operating income, was paid on December 31, 19X1.

The events and transactions (excluding replacement cost information) described in items 1 through 8 are recognized according to conventional accounting on lines 1 through 8 of the financial position worksheet appearing in Exhibit 14-3. The dividends paid (item 11 of Example 14-7) are based upon replacement-cost-based current operating income for the period. This amount is verified in the replacement-cost-based income statement for 19X1 (Exhibit 14-6). Pre- and post-dividend ending owners' equity figures are displayed in the financial position worksheet to facilitate the calculation of replacement-cost-based net income by means of the dividend-adjusted change in owners' equity. This calculation appears in Exhibit 14-4.

The measurement of replacement-cost-based net income in Exhibit 14-4 requires the determination of owners' equity at the beginning and the end of the period, using replacement costs at each point in time to value the assets on hand. As a consequence of the definition of unrealized holding gains, we note that at any point in time replacement-cost-based owners' equity is equal to the sum of conventional accounting owners' equity and the unrealized holding gains. This relationship is used in Exhibit 14-4 to derive 12/31/X1 replacement-cost-based owners' equity (before dividends). Data for determining the end-of-period replacement costs is given in items 9 and 10 of Example 14-7. Cash, the only asset on hand at the beginning of the period, is valued the same under both the conventional accounting and the replacement cost models. Therefore, owners' equity at 1/1/X1 is the same under both models, and no additional calculations need be made in determining replacement-cost-based beginning owners' equity.

Exhibit 14-3

PANOZZO LABS, INC.

Financial Position Worksheet
For 19X1
(amounts in thousands)

	Cash	Inventory	Equipment	Accumulated Depreciation	Accounts Payable	Owners' Equity
1. Original investment	10,000					10,000
2. Purchase equipment	(8,000)		8,000			
3. Purchase inventory on account		3,600			3,600	
4. Revenue	6,000					6,000
5. Operating expenses	(1,000)					(1,000)
6. Payments on account	(2,800)				(2,800)	
7. Cost of sales		(3,000)				(3,000)
8. Depreciation expense				(800)		(800)
Pre-dividend ending balances	4,200	600	8,000	(800)	800	11,200
Dividends paid	(650)					(650)
Ending balances	3,550	600	8,000	(800)	800	10,550

Exhibit 14-4

PANOZZO LABS, INC.

Calculation of Replacement-Cost-Based Net Income for 19X1
(amounts in thousands)

Replacement-cost ending owners' equity (before dividends):			
Conventional accounting ending owners' equity (before dividends)		$11,200	
Add 12/31/X1 unrealized holding gains* on:			
Inventory	$ 100		
Equipment (net of accumulated depreciation)	1,350	1,450	$12,650
Replacement-cost beginning owners' equity—			
For 19X1, equal to conventional accounting beginning owners' equity			10,000
Replacement-cost-based net income for 19X1			$ 2,650

		12/31/X1 Equipment (net)		
	12/31/X1 Inventory	Equipment (Gross)	Accumulated Depreciation	Equipment (Net)
Replacement Cost	$700	$9,500	$(950)	$8,550
Original Transaction Value	600	8,000	(800)	7,200
Unrealized Holding Gains, 12/31/X1	$100			$1,350

*Calculation of 12/31/X1 unrealized holding gains:

   The effect of recognizing current replacement costs on the financial position of Panozzo Labs, Inc. as of December 31, 19X1 is reflected in the comparative statements of financial position shown in Exhibit 14-5. Note that the owners' equity section of the replacement-cost-based statement of financial position is separated into two parts—conventional accounting owners' equity and total unrealized holding gains. Note also that the owners' equity figures in both statements are *post*-dividend amounts, whereas the figures used in Exhibit 14-4 in determining replacement-cost-based net income are adjusted for the $650,000 dividend.

   In developing an income statement for Panozzo Labs, Inc. for 19X1, we rely upon our definition of replacement-cost-based net income as the sum of replacement-cost-based current operating income, realized holding gains, and the change in unrealized holding gains over the year. Comparative income statements under the conventional accounting and replacement cost models, and the relationships between them, are presented in Exhibit 14-6. In the upper part of the statement, current operating income for 19X1 is determined. The data for the conventional accounting column come directly from the financial position worksheet in Exhibit 14-3. The replacement cost values for cost of sales and depreciation expense are given in items 7 and 8 of Example 14-7. The middle column, labeled "replacement cost adjustments" or "realized holding gains," reflects the differences between expenses based upon original transaction values and expenses based upon the current cost to replace resources *at the time that they were used* in producing the current period's revenue. Since the replacement cost model seeks to match the current cost of consumed resources against

Exhibit 14-5

PANOZZO LABS, INC.

Statement of Financial Position
(Calculated for Both Conventional Accounting and Replacement Cost Models)
As of December 31, 19X1
(amounts in thousands)

	Original Transaction Value	Replacement Cost
Cash	$ 3,550	$ 3,550
Inventory	600	700
Equipment	8,000	9,500
Less: Accumulated depreciation	(800)	(950)
	$11,350	$12,800

	Original Transaction Value	Replacement Cost
Accounts payable	$ 800	$ 800
Owners' equity:		
Conventional	$10,550	$10,550
Unrealized holding gains	—	1,450
Total owners' equity	$10,550	$12,000
	$11,350	$12,800

Exhibit 14-6

PANOZZO LABS, INC.

Income Statement
for the Year Ended December 31, 19X1
(amounts in thousands)

	Conventional Accounting	Replacement Cost Adjustments (Realized Holding Gains)	Replacement Cost
Revenues	$6,000	—	$6,000
Expenses:			
Cost of sales	$3,000	$400	$3,400
Depreciation expense	800	150	950
Other operating expenses	1,000	-0-	1,000
Total expenses	$4,800	$550	$5,350
Current operating income:			
Conventional	$1,200		
Replacement cost			$ 650
Realized holding gains	—		550
Realized income (conventional net income)	$1,200		$1,200
Change in unrealized holding gains	—		1,450*
Net income:			
Conventional	$1,200		
Replacement Cost			$2,650

*Note that the *change* in unrealized holding gains shown here equals the sum of unrealized holding gains at the end of 19X1 because there were no unrealized holding gains as of the beginning of 19X1 (that is, the net assets then consisted solely of cash). See Exhibit 14-4 for details of the year-end unrealized holding gains.

revenue as it is realized, the revenue figure in the statement is, of course, not adjusted. We are only *assuming* in this illustration, for reasons of simplicity, that all of the "other operating expenses" had current replacement costs at the time they were incurred equal to their original transaction values.

The replacement-cost-based cost of sales value in Exhibit 14-6 presumably reflects the aggregation of the current replacement costs of supplies as they were consumed throughout the period. The replacement cost value for depreciation expense, however, reflects the application of one of two alternative methods of measuring this expense. The information provided in the example indicates that the equipment has an estimated service life of ten years, with no salvage value, and a current replacement cost *at December 31, 19X1* of $9,500,000. Hence, the depreciation expense on a replacement cost basis of $950,000 in this example is calculated using this *year-end* replacement cost of the equipment. We should note that one can make a case for the alternative method of using the *average* replacement cost of the equipment during the year as the basis for calculation of replacement-cost depreciation expense. Though such a choice involves more effort and possibly more cost (to obtain a weighted average cost for the year rather than a single year-end cost) it affords comparable treatment to inventory and equipment. We therefore use end-of-period replacement cost in Example 14-7 only to simplify the calculations—not because it is clearly preferable. Note however that replacement-cost-based net income is unaffected by this choice. If use of average replacement cost produces a measure of depreciation expense for the year that is lower (higher) than that calculated using end-of-period replacement prices, then replacement-cost-based current operating income would be higher (lower) than measured, *and* realized holding gains would be lower (higher) by the same amount. Unrealized holding gains are unaffected, because they are a function of the values assigned to the assets, and these values are determined using end-of-period replacement prices. This is not to argue, however, that possible misstatement of the current operating income (with an equal and offsetting misstatement of realized holding gains) is unimportant, because we have previously suggested (and will discuss more fully later) that current operating income may serve as an appropriate measure of performance and/or disposable wealth.

Thus, *replacement-cost-based current operating income*, which is the first component of replacement-cost-based net income, is determined to be $650,000. The presumption in this example, and in our discussion to this point, is this income component best measures the disposable wealth of the firm—from a physical capital point of view. The increase in wealth in the form of holding gains must, from this perspective, be retained by the firm in order to have sufficient resources to replace the physical assets when replacement is necessary.

When the second component, realized holding gains for 19X1 of $550,000, is added to replacement-cost-based current operating income, we determine *replacement-cost-based realized income* for 19X1 to be $1.2 million. This measure of income is always equal to conventional accounting net income, because the difference between the two current operating income measures—the realized holding gains—has been added to the replacement-cost-based current operating income. Thus, realized income provides a potential measure of disposable wealth based upon a money capital point of view and a realization test (through sale or use) on changes in the replacement prices of assets.

Adding the third component, changes in the unrealized holding gains of $1,450,000, to realized income produces *replacement-cost-based net income* for 19X1 of $2,650,000. This amount is of course equal to the amount determined in Exhibit 14-4 in which we work with owners' equity at the beginning and end of the period, and thus reinforces the equivalence of the two definitions of replacement-cost-based net income. Use of replacement-cost-based net income as a measure of disposable wealth requires a commitment to the following: (1) a replacement cost basis for value determination, (2) money capital as the capital maintenance criterion, and (3) no requirement that the gains or losses resulting from fluctuations in the replacement costs of resources be realized through sale or use of the resources.

Application of Replacement Cost Model Extended

Having completed the analysis of Panozzo Labs' first year of operations, we now extend the example to a second year.

Example 14-8

The transactions and relevant replacement costs for Panozzo Labs, Inc. for the year 19X2 are as follows:

1. During 19X2 the firm purchased inventory (supplies) of $3.5 million on account.
2. Revenue for 19X2, all in cash, amounted to $6.5 million.
3. The firm made cash payments of $1 million for various types of operating expenses in 19X2.
4. Payments on account to trade creditors during 19X2 amounted to $3.7 million.
5. Cost of sales for the year were:

    On original transaction value basis—$3.2 million

    On replacement cost basis—$3.7 million

6. Depreciation expense for the year on the basis of original transaction value was again $800,000, but on a replacement cost basis (again using end-of-year replacement prices—see number 8 below) it amounted to $1 million.
7. The replacement cost of the ending inventory was $1.2 million.
8. The replacement cost (new) of the laboratory equipment at the end of 19X2 was $10 million.
9. A cash dividend of $800,000, equal to the replacement-cost-based current operating profit, was paid on December 31, 19X2.

Following the same method of analysis that we employed for the first year of operations, the transactions that are recognized under the conventional accounting model are entered in the financial position worksheet in Exhibit 14-7. The beginning balances are of course obtained from the financial position worksheet for 19X1. The owners' equity values from the 19X2 financial position worksheet and the December 31, 19X2 replacement costs for inventory and equipment are used as before to calculate replacement-cost-based net income (See Exhibit 14-8). Note that in this second year of operations, the beginning owners' equity has to be adjusted for unrealized holding gains in the same manner as we adjust the ending owners' equity.

Comparative statements of financial position as of December 31, 19X2 are shown in Exhibit 14-9. The format of the owners' equity section of the replacement cost statement is the same as in 19X1, emphasizing again that the total difference in asset values between the two models at any point in time is reflected in the amount of unrealized holding gains.

Finally, comparative income statements for 19X2 under the conventional accounting and replacement cost models, and the relationships between them, are presented in Exhibit 14-10. Since unrealized holding gains existed at both the beginning and the end of 19X2, the change in unrealized holding gains for 19X2 reflects the increase from $1,450,000 to $1.9 million. If the unrealized holding gains had decreased over the year, this component would have been deducted from realized income. All of the remaining measurements in the income statement are equivalent in concept and mechanics to those discussed for 19X1.

Exhibit 14-7

PANOZZO LABS, INC.

Financial Position Worksheet
for 19X2
(amounts in thousands)

	Cash	Inventory	Equipment	Accumulated Depreciation	Accounts Payable	Owners' Equity
Beginning Balances	3,550	600	8,000	(800)	800	10,550
1. Purchase inventory on account		3,500			3,500	
2. Revenue	6,500					6,500
3. Operating expenses	(1,000)					(1,000)
4. Payments on account	(3,700)				(3,700)	
5. Cost of sales		(3,200)				(3,200)
6. Depreciation expense				(800)		(800)
Pre-dividend ending balances	5,350	900	8,000	(1,600)	600	12,050
Dividends paid	(800)					(800)
Ending balances	4,550	900	8,000	(1,600)	600	11,250

Exhibit 14-8

PANOZZO LABS, INC.

Calculation of Replacement-Cost-Based Net Income for 19X2
(amounts in thousands)

Replacement-cost ending owners' equity (before dividends):				
Conventional accounting ending owners' equity (before dividends)			$12,050	
Add 12/31/X2 unrealized holding gains* on:				
Inventory		$ 300		
Equipment (net of accumulated depreciation)		1,600	1,900	$13,950
Replacement-cost beginning owners' equity:				
Conventional accounting beginning owners' equity			10,550	
Add 1/1/X2 unrealized holding gains** on:				
Inventory		100		
Equipment (net of accumulated depreciation)		1,350	1,450	12,000
Replacement-cost based net income for 19X2				$ 1,950

		12/31/X2 Equipment (net)		
	12/31/X2 Inventory	Equipment (Gross)	Accumulated Depreciation	Equipment (Net)
Replacement Cost	$1,200	$10,000	$2,000	$8,000
Original Transaction Value	900	8,000	1,600	6,400
Unrealized Holding Gains, 12/31/X2	$ 300			$1,600

*Calculation of 12/31/X2 unrealized holding gains:
**See Exhibit 14-4

Exhibit 14-9

PANOZZO LABS, INC.

Statement of Financial Position
(Calculated for both Conventional Accounting and Replacement Cost Models)
As of December 31, 19X2
(amounts in thousands)

	Original Transaction Value	Replacement Cost		Original Transaction Value	Replacement Cost
Cash	$ 4,550	$ 4,550	Accounts payable	$ 600	$ 60
Inventory	900	1,200	Owners' equity:		
Equipment	8,000	10,000	Conventional		$11,25
Less: Accumulated depreciation	(1,600)	(2,000)	Unrealized holding gains	$11,250	1,90
	$11,850	$13,750	Total owners' equity	$11,250	$13,15
				$11,850	$13,75

Exhibit 14-10

PANOZZO LABS, INC.

Income Statement
For the Year Ended December 31, 19X2
(amounts in thousands)

	Conventional Accounting	Replacement Cost Adjustments (Realized Holding Gains)	Replacement Cost
Revenues	$6,500	—	$6,500
Expenses:			
Cost of sales	$3,200	$500	$3,700
Depreciation expense	800	200	1,000
Other operating expenses	1,000	-0-	1,000
Total expenses	$5,000	$700	$5,700
Current Operating income:			
Conventional	$1,500		
Replacement cost			800
Realized holding gains			700
Realized income			
(conventional net income)	$1,500		$1,500
Change in unrealized			
holding gains	—		450*
Net income:			
Conventional	$1,500		
Replacement Cost			$1,950

*12/31/X2 Unrealized Holding Gains (See Exhibit 14-8) $1,900
12/31/X1 Unrealized Holding Gains (See Exhibit 14-8) 1,450
Increase in Unrealized Holding Gains $ 450

Replacement Costs and Disposable Wealth Measurement

Whether or not the use of the replacement cost model improves disposable wealth measurement in times of changing prices is a question that must be examined in the context of the capital maintenance and realization criteria that are adopted. As we have seen in our example, if the money capital view is adopted and a strict realization test imposed, nothing is gained over conventional accounting *with respect to disposable wealth measurement* because realized income equals conventional accounting net income. Of course the measure of the value of the assets employed during the period to produce this income will be different under the two models, and thus the user may gain additional analytical insights even though the disposable wealth measure is unchanged.[2] If the realization test is dropped, then the logical candidate for our measure of disposable wealth would be replacement-cost-based net income, and

[2] The analysis of relationships between values in the income statement and the statement of financial position is part of the broader topic of financial statement analysis, which is examined in Chapter 18.

this value normally would be significantly different from other competing disposable wealth values. However, because the unrealized holding gains are, in a sense, still "tied up" in inventory and long-lived assets (without any management decision during the period to reinvest them as may be the case with *realized* holding gains), few accountants or statement users have proposed the adoption of replacement-cost-based net income as a measure of disposable wealth. Therefore, since its primary appeal *for disposable wealth measurement purposes* seems to be derived from the physical capital point of view, we now examine the general adequacy of the replacement cost model as a means of preserving a firm's endowment of physical resources.

The income concept we have been using as a measure of disposable wealth under the physical capital maintenance criterion is replacement-cost-based current operating income. This choice is consistent with much of the developing accounting literature in the United States on the replacement cost model. Indeed, many authors refer to this measure of income as *sustainable,* or *distributable, income.* How well does it meet the underlying objective? We have previously noted that use of this income number implicitly assigns all of the required investment due to increasing prices to the equity shareholders. To the extent that this is unrealistic, replacement-cost-based current operating income tends to understate the amount that can be distributed as a result of the current period's activities. Some correction could of course be made for this factor, but since choice of financing policy is a management, not an accounting, issue, it is impossible to envision a satisfactory accounting response that is not strictly arbitrary.

Another important issue is whether exclusion of the holding gains from disposable wealth is reasonable and accurate for the purpose at hand. Let us first consider the holding gains on inventory. If the inventory is replaced as consumed, the level of holding gains will accurately measure the necessary additional investment. But if the firm replaces its inventory at periodic intervals, as most do, and if the replacement price fluctuates between the date of consumption and the date of replacement, the equivalence of the holding gains and the required additional investment will suffer. There may be no greater reason to expect the replacement price to go up between the dates of consumption and replacement than to expect it to go down. If this is the case, we should have offsetting effects over time and over many different inventory items, and therefore measured holding gains may provide a reasonably good measure of required additional investment. However, should there be a general trend upward in replacement prices (due, for example, to an increasing general price level), then each year our holding gains measure may be slightly understated as an indication of additional investment. In this case, management may have to react conservatively in dividend and other wealth distribution decisions (to the extent that it can take the initiative) and reserve a portion of the current operating income for future investment.

Now let us consider the holding gains on plant and equipment. Here we encounter a possibly significant problem in terms of maintaining physical capital. Because of the long lives of assets in this category, the period of time between the recognition of depreciation expense (and the related holding gains) and the replacement of the productive capacity may be substantial. And if replacement prices are moving, say, upward over the life of the asset, the total holding gains realized on the use of the asset will be less (often much less) than the required additional investment.

Example 14-9

In Example 14-4 it was assumed that the Abney Company acquired on January 1, 19X1, a new machine for $3,000, with an expected service life of three years and no salvage value. Assume now that the replacement cost (new) at the end of each of the three years of its service life was as follows:

Year	Replacement Cost (New)
19X1	$4,500
19X2	6,000
19X3	7,500

With this information we can determine the accounting values that would be generated under the replacement cost model (using end-of-period prices):

Year	Depreciation Expense	Realized Holding Gains	Unrealized Holding Gains— End of the Year	Change in Unrealized Holding Gains
19X1	$1,500	$ 500	$1,000	$1,000
19X2	2,000	1,000	1,000	-0-
19X3	2,500	1,500	-0-	(1,000)
	$6,000	$3,000		$ -0-

The total realized holding gains for the three years amounts to $3,000, and thus replacement-cost-based current operating income will, in sum over the three years, be $3,000 less than the sum of the conventional accounting net income measures. But the additional investment over the original $3,000 purchase price that is necessary at the end of 19X3 when the machine is worn out is $4,500 ($7,500 − $3,000). Hence, in this case, the holding gains understate the amount that would be necessary in the future to replace the physical asset.

The result obtained in Example 14-9 is indicative of a pervasive problem in the application of the replacement cost model to long-lived assets in times of generally increasing prices. Even though the calculations drew upon the most current prices at the end of each year, they could not anticipate the effects of price changes in subsequent periods. To alleviate the inherent problem illustrated in this example, some authors and practitioners argue that an additional provision for "catch-up depreciation" should be recognized as an expense each period. For example, at the end of 19X2 the current replacement cost (new) of the machine is $6,000. On the basis of this price, we should have recognized an annual depreciation expense of $2,000 for each of the past two years. But in 19X1, depreciation expense on a replacement cost basis was only $1,500, using the replacement cost (new) of $4,500 prevailing at the end of that year. Therefore the "catch-up depreciation" to be recognized in 19X2 for the understated depreciation expense in 19X1 would be $500 ($2,000 − $1,500). A similar analysis of 19X3 would show a required adjustment for "catch-up depreciation" for the years 19X1 and 19X2 of $1,000. Recognition of these adjustments would result in additional cumulative realized holdings gains of $1,500 and would reestablish the desired equivalence between this measure and the necessary additional investment.

Other circumstances could also affect the relationship between the realized holding gains and the necessary additional investment. For example, if management actively speculates in the future replacement cost of inventory by acquiring a greater than normal quantity, any holding gain or loss should probably not be treated the same as the holding gains on the normal levels of the firm's productive capacity. Hence we cannot be certain whether the replacement cost model, and specifically the use of current operating income as the measure of disposable wealth, will satisfy the objective of maintaining a firm's physical capital. It does seem reasonable to conclude, however, that in many cases this disposable wealth measure will be an improvement over conventional accounting net income when the goal is to maintain physical capital.

Replacement Costs and Performance Measurement

The principal orientation of this chapter has been toward the two alternative capital maintenance criteria and the related measures of disposable wealth. But an equally important objective of income measurement is the determination of a measure of performance for the period that can be used by the investor to estimate a firm's long-run cash-generating ability. A logical question, then, is, How well does the replacement cost model satisfy this objective?

As a basis for our consideration of this issue, it may be helpful to review briefly the motivation originally developed in Chapter 3 for introducing measures of performance based on past and present activities. Recall that in making investment decisions, investors presumably use some estimates of the future cash flows and attendant risk associated with an investment in a business. Whether management provides forecasts of future cash flows or investors produce their own forecasts, measures of the enterprise's demonstrated ability to generate cash in the immediate past are assumed to be useful in testing the credibility of such forecasts. This is an objective that conventional accounting performance measure is intended to serve by focusing on the set of products that were sold in the current period and the set of productive activities that produced them. By matching the prices received for the products sold against the prices paid for the resources consumed, net operating income attempts to measure the contribution *of that set of activities* to the long-run cash flow of the enterprise. Presumably if the enterprise were to engage in an identical set of activities in the future, with the same efficiency as demonstrated in the past, *on average* the same contribution to long-run cash flows would result. Accountants recognize, of course, that sets of activities will virtually never repeat themselves exactly. But that does not mean that measurement of past performance is futile. It simply means that a measure of past performance is not a forecast *per se*. Instead, it may only provide a starting point for forecasting (assuming that the forecaster attempts to predict first the ways that future activities will differ from past activities, and then the amounts by which the resulting future performance will depart from past performance).

With this motivation in mind, we now consider the relevance of current replacement costs in measuring the firm's performance for the period. When replacement prices differ from the prices paid for resources that were consumed during the period, we are put on notice of an almost certain difference between the cash-flow implications of past and future activities. Assuming that the operating activities of the current period are repeated exactly in the future, the presumption of the replacement cost model is that the operating margin measured by matching current replacement prices against realized revenue is more closely related to the cash flows that the firm will realize (on average) in the future than is the margin based on past transaction costs. Stated another way, matching current replacement costs against realized revenues for the period is presumed to indicate the extent of the firm's ability to generate *real* economic value through its productive activities, where real economic value is measured by the difference between the market price for the firm's product and the current market prices for the factors of production that are consumed in the production of the product.

Use of *replacement-cost-based current operating income* as a performance measure is based upon at least two important assumptions. First, it assumes that the market price for the output of a firm adjusts contemporaneously with changes in the current entry prices for the factors of production, as opposed to a price adjustment only after the new prices have been paid in an exchange transaction. In general, this assumption seems reasonable; within an industry some firms will use resources purchased at the old price and other firms will consume resources acquired at the new price, and we would expect the market-determined price to reflect the current economic cost of the resources consumed. Second, by excluding the holding gains from the measure of performance, we assume that a firm's past ability to generate holding gains cannot be replicated in the future. This is certainly not true in all circumstances, but whether the exceptions are sufficiently important to negate the predictive ability of current operating income is still an open question. It should also be noted in this regard that use of the performance measure by the investor is essentially an individual analytical exercise, and should an investor believe that holding gains can be replicated in the future, he is free to make whatever adjustment he wishes in his conversion of this measure of past performance into an estimate (forecast) of future performance. A related issue that we should mention is that if an investor believes that a firm has engaged in speculative purchasing activities, the holding gains measurement illustrated earlier may not capture accurately the gain or loss actually realized. For example, if an above-normal inventory purchase is made in anticipation of a price increase, the holding gain reflects only the difference between the two prices of the resource. The cost of holding the extra inventory, which is properly treated as a cost of the price speculation activity, is included with the other operating expenses of the period. Thus, current operating income may be understated and holding gains overstated.

In summary, by restating current period performance in terms of the current replacement costs of resources used, we take into account the expected difference, due to price changes that have actually occurred, between present and future performance. We do not, however, preempt the function of forecasting *per se,* since we still reflect the same past productive activities (but in terms of a more current set of prices).

Replacement Costs and General Price-Level Adjustments

Although we observed at the outset of this chapter that the replacement cost model and the general price-level-adjusted conventional accounting model differ significantly in what they seek to measure, we should remember that general price-level adjustments also are a means of converting all the dollar measures into a *common unit of measurement.* Therefore it is reasonable to inquire whether some form of general price-level adjustments are (1) compatible with replacement cost measurement techniques and (2) useful in the interpretation of statements produced by the replacement cost model. To answer this question, we must examine the individual purpose and characteristics of the measure of performance and the measure of disposable wealth.

The measure of performance (under any valuation model) seeks to provide an indication of a firm's long-run cash-generating ability. Using the replacement cost model, we have, with some qualifications, interpreted replacement-cost-based current operating income as the performance measure. Current operating income is calculated by matching realized revenues for the period against the current replacement prices of the resources consumed. Thus, for the current period, the dollar measures are all in *relatively* homogeneous units—i.e., a mix of dollars of the current period. Some additional precision could be obtained by converting this mix of within-period dollars to a common dollar—say the dollars at the end of the period—but unless inflation was very high during the year, this improvement in measurement accuracy would probably not be significant to users. However, when the current operating income of prior periods is compared with the current operating income of the current period, or when the current period's income is extrapolated to future periods, adjustment for interperiod changes in the value of the dollar may be useful.

One additional factor that should be taken into account in deciding whether it is desirable to apply general price-level adjustments to the measure of performance is the probable magnitude of the monetary gain or loss from holding monetary assets and liabilities. If this measure is significant, and if it is interpreted as a recurring factor in the environment in which the firm is operating, the case for general price-level adjustment of current operating income is strengthened.

The disposable wealth measure (under any valuation model) seeks to provide an indication of the amount that can be distributed to parties having an economic interest in an enterprise and still leave the firm as well-off after the distribution as it was at the beginning of the period. The interpretation of the meaning of "well-offness" is a principal motivation for consideration of the replacement cost model, because when "well-offness" is interpreted in terms of equivalent physical resources or physical operating capability, the conventional accounting measure of disposable wealth appears to be subject to some major deficiencies. The replacement cost model seeks to alleviate these weaknesses by excluding from income the value changes that are the result of fluctuations in the purchase prices of resources. Hence we concluded, with some qualifications, that replacement-cost-based current operating income serves as the measure of disposable wealth when the intent is to maintain physical capital. With this capital maintenance criterion, general price-level adjustments of the disposable wealth measure are *not* appropriate. In essence, the physical capital point of view shifts the unit of capital measurement from dollars to physical resources, and current operating income merely expresses the amount of physical resources that can be distributed at the end of the period in end-of-period prices (dollars).

However, if the money capital criterion of "well-offness" is adopted together with the use of the replacement cost model, then general price-level adjustments are appropriate—assuming that the money capital orientation is toward the purchasing power of dollars, and not the number of dollars *per se*. If a realization test is imposed on the measure of disposable wealth for the period, then general price-level-adjusted realized income serves as the disposable wealth measure. This value is, of course, equal to general price-level-adjusted net income under the conventional accounting model. If the realization test is not imposed, however, then price-level-adjusted, replacement-cost-based net income is the disposable wealth measure. Since this value reflects all changes in the components of owners' equity under the replacement cost model, we can calculate it by computing the general price-level-adjusted change in owners' equity and adjusting for investments and dividends during the period. In making this calculation, note that all the assets and liabilities at the end of the period are valued at end-of-period prices, and thus end-of-period dollars; hence the recorded value of total owners' equity at the end of the period can be used without adjustment. On the other hand, the beginning-of-period owners' equity is the difference between assets and liabilities valued at beginning-of-period prices; thus the value of beginning owners' equity is a meaningful combination of resources valued in a common unit of measurement, but it must be adjusted to end-of-period dollars before it can be compared with ending owners' equity.

Example 14-10

Referring back to Exhibit 14-8 which discloses the 19X2 beginning and ending owners' equity of Panozzo Labs, Inc., assume that the index of the general level of prices was 110 on January 1 and 120 on December 31. Note also that the $800,000 cash dividend was paid on December 31, 19X2, and therefore is measured in end-of-period dollars. With this information, general price-level-adjusted, replacement-cost-based net income for 19X2 (in end-of-period dollars) can be calculated as follows:

	(000 omitted)
Owners' equity, 12/31/X2 (after cash dividend)	$ 13,150
Owners' equity, 1/1/X2 ($12,000 × 120/110)	13,091
Change in owners' equity in 19X2	$ 59
Cash dividends, December 31, 19X2	800
General price-level-adjusted, replacement-cost-based net income (in 12/31/X2 dollars)	$ 859

No general price-level adjustments are required in the current end-of-period statement of financial position prepared on the basis of the replacement cost model, because all assets and liabilities are measured in terms of end-of-period prices. This was, of course, the reason why we did not have to make any adjustment to ending owners' equity in the income calculation in Example 14-10. But for the same reason that we adjusted beginning owners' equity in that calculation, all the values in the statement of financial position of a prior period would have to be restated in the current period's dollars if the two statements were to be compared. Note that since all the assets and liabilities in a prior period's statement are measured in the same dollars, the restatement (or rollforward) would be accomplished by multiplying each asset and liability value by a single (unchanging) ratio of two index numbers. In Example 14-10 the statement of financial position at December 31, 19X1, would be restated in December 31, 19X2, dollars by multiplying every number in the statement by the ratio 120/110.

Current Replacement Cost Reporting

As was discussed in the preceding chapter, interest in alternatives to the conventional accounting model has increased appreciably over the past ten to fifteen years as the pace of inflation first increased and then remained at a higher level than in earlier years. In the early 1970s, accounting policy-making bodies in the United States, the United Kingdom, Australia, and Canada all released *proposed* standards that would have essentially implemented the general price-level-adjusted conventional accounting model in corporate financial reports (at least as supplementary information). But before these proposed standards were officially adopted, several events occurred that caused reconsideration of the appropriateness of this course of action. In the United Kingdom the government established a committee to study the effect of this proposed change in accounting on the British economy, and the report of the committee advocated current (replacement) cost accounting rather than general price-level-adjusted accounting. At about the same time the Australian accounting policy-making body also shifted its position to current (replacement) cost accounting. The final coup de grace from the point of view of accountants in the United States came on March 23, 1976, when the U.S. Securities and Exchange Commission (SEC) adopted a new reporting rule (for the approximately one thousand largest U.S. corporations) requiring the supplementary disclosure of certain replacement cost information. In view of these developments the Financial Accounting Standards Board (FASB) in the United States, as well as the policy-making bodies in Canada and the United Kingdom, suspended action on the proposed general price-level standards.

At present, accounting policy makers in all of the countries mentioned are actively involved in considering or implementing some form of current replacement cost reporting system. In the United States, two replacement cost reporting systems have been adopted or proposed—the SEC requirement in 1976 and the FASB proposed financial accounting standard in late 1978. Both are viewed as experimental in nature by the accounting policy makers, and both are also limited in applicability to large companies. The main features of each are now discussed, beginning with the SEC requirement.

SEC Reporting Requirement. The SEC reporting requirement is applicable only to the required annual filings (on Form 10-K) with the Commission and is limited to firms with inventories and *gross* property, plant, and equipment amounting to more than $100 million. For firms subject to this ruling (approximately one thousand), the following information (unaudited) must be reported as supplementary information:

a. Current replacement cost of inventories.

b. Current replacement cost (new) of the productive capacity, and current depreciated cost of the productive capacity.

c. Estimated cost of sales that would have been calculated if resources consumed had been valued at their replacement prices at the time they were consumed.

d. Estimated depreciation expense on the basis of the average current replacement cost of productive capacity.

e. Description of the methods used to estimate the above values.

f. Any additional information of which management is aware that it believes is necessary to prevent the above disclosures from being misleading.[3]

In terms of the estimated replacement cost information, the required disclosures are based upon essentially the same methods as those described in this chapter, except that *d* calls for depreciation expense to be based upon average rather than end-of-period replacement prices.

These disclosures were first made in 1976 financial statements. An example of the disclosures (for PPG Industries in 1977) is given in Exhibit 14-11 at the end of the chapter.

These data represent an early experimental stage in the provision of replacement cost information to investors in the United States. Because of the many unresolved measurement issues, specific standards and guidelines were not promulgated. Rather, companies were encouraged to supplement the disclosures with whatever additional information management believed would be necessary for the investor to understand the impact of changing prices on the firm's operations. Further, the SEC added the following caveat:

> The Commission cautions investors and analysts against simplistic use of the data presented. It intentionally determined not to require the disclosure of the effect on net income of calculating cost of sales and depreciation on a current replacement cost basis, both because there are substantial theoretical problems in determining an income effect and because it did not believe that users should be encouraged to convert the data into a single revised net income figure. The data are not designed to be a simple road map to the determination of "true income." In addition, investors must understand that due to the subjective judgments and the many different specific factual circumstances involved, the data will not be fully comparable among companies and will be subject to errors of estimation.[4]

[3] Securities and Exchange Commission, "Notice of Adoption of Amendments of Regulation S-X Requiring Disclosure of Certain Replacement Cost Data," *Accounting Series Release No. 190.*

[4] Ibid.

Notwithstanding this caveat, many analysts calculated revised income figures immediately upon the release of the first replacement cost disclosures, and one would suppose that many individual investors made similar calculations. We propose to briefly examine how the disclosures can be used to estimate replacement-cost-based current operating profit and replacement-cost-based net income for three reasons. First, use of the data in this manner should reinforce the reader's understanding of the basic concepts of the replacement cost model. Second, we have previously discussed many of the theoretical issues associated with the calculation of replacement-cost-based income numbers and believe that this permits the reader to use the additional information judiciously. And third, the subjectivity and lack of comparability that the SEC is now concerned about is in large measure a product of the novelty of replacement cost measures. As experience is gained, we would expect the measurements to become more reliable; if they do not, that may be a sufficient reason to discontinue replacement cost disclosures.

Example 14-11

> To illustrate the use of the replacement cost disclosures in estimating the various components in an income statement prepared using the replacement cost model, we will draw upon the disclosures made by PPG Industries in Exhibit 14-11. Additionally, we note that the firm reported conventional accounting net income of $91.7 million for 1977 in its 1977 annual report to shareholders.

In order to calculate replacement-cost-based current operating income, given that we know conventional accounting net income, we must estimate the realized holding gains for the year. Realized holding gains are measured by calculating the difference between cost of sales and depreciation expense valued at replacement prices and the same expenses valued at original transaction costs. This information is available in the replacement cost disclosures in Exhibit 14-11, and realized holding gains can accordingly be calculated as follows:

	1977 Cost of Sales	*1977 Depreciation Expense*
	(in millions)	
Replacement cost basis	$1,654.0	$139.0
Original transaction value basis	1,653.9	90.9
Realized holding gains	$ 0.1	$ 48.1
Total realized holding gains for 1977	$48.2	

The unrealized holding gains at the end of any year are measured by the difference between the value of an asset (inventory and property in this case) using replacement prices at the end of the year and its value using original transaction costs. Again, sufficient information is available in the replacement cost disclosure to make this calculation:

	(in millions)			
	Inventories		*Property (net)*	
	12/31/76	*12/31/77*	*12/31/76*	*12/31/77*
Replacement cost basis	$418.5	$445.7	$1,182.2	$1,473.0
Original transaction value basis	327.8	327.5	833.7	950.1
Unrealized holding gains	$ 90.7	$118.2	$ 348.5	$ 522.9
Increase (decrease) in unrealized holding gains in 1977		$27.5		$174.4
Total increase (decrease) in unrealized holding gains in 1977			$201.9	

With these values we can produce the major components of a replacement-cost-based income statement for PPG Industries for 1977 as follows:

Replacement-cost-based current operating income	$ 43.5
Realized holding gains	48.2
Realized income (conventional accounting net income for 1977)	91.7
Change in unrealized holding gains	201.9
Replacement-cost-based net income	$293.6

If desired, the adjustments can be made to the reported expenses for the year, thus producing a complete income statement on an estimated replacement cost basis.

These data, and the related narrative in Exhibit 14-11, illustrate an important property of the Fifo/Lifo inventory costing alternatives under the conventional accounting model. We have previously observed that use of Fifo produces an ending inventory value that approximates replacement cost, and use of Lifo yields a cost-of-sales figure that approximates replacement costing. But under the conventional accounting model, both approximations cannot be obtained simultaneously. Because of these properties, the SEC has authorized companies to use Fifo (Lifo) values in estimating the replacement costs of ending inventories (cost of sales) if these values are reasonably good approximations of the values that would be derived from a direct application of replacement prices. Without going into how this test of reasonableness would be determined, we note from Exhibit 14-11 that PPG Industries availed itself of this option. Further, we observe from our calculations above that the realized holding gains from inventory consumption (cost of sales) are fairly small, while the unrealized holding gains associated with inventory on hand are large. This implies that PPG Industries used Lifo in determining its original transaction values. If a firm used Fifo to determine inventory values, the unrealized holding gains on inventory would be fairly small, and the realized holding gains from the use of inventory would be somewhat larger.

Proposed FASB Reporting Requirement. On December 28, 1978, the Financial Accounting Standards Board issued a proposed financial accounting standard calling for the following minimum supplementary information from publicly held enterprises that have inventories and *gross* property, plant, and equipment amounting to more than $125 million *or* total assets amounting to more than $1 billion (both amounts measured in accordance with the conventional accounting model):[5]

a. (1) Income from continuing operations on a current cost basis, and holding gains or losses net of inflation; *or*

(2) Income from continuing operations on the basis of the general price-level-adjusted conventional accounting model (in FASB terminology, on a historical cost/constant dollar basis).

b. Inflation gain or loss on net monetary items.

c. A five-year summary of selected accounting data measured on the basis of current cost or historical cost/constant dollars. Among the data required are income from continuing operations, holding gains or losses net of inflation (when current cost is the selected measurement basis from *a* above), inflation gain or loss on net monetary items, and net assets at fiscal year-end.

The current cost basis (which the FASB seems to prefer) referred to in this proposed standard relies primarily upon replacement cost measures, although in certain circumstances, alternative measurement bases are employed. These circumstances and the alternatives are discussed in Chapter 16. Additionally, the holding gains and losses that are to be disclosed are the total holding gains and losses for the period—i.e., the sum of the realized holding gains and losses for the period and the change in the unrealized holding gains and losses over the period. The inflation adjustment of the holding gains and losses recognizes that the two components of the computation of a holding gain (loss) are not measured in the same dollars. The computation of the inflation gain or loss on net monetary items uses the principles described in Chapter 13 for the calculation of the net monetary gain or loss. Finally, the general price-level adjustments that are necessary are based upon the *Consumer Price Index for All Urban Consumers,* published by the Bureau of Labor Statistics of the U.S. Department of Labor.

In summary, the prospects for continued reporting of replacement cost information of the type required by the SEC and illustrated in Exhibit 14-11, and/or the more comprehensive set of replacement cost disclosures (and related adjustments for changes in the general price level) proposed by the FASB, are still under deliberation. There are many unresolved theoretical and practical issues, but the experience that will be gained over the next several years both in the measurement and in the use of the data should provide a sounder basis for the ultimate decision on the replacement cost model.

[5] Financial Accounting Standards Board, "Financial Reporting and Changing Prices," *Proposed Statement of Financial Accounting Standards,* December 28, 1978.

Exhibit 14-11

PPG INDUSTRIES

Replacement Cost Disclosure in Annual Report to SEC
For Year Ended December 31, 1977

20. REPLACEMENT COST INFORMATION (UNAUDITED)

In compliance with the rules of the Securities and Exchange Commission, PPG has prepared certain estimated replacement cost information for inventories, property, cost of sales and depreciation of plant and equipment. Such amounts are not indicative of either the amounts for which such inventories or existing productive capacity could be sold or management's intent to replace existing productive capacity and, even if replaced in the manner described, may not represent the actual future costs of replacement. Rather, such amounts represent management's estimate of the cost of replacement that would be incurred at December 31, 1977, if such assets were replaced in total at that time. While the estimate assumes a one-time replacement, most of these assets will be replaced over a period of time and actual events probably will be different from the assumptions used to prepare this estimate. Replacement cost information is excluded for PPG's productive capacity which, in management's current opinion, would not be replaced. However, conditions could subsequently change which would cause management to modify its current opinion.

For purposes of estimating the replacement cost of inventories, the first-in, first-out method utilizing either average or standard factory costs, which approximate actual costs at year end, has been applied. The replacement cost for cost of sales is based on the last-in, first-out method of valuing ending inventories. The replacement costs for cost of sales and inventories do not reflect any improved efficiency or reduced operating cost which might occur if all productive capacity were replaced. PPG believes that the replacement costs provided are reasonably representative of the approximate replacement cost of year-end inventories and the approximate replacement cost of sales, determined at cost levels experienced during the periods in which the products were sold.

For purposes of estimating the replacement cost of productive capacity, several approaches were utilized. In those instances in which the latest available technology is being used, replacement costs were estimated by applying indexes to the historic cost or using quoted market prices for new machinery of equivalent capacity. PPG believes that these indexes, which are published by various governmental and private organizations, provide a reasonable basis for the estimation of the replacement cost of productive capacity. For facilities in which the latest available technological developments are not being used, but would be utilized in replacing current productive capacity, the estimated replacement cost was developed using a functional approach. This method utilized engineering estimates or recent experience in replacing similar assets to derive a cost per unit of productive capacity. The cost per unit of such productive capacity was extrapolated to an estimated replacement cost of the existing productive capacity.

Exhibit 14-11 (cont.)

In each approach, no attempt was made to totally reengineer or to consolidate the entire productive capacity into larger units than those currently in existence. Also, the replacement cost estimates do not comprehend relocation of existing productive capacity and the resulting effects of items such as environmental regulations, cost and availability of labor, raw materials and energy. All of these and other matters would be considered in depth before such replacement were undertaken. The results of these considerations might significantly alter the costs of productive capacity replacement and PPG's manner of capacity replacement contemplated by this disclosure.

The accumulated depreciation related to the replacement cost of productive capacity was estimated using the relationship of the expired service to total service lives of existing productive facilities assumed to be replaced. Asset service lives were not extended for purposes of determining accumulated depreciation.

Basically, two methods were employed to calculate replacement cost depreciation expense. Where the replacement cost of productive capacity was developed using indexes, the replacement cost depreciation expense was calculated by indexing the related historical cost depreciation expense. Where the replacement cost of productive capacity was estimated using a functional approach, the replacement cost depreciation expense was developed by using the relationship of the historical cost depreciation expense to the historical cost of the assets.

Replacement cost information for PPG's foreign operations was determined by the use of the same procedures as described above for domestic operations. Amounts related to foreign assets have been translated to United States dollars at exchange rates in effect at December 31, 1977; amounts related to foreign cost of sales and depreciation expense have been translated to United States dollars using average exchange rates.

In PPG's view, the replacement cost information presented herein represents a reasonable estimate of such data. However, the replacement cost data have inherent imprecisions because of the need to make substantial subjective judgments in the estimating process. Additionally, all inflationary effects have not been comprehended in the replacement cost information. These additional effects would include, but not be limited to, the holding gain from being a net borrower in times of inflation or the holding losses from holding monetary assets. Accordingly, the data should not be used to determine the effect of inflation on PPG's net earnings as reported. Additionally this information may not be comparable to other companies and should not be used to adjust and compare PPG's financial statements with those of other companies.

PPG has not attempted to quantify the total impact of inflation and changes in other economic factors on its business because of the many unresolved conceptual problems related thereto. In order to recognize the impact of inflationary cost increases, the Company has increased sales prices as competitive conditions have permitted. PPG expects to continue to modify its sales prices to recognize future cost changes.

The following represents PPG's replacement cost information:

	Estimated Replacement Cost		Related Historical Cost	
	1977	1976	1977	1976
	(Millions)			
Inventories	$ 445.7	$ 418.5	$ 327.5	$ 327.8
Property	$3,400.3	$2,945.2	$1,882.9	$1,663.8
Less accumulated depreciation	1,927.3	1,763.0	932.8	830.1
Property—net	$1,473.0	$1,182.2	$ 950.1	$ 833.7
Cost of sales	$1,654.0	$1,443.6	$1,653.9	$1,440.1
Depreciation expense	$ 139.0	$ 137.5	$ 90.9	$ 89.9

The 1976 information has been restated for the effect of recording capital leases and for correction of the replacement cost of property.

The following table reconciles the historical cost amounts for which replacement cost data are provided to the related totals shown in the accompanying balance sheets and statements of earnings.

	Inventories	Property	Accumulated Depreciation	Cost of Sales	Depreciation Expense
1977 Historical costs:					
Amounts for which replacement cost information is provided	$327.5	$1,882.9	$ 932.8	$1,653.9	$90.9
Land, mineral deposits and construction in progress	—	142.7	3.4	—	1.7
Operations which will not be replaced at the end of their economic lives	—	93.1	80.2	—	6.0
Totals as shown in the accompanying financial statements	$327.5	$2,118.7	$1,016.4	$1,653.9	$98.6
1976 Historical costs:					
Amounts for which replacement cost information is provided	$327.8	$1,663.8	$ 830.1	$1,440.1	$89.9
Land, mineral deposits, and construction in progress	—	209.0	1.2	—	.5
Operations which will not be replaced at the end of their economic lives	—	80.7	68.4	—	2.4
Totals as shown in the accompanying financial statements	$327.8	$1,953.5	$ 899.7	$1,440.1	$92.8

Accumulated depreciation as of December 31, 1977, includes $50.7 million related to the write-down of certain assets of the Company's Puerto Rico operations.

Questions for Review and Discussion

14-1. Define:
   a. Current exchange price
   b. Current entry price (replacement cost)
   c. Current exit price (market value)
   d. Realized holding gains
   e. Unrealized holding gains
   f. Replacement-cost-based current operating income
   g. Replacement-cost-based realized income
   h. Replacement-cost-based net income

14-2. It is asserted that general price-level accounting (as described in Chapter 13) does not depart in principle from the conventional accounting model, but that the replacement cost model does. Explain the basis for this proposition.

14-3. Explain the distinction between the money capital and the physical capital points of view, and indicate how they impact upon the accounting measure of disposable wealth.

14-4. The proposition has been advanced that investors in general may prefer the money capital point of view to the physical capital point of view. Explain the reasoning underlying this assertion.

14-5. Explain how the disposable wealth measure under the physical capital maintenance criterion assumes that all the additional investment that is required due to increasing prices should come from the equity shareholders.

14-6. Assume that the income tax law is changed such that holding gains realized by a going concern are excluded from taxable income in order to allow the firm to maintain its physical capital. What tax treatment would you propose for the accumulated holding gains at the time the firm decides to liquidate its operations and distribute all of its assets (presumably in the form of cash after liquidation) to the shareholders?

14-7. Under the replacement cost model, what values should be assigned to (*a*) monetary assets and liabilities, (*b*) inventory, and (*c*) plant and equipment?

14-8. When it is no longer possible to replace an asset with an identical asset, and assuming no secondhand market exists, what alternative approaches might be used to estimate the replacement cost of the asset?

14-9. Explain why the change in unrealized holding gains for the period is added to the realized holding gains for the period in the calculation of replacement-cost-based net income.

14-10. Explain the relationship between replacement-cost-based net income and the change in owners' equity, where assets and liabilities have been valued at current replacement costs.

14-11. The financial vice-president of a company has just returned from a meeting where he learned that the trade association of which the company is a member is recommending that replacement cost depreciation for the period be calculated on the basis of the average replacement cost of productive capital for the period. He observes that this will result in a value for depreciation expense for the company that will be approximately $500,000 less per period than would have been reported had the company continued to use end-of period prices for equipment. He asks you to explain what effect this proposed change will have on the company's reported net income on a replacement cost basis.

14-12. Assuming the acceptance of a physical capital maintenance criterion, evaluate the validity of replacement-cost-based current operating income as the measure of disposable wealth.

14-13. Evaluate the validity of replacement-cost-based current operating income as the measure of performance.

14-14. Explain what general price-level adjustments might be appropriate in an income statement prepared using current replacement costs.

14-15. Explain what general price-level adjustments might be appropriate in a statement of financial position prepared using current replacement costs.

14-16. Summarize the replacement cost information that must be reported by companies subject to the 1976 SEC replacement cost reporting requirement.

Exercises

14-1. Comparing Disposable Wealth Measures. Morriss Enterprises was incorporated on January 1, 19X1 with an initial cash endowment of $1 million for the purpose of buying and selling turquoise rings. The rings will be purchased in New Mexico and Arizona and will be sold in New York City. The company's operating expenses will only consist of a sales commission amounting to 20 percent of selling price.

On January 1, 19X1, Morriss purchased 50,000 rings at a price of $20 per ring. During the year, the rings were sold at the expected 150 percent markup, or $30 per ring. On January 1, 19X2, Morriss replaced its stock of 50,000 rings at the same $20 unit cost. But shortly after this purchase, the replacement cost of the rings increased to $25 per ring, and accordingly the selling price went up to $37.50 per ring. All of the rings were sold during 19X2 at the $37.50 price. At the end of 19X2, the replacement cost of the rings remained at $25, and no further price changes occurred in 19X3. On January 1, 19X3, Morriss purchased as many rings as it could with the cash available.

Required:

1. Prepare conventional accounting income statements for 19X1, 19X2, and 19X3, assuming that Morriss Enterprises distributed a cash dividend at the end of each year equal in amount to conventional accounting net income.

2. Prepare replacement cost income statements for 19X1, 19X2, and 19X3, assuming that Morriss Enterprises distributed a cash dividend at

the end of each year equal in amount to replacement-cost-based current operating income.

3. Calculate the return on investment (i.e., net income divided by the dollar investment in inventory at the start of the year) for 19X3 under the two alternative dividend policies, and relate these calculations to the amounts of net income realized in 19X3 in the two different circumstances.

14-2. Comparing Disposable Wealth Measures. Purmer Company is in the business of producing and selling calendars. Because most of the calendars are sold between October and April, the company determines its results of operations on a fiscal year basis running from July 1 to June 30. The company has experienced fairly stable prices over the past few years and thus has been able to operate on a constant financial capital of $500,000. The company has no debt.

During the period July 1–September 30, 1980, the company produced 1 million calendars for 1981 at a unit cost of $0.50. During this production period, the replacement cost of paper increased dramatically. Fortunately, Purmer had acquired a sufficient supply of paper before the price increase, but Mary Purmer, the president of the company, estimates that the present replacement cost of the calendars (using the current price for paper) is $0.75. Most other companies in the industry were not as fortunate as Purmer Company, and they had to purchase their paper stock for the 1980 production run at the new (higher) price. Accordingly, the selling price for the calendars has increased from $1.00 to $1.25. On June 30, 1981, the company has sold all of the calendars at the $1.25 price, and all of its assets are in the form of cash.

Required:

1. Prepare an income statement for Purmer Company for fiscal year 1981 using the replacement cost model.

2. In the past, Mary Purmer has always had the company pay a cash dividend on June 30 equal to conventional accounting net income for the fiscal year. In view of the increase in the price of paper, she asks your advice as to dividend policy for the current year. You may assume that prices have stabilized at the new, higher level, and that no further increases appear imminent.

14-3. Valuing Long-lived Assets. On January 1, 1975, Hudson Company purchased equipment with an expected service life of ten years and no salvage value at a cost of $400,000. On December 31, 1980, the equipment was determined to have a replacement cost (new) of $700,000.

Required:

1. What values would be shown for the equipment in a statement of financial position at December 31, 1980, under the conventional accounting model and the replacement cost model?

2. Determine depreciation expense on the equipment for 1980 on a re-

placement cost basis (using end-of-period replacement prices for this purpose).

3. Determine the realized holding gains for 1980, and the balance of the unrealized holding gains at December 31, 1980.

14-4. Applying Replacement Costs to Long-lived Assets. On January 1, 1976, Johnson Corporation acquired a warehouse with an expected service life of twenty years and no salvage value at a cost of $2 million. The warehouse was determined to have a replacement cost (new) of $2.8 million on December 31, 1979, and $3.2 million on December 31, 1980.

Required:

1. What values would be shown for the warehouse in a statement of financial position at December 31, 1979, and December 31, 1980, under both the conventional accounting model and the replacement cost model?
2. Determine depreciation expense on the warehouse for 1980 on a replacement cost basis using the *average* 1980 replacement cost for the warehouse (assume the average 1980 replacement cost can be validly computed by taking the simple average of the beginning and ending replacement costs).
3. Calculate the realized holding gains for 1980.
4. Determine the balance of the unrealized holding gains at December 31, 1979, and December 31, 1980.
5. Assuming that Johnson Corporation has no other assets or expenses that are affected by the application of replacement costs (i.e., all other original transaction values are equal to replacement costs), and that conventional accounting net income for 1980 has been determined to be $180,000, calculate replacement-cost-based current operating income, realized income, and net income for 1980.

14-5. Applying Replacement Costs to Long-lived Assets. On January 1, 1979, Todd Corporation purchased machinery with an expected service life of ten years and no salvage value at a cost of $500,000. It was determined that the machinery had a replacement cost (new) of $700,000 on December 31, 1979, and $720,000 on December 31, 1980.

Required:

1. What values would be shown for the machinery in a statement of financial position at December 31, 1979, and December 31, 1980, under both the conventional accounting model and the replacement cost model?
2. Determine depreciation expense on the machinery for 1979 and 1980 on a replacement cost basis using the end-of-period replacement price.
3. Calculate the realized holding gains for 1979 and 1980.
4. Determine the balance of the unrealized holding gains at December 31, 1979, and December 31, 1980.

5. Assuming that Todd Corporation has no other assets or expenses that are affected by the application of replacement costs (i.e., all other original transaction values are equal to replacement costs), and that conventional accounting net income for 1980 has been determined to be $90,000, calculate replacement-cost-based current operating income, realized income, and net income for 1980.

14-6. Applying Replacement Costs to Inventory and Long-lived Assets. Hillrise Company began operations on January 1, 1979. At the end of 1979 and 1980, the firm compiled the following information:

	1979		1980	
	Original Transaction Value	Replacement Cost	Original Transaction Value	Replacement Cost
Cost of sales	$1,800,000	$2,100,000	$1,900,000	$2,300,000
Inventory, December 31	600,000	670,000	400,000	420,000
Plant and equipment (all purchased 1/1/79 with expected service life of 20 years and no salvage value)	5,000,000	6,000,000*	5,000,000	6,000,000*

*Replacement cost (*new*).

Required:

1. What values would be shown for the inventory and the plant and equipment in a statement of financial position at December 31, 1979, and December 31, 1980, under both the conventional accounting model and the replacement cost model?

2. Calculate the realized holding gains for 1979 and 1980. (Use end-of-period replacement costs in calculating depreciation expense on a replacement-cost basis).

3. Determine the balance of the unrealized holding gains at December 31, 1979, and December 31, 1980.

4. Assuming that Hillrise Company's sales were $2.8 million in 1979 and $3 million in 1980, and that the firm's only operating expenses were cost of sales and depreciation expense, prepare replacement cost income statements for 1979 and 1980.

14-7. Preparing Replacement Cost Financial Statements. Capital Computer Company is engaged in providing computer services to small businesses that do not have computers of their own. CCC, as it is called, has been in business for three years. Its very simple balance sheet at the end of year three and its income statement depicting results of year three's operations follow (both calculated under the conventional accounting model).

CAPITAL COMPUTER CORPORATION

Balance Sheet
As of the End of Year Three

Assets:			Liabilities and Owners' Equity:		
Cash		$ 900,000	Accounts payable		$ 50,000
Accounts receivable		300,000	Owners' equity:		
Supplies		50,000	Capital stock	$1,000,000	
Computer equipment	$1,500,000		Retained earnings	800,000	1,800,000
Less accumulated depreciation	(900,000)	600,000	Total liabilities and		
Total assets		$1,850,000	owners' equity		$1,850,000

CAPITAL COMPUTER CORPORATION

Income Statement
For Third Year of Operations

Revenue (service fees)		$1,200,000
Expenses:		
Wages and salaries	$400,000	
Supplies	50,000	
Rent (office and equipment)	10,000	
Depreciation of computers	300,000	760,000
Net income		$ 440,000

Through the end of year two no changes in the replacement cost of computer equipment took place. But during year three it became known that the replacement cost of the computer equipment increased to $2 million. When the equipment was purchased three years ago, it was expected to last five years and have no salvage value. The firm had the same expectations at the end of year three.

Required:

1. Prepare a balance sheet at the end of year three and an income statement for year three using the replacement cost model (assume that all assets, liabilities, revenues, and expenses other than the computer equipment and the related depreciation expense do not require any adjustment for replacement costs, and use end-of-year replacement cost in computing depreciation expense for the year).

2. Evaluate the validity of replacement-cost-based current operating income as a measure of disposable wealth (assuming a physical capital maintenance criterion).

14-8. **Effect of Inventory Costing Choices.** The inventory records of Madison Company disclose the following information for 1980:

	Units	Unit Cost
Beginning inventory	60,000	(a) Lifo: $ 5
		(b) Fifo: $10
Purchases:		
First quarter	80,000	$10
Second quarter	70,000	11
Third quarter	90,000	12
Fourth quarter	100,000	13
	340,000	
Ending inventory	70,000	

Required:

1. Calculate 1980 cost of sales and the value of the inventory at December 31, 1980, using (*a*) Lifo and (*b*) Fifo.

2. Assuming that Madison Company uses Lifo to estimate replacement-cost-based cost of sales and Fifo to estimate the replacement cost of the ending inventory, calculate the realized holding gains for 1980 and the unrealized holding gains at December 31, 1979, and December 31, 1980:

    (a) Assuming the firm's conventional accounting values are based upon Lifo

    (b) Assuming the firm's conventional accounting values are based upon Fifo

14-9. Preparing Replacement Cost Income Statement. Desk Lighting Company assembles and distributes a single fluorescent desk lamp model that is popular with department stores and office equipment dealers. The company consistently assembles 3,000 lamps per month from standardized parts. Parts are ordered at the end of each month in amounts equal to the parts used. The supplier is informed of each part used and the quantity required for one lamp, plus the number of lamps for which the company wants parts. The supplier then delivers the right quantity of each type of part, billing the company at a single "per lamp" price for the parts. When an order is received, the stock on hand is rotated so that the older parts are used first.

The company started 19X4 with 6,000 sets of lamp parts, all purchased at $4.00 per lamp set. During the year, 3,000 lamps were assembled and sold each month, and 3,000 part sets were ordered to replace those used. Selling prices and parts costs for the year (by quarter) were as follows:

	Jan.-Mar.	Apr.-June	July-Sept.	Oct.-Dec.
Selling price	$9.00	$9.50	$10.00	$10.50
Parts cost	4.00	4.25	4.75	5.00

The replacement cost of a set of parts as of December 31, 19X4, is $5.20. The company anticipates raising its price to customers to $10.75 as of January 1, 19X5.

In addition to the parts used in the lamps, certain tools and equipment are used in the assembly operation. The tools and equipment currently in use were purchased on January 1, 19X1, for $200,000. They are expected to last five years in all and have a zero net salvage value. During 19X4 the cost of replacing the tools and equipment started at $230,000 and reached $260,000 by year-end. The average of month-end price quotations for the year was $240,000.

During 19X4 rent, wages, and other expenses amounted to $50,000. There was no increase in these expenses during the year, and none is anticipated for the foreseeable future.

Required:

Prepare a replacement-cost-based income statement for the year 19X4 for Desk Lighting Company. Assume (*a*) that the company uses Fifo to calculate its original transaction values for inventory, (*b*) that the parts cost for a quarter is a good estimate of the replacement costs prevailing during the quarter, and (*c*) that depreciation expense on a replacement cost basis is computed using the average 19X4 replacement cost for the tools and equipment.

14-10. Analyzing SEC Replacement Cost Disclosures. The following information was extracted from Dow Chemical Company's 1977 report to the SEC:

U—Estimated Replacement Cost (Unaudited):

The relatively high rates of inflation experienced worldwide in recent years have focused attention on the propriety of using historical cost as the basis for valuation of assets and liabilities and for determination of income from operations. A number of government and independent bodies are considering the need for appropriate alternatives. To date, no single method has earned general acceptance as a satisfactory alternate.

The Securities and Exchange Commission has mandated that beginning in 1976 certain companies must submit, as a part of their annual reports to the Commission, selected items of information stated on the basis of estimated replacement costs. Management's estimates of the replacement cost of the inventories and productive capacity of the Company and its subsidiaries as of December 31, 1976 and 1977, together with estimates of cost of sales and depreciation on the basis of replacement cost for the years then ended, are presented below.

The estimated replacement cost of finished goods and work-in-process inventories was calculated by using the Company's standard costs at December 31 of each year. Standard cost includes labor, materials, depreciation and other overhead, which, except for depreciation, are all stated at then current purchase prices and labor rates. Inventories have not been adjusted for depreciation calculated on the replacement cost basis. Raw materials and supplies are stated at then current cost.

	1976		1977	
	Estimated Replacement Cost	*Comparable Historical Cost*	*Estimated Replacement Cost*	*Comparable Historical Cost*
	(In millions)			
As of December 31:				
Inventories	$1,338	$ 999	$ 1,477	$1,068
Property, plant and equipment	$9,739	$6,479	$11,089	$7,437
Less accumulated depreciation and depletion	4,832	2,925	5,427	3,237
Net property, plant and equipment	$4,907	$3,554	$ 5,662	$4,200
For the year ended December 31:				
Cost of sales excluding depreciation	$3,752	$3,742	$ 4,292	$4,278
Depreciation expense	435	392	492	464
Total cost of sales	$4,187	$4,134	$ 4,784	$4,742
Depreciation (inclusive of amounts allocated to cost of sales)	$ 449	$ 404	$ 508	$ 479

For purposes of calculating the replacement cost of property, plant and equipment, appropriate indexes were applied to the historical cost of the assets, which include fully depreciated assets that are still in use. It is believed that the resulting replacement costs are reasonably representative of changes in construction costs for those assets. It is assumed that the benefits of technological improvements in replacement of productive capacity would be offset by cost of additional support facilities. Estimated replacement costs for the years ended December 31, 1976 and 1977 include oil and gas properties, land and construction in progress at historical costs of $1,434 and $1,636 million and historical accumulated depreciation in the amounts of $67 and $72 million, respectively.

Cost of sales at replacement cost was calculated by applying the last-in, first-out method to all inventories. No attempt has been made to measure reduced operating cost which might occur if manufacturing facilities were replaced.

The provision for depreciation for 1976 and 1977 based on the average replacement cost of productive capacity and accumulated depreciation at the end of each year have been estimated on a straight-line basis, using the same estimates of useful life and salvage value utilized in preparing the historical cost financial statements on the double-declining balance basis.

Replacement costs for companies outside the United States were determined in local currency. All replacement cost amounts related to foreign inventories and productive capacity were translated into U.S. dollars at exchange rates in effect at each year-end. Cost of sales and depreciation expense in foreign currencies were translated at the average rate for each year.

The amounts reported are the result of procedures described and should not be interpreted to indicate that the Company actually has present plans to replace such assets, nor that actual replacement would take place in the manner assumed in developing these estimates. In the normal course of business, the Company will replace its production capacity over an extended period of time. Decisions concerning replacement will be made in the light of economic, regulatory and competitive conditions, as well as other considerations existing on the dates such determinations are made and could differ substantially from the assumptions on which the data included herein are based.

These replacement cost data are predicated upon certain assumptions and subjective judgments. They are not representative of the current value of existing inventory and productive capacity. Rather, they represent management's estimates of the cost that would be incurred at December 31, 1976 and 1977 if such assets were replaced at those dates. Further, it must be recognized that the difference between the replacement cost and the historical cost of inventory and productive capacity does not represent additional book value of the Company. The difference between depreciation based on historical cost and depreciation based on estimated replacement cost, which difference is not deductible in determining income tax expense, is not truly an additional amount of depreciation expense. Also, because of the lack of established criteria and standards for estimating, the replacement cost data presented herein may not be fully comparable with that of other companies.

No attempt has been made to show the effect of price level changes on liabilities or on assets other than inventory and certain properties. Accordingly, it is management's view that the replacement cost data presented herein cannot be used alone to impute the total effect of inflation on reported operating results.

Additionally, the following income statement information (prepared on the basis of the conventional accounting model) has been extracted from Dow's 1977 annual report to shareholders:

	(in millions)
Sales	$6,234.3
Expenses:	
Cost of sales (including depreciation expense of $464.0)	4,742.0
Additional depreciation expense	15.0
Income tax expense	372.6
Other expenses (net of miscellaneous income items)	549.0
	$5,678.6
Net income for 1977	$ 555.7

Required:

1. Calculate the realized holding gains for 1977.
2. Calculate the balance of unrealized holding gains at December 31, 1976, and December 31, 1977.
3. Prepare a replacement-cost-based income statement for 1977 for Dow Chemical Company.

14-11. Analyzing SEC Replacement Cost Disclosures. The following information was extracted from Westinghouse Electric Corporation's 1977 report to the SEC:

> Replacement Cost estimates for inventories, productive capacity, cost of sales and depreciation are presented for the Corporation and its consolidated subsidiaries as of December 31, 1977 and 1976.
>
> Management advises that the replacement cost data presented are not necessarily the current market values of existing inventories and productive capacity or the amount for which they could be sold. Also, the difference between historical and replacement cost does not represent additional book value of the Corporation's common stock.
>
> In the opinion of management, use of replacement cost data to estimate revised net income would be erroneous. Management replaces elements of productive capacity from time to time in the ordinary course of business when sufficient potential cost savings or appropriate competitive conditions exist. The data do not represent the intention of management to replace the productive capacity at one time. Therefore, the replacement cost data may not represent the cost of replacement because of future changes in cost levels and continued advances in technology. The basic data do not reflect the significant operating cost savings which should result from the replacement of existing assets. Finally, the inflationary effects on the Corporation's other assets and liabilities have not been calculated.
>
> Because it was necessary to make subjective judgments and due to differences in the methodology used, the data may not be comparable among companies with which the Corporation competes.

	1977		1976	
	Estimated Replacement Cost	Comparable Historical Cost	Estimated Replacement Cost	Comparable Historical Cost
	(Amounts in Thousands)			
At December 31,				
Inventories	$1,351,000	$ 822,555	$1,242,000	$ 769,557
Productive capacity—gross	4,780,000	2,369,314	4,583,000	2,288,278
Productive capacity—net of depreciation	1,688,000	1,091,704	1,692,000	1,093,669
For the year ended December 31,				
Cost of sales, excluding depreciation	$4,736,000	$4,676,402	$4,355,000	$4,299,587
Depreciation	196,000	134,893	185,000	126,722

Methodology

Replacement cost for inventories, productive capacity, cost of sales and depreciation was estimated on a worldwide basis, and the methods described below were applied for both 1977 and 1976 data. Replacement cost estimates as included herein were not made for amounts permitted to be excluded by the regulations, principally ACEC in 1976 (See Note 9 to the financial statements of the 1977 Annual Report to Stockholders incorporated herein in Exhibit I), and other divestitures. The foreign subsidiaries' inventories and productive capacity were translated to U.S. dollars at current exchange rates, cost of sales at the exchange rates in effect at the time of sale and depreciation at the average exchange rates for the period.

Inventories

The estimated replacement cost of inventories was based primarily on revised standard costs as of year-end. As permitted by regulations the comparable historical amount excludes $92,945,000 and $222,995,000 for 1977 and 1976, respectively.

Cost of Sales

The LIFO method of valuing inventories is used for the majority of operating units and consequently the cost levels cleared to cost of sales approximate replacement cost of sales. For the remaining operating units, historical cost of sales values were adjusted to reflect costs that would have been experienced at the time of sale. As permitted by regulations the comparable historical amount excludes $90,936,000 and $486,599,000 for 1977 and 1976, respectively.

Productive Capacity

The replacement cost of buildings at gross was estimated by applying Department of Commerce construction cost indices, supplemented by recognized indices available for years prior to government-developed indices, to acquisition prices of these assets. Appropriate tests confirmed that these indices as applied reflect changes in construction methods and modern materials. Current years' additions are stated at acquisition prices.

The replacement cost of machinery and equipment at gross was estimated by applying internally developed index numbers to acquisition prices. The index numbers were derived, using generally accepted statistical sampling techniques, from current cost data reflecting technological and environmental factors compared to acquisition prices for randomly selected items to produce equivalent productive capacity. These indices were then applied to homogeneous groupings of machinery and equipment acquisition prices. Current years' additions are stated at acquisition prices.

The comparable historical amount for gross productive capacity excludes $45,993,000 for 1977 and $168,239,000 for 1976 primarily due to divestitures, and $241,226,000 for 1977 and $182,342,000 for 1976 of land and construction in progress which are specifically excludable by the regulations.

The replacement cost of productive capacity net of depreciation results from applying straight-line depreciation on the same service lives as were used in preparing the historical financial statements.

Depreciation

Replacement cost depreciation has been estimated using straight-line depreciation based on the same service lives as were used in preparing the financial statements. No depreciation is included on fully depreciated assets. Average replacement cost of productive capacity at the beginning and end of the year, exclusive of current years' additions, was the basis upon which depreciation expense was computed. Depreciation expense for current years' additions is stated at historical cost. As permitted by regulations the comparable historical amount excludes $3,024,000 and $12,928,000 for 1977 and 1976, respectively.

Additionally, the following information was extracted from Westinghouse's 1977 annual report to shareholders:

Net income before extraordinary loss	$ 271,329,000
Extraordinary loss—1977 uranium contract litigation settlements, net of income taxes of $18,970,000	20,550,000
Net income for 1977	$ 250,779,000

Required:

1. Calculate the realized holding gains for 1977.

2. Calculate the balance of unrealized holding gains at December 31, 1976, and December 31, 1977.

3. Calculate replacement-cost-based current operating income, realized income, and net income for 1977.

Alternative Financial Accounting Models: Current Exit Prices (Market Values)

In Chapter 14 we examine the first of two alternative financial accounting models of the firm that use current exchange prices—the replacement cost model. In this chapter we complete our discussion of current exchange price models with the current exit price, or market-value, model.

From an income determination point of view, an important difference between the market-value model and the conventional accounting model is the point in time at which revenue is to be recognized. Accordingly, we begin with a brief review of the conventional accounting rationale for its realization principle. The limitations inherent in this principle provide a point of reference for subsequent analysis and evaluation of the market-value model.

The Realization Principle Reconsidered

When we first introduced conventional accounting net income as a measure of enterprise performance in Chapter 3, we described it as the difference between recognized revenues and expenses. *Revenue* is the money representation of the recognized accomplishment of the enterprise for an accounting period; *expense* is the money representation of the *related* sacrifice. Because of the desirability of relative objectivity in measuring performance for the benefit of outside investors, conventional accounting is very selective in the way that it recognizes accomplishment. The realization principle generally restricts our measure of the accomplishment of an enterprise to the prices agreed to be paid by customers for the completed products *actually sold* and services *actually performed* during the period. But, of course, the value of those completed products and services *sold* during the current accounting period may be the result of the actual production activity of some past accounting period (or perhaps many past periods). Furthermore, current period production activity may go unrecognized, at least in part, during the current accounting period because the products and services produced will not all be brought to completion and sold until a future accounting period.

This does not necessarily mean that the recognition of efforts and accomplishment is not synchronized. On the contrary, the matching principle requires that insofar as possible the efforts expended (assets expired) in production activity be recognized as expenses in the period in which the total related accomplishment is recognized—usually the period of sale. But because the recognition of accomplishment and effort is postponed until the period of sale, the "performance" embodied in conventional accounting net income may be out of synchronization with the real productive activities that took place during the current period.

Perhaps in the many manufacturing and service operations where there is a relatively short lag from the beginning of production or service to completion and sale, the potential for measured performance to be greatly out of synchronization with the bulk of current productive activity is slight. But in some types of business enterprises where production-to-sales lags are long or sales are infrequent or sporadic due to the nature of the business, conventional accounting revenue based on the realization principle may be a very untimely measure of periodic accomplishment of the enterprise.[1] This point can be illustrated as follows:

Example 15-1

Suppose several friends pooled their cash to form an investment company several years ago. Five individuals each contributed $20,000 for a total of $100,000. The whole amount was immediately invested in common stocks of some large publicly held corporations whose stocks are traded on a major securities exchange. These investments were expected to pay regular dividends and appreciate in value as well.

The common stocks were held for three years and were then sold for $160,000. In the meantime $5,000 in total dividends was received each year, including year three. Furthermore, the prices at which the stocks could have been sold went up to $120,000 by the end of year one and $145,000 by the end of year two. The cash on hand at the end of each year was put into a savings certificate at 6 percent annual interest pending the accumulation of a sufficient amount to purchase another substantial block of common stock. After sale of the initial block of securities and receipt of dividends and interest for year three, $175,000 was reinvested in common stocks at the end of the year. The conventional accounting treatment of these facts appears in Exhibit 15-1.

[1] This deficiency of the conventional accounting model is recognized in the case of long-term construction contracts, where revenue recognition can be accelerated by applying the percentage-of-completion method when certain conditions are satisfied (see Chapter 8). This is but a partial solution to the problem, however, and does not apply to the type of situation described in Example 15-1.

Notice that the original common stock investments continue to be valued at their original transaction cost of $100,000 up to the time of their sale, the point at which a higher value is actually "realized." This conventional accounting treatment of the facts results in the net income figures for the first three years of Investment Company's operations shown in Exhibit 15-2.

Exhibit 15–1

INVESTMENT COMPANY

Financial Position Worksheet—Conventional Accounting Basis
For the First Three Years of Operation

Description	Cash	Stock Investments	Owners' Equity
Original Investment	100,000		100,000
Year 1			
Bought stock	(100,000)	100,000	
Received dividends	5,000		5,000 (R)
Ending (Beginning) Position	5,000	100,000	105,000
Year 2			
Received dividends	5,000		5,000 (R)
Received interest (6% × $5,000)	300		300 (R)
Ending (Beginning) Position	10,300	100,000	110,300
Year 3			
Received dividends	5,000		5,000 (R)
Received interest (6% × $10,300)	618		618 (R)
Sold stock	160,000	(100,000)	60,000 (G)
Bought stock	(175,000)	175,000	
Ending (Beginning) Position	918	175,000	175,918

Exhibit 15–2

INVESTMENT COMPANY

Comparative Statements of Net Income
For the First Three Years of Operations

	Year 1	Year 2	Year 3
Dividend income	$5,000	$5,000	$ 5,000
Interest income		300	618
Gain from sale of stock			60,000
Net income	$5,000	$5,300	$65,618

Although this accounting treatment is a strict application of the realization principle as it is traditionally interpreted, there is something troubling about the pattern of the amounts of net income recognized for the first three years. Using net income as an index of performance implies that the year three performance of the Investment Company was more than ten times "better" than either year one or year two. But the principal difference between year three and years one and two is the single transaction that took place in which the company gave up one asset, common stock, in exchange for another asset, cash. The question is whether the transaction itself was of sufficient economic significance that all the difference between the final selling price and the original transaction cost of the common stock ($60,000) should be assigned as income to the period in which that event took place. A traditional interpretation of the realization principle implies that the answer is yes, since the period of actual sale is the first time period in which the increase in value of the common stock was affirmed in an actual transaction with an independent economic unit (the purchaser). The third year is, furthermore, the first time in which the increase in value was "realized" in the form of a flow of new cash or claim to cash (the selling price).

The Value-Added, or Accretion, Concept of Accomplishment

There is reason to object to the traditional view that a sale transaction is the dominant or "critical" event in determining the period in which the accomplishment embodied in a particular asset is recognized. The purpose of net income as a performance measure is to characterize the results of the productive activity of the enterprise for a period of time. But the productive activity of the enterprise includes all activity within the enterprise that advances or adds to the value of the goods or services that the company produces or holds for sale. To measure actual performance for a period, then, it is necessary to measure the advance toward ultimate sale value of all assets of the enterprise during a period, not just those that were actually brought to completion and sale. This is known as the value-added, or accretion, concept of income.

Typically, the problem in applying the value-added concept of income is to measure objectively the advances in asset values that were created during a period. This is particularly difficult in the case of partially complete manufactured goods, which are sufficiently specialized that they are not very usable or salable in any but final or complete form. It would be a matter of judgment on the part of management as to how much increase in value should be ascribed to such an asset (say, an automobile) at the end of a period in which it was brought from zero to only 50 percent completion. Less difficulty is encountered in applying the value-added concept of income when the principal economic activity of the enterprise is the production of products that are readily salable in all stages of completion, or merely the holding of readily marketable final goods for sale—provided the relevant market values (current exchange exit values) are available.

Market Values and the Value-added Concept. The Investment Company example fits into the latter category. The enterprise's principal activity is the holding of marketable securities not only for regular dividend returns but also on the expectation that they will increase in value. Furthermore, since the common stocks bought and sold by Investment Company are traded on a well-organized securities exchange, their exit values at virtually any time can be determined from the prices at which those stocks are then selling on the exchange. Thus the Investment Company is a good case for illustrating how current market values can be used to implement the value-added concept of income.

Example 15-2

The worksheet in Exhibit 15-3 showing year-by-year recognition of current market values contrasts with the conventional accounting treatment of Investment Company's first three years of operations illustrated earlier (Exhibit 15-1).

Exhibit 15-3

INVESTMENT COMPANY

Financial Position Worksheet—Current Market Value Basis
For the First Three Years of Operations

Description	Cash	Stock Investments	Owners' Equity
Original Investment	100,000		100,000
Year 1			
Bought stock	(100,000)	100,000	
Received dividends	5,000		5,000 (R)
Increase in market value of stock		20,000	20,000 (G)
Ending (Beginning) Position	5,000	120,000	125,000
Year 2			
Received dividends	5,000		5,000 (R)
Received interest (6% × $5,000)	300		300 (R)
Increase in market value of stock		25,000	25,000 (G)
Ending (Beginning) Position	10,300	145,000	155,300
Year 3			
Received dividends	5,000		5,000 (R)
Received interest (6% × $10,300)	618		618 (R)
Increase in market value of stock		15,000	15,000 (G)
Sold stock	160,000	(160,000)	
Bought stock	(175,000)	175,000	
Ending (Beginning) Position	918	175,000	175,918

Unrealized Gains and Losses—Interpretation. The first departure from conventional accounting in Exhibit 15-3 appears at the end of year one when the then-current market values of the common stock are recognized. The line on the worksheet labeled "Increase in market value of stock" shows a $20,000 increase in Stock Investments and a concurrent $20,000 increase in Owners'

Equity, labeled *G* for *gain*. This gain or income is recognized at the end of year one, even though it has *not yet been realized* in the form of cash or claims to cash. The reasoning is as follows:

> The process or activity of holding securities in anticipation of an increase in their value was carried on throughout year one. If the securities had been sold at the end of year one, their sale would have yielded $120,000, or $20,000 in excess of their original transaction costs. Therefore, $20,000 is the increase in value brought about by the first year's holding activity. In the event that the securities had actually been sold at the end of year one, the $20,000 income or gain would have actually been "realized" in the conventional sense. That the enterprise did not actually sell at the $120,000 price should not alter our view of the first year's holding activity. It only indicates that the enterprise expected additional gains from additional years' holding activities.

The same reasoning applies to the recognition of the additional increase in value to $145,000 during year two, a further gain of $25,000. Finally, in year three, before the securities were sold, the additional gain recognized is only $15,000, the excess of the $160,000 then-current market value (selling price) over the end-of-year-two market value of $145,000.

Recognition of Market Values and the Timing of Income. We compare in Exhibit 15-4 the *pattern* of recognized net income that accompanies recognition of the current market value of the securities with the conventional accounting pattern depicted earlier.

Exhibit 15-4

INVESTMENT COMPANY

Comparative Income Statements
For the First Three Years of Operations

	Year 1	Year 2	Year 3	Total
Conventional Accounting				
Dividend income	$ 5,000	$ 5,000	$ 5,000	$15,000
Interest income		300	618	918
Gain from sale of stock			60,000	60,000
Total net income	$ 5,000	$ 5,300	$65,618	$75,918
Current Market Values Recognized				
Securities gains	$20,000	$25,000	$15,000	$60,000
Interest income		300	618	918
Dividend income	5,000	5,000	5,000	15,000
Total net income	$25,000	$30,300	$20,618	$75,918

Period-by-period recognition of the current market value of the securities leads to a more even spread of the total gain from holding the securities over all three years that they were held. But the smoothness or evenness of the pattern is not the important difference. That simply follows our contrived facts which specified that the price of the securities rose in each year of the total holding period. We could have just as readily supposed that after rising to $120,000 by the end of year one, the prices of the securities fell to $90,000 by the end of year two but recovered and rose to $160,000 by the end of year three when they were sold.

The conventional accounting treatment of this alternate set of facts would be identical to the conventional accounting treatment of the original set of facts, since all market prices or price changes would be ignored until the securities were sold at the end of year three. But recognizing current market values of the securities year by year gives quite a different picture.

Exhibit 15-5

INVESTMENT COMPANY

Comparative Income Statements
For the First Three Years of Operations

	Year 1	Year 2	Year 3	Total
Current Market Values Recognized				
Securities gains (losses)	$20,000	($30,000)	$70,000	$60,000
Interest income		300	618	918
Dividend income	5,000	5,000	5,000	15,000
Total net income	$25,000	($24,700)	$75,618	$75,918

The picture in Exhibit 15-5 is very uneven—but so are the facts. That is the important point. The recognition of current market values permits us to recognize changes in value between the point (in time) of entry of resources into the enterprise and the point of their final exit in a sale transaction.

Incidentally, it is important to note one common feature of both conventional accounting and the recognition of current market values. Notice in the comparative statements in Exhibit 15-4 that the total net income for all three years is the same amount, $75,918, for both conventional and market-value accounting. This is no coincidence. The total increase in the value of the enterprise from the investment in the securities is ultimately governed by the difference between the price paid originally to acquire the securities and the price finally received from the sale (plus dividends received). But the recognition of current market values of the securities in the periods between purchase and sale assigns portions of that total to accounting periods between the point of purchase and the point of sale. Conventional accounting recognizes the total change between the actual entry and exit prices of the securities in the period of sale.

Market Values of Assets Not Held for Eventual Sale

Our use of the Investment Company example above made it easier to develop a strong case for market-value accounting. However, we should recognize that such a simple example leaves untouched some important issues in applying market-value accounting. In particular, the example purposely omitted consideration of the valuation and related income effects of assets held for use in a business (as opposed to assets like marketable securities held for sale) and of the problems of matching efforts and accomplishments in measuring performance. The application of exit prices to assets held for use in production raises a problem. Here, rather than using depreciation based on (1) original transaction cost, or (2) price-level-adjusted cost, or (3) replacement cost as a measure of services consumed, the change in the market value of assets used in production is the measure of sacrifice (expense) for a period. Because enterprises generally do not engage in regularly trading the kinds of assets they use in production, they typically must buy such assets at higher (retail) prices than the prices (wholesale) at which they can sell the same assets. Hence there is usually a significant drop immediately after acquisition in the value of such assets. If the acquisition of a productive asset involves a large expenditure, as is often the case when a firm acquires plant and equipment, this dual-market phenomenon may in fact produce a distortion in the measure of performance for the first period of use. For this reason (as well as some others), current market exit prices are frequently not advocated for use by firms with large investments in productive plant and equipment (assets not held for sale).

A Format for Reporting Market-Value-Based Operating Income

Even though market-value accounting relies on a valuation base different from that of conventional accounting (and replacement cost accounting), the attempt to match efforts and accomplishments in measuring performance is still relevant. This is based on the assumption that investors interested in the long-run cash-generating ability of the enterprise are interested not just in the final operating income figure but also in the significant positive and negative components that make it up. However, since we wish to recognize increases in values of assets as income in the period in which they take place rather than the period in which revenue is realized, the conventional income statement format must be modified. An alternative format is suggested in Exhibit 15-6.

Exhibit 15-6

MARKET-VALUE-BASED INCOME STATEMENT FORMAT

Net increase (or decrease) in market values of assets held or produced for sale
Plus other income:
  Dividends
  Interest
  Increases in market values of assets held for use in the business
Less expenses:
  Wages and salaries
  Selling and administrative expense
  Interest
  Decreases in market values of assets held for use in the business
  Other expense
Operating income

Notice that the format recognizes that the primary positive component of income, in the long-run sense, is the increase in the value of assets that the enterprise buys and holds (or produces) for sale to customers. Although in any given period the enterprise may experience income from other sources, in the long run its "stock-in-trade" will presumably be the most important source of cash flows. Thus the format begins with the increase (or decrease) in value of "stock-in-trade" assets (rather than revenue) and then continues with much the same organization as a conventional income statement.

The only other exception is the treatment accorded assets held *for use in the business* rather than for sale. Besides the conceptual problem (noted in the preceding section) with the often dramatic decline in value when such assets are placed in use, they present another problem in reporting income. Although they are held for consumption in operating the business, in some periods their market values may increase (appreciate) rather than decrease (depreciate). When the values of such assets increase, they contribute to the income of the period, though they are not primary sources of income. When the values decrease (as would be expected in the long run for all such assets other than land), the decreases are expenses. The format recognizes these possibilities with a heading for possible increases in the values of such assets under "other income" and one for decreases under "expenses."

Example 15-3

Wilderness Tents, Inc., is a retail tent store. It buys a single tent model made to its specifications for $250 each and sells all it can handle (about 1,000 per year) at $500 each. Its status and operations for a recent year, 19X3, are shown in the worksheet in Exhibit 15-7. The income statement in Exhibit 15-8 is prepared from the information in the worksheet according to the format shown in Exhibit 15-6.

Exhibit 15-7

WILDERNESS TENTS, INC.

Financial Position Worksheet—Current Market Value Basis
For the Year 19X3

Description	Cash	Tents	Equipment	Buildings	Land	Owners' Equity
Beginning Position	5,000	15,000	16,000	24,000	20,000	80,000
Purchased tents	(250,000)	250,000				
Increase in market value of tents		250,000				250,000 (G)
Tent sales	475,000	(475,000)				
Wages and salaries	(100,000)					(100,000) (E)
Other expenses	(50,000)					(50,000) (E)
Decrease in market value of equipment and buildings			(4,000)	(6,000)		(10,000) (E)
Increase in market value of land					5,000	5,000 (G)
Ending Position	80,000	40,000	12,000	18,000	25,000	175,000

Exhibit 15-8

WILDERNESS TENTS, INC.

Market-Value-Based Income Statement
For 19X3

Increase in value of tents held for sale		$250,000
Plus increase in value of land		5,000
		$255,000
Less expenses:		
Wages and salaries	$100,000	
Decrease in market value of buildings	6,000	
Decrease in market value of equipment	4,000	
Other expenses	50,000	160,000
Net operating income		$ 95,000

Recognition of Market Values and Measurement of Disposable Wealth

As in the case of recognition of current replacement cost, recognition of exit prices results in a concept of disposable wealth that contrasts period by period with disposable wealth measured under conventional accounting. Under conventional accounting, periodic net income is the difference between ending owners' equity (net assets), adjusted for additional investments or withdrawals, and beginning owners' equity (net assets). Thus net income is equal to the advance in recognized net assets of the enterprise over the unexpired original transaction costs (original money invested) of assets as of the beginning of the period. Disposing of assets equal to conventional accounting net income therefore sets the enterprise back to a position of having recognized net assets equal in amount to the unexpired original cost of assets as of the beginning of the period.

When assets are valued at their current selling prices, on the other hand, something different happens. Of course, net income still equals the difference between beginning and ending owners' equity for the period (adjusted appropriately for additional investments or withdrawals). But with the individual assets valued at their beginning and end-of-period market values, *owners' equity has a different interpretation* than under conventional accounting. Essentially, it is the amount of cash that can be realized by the enterprise or its owners as of a given point in time through immediate disposal of its net assets. Thus, beginning owners' equity is the amount of cash proceeds from the sale of net assets that the owners could have enjoyed at the beginning of the period, and ending owners' equity represents the amount of cash value that could be realized at the end of the period. The difference between the two figures is therefore the amount of cash (or other assets) that can be distributed to owners without setting the enterprise back below the beginning-of-year cash value of its net assets.

It is important to note, however, that in order for the above interpretation of market-value-based owners' equity to be completely valid, the enterprise's liabilities must be valued not at their original transaction values, but at the amount that would be accepted in full payment as of the given balance sheet date. Only if the liabilities are so valued will the excess of (1) the sum of the asset values over (2) the sum of the liability values actually represent the net proceeds from disposal of the enterprise's assets and discharge of its liabilities.

It is also noteworthy that in market-value-based disposable wealth measurement we are again concerned (as we were in conventional accounting) with a purely money-oriented (financial capital) concept of enterprise wealth. That is, the criterion level of wealth is the beginning cash equivalent (upon sale) of the enterprise's net assets.

One significant implication of this money-wealth orientation is that if the enterprise consistently distributes assets to owners equal to market-value-based net income in every period from the inception of the business, the enterprise will retain net assets equal to the original money capital contributed by the owners—the same result as obtained under conventional accounting (though at any point in time, the net asset composition would differ between the two models).

Another significant implication of the money-wealth orientation of market-value accounting is that in times of generally changing prices, general price-level adjustments are as applicable to market-value accounting measures as they are to conventional accounting. (Recall from our Chapter 13 discussion that general price-level adjustments do not change the values used to represent the enterprise and its activities but are simply a means of expressing those values in the purchasing power units in existence at year-end.) As in conventional accounting, when market-value accounting is adjusted for changes in the general price level, a difference (net monetary gain or loss) emerges between (adjusted) market-value net income and net operating income.

Example 15-4

> Refer back to the case of the Investment Company whose activities for its first three years of operations are depicted according to market-value accounting in Exhibit 15-3. Suppose that during years one and two no change in the general level of prices took place, but during year three the price level rose uniformly from 100 to 110. Suppose further that the interest and dividends were received throughout the year and that the transactions in common stock took place at year-end. Exhibit 15-9 shows the general price-level-adjusted, market-value-based income calculations for year three.

The procedures used to make the price-level adjustments in Exhibit 15-9 are similar in principle to those discussed in Chapter 13, but a few unique properties of the market-value-based financial statements are worth noting. First, the statement of financial position is always measured in end-of-period dollars, since all assets and liabilities are valued at their end-of-period exit prices. Therefore no adjustment is required for ending owners' equity, and beginning owners' equity is restated without having to examine the valuation bases of individual assets and liabilities. Second, the income statement contains a component for changes in the value of assets and liabilities—in this case, increase in value of securities held. This component is the net result of subtracting the beginning value of the asset (or liability) from the ending value of the asset (or liability). Each of these two values must be individually adjusted in order to recognize applicable general price-level changes. The end-of-year

Exhibit 15-9

INVESTMENT COMPANY

General Price-Level-Adjusted Income Calculations
Year Three

Net Income:
Ending owners' equity from Exhibit 15-3 (all elements of ending financial position are already stated in end-of-year dollars) $175,918
Beginning owners' equity from Exhibit 15-3 adjusted for price-level change $155,300 × $\frac{110}{100}$ 170,830
Price-level-adjusted, market-value-based net income .... $ 5,088

Operating Income:
Increase in value of securities held:
  End-of-year value $160,000
  Less adjusted beginning-of-year value
    $145,000 × $\frac{110}{100}$ .... 159,500 $ 500
Dividends and interest $5,618 × $\frac{110}{105}$ 5,886
Price-level-adjusted, market-value-based operating income ...... $ 6,386

Monetary Loss from Holding Cash:	Actual		Adjusted
Beginning balance	$ 10,300 × $\frac{110}{100}$		$ 11,330
Dividends and interest	5,618 × $\frac{110}{105}$		5,886
Sale of stock	160,000 × $\frac{110}{110}$		160,000
Purchase of stock	(175,000) × $\frac{110}{110}$		(175,000)
Ending balance	$918		$ 2,216
			918
Monetary loss			$ 1,298

Reconcilement:
Price-level-adjusted operating income .... $ 6,386
Less monetary loss 1,298
Price-level-adjusted net income .... $ 5,088

value of the securities in the example is $160,000, and since this is measured in end-of-period dollars, it is not further adjusted. The beginning-of-year value of the securities is $145,000, measured in beginning-of-year dollars, and it is restated to $159,500 end-of-year dollars. *The difference of $500 is the general price-level-adjusted increase in value, measured in end-of-period dollars.* Finally, notice that the monetary loss is calculated in this example in the same way that it would be calculated under the price-level-adjusted conventional accounting model because the only monetary asset (cash) is valued the same under both the conventional accounting model and the market-value model. Should a different value be assigned to a monetary asset or liability under the market-value model, as might be the case for some receivables and payables, different amounts of monetary gain or loss would result. But whichever model is used, the algebraic sum of price-level-adjusted operating income and the monetary gain or loss always equals the price-level-adjusted net income figure.

The Relevance of Market-Value-Based Net Assets

We began our examination of the market-value model by contrasting the properties of the income measures produced by this model with those of the conventional accounting model. Another important aspect of the market-value model is the special decision relevance in certain circumstances of market-value-based net assets. Three special classes of usage are important.

Measure of Market Value of Firm. Overall a firm may be worth more or less than the sum of the market values of its individual (recognized) assets and liabilities. Nonetheless this sum can be a useful piece of information in estimating the total value of the firm as a whole. Circumstances in which market-value-based measures of net assets could be particularly useful might include negotiations for the purchase (sale) of a small firm whose ownership shares are not traded actively in an organized market, or establishment of the value of an ownership interest in a closely held family business for federal and state estate tax purposes. In the case of mutual funds, or open-end investment trusts, the market value of net assets assumes a special importance—it is the sole basis for the determination of buy or sell prices for ownership interests. Therefore, daily measures of the current exit value of the fund's net assets must be calculated. Illustrative financial statements for one such firm—Massachusetts Investors Trust—are shown in Exhibit 15-10. The single most important asset item—investments—in the statement of financial position is further elaborated in a supplementary schedule, in which (for each individual investment) the number of shares, the cost, and the market value are disclosed. Notice also in the statement of operations that the change in the value of the investments is divided into realized and unrealized components, where the test of realization is sale of the investment. Thus, in the year of sale, the entire difference between the selling price and the original cost is recognized as a *realized* gain or loss. Any *unrealized* gain or loss recognized in prior years is (implicitly) deducted therefrom by including the change in the unrealized market values of investments during the year as a second element of "change in value."

Measure of Viability of Firm. One question that the present owners and the management of any firm should ask themselves from time to time is whether the firm should stay in business. Resolution of this question essentially boils down to a simple comparison of two values: (1) the present value of future cash flows from operation of the business, and (2) the current market value of the firm's net assets. If the present value of future cash flows is larger, the firm is more valuable as a going concern (i.e., a generator of cash flows through production of products and services). However, if the current market value of the firm's net assets is the larger of the two values, the best course of action is

Exhibit 15-10

MASSACHUSETTS INVESTORS TRUST

Statement of Assets and Liabilities
December 31, 1977

ASSETS

Investments, at value (average cost, $980,355,082)	$1,164,640,341
Cash	411,887
Receivable for investments sold	4,253,318
Receivable for shares sold	172,904
Dividends and interest receivable	3,300,346
Total assets	$1,172,778,796

LIABILITIES

Capital gain distribution ($0.155 a share) on shares requesting payment in cash, payable February 3, 1978	$7,122,794	
Payable for investments purchased	1,134,268	
Payable for shares reacquired	1,985,394	
Accrued expenses	147,979	
Total liabilities		10,390,435
Net assets for 123,258,702 shares of beneficial interest outstanding (including 1,250,990 shares to be issued on February 3, 1978 in payment of capital gain distribution)		$1,162,388,361
Net asset value and redemption price per share ($1,162,388,361 ÷ 123,258,702 shares of beneficial interest outstanding)		$ 9.43
Computation of offering price: Offering price per share (100/92.75 of $9.43)		$10.17

On sales of $10,000 or more, the offering price is reduced.

to liquidate the firm and invest the cash proceeds in the owners' best available investment opportunity.

Measure of Ability to Satisfy Creditors. Although credit is extended primarily on the basis of a firm's or an individual's prospective earning power, creditors are also interested in the amount that could be realized from the sale of all or a portion of the borrower's assets should the need for this action arise. Therefore financial statements indicating the exit values of a borrower's assets are often an important information source in the credit decision, particularly in the case of individuals. In recognition of this fact, the American Institute of Certified Public Accountants issued in 1968 an audit guide entitled "Audits of Personal Financial Statements." This guide recommends the presentation of financial information on both a cost and an exit value basis. Illustrative financial statements included in this guide are presented in Exhibit 15-11.

Several aspects of the recommended statements are worth noting. First, the recommended format involves presentation of both the cost and the exit values (estimated value basis) for the assets and liabilities in adjacent columns. In this way, the amount of "unrealized appreciation" incorporated into the market-value statements is highlighted for each individual asset and liability. Second,

Exhibit 15-10 (cont.)

Statement of Operations
For the Year Ended December 31, 1977

Investment Income:		
Income—		
Dividends		$ 55,716,944
Interest		3,448,335
Total income		$ 59,165,279
Expenses (representing 9.7% of gross income)—		
Investment advisory fee	$ 4,314,369	
Compensation of Trustees not affiliated with the investment adviser	39,091	
Transfer and dividend disbursing agent fees	744,626	
Custodian fee	75,155	
Printing and postage	374,331	
Legal and auditing services	51,515	
Miscellaneous	154,171	
Total expenses		5,753,258
Net investment income		$ 53,412,021
Realized and Unrealized Gain (Loss) on Investments:		
Realized gain from investment transactions (average cost basis)—		
Proceeds from sales	$273,004,535	
Cost of investments sold	255,575,402	
Net realized gain		$ 17,429,133
Unrealized appreciation of investments—		
Beginning of year	$415,597,842	
End of year	184,285,259	
Decrease in unrealized appreciation		(231,312,583)
Net realized and unrealized gain (loss) on investments		$(213,883,450)

the basis for the estimate of current market value for each asset is described in the notes to the financial statements so that the user can evaluate the reasonableness of the estimate. Third, individuals often possess certain interests that may with the passage of time become valuable assets, but which do not at the financial statement date meet the tests for recognition of an asset. These interests, labeled contingent assets, are enumerated on the face of the statement of assets and liabilities without any values and are described in more detail in the notes to the statements (see, for example, note 9). Finally, recognition of the exit values of assets is based upon the assumption that the assets will be sold, and such action often generates a tax liability under current U.S. income tax law. Therefore, in order to reflect the "net" effect of the hypothetical sale transaction, it is necessary to recognize a liability for the "accrued income taxes on unrealized asset appreciation." This estimated liability is generally calculated by multiplying the "unrealized appreciation"—i.e., the difference between the estimated exit value and the cost (or other tax basis)—by the appropriate tax rate (ordinary income or capital gains rate).

In addition to the use of market values in statements prepared as a basis for obtaining credit, we should also note that this valuation basis is common for financial statements prepared for firms that are under the jurisdiction of creditor committees or bankruptcy courts.

Exhibit 15-11

MR. AND MRS. INDIVIDUAL

Statement of Assets and Liabilities
December 31, 1980

	Column A Cost Basis	Column B Estimated Value Basis
ASSETS		
Cash	$ 11,079	$ 11,079
Marketable securities (Note 2)	29,578	42,227
Cash value of life insurance	4,647	4,647
Net assets of ABC Proprietorship (Notes 1 and 3)	47,970	65,280
Interest in net assets of XYZ Corp. (Note 4)	3,000	4,730
Residence, pledged on mortgage note (Note 6)	42,000	67,000
Automobiles	3,000	3,000
Jewelry (Note 6)	6,300	8,400
Paintings (Note 5)	10,000	20,000
Household furnishings	2,000	2,000
Vested interest in QM Corp. Pension Trust	—	17,810
Investment in real estate (Note 6)	30,678	41,000
Contingent asset (Notes 8 and 9)	—	—
Total Assets	190,252	287,173
LIABILITIES		
Accounts payable and accrued expenses	3,290	3,290
6% note payable, unsecured, due January 15, 1982	15,000	15,000
5½% mortgage, maturing in 1987, secured by residence (Annual amortization and interest payments amount to $2,680)	19,790	19,790
Accrued income taxes payable, net of prepayments	2,400	2,400
Accrued income taxes on unrealized asset appreciation (Note 7)	—	24,230
Total Liabilities	40,480	64,710
EXCESS OF ASSETS OVER LIABILITIES	$149,772	$222,463

The Notes to the Financial Statements are an integral part of this statement.

MR. AND MRS. INDIVIDUAL

Statement of Changes in Net Assets
Year Ended December 31, 1980

	Column A Cost Basis	Column B Estimated Value Basis
NET ASSETS		
January 1, 1980	$146,046	$215,998
Add—Income and Other Increases in Net Assets		
Dividends on stock	1,565	1,565
Interest income	845	845
Salaries and bonuses XYZ Corp.	4,040	4,040
Drawings from ABC Proprietorship	16,000	16,000
Gain on the sale of securities	3,989	1,743
Increase in value since January 1, 1980:		
Marketable securities	—	2,936
Net assets of ABC Proprietorship (net of drawings)	3,618	4,300
Interest in net assets of XYZ Corp.	—	613
Vested Interest in QM Corp. Pension Trust	—	547
Residence	—	1,120
Total	30,057	33,709
Deduct—Expenses and Other Decreases in Net Assets		
Interest expense	1,870	1,870
Decrease in value of automobiles	1,125	1,125
Income taxes	4,000	4,000
Real estate taxes	1,873	1,873
Personal expenditures	17,463	17,463
Provision for income taxes on unrealized asset appreciation	—	913
Total	26,331	27,244
NET ASSETS, December 31, 1980	$149,772	$222,463

The Notes to the Financial Statements are an integral part of this statement.

Notes to the Financial Statements
December 31, 1980

COST BASIS COLUMN

Note 1—Net Assets of ABC Proprietorship

A summary statement of the net assets of the proprietorship as of December 31, 1980, follows:

Current Assets	$37,694
Land, Building and Equipment, net	25,570
Other Assets	2,110
Total	65,374
Current Liabilities	5,790
Deferred Items	3,094
Long-Term Debt	8,520
Total	17,404
NET ASSETS	$47,970

Income before provision for income taxes for the year ended December 31, 1980 amounted to $19,618. Drawings by Mr. Individual during the year were $16,000.

A certified public accounting firm has examined the financial statements of the proprietorship as of December 31, 1980 and expressed an unqualified opinion on them.

Exhibit 15-11 (cont.)

ESTIMATED VALUE COLUMN

Note 2—Marketable Securities
  The amounts shown as market value at December 31, 1980, were arrived at as follows:

  Stocks—Quoted closing or latest bid prices
  Bonds, U.S.—Quoted latest bid prices
  Bonds, Other—Quoted latest bid prices

  Marketable securities consist of the following:

STOCK:	Shares	Cost	Market Value
American Industries, Inc.	100	$ 1,647	$ 4,003
Colleen Fabrics Corp.	1000	9,696	15,322
Do-All Manufacturing, Ltd.	50	913	401
Thomas Lighting Company	75	1,097	4,243
Maureen Fashions, Inc.	225	7,674	8,949
United Products	500	2,312	1,676
U.S. Equipment Rentals	100	239	920
		23,578	35,514
BONDS:			
United Products 6¼% due 7-1-97		2,000	2,713
U.S. Government 5½% due 11-15-89		4,000	4,000
		6,000	6,713
		$29,578	$42,227

Note 3—ABC Proprietorship
  Estimated value is based on an offer to purchase the net assets of the business, dated September 17, 1980. Mr. Individual has refused the offer.

Note 4—Interest in Net Assets of XYZ Corp.
  Estimated value of the 25% interest in the net assets of the corporation is based on unaudited financial statements as of September 30, 1980. Management of XYZ Corp. has reported that no material financial changes have occurred since that date.

Note 5—Paintings
  Estimated value is based upon a bona fide offer to purchase the paintings by Modern Galleries, Inc. on December 16, 1980.

Note 6—Appraisals
  Estimated value is based upon independent appraisals obtained from individuals and/or firms (could be named) for the following assets:

Residence	$67,000 (1)
Jewelry	8,400 (2)
Real Estate	41,000 (3)

  (1) Recent purchases of homes within the same general area approximate the appraised valuation. The assessed real estate value (100% valuation) was determined in 1979 to be $61,000.

  (2) Mrs. Individual's jewelry has been insured in the amount of $8,400.

  (3) The assessed real estate value (100% valuation) was determined in 1978 to be $38,000.

Exhibit 15-11 (cont.)

Note 7—Accrued Income Taxes on Unrealized Appreciation
Unrealized appreciation in value of assets would, if realized, require payment of taxes at capital gains rates. Therefore, the accrual has been made on that basis.

CONTINGENT ASSETS

Note 8—Stock Option
Mr. Individual has been granted an option to purchase 300 shares, or any part thereof, of QM Corp. common stock at a price of $9 per share. The option expires on August 31, 1983. The market value of QM Corp. common stock is approximately $10 per share.

Note 9—Interest in Property Subject to Life Estate
Mrs. Individual is the beneficiary of the estate of John Smith, her father, remaining at the time of the death of her mother. Contingencies within the bequest preclude the actuarial determination of a present value.

Source: Adapted from AICPA *Audits of Personal Financial Statements* (1968).

Measurement of Current Exit Values

In Chapter 14 we defined the current exit price, or market value, of a resource as the amount that would be received in exchange for the resource. Throughout this chapter we have continued to rely on the same notion. But we should observe now that determination of the price that would be received upon the sale of a resource involves a judgment regarding the *timing* of the sale—all within the context of some type of reasonably "current" price. If we adhere strictly to the notion of "current price," *immediate sale or liquidation* of the resources of the firm is implied. The amount realized in a "forced liquidation" situation is often drastically less than a rational person would accept for his resources even under extreme conditions. For this reason, most advocates of the current market-value model reject the establishment of values on the basis of immediate liquidation. Rather, the normal assumption made in determining exit values is that the firm will sell or dispose of its resources in an *orderly liquidation*. The values estimated under this type of situation are usually less than might be realized if the firm could dispose of the resources under normal business conditions. But orderly liquidation values are judged the best estimate of the concept of value inherent in the market-value model. Thus the estimated exit values under a circumstance of orderly liquidation are referred to in the current accounting literature as *current exit values*. The expected exit values in the normal course of business, less any additional costs of completion and disposal, are referred to as *net realizable values*. Net realizable values currently play a minor role in accounting under the conventional accounting model, as they establish a floor (or lowest possible value) for the value to be assigned to inventories under the "lower of cost or market" rule (see Chapter 10 for a discussion of this valuation method). Note also that for some types of assets held for sale—e.g., marketable securities—there may be no difference between the current exit value and the net realizable value.

Some Limitations Associated with Recognizing Market Values

As was true of recognition of replacement costs, recognition of market output values is subject to some significant limitations. Whereas our primary example, Investment Company, dealt with readily marketable securities for which "realizable" current prices existed, many firms' assets may not have well-established and accessible markets. It may not be clear at all that a particular enterprise can actually realize the current prices if it decides to enter the market and sell. If the firm produces a unique or "differentiated" product, it may be difficult to estimate accurately what price a particular quantity or supply of that product will bring without actually selling it. Furthermore, it may take considerable time before it can be sold, or there may be additional operations required before the product is in condition for sale. In the former case it may be necessary to arrive at a present value of the more distant future proceeds of sale as a means of recognizing the current value of assets of the enterprise. In the latter case it is necessary to estimate the costs of completion and sale of the asset and deduct that amount from what it would currently sell for if complete and ready for sale, that is, the net realizable value of the asset.

What all these reservations mean is that the decision relevance that can be achieved potentially by recognition of current market values is accompanied by a whole range of problems that have something in common. There is an element of subjective judgment required that is not present in the same form in conventional accounting (though we recognize that there are areas of judgment in conventional accounting). And since subjective judgments are less susceptible to verification by outside independent parties, they open up opportunities for personal bias or manipulation that might not be present otherwise.

Present Status of Market-Value Accounting

At the present time, primary applications of market-value accounting are limited to mutual funds, personal financial statements, and some of the special applications discussed above for small, closely held companies. In addition, firms that hold marketable securities apply a modified form of market-value accounting to these particular assets.[2] But for the bulk of the companies in the United States, there is little if any use of current exit values in present financial statements. Perhaps this is a reflection that such information (1) is not now required by accounting policy, (2) is costly to prepare, and (3) is subject to the limitations noted above.

Questions for Review and Discussion

15-1. Recognition of current market values is a means of avoiding a limitation on the income measure produced by a strict application of the realization principle. Describe the limitation and explain how recognition of market values may overcome it.

[2] See FASB Standard No. 12.

15-2. Explain the value-added, or accretion, concept of accomplishment.

15-3. Discuss briefly the general problem that is encountered in applying the value-added concept of income.

15-4. Provide an interpretation of unrealized gains and losses in the income statement on assets held for the entire period.

15-5. In applying the market-value model, assets held for use in the business present some conceptual difficulties. Describe the difficulties.

15-6. The market-value model, like the conventional accounting model, is oriented toward a money, or financial, capital concept. True or false? Defend your position.

15-7. In applying general price-level adjustments to a market-value-based statement of financial position, which assets on hand or liabilities owed at the end of the period are adjusted?

15-8. In applying general price-level adjustments to a market-value-based income statement, how is the component "changes in value of assets" adjusted?

15-9. Contrast the measure of the monetary gain or loss produced under the general price-level-adjusted conventional accounting model and the general price-level-adjusted market-value-model.

15-10. Describe three general types of decision situations in which market-value-based net assets may have a special decision relevance.

15-11. Explain the reason for including a liability for "accrued income taxes on unrealized asset appreciation" in personal financial statements prepared using market values.

15-12. What timing and type of sale situation is assumed in estimating the current market value of an asset?

15-13. Distinguish between the current exit value and the net realizable value of an asset.

15-14. In this and the preceding chapter, alternative valuation bases (current exchange values) have been introduced to illustrate financial accounting models of the enterprise that are potentially more decision relevant than the conventional accounting model. Does this mean that the replacement cost model and market-value model are clearly superior to the conventional accounting model? Support your answer.

15-15. Teachers Pension Fund is an independent investment company owned by teachers all across the country. It is designed so that the teachers and their employers can make contributions to one ongoing retirement plan, regardless of where or for what school the teacher works. When contributions are made, they are used to purchase shares in the company in the name of the teacher on whose behalf they are made. The company invests contributed funds in securities of various kinds. When a teacher retires, the company buys an annuity policy (a set of monthly payments) with an insurance company for an amount equal to the teacher's share in the net assets of the company at the time of retirement. What accounting valuation basis should be used for measuring the net assets of the company—original transaction values, replacement cost, or market value? Defend your choice.

15-16. Discussion in this chapter noted that recognition of market values of assets is one means of implementing the value-added concept of income. However, recognizing market values will approximate the value-added concept *more or less* depending on the circumstances faced by the individual enterprise. What circumstances are particularly important in this respect?

Exercises

15-1. Market-Value Net Income and General Price-Level Changes. The Low-Turnover Investment Company was formed at the beginning of 1978 with $20,000 cash contributed by the partners. Immediately thereafter, the company purchased 5,000 shares of Eastern Central Railroad for $8,000, and 100 shares of Western Satellite Corporation for $12,000. The partners believed this constituted a balanced portfolio and decided to ignore the day-by-day fluctuations in market prices and hold on to the stock for long-term growth. On December 31, 1980, the stock was sold: Eastern Central for $10,000, and Western Satellite for $15,000.

The market value of the stock at the end of each of the previous two years follows:

	December 31, 1978	*December 31, 1979*
Eastern Central Railroad	$ 6,000	$ 9,000
Western Satellite Corporation	10,000	25,000

Required:

1. What will be the net income for each of the three years and in total under (*a*) conventional accounting and (*b*) market-value-based accounting?

2. The partners took issue with the income measures you came up with under the market-value-based model. They argued that the numbers were "merely paper profits or losses," and for that reason they intended to ignore the numbers in a retrospective assessment of their performance as investment fund managers. Assuming that you were one of the advocates for market-value-based accounting, indicate *briefly* how you would reply to this argument.

3. If the general price level was at 100 on January 1, 1978, but had reached 120 by December 31, 1980, what would *total* price-level-adjusted net income be for the three-year period?

15-2. Market Value Net Income and General Price-Level Changes. The Long Horizon Investment Company was formed on January 1, 1980, with a cash investment by owners of $1 million. On January 2, 1980, a portfolio of securities was acquired at a cost of $980,000. During 1980 the firm received cash dividends of $50,000 uniformly over the year. The firm's cash was maintained in a non-interest-bearing checking account. On July 1, 1980, additional securities were acquired at a cost of $45,000. No securities were sold during 1980. On December 31, 1980, the portfolio of securities held by the company at that time had a market value of $900,000.

Required:

1. Using the market-value model, prepare a financial position worksheet to reflect the firm's transactions for 1980.

2. Using the market-value model, calculate net income for 1980.

3. Using the general price-level-adjusted market-value model, calculate net operating income, net income, and the monetary gain or loss for 1980. The applicable price-level indexes are as follows:

January 1, 1980	200
July 1, 1980 (average for year)	210
December 31, 1980	220

15-3. Personal Financial Statements. John Marian has decided to start a construction business and wishes to establish a line of credit at the First National Bank for future construction loans. The bank asks for a financial statement from John and his wife, Jill, enumerating all of their assets and liabilities as of September 1, 1980. John asks you to prepare the statement for him and provides the following information concerning the Marians' resources and obligations on September 1, 1980:

a. The Marians have $1,800 in their checking account, and Jill has a regular savings account with a balance of $8,000.

b. John owns a two-year-old truck that cost $7,000 and has an estimated sales value of $4,500. Jill recently purchased a new car that cost $5,800 and has an estimated sales value of $5,200.

c. The Marians' home was purchased five years ago at a cost of $64,000. Recent sales of houses within the general area of the Marians' home have been for prices approximately 150 percent of the appraisals for local tax purposes. The 1980 tax appraisal on the Marians' home is $70,000. The balance of the mortgage note on the home as of September 1, 1980, is $48,000.

d. Jill owns the following securities, all of which are listed on a national stock exchange:

	Shares	Cost	Market Value, September 1, 1980
Dane County Steel	100	$1,800	$2,600
Meyer Industries	50	3,000	4,400
Northern Mines, Inc.	200	2,200	1,400
		$7,000	$8,400

    e. The Marians' household furnishings cost $5,000 and have an estimated sales value of $2,000.
    f. John owns five lots in a new subdivision that cost $75,000 and have a current market value of $100,000. John currently owes Mutual Savings & Loan $50,000 on a note he signed when he purchased the lots.
    g. The current balance (as of September 1) on the Marians' Quick Charge credit card is $1,500.
    h. After consultation with his tax accountant, John learned that the Marians would have a tax liability of approximately $17,000 if they sold all their assets.
    i. John and Jill have both given up their jobs to devote full time to the new business.

Required:

Prepare a statement of assets and liabilities for John and Jill Marian as of September 1, 1980, with columns for "Cost Basis" and "Estimated Value Basis."

15-4. Market Value and General Price-Level Changes. New Deal Leases is in the business of buying, selling, and leasing land. Its financial position on January 1, 1980, was as follows:

Cash	Accounts Receivable	Land	Owners' Equity
5,000	2,000	35,000	42,000

During the first six months of 1980 the following events occurred:

    a. The amount due from customers at the beginning of the period was received.
    b. Lease rentals earned throughout the period (all of which have been collected) amounted to $3,000.
    c. Wages incurred and paid throughout the period, $1,800.
    d. Advertising expense (paid on January 2, 1980), $400.
    e. On June 30 a number of buyers made firm offers to buy the land for a price of $38,000. The land was not sold, however.

Required:

1. Prepare income statements for the period ended June 30, 1980, according to (*a*) the conventional accounting model and (*b*) the market-value model.

2. In your judgment, which income figure better represents the company's performance? Explain.

3. Repeat number 1, assuming that the price level went up by 8 percent for the whole six-month period, but the ending price level was up only 5 percent over the average for the six-month period. Assume further that no changes in prices have taken place in prior years.

15-5. Market Value and Conventional Accounting Contrasted. On December 15, 1978, you donated a valuable painting to a charitable institution, and with the large tax saving you realized, you invested in marketable securities on December 31, 1978. The investment portfolio that you formed consisted of a municipal bond, stock in an oil exploration company, and stock in a large durables manufacturing company. At December 31, 1980, you still held all of the securities. The following charts that you have maintained on your investments (data as of end of the year) reflect their price and dividend (or interest) behavior during the two-year period:

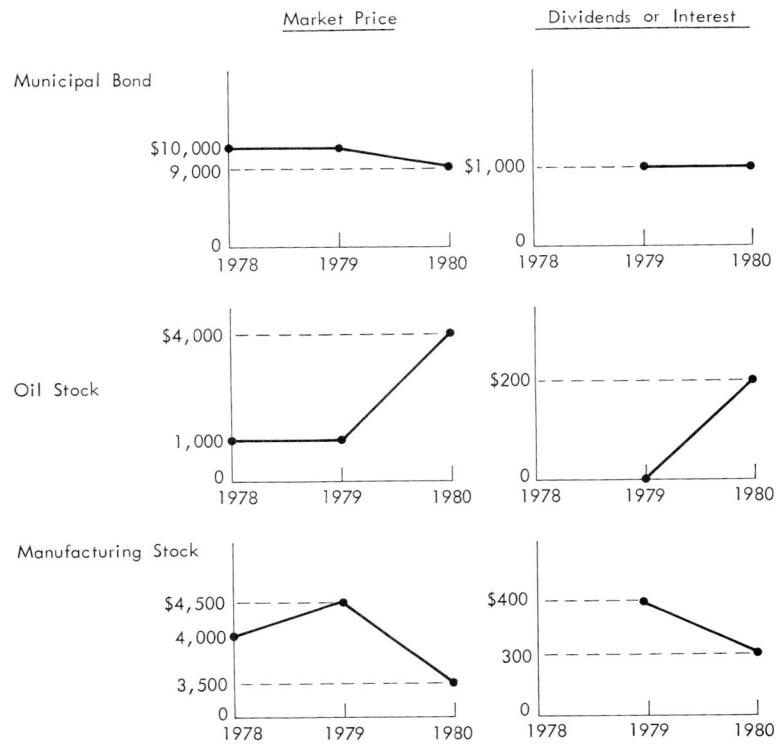

Required:

Prepare income statements for 1979 and 1980 using (*a*) the conventional accounting model, and (*b*) the market-value model.

15-6. Market Value and Conventional Accounting Contrasted. The chairman of Razzle-Dazzle Investment Corporation has just attended a professional development course run by the Sharftville Chamber of Commerce and has learned that conventional accounting has certain limitations for financial reporting by investment companies.

He sends you a memorandum asking for a report on the conventional accounting model versus the current-exchange-output accounting model. He specifically asks you to include in your report a discussion of the effects a change from the conventional model to the current-exchange-output model would have on the reported profit of Razzle-Dazzle Investment Corporation. From the accounting records and external sources, you gather the following information about the years 1979, 1980, and 1981:

    a. Razzle-Dazzle Investment Corporation was set up in 1979 with an investment by the owners of $100,000 in exchange for stock in Razzle-Dazzle.

    b. Early in January 1979, and immediately after the corporation was set up, $70,000 was invested by Razzle-Dazzle in common stocks and $20,000 in bonds (paying 10 percent interest per annum). The stocks and bonds purchased are listed on the Sharftville Exchange.

    c. Administrative expenses were as follows:

1979	$5,000
1980	1,250
1981	2,000

    d. Toward the end of December 1979, dividends on the common stocks totaling $4,000 as well as the interest on the bonds were received.

    e. There were *no* transactions in 1980 other than the receipt toward the end of December of dividends on the common stock totaling $4,500 and the interest on the bonds.

    f. Early in July 1981, before any dividends or interest had been received, the common stocks were sold for $90,000 and the bonds for $18,000. No further transactions took place in 1981.

    g. From stock exchange records you find that the market values of the common stocks and bonds held were as follows:

December 31, 1979:	Common stock	$82,000
	Bonds	19,000
December 31, 1980:	Common stock	89,000
	Bonds	18,000

Closing notes:

1. Assume for the sake of simplicity that no interest was earned on the balance of cash held at any time by the corporation.

2. No withdrawals were made over the three years. You should, however, include in your report an explanation of the amount technically disposable each year from an accounting viewpoint and any financial constraints that might hamper such a withdrawal.

3. Append worksheets to your report.

15-7. Market Value and Conventional Accounting Contrasted. Speculation Corporation is an investment company formed by members of several well-acquainted families who together own all outstanding common stock. The company has been in existence for only three years. It started with a total cash investment by all the shareholders of $100,000. The elected officers immediately purchased a plot of land for $40,000 in cash, and marketable securities for $40,000. The remaining $20,000 was invested for the first year in savings certificates at 6 percent. The $20,000 plus interest was returned to the business just before the end of the first year. At the start of each subsequent year any cash remaining in the business after dividend payments (withdrawals) was again invested in one-year savings certificates at 6 percent. There was general agreement among the shareholders right from the beginning that cash dividends to the shareholders (withdrawals) *would equal income each year.* The shareholder-elected officers have accounted for the company from the start according to conventional accounting. Each year they have reported conventional accounting income and financial position, have made the appropriate payments of cash dividends to the shareholders, and, for the information of other shareholders, have obtained appraisals and market prices on the land and securities held at the end of each year.

This latter practice has caused some dissent among the shareholders, particularly the younger ones. They agree with the policy of distributing cash dividends only to the extent of net income. But they also feel that increases in the market values of the land and securities ought to be included in net income.

The following facts relate to the first three years of operations of Speculation Corporation:

	Dividends Earned on Securities	Rent from Land	Year-end Market or Appraisal Values	
			Securities	Land
Year 1	$4,000	$5,000	$39,000	$45,000
Year 2	4,000	6,000	38,000	55,000
Year 3	3,700	6,500		

Just before the end of year three, the land purchased at the outset was sold for $54,000, and the marketable securities for $41,000.

Required:

1. In worksheet form, record the effects on financial position of Speculation Corporation of all the above facts for each of the first three years *as if* current market and appraisal values had been used by the company. Assume that dividends to owners were based on market-value-based income. (Do not forget the interest on the savings certificate that will be received at the end of each year.)

2. Make up a comparative schedule of net income for each of the three years and in total according to
   (a) Conventional accounting,
   (b) Recognition of market and appraisal values.

3. Repeat number 2, assuming that there were no cash dividends to shareholders of Speculation Corporation in any of the years. Explain the differences between your answer under this assumption and your earlier answers.

4. Comment on what you feel are the pros and cons of the two systems in terms of how well they measure the performance of Speculation Corporation for the long and short runs and in terms of which system provides the "best" measure of disposable wealth in your estimation.

15-8. Unrealized Gains and Disposable Wealth. The Ayers Rock Land Corporation was formed two years ago for the primary purposes of real estate development and land speculation. The principals of the corporation are N. Kelly and R. Hood. N. Kelly contributed the assets of his business, N. Kelly and Associates, which had an appraised value of $300,000 made up as follows:

Cash	$230,000
Land	50,000 (1,000 acres in the vicinity of Ayers Rock)
Office buildings	20,000

R. Hood contributed his substantial land holdings of 30,000 acres with an appraised market value of $300,000.

During 19X0, the first year of operation, the following events took place:

    a. The 30,000 acres contributed by R. Hood were leased to a rancher for $.60 per acre per annum.
    b. Some 4,000 acres were purchased in the vicinity of Muckawilla Springs for speculative purposes at $20 per acre.
    c. Plans were drawn up for a motel and dude ranch on the 1,000 acres near Ayers Rock. Construction had been completed by the end of the year at a cost of $75,000.
    d. Administrative expenses amounted to $4,000 for the year, and office salaries were $6,000.
    e. At the end of the year the market value of the 30,000 acres leased to the rancher remained unchanged; however, several offers had been received for the 4,000 acres at Muckawilla

Springs. The highest of these offers was $130,000. An appraiser estimated the market value of the motel and dude ranch, together with the 1,000 acres, at $150,000. The market value of the office buildings was $20,000.

During 19X1, the following events took place:
  a. Early in 19X1 the rancher made an offer to purchase the 30,000 acres he was currently leasing for $13 per acre. This offer was accepted, and a check for the full amount was received by Ayers Rock Land Corporation. The lease was canceled retroactive to January 1, 19X1.
  b. Of the 4,000 acres at Muckawilla Springs, 2,000 acres were sold at $40 per acre. Interest in the remaining 2,000 acres was high, and the partners were confident that they could at this time realize at least $40 per acre.
  c. The motel and dude ranch proved to be a successful undertaking. Revenues (all in cash) totaled $80,000 for the year; operating expenses (all of which had been paid by year-end) came to $50,000. An offer of $200,000 was received for the motel and dude ranch but was declined.
  d. In June N. Kelly heard rumors that a large mining company had discovered a significant reserve of nickel on a nearby property. On the basis of this rumor the partners bought $100,000 of the company's common stocks.
    The market value of the shares rose rapidly as other investors reacted to the rumors, but a report from the company's directors toward the end of 19X1 indicated that the find was not as extensive as rumored and the market value of the common stock fell rapidly. At year-end the market value of the partners' holding was $70,000.
  e. Administrative expenses and office salaries were the same as in 19X0.
  f. There was no change in the market value of the office buildings.

Required:

Using the market value model:

1. Prepare worksheets for each of the two years.
2. Prepare income statements for 19X0 and for 19X1.
3. Discuss any difficulties that might be encountered in distributing, in cash, the full amount of net income to owners each year.

15-9. Personal Financial Statements. James Nolan, M.D., and Louis Ferrara, M.D., are applying for a $115,000 loan to purchase additional equipment for their medical practice. The bank has requested a personal statement of assets and liabilities as of June 30, 1980, from Dr. and Mrs. Nolan. Pertinent facts about the Nolans follow (unless stated otherwise, all facts are presented as of June 30, 1980):
  a. The Nolans have $8,000 in a checking account and $30,000, including interest through June 30, 1980, in a savings account.

b. The Nolans paid $7,500 in 1978 for a 15 percent interest in Crown Corporation which has 100,000 shares outstanding. The stock is traded on a midwestern exchange. In recent months the stock has traded in blocks of 100 shares or less at $1.50 per share. Dr. Nolan was offered $1.10 per share for all his shares on June 22, 1980. The offer is still outstanding.
c. Dr. Nolan and Dr. Ferrara each own a 50 percent interest in the Suburban Medical Group, a partnership. The balance sheet of Suburban Medical Group prepared on a modified cash basis follows:

Assets

Cash (in non-interest-bearing account)	$ 10,400
30-day treasury bills (maturing July 30, 1980)	11,000
Drugs and supplies inventory	6,100
Equipment and office furniture (net of $14,000 accumulated depreciation)	66,000
Automobiles (net of $1,150 accumulated depreciation)	10,800
Building (purchased June 28, 1980)	55,000
Total	$159,300

Liabilities

9% notes payable (principal and interest payable monthly until 1987)	$ 39,000
Capital	120,300
Total	$159,300

Other data: As of June 30, 1980, there were unrecorded accounts receivable of $12,451 and unrecorded accounts payable of $1,327. Payments on the notes are current.

d. Dr. Ferrara and Dr. Nolan were offered $260,000 for their practice by the Rural Medical Center. The offer is still outstanding.
e. The Nolans purchased their residence in 1977 for $85,000. The balance of the 30-year, 8¾ percent mortgage is $64,498. The current rate charged on similar mortgages is 8¾ percent. Payments on the mortgage are current. Similar homes in the area have increased in value approximately 30 percent since 1977. The assessed real-estate value was determined in March 1980 to be $108,500 based on fair value.
f. Mrs. Nolan owns a 1979 automobile which cost $5,950. Current newspaper advertisements indicate that her car could be sold for $4,800.

g. In 1971 the Nolans received a painting as a wedding present from Mrs. Nolan's aunt, an internationally known artist. At the date of gift, the painting was appraised at $6,000. The painting was appraised in June 1980 at $16,000.
h. The Nolans have maintained cost records on their major household effects. The costs aggregate $27,500. A local business which specializes in auctioning this type of merchandise estimated in July 1980 that the household effects have a net realizable value of $12,000. Other household effects are of nominal value.
i. Dr. Nolan has a vested interest of $14,175 in a group-participating pension plan. The present value of the vested benefits is $6,818. Dr. Nolan's contributions to the plan (tax basis) have been $5,432.
j. On July 1, 1977, Dr. Nolan paid $9,000 for 25 percent of the capital stock of Medical Instruments, Inc., a closely held business which designs medical instruments. A summary of financial data of the corporation follows:

	Balance Sheet at June 30, 1979	Earnings Summary for the Years Ended June 30,		Dividends Paid	
Assets	$112,800				
Liabilities	46,650	1978	$12,050		
Equity	66,150	1979	18,100		
	$112,800	1980	28,050	$6,200	June 10

Similar businesses in the area have been sold recently for ten times the average of the last three-years' earnings.
k. The Nolans owed $810 on charge accounts and $220 on a national credit card account at June 30, 1980.
l. In early July 1980 the Nolans estimated their federal income tax for their 1980 return to be $26,000. Estimated tax payments of $8,000 had been made as of June 30, 1980.
m. A tax accountant has advised that if all the assets were sold, there would be a tax liability on the currently unrealized appreciation of approximately $43,000.

Required:

Present a personal statement of assets and liabilities as of June 30, 1980, for Dr. and Mrs. Nolan. Supporting calculations should be in good form. Footnotes are not required.

(AICPA adapted)

15-10. Reporting Fair Values as Supplementary Information. The following information was taken from the 1976 annual report of Hilton Hotels Corporation:

[10] Information on Replacement Cost (Unaudited) and Fair Market Value of Property and Equipment

As part of the Company's compliance with the Securities and Exchange Commission's Accounting Series Release 190 (ASR 190), the Company had appraisals made of each of its major wholly-owned and 17% to 50% owned properties. The appraisals were made by Joseph J. Blake and Associates, Inc., Valuation Counselors, Inc., and Real Estate Research Corporation.

Although ASR 190 requires replacement cost data only for depreciable property, the appraisers were requested also to estimate the fair market value of the same properties as well as that of the underlying land.

The replacement cost information represents estimates of the cost to be incurred at December 31, 1976, if such assets were replaced at that time. The replacement cost of buildings, leaseholds and improvements was developed by estimating construction costs to obtain comparable facilities; replacement cost for furniture and equipment, representing all personal property, was arrived at by applying current furnishing costs per room to the existing number of rooms. Replacement cost was developed by the use of indices, units of capacity, and component costing techniques.

Fair market value is frequently referred to as the price at which a willing seller would sell and a willing buyer would buy, neither being compelled to sell or buy. Fair market value was arrived at by calculating the present worth of estimated future income streams accruing to the owner utilizing rates of return ranging from 9 to 12 percent, and various terms of financing, and conditions of sale and profitability factors with respect to individual properties. It was assumed that the buyers of the hotel properties would retain management companies to operate the properties and therefore $3,965,000 in annual pro-forma management fees were deducted from the estimated future earnings stream used to value the hotel properties. No management fee was assumed for the Las Vegas properties since it is not customary for owners of hotel-casinos to employ third party management firms.

In the development of the information on replacement cost and fair market value, various critical estimates and assumptions were made. Although these estimates and assumptions are believed to be reasonable in the circumstances, they nevertheless are subjective judgments of management and the appraisers relevant only to the time as of which the information is furnished. The resulting estimated replacement cost and fair market value information may vary therefore from actual future replacement cost or fair market value because of changed conditions.

The basic replacement cost data presented does not take into consideration any operating cost savings or additional revenues which may result from the replacement of existing properties with properties having improved technology and facilities. If the Company's income producing properties were to be replaced in the manner assumed in the calculation of replacement cost of existing properties, many costs other than depreciation, such as labor costs, repairs and maintenance and heat, light and power, would be affected. Although these probable cost changes cannot be quantified with any precision, the current level of operating costs other than depreciation and possibly property taxes may be reduced as a result of the technological improvements assumed in the hypothetical replacement.

Replacement cost depreciation was calculated on the straight-line method generally over the historical depreciation lives. The exceptions were those properties which had been operating prior to the time they were acquired by the Company. Such properties are depreciated for replacement cost purposes as new property from the date of construction including the estimated remaining life at December 31, 1976, versus a shorter term as used property for historical cost purposes.

The following table represents the summary of data described above as of December 31, 1976:

HILTON HOTELS CORPORATION AND SUBSIDIARIES

(In thousands of dollars)	Historical Cost	Estimated Replacement Cost Exclusive of Land (Unaudited)	Estimated Fair Market Value Inclusive of Land
December 31, 1976			
Depreciable property, buildings, leaseholds and improvements	$233,851	634,029	
Furniture and equipment	77,041	118,399	
Total	310,892	752,428	
Less accumulated depreciation	130,651	422,689	
Net depreciable property	180,241	329,739	
Land	56,720		
Net property	236,961		466,937
Reconciliation to Consolidated Balance Sheet:			
Add operating equipment at cost	1,908		
Less cost to acquire leasehold interest in the Waldorf Corporation included in above costs	(35,000)		
Total as shown on the accompanying consolidated balance sheet	$203,869		
Year ended December 31, 1976			
Depreciation expense	$ 16,499	27,302	

HILTON HOTELS CORPORATION AND SUBSIDIARIES (cont.)

17% to 50% Owned Companies

(In thousands of dollars)	Historical Cost	Estimated Replacement Cost Exclusive of Land (Unaudited)	Estimated Fair Market Value Inclusive of Land
December 31, 1976			
Depreciable property, buildings, leaseholds and improvements	$125,353	238,100	
Furniture and equipment	21,412	33,247	
Total	146,765	271,347	
Less accumulated depreciation	47,250	101,789	
Net depreciable property	99,515	169,558	
Land	34,426		
Net property	$133,941		250,708
Year ended December 31, 1976			
Depreciation expense	$ 6,531	9,969	

The excess of the estimated fair market value of wholly-owned and 17% to 50% owned property over historical cost is $346,743,000. The presentation of this information does not imply management's intent to replace or sell existing properties.

Required:

1. Is the estimated "fair market value" described in this footnote essentially equivalent to the concept of current exit value discussed in this chapter?

2. How might the estimated fair market value be used in assessing the viability of the firm?

3. How might the estimated fair market value be used in assessing the market value of the firm?

4. How might the estimated fair market value be used in assessing Hilton Hotels Corporation's ability to satisfy creditors?

Financial Accounting Models in Perspective

16

Our consideration of the alternative financial accounting models in Chapters 13, 14, and 15 was motivated by some possible shortcomings in the conventional accounting model in a period of changing prices. Although motivated by a common issue, the models differ substantially in the attributes they seek to measure and the units in which the measurements are expressed. As a consequence, each of the models provides different wealth assessments and measures of performance and disposable wealth. Final judgment on the appropriateness of a particular model for a particular class of decisions must ultimately be based on the costs and benefits associated with its use in those decisions. This raises the question of whether the models can, in general, be ranked in some kind of "order of preference" so that a choice of the "best" model can be made. This question is one of the most difficult to answer for anyone interested in financial accounting. The reason for the difficulty is that the selection from among financial accounting alternatives has consequences that transcend the use of information by individuals. It is, in essence, a problem of social choice. Our first order of business in this chapter is to examine in fairly general terms the nature and present means of resolving this choice problem.

Having provided some insight into the accounting choice mechanism, we examine the alternative models from the perspective of three basic accounting measurement issues (choices): (1) What unit of measurement is appropriate? (2) What attribute(s) of assets and liabilities do we wish to measure? and (3) Which capital maintenance concept is appropriate? Finally, we highlight the important operational characteristics of the conventional accounting model and the alternative financial accounting models developed in Chapters 13, 14, and 15 by means of a simple illustration to which each of the models is applied for contrast.

CHOICE AMONG ACCOUNTING ALTERNATIVES

A Problem of Social Choice

At the individual level, the selection of a financial accounting model of the enterprise is a simple matter—at least in principle. We know from Chapter 1 that the individual should seek all information for which the expected benefit (from improved expected decision outcomes) exceeds the expected cost. As long as a particular individual is the exclusive producer (or buyer) and consumer of information about the business enterprise, the choice is his (or hers). We have no interest in preempting such individual choice here.

However, one of the most important features of financial accounting (also noted in Chapter 1) is that it goes beyond the level of strictly individual production and consumption of information. As a result, financial accounting involves a number of complications. Because the enterprise management has a comparative advantage in observing, recording, and determining the effects of enterprise activities, resources, obligations, and so forth, there is a clear benefit in having the enterprise be the primary producer of accounting information about itself. But to exploit this advantage means that many individuals may experience benefits from the information while not necessarily bearing any of the cost of its production. The costs of production are borne by the enterprise—and, through it, by its present shareholders.

In addition to *uneven* distribution among many individuals of the costs and benefits from the production of information by a given enterprise, financial accounting is thought by many to have potential for producing certain "externalities." Externalities occur in general when a number of individuals (or other entities), acting independently, create a positive or a negative *joint effect* of their actions as well as the expected individual consequences. Currently, the most familiar examples of externalities are the negative effects on the environment of various forms of pollution. No single individual produces so many pollutants that these cannot be readily absorbed by the biosphere. But together the effect can be significant.

In financial accounting the potential for positive (and perhaps negative) externalities is usually thought to arise because decision makers are interested in making choices among investments in a number of different enterprises. This obviously involves interfirm comparisons of expected future returns (cash flows) and risk. Thus, if a particular type of accounting is selected for just one enterprise, it may not be as helpful (valuable) to decision makers as it would be if it were used by all enterprises—thus facilitating comparisons between enterprises.

We have noted above three complications in the financial accounting information choice situation not present in strictly individual information choice problems: (1) multiple users of information, (2) uneven distribution of costs and benefits, and (3) positive (and perhaps negative) external effects of financial accounting information. The implication of these three complications is that *the choice of financial accounting alternative(s) is a social choice*. Although the actual selection of accounting alternatives may be made by one or at most a few individuals, the outcome affects the flow of costs and benefits to many. The important questions, then, are, How should such choices be made (how should the alternatives be ranked)? and By whom? Unfortunately, no one can answer these questions unequivocally. However, we attempt below to describe how accountants have traditionally tried to rank the alternatives, and some of the problems with the traditional criteria.

Traditional Criteria for the Financial Accounting Choice Problem

Perhaps the one widely accepted assumption about the selection of accounting alternatives is that it is probably not optimal to have business enterprises report according to *all feasible* financial accounting alternatives. The assumption is very likely to be true in the extreme, that is, the number of information alternatives could be expanded almost indefinitely (at a cost), and further benefits of additional information would eventually be exhausted. There is some question, of course, as to whether sufficient financial accounting alternatives have been suggested to date so that the costs of reporting under all the alternatives would clearly outweigh the benefits. However, there seems to be a pervasive belief to this effect.

Usefulness of Information for Decisions. If we cannot simultaneously have accounting information based on all feasible financial accounting models of the enterprise, how do we choose a more limited ideal or optimal set? In recent years a single primary criterion has been more and more widely acknowledged as very important in ranking alternative models. That criterion is the usefulness *to decision makers* of the information produced. However, since financial accounting goes beyond the individual level, usefulness is usually translated into a number of criteria or characteristics that may be possessed to varying degrees by the information produced under each model. The most important (and perhaps the most widely acknowledged) of the criteria is decision relevance.

Decision Relevance. Decision relevance is, in a general sense, the obvious requirement that an individual user would impose on any information request. Does it enable him, in some measure, to better predict the outcomes that would result from various courses of action?

Example 16-1

> If you were considering a career in either the legal profession or the accounting profession, the receipt of the information that the probability of rain that day is 60 percent would probably not be conceived of as decision-relevant information. On the other hand, if from another source you received information that reflected the average salaries of lawyers and accountants at various points in their careers, this would undoubtedly be considered highly decision relevant to the question at hand.

To date, the assessment by accounting researchers of the decision relevance of the various financial accounting models has taken one of two general forms:

1. The use of logic and examples to explore structural relationships between accounting information and the information requirements implied by specified decision situations.

2. Empirical tests of either (a) the ability of accounting information to predict future phenomena (like future earnings or cash flows) of interest in decision situations, or (b) the association between accounting information and the apparent risk and return characteristics of firms' securities as reflected by the market values of those securities.

It is beyond the scope of this book to review each of these methods exhaustively. Of course the first method (using logic and examples) has actually been used in our own earlier discussion, but the authors have not gone so far as to attempt to show logically which model is most relevant for investment and wealth distribution decisions. Rather, our purpose has been to introduce each model by showing (primarily through example) how its outputs relate to certain classes of decision situations. We have used this method only because it is the more efficient and flexible for introducing students to some of the important characteristics of each model.

Unfortunately, neither of the two relevance-assessment methods has proved particularly conclusive in ranking the alternative models in the past. Often a logical argument (or empirical evidence) that one model produces more relevant (predictive) information than another is countered by arguments that it possesses less of another "useful" characteristic. The most frequently mentioned of these other useful characteristics is objectivity.

Objectivity. In our discussion in earlier chapters, the criterion of objectivity was introduced as the intuitive notion that financial accounting information should be largely based on fact. While this notion is reflective of the general thrust of the criterion, some elaboration may be helpful.

It is sometimes suggested that the objectivity criterion be applied in accounting in the form of a degree-of-precision measure (degree-of-precision being the amount of variation that one might reasonably expect if a number of accountants made independent measurements of the same phenomenon). Accordingly, an accounting measure that is high on this aspect of objectivity would be one that does not exhibit much variation in the values assigned by different accountants to the same set of observations. Presumably, if an accounting measurement is low in precision, it is also apt to be low in terms of the expectation that users of the accounting measurement will gain the same perception from it that the preparer had in mind when making the measurement. This latter characteristic, called "shared meaning" or "transferability" of information, is what accountants are really concerned about when they talk about objectivity.

Problems with the Traditional Criteria

Although more than one characteristic (e.g., relevance and objectivity) is thought to have a bearing on the usefulness of accounting information to various classes of decision makers, this is not, in and of itself, a barrier to ranking accounting information models. For instance, one model could conceivably be acknowledged by everyone to be better than any other model with respect to every characteristic. Unfortunately, however, none of the financial accounting models put forth to date clearly dominates the others in this way. In the absence of a clearly dominant alternative, it is necessary to measure the extent to which each characteristic is possessed by each alternative, and then to be able to combine the scores on each measurement scale into a single score for each information model.

Of course we have not formally specified (and cannot specify at present) scales on which to measure the extent to which a particular valuation model possesses each characteristic. In the case of the objectivity criterion, the degree-of-precision notion provides a good deal of guidance of this type; even here, however, precision is but part of the larger question of how much shared meaning (and thus potential transferability) exists. Furthermore, even if we could specify scales measuring relevance and objectivity, we would still lack a common scale on which to combine the separate measures (according to some trade-off system). Because of the absence of these bases for comparison, it is impossible to make direct assessments of the relative usefulness of the alternative valuation models.

Furthermore, financial accounting is concerned with information produced by one group of economic units (business enterprises) for use by other groups (external decision makers). As a result, decisions as to how to go about the financial accounting process (including the choice among accounting models) inevitably affect the distribution of costs and benefits (and therefore wealth) among the individuals in the economy. Unfortunately, few social choices involve one alternative under which everyone would clearly be better off (or at least not worse off) than under the other alternatives. This means that there will seldom be unanimous agreement to a particular social choice among all the individuals affected. Thus, since whatever choice is made will tend to favor some and be unfavorable to others, the question of what is "equitable" or fair inevitably becomes an issue. Traditionally, accounting researchers, theoreticians, and practitioners have not addressed themselves to this issue directly. As a result, relatively little is known about the possible effects of different financial accounting models on the distribution of wealth (and the fairness of the distribution) among the members of society.

The Present Social Choice Mechanism

The problems identified above are not unique to the financial accounting choice question. Virtually every decision made by governmental bodies (agencies, legislative bodies, etc.) involves the same difficult considerations. Whatever the choice, one group will probably benefit to the detriment of another group. Furthermore, prior to the decision (and often after the decision), the effects that the choice will have on the various parties is seldom clear. But such decisions are continuously made by individuals and institutions entrusted with the authority to do so. A similar situation prevails in respect to the financial accounting function. The particular institutional forces that play a significant role in deciding how the financial accounting function is carried out are examined in some detail in Chapter 17. What is important to note at this point, however, is that individuals within the institutions are ultimately making the choices, and they are confronted by the same (probably an even broader) kaleidoscopic pattern of model characteristics, information requirements, and alleged costs of preparing and revealing information. How do they reach a final judgment? They probably evaluate the issues by using a mode of analysis similar to that specified by the traditional criteria, recognizing the inherent limitations and subjectively making the required cost/benefit trade-offs. Thus, while final evaluation of the relative merits of the alternative financial accounting models is an individual decision, the decision is strongly influenced by an understanding of the strengths and weaknesses of each of the models, and the types of decision contexts in which they are most appropriate. This is, of course, the perspective we have attempted to provide for each of the models.

ACCOUNTING MEASUREMENT ISSUES

The different wealth assessments and measures of performance and disposable wealth that are produced by the alternative financial accounting models are a consequence of the choices that are made on three basic accounting measurement issues:

1. What is the unit of measurement?
2. What is the attribute of assets and liabilities that is measured?
3. Which capital maintenance concept has been adopted?

In the following review of the choices that are generally considered for each of these issues, we seek to provide a broader perspective on the alternative measurement systems that we have previously examined (and a few alternatives not explicitly considered).

Unit of Measurement

Economic resources can be measured in terms of many different units of measure. For example, the output of General Motors Corporation could be measured in terms of the number of automobiles as well as the number of dollars received from their sale. But as was pointed out in Chapter 1, decision making is facilitated by choosing a single common denominator, and the choice that has been made in the financial accounting system (whatever the model) is the dollar. This does not preclude providing additional information measured, say, in physical terms, but the measures of performance, disposable wealth, and resources and obligations within the financial accounting system are all expressed in the common unit of measure—dollars.

The issue that has become increasingly controversial over the past ten to twenty years is whether financial accounting measurements should be expressed merely in units of money or in units of purchasing power (general price-level-adjusted, or common, dollars). The status of this debate was briefly reviewed in Chapter 13 and will not be repeated here. But whatever the outcome of the debate, the choice is an important determinant of the types of measurements that will be provided.

Attribute to Be Measured

The second major determinant of the types of measurements that will be provided by financial accounting is the *attribute* that is measured. The Financial Accounting Standards Board has identified five attributes, or properties, of assets and liabilities that received some, or much, support from those interested in the financial accounting process:

1. Historical cost/historical proceeds
2. Current cost/current proceeds
3. Current exit value in orderly liquidation
4. Expected exit value in due course of business
5. Present value of expected cash flows[1]

A summary of the interpretations, or meanings, of measures of these attributes for both assets and liabilities is given in Exhibit 16-1. Identification of alternative attributes of, say, an asset is equivalent to the commonly recognized fact that, say, a table can be viewed (or measured) from many different points of view—height, width, weight, etc. None of these attributes of the table is inherently "superior" to any other attribute independent of an intended use for the measurement. The same is true of the accounting measures of attributes of assets and liabilities, and underscores our emphasis throughout the book on the decision context for accounting information.

The choices for the attribute to be measured and the unit of measurement jointly determine what we have called in this book a financial accounting model. Exhibit 16-2 summarizes the alternative financial accounting models that we have examined in terms of the choices that are made on these two dimensions. Recognition of the joint effect of the two independent decisions reinforces a point we made when general price-level adjustments were first introduced in Chapter 13. In that chapter we asserted that the general price-level-adjusted conventional accounting model measures would have the same characteristics in times of generally changing prices that the conventional accounting model measures have in times of static prices. The reason for this assertion is clearly explained by Exhibit 16-2. The attribute to be measured—historical cost/historical proceeds—is not changed; only the unit of measurement is changed. Therefore the resulting measures will have all of the same properties that the original measures had, but they are expressed in different units. The same conclusion is drawn when general price-level adjustments are applied to the other alternative models; the properties of the model remain unchanged, but the unit in which the measurements are expressed is changed from units of money to units of purchasing power.

Additional understanding of the attributes (and the financial accounting models they imply) may be gained by viewing them from several different clas-

---

[1] Financial Accounting Standards Board Discussion Memorandum, "Conceptual Framework for Financial Accounting and Reporting: Elements of Financial Statements and Their Measurement," Chap. 8.

Exhibit 16-1

ATTRIBUTES OF ASSETS AND LIABILITIES

Attribute	Assets	Liabilities
1. Historical cost/historical proceeds	Initially, the amount of cash (or its equivalent) paid to acquire an asset (historical cost); subsequent to acquisition, the historical amount may be adjusted for amortization	Initially, the amount of cash (or its equivalent) received when an obligation was incurred (historical proceeds); subsequent to incurrence, the historical amount may be adjusted for amortization
2. Current cost/current proceeds	Amount of cash (or its equivalent) that would have to be paid if the same asset were acquired currently (current cost) 2.1 The "same asset" may be an identical asset ("current reproduction cost" or "current cost of replacement in kind") 2.2 The "same asset" may be an asset with equivalent production capacity ("current replacement cost")	Amount of proceeds that would be obtained if the same obligation were incurred currently (current proceeds)
3. Current exit value in orderly liquidation	Amount of cash that could be obtained currently by selling the asset in orderly liquidation (current market value)	Cash outlay that would be required currently to eliminate the liability (current market value)
4. Expected exit value in due course of business	Amount of cash (or its equivalent) into which asset is expected to be converted in due course of business less direct costs necessary to make that conversion (this attribute of accounts receivable and inventories has customarily been referred to as "net realizable value")	Amount of cash (or its equivalent) expected to be paid to eliminate liability in due course of business including direct costs necessary to make those payments (nondiscounted amount of expected cash outlays)
5. Present value of expected cash flows	Present value of future cash inflows into which asset is expected to be converted in due course of business less present value of cash outflows necessary to obtain those inflows. Rate of discount may be: 5.1 Historical rate 5.2 Current rate 5.3 Other rate (for example, average expected rate or weighted average cost of capital)	Present value of future cash outflows to eliminate liability in due course of business including cash outflows necessary to make those payments. Rate of discount may be: 5.1 Historical rate 5.2 Current rate 5.3 Other rate (for example, average expected rate or incremental borrowing rate)

Source: Financial Accounting Standards Board Discussion Memorandum, "Conceptual Framework for Financial Accounting and Reporting: Elements of Financial Statements and Their Measurement," p. 193.

Exhibit 16-2

CLASSIFICATION OF FINANCIAL ACCOUNTING MODELS IN TERMS OF ATTRIBUTE TO BE MEASURED AND UNIT OF MEASUREMENT

	Unit of Measurement	
	Nominal Dollars	*General Price-Level-Adjusted Dollars (Purchasing Power)*
Attribute To Be Measured:		
Historical cost/historical proceeds	Conventional Accounting Model (Chapters 3-12)	General Price-Level-Adjusted Conventional Accounting Model (Chapter 13)
Current cost/current proceeds	Replacement Cost Model (Chapter 14)	General Price-Level-Adjusted Replacement Cost Model (Chapter 14)
Current exit value in orderly liquidation	Market-Value Model (Chapter 15)	General Price-Level-Adjusted Market-Value Model (Chapter 15)
Expected exit value in due course of business	General model not discussed; when applied to a single asset, referred to as net realizable value	Not discussed
Present value of expected cash flows	Present Value Model (Chapter 2)	Not discussed

sificational perspectives.[2] First, from the point of view of the *timing* of the prices or cash flows used in the measurement, we obtain the following classification:

Past Prices
  Historical cost/historical proceeds

Present Prices
  Current cost/current proceeds
  Current exit value in orderly liquidation

Future Prices
  Expected exit value in due course of business
  Present value of expected cash flows

A second way of looking at the different attributes is to focus on the *kind of transaction*—purchase or sale—that is assumed. We have previously emphasized this point in our discussion of the current exchange price models, but note here that the distinction applies across the attributes:

Purchase (Entry) Values
  Historical cost/historical proceeds
  Current cost/current proceeds

---

[2] This set of alternative classifications is presented in FASB Discussion Memorandum, "Conceptual Framework," pp. 192-194.

Sale (Exit) Values
    Current exit value in orderly liquidation
    Expected exit value in due course of business
    Present value of expected cash flows

Finally, the attributes can be classified according to the *type of event*—actual, expected, or hypothetical—that is assumed:

Actual Event
    Historical cost/historical proceeds

Expected Event
    Expected exit value in due course of business
    Present value of expected cash flows

Hypothetical Event
    Current cost/current proceeds
    Current exit value in orderly liquidation

The different classifications do not, of course, provide a basis for accepting or rejecting any particular attribute. But they may be helpful in identifying critical differences in the attributes that would be relevant in particular decision contexts. We might note that the last two attributes listed in Exhibit 16-2—expected exit values and present values of expected cash flows—do not differ on any of the three dimensions. This emphasizes that they are indeed quite similar and that they differ only in whether or not a discount rate is applied to the expected future cash flows.

Capital Maintenance Concept

Although the alternative financial accounting models are fully identified by the joint choices of the attribute to be measured and the unit of measurement, the capital maintenance concept that is adopted is an important related decision. Two capital maintenance concepts have been discussed—financial capital and physical capital. These alternative concepts of capital are in fact alternative ways of viewing the beginning-of-period wealth position of the firm that is used as the criterion for determining disposable wealth. When we seek to maintain physical capital, the firm must retain sufficient net assets at the end of the period to have the same level of physical operating capability that it possessed at the beginning of the period; any assets above this level may be distributed to parties with an equitable interest in the firm (owners, taxing authorities, etc.). On the other hand, when we seek to maintain financial capital, the firm must retain net assets at the end of the period in an amount equal to its money capital (in either dollars or purchasing power) at the beginning of the period. Depending upon the types of price changes that the firm faced during the period, these alternative capital maintenance concepts may produce quite different measures of disposable wealth.

    The relationship of the capital maintenance decision to the choice of an attribute to be measured is conditional upon the capital maintenance concept adopted. If the physical capital concept is adopted, then the current cost/current proceeds (replacement cost model) attribute is the only choice that will facilitate the desired result in times of changing prices. That is, maintenance of physical capital implies that the firm retains sufficient resources to replace its physical assets as they are consumed, and this notion is implemented in the replacement cost model by valuing consumed resources (expenses) at their current replacement prices. As was pointed out in Chapter 14, some additional adjustments to current operating income may be necessary in arriving at the desired measure of disposable wealth, but nonetheless the attribute measured in the replacement cost model is uniquely related to the physical capital maintenance concept. If the decision is made to adopt financial capital as the capital to be maintained, none of the five possible attributes are automatically selected or rejected. Any of the attributes, including current cost/current proceeds, may be used in conjunction with the financial capital concept of capital maintenance. Recall, however, that the periodic measures of disposable wealth will generally be different for the alternative attributes because the financial accounting model associated with each attribute recognizes value increments in different forms and at different times. Thus the choice of a preferred attribute must be based upon an evaluation of each attribute in terms of the properties of its disposable wealth measure, the expected usefulness of the performance measure, and possibly the types of values assigned to assets and liabilities in the statement of financial position.

FASB Choices in "Financial Reporting and Changes Prices"

The FASB is now studying the above issues in the context of its attempt to develop a "conceptual framework for financial accounting and reporting," but no final decisions on the project have yet been made.[3] However, as was pointed out in Chapter 14, in late 1978 the FASB issued a proposed standard calling for supplementary disclosures to reflect the effects of changing prices. Summarizing this proposal again, it calls for the following minimum supplementary information:[4]

a. (1) Income from continuing operations on a current cost basis, and holding gains or losses net of inflation; *or*
   (2) Income from continuing operations on the basis of the general price-level-adjusted conventional accounting model (in FASB terminology, on a historical cost/constant dollar basis).
b. Inflation gain or loss on net monetary items.
c. A five-year summary of selected accounting data measured on the basis

---

[3] FASB Discussion Memorandum, "Conceptual Framework."

[4] Financial Accounting Standards Board, "Financial Reporting and Changing Prices," *Proposed Statement of Financial Accounting Standards,* December 28, 1978. Recall that the proposed standard is applicable only to publicly held enterprises that have inventories and *gross* property, plant, and equipment amounting to more than $125 million *or* total assets amounting to more than $1 billion (both amounts measured in accordance with the conventional accounting model).

of current cost or historical cost/constant dollars. Among the data required are income from continuing operations, holding gains or losses net of inflation (when current cost is the selected measurement basis from *a* above), inflation gain or loss on net monetary items, and net assets at fiscal year-end.

In arriving at this proposed standard, the FASB of necessity had to make choices, at least tentatively, on each of the measurement issues. These choices, and the decision context that was assumed, are summarized below.

The decision context assumed by the board is reflected in *FASB Statement of Financial Accounting Concepts No. 1,* "Objectives of Financial Reporting by Business Enterprises." Two major financial reporting objectives that the board drew from the overall set of objectives follow:

1. Information should be provided that will help investors, creditors, and other interested parties assess the amounts, timing, and uncertainty of prospective net cash inflows; and

2. Information should be provided that will help discharge management's accountability to owners to protect them to the extent possible against unfavorable economic impacts of factors such as inflation or deflation.

The first objective is obviously responsive to what we have referred to in this book as the investment decision, and thus it establishes the measurement of performance (and related asset and liability valuation) as a criterion to be used in making the choices of unit of measurement, attribute to be measured, and capital maintenance concept. The second objective focuses on existing owners and thus might be interpreted to encompass both the investment decision (the present owners' decision to sell, maintain existing holdings, or purchase additional holdings) and the distribution-of-benefits decision.

Financial Concept of Capital. The FASB opted for a financial concept of capital primarily because it believed that this concept of capital was "consistent with the basic investment objective of preserving and increasing the individual investor's purchasing power regardless of the physical form or quantity of assets held."[5] This reasoning is similar to our discussion in Chapter 14 in which we drew a distinction between management's highly probable interest in preserving the firm's operating capability and investors' *possible* interest in only the financial investment in the firm. In its selection, the board focused on the needs of investors (consistent with the overall financial reporting objectives) and assumed that their interest was indeed in maintaining their financial investment. The board also noted that this choice eliminates the issue of whether distributable earnings can be generated (and measured) by the wise timing of purchase decisions, and the measurement complexities of a dynamic environment involving changing methods of production and mixes of activities.

Constant Dollar Accounting. The FASB chose purchasing power as the unit of measurement for several reasons. First, it was assumed that investors desire to preserve and increase their purchasing power, and that by measuring the results of operations of the firm in constant units of purchasing power the

---

[5] Ibid., p. 35.

investors will be able to judge management's success in achieving this goal. Such measurements also permit the calculation of the amount of disposable wealth for a period so as to preserve the invested purchasing power at the beginning of the period. Second, with income measured in constant dollars, investors can compare the performance of different firms. Third, use of constant dollars provides a common denominator that can be properly added, subtracted, and otherwise combined. Fourth, the economic gain or loss that arises as a consequence of holding monetary items during a period of inflation or deflation is unreported when the unit of measurement is nominal dollars. Identification of this important consequence of a changing general price level is believed to be another important reason for adopting purchasing power as the unit of measurement. Fifth, use of constant dollars permits comparison of measurements over time. And finally, all of the above reasons "in principle" are supported also in terms of practicality by the amount of inflation that has occurred in the recent past. In a period of mild inflation, the adjustments that would be introduced by use of general price-level techniques may not be significant enough to justify the costs involved. But the board believes that its field tests indicate that the adjustments are sufficiently material to justify the additional information-processing costs.

Current Cost Accounting. Although the required disclosures summarized above provide for a choice between the current cost and the historical cost attributes, the guidelines presented by the FASB for making this choice seem to reflect a clear preference under most circumstances for the current cost attribute. Application of this measurement basis for purposes of computing income from continuing operations and holding gains or losses is required only for inventories and property, plant, and equipment, and the related measures of cost of sales and depreciation expense. Other assets and liabilities may continue to be measured by using conventional accounting principles. The board apparently believes that most of the effects of changing prices can be captured in this experimental stage by merely revaluing these two important classes of assets.

For application of the current cost option, the board presents the following general valuation rule for assets:

1. Current cost, or *if lower,*
2. Net realizable value or value in use (whichever is applicable in the circumstances)

The reason for this alternative to current cost valuation is that in certain cases, presumably infrequent, the replacement cost of an asset exceeds its "value to the business." The value of a presently owned asset to the business, it is argued, cannot exceed the maximum amount that the firm would be willing to pay to possess the asset. Normally, this maximum amount is the current replacement cost of the asset, because the firm could obtain the same future cash flows by purchasing the asset. However, in some circumstances, the cash-flow potential of an asset *in the possession of the firm* has been impaired to the extent that the firm would not wish to purchase it at the current entry price. Such a situation implies that the current purchase (or production) price of the asset exceeds its net realizable value (presumably adjusted for the time value of money, if material) for an asset held for sale, or the value in use (present value) for an asset to be used in the business. Therefore, in such circumstances, it seems appropriate to value the asset at net realizable value or value in use, depending upon whether the asset in question is held for sale or use.

The principal reason for the board's preference for current cost accounting seems to be an anticipated improvement in the investor's ability to assess the amounts, timing, and risk of future cash flows. The operating margins reflected by the "current matching" of sales revenue against current costs of resources consumed are assumed to have some degree of stability over time and thus should provide a better basis for assessing future cash flows. Additionally, it is assumed that the current cost of resources on hand reflects a type of market judgment of their current cash-flow potential because current buyers are presumably comparing this price against their estimates of the present value of the cash flows that will be generated by the asset. Thus, valuing the assets at current cost provides additional assistance to the investor wishing to assess the firm's long-run cash-generating ability.

These choices that the board has made in proposing supplementary information to reflect the effects of changing prices are embedded in an assumed decision context (similar to the one developed in this text) and are supported by some persuasive reasoning. Of course the assumed decision context may be incomplete or improperly developed, and the reasoning involves many assumptions, value judgments, and trade-offs between conflicting qualities of information (e.g., relevance and objectivity). But as we have pointed out in this chapter, such characteristics are a necessary ingredient of the mechanism by which accounting policies are established. Further, the choice mechanism is a dynamic process, and continuing adjustments, modifications, and adaptations are to be expected in a changing environment.

COMPARATIVE ACCOUNTING MODELS: AN ILLUSTRATION

The purpose of the following illustration is to highlight and contrast the alternative financial models of the business enterprise. Therefore the situation constructed for our example is deliberately as simple as possible in order to avoid obscuring the basic characteristics of the models with unnecessary computational complexity. Additionally, we have chosen a situation that begins with an initial investment of cash and after two periods of operations is back to a "cash only" condition. This allows us to contrast the *periodic* measures of performance and disposable wealth in a clear-cut way because we are thus able to achieve a "total life" perspective on the operations of the firm. While the more realistic case of a business engaged in continuing operations tends to mask some of the numerical differences between the models that are created in this example, the conceptual differences between the models nonetheless remain.

Basic Case Data

Example 16-2

Bill Flicker had operated a marina in Corpus Christi, Texas, for a number of years, but he had not engaged in the business of selling sailboats because of the large investment that was required in each boat. In view of a substantial increase in interest among the population in the immediate area in sailboats in the 25- to 35-foot range, Bill decided late in 19X0 that he would enter this business. On December 31, 19X0, Bill formed Blue Water Yacht Sales, Inc., and entered the sailboat business as a distributor for PW-30s.

Bill did not want to get too heavily committed to this area immediately, and thus he decided to start the business with a $40,000 investment. With a current wholesale cost of $20,000 for each PW-30, Bill was restricted to an inventory of two boats. He then made the decision that he would not replace his inventory until he had sold both boats—a policy that somewhat inhibited his sales potential but at the same time provided, in Bill's opinion, less financial risk.

The operations of the company were only moderately successful. It took two years for Bill to sell both boats. (The PW-30 was a popular yacht, but it seemed that every serious customer wanted a color that Bill did not have in stock.) The activities of Blue Water Yacht Sales, and related environmental events, can be summarized as follows:

19X1

Purchased two PW-30s at start of year for $40,000. Sold one PW-30 in middle of year for $30,000, at which time the replacement cost for a PW-30 was $24,000.

Relevant price data at end of year:
  Estimated replacement cost—$26,000.
  Estimated immediate-sale (orderly liquidation) price—$28,000.
  Expected 19X2 selling price—$32,500.
  General price-level index increased uniformly over the period from 200 to 220, with an average for the period of 210.

19X2

Sold second PW-30 at end of year for $37,500, at which time the replacement cost for a PW-30 was $30,000.

General price-level index increased uniformly over the period from 220 to 240, with an average for the period of 230.

We will assume that Blue Water Yacht Sales, Inc., did not have other operating expenses during the two years, as the marina operation provided the necessary selling environment without charge. Furthermore, to simplify our calculations, we will assume that Bill made no withdrawals during the two years, leaving any cash in a non-interest-bearing checking account.

Conventional Accounting Model—Nominal Dollars

The effect of these events on the financial position of Blue Water Yacht Sales, Inc., from its inception through the end of 19X2 based on conventional accounting, measured in nominal dollars, is summarized in Exhibit 16-3.

The conventional accounting income statement for the two years of operations is presented in Exhibit 16-4. Since there are no extraordinary gains or losses during the period, net operating income and net income are equal, and the single income measure serves as the measure of performance and disposable

Exhibit 16-3

BLUE WATER YACHT SALES, INC.

Financial Position Worksheet—Conventional Accounting

Description	Cash	Inventory	Owners' Equity
Initial Investment	40,000		40,000
19X1			
Purchased two sailboats	(40,000)	40,000	
Sold one sailboat	30,000		30,000 (R)
Cost of sailboat sold		(20,000)	(20,000) (E)
Ending (Beginning) Position	30,000	20,000	50,000
19X2			
Sold one sailboat	37,500		37,500 (R)
Cost of sailboat sold		(20,000)	(20,000) (E)
Ending Position	67,500	-0-	67,500

Exhibit 16-4

BLUE WATER YACHT SALES, INC.

Income Statements
(Conventional Accounting Model—Nominal Dollars)
For the First Two Years of Operations

	19X1	19X2	Total
Sales	$30,000	$37,500	$67,500
Cost of sales	20,000	20,000	40,000
Net income	$10,000	$17,500	$27,500

wealth. Whether the measure is adequate for either of these purposes in the face of changing specific and general prices is the crucial question that motivated the introduction of the alternative financial accounting models in Chapters 13, 14, and 15.

With this in mind, we now turn to an application of the general price-level-adjusted conventional accounting model to the facts of this example. Recall that since we are changing *only* the unit of measure, from nominal dollars to units of purchasing power, the resulting "adjusted" measures of performance and disposable wealth should possess essentially the same characteristics in times of generally changing prices that the conventional accounting measures (in nominal dollars) have in times of static prices.

Conventional Accounting Model—Units of Purchasing Power

The concepts of disposable wealth and performance in the conventional accounting model are intuitively appealing—but the strength of the appeal depends on a price environment that is static. Essentially, the conventional accounting view (implicitly) is that the business enterprise is a reservoir of money capital. Hence, so long as net assets equal in amount to the money investment in the business are preserved, it is assumed that the wealth of the enterprise will not have been diminished. Under static price conditions, this assumption has some validity. However, in times of generally changing prices, original dollar amounts cease to have the power to represent the original economic "meaning" of the original money capital. Hence, the objective underlying general price-level adjustments of amounts otherwise determined in accordance with the conventional accounting model is clear. Original transaction values are adjusted to the current dollar equivalent of their general purchasing power at the date they were given recognition—in an attempt to recapture and preserve the economic significance (meaning) of the various original transactions.

The general price-level-adjusted income measures for Blue Water Yacht Sales, Inc., are calculated in Exhibit 16-5. The calculation of general price-level-adjusted net income is based upon the difference between owner's equity at the beginning and end of the period, both expressed in end-of-year dollars. General price-level-adjusted net operating income is determined by adjusting the sales and cost of sales as measured under the conventional accounting model, and the determination of the monetary loss from holding cash reconciles the two price-level-adjusted income measures. The final section of this exhibit presents a calculation of the income measures for the entire two-year period, measured in December 31, 19X2, dollars. In the reconciliation of the individual 19X1 and 19X2 calculations with this overall two-year calculation, the only adjustment that is required is the restatement of the 19X1 measures in 19X1 dollars into 19X2 dollars. After this restatement, the 19X1 and 19X2 measures of income are both measured in the same dollars (end-of-19X2 dollars), and they can be added to produce the two-year income numbers, measured in December 31, 19X2, dollars.

The measure of disposable wealth under this financial accounting model is given by general price-level-adjusted net income. In this example, disposable wealth for the two-year period is $19,500. A withdrawal of this amount would leave owner's equity of $48,000, which represents the same purchasing power in December 31, 19X2, dollars as did the original $40,000 investment of January 1, 19X1, dollars. This measure of disposable wealth is in contrast to the $27,500 indicated when the beginning-of-period financial capital is viewed in terms of nominal dollars.

Determination of the measure of performance for the two years depends upon our interpretation of the long-run permanence of inflation and the representativeness of the net monetary position of the business during this period of time. If inflation is considered to be a transient factor, then general price-level-adjusted net operating income would be used as the measure of performance. However, if inflation is regarded as a relatively constant environmental factor, then the monetary gain or loss must be taken into account in projecting the long-run cash-generating ability (in units of purchasing power) of the firm. One might modify the measure of the monetary loss in this example if the accumulation of cash in the firm during these first two years of operation was not considered representative of the financial management policies that would be followed in the future.

Exhibit 16-5

BLUE WATER YACHT SALES, INC.

Calculation of Income Measures
(Conventional Accounting Model—Units of Purchasing Power)
For the First Two Years of Operations

19X1

			12/31/X1 Dollars
General Price-Level-Adjusted Net Income:			
Ending owners' equity, in 12/31/X1 dollars:			
Cash			$30,000
Inventory ($20,000 × 220/200)			22,000
			$52,000
Beginning owners' equity, in 12/31/X1 dollars:			
$40,000 × 220/200			$44,000
General price-level-adjusted net income			$ 8,000

	Original Transaction Value	Translation Factor	12/31/X1 Dollars
General Price-Level-Adjusted Net Operating Income:			
Sales	$30,000	220/210	$31,429
Cost of sales	20,000	220/200	22,000
Net operating income	$10,000		$ 9,429
Monetary loss from cash:			
Beginning balance	$40,000	220/200	$44,000
Purchase of inventory	(40,000)	220/200	(44,000)
Receipt from sales	30,000	220/210	31,429
Ending balance	$30,000		$31,429
			30,000
Monetary loss			$ 1,429
Reconciliation:			
Net operating income			$ 9,429
Monetary loss			1,429
Net income			$ 8,000

19X2

	12/31/X2 Dollars
General Price-Level-Adjusted Net Income:	
Ending owners' equity, in 12/31/X2 dollars (all cash)	$67,500
Beginning owners' equity, in 12/31/X2 dollars:	
Cash ($30,000 × 240/220)	$32,727
Inventory ($20,000 × 240/200)	24,000
	$56,727*
General price-level-adjusted net income	$10,773

*Can also be calculated by restating price-level adjusted 12/31/X1 owners' equity, i.e., $52,000 × 240/220 = $56,727.

Exhibit 16-5 (cont.)

19X2

General Price-Level-Adjusted Net Operating Income:

	Original Transaction Value	Translation Factor	12/31/X2 Dollars
Sales	$37,500	240/240	$37,500
Cost of sales	20,000	240/200	24,000
Net operating income	$17,500		$13,500

Monetary loss from cash:

Beginning balance	$30,000	240/220	$32,727
Receipts from sales	37,500	240/240	37,500
Ending balance	$67,500		$70,227
			67,500
Monetary loss			$ 2,727

Reconciliation:

Net operating income	$13,500
Monetary loss	2,727
Net income	$10,773

Total for 19X1 and 19X2

	12/31/X2 Dollars
General Price-Level-Adjusted Net Income:	
Ending owners' equity, in 12/31/X2 dollars	$67,500
Beginning owners' equity, in 12/31/X2 dollars ($40,000 × 240/200)	48,000
Net income	$19,500

Reconciliation with 19X1 and 19X2 Calculations:

	19X1			19X2	Total
	As Measured, 12/31/X1 Dollars	Translation Factor	Restated, 12/31/X2 Dollars	As Measured, 12/31/X2 Dollars	12/31/X2 Dollars
Net operating income	$9,429	240/220	$10,286	$13,500	$23,786
Monetary loss	1,429	240/220	1,559	2,727	4,286
Net income	$8,000	240/220	$ 8,727	$10,773	$19,500

Replacent Cost Model—Nominal Dollars

Since the valuation alternative reviewed above is concerned with "correcting" conventional accounting valuations for changes in the general purchasing power (i.e., the size) of the monetary unit, it focuses on changes in the general level of prices. In view of the concern only with the size of the monetary unit, general price-level-adjusted conventional accounting quite properly ignores the differences between price changes for specific assets and the change in the general price-level index. We now turn our attention to the replacement cost model, which focuses on one form of *specific price changes*.

If the assets and liabilities of a firm are valued at their end-of-period replacement costs each period, and assuming no transactions with owners during the period, replacement-cost-based net income for a period is the difference between beginning and ending owners' equity. For our example, this is calculated as follows:

	19X1	19X2
Ending owners' equity:		
Cash	$30,000	$67,500
Inventory	26,000	-0-
	$56,000	$67,500
Beginning owners' equity:		
Cash	$40,000	$30,000
Inventory	-0-	26,000
	$40,000	$56,000
Replacement-cost-based net income	$16,000	$11,500

The total net income for the two years, $27,500, is equal to the amount calculated under the conventional accounting model (in nominal dollars). This equivalence is the result of constructing the example so that the firm is back to a "cash-only" position at the end of the second year. Selection of a different attribute to be measured produces different asset values, and thus different measures of income (as is illustrated by comparing the income measures for the individual years). But when the firm is in a "cash-only" position, the net assets of the firm are valued the same under all of the alternative models and equivalence of income measures *over the total period* results.

In addition to measuring net income in terms of the change in net assets, we can also calculate net income in terms of the various income statement components. To do this, we need the values for realized holding gains during 19X1 and 19X2, and the change in unrealized holding gains over each of the years. These are calculated as follows:

	Original Transaction Value	Replacement Cost	Holding Gain
Realized holding gain on cost of sales:			
19X1	$20,000	$24,000	$ 4,000
19X2	20,000	30,000	10,000
	$40,000	$54,000	$14,000

continued from page 646

	Original Transaction Value	Replacement Cost	Holding Gain
Unrealized holding gain on ending inventory at:			
12/31/X1	$20,000	$26,000	$ 6,000
12/31/X2	$ -0-	$ -0-	$ -0-
Change in unrealized holding gain for:			
19X1 ($6,000 − $ -0-) = $6,000			
19X2 ($ -0- − $6,000) = $(6,000)			

With these values in hand, and noting that the cost of sales for each of the years on a replacement cost basis is also provided above, the replacement-cost-based income statements for 19X1 and 19X2 are constructed in Exhibit 16-6. As we noted in Chapter 14, the replacement cost income statement divides conventional accounting net income into two major components: (1) current operating income, which is the difference between realized revenues and expenses valued at their replacement costs at time of consumption, and (2) realized holding gains, which is the difference between expenses valued at replacement costs and expenses valued at original transaction values. When the change in the unrealized holding gains over the period is added (or subtracted), we obtain replacement-cost-based net income. Observe that over the life of any particular asset, or set of assets, the change in unrealized holding gains will sum to zero. Additionally, recall that the sum of the realized holding gains and the change in the unrealized holding gains for any period will measure the total holding gains that were generated during the period.

The measure of performance for the period is normally assumed to be given by current operating income. Use of this value for the performance measurement is based upon two important assumptions. First, we assume that the market price for the output of a firm adjusts contemporaneously with changes in the current entry prices for the factors of production, as opposed to a price

Exhibit 16-6

BLUE WATER YACHT SALES, INC.

Income Statements
(Replacement Cost Model—Nominal Dollars)
For the First Two Years of Operations

	19X1	19X2	Total
Sales	$30,000	$37,500	$67,500
Cost of sales	24,000	30,000	54,000
Current operating income	$ 6,000	$ 7,500	$13,500
Realized holding gains	4,000	10,000	14,000
Realized income (conventional accounting net income)	$10,000	$17,500	$27,500
Change in unrealized holding gains	6,000	(6,000)	-0-
Net income	$16,000	$11,500	$27,500

adjustment only after the new prices have been paid in an exchange transaction. In this example, that assumption seems justified. Second, by excluding the holding gains from our performance measurement, we are assuming that a firm's past ability to generate holding gains cannot be consistently replicated in the future. The validity of this assumption cannot be judged in this example. Furthermore, in general, this is an assessment that the investor must make for each firm he or she is evaluating.

Choice of the income statement component to be used as the measure of disposable wealth depends first upon the capital maintenance concept that has been adopted. If the capital maintenance concept adopted is physical capital, then the measure of disposable wealth should indicate how much can be distributed and still maintain the physical operating capability that the firm possessed at the start of the period. Viewing our example in terms of the total two-year period, Blue Water Yacht Sales began with an inventory of two PW-30s. Thus, any distribution of wealth at December 31, 19X2, should leave sufficient resources to acquire two new boats for inventory. Normally, current operating income is considered to provide such a measure. However, we observed in Chapter 14 that this value sometimes overstates the actual distributable wealth because of increases in the replacement cost of assets (usually property, plant, and equipment) subsequent to the time that they were consumed but before they were actually replaced. Because of the simplifying assumptions that were invoked in this example, that phenomenon is present here. The total current operating income for the two-year period is $13,500. But if that amount were distributed, the firm would have cash of only $54,000 remaining, and this would be insufficient to acquire two new PW-30s at $30,000 each. This situation arose because Blue Water Yacht Sales did not replace the first PW-30 at the time it was sold in 19X1. Thus the indicated disposable wealth of $13,500 would have to be further adjusted downward for the additional $6,000 needed to replace the two boats at this time. The necessity for annual remedial adjustments of this type is one of the practical problems associated with adoption of the physical capital concept of the firm.

If the financial capital concept is adopted, the disposable wealth for the two-year period is $27,500, the same as it is under the conventional accounting model measured in nominal dollars. This equivalence is due to the "cash-only" condition at the end of the two years. However, when the individual years are examined, choice of the disposable wealth measure depends upon whether the test of realization is imposed. If it is, then replacement-cost-based realized income, which is equal to conventional accounting net income, provides the measure of disposable wealth. However, if no realization test is imposed upon the distributability of the holding gains, then replacement-cost-based net income provides the measure of disposable wealth and, in this example, would indicate distributable income of $16,000 and $11,500 in 19X1 and 19X2, respectively.

Replacement Cost Model—Units of Purchasing Power

Adjustment of the replacement-cost-based income statements for changes in the value of the dollar is illustrated in Exhibit 16-7. In this example we are able to identify precisely the dollars in which each revenue and expense item is measured, and we can adjust them correspondingly. In most practical applications we would expect that revenues and replacement-cost-based expenses would normally be measured in average dollars of the current period, assuming that there is relatively uniform economic activity and changes in replacement prices over the period. If either of these assumptions is not warranted, the typical practical response would be to make adjustments based on average price changes to quarterly or monthly data, the assumption being that averages for such shorter periods would probably be justified.

A special type of adjustment procedure has to be applied to the unrealized and realized holding gains in Exhibit 16-7 because each of these measures is the result of taking the difference between two values—the replacement cost value of the asset or expense, and the corresponding original transaction value. Thus, each of the components of the measure has to be individually adjusted for changes in the value of the dollar. Once the individual components have been adjusted, the difference is measured in dollars of the desired point in time, and it can then be adjusted to dollars of some other point in time without readjusting the components. This property is utilized in restating the unrealized holding gain at December 31, 19X1, in 19X1 dollars into the unrealized holding gain at January 1, 19X2, in 19X2 dollars (the same unrealized gain restated from 19X1 to 19X2 dollars), and also in restating the 19X1 income statement in 19X1 dollars into 19X2 dollars.

Note also that when the unit of measure is purchasing power, the gain or loss from holding monetary items is an economic fact that must be measured and reported in the income statement. Since the only monetary asset held by Blue Water Yacht Sales is cash, and it is valued the same under all the alternative valuation models, the measure of the monetary loss for the period will be same in all the models. Thus the monetary loss of $1,429 for 19X1 and $2,727 for 19X2 calculated in Exhibit 16-5 is included in the income statements in Exhibit 16-7 prepared under the replacement cost model using units of purchasing power. Also, as was the case for the two-year totals measured in nominal dollars, the two-year net income in units of purchasing power (in 12/31/X2 dollars) under the replacement cost model, $19,500, is equal to the two-year net income under the conventional accounting model measured in units of purchasing power (see Exhibit 16-5). This equivalence is again the result of the now-familiar reason—an ending "cash-only" condition.

It will be recalled from our discussion in Chapter 14 that the purpose of restating the performance measure from prior periods into dollars of the current period is to enhance the comparability of the performance measurement—a factor that may be important in evaluating the trend of a firm's indicated long-run cash-generating ability. Adjustment of the replacement cost values for purposes of assessing disposable wealth again depends upon the capital maintenance concept. When the physical capital of the firm is the criterion wealth level that we wish to preserve, general price-level adjustments are unnecessary because this capital maintenance point of view essentially shifts the unit of measure from dollars to physical resources, and current operating income is regarded as an estimate of the amount of physical resources that can be distributed at the end of the period in end-of-period prices (dollars). If, however, we are working with a criterion wealth level of financial capital, adjustment for changes in the general price level would be justified under the same circumstances as under the conventional accounting model—i.e., when the focus of interest is purchasing power rather than nominal dollars.

Exhibit 16-7

BLUE WATER YACHT SALES, INC.

Income Statements
(Replacement Cost Model—Units of Purchasing Power)
For the First Two Years of Operations

	19X1 (Measured in 12/31/X1 Dollars)			19X2 (Measured in 12/31/X2 Dollars)		
Sales	($30,000 × 220/210)		$31,429	($37,500 × 240/240)		$37,500
Cost of sales	($24,000 × 220/210)		25,143	($30,000 × 240/240)		30,000
Current operating income			$ 6,286			$ 7,500
Realized holding gains:						
Current replacement cost	($24,000 × 220/210)	$25,143		($30,000 × 240/240)	$30,000	
Original transaction value	($20,000 × 220/200)	22,000	3,143	($20,000 × 240/200)	24,000	6,000
Monetary loss (from Exhibit 16-5)			(1,429)			(2,727)
Realized income (general price-level-adjusted conventional accounting net income)			$ 8,000			$10,773
Change in unrealized holding gains (see below)			4,000			(4,364)
Net income			$12,000			$ 6,409

Change in Unrealized Holding Gains:

	19X1 (Measured in 12/31/X1 Dollars)			19X2 (Measured in 12/31/X2 Dollars)		
Unrealized holding gain, 1/1			$ -0-	($ 4,000 × 240/220)		$ 4,364
Unrealized holding gain, 12/31:						
Inventory, at current replacement cost	($26,000 × 220/220)		$26,000			$ -0-
Inventory, at original transaction value	($20,000 × 220/200)		22,000			-0-
			$ 4,000			$ -0-
Change in unrealized holding gains			$ 4,000			$(4,364)

650

Exhibit 16-7 (cont.)

Net income, in 12/31/X2 dollars:

Ending owners' equity, in 12/31/X2 dollars	$67,500
Beginning owners' equity, in 12/31/X2 dollars ($40,000 × 240/200)	48,000
Net income	$19,500

Reconciliation with 19X1 and 19X2 Calculations:

	19X1			19X2	Total for 19X1 and 19X2
	As Measured, 12/31/X1 Dollars	Translation Factor	Restated 12/31/X2 Dollars	As Measured, 12/31/X2 Dollars	Total 12/31/X2 Dollars
Sales	$31,429	240/220	$34,286	$37,500	$71,786
Cost of sales	25,143	240/220	27,429	30,000	57,429
Current operating income	$ 6,286	240/220	$ 6,857	$ 7,500	$14,357
Realized holding gains	3,143	240/220	3,429	6,000	9,429
Monetary loss	(1,429)	240/220	(1,559)	(2,727)	(4,286)
Realized income (general price-level-adjusted conventional accounting net income)	$ 8,000	240/220	$ 8,727	$10,773	$19,500
Change in unrealized holding gains	4,000	240/220	4,364	(4,364)	-0-
Net income	$12,000		$13,091	$ 6,409	$19,500

Current Market-Value Model—Nominal Dollars

The second form of current exchange price that is used as the basis of an accounting model is the current exit price (market value) of an asset. Use of exit prices is largely motivated by a dissatisfaction with the conventional model view that a sale transaction is the "critical event" in determining the period in which the value produced by the enterprise is recognized. Advocates of the market-value model argue that to measure actual performance for a period, it is necessary to measure *all increases (or decreases)* in the value of a firm's resources—evidenced by current market values of those resources—not just those that were confirmed by a sale to outside parties or recognized as replacement costs change. When applied to assets held for investment that are readily marketable in an organized market, this notion of performance is appealing. Whether it is equally appealing when applied to assets held for sale, particularly where the market is "thin" as is the case for the sailboats held by Blue Water Yacht Sales, is a questionable matter.

The current market-value-based income statements for Blue Water Yacht Sales, Inc., are presented in Exhibit 16-8. Note that two "exit" prices are provided for the PW-30 on hand at the end of 19X1: (1) an estimated immediate-sale (orderly liquidation) price of $28,000, and (2) an expected 19X2 selling price of $32,500. As was discussed in Chapter 15, the current market-value model is based upon exit prices in orderly liquidation, and thus the $28,000 value is used in the 19X1 income statement in arriving at the "increase in market value of inventory" of $8,000. Also, with regard to statement format, the boat sold each year is reported in "sales" and "cost of sales" to provide comparability with the other valuation alternatives. Thus the "increase in market value" component of a current market-value income statement relates only to inventory on hand at the end of the period. In this example, inventory was on hand only at the end of 19X1. But since the income statement for 19X1 recognized the increase in value of the PW-30 on hand at the end of the year from $20,000 to $28,000, the cost of sales for this boat in 19X2 reflected this higher recognized value. Thus, for both years, the excess of sales over cost of sales shows the increase in value from the beginning of the year to the date of sale for the boat sold.

Under the current market-value model, the measures of performance and disposable wealth are provided by the net income for the year (assuming no

Exhibit 16-8

BLUE WATER YACHT SALES, INC.

Income Statements
(Current Market-Value Model—Nominal Dollars)
For the First Two Years of Operations

	19X1	19X2	Total
Sales	$30,000	$37,500	$67,500
Cost of sales	20,000	28,000	48,000
	$10,000	$ 9,500	$19,500
Increase in market value of inventory	8,000	-0-	8,000
Net income	$18,000	$ 9,500	$27,500

extraordinary gains or losses). This choice incorporates increases (or decreases) that have not been "realized" through sale transactions, but this seems reasonable since it is dissatisfaction with the sale as a critical event in measuring performance of the firm that motivates the use of the model. As in the replacement cost model measured in nominal dollars, the total net income for the two years is equal to the amount measured under the conventional accounting model because of the ending "cash-only" condition. But the net income for each of the two individual years differs from the conventional accounting and replacement cost models because we are measuring a different attribute of assets and taking a different point of view as to what constitutes performance.

Current Market Value—Units of Purchasing Power

Adjustment of the current market-value-based income statements for changes in the value of the dollar is illustrated in Exhibit 16-10. Most of the characteristics of this adjustment process that were noted earlier in the discussion of adjusting the replacement cost model for changes in the value of the dollar are again present. Shifting the unit of measure to units of purchasing power introduces the monetary loss from holding cash. Additionally, the total net income for the two-year period, $19,500 measured in 12/31/X2 dollars, is the same under the current market-value model as it was for the conventional accounting and the replacement cost models because of the ending "cash-only" position. But of course the measure of net income for the individual years is different from that produced by the other models.

Recap of Income Measures

The income measures produced for this illustration under the alternative valuation models are summarized in Exhibit 16-9. The summary highlights the variation that can result in each of the two years depending upon which valua-

Exhibit 16-9

BLUE WATER YACHT SALES, INC.

Comparison of Income Measures

	Nominal Dollars			Units of Purchasing Power			
				19X1		19X2	Total
	19X1	19X2	Total	12/31/X1 Dollars	12/31/X2 Dollars	12/31/X2 Dollars	12/31/X2 Dollars
Conventional accounting model net income	$10,000	$17,500	$27,500	$ 8,000	$ 8,727	$10,773	$19,500
Replacement cost model:							
Current operating income	6,000	7,500	13,500	6,286	6,857	7,500	14,357
Realized income	10,000	17,500	27,500	8,000	8,727	10,773	19,500
Net income	16,000	11,500	27,500	12,000	13,091	6,409	19,500
Current market-value model net income	18,000	9,500	27,500	14,000	15,273	4,227	19,500

Exhibit 16-10

BLUE WATER YACHT SALES, INC.

Income Statements
(Current Market-Value Model—Units of Purchasing Power)
For the First Two Years of Operations

	19X1 (Measured in 12/31/X1 Dollars)		19X2 (Measured in 12/31/X2 Dollars)	
Sales	($30,000 × 220/210)	$31,429	($37,500 × 240/240)	$37,500
Cost of sales	($20,000 × 220/200)	22,000	($28,000 × 240/220)	30,546
		$ 9,429		$ 6,954
Increase in market value of inventory:				
December 31 value	($28,000 × 220/220)	$28,000		
January 1 value	($20,000 × 220/200)	22,000		
		6,000		-0-
Monetary loss (from Exhibit 16-5)		(1,429)		(2,727)
Net income		$14,000		$ 4,227

Total for 19X1 and 19X2

Net income, in 12/31/X2 dollars:
Ending owners' equity, in 12/31/X2 dollars: $67,500
Beginning owners' equity, in 12/31/X2 dollars (40,000 × 240/200) 48,000
Net income $19,500

Reconciliation with 19X1 and 19X2 Calculations:

	19X1			19X2	
	As Measured, 12/31/X1 Dollars	Translation Factor	Restated 12/31/X2 Dollars	As Measured, 12/31/X2 Dollars	Total 12/31/X2 Dollars
Sales	$31,429	240/220	$34,287	$37,500	$71,787
Cost of sales	22,000	240/220	24,000	30,546	54,546
	$ 9,429	240/220	$10,287	$ 6,954	$17,241
Increase in market value of inventory	6,000	240/220	6,545	-0-	6,545
Monetary loss	(1,429)	240/220	(1,559)	(2,727)	(4,286)
Net income	$14,000	240/220	$15,273	$ 4,227	$19,500

tion model is chosen. The equality of the two-year totals for each of the units of measure is a consequence of the particular circumstances of the example and would not occur in most practical situations. Additionally, the relative size of the income measures under the various alternatives is also a consequence of the price-change assumptions of the case. Under a different set of facts, a valuation methodology that produced lower measures of net income in this illustration might generate higher measures. When the income measures differ between valuation alternatives, we know that the values reflected in the statement of financial position will also differ, although such statements were not summarized in this example.

Questions for Review and Discussion

16-1. The choice among alternative financial accounting models is a social choice problem. Explain what this means. What are the implications for choosing the optimum alternative (or set of alternatives)?

16-2. In attempting to select one of the valuation models for a particular application, the usefulness criterion has often been invoked. Explain briefly the problems associated with this approach.

16-3. For each alternative valuation model, try to construct one simple, hypothetical business circumstance for which that model would seem to be poorly suited to investment decisions based on the decision-relevance criterion. For each of these circumstances, which of the valuation models seems to be most decision relevant? How would the objectivity criterion influence your choice?

16-4. Under the logical approach to selecting an optimum financial accounting model, the concepts underlying the production of information under the model presumably have to be in harmony, to some degree at least, with the specific needs of specific decision problems. Some people believe that this requirement precludes accountants from producing aggregate information that is applicable to a broad general class of decision problems. By aggregating or summarizing the results of individual transactions under a particular set of concepts, the accountant does not give the user the opportunity to "reassemble" the data under a different set of concepts. One possible alternative is, of course, to communicate a large volume of less highly summarized transaction data (the extreme form of which is sometimes disparagingly referred to as a "memory dump"). Evaluate this alternative in the context of the "choice among accounting alternatives" dilemma.

16-5. This chapter discusses the problems of choice among financial accounting models but does not resolve the problem. Do you see any social advantages or disadvantages of simply *not* resolving the problem in favor of one model or set of models under which all similar businesses must report?

16-6. The different wealth assessments and measures of performance and disposable wealth that are produced by the alternative financial accounting models are a consequence of the choices that are made on three basic accounting measurement issues. Explain briefly these three issues.

16-7. Enumerate the five attributes, or properties, of assets and liabilities that have been identified by the Financial Accounting Standards Board as having some support from those interested in the financial accounting process.

16-8. The alternative attributes of assets and liabilities that might be selected for measurement can be viewed from three different classificational perspectives. Describe briefly these three classificational schemes.

16-9. Identify the financial accounting model that results from combining each of the five alternative attributes being considered by the Financial Accounting Standards Board with the two alternative units of measure under consideration.

16-10. Describe briefly the two capital maintenance concepts that have been considered in this book.

16-11. Explain the relationship between the choice of a capital maintenance concept and the choice of an attribute to be measured.

16-12. The Financial Accounting Standards Board has tentatively made certain choices on the basic measurement issues in its proposed standard "Financial Reporting and Changing Prices." Explain briefly these choices.

16-13. Explain briefly the basic asset valuation concept labeled "value to the business." How is it implemented in the Financial Accounting Standards Board's proposed standard "Financial Reporting and Changing Prices"?

16-14. Valuation of assets is an important topic in accounting theory. Suggested valuation methods include the following:
    a. Historical cost (past purchase price)
    b. Historical cost adjusted to reflect general price-level changes
    c. Discounted cash flow (future exchange prices)
    d. Market price (current selling prices)
    e. Replacement cost (current purchase prices)

Why is the valuation of assets a significant issue? Explain the basic theory underlying *each* of the valuation methods cited above. (Do *not* discuss advantages and disadvantages of each method.)

(AICPA adapted)

16-15. Published financial statements of United States companies are currently prepared on a stable-dollar assumption even though the general purchasing power of the dollar has declined considerably because of inflation in recent years. To account for this changing value of the dollar, many accountants suggest that financial statements should be adjusted for general price-level changes. Three independent, unrelated statements regarding general price-level-adjusted financial statements follow. Each statement contains some fallacious reasoning.

Statement I

The accounting profession has not seriously considered price-level-adjusted financial statements before because the rate of inflation usually has been so small from year to year that the adjustments would have been immaterial in amount. Price-level-adjusted financial statements represent a departure from the historical-cost basis of accounting. Financial statements should be prepared from facts, not estimates.

Statement II

If financial statements were adjusted for general price-level changes, depreciation charges in the earnings statement would permit the recovery of dollars of current purchasing power and, thereby, equal the cost of new assets to replace the old ones. General price-level-adjusted data would yield statement-of-financial-position amounts closely approximating current values. Furthermore, management can make better decisions if general price-level-adjusted financial statements are published.

Statement III

When adjusting financial data for general price-level changes, a distinction must be made between monetary and nonmonetary assets and liabilities, which, under the historical-cost basis of accounting, have been identified as "current" and "noncurrent." When using the historical-cost basis of accounting, no purchasing-power gain or loss is recognized in the accounting process, but when financial statements are adjusted for general price-level changes, a purchasing-power gain or loss will be recognized on monetary and nonmonetary items.

Evaluate each of the independent statements and identify the areas of fallacious reasoning in each and explain why the reasoning is incorrect.

(AICPA adapted)

16-16. *Part a.* Advocates of current value accounting propose several methods for determining the valuation of assets to approximate current values. Two of the methods proposed are replacement cost and present value of future cash flows.

Required:

Describe each of the two methods cited above and discuss the pros and cons of the various procedures used to arrive at the valuation for each method.

Part b. The financial statements of a business entity could be prepared by using historical cost or current value as a basis. In addition, the basis could be stated in terms of unadjusted dollars or dollars restated for changes in purchasing power. The various permutations of these two separate and distinct areas are shown in the following matrix:

	Unadjusted Dollars	Dollars Restated for Changes in Purchasing Power
Historical cost	1	2
Current value	3	4

Block number 1 of the matrix represents the traditional method of accounting for transactions in accounting today, wherein the absolute (unadjusted) amount of dollars given up or received is recorded for the asset or liability obtained (*relationship between resources*). Amounts recorded in the method described in block number 1 reflect the original cost of the asset or liability and do not give effect to any change in value of the unit of measure (*standard of comparison*). This method assumes the validity of the accounting concepts of going concern and stable monetary unit. Any gain or loss (including holding and purchasing power gains or losses) resulting from the sale or satisfaction of amounts recorded under this method is deferred in its entirety until sale or satisfaction.

Required:

For each of the remaining matrix blocks (2, 3 and 4) respond to the following questions. *Limit your discussion to nonmonetary assets only.*

1. How will this method of recording assets affect the relationship between resources and the standard of comparison?
2. What is the theoretic justification for using each method?
3. How will each method of asset valuation affect the recognition of gain or loss during the life of the asset and ultimately from the sale or abandonment of the asset? Your response should include a discussion of the timing and magnitude of the gain or loss and conceptual reasons for any difference from the gain or loss computed using the traditional method.

(AICPA adapted)

16-17. Select the best answer for each of the following questions:
   1. Following are four observations regarding the amounts reported in financial statements that have been adjusted for general price-level changes. Which observation is valid?
      a. The amount obtained by adjusting an asset's cost for general price-level changes usually approximates its current fair value.
      b. The amounts adjusted for general price-level changes are *not* departures from historical cost.
      c. When inventory increases and prices are rising, last-in, first-out (Lifo) inventory accounting has the same effect on financial statements as amounts adjusted for general price-level changes.

d. When inventory remains constant and prices are rising, Lifo inventory accounting has the same effect on financial statements as amounts adjusted for general price-level changes.
2. An accountant who recommends the adjustment of financial statements for general price-level changes should *not* support his recommendation by stating that
   a. Purchasing power gains or losses should be recognized.
   b. Historical dollars are not comparable to present-day dollars.
   c. The conversion of asset costs to a common-dollar basis is a useful extension of the original cost basis of asset valuation.
   d. Assets should be valued at their replacement cost.

(AICPA adapted)

Exercises

16-1. Replacement Cost and General Price-Level Conventional Accounting Contrasted. Valuation to reflect general price-level adjustments of conventional accounting measures, as opposed to replacement cost measures, would yield differing amounts on a firm's financial statements.

Several transactions concerning one asset of a calendar-year company are summarized as follows:

1978	Purchased land for $40,000 cash on December 31. Replacement cost at year-end was $40,000.
1979	Held this land all year. Replacement cost at year-end was $52,000.
1980	Sold this land for $68,000 on December 31.

General price-level index:

December 31, 1978	100
December 31, 1979	110
December 31, 1980	120

Required:

Duplicate the following schedules and complete the information required based upon the transactions and events described above.

Valuation of Land on Statement of Financial Position	Historical Cost (Units of Purchasing Power)	Replacement Cost (Nominal Dollars)
December 31, 1978		
December 31, 1979		

Gains (Realized or Unrealized) on Income Statement	Historical Cost (Units of Purchasing Power)	Replacement Cost (Nominal Dollars)
1978		
1979		
1980		
Total		

(AICFA adapted)

16-2. Replacement Cost versus Market Value. Phil McCavity graduated from dental school two years ago. After one year of working with another dentist, he decided to set up his own practice. His transactions during the first year of his practice are as follows:
- a. Opened a bank account for his practice and deposited $5,000. At the same time he negotiated a loan of $25,000 to be repaid over the next ten years at $2,500 at year-end each year. Interest on the loan is 10 percent per annum on the beginning-of-year balance, payable as of the end of each year.
- b. Purchased dental tools and equipment with an expected useful life of ten years and zero salvage value for $20,000.
- c. Purchased office furniture with an expected useful life of five years and zero salvage value for $5,000.
- d. Paid rent monthly at $500 per month.
- e. Paid receptionist $625 per month.
- f. Purchased general dental supplies for $2,000, all of which were used during the year.
- g. Billed patients $30,000. Of this amount, $2,000 was outstanding (i.e., unpaid) at year-end.
- h. Repaid $2,500 on loan, together with the interest due.

No general price change occurred throughout the year. However, if McCavity wished to replace (new) his tools and equipment and his office furniture at year-end, it would cost him $24,000 and $6,000 respectively, to do so. On the other hand, if he wished to sell his tools and equipment and his office furniture at year-end, he could expect to realize $14,000 and $2,500, respectively.

Required:

1. (a) If McCavity were to use the current replacement cost model for accounting purposes, at what amount would the dental tools and equipment and the office furniture be shown in the ending balance sheet?
   (b) Prepare a replacement-cost-based income statement for the year. (Calculate depreciation expense on the basis of the replacement cost at the end of the year.)
2. (a) If McCavity were to use the current market-value model for accounting purposes, at what amount would the dental tools and equipment and the office furniture be shown in the ending balance sheet?

(b) Prepare a market-value-based income statement for the year. (*Hint: Base depreciation on the decline in market values.*)

16-3. Conventional Accounting, Market Value Accounting, and General Price-Level Adjustments. At the beginning of 1975 the Small Investment Company invested $100,000 (all of its owners' equity) in bonds that paid 8 percent interest at the end of each year, with the principal of $100,000 to be returned at the end of 1990. It held the bonds as market interest rates gradually rose until finally it sold the bonds at the end of 1979 for $90,000. The market values of the bonds at the end of each of the intervening years were as follows:

Year	Market Value
1975	$ 101,000
1976	100,000
1977	93,000
1978	88,000

Assume that the cash received as interest income is immediately distributed to the owners of Small Investment Company as a dividend at the end of each year.

Required:

1. Calculate the net income that would have been recognized in each year and in total for the five-year period under (*a*) conventional accounting and (*b*) the market-value model.

2. During the period that this investment was held, the general price-level index took on the following values:

Beginning of 1975	100
End of:	
1975	100
1976	100
1977	110
1978	110
1979	125

Assume that Small Investment Company demanded an 8 percent rate of return at the beginning of 1975, based on the assumption of no inflation. In retrospect, how much would it have paid at the beginning of 1975 for the bonds if it knew it was going to collect $8,000 interest each year and sell the bonds at the end of 1979 for $90,000 of lesser purchasing power?

3. Assuming again that Small Investment Company paid $100,000 for the bonds, and using the general price-level index numbers from number 2 above, calculate the net income that would have been recognized in each year and in total for the five-year period under (*a*) conventional accounting and (*b*) the market-value model, *both adjusted for changes in the purchasing power of the dollar.*

16-4. Comprehensive Comparative Accounting Exercise. During her first year of practice, Wilma Jones, M.D., prepared the following conventional accounting worksheet:

Date	Description	Cash	Supplies Inventory	Equipment	Accumulated Depreciation	Owners' Equity
1/1	Original investment	100,000				100,000
1/1	Purchased equipment	(60,000)		60,000		
1/1	Purchased initial stock of medical supplies	(20,000)	20,000			
1/1–12/31	Fees for medical services received uniformly throughout year	90,000				90,000 (R)
1/1–12/31	Paid employee wages uniformly throughout year	(27,000)				(27,000) (E)
12/31	Cost of supplies used		(12,000)			(12,000) (E)
12/31	Depreciation expense				(12,000)	(12,000) (E)
	Balances	83,000	8,000	60,000	(12,000)	139,000

Required:

1. What is the conventional accounting net income for Dr. Jones's first year of operations?

2. The general price-level index was 80 at the start of the year and 100 at the end of the year, and the average index for the year was 90.
   (a) What is the price-level-adjusted net income for the year?
   (b) What is the price-level-adjusted operating income for the year?
   (c) What is the amount of monetary gain or loss for the year? Indicate whether it is a gain or a loss.

3. On December 31 the replacement cost (new) for the equipment was $90,000, and there was no change in the price of the medical supplies. Prepare replacement-cost-based income statements for the year, expressed in (a) nominal dollars and (b) units of purchasing power (using end-of-year dollars). Calculate depreciation expense for the year on the basis of the end-of-year replacement cost. (Hint: In the units of purchasing power calculation, note that since the replacement price of supplies did not change during the year, the cost of supplies used on a replacement cost basis equals the cost of supplies used on an original transaction value basis, but the replacement-cost-based cost is expressed in *average* dollars of the period.)

4. On December 31 the estimated current exit prices were $5,000 for the inventory of medical supplies and $30,000 for the equipment. Prepare market-value-based income statements for the year, expressed in (a) nominal dollars and (b) purchasing power units (in end-of-year dollars).

16-5. Comprehensive Comparative Accounting Exercise. During her first year of business Joan Smith, who repairs jewelry and watches, prepared the following conventional accounting worksheet:

Date	Description	Cash	Supplies Inventory	Equipment	Accumulated Depreciation	Owners' Equity
1/1	Original investment	100,000				100,000
1/1	Purchased equipment	(60,000)		60,000		
1/1	Purchased initial stock of supplies	(20,000)	20,000			
1/1–12/31	Fees for repair services received uniformly throughout year	135,000				135,000 (R)
1/1–12/31	Purchased supplies uniformly throughout year	(40,000)	40,000			
1/1–12/31	Paid employee wages uniformly throughout year	(27,000)				(27,000) (E)
12/31	Cost of supplies used		(51,000)			(51,000) (E)
12/31	Depreciation expense				(12,000)	(12,000) (E)
	Balances	88,000	9,000	60,000	(12,000)	145,000

Required:

1. What is the conventional accounting net income for Ms. Smith's first year of operations?

2. The general price-level index was 90 at the start of the year and 120 at the end of the year, and the average index for the year was 100. Assume the ending inventory of supplies consists of supplies purchased at the average index for the year. (*Hint:* This means that the cost of supplies used consists of a *mixture* of beginning-of-year index dollars *and* average index dollars.)
   (a) What is the price-level-adjusted net income for the year?
   (b) What is the price-level-adjusted operating income for the year?
   (c) What is the amount of monetary gain or loss for the year? Indicate whether it is a gain or a loss.

3. The following replacement cost information was compiled:

   Replacement cost at December 31:

   Supplies inventory $10,000
   Equipment (new) $80,000

   Replacement-cost-based cost of supplies used for the year was $53,000.

   Using this information, prepare a replacement-cost-based income statement for the year measured in nominal dollars. Calculate depreciation expense on the basis of the average replacement cost of equipment, assuming that the replacement price increased uniformly over the year.

4. On December 31 the estimated current exit prices were $6,000 for the

inventory of supplies and $30,000 for the equipment. Calculate market-value-based net income for the year, measured both in nominal dollars and in units of purchasing power.

5. Which of the two current-exchange-price valuation models do you believe provides the more useful and relevant measure of income for Ms. Smith's first year of operations? Why?

16-6. Comprehensive Comparative Accounting Exercise. On January 1, 19X1, David Wilson signed an agreement with Executive Aircraft, Inc., to market its new airplane in the Houston, Texas, area. As part of the agreement, David purchased two of the planes at a price of $125,000 each. The planes were to be delivered within ten days to Wilson, Inc., which David had incorporated in late December with an initial cash investment of $250,000.

Relevant 19X1 transactions and price information are as follows:

Sold one plane in the middle of the year for $200,000, at which time the replacement cost for the plane was $140,000.

Price data at end of year:

Estimated replacement cost—$150,000
Estimated immediate-sale (orderly liquidation) price—$180,000
Expected 19X2 selling price—$225,000

General price-level index increased uniformly over the period from 180 to 198, with an average for the period of 190

Assume that Wilson, Inc., did not have any operating expenses for the year, and that the cash received from the sale of the plane was deposited in a non-interest-bearing checking account. No dividends were paid during the year.

Required:

Prepare income statements for 19X1 for Wilson, Inc., measured in *both* nominal dollars and units of purchasing power (expressed in December 31, 19X1, dollars), under (a) the conventional accounting model, (b) the replacement cost model, and (c) the market-value model.

16-7. Comprehensive Comparative Accounting Exercise. Referring to the data in Exercise 16-6, assume that the relevant 19X2 transactions and price information for Wilson, Inc., are as follows:

Sold the second plane at the end of 19X2 for $240,000, at which time the replacement cost for the plane was $190,000.

General price-level index increased uniformly over the period from 198 to 216, with an average for the period of 207.

Assume again that Wilson, Inc., did not have any operating expenses for the year, and that the cash received from the sale of the plane in 19X1 was left in the non-interest-bearing checking account. Also, no dividends were paid in 19X2.

Required:

Prepare income statements for 19X2 and for the two-year period for Wilson, Inc., measured in *both* nominal dollars and units of purchasing power (expressed in December 31, 19X2 dollars), under (*a*) the conventional accounting model, (*b*) the replacement cost model, and (*c*) the market-value model.

16-8. Comprehensive Comparative Accounting Exercise. On January 1, 1980, the A & B Company was incorporated with an initial cash investment of $45,000, with the purpose of marketing a new limited-production sports car. The company took delivery of three cars (all identical) on January 15 at a price of $15,000 each. Relevant 1980 transactions and price information are summarized below.

Sold two cars, as follows:

	Replacement Cost at Date of Sale	Selling Price
July 1, 1980	$ 16,000	$ 22,500
December 24, 1980	17,500	24,000

Price data at end of year:

Estimated replacement cost—$17,500

Estimated current exit price—$21,500

General price-level index increased uniformly over the period from 150 to 165, with an average for the period of 157.

At December 31, 1980, the company had not replaced either of the two cars that it had sold, and the proceeds of sale remained in the firm's checking account. No dividends were paid in 1980, and the company had no operating expenses.

Required:

Prepare income statements for 1980 for A & B Company, measured in *both* nominal dollars and units of purchasing power (expressed in December 31, 1980, dollars), under (*a*) the conventional accounting model, (*b*) the replacement cost model, and (*c*) the market-value model.

16-9. Price-Level Depreciation and Maintenance of Capital. The income statement from an annual report of Indiana Telephone Corporation appears on pages 667–8. The "Column B" figures on the statement constitute historical cost (original transaction cost) figures adjusted for changes in the purchasing power of the dollar, stated in end-of-year dollars. Following is Note 2 to the financial statements from the same annual report.

2. Recovery of Capital and Return on Capital

Under the law of Indiana, the Corporation is entitled to recover the fair value of its property used and useful in public service by accruing depreciation based on the "fair value" thereof and is entitled to earn a fair return on such "fair value." The amount shown in Column B for telephone plant approximates the fair value of the property as determined based on the principles followed by the Public Service Commission of Indiana in an order dated September 1, 1967, authorizing the Corporation to increase its subscriber rates.

In the accompanying financial statements, Column A includes depreciation expense based on historical cost and Column B includes depreciation expense, as well as other expenses, on the basis of historical cost repriced in current dollars to reflect the changes in the purchasing power of the dollar. Also, the annual reports to the Indiana Commission are in the same basic form shown herein.

It must be kept in mind that this determination of depreciation expense is a year-to-year estimate and there are involved the questions of obsolescence, foresight, and judgment giving due consideration to maintenance but the regulatory process does not adjust even to this accurately.

If use of property, obsolescence and current denominators (in the case of monetary inflation) are used accurately by way of keeping the allowable expense of depreciation current and rates sufficient to return it along with a fair return, and the proceeds are immediately invested in property used and useful in the public service, there more likely will be a real return of capital and a fair return thereon. However, if monetary inflation continues, as it usually does, purchasing power of capital is unlikely ever to be truly returned. It must be observed there is a substantial lag in the regulatory process. In rate making there is no guarantee of recovery of capital or of an adequate rate of return to the Corporation. This is an added risk which should be considered in estimating a fair return.

Since the present Internal Revenue Code does not recognize the costs measured in current dollars, they are not deductible for computing Federal income tax payments, and the Corporation in fact pays taxes on alleged earnings which do not exist in true purchasing power. If they were deductible, as they should be, reductions in Federal income taxes as shown in Column B of $266,000 in 19X1 and $252,000 in 19X0 would result. By requiring the use of the Uniform System of Accounts for utility accounting and by virtue of the Internal Revenue Code, the Government has condemned and confiscated during the last 7 years over $1 million (in terms of the dollars of the years in which they were paid) of the assets of this Corporation through taxation of overstated earnings. This is true to a greater or lesser extent in each case where we have been able to ascertain the facts. We do not understand why this is currently concealed by management and accountants—to their detriment.

For book and financial reporting purposes, the Corporation provides for depreciation on a straight-line basis over the average service lives of the various classes of depreciable plant. In 19X1, the overall rate was 6.3%. For Federal income tax purposes, beginning in 1967, an accelerated depreciation method is used and a provision is made in the Statement of Income for the taxes deferred as a result thereof.

Required:

Assume you are attending the annual meeting of Indiana Telephone and several shareholders, completely unfamiliar with accounting, ask you the following questions. Answer these questions as clearly as you can.

1. Briefly, what is management trying to say in Note 2 to the financial statements?
2. The bulk of the assets of ITC consists of telephone plant and equipment. Assume that the Column B figures were used consistently for such things as the basis for income tax assessment and dividend policy. Under such circumstances, would recognition of the depreciation expense figures appearing in Column B generally ensure that the telephone plant and equipment can be replaced when they wear out? Explain (defend) your answer.

INDIANA TELEPHONE CORPORATION

Statement of Income

	Column A Historical Cost		Column B Historical Cost Restated for Changes in Purchasing Power of Dollar	
	19X1	19X0	19X1	19X0
OPERATING REVENUES:				
Local service	$ 5,744,356	$5,384,154	$ 5,788,990	$ 5,695,270
Toll service	4,852,156	4,350,496	4,889,858	4,601,883
Miscellaneous	304,522	234,979	306,888	248,557
Total operating revenues	10,901,034	9,969,629	10,985,736	10,545,710
OPERATING EXPENSES:				
Depreciation provision, Note 2	1,943,551	1,541,560	2,497,078	2,026,211
Maintenance	1,486,495	1,427,487	1,505,457	1,523,311
Traffic	1,226,906	1,157,565	1,237,139	1,224,453
Commercial	511,661	449,104	515,637	475,054
General and administrative	1,055,318	1,170,198	1,068,682	1,278,407
State, local and miscellaneous Federal taxes	912,601	648,996	919,692	686,497
Federal income taxes, Note 2				
Currently payable	1,132,500	1,127,087	1,141,300	1,192,215
Deferred until future years	315,800	295,000	318,254	312,047
Deferred investment tax credit (net)	9,708	(14,997)	3,262	(21,018)
Total operating expenses	8,594,540	7,802,000	9,206,501	8,697,177
OPERATING INCOME	2,306,494	2,167,629	1,779,235	1,848,533
INCOME DEDUCTIONS:				
Interest on funded debt	651,195	659,567	656,255	697,679
Other deductions	36,828	21,355	40,229	24,583
Interest charged to construction (credit)	(63,905)	(30,442)	(64,402)	(32,201)

INDIANA TELEPHONE CORPORATION (cont.)

Statement of Income

	Column A Historical Cost		Column B Historical Cost Restated for Changes in Purchasing Power of Dollar	
	19X1	19X0	19X1	19X0
Other income (credit)	(95,974)	(98,759)	(96,720)	(104,466)
Gain from retirement of long-term debt through operation of sinking fund (credit)	(15,192)	(15,865)	(15,310)	(16,781)
Price level gain from retirement of long-term debt (credit)	—	—	(61,137)	(55,175)
Gain from retirement of preferred stock through operation of sinking fund (credit)	(5,055)	(5,515)	(5,094)	(5,834)
Price level gain from retirement of preferred stock (credit)	—	—	(12,908)	(12,029)
Price level loss from other monetary items	—	—	87,508	118,125
Total income deductions	507,897	530,341	528,421	613,901
NET INCOME	1,798,597	1,637,288	1,250,814	1,234,632
Preferred stock dividends applicable to the period	96,209	97,541	96,957	103,178
EARNINGS APPLICABLE TO COMMON STOCK	$ 1,702,388	$1,539,747	$ 1,153,857	$ 1,131,454
EARNINGS PER COMMON SHARE	$ 3.49	$ 3.16	$ 2.37	$ 2.32
BOOK VALUE PER SHARE	$ 21.45	$ 18.29	$ 20.19	$ 18.14
Stations in service at end of year	75,015	72,569	75,015	72,569

16-10. **Comprehensive Comparative Accounting Exercise.** Sam Shovel is the sole owner of Shovel Leasing, which specializes in the leasing of construction equipment to local contractors. It has been in operation since January 1, 19X0, and its balance sheet at the end of the first year of operations is as follows.

SHOVEL LEASING

Balance Sheet
As of December 31, 19X0

Assets:			Liabilities and Owners' Equity:	
Cash		$ 50,000	Accounts payable	$ 30,000
Accounts receivable		30,000		
Fuel		15,000		
Parts		20,000		
Supplies		5,000		
Equipment for lease*	$200,000			
Less accumulated depreciation	(40,000)	160,000	Owners' equity	250,000
Total assets		$280,000	Total liabilities and owners' equity	$280,000

*See table at top of page 669.

INFORMATION ON EQUIPMENT AVAILABLE FOR LEASE

Item	No.	Date of Purchase	Expected Useful Life (in years)	Original Cost per Unit	Expected Salvage Value	Replacement Cost (New) as of Dec. 31, 19X1, per Unit	Current Market Value as of Dec. 31, 19X1, per Unit
Bulldozer	4	1/1/X0	5	$20,000	-0-	$25,000	$13,000
Compressor	4	1/1/X0	5	7,500	-0-	7,500	4,000
Pneumatic drill	10	1/1/X0	5	1,000	-0-	1,000	700
Mechanized ditchdigger	5	1/1/X0	5	10,000	-0-	11,000	7,500
Mobile crane	2	1/1/X0	5	15,000	-0-	17,500	10,000

The enterprise's transactions for the year ended December 31, 19X1, were as follows:

    a. Rental payments on business location, $5,000. Paid at the beginning of the year.
    b. Wages and salaries paid throughout the year, $14,000.
    c. Purchased on account *at the beginning of the year*—fuel, $55,000; parts, $30,000; and supplies, $15,000.
    d. Payments made on accounts payable throughout the year, $80,000.
    e. Billed customers $200,000 throughout the year, and by year-end had received $190,000 from customers.
    f. Inventory was taken at year-end. On hand was fuel, $20,000; parts, $10,000; and supplies, $5,000.

Additional information:

a. There has been no movement in the cost of fuel, parts, and supplies.

b. It is estimated by Sam that if he should attempt to sell the fuel, parts, and supplies on hand at December 31, 19X1, their current market values would be as follows:

        Fuel $20,000
        Parts   9,000
        Supplies   4,500

c. The general price index has risen from 100 at the beginning of the year to 120 at the end of the year. The price index averaged about 110 for the year. There had been no movement in the general price index in 19X0.

d. Market values and replacement costs of the equipment, fuel, parts, and supplies all equaled unexpired historical cost at the beginning of 19X1.

e. Replacement-cost-based depreciation expense should be calculated on the basis of the replacement cost of the equipment at the end of the year.

Required:

1. Prepare an income statement for 19X1 for Shovel Leasing under each of the following financial accounting models:
   (a) Conventional accounting
   (b) Conventional accounting adjusted for general price-level changes
   (c) Current replacement cost accounting (nominal dollars)
   (d) Current market-value accounting, adjusted for general price-level changes

2. Calculate comparative net values at December 31, 19X1, for the equipment for lease under each of the above models.

CONTEMPORARY FINANCIAL REPORTING ENVIRONMENT

Capital Market Institutions and the Accounting Policy-Making Process

17

RESOLVING THE COMPETING ALTERNATIVES DILEMMA: ACCOUNTING POLICY

As is pointed out in Chapter 16, we have examined in Chapters 13, 14, and 15 several alternative financial accounting models, each having certain alleged advantages and disadvantages. It was observed that the choice between these (and still other) alternatives is complicated by a number of factors not present in simple, individual problems of choosing the most desirable information alternative. The complicating factors include the following: (1) there are multiple users of financial accounting information, (2) the costs of producing financial accounting information may be borne by entities (enterprises) other than those who experience the benefits (external users), and (3) the possibility exists for external effects of financial accounting information when all reporting entities are considered together.

The fact that different economic entities are affected by the financial reporting process in different ways and to different degrees (in terms of costs and benefits) means that different choices among financial accounting alternatives can lead to different distributions of wealth among the various entities (including individuals) in the economy. Furthermore, since different entities may be better off or worse off under one model than under another, there is no unanimity as to which is the best model on which to base present-day financial reporting practice.

Unfortunately, even if there were unanimity as to which financial accounting model (or combination of models) would be most appropriate, there need not be agreement as to how to solve all the measurement problems that emerge in applying it to various situations arising in practice. That is, there would be (and is) disagreement over the appropriate *measurement rules* to be employed at the operational level in applying any given financial accounting model. Indeed, many of the issues discussed in Chapters 8 through 12 (applied conventional accounting) focus on alternative methods of dealing with measurement problems. Further, although the examination of the alternative financial accounting models in Chapters 13 through 16 emphasized broad principles, nonetheless a number of measurement problems are identified (e.g., Does the replacement cost of an asset presume replacement in kind or replacement of equivalent service potential?). Implementation of one or more of those models would of course raise a set of operational issues analogous to those discussed in detail for the conventional accounting model.

Because of (1) the lack of unanimity as to the most appropriate financial accounting model and measurement rules and (2) the implication that different alternatives may lead to different distributions of wealth in the economy, the question of what is the optimum *financial accounting policy* (the set of acceptable measurement concepts and rules at any point in time) is a socioeconomic question rather than a question of accounting theory *per se*. All such questions are, of course, ultimately decided, directly or indirectly, within some type of political mechanism.

Understandably, then, accounting policy is the result of many economic, social, and political influences, past and present. These influences are exerted by individuals and organizations of two types: (1) those stimulated by an interest in the outcomes of the decision-making process and (2) those legally vested with the power to determine the outcomes. With respect to the former type of influence, as new financial accounting concepts or measurement rules come up for consideration, many individuals and organizations, reflecting varying points of view and degrees of economic interest in the particular issues, try to bring their points of view to bear on the decision-making process. Such individuals and organizations include, among others, industry associations, professional accountants, the major stock exchanges, and financial analysts.

Our political and economic system being what it is, one might expect that the final determination of what financial accounting concepts and measurement rules are adopted by particular firms would be left to purely economic forces (i.e., the "market mechanism" would shape accounting practice). But this is not the case. As in so many areas of modern market-based economies, a government agency has been established to regulate an activity that is thought to involve elements of public interest not adequately handled by a completely free market mechanism. This agency, the Securities and Exchange Commission (SEC), has possessed (federal) statutory authority over financial accounting practice for most business enterprises of any size in the United States ever since the mid-1930s.

The Securities and Exchange Commission was established by the Securities Exchange Act of 1934. This act and the Securities Act of 1933 are the major sources of the SEC's authority over accounting for business enterprises. But the SEC derives additional authority under five other statutes. The full list of this statutory authority is as follows:

1. The Securities Act of 1933 (originally administered by the Federal Trade Commission)

2. The Securities Exchange Act of 1934 (established the Securities and Exchange Commission with authority to regulate securities exchanges and trading of securities)
3. The Public Utility Holding Company Act of 1934
4. The Trust Indenture Act of 1939
5. The Investment Company Act of 1940
6. The Investment Advisors Act of 1940
7. The National Bankruptcy Act of 1938, Chapter X (advisory capacity to the federal courts)

None of the above legislation is devoted exclusively to corporate financial reporting. But all of the above statutes are concerned with interrelated elements of the same focal point of public interest: the process of capital formation by business enterprises and the capital markets that facilitate that process. That the public has an interest in corporate financial reporting and accounting policy making is, however, an integral part of this larger interest. To understand why and how institutions (particularly the SEC) are so influential in present-day accounting policy, we need to examine a set of related topics:

1. Capital formation in a market economy (including why the process is vested with the public interest)
2. The social demands on the corporate securities markets
3. The historical and economic reasons that stimulated government regulation which embraced accounting matters as well as other aspects of corporate capital formation
4. The evolution of accounting policy-making institutions from 1935 to the present (including the relationship between the SEC and the policy-making bodies of the accounting profession)
5. Some important environmental influences on the formulation of accounting policy

This chapter deals with each of these topics in turn.

Capital Formation in a Market Economy

The *material* standard of living of an individual or a whole society is dependent on how many goods and services can be produced in any period of time with the available supply of resources. The only way to improve the standard of living of a given population without increasing the hours of labor required is to improve the level of output of the given supply of labor hours. The efficiency of labor is improved by augmenting it with physical, technical, and human capital. In order for a high standard of living to be sustained, a high level of capital must be built up and maintained whether on an individual or a societal level.

Consumption Postponement. The prerequisite to capital formation is a sacrifice of current consumption. Hence, to form capital, some of the currently available supply of productive resources must be diverted from current production of final consumer goods and services to the production of capital.

For primitive people the transfer was direct and simple. The hunter, for instance, could simply pause in the middle of an expedition to fashion a weapon, thereby sacrificing the immediate bounty that might have been secured for improved performance later. But in a modern market economy the relationship between sacrificed consumption and capital formation is not so simple and direct. Here consumption is postponed through the direct or indirect savings of consumption units. Direct saving takes place when an individual, a family, or some other consumption unit does not spend all the funds it currently receives from employment of its factors of production. Indirect saving takes place when business enterprises distribute cash to their owners in amounts less than the current income of the enterprises. In either case, some of the cash flow from production of goods and services is not spent for current consumption.

Demand for Capital. By itself, however, direct or indirect savings is not enough. The funds not spent on current consumption by savers must be spent on new capital or replacements for capital exhausted in current production.

Savings not spent by a given economic unit represent a lack of demand for consumer goods and services, perhaps leading to unemployment of some of the resources previously committed to their production (and, in the extreme, possible economic recession). This is what is known as the "paradox of thrift." The constituents of a society, by being frugal and not spending large amounts of their incomes, can save themselves into unemployment and economic recession. Savings devoted to capital formation, however, result in employment of some of the productive resources of the economy in the production of goods and services for nonconsumption purposes.

But a balance is important. Just as an excess of savings can lead to unemployment, an excess in the other direction means that the combined demand for both consumer and capital goods and services will exceed the productive capacity of the economy, leading to inflation. The balance not only is important but also can be very delicate, as there is a somewhat natural imbalancing force at work. This imbalancing force is explained below.

Transfer of Funds Between Economic Units. A particular consumer unit that has saved part of its income may dispose of its excess funds by investing directly in some form of capital, such as buildings, implements, or education. But this need not always be so, and most often it is not. Another economic unit may wish to buy something now for which it currently has insufficient funds, such as a house or a car for a consumer, or a factory or equipment for a business. Thus there is a tendency toward imbalance in the saving-spending desires of individual economic units.

If a market economy is to avoid serious unemployment or inflation, it is necessary that there be some systematic way of transferring funds from savers to those interested in using those funds currently. Furthermore, if the economy is to maintain (or increase) its standard of living, a sufficient amount of the funds saved must be spent to replace that amount of capital currently exhausted in production (or more). In a market economy the capital market serves these purposes.

Capital Market. The capital market consists of all the individuals and institutions that together accomplish the transfer of funds from savers to economic units that wish to spend additional funds on capital goods and services.

Capital Market Participants and Transactions. The capital market of an economy like that of the United States is a very broad economic phenomenon, having many participants and many types of transactions and places of exchange. In general, the relationship between participants is represented in Exhibit 17-1.

Exhibit 17-1

CAPITAL MARKET RELATIONSHIPS IN NEW CAPITAL FORMATION

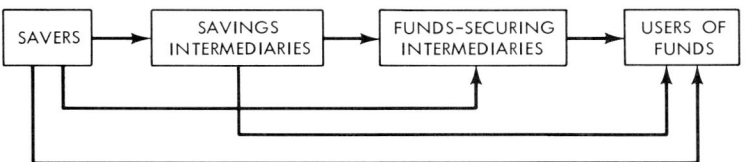

Economic units that wish to save may place their funds directly in the possession of an economic unit that will put them to use. The saver will receive some claim in return, ranging from (1) an unconditional promise on the part of the user to return the funds with interest, such as a mortgage note of a borrower who wants to purchase a home, to (2) a share of common stock in a corporation or a partnership interest, promising only a share in any earnings that are generated thereafter.

Capital Market Intermediaries. Direct transfers would satisfy the needs of only a small fraction of the total savers and users of funds. Thus there are many types of capital market intermediaries working to satisfy demand initiated by either savers or users of funds.

On the savings side, there exist commercial banks, savings banks, savings and loan associations, mutual funds, insurance companies, and pension funds. All of these types of savings intermediaries exist as outlets or opportunities for vast numbers of consumers to put their funds to work as they save, without worrying about who will actually use the funds and for what purpose. In exchange for control over their savings, the financial intermediaries pay interest, dividends, or deferred payments (in the case of insurance companies and pension funds) to savers. The savings intermediaries, in turn, lend large blocks of pooled savings or invest them in ownership shares in various kinds of users of funds, in return for interest or dividends, presumably in excess of what they are obligated to pay their creditors (the savers).

From the other side, a potential user of funds, such as a large corporation (or a governmental unit) whose management wants to expand its operations with new plant and equipment that will cost several hundred million dollars, may find it difficult, time consuming, and costly to seek out the savings of individuals. But, fortunately, it can call upon the services of a funds-securing intermediary, usually an investment banker. The investment banker will form a syndicate with other investment bankers, and together they will buy all the securities that the corporation needs to issue in order to carry out its capital expansion. The investment bankers, in turn, sell the securities, often in much smaller blocks, to savers and savings intermediaries. The amount the investment bankers pay to the user of funds will be somewhat less than they estimate they will collect from the savers and/or the various savings intermediaries for the securities.

Sources of Funds for Business Enterprises—The Corporate Securities Markets. The foregoing description of participants and relationships holds for the capital market in general. But since our area of interest is society's regulatory interest in accounting for business enterprises, we need only be concerned hereafter with that portion of the total capital market in which significant numbers of business enterprises (mainly corporations) raise the funds with which they acquire capital goods and services. We call this segment "the markets for corporate securities." From this point on we will ignore other segments of the capital market, such as the market for mortgage loans and the government securities markets.

Social Demands on the Corporate Securities Markets

In a market economy, the public interest embraces all segments of the capital market, including the markets for corporate securities. Why? Because a healthy market economy requires a capital market that performs the functions and exhibits the characteristics that are listed below and discussed in the paragraphs that follow.

1. As mentioned earlier, for economic stability it is necessary that the supply of funds from savers be matched against the demand for funds of potential users.
2. If society is to maintain a high and growing standard of living, there must be a sufficient supply of funds at a low enough cost to business enterprises to ensure that it will be worthwhile to replace worn-out capital and add new capital to the total stock of capital in the economy. This in turn is dependent on two additional requirements:
   a. The markets must be operationally efficient.
   b. The markets must be reasonably fair, meaning free from fraud, deception, and manipulation by any participants. (This requirement is the principal motivation for a public interest in and related regulation of corporate financial reporting.)

Matching Supply and Demand for Funds in the Corporate Securities Markets. The two major aspects of matching supply and demand for funds in the corporate securities markets are size and time. Businesses are often interested in investing in capital goods that cost enormous amounts and last many years. Savers, on the other hand, are usually interested in committing relatively small amounts and maintaining flexibility with respect to when they may recover funds committed.

The problem of size is, of course, partly solved when corporations issue large numbers of securities in small denominations in exchange for savings funds.

Furthermore, savings intermediaries make available opportunities for savers to save in small amounts, completely unrelated to the denominations of securities purchased with the funds pooled from many individuals by the bank or other intermediary.

Savings intermediaries also serve as a buffer with respect to the duration of savings relative to the duration of investment in capital goods on the part of users of savings funds. An individual saver may make deposits and withdrawals from a savings or mutual fund account usually on demand, independent of the duration of investment in capital assets made by a corporation with funds received from the savings intermediary. The intermediary is in a position to match the deposits of an individual against the withdrawals of others. But what about individual savers who prefer not to save through savings intermediaries, and what about the savings intermediaries themselves? Will they not want to commit funds for intervals less than the duration of business enterprises' investments in capital goods? The answer is clearly yes. For them there exist the opportunities provided by the *secondary* market in corporate securities.

Primary and Secondary Securities Markets. The markets for corporate securities may be separated into two kinds, based on the effects that transactions in those markets have on the money capital or funds of business enterprises. The two kinds of corporate securities markets are called primary and secondary.

Primary Corporate Securities Market. The primary corporate securities market consists of all transactions in which the money capital of business enterprises is expanded through the issue of new securities or contracted through the redemption, retirement, or liquidation of previously outstanding securities of the enterprises.

Secondary Corporate Securities Market. The secondary corporate securities market consists of all exchanges involving corporate securities *except* those in which a business enterprise is selling (issuing) or buying (redeeming, retiring, or liquidating) its own securities.

Clearly, it is only in the primary market that business enterprises can acquire the necessary new funds for capital formation. This does not mean that the secondary market (including national securities exchanges like the New York Stock Exchange) is unimportant merely because the secondary market does not *directly* affect the flow of new funds to business enterprises. On the contrary, were it not for the ability to buy and sell corporate securities independent of the lives of capital assets, the securities would be less attractive at the time of issue, and thus it would be more difficult for enterprises to raise new funds.

Adequacy of the Supply of Funds for Capital Formation. Savers forgo consumption because, by investing in some form of saving opportunity, they expect to have a greater ability to consume in the future. Such opportunities exist, however, only because someone will put the saved funds to use in acquiring real capital goods and services with which they can earn sufficient amounts to reward savers adequately for supplying their funds, as well as provide a return for their own efforts. But the opportunities are really reciprocal. Investors need savers willing to supply funds for returns that are not so large as to deny them (the investors) an attractive residual return on their investment and production efforts. Two things discourage the level of reciprocal opportunities generated by savers and capital formers: (1) intermediaries that require too large a share of the funds that flow into both the primary and secondary markets and (2) fraud, deception, and manipulation by primary or secondary market participants.

The Operational Efficiency of the Securities Markets. In order for the economy to generate a high level of reciprocal opportunities between savers and capital formers, and so enjoy a high and growing standard of living, the securities markets must be operationally efficient.

> **Operational Efficiency.** A securities market is operationally efficient when all the intermediaries and others who participate in the transfer of funds from savers to users earn no more than is necessary to induce them to provide their services.

Primary Market Efficiency. The level of operational efficiency of both the primary and secondary capital markets can greatly influence the volume of funds that flow from savers to users and hence the level of capital formation. In the primary securities market the influence is quite direct, as the following hypothetical example illustrates:

Example 17-1

> MMW Corporation's management has an opportunity to invest in new capital equipment, which, after labor and other operating costs, will return, through sales of products and services, enough to recover the invested funds in twenty years, plus 10 percent per year on the original investment. To raise the necessary funds, the company is planning to offer twenty-year, $1,000 bonds on which it will pay 6 percent, or $60 per year, to savers in addition to $1,000 at the end of the twentieth year. It is looking forward to the deal, since it only needs to make for itself $35 per $1,000 borrowed to justify its efforts in organizing the necessary resources and taking the risk that things might not work out as well as expected. But upon talking to investment bankers the company managers are disappointed.
>
> The bankers are convinced that savers will pay $1,000 each for the bonds. But, since the investment bankers will have to incur various promotional expenses and some risk in underwriting and "floating" a large issue of the bonds, they will remit only $930 per bond to MMW Corporation, taking an estimated $70 per bond for themselves. Unfortunately, if they went ahead with the deal the management would be faced with having to pay $60 per year plus $1,000 principal after twenty years to each bondholder, while the company would earn only $93 (10 percent of $930) per year on the proceeds of each bond, plus recovering the investment of only $930 by the end of twenty years. This would leave it less than the $35 annual, residual return that it requires to justify its efforts in the expansion. Additionally, the company would need to make up the $70 difference between its recovery of $930 and the $1,000 that it will have to return to the bondholders at the end of twenty years.
>
> Thus management may decide to forgo the contemplated expansion. But this need not have been the case if the demands of the underwriters had not been so great. If the underwriters had agreed to remit, say, $970 per bond instead of $930, the expansion might have remained attractive to management. New capital would have been formed, additional employees might have been hired, and the total production of products and services of the economy possibly expanded.

Secondary Market Efficiency. Inefficiency in the secondary market for securities can also discourage capital formation, but in a different way.

Example 17-2

> Suppose that MMW Corporation found underwriters that were highly efficient and willing to "float" MMW's bonds for a fee of only $30 per bond, or 3 percent of face value. In spite of the reasonable efficiency of the primary market, the level of efficiency in the secondary market for securities might still discourage MMW from making its capital expansion.
>
> For instance, suppose that brokers who actually place the buy-and-sell orders and complete the exchanges of securities in the secondary market charge exorbitant brokerage fees—say 3 percent of the selling price in a given transaction. Many savers who are willing to buy an MMW bond at the time it is issued, but who are not necessarily willing to hold it twenty years to maturity, would have to sell through brokers. If they thought that in the future, when they wanted to sell, the bonds would sell for $1,000, they would expect to receive only $970 after the broker's fee. Faced with this prospect, they might not value the bonds at their principal or face value of $1,000 at the time of issue. So if they will only pay, say, $985 per bond at the time of issue because of high broker's fees for resale, then, even with low underwriting fees of $30 per bond, MMW will only receive $955 per bond from the underwriters ($985 - $30). This, again, may be too little to make the capital expansion worthwhile to the management of MMW Corporation.

In both examples, the key issue is not that any particular level of fees is too high. But, if the level of fees prevailing at any time is higher than necessary to induce the participants to perform their services, it will unnecessarily inhibit the flow of funds between savers and capital formers, and thereby unnecessarily inhibit the formation of capital.

Presumably, the best insurance against excessive fees for intermediaries in either the primary or the secondary market is the rigor of competition. Provided no intermediary or group of intermediaries can bar entry of competitors or otherwise monopolize a part of the market, fees will be competitively low. But in the absence of rigorous competition, on the other hand, there is a definite societal interest in regulating or supervising the activities and fee structures of intermediaries.

Fairness of Markets—The Source of the Public Interest in Corporate Financial Reporting. Savers invest their funds in corporate securities directly or through intermediaries, in the expectation that the value of the returns they will receive in the future will exceed the value of the funds they give up. The actual returns that savers receive and/or the risks actually associated with those returns depend upon the performance of the user of the funds—the business enterprise. Hence the values, and therefore the prices, of corporate securities at the time of issue or in later trading in the secondary market are dependent on expectations of the returns the corporation will generate and the perceived risk associated with the expected returns. It is through influence on investors' expectations and risk perceptions that fraud, deception, and manipulation by market participants can seriously retard the flow of funds to business enterprises (capital formers).

Fraud, deception, and manipulation by some market participants increase the general level of risk associated with investment in corporate securities.

Along with the potential for less-than-expected returns inherent in the economic pursuits of any business enterprise, each investor faces the additional possibility that his expectations will turn out to be completely unrealistic because he has been deceived in some manner. This addition to the risk associated with investing in corporate securities means that the values placed on those securities by investors will be less than they would be without the threat of fraud or deception. (Recall the discussion in Chapter 2 of the relationship between risk and the present value of an investment.) But if the expected prices that securities will bring from investors at time of issue are too low, it may discourage corporations from securing the necessary funds for capital formation—as was pointed out in the earlier examples concerning the fees charged by market intermediaries.

Thus, in order for society to enjoy a high and growing standard of living, it may be essential to minimize deceptive and manipulative practices on the part of market participants. This objective is achieved, to a significant extent, through requirements for fair and accurate reporting of all material facts—a major source of which is the corporate financial report.

Historical Perspective on Govenment Regulation of Accounting Practice

Today the corporate securities markets appear to be characterized by a reasonably high level of operational efficiency (although some brokerage fees and the administrative costs of some mutual funds have received critical public scrutiny recently). They are also characterized by a reasonably low level of fraud, deception, and manipulation. But this has not always been the case. The excesses of the decade preceding the stock market debacle in 1929 contrast sharply with today's securities markets. In the October 1959 *George Washington Law Review,* the chairman of the SEC recalled this observation from a 1938 congressional report:

> During the post-war (W.W. I) decade some $50 billion of new securities were floated in the United States. Fully half or $25 billion worth of securities floated during this period have been proven to be worthless. These cold figures spell tragedy in the lives of thousands of individuals who invested their life savings, accumulated after years of effort, in these worthless securities. The flotation of such a mass of worthless securities was made possible because of the complete abandonment by many underwriters and dealers in securities of those standards of fair, honest, and prudent dealing that should be basic to the encouragement of investment in any enterprise. Alluring promises of easy wealth were freely made with little or no attempt to bring to the investors' attention those facts essential to estimating the worth of any security.

Often based on the kind of promotion implied in the observation above, prices of corporate stocks rose in meteoric fashion during the middle and late 1920s. The *New York Times* simple average of the prices of the common stocks of twenty-five industrial corporations rose from 106 at the end of May 1924 to 449 at the end of August 1929. But in 1929 the Great Crash began, dashing the hopes and fortunes of so many who were victims of manipulation, or were denied access to sound information about the corporations whose securities they bought, or were just caught up in the atmosphere of greed and self-delusion encouraged by the dearth of such information. Between the end of August and November 13, 1929, the *Times* average fell from 449 to 224, or roughly 50 percent. The ensuing, relentless fall in securities prices that ushered in the Great Depression left the *Times* average at only 58 on July 8, 1932, or a total fall of more than 87 percent from the August 1929 level of 449.

In the aftermath of the Crash, during the economic doldrums of the Great Depression, many investigations were conducted to discover the causes of both the Crash and the Depression. No completely conclusive findings were possible, but several forms of actions were highly suspect, and public support to put an end to them was running high. Among the suspect actions were various manipulations and acts of fraud by both market intermediaries and corporate executives and promoters. Perhaps one of the most conspicuous was the lack of any consistent "hard" information on the financial standing and results of operations of many public corporations. This fact was lamented in print as early as 1927 by William Z. Ripley, a Harvard University professor of political economy and critic of American corporate reporting practices. In his book *Main Street and Wall Street*, Ripley describes his review of corporate annual reports of the time:

> Confronted with a great pile of recent corporate pamphlets on my table, the first impression is of their extraordinary diversity, in appearance, size, content, and intent. One premier concern, the Royal Baking Powder Company, fails to register any fiscal information at all, in as much as it has never issued a balance sheet or financial statement of any kind whatsoever for more than a quarter of a century.... Akin to it is the Singer Manufacturing Company, which handles 80 percent of the world's output of sewing machines. Neither hide nor hair of financial data for this firm is discoverable in the usual sources of information. The dance-card, bald balance-sheet, or picture-book variety of corporation report follows hard upon these examples of complete reticence.... Yet colored pictures of factories, brightly lighted at night,—as some of these must well have been in view of their extraordinary success,—tell no tales....
>
> Then there is the leaflet type, done on a single folded sheet of paper. This "tuppence ha' penny" variety, once common, is happily by way of passing out. Cotton mills are still in this stage, again with nothing but a balance sheet, and no income statement at all.... Or there is the pompous but empty type, suggestive of President Wilson's pithy distinction between men who grow and those who merely swell with the advance of years.... Other reports may well be designated the "business condition" type, devoting much attention to things in general and but little to their own affairs in particular.... And then there are the reports ..., "all obfuscated and darkened over with fuliginous matter."[1]

The two events that did more than any others to bring about fuller corporate financial disclosure occurred some six years after Ripley's book was published. They were passage of the Securities Act of 1933 and the Securities Exchange Act of 1934.

The Securities Act of 1933. The two principal objectives of the Securities Act of 1933 are (1) to require adequate and accurate disclosure of material

---

[1] William Z. Ripley, *Main Street and Wall Street* (Lawrence, Kans.: Scholars Book Co., 1972), pp. 162-64.

data, financial or otherwise, concerning securities to be sold in interstate commerce or through the mail, and (2) to specifically outlaw fraud in the sale of securities whether or not newly issued, and to provide criminal penalties for offending parties, and remedies for injured parties. The law clearly stops short of directly rationing the flow of funds in the corporate securities market, that is, determining which enterprises are worthy of funds and/or the prices at which their securities may be fairly and equitably issued. Instead, the 1933 act is premised on full disclosure of all material facts about the issuer, leaving to a "free" market the determination of worth.

The principal means by which the first objective of the act is pursued is the requirement that before any security is sold or delivered across state lines or through the mail, the management of the issuing enterprise must file the following:

1. All notices to be used to publicly announce the intent to sell securities
2. A registration statement
3. Circulars to be used to offer the securities for sale
4. Prospectuses to be used to describe the securities and the enterprise to prospective buyers
5. Advertising and promotional material

Both the registration statement and the prospectus required under the act must contain a recent balance sheet and several years' comparative income statements, audited by independent certified public accountants, "... in such detail and in such form as the Commission shall prescribe...." It is this latter clause that gave first the Federal Trade Commission and later the Securities and Exchange Commission sweeping power over accounting principles and procedures. If the commission finds any part of the filings for a particular security objectionable, including any accounting practice incorporated into the statements, it may issue a "stop order" rendering the registration ineffective and the sale of the securities illegal.

The Securities Exchange Act of 1934. The Securities Exchange Act of 1934 established the Securities and Exchange Commission and gives it authority to regulate trading in securities, securities exchanges, and the conduct and financial affairs of members of national securities exchanges along with other brokers and dealers. To accomplish its major objective of regulating trading in securities, however, the 1934 act extends the power of the commission over the accounting practices of business enterprises.

Along with requiring that trading on national securities exchanges be limited to securities registered with the commission, certain other provisions are directed toward the issues of securities "listed" (traded) on a national securities exchange. Among other things, the act requires that the issuers of listed securities file with the commission such annual reports (to be audited by independent certified public accountants if required by the commission) and such quarterly reports as the commission may prescribe. Furthermore, "... the Commission may prescribe, in regard to reports made pursuant to this title [law], the form or forms in which the required information shall be set forth, the items or details to be shown in the balance sheet and the earnings statement, and the methods to be followed in the preparation of reports. . . ."

Thus, as a matter of law, any business enterprise that wishes to have its securities traded on a national exchange is subject to the prescriptions of the SEC in accounting for its financial status and activities, both at the time of first listing on the exchange (registration) and thereafter. Any issuer of securities listed on a national exchange that violates the requirements of the 1934 act may have trading in its securities summarily suspended for up to ten days by the commission or up to ninety days with the approval of the president. Or, after appropriate notice and hearing, the commission may suspend for up to twelve months, or withdraw altogether, the registration of the enterprise's securities.

Evolution of Accounting Policy-Making Institutions

Although the 1933 and 1934 Securities Acts clearly gave the SEC the power to prescribe acceptable measurement concepts and rules right down to the last detail, the SEC has never directly done so. Some of the original commissioners favored an SEC-prescribed set of accepted accounting policies, but others were unconvinced as to the desirability of that approach. Instead the commission has historically exercised a kind of veto power over objectionable accounting practice, otherwise accepting practices that have substantial authoritative support from the accounting profession. To facilitate this approach, there has been an informal working relationship ever since the late 1930s between the SEC and the American Institute of Certified Public Accountants (AICPA). The AICPA, which represents about two-thirds of the CPAs in the United States, has from time to time made authoritative statements as to the acceptability of various aspects of accounting for business enterprises; for the most part these have been understood by all concerned parties to be supported by or acceptable to the SEC.

This informal working arrangement seemed to be advantageous to both groups over the years from 1938 to 1973. The SEC had the advantage of the combined expertise of many of the most successful members of the accounting profession, who served at no cost on either the AICPA's Committee on Accounting Procedure (1938–59) or its successor body, the Accounting Principles Board (1959–73). In addition, the SEC has automatically had the official backing, in most accounting matters, of the major national organization of the professionals who perform the audits (required under the Securities Acts) of listed companies' financial statements. And, for its part, the accounting profession has enjoyed the greater stature of being a self-regulating profession, presumably mature enough to not require governmental codification of acceptable accounting practices.

In response to growing pressure from other interested organizations, however, the AICPA in 1972 approved a plan to place its traditional role of making authoritative pronouncements on the acceptability of accounting principles and procedures under the authority of a new organization, the Financial Accounting Foundation (FAF). The foundation is designed to be broadly representative of groups with an interest in the financial reporting process. Trustees of the foundation are appointed by a board of six electors, each representing one of the six organizations sponsoring the foundation (American Accounting Association, American Institute of Certified Public Accountants, Financial Analysts Federation, Financial Executives Institute, National Association of Accountants, and Securities Industry Association). The trustees of the foundation have among their principal tasks the appointment and financial support of the newest accounting policy-making body, the Financial Accounting Standards Board (FASB). This board, which began operations in 1973, makes authoritative pronouncements on financial accounting matters. Although originally four of the seven board members were required to have had a majority of their professional experience in public accounting practice, the present standard is to seek the most highly qualified individuals in the area of financial accounting. Presumably, this move away from near exclusion of non-CPAs in generating authoritative pronouncements concerning accounting practice will promote wider support in the financial community than had been enjoyed by the predecessor Accounting Principles Board.

Some Important Environmental Influences on the Formulation of Accounting Policy

Three major influences on the development, *by authority,* of acceptable accounting policy have been (1) the state of accounting practice prior to 1935, (2) the dynamic change in the business environment since World War II, and (3) the increasing "intervention" of (often conflicting) special interest groups.

Effect of Pre-1935 Accounting Practices. Accounting practice prior to 1935 was marked by two compelling features. First, the procedures and practices followed by business enterprises in representing their status and activities through financial statements varied greatly from enterprise to enterprise. This great diversity was uncovered early in 1935 when some twenty-five hundred enterprises listed on twenty national securities exchanges registered their securities for the first time under the 1933 and 1934 acts. The impression created was described in an accounting symposium at the University of California, Berkeley, in 1967 by Carman G. Blough, chief accountant for the SEC during those critical early years:

> Never before had so much information regarding the accounting principles, methods and procedures of business concerns been made known as that which became public during the first six months of 1935.
>
> For the first time it was possible to know of the many areas of differences that actually existed among the accounting practices followed by well known business enterprises. These differences soon became the subject of discussion, criticism, defense and analysis.

The second compelling feature of pre-1935 accounting practice was what seemed, in retrospect, widespread abuse by management of the rather liberal latitude it had in selecting and disclosing its accounting methods. Dissatisfaction with this degree of latitude was expressed as early as 1927 by William Z. Ripley in *Main Street and Wall Street:*

... one turns in vain to many otherwise excellent statements for light as to whether the appraisal is based upon prices paid, upon the market value, upon reproduction cost, "prudent investment," or what not. The great packing concerns, now so largely publicly owned, have always been cryptic in their statements. The Federal Trade Commission in 1920 squarely criticized their inventories as invariably appraised on a market basis when sound accounting principles required a basis of cost. This criticism concludes with the broadside condemnation that this accounting practice "casts doubt upon all the public statements and advertisements of the great packers." Nor may there be question that the virtual theft by bankers and the dominant stockholders from the public shareholders of the entire increment in value of their real-estate holdings in the stockyard district over a number of years, by misuse of the holding company device in 1911, was due to a deliberate and willful failure to reflect the true state of affairs in the balance sheet. Whether such misrepresentation be understatement, as in this instance, or an overestimate, is immaterial for the purposes of this presentment. The wrong worked upon the shareholders and the public is as great one way as the other.[2]

The development of accounting principles after the inception of the SEC was marked by two responses to the state of prior accounting practice. An immediate but long-lasting response to management's latitude and apparent abuse of selection of a valuation basis for assets was recalled by Carman Blough as follows:

One of the first members of the newly formed SEC to be appointed was a former General Counsel for the Federal Trade Commission who had been in charge of that Commission's very comprehensive investigation of the public utility holding companies. During that study the flagrant write-up policies of the holding companies and their subsidiaries and the havoc they caused when the crash came in 1929 and 1930 kept impressing themselves on the chief investigator to the point that their end became almost an obsession with him. It was only logical to expect that when he had an opportunity to outlaw write-ups he would do so. So strong were his convictions and so convincing were his arguments against write-ups that all of the other members of the Commission were persuaded to take a positive stand against them from the very first case in which the question arose.

Thus the principle that assets must never be valued at more than their original transaction cost became firmly established as acceptable accounting practice in SEC-related matters. Partly due to this early entrenchment, the conventional accounting model has dominated accounting policy to the present. As a result, the vast majority of present corporate financial reports are largely based on this measurement model. But the acceptance of this model is not without exception. For instance, due to the nature of their business and the character of the assets they hold, it is accepted accounting practice for mutual funds to value assets at current market (selling) prices. Nor is the conventional model accepted without challenge. That exceptions and debate exist is understandable, since no single model can be expected to apply equally well to all circumstances, nor to appeal equally to all interested parties.

An alternative to selecting a single model for all corporate reporting (one that seems to be increasingly important) is the specification of different models (measurement concepts) for different types of resources and/or obligations. Sometimes the use of different measurement concepts is prompted by the

[2] Ripley, *Main Street and Wall Street*, pp. 191-92.

nature of the resource or obligation and thus applies to all business enterprises. In other instances, the differences are the result of situations experienced by particular firms, in which case they will only be evident on the financial statements of those firms. For example, it has been proposed that inventories held for sale be valued at current market (selling) prices, and that inventories held for use in production be valued at current replacement costs.

Many other illustrations of this *eclectic approach* to accounting policy exist, and the trend in the past few years in the formulation of accounting policy seems to be in this direction. Such an approach has the positive feature of associating measurement concepts with particular economic resources and obligations which correspond fairly closely to the assumptions and objectives of the particular conceptual model. By focusing on more homogeneous clusters of items, the analysis of the appropriate model is clearly enhanced. However, the financial model of the firm (at least in current practice) requires that these individual valuations be summed, and income for the period determined. While no difficulty is encountered in generating a "number," what can such a single aggregate value represent? It is an amalgam of all the concepts underlying the individual valuations and thus may itself defy explanation. Whether this deficiency is a more serious one than the problem of attempting to associate a single measurement concept with all items within financial statements is something that future experience may reveal. In any event, eclecticism seems to be in fashion at the moment.

Another variation that has been proposed by some policy-setting bodies, but has not yet been incorporated into many corporate reports, is the presentation of financial statements of the firm prepared under one measurement concept side by side with the presentation of financial statements of the same firm prepared under a different measurement concept. For example, one proposal urges the presentation of financial statements based on the conventional accounting model side by side with a set of statements that incorporate general price-level adjustments. Another proposal is to present two corresponding sets of statements, one using the conventional model and the other using current replacement costs. A variation on this proposal is illustrated by the current SEC reporting requirement for replacement cost data on inventories and property, plant, and equipment and the FASB proposed standard for current cost or constant dollar data for the same assets as *supplementary information.* Obviously, these alternatives to the choice of a single measurement concept, or more precisely the presentation of one set of statements using a single measurement concept, could be extended to more than two measurement concepts. Whether this type of variation will endure in accounting policy is yet to be seen. It does seem fairly clear that it is itself merely a variation of the eclecticism theme mentioned above. Thus we can characterize the current status of this type of accounting policy choice (i.e., choice of the appropriate financial accounting model, or measurement concept) as being one of "mixing and matching" different concepts with different types of situations and/or resources and obligations.

In the years immediately following 1935, the diversity and abuses in pre-1935 accounting practice created still another response whose influence is also still with us. From the first registration of so many companies' securities in 1935 and the discovery of tremendous diversity in accounting methods, the pressure was felt by the SEC and later, through the SEC, by the AICPA Committee on Accounting Procedure, to determine which methods (measurement rules) were acceptable and which were not. As a result, early in its life the Committee on Accounting Procedure decided to devote its attention to pressing current problems, reluctantly sidelining any immediate effort to develop a comprehensive and cohesive statement of broader measurement issues. The effect of this decision was (and continues to be) to limit, but not eliminate, management discretion in the choice of accounting alternatives.

Effect of Changes in the Business Environment. If the backlog of diversity and abuse originally distracted the Committee on Accounting Procedure from a broad and comprehensive approach, matters did not get better as time passed. After World War II, the tremendous growth in the economy and the change in many business practices put new pressure on certain areas of accepted accounting practice, and new and pressing problems were continually raised. Thus neither the Committee on Accounting Procedure nor its successor, the Accounting Principles Board, was able to devote much attention to a broad foundation for accounting for business enterprises—though the resolution to do so was renewed from time to time, and the FASB is currently near the decision point in a major effort to establish a broad conceptual framework for financial accounting and reporting that is acceptable to the various interested parties.

Effect of Special Interest Groups. We have seen that the development of accounting policy up to 1960 was largely a product of forces coming out of the Depression and the related federal and state legislation. While disagreements over proper accounting policy existed among accountants, regulatory officials, and businessmen, they were largely resolved in a low-key manner. The period after 1960, however, has been as turbulent for the accounting policy process as it has been for the nation. Disputes over permissible accounting procedures and methods burst onto the public scene as various interest groups pleaded their cases through whatever avenues seemed most promising, and the news media reacted in response to this purported exploitation of the investing public.

The power and influence of various interest groups within the business community created strong, and some argue inhibiting, pressure on the Accounting Principles Board. At the time the new Financial Accounting Standards Board was proposed, the following assessment of the climate surrounding the development of accounting policy was made:

> In several areas in which it [APB] proposed substantial changes . . . the Board bit off more than it could chew. It had to back down from ambitious preliminary positions.
>
> If an industry really got its back up, the Board proved unwilling or unable to override it. In oil-and-gas accounting, for instance, the major oil companies were already following the financial reporting the Board preferred. But a proposal to eliminate something called "full cost" accounting was regarded by newer and smaller companies as a life-or-death threat. *Their bitter opposition prevailed.*
>
> With industry assured a role in the proposed . . . [FASB], it's doubtful that panel would lightly regard the practical impact of its pronouncements. It would probably draw some lessons from the current Board's woes. "We have found compromise is the only way out of many of these things, and perhaps the only way to make progress," Mr. Defliese [Chairman of the APB] declares. "The Board can't opt for high theory and come out with answers totally unacceptable to business and government."

Lately, the accountants have new worries from Washington. Last November, Congress stunned accounting authorities by denying them the power to decide how companies must account for the investment tax credit. The Principles Board had embarked on a course opposed by most of industry and many accountants. Urged on by industry lobbyists, *Congress passed a law allowing taxpayers to account for the credit as they preferred.*

The accountants are fearful other interests will continue to appeal over their heads to Washington. One reason the oil companies prevailed is that they are known to have powerful friends. Already some opponents of proposed stiffer rules on leasing have prompted at least 30 Congressmen and Senators to write inquiries to the Principles Board.

Typically, those who intervene from Washington aren't concerned with the niceties of accounting theory. One letter-writer was Rep. Chet Holifield, an influential member of the Joint Committee on Atomic Energy. He was upset about the impact on nuclear-fuel leasing. Similarly, the Federal Power Commission recently preempted the Principles Board by specifically requiring of natural-gas companies a liberal accounting treatment the Board was moving to prohibit. *The regulatory commission apparently intended to encourage exploration for natural gas.*

This problem is bound to afflict the proposed Standards Board.... [The report creating it] urged that the private standards body become "more actively and intimately involved" with the needs of federal agencies capable of overriding it. The idea, the [report] said, was to educate the regulatory agencies about the importance of good accounting. But the federal agencies, with distinct priorities of their own, may prove difficult to "educate."[3]

The apparent success of special interest groups can only encourage them and others to continue their pressure on the accounting policy process. Thus the APB in the past, and now the Financial Accounting Standards Board, seem to function as a quasi-legislative, quasi-judicial body. The needs of various groups are acknowledged, and the board attempts to formulate propositions that are acceptable (and, it is hoped, equitable) to private individuals and the public as a whole.

But who speaks for the public? There is no question that the organized interest groups make their needs and concerns known. In a sense the APB, and now the FASB, have tried to assume the role of spokesman for the public. The members of these boards have been and are aware of the possible inequities that could be wrought upon the investing public, as well as the allocation of resources within the nation, if inappropriate accounting procedures are permitted to exist. Also, by law, the various regulatory commissions (including importantly the SEC) are charged with responsibility for the "public interest." This responsibility is, however, a formidable task for both groups.

Whether the Financial Accounting Standards Board will ultimately be successful in convincing the public that it is giving proper attention to the public interest still remains to be seen. The board has continued to operate under increasing pressures from a variety of sources, including more intense public scrutiny of its efforts. A system of countervailing powers seems to be taking shape in the accounting policy process. Whether the "power" of the public

---

[3] "Overhaul of Accounting Rule-Making Unit, Expected Today, Is Seen Reducing Conflicts," *Wall Street Journal*, May 2, 1972. Reprinted with the permission of The Wall Street Journal, © Dow Jones & Company, Inc., 1972. Emphasis supplied.

will become sufficiently strong to adequately represent this important, yet highly diffused, interest is as yet uncertain.

Questions for Review and Discussion

17-1. Define:
a. Capital market
b. Primary corporate securities market
c. Secondary corporate securities market
d. Operational efficiency (of a securities market)

17-2. Enumerate three factors that make the selection of one of the alternative financial accounting models for general use in present-day financial reporting more difficult than an individual information choice problem.

17-3. Distinguish between financial accounting models (measurement concepts) and accounting measurement rules.

17-4. Accounting policy is influenced by many different individuals and organizations, which for our purposes have been grouped into two broad types. Name the two types, and give an example of individuals or organizations that fall within each type.

17-5. What are the consequences for society when there are imbalances between the level of savings and the demand for capital in the economy?

17-6. A healthy market economy requires a capital market that performs two basic functions. Describe these functions.

17-7. Why is regulation of corporate financial reporting—keeping it free from fraud and deception—in the public interest?

17-8. Summarize briefly the principal objectives of the Securities Act of 1933 and the Securities Exchange Act of 1934, and describe the authority over accounting practice provided to the SEC by the acts.

17-9. Enumerate the accounting policy-making bodies that have been set up by the accounting profession since 1935. What has been their relationship with the SEC?

17-10. There have been three major environmental influences on the development, *by authority*, of acceptable accounting policy. Enumerate these influences.

17-11. In the view of the authors, two features of pre-1935 accounting practice have influenced post-1935 accounting policy. What are those features and how has their influence been felt in recent years on accounting policy making?

17-12. It has been said that the philosophy of the Securities Acts is to regulate the processes of capital formation and securities trading, but not to determine directly the allocation of money capital to firms. Explain.

17-13. The president of a large public corporation, a prominent member of the business community, has buttonholed you at a social gathering and is complaining bitterly about SEC regulation of financial reporting. He contends that government regulation of the capital markets, or indeed any other markets, is very unhealthy for a free-enterprise system. In his opinion buyers and sellers of securities ought to be mature enough to look after their own interests without "big brother" watching over them. Furthermore, he asserts that society has no right to interfere if the individual does not want its protection. How would you rebut his contentions, assuming you chose to do so?

17-14. Do you believe that accounting policy-making authority should be in the public or the private sector? Explain.

17-15. As a special project, go to your library reference desk and ask for the index to the *Wall Street Journal* for a recent year. The front half of the index is a directory of companies whose names are followed by annotated lists of news items that appeared in the *Wall Street Journal* during the year covered by the index. Pick a company with only thirty to forty news items for the year.

1. How many of the news items contained accounting information?
2. Would you expect the same percentage of *accounting* news items for a company with more total news items?
3. Do you believe that some of the news events are irrelevant to external decision makers who have an investment or other interest in the company? If so, which ones? (Describe them.)
4. After seeing accounting news items in the context of the total news items for a company, what additional insight into the role of financial accounting do you feel you have?
5. Do you see some informational role for accounting outside the context of "news releases"?
6. Do you see some noninformational role for corporate financial reporting in the context of the capital formation process?

Exercises

17-1. **The Investment Credit Controversy.** From time to time over the last two decades Congress has included in income tax legislation a provision that permits companies making expenditures for certain kinds of capital assets (e.g., machinery and equipment) to reduce their income tax payments (usually in the year of acquisition) equal to a percentage of the cost of such assets. The intent of this particular "tax break" is, of course, to reduce the cost of capital assets relative to the expected benefits and thereby encourage companies to expand. This, in turn, presumably increases employment.

Accountants and managements have disagreed over the years as to how to account for the "investment tax credit," as it is called. Many accountants argue that the investment tax credit is a reduction in the cost of the assets acquired and should therefore be recognized as a reduction in expense (related to the use of the asset) over the asset's life. Others (including the managements of many companies), on the other hand, have argued that the credit is clearly a reduction of the income tax expense of the year in which it is recognized on the company's tax return.

In the first official accounting response to this issue in December 1962, the APB issued its Opinion No. 2 supporting the former position based on the following arguments:

> 12. In concluding that the cost reduction concept is based upon existing accounting principles we attach substantial weight to two points in particular. First, in our opinion, earnings arise from the use of facilities, not from their acquisition. Second, the ultimate realization of the credit is contingent to some degree on future developments. Where the incidence of realization of income is uncertain, as in the present circumstances, we believe the record does not support the treatment of the investment credit as income at the earliest possible point of time. In our opinion the alternative choice of spreading the income in some rational manner over a series of future accounting periods is more logical and supportable. [Copyright © 1962 by the American Institute of Certified Public Accountants, Inc.]

As the result of this reasoning, the board reached the following decision:

> 13. We conclude that the allowable investment credit should be reflected in net income over the productive life of acquired property and not in the year in which it is placed in service.
>
> 14. A number of alternative choices for recording the credit on the balance sheet has been considered. While we believe the reflection of the allowable credit as a reduction in the net amount at which the acquired property is stated (either directly or by inclusion in an offsetting account) may be preferable in many cases, we recognize as equally appropriate the treatment of the credit as deferred income, provided it is amortized over the productive life of the acquired property. [Copyright © 1962 by the American Institute of Certified Public Accountants, Inc.]

Unfortunately (for the prestige of the APB), in the months following Opinion No. 2 the SEC did not support the board, eventually announcing its official acceptance of the alternative treatment of the investment tax credit as an element of income (expense reduction) in the year in which it is applied to a company's tax bill. The APB was, therefore, forced to reconsider its position—resulting in Opinion No. 4, which was marked by dissent among members of the board but through which a majority of the board modified Opinion No. 2 as follows:

> 8. It is the conclusion of this Board that the Revenue Act of 1964 does not change the essential nature of the investment credit and, hence, of itself affords no basis for revising our Opinion as to the method of accounting for the investment credit.
>
> 9. However, the authority of Opinions of this Board rests upon their general acceptability. The Board, in the light of events and developments occurring since the issuance of Opinion No. 2, has determined that its conclusions as there expressed have not attained the degree of acceptability which it believes is necessary to make the Opinion effective.

10. In the circumstances the Board believes that, while the method of accounting for the investment credit recommended in paragraph 13 of Opinion No. 2 should be considered to be preferable, the alternative method of treating the credit as a reduction of Federal income taxes of the year in which the credit arises is also acceptable. [Copyright © 1964 by the American Institute of Certified Public Accountants, Inc.]

Although Opinion No. 4 represented a setback to the board's original position on the investment tax credit, some years later the board (with the composition of its members changed) revisited the issue. After conferring with SEC representatives to ensure support, the APB was about to reaffirm the basic position originally taken in Opinion No. 2 when the unprecedented action referred to in the following editorial appearing in the *Wall Street Journal* of November 23, 1971, preempted any further action by the APB or the SEC:

A Vote for Gimmickry

Over the years, the accounting profession has had to cope with two forces that sometimes are in conflict.

On the one hand, it has professional and certain legal obligations to set and maintain acceptable and consistent standards for certifying the fairness and accuracy of corporate financial reports. On the other, it is faced with pressures from clients seeking to present their reports in ways most convenient to their own purposes.

Now, it would appear, yet another force, the United States government, is involving itself more heavily in the delicate balance of interests. From all appearances, moreover, the government is entering the lists not on the side of consistent standards but on the side of short-term convenience.

The argument is over how companies and their accountants should handle the proposed 7% tax credit on capital investment which President Nixon is pushing as an economic stimulant. The accounting profession, through its rule-making Accounting Principles Board, wants the tax-saving effect of the credit spread over the life of the capital equipment purchased, on the ground that this single method would make earnings reports consistent with each other and reduce year-to-year distortions.

The administration, on the other hand, fears that the APB approach would weaken the stimulative effect of the tax credit by preventing a quick recovery of the full 7% by companies that wanted to apply it to their earnings immediately.

Last week, the Senate sided with the administration, voting a provision into its version of the tax bill that would prohibit application of the APB rule. The APB says this could leave companies with a choice of three or more different ways of accounting for the tax credit and represents a decided step backwards "for the long, hard effort to achieve uniformity in financial reporting."

Indeed it does. And the reason all this comes about is the government's effort to make the economy, and its own record, look good through employment of a tax gimmick. In other words, the government is trying to do much the same thing responsible accountants have been trying to get corporations not to do for so many years.

The tax law still hasn't passed both houses of Congress. The APB may still win its point, but the chances don't look particularly bright. It is one thing to persuade a corporation to abide by "generally accepted accounting procedures." But it is something else again to persuade a government.[4]

Required:

1. Based on the above discussion and quotations, contrive a simplified example covering a two-year period in which a business enterprise acquires a long-lived asset to which a 7 percent investment credit applies. Make the following assumptions:
   (a) That all "other" revenues and expenses are alike for the two years
   (b) That income tax expense without regard to the investment tax credit is equal to 50 percent of the excess of revenue over all expenses other than income tax expense
   (c) That the new asset acquired in year one is expected to last ten years.
   Using these assumptions, draw up income statements for the two years according to the two methods alluded to above.

2. In the *Wall Street Journal* editorial it was noted that the administration feared that the APB's position, if imposed on companies, would blunt the stimulating effect of the investment credit. Do you feel that such fears were warranted? In what sense, if any?

3. The *Wall Street Journal* editorial also expressed dismay that Congress had intervened in the process of determining accounting policy. Do you find such intervention surprising? Why or why not? Is such intervention justified in general (i.e., disregarding the facts in this particular case)?

17-2. The Oil Industry Accounting Controversy. Following is an article from the *Wall Street Journal* describing one stage in the controversy over accounting policy for companies in the oil industry.

> The accounting profession's rule-making body, already typecast as Caspar Milquetoast for repeatedly watering down stiff accounting proposals in recent years, appears ready to play the same role in a new drama.
>
> Under heavy pressure from the oil industry, the Accounting Principles Board seems likely to reverse a tentatively proposed accounting change that would have sharply lowered the reported earnings of many oil companies, particularly smaller ones.
>
> The board's Committee on Extractive Industries has decided to recommend to the board next month that the oil companies be allowed to continue using the controversial "full-cost" method of accounting. Insiders believe the board will concur.
>
> The full-cost method gives a boost to current reported earnings of oil companies

---

[4] "A Vote for Gimmickry," *Wall Street Journal*, November 23, 1971. Reprinted with the permission of The Wall Street Journal, © Dow Jones & Company, Inc., 1971.

choosing to use the system because it permits them to stretch over a period of years such current costs as unsuccessful exploration and drilling expenses. Thus, they can report much higher earnings in the early years of an exploration program than they could if they charged off the expenses as incurred.

Most major oil companies shun the full-cost system and instead charge off these costs as they are incurred. But roughly half of the publicly held oil-exploration companies use the full-cost system, including Occidental Petroleum Corp., Tenneco Inc., Texaco Inc. and Texas Oil & Gas Corp.

Reflecting the importance of the accounting method to these companies, their stocks generally took a nosedive when the accountants' Extractive Industries Committee in November announced a "highly tentative position" withdrawing most benefits of full-cost accounting as practiced by companies operating in the U.S. and Canada.

Battle Lines Drawn

Not surprisingly, these companies leapt into battle with the accountants. And not surprisingly in view of recent accounting board history, the companies apparently have succeeded in winning a reversal.

The board still bears scars from its protracted controversy over tighter rules for merger accounting. Over much of 1970, the board, badly split and under heavy pressure from industry, repeatedly weakened its proposals before reaching a compromise. (But the board has taken on a tremendous number of industries in recent years in attempts to make accounting rules more consistent. Currently keeping the board especially busy are guidelines for life insurers.)

Under regulations of the Securities and Exchange Commission and the major stock exchanges, corporate financial reports must be certified as conforming to "generally accepted accounting principles." It's the job of the 18-member Accounting Principles Board to set these principles.

Severely criticized for its sometimes bewildering and contradictory array of principles, the board in recent years has been trying to narrow the choices of accounting methods. In many cases, such as in accounting for oil-drilling expenses, the same basic costs may be reflected in shareholder reports in several different ways, to the confusion of shareholders and securities analysts. But the board's efforts, as in the current oil case, have often riled corporate treasurers, bringing reversals or compromises.

Anguished Outcry from Some

The vehemence of the attack by oil companies using the full-cost method stunned some accountants at hearings in November. Occidental called the committee proposal attacking full-cost "truly incredible." Underwriters said the proposed new rule would make it extremely difficult for smaller companies to get financing, especially in stock sales, because their earnings would be "distorted" downward.

A parade of companies using the full-cost method, their analysts, auditors and others, testified that the overall impact of adopting such restrictive proposals would be to discourage aggressive exploration just as the U.S. faces an energy crisis and just as U.S. oil and gas companies face the need to raise some $150 billion in the next decade for capital and exploratory spending.

Officials of "full-cost companies" that have already learned of the committee's reversal consider the battle won. But not all the analysts or accountants involved are happy about the reversal, and some complain that the committee caved in abysmally under pressure. "The whole thing was outrageous," fumes David Norr, a securities analyst, a committee member, and a partner in First Manhattan Co. "This was the howl of the mob determining accounting principles."

"Interesting Exchanges"

Joseph Cummings, committee chairman and a partner in Peat, Marwick, Mitchell & Co. in New York, concedes the companies using the full-cost method were quite upset and "a few interesting exchanges" took place. But he says the companies' arguments persuaded the committee to change course.

Committee members now are drafting their recommendations on oil accounting, for presentation to the Accounting Principles Board at a meeting March 8 to 10. Mr. Cummings says the recommendations will place certain restraints on full-cost accounting. But in effect the companies will be allowed to amortize, or spread out, their exploration and other costs pretty much as they have been, because they can still use an entire country or continent as a "cost center."

In accounting jargon, the "cost center" is the geographic area within which drilling and other exploratory costs may be balanced off against the income from reserves in that area. Under the present full-cost procedure, companies using the method have considered all of the U.S. and even all of North America as their "cost center"—meaning that they could capitalize all of the costs involved in a fruitless search for oil in, say, Louisiana, and balance them off against income from reserves in California over a period of years.

The harshly criticized November proposal of the Extractive Industries Committee would have narrowed the cost center down to a single producing field. Some oil analysts viewed this position as a compromise of sorts between full-cost advocates and those who favored immediate write-offs, because it did allow costs within the field to be accounted for as capital items.

Support from the Opposition

But to most companies using the full-cost method, the decision was clearly a death blow to their way of accounting. Even Robert Mays, comptroller of Standard Oil Co. (New Jersey), who as a mild critic of the full-cost method and whose company uses more conservative accounting, agrees that the proposal amounted to a rescission of most full-cost benefits.

"Companies frequently start out working within a broad geographic area of interest," he says, "and spend a lot of time and money identifying prospects in the area without locating a producing field. What do you do with all of the costs involved in working the whole area, the costs that can't be associated with a given field? The inference of the original (accounting panel) memorandum is that you would write them off" against current earnings rather than making them capital items to be amortized over several years.

In its review of oil industry accounting methods, the Accounting Principles Board is seeking to arrive at a set of principles to make the earnings of separate oil companies a good deal more uniform. But the uproar over the November proposals and the switch in position by the Extractive Industry Committee apparently are resulting in a continuation of two basically different ways of accounting for key expenses of oil companies.

There would, however, be some steps toward uniformity, if the committee recommendations are adopted. For example, all oil and gas companies would be required to capitalize (and therefore spread out) their costs for geological and geophysical work, property acquisition, carrying costs and several other expenses—practically all costs leading up to drilling.

Once drilling occurs, however, a company could go in either of two directions. If the well is a dry hole, a company could conservatively write off the cost of drilling it immediately, considering that field its cost center. But if a "full-cost company" drills a dry well, it will be permitted to consider the whole country its cost center, just as it does now. So it can stretch out the cost of that dry hole instead of writing it off immediately, provided it has offsetting revenues from enough proven reserves somewhere else in the country.

But critics of the plan say drilling costs generally represent a huge chunk of total expenses in exploration, and only a small percentage of wildcat wells strike oil in commercial quantities. They feel that allowing separate oil companies to treat such an important cost item in two different ways perpetuates a confusing dual system.

Choices in Oil Discoveries

Under the new committee proposals, a company finding oil also would have a dual choice. Under conservative accounting, companies could write off all costs, including predrilling costs, not associated with that specific find. A concern using full-cost accounting could treat that discovery exactly as it always has, capitalizing all the costs and lumping the reserves found into its total, nationwide pool.

The "full-cost companies," however, wouldn't be allowed to capitalize exploration and drilling expenses in an amount beyond the value of their existing national reserves (currently, there is no such limit). Also, under the new recommendations, oil companies would have to fully disclose expenditures on separate unsuccessful explorations, the amount of capitalization of these expenses, what reserves were discovered in given areas, and the quality of those reserves.

Richard Lemmon, adviser to the Extractive Industry Committee chairman, believes the new recommendations will bring a measure of uniformity to oil accounting. "Actually, we don't have just two accounting methods right now, but more like 200, because each method is applied with many variations," he says. "I think now we will have one accounting method, requiring the same capital expense decisions before discovery but allowing some flexibility afterward."

Others aren't so sure. Says one puzzled executive of a major oil concern, "None of it makes sense unless you've got a darn good astrologer on your staff." An accountant specializing in oil concerns says the Accounting Principles Board has "suffered through some big battles lately with the insurance industry and over investment tax credits." He adds, "So maybe they're trying some sort of compromise here. But any compromise which permits the two systems to exist is no compromise. It's simply walking away from the problem."[5]

Required:

1. At the time the article was written there were basically two widely practiced methods for matching the costs of unsuccessful oil and gas exploration efforts (which are presumably necessary costs of discovering oil and gas deposits) against the revenues of present and future periods. Describe the two methods as best you can, and, if possible, contrive a simple example to contrast the effects of the two methods on financial position and income.

2. The Accounting Principles Board initially favored one of the methods. Which one did it favor?

3. Some parties (entities) thought they would be penalized by limitation of acceptable accounting practice to the method initially favored by the board. Name the parties (entities), and explain why they felt as they did.

4. What benefits were alleged to be associated with limiting the acceptable alternatives for accounting for unsuccessful exploration costs?

5. The board ultimately changed its position. Did the change apparently take place exclusively because the board felt it was initially wrong on theoretical grounds? If not, what other grounds for the change are alluded to?

6. Do you feel that the board was right or that it was wrong in its decision? If you cannot decide, state "in principle" why not.

17-3. The Home-Stake's Ponzi Caper. Following are some excerpts from the *Wall Street Journal* describing an investment scheme in which a number of prominent business, government, and entertainment figures might lose up to $100 million.

Walter B. Wriston is chairman of First National City Bank, the nation's second largest. Fred J. Borch is former chairman of General Electric Co. Russell W. McFall is chairman and president of Western Union. George J.W. Goodman is the pseudonymous financial supersophisticate, "Adam Smith," who wrote "The Money Game." Murray I. Gurfein is the U.S. district judge who wrote the "Pentagon

---

[5] G. Christian Hill, "Wildcatter Wrangle," *Wall Street Journal,* February 16, 1972. Reprinted with the permission of The Wall Street Journal, © Dow Jones & Company, Inc., 1972.

Papers" decision. You already know Jack Benny, Liza Minnelli, Walter Matthau and Barbra Streisand.

Along with some 2,000 other rich and not-so-rich Americans, they appear to have fallen victim to what the Securities and Exchange Commission alleges is a classic swindle: a Ponzi scheme.

This may be the biggest swindle of its kind in history. The investors, whose stakes in some cases exceed $500,000, are estimated to have put into it a total of more than $130 million. Of that, possibly $100 million or more has gone astray.

It has vanished into a now-bankrupt oil-drilling operation whose cast of characters, and props, includes a persuasive Oklahoma oil lawyer, Robert S. Trippet; a California vegetable farm's irrigation piping, painted oil-field orange; an Oxford-accented salesman and his well-placed colleagues, who wined and dined prospects at places like the Twenty One Club; and a bevy of accountants and lawyers, including a partner in one of Wall Street's biggest and most prestigious old firms, Simpson Thacher & Bartlett, whose presence allegedly helped assure everybody that everything was proper.

A Criminal Investigation

Persuasive, also, were handsome payouts to some early investors, who thus were encouraged to increase their stakes unaware that most of the money really was coming from their own or other investors' funds rather than from legitimate business activity. And that is what makes a Ponzi scheme. It's named after Charles Ponzi, a Boston confidence man active in 1919 and 1920, who promised $1.40 in 90 days for every $1 invested and, for a while, delivered. He took in $10 million before he was arrested, tried and imprisoned for more than five years for fraud and larceny.

The current case centers on Home-Stake Production Co., a Tulsa tax-shelter oil-drilling company, unrelated to Homestake Mining Co. of San Francisco. The Securities and Exchange Commission, which first took action against it in 1971, declared it insolvent in a little-noticed proceeding last September. The SEC is conducting an intense criminal investigation of its affairs. At least one federal grand jury is expected to convene soon, probably in Los Angeles or in New York, to hear evidence. Meanwhile, the trustee in Home-Stake's bankruptcy and four groups of Home-Stake investors have filed suits in federal and state courts in Tulsa accusing the principals of wrongdoing.

The principals generally deny having done anything wrong. Lawyer Trippet, who founded Home-Stake in 1955, took its drilling programs public in 1964 and ran it until he resigned last summer, has consented to a court injunction against securities-law violations without admitting or denying any charges by the SEC. He says he acted in "good faith" in raising money for oil drilling and warned investors that the ventures were risky. He denies charges by the SEC and others that false statements were made to investors. He notes that no court has resolved any of the factual or legal questions raised. Otherwise, he declines to discuss any specific charges on the ground that the issues are in litigation.

Some Refunds

The four groups of Home-Stake investors, in their suits, have accused Harry Heller, partner in charge of Simpson Thacher's Washington office, of either knowing or failing to exercise enough care to know, that Home-Stake was engaged in illegal activities. In each year from 1964 through 1971, Mr. Heller passed upon the legality—and thus, according to the investors, lent his reputation to the veracity—of the Home-Stake circulars that offered them participations in its subsidiaries' yearly oil-drilling programs.

Mr. Heller denies any impropriety. Simpson Thacher is a defendant, too, though there's no evidence that the firm's other partners had anything to do with Home-Stake.

The story is incomplete. But investigators have turned up evidence to suggest that Home-Stake used little, of the $130 million or so it took in, for drilling. In one year, for example—1970—the Internal Revenue Service has alleged that the company used less than $3 million to drill for oil of the $23 million it raised from the sale of participation units, or shares, in its drilling program.

For that year the company did refund about $5 million to unhappy investors made wary by an SEC complaint that the offering was misleading. What happened to the rest of the money that year and other years is unclear. Royce H. Savage, Home-Stake's court-appointed trustee, has accused Mr. Trippet of diverting more than $3 million to his own use and, among other things, causing Home-Stake to provide members of his family with cars and credit cards for personal use.

Home-Stake's selling expenses clearly were very high. And some money was handed out in loans (which haven't all been repaid) and other payments to lawyers and accountants who encouraged their clients to invest in the drilling programs. This isn't necessarily illegal, but in some circumstances it can be. It also can be unethical.

Mr. Trippet, 56 years old, a graduate of the University of Oklahoma, is said to be one of the first men in the U.S. to discern the appeal of oil-drilling ventures as tax shelters for wealthy people. The total investment in them usually is tax-deductible right away. The typical investor buys in near year-end, when he gets around to tax planning. Mainly seeking a fast write-off, he doesn't necessarily expect a fast profit.

So the investor isn't especially suspicious when initial returns come slowly, and he is pleasantly surprised when big returns come fast. One group of New Yorkers invested $200,000 in Home-Stake's 1966 drilling program and $365,750 in 1967. When early returns proved better than expected, they stepped up their investment to $2.2 million in 1968 and $1.3 million in 1969. Then returns began to fall far short of projections. Some investors had been told their total return, taking tax breaks into account, might reach 700%.

There was an additional twist. The returns were distributed unequally, apparently sized to keep individual investors happy. For example, John D. Lockton, former treasurer of GE, invested $50,000 in the 1970 Home-Stake drilling program. He got a return of $2,418, or 4.8%. Western Union's Mr. McFall invested $60,000 in the same program and got a return of $6,220—or 10.4%.

Mr. McFall had made his first investment of $38,000 in 1966. His yearly outlay rose to $60,000 in 1969 and 1970, and $140,000 in 1971. By 1972, returns had dwindled and Mr. McFall kicked in only $20,000. He won't discuss his losses.

The programs were sold most intensively in Los Angeles and in New York, where early key contacts for Home-Stake Chairman Trippet were William E. Murray, a well-known tax and estate lawyer, and high GE officials. Mr. Trippet already had known a few of the GE officers; others he met through Mr. Murray, who had done legal work for some of them. Back in 1960, Mr. Borch, then a GE vice president, invested $28,000. He increased his investments to $31,360 in 1961, to $132,160 in 1964 and to $209,000 in 1965.

Eventually, at least two dozen present and former GE officials poured a total of more than $3.7 million into Home-Stake drilling programs. Mr. Lockton invested $567,000; Herman L. Weiss, now a vice chairman, invested $570,180.

Another fat New York target was the high command of First National City Bank. George S. Moore, then president and later chairman, invested $56,400 in 1964 and $256,500 in 1965, cutting back to $57,000 in 1967 and $38,000 in 1968. The current chairman, Mr. Wriston, started with an $18,800 outlay in 1964 and invested $38,000 to $40,000 in each of the next five years.

"I Should Have Listened"

Home-Stake men dropped the names of GE and Citibank investors to attract others. Hoyt Ammidon, chairman of New York's U.S. Trust Co., recalls that Mr. Murray introduced Robert Trippet to him, and the two stressed that GE and Citibank officers had invested.

"Because these two organizations, including the head of the oil department at Citibank (William I. Spencer, now president), liked it, it appeared to me to have merit," Mr. Ammidon says. He invested more than $114,000 from 1966 through 1969. "The people in our own oil department were against it from the beginning," he says. "Had I been smarter I would have listened to them."

Mr. Ammidon's name helped attract still other investors: among them, Howard D. Brundage, executive vice president of J. Walter Thompson Co., the advertising agency, and Chester W. Nimitz Jr., chairman of a Connecticut scientific-instruments concern, son of the World War II Navy hero and himself a retired rear admiral. Many other major investors relied on the example of trusted peers and made little effort to investigate Home-Stake on their own.

Had they done so, however, they might have shared the experience of some investors who did look at Home-Stake's oil operations in Central California in the late 1960s. Harvey L. Garland, then operations manager, says the company had drilled five wells on a vegetable farm near the small town of Santa Maria. To make things look more impressive, he says, Home-Stake officials got permission from the farmer to paint some of his gray concrete irrigation pipes orange and code them with oilfield markings. Wells hadn't even been drilled at these locations, Mr. Garland says.

* * *

Tardy Tax Sleuths

The IRS and the SEC, both understaffed and lacking tax-shelter expertise, were slow to investigate Home-Stake and other shelters thoroughly. This was well-known among people selling them, and there's reason to believe that it encouraged shabby practices. Now that the IRS has moved, it is barred in many cases by a three-year statute of limitations from challenging deductions and collecting extra taxes for years prior to 1970. Generally, investors didn't criminally falsify their deductions, because they didn't know their money was being used questionably. Thus they aren't subject to fraud proceedings, on which the statute of limitations runs longer.

Before last April 15, however, the three-year deadline for action on 1970 returns, the IRS got waivers of the deadline from many investors, and it is moving to get waivers for later years. Taxpayers can be induced to waive the protection of the statute of limitations by an IRS threat to immediately assess whatever extra tax the IRS thinks is due.

If deductions for 1970 and later are barred by the IRS, some tax lawyers believe, investors still will be able to take theft loss deductions for their initial outlays on the ground that the investments were obtained by fraud.

In any event the Treasury is out many millions of dollars, which will eventually have to be made up by other taxpayers. The IRS and state tax men have claims against Home-Stake itself exceeding $30 million, according to Home-Stake's bankruptcy trustee. The tax claims alone far exceed the company's $18.6 million in assets estimated by a recent audit by Coopers & Lybrand, the big accounting firm.

Nobody has determined the total dimensions of the Home-Stake disaster with any real precision. Estimates have it that the company sold $3 million in common stock as well as roughly $130 million in drilling units since the late 1950s. The stock is considered by many to be practically worthless. The company is believed to have returned roughly $30 million to investors in one form or another, thus indicating a total loss of more than $100 million, excluding tax savings to investors that the IRS was too late to challenge.

Some investors now concede they should have been more careful. In 1967 Home-Stake parted company with its auditing firm, Arthur Andersen & Co., after Andersen qualified its certification of Home-Stake's 1966 annual report. "I became suspicious a couple of times, when they fired their auditors and one thing and another," says Ralph A. Hart, former chairman of Heublein Inc. "But he"—Mr. Trippet—"was such a good salesman I just kept on buying."

From 1961 through 1970 Mr. Hart put more than $322,000 into Home-Stake. He is among those suing for his losses.[6]

Required:

1. How did the promoters manage to lure so much money out of so many people?

---

[6] David McClintick, "The Big Write-off," *Wall Street Journal,* June 26, 1974. Reprinted with the permission of The Wall Street Journal, © Dow Jones & Company, Inc., 1974.

2. Many of the people involved apparently did not attempt to obtain or evaluate any accounting information about the concern in question. Was that wrong or irrational on their part?

3. There are civil and criminal penalties for the kinds of wrongdoing allegedly engaged in by the promoters in this case which may be applied to satisfy (at least in part) the complaints of people who lost money. Are there any other victims besides those who invested directly in this particular case? Explain your position.

4. Besides the penalties for wrongdoers in such cases (which no doubt act as deterrents), is there any reason for society to actually prevent the wrongdoing from taking place? If so, what steps might have been taken in this case?

17-4. The Fair Market Value Controversy. We have seen that current accounting policy embraces, in the main, the conventional accounting model as its guiding measurement concept. It was noted, however, that certain exceptions are made for specific industries or specific types of resources or obligations.

In early 1971 the Accounting Principles Board considered a possible exception. It seemed at that time tentatively inclined to recommend that investments by an enterprise in the stock of another company should be valued at current market value (selling prices) rather than at historical cost. This valuation method was to apply only where the company held investments of less than 20 percent of another company's stock; where a greater interest prevails, different (other than historical cost) accounting methods already prevail.

The treatment of the value increment that results from adopting market value and thereby adjusting the cost price of the equity investments to a larger or smaller value was not fully resolved. As indicated in our examination of the current market-value concept in Chapter 15, the value increment may be regarded as income of the period. Indeed, this recognition of income at the time of the corresponding change in the value of the asset is a major objective of applying the market-value concept. However, other possible treatments of the value increment had been considered by the board.

To permit various interest groups to express their position on this proposed change in accounting policy, the Accounting Principles Board held a public hearing in May 1971. This open hearing, which was the first such forum open to interested parties before opinions were issued, has now become a standard part of the policy formulation process.

If any asset on the corporate balance sheet should be amenable to valuation at current market prices, one would speculate that it would be marketable securities held by the firm. Thus one would not have expected this proposed change to have generated much discord. However, the public hearing revealed significant divergence in the opinions of various government and industry representatives. Exhibit 17-2 contains selected excerpts from the testimony, both written and oral, that was presented to the board on the subject.

Required:

1. Several different proposals for accounting for equity securities (asset valuation and related income recognition) were expressed in the public hearing. Based upon your review of the testimony in Exhibit 17-2, enumerate as many of these proposals as you can identify. For each of these positions, state briefly the rationale you believe supports it.

2. Summarize the general positions of the various interest groups identified in Exhibit 17-2.

3. If you were a member of the accounting policy-making body dealing with this question, what position would you support? Why?

Exhibit 17-2
SELECTED EXCERPTS FROM THE PROCEEDINGS
OF THE "PUBLIC HEARING ON ACCOUNTING
FOR EQUITY SECURITIES," MAY 25–26, 1971

1. *Position expressed by Securities and Exchange Commission:*

. . . while . . . the Commission is not unmindful of the changing nature of the environment in which accounting is required to perform its function, the Commission feels that the continuing weight of authority for continued adherence to historical (acquisition) costs should not, and cannot, be lightly disregarded. In this respect, the Commission is not yet persuaded that a convincing case for an across-the-board current value basis of presentation of marketable securities has been made. (From SEC Position Paper, p. 354.)

2. *Position expressed by Financial Executives Institute:*

Referring back to the Committee on Corporate Reporting of the FEI, I stated that we had a great divergence of opinion within that group on two points. However, we were almost unanimous, first, that there was an inherent danger in embarking on an isolated phase, such as marketable equity securities, of the broad question of fair value accounting; and second, there does not appear to be an urgent and pressing need to concentrate on this subject at this time, to the extent of issuing an Opinion of the Accounting Principles Board. I must add that I have not noted anything at these hearings to suggest any urgency. (From public testimony of Donald Hibbert, vice-president for finance for Kimberly-Clark Corporation and representative of the Subcommittee on Accounting for Marketable Securities of the Committee on Corporate Reporting of the Financial Executives Institute, p. 102.)

3. *Position expressed by Financial Analysts Federation:*

I will preface my remarks by describing the Federation briefly. The Financial Analysts Federation is composed of 42 societies in the United States and Canada which have an aggregate membership of some 30,000 financial analysts, and of these some 2,570 have earned the designation of Chartered Financial Analysts.

"Financial analyst" is a broad term which encompasses security analysts, portfolio managers, and executives who have responsibility for the overall direction of the investment function. Approximately two-thirds of our members are employed by institutional investors, and about one-third by brokers and investment dealers.

The position of the Federation on accounting for marketable securities has been prepared by our Financial Accounting Policy Committee, which is composed of twenty members. Mrs. Rosemarie Tevelow was Chairman of the Subcommittee on this subject and wrote the position paper, which has already been submitted. Unfortunately, Mrs. Tevelow had to be at another meeting today, or she would be here with me to present our views.

There were two dissents within the Committee on this paper. This position paper has been discussed by the Board of Directors of the Federation since its submission to the APB, but the Board has not formally approved or disapproved the paper. There has not been any opportunity to circulate the statement to the membership as a whole.

I will not read the paper, but I will summarize some of the key points. First, I think there is agreement that the conventional accounting concepts based on historical costs are not applicable to marketable securities. We feel that current values based on quotations in active markets are a far more accurate representation of worth than historical cost, which is really an incidental product of the timing of transactions. Consequently, we favor marking marketable securities to current prices, net of tax effect, as of the statement date.

While not within the purview of the present hearing, we favor also the treatment of marketable fixed income securities on the same basis as equities. Those securities are a major part of many portfolios, and are managed along with equities to achieve a maximum investment return within an acceptable limit of risk. While high quality bonds may differ from equities in their fixed return and repayment at maturity, they have, in fact, fluctuated widely in price in recent years. We consider them an inseparable aspect of total portfolio management.

Now, I should say that we have not made a study of the implications of this recommendation on life insurance companies. I think this would have to be considered, because of the substantial bond portfolios characteristic of this industry.

Our position paper favors the reporting of both realized and unrealized capital gains and losses in the income statement. The differentiation of realized and unrealized gains and losses in the income statement is meaningless when applied to securities which have liquidity and continuous quotations. An unrealized gain, sometimes referred to as a paper profit, can be realized quickly upon a call to a broker, or perhaps, if it is a very large holding, within a few days by a call to an underwriter. Furthermore, such accounting developments would be more nearly consistent with modern portfolio practice, which aims for a total return including both income and capital appreciation.

In recent years some insurance companies have begun reporting realized gains in current income, especially if they have been acquired by noninsurance holding companies. These realizations sometimes appear to be keyed to the management of total reported earnings, and therefore are not indicative of total investment performance for either the current year or for some longer period. Financial analysts have great reservations about managed earnings. I might add here that some insurance companies, possibly in trying to defend themselves against acquisition by other companies, have begun to resort to that type of reporting, presumably, in order to influence the price of their stock in the market.

We recommend that total portfolio changes, net of tax, be shown separately in the income statement. That is, they should maintain their separate character. This would mean, potentially, three segments of net income; that is, operating income, investment portfolio change, and extraordinary gains and losses. The sum of these would be net income.

We also recommend that for subsidiary companies portfolio changes in each period should keep their separate identity in consolidation at the parent company level.

The Committee could see no strong justification for industry exceptions, except for mutual funds, which are deemed to report satisfactorily on the present basis. If, however, a company which owns a few incidental securities but does not manage an investment portfolio is exempted by APB Opinion, we believe it should make disclosure of current market values nonetheless.

Two members dissent from the Committee's statement, and one statement of dissent has been submitted with the position paper. In addition, a number of our directors, who are all experienced investment men, showed some disagreement with the paper, although no formal vote was taken. I would like to summarize some of these objections.

The primary reservation was related to the significance and utility of a total net income per share figure which includes both realized and unrealized portfolio gains. It was felt that such a figure would be too volatile on a year-to-year basis to be of much use for true valuation of a company or its securities. Some expressed the view that they would have to "work around" such a figure, probably concentrating on operating earnings, as has happened with bank stocks. They believe they would be able to take care of themselves, so to speak, but wondered whether the individual with less time and knowledge could cope with the proposed reporting equally well. I think that consideration must be given to the reporting procedure in newspapers as well as in annual reports in this connection. However, the Federation has made no studies or surveys to predict the effect of portfolio change volatility on security valuation.

In general, all felt that current market value was the proper balance sheet representation, not historical cost. Also, with two exceptions, all felt that inclusion of only realized gains in net income was unsatisfactory, because of the opportunity for managing earnings. Two dissenters felt that volatility of earnings which included all portfolio changes would be too great, and favored essentially the present practice. (From public testimony of William C. Norby, executive director of the Financial Analysts Federation, pp. 108-10.)

4. *Position expressed by the insurance industry:*

Mr. Jones, the President of our Association [American Insurance Association], has just outlined our position relating to the reporting of equity securities. The philosophy and underlying reasons on which this position is based are clearly and completely described in the paper which we submitted to the Accounting Principles Board. However, there are certain aspects of this problem which are so important that I would like to take a few minutes to review them with you.

Accounting for equity securities has very significant effects for insurance companies. There are few if any other industries affected to the same extent. Insurance companies invest in equities in order to obtain favorable investment returns over a long period of time, and they do not invest—and, in fact, in some instances are prohibited from investing—in these securities for short-term speculative purposes.

Insurance companies invest large amounts in equities. For many companies the carrying value of equities in the portfolio is measured in hundreds of millions of dollars, and for some companies the amount may approach or even exceed a billion dollars. The capital gains and losses arising from these large portfolios are sizable, and fluctuate widely from year to year. The largest portion of these capital gains is unrealized.

It is apparent that this problem of accounting for equity securities cannot be viewed lightly by the insurance industry. Perhaps the most difficult portion of this accounting problem is the assignment of these capital gains and losses to the proper accounting period. A comparison of characteristics of fixed income obligations, such as bonds, with that of stocks clearly illustrates this problem.

The purchase price of a bond is determined so that the investor will achieve a certain determinable yield over the life of the investment. At the time of purchase the interest payments, or coupon amounts, are known, and there are definite commitments that such payments will be made. The period of the investment is readily determinable, and the appreciation can easily be computed by comparing the maturity value with the cost. Thus it is a simple matter to not only assign the interest payments but also the precise portion of the appreciation attributable to any one accounting period in a manner consistent with the underlying philosophy and objectives under which the investment was made.

For common stocks the situation is entirely different. There is no single rate of return which serves as the basis for determining the cost. There is no commitment that the dividend will be paid each year. The length of the investment period is indefinite, and the ultimate amount of the appreciation is not determinable. Therefore, it is impossible to accurately assign among an unknown number of accounting periods appreciation which cannot be determined, although a number of methods of accomplishing this have been suggested.

One method includes as part of net income only the realized portion of capital gains and losses attributable to equitable securities. Thus it is implied that all such gains and losses over a long period of time become part of the earned income at the instant a sale is consummated. We know this is not correct.

Another method includes the net income and both realized and unrealized capital gains and losses as they occur. This implies that the instantaneous market values at the beginning and end of the accounting period have a significant relationship to the long-term investment policy. We know this also is not correct.

Then, finally, there is the formula basis by which these capital gains and losses are included in net income. This method creates an appearance of accuracy which is more apparent than real, and tends to camouflage with mathematical detail the real problem of assigning income to the proper accounting period.

There is even some disagreement among advocates of this method. Some, in order to reflect long-term trends, favor a formula involving a long period of time—say, ten or fifteen years. Others feel that a formula involving, say, more than five years tends to obscure current trends, but they recognize that a formula involving less than five years—say, three years—encounters problems because of severe annual fluctuations.

Because of the nature of these gains and losses and the associated common difficulties, there has never been the same degree of credibility attached to capital gains and losses as has been attached to income arising from other sources. For example, financial analysts, when assessing the potential of a corporation, often give little or no weight to the appreciation in equity securities. It is apparent from the position taken by the various insurance industry associations that most managements favor a separate statement approach in reporting capital gains and losses. Regulatory authorities often require the subsequent reporting of capital gains and losses in financial statements.

These are some of the considerations which led our Association to take the position that appreciation of equity securities is a part of total gains, but the characteristics of this portion of our reports are so different from the characteristics of that portion derived from other sources that it should be reported separately, so that meaningful analysis can be made. (From public testimony of Robert McMillen, vice-president and actuary for the Travelers Insurance Companies and speaking as chairman of the Accounting Committee of the American Insurance Association, pp. 6-7.)

18

Dissemination and Content of Corporate Financial Reports

Corporate financial reports are the end product of the accounting data accumulation process (the accounting information system) and the set of accounting measurement rules selected from the alternatives examined in previous chapters. These reports are distributed to many external decision makers with an interest in the corporation through a variety of communication channels. The purpose of this chapter is to describe the nature of this public dissemination process for corporate financial information, and to review briefly some general considerations relating to use of the information.

INFORMATION DISSEMINATION (THE REPORTING PROCESS)

The ultimate objective of financial accounting is the dissemination of relevant financial information on a timely basis to interested external parties. The reporting process is a complex one, involving a variety of reporting formats and numerous legal requirements. While the financial statements *per se* contain the core information that is transmitted, they are not the sole vehicles. The financial statements included in the annual (and often quarterly) reports of corporations are, when issued, usually accompanied by a large amount of supporting statistics and explanatory information. In addition, selected pieces of information that are eventually included in the financial statements (for example, sales and net income) are often communicated on a more timely basis through media other than the annual reports. In this section, we provide some perspective on the various types of information that are made available and describe some of the important properties of this information. In the following section, we consider ways in which this package of financial information presumably can be used by the decision maker.

Some Typical Reports to External Parties

Annual Financial Reports. A corporation receives a charter to do business from a state, and one of the responsibilities often imposed by law on that corporation is to report at least annually to the shareholders. This accountability obligation often includes the distribution of copies of the corporation's annual financial report to each of the shareholders. Besides this general statutory responsibility, if the corporation's shares are listed and traded on an organized stock exchange, such as the New York Stock Exchange (NYSE), additional requirements may be imposed. For example, a corporation listed on the New York Stock Exchange must submit its annual financial report to shareholders not later than 120 days following the end of its fiscal year, or 30 days prior to the annual stockholders' meeting, whichever comes first.

The content of the annual financial report will vary among corporations, but for corporations that are "publicly held," certain inclusions have evolved as a matter of law, listing requirements, and/or accounting policy. The corporate financial report will typically include three primary statements: (1) a statement of financial position, (2) an income statement, and (3) a statement of changes in financial position. As an integral part of these financial reports, there will be a number of "notes" appended to the statements. The notes contain important explanatory information that enables the reader to understand the underlying economic circumstances and the related accounting policy choices that have been made in arriving at certain monetary representations in the financial statements. Corporations will also often include five- or ten-year summaries of selected financial statistics so that the reader will have a time-based perspective on the current figures (NYSE-listed companies are required to provide at least a five-year summary). If the financial statements are attested to (audited) by an independent certified public accountant (as are most of the financial reports of large publicly held corporations), the auditor's opinion will be included in the annual report. This audit opinion normally covers most of the accounting representations of the corporation described above. (Chapter 19 is an introduction to the attest function as it applies to present-day financial reporting.)

The corporation's annual report often includes not only financial statement information but also descriptive information about its activities and product lines, as well as some summary comments and prognostications by the chief executive officer of the corporation. Frequently, a summary of the financial information included in the financial statements will be presented in the form of an unaudited "financial review."

As an illustration, the financial statement information included in the 1978 annual report of United States Steel Corporation is reproduced in the Appendix to this chapter.

Interim Financial Reports. The information contained in the annual financial report is probably the most complete package of financial data that is given to the shareholder and other interested external parties. Thus, annually, the decision maker can use this information to evaluate that particular business enterprise and reconsider his or her objectives. It may be useful, however, to have more current readings on the financial progress of a corporation. Such readings are provided by *interim financial statements*.

Typically, interim financial statements are submitted to shareholders quarterly (a requirement for most corporations listed on major securities exchanges) and are restricted to financial statement information only—they do not include the more elaborate discussion of the corporation's activities that is included in the annual report. Because the time period involved is shorter, additional measurement problems exist (for example, the impact of seasonal activity), and as a result the reports are generally considered somewhat less reliable (less objective) than the annual reports. While improvements have recently been made in the methods of adapting the conventional accounting model to these quarterly time periods, the inevitable consequence of the shortened time period on the reliability of the reports means that the decision maker may find it advantageous to make additional adjustments in using the information to predict the future cash-generating ability of the business. Yet the trade-off between timeliness and reliability seems increasingly in favor of more frequent reporting.

SEC Reporting. Besides the annual financial reports that are sent to shareholders and certain other interested parties, such as security analysts, the Securities and Exchange Commission requires that all corporations subject to its jurisdiction file audited annual reports with the Commission. These annual reports are filed in 10-K Form (and are usually referred to in the financial community as 10-Ks). The SEC 10-K report includes financial information that is similar to that included in the annual financial report to shareholders, but it also includes some additional information. In general, the additional information expands upon the amount of detail included in a typical annual report. For example, the replacement cost data reported to the SEC (illustrated in Chapter 14) are usually summarized in one or two paragraphs in the annual financial report. Thus, if the external investor wishes to probe more deeply into the diverse activities of a corporation, it may be useful to obtain a copy of the 10-K annual report. The 10-K report is a document of public record and may be obtained at SEC offices (as well as at selected quasi-public repositories, such as the NYSE library). At least one commercial financial service makes available, on a subscription basis, copies of 10-Ks and other filings with the SEC.

In addition to the 10-K report that corporations file annually with the SEC, there are several other types of filings of financial information that are triggered by specified corporation activities. For example, if a corporation (under SEC jursidiction) plans to make a public offering of a new stock issue, it must file in a registration statement (called an S-1) an extensive description of its financial and economic affairs (including the prospectus it plans to issue offering the shares to the public). The SEC explicitly disclaims any endorsement of the value of the stock issue, leaving this assessment of the company's future prospects to the prospective investor; but the Commission does attempt to monitor the accuracy of the factual representations included in the prospectus and other promotional material. Another SEC filing that is made by "widely held" public companies is the unaudited quarterly financial report (Form 10-Q). Thus, for the investor who is prepared and able to seek out and obtain the reports on file with the Commission, a considerable amount of information is publicly available.

News Announcements. Along with the formal financial statements included in the annual and interim financial reports sent to shareholders, and the annual 10-K report and other reports filed with the SEC, corporations also release selected financial information at various times throughout the year through the financial press. The large publicly held corporations whose securities are listed on national exchanges are actually required to release certain financial information to the press and newswire services as soon as it is accurately measured. In this sense such information is always assumed to have significant newsworthiness. Typically, this information consists of data on sales and earnings for the quarter or the year. An example of this type of information dissemination is presented in Exhibit 18-1. While these news announcements contain highly aggregated data and primarily focus on revenue and earnings for the year, they are generally available up to thirty days prior to the release of the annual or interim reports and thus represent a more timely source of information for the external investor.

Exhibit 18-1

ILLUSTRATIVE NEWS ANNOUNCEMENT EXCERPT

Wall Street Journal Report of Fourth Quarter, 1978, and 1978 Annual Earnings for U.S. Steel Corporation

	1978	*1977*
Year Dec. 31:		
Sales	$11,049,500,000	$9,609,900,000
Net Income	242,000,000	137,900,000
Share earnings (primary):		
Net Income	2.85	1.66
Share earnings (fully diluted):		
Net Income	2.78	1.66
Quarter:		
Sales	2,955,400,000	2,448,600,000
Net Income	94,600,000	9,000,000
Share earnings (primary):		
Net Income	1.11	.11
Share earnings (fully diluted):		
Net Income	1.07	.11

Source: "Digest of Corporate Earnings Reports," *The Wall Street Journal*, January 31, 1979, p. 24. (Reprinted with the permission of The Wall Street Journal, © Dow Jones & Company, Inc. (1979)).

Financial Services. In addition to the information that is made publicly available by the corporation, the interested external investor may also have recourse to one or more of the several commercial financial services that tabulate information for a large number of corporations and compile it in an easily usable form. Such digests will normally include more detail than is contained in the news announcements released by the corporation, but less information than will be found in the quarterly and annual reports. An example of commercial financial service information is presented in Exhibit 18-2.

Exhibit 18-2

ILLUSTRATIVE COMMERCIAL FINANCIAL SERVICE REPORT

UNITED STATES STEEL CORPORATION

LISTED	SYMBOL	INDICATED DIV.	RECENT PRICE	PRICE RANGE (1978)	YIELD
NYSE	X	$1.60*	24	33 - 23	6.7%

UPPER MEDIUM GRADE. LARGE CAPITAL EXPENDITURES HAVE HELPED PROFIT MARGINS OF THIS MAJOR STEEL PRODUCER. EARNINGS REMAIN HIGHLY CYCLICAL.

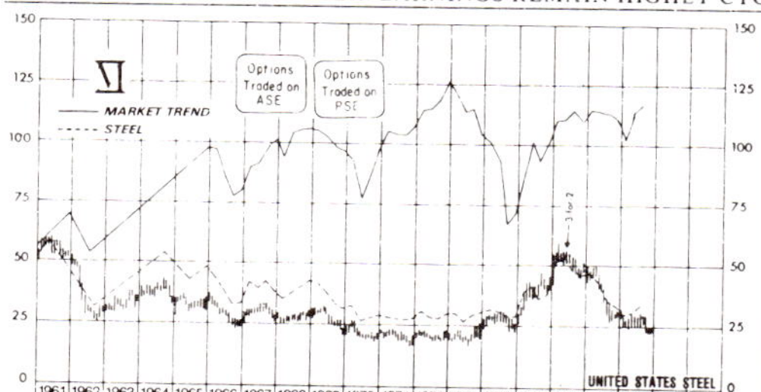

	1961	1962	1963	1964	1965	1966	1967	1968	1969	1970	1971	1972	1973	1974	1975	1976	1977	1978	1979	1980
EARN	2 03	1 7 :	2 20	2 61	3 08	3 07	2 13	3 13	2 67	1 81	1 90	1 93	4 01	7 81	6 34	5 03	1 66			
DIV	2 00	1 83	1 33	1 33	1 33	1 33	1 60	1 60	1 60	1 60	1 33	1 07	1 07	1 47	1 87	2 12	2 20			

CAPITALIZATION: (12/31/77)

	(000)	(%)
Debt	$2,300,200	29.2
Defer. inc. tax	445,800	5.6
Com. & Surp.	5,141,700	65.2
Total	$7,887,700	100.0

Shs. ($1)-84,169,399

INTERIM EARNINGS:

Qu.	3/31	6/39	9/30	12/31
75a	1.69	1.59	1.62	1.44
76	1.20	1.47	1.38	0.98
77	0.33	0.91	0.38	0.11
78	d0.70	1.38	1.04	

DIVIDENDS:	RECORD	PAYABLE
0.55Q	11/4/77	12/10/77
0.40Q	2/10/78	3/10/78
0.40Q	5/5	6/10
0.40Q	8/4	9/9
0.40Q	:1/10	12/9

BACKGROUND:

U.S. Steel, the largest domestic steelmaker, produced 28.8 million tons of steel in 1977 and shipped 19.7 million tons of steel products (approximately 23.1% of industry). In 1977 revenues (and operating income) were derived as follows: steel manufacturing, 72% (-27%); chemicals, 6% (20%); resource development, 4% (16%); fabricating and engineering, 14% (48%); domestic transportation and utility subsidiaries, 4% (43%). Raw steel production capability is 38 million tons; during 1977, the average utilization was 76%. The Company operates 29 service centers. U.S. steel also ownes or leases coal, limestone and iron ore properties.

RECENT DEVELOPMENTS:

In the nine months ended 9/30/78, net income climbed 14% to $147.4 million on a 13% advance in revenues to $8.09 billion. In the quarter, net income jumped to $88.8 million from $25.2 million in the prior year's period. Revenues totaled $2.79 billion, up 18%. Costs of production and services sold benefited from a gain of $90.1 million in the year-to-date ($15.4 million in the quarter) from LIFO inventory liquidation. Although shipments were higher, gains in productive efficiency and income were partially offset by increased repair and maintenance costs and the railroad strike.

PROSPECTS:

Although the demand for flat-rolled sheet has strengthened, a resurgence in the capital goods industry where higher margin heavy steel is used, is needed to restore a suitable level of profitability. Recent price increases on flat-rolled products should help offset escalating costs in this area. In the near term, the effects of the level of foreign steel imports and the government's plan to alleviate the resulting pressures will have an uncertain impact on the Company's performance.

STATISTICS:

YEAR	GROSS REVS ($mill.)	OPER PROFIT MARGIN %	NET INCOME ($000)	WORK CAP ($mill.)	SENIOR CAPITAL ($mill.)	SHARES (000)	EARN PER SH $	DIV PER SH $	DIV PAY %	PRICE RANGE	P/E RATIO	AVG YIELD %
68	4,609.2	9.1	253,676	875	1,571.3	81,218	3.13	1.60	51	30⅜ - 25⅜	8.9	5.7
69	4,825.1	7.4	217,207	534	1,434.7	81,254	2.67	1.60	60	32⅝ - 21⅞	10.2	5.9
70	4,883.2	4.7	147,491	697	1,398.7	81,254	1.81	1.60	88	26⅜ - 18¾	12.4	7.1
71	4,963.2	4.6	154,515	569	1,444.1	81,254	1.90	1.33	70	23⅞ - 16⅝	10.7	6.6
72	5,428.9	7.8	156,988	556	1,539.7	81,254	1.93	1.07	55	23⅛ - 18¼	10.7	5.2
73	7,044.7	10.7	325,758	583	1,420.3	81,254	4.01	1.07	27	25½ - 17⅞	5.4	4.9
74	9,186.4	12.5	634,900	1,152	1,323.4	81,254	7.81	1.47	19	32⅜ - 23⅝	3.6	5.3
75	8,380.8	10.7	a495,000	1,203	1,389.3	81,386	a6.34	1.87	29	47⅝ - 25½	5.8	5.1
76	8,747.7	8.2	410,300	1,154	1,959.9	82,206	5.03	2.12	42	59⅜ - 43⅜	10.2	4.1
77	9,610.0	9.8	137,900	1,328	2,300.2	84,169	1.66	2.20	32	50 - 27	23.2	5.7

Adjusted for 3-for-2 split 6/76. a-Before extraordinary gain of $44.6 million (55c a share).

INCORPORATED:
Sept. 13, 1965 – Del.

PRINCIPAL OFFICE:
600 Grant Street,
Pittsburgh, Pa. 15230

ANNUAL MEETING:
First Monday in May

NUMBER OF STOCKHOLDERS:
248,896

TRANSFER AGENT(S):
Company office

REGISTRAR(S):
Morgan Guaranty Trust Co., New York
Mellon Bank, N.A.,
Pittsburgh, Pennsylvania

INSTITUTIONAL HOLDINGS:
No. of Institutions: 268
Shares Held: 14,404,276

OFFICERS:
Chairman
E.B. Speer
President
D.M. Roderick
Secretary
C.G. Schwartz
Treasurer
R.D. Ryan

Source: Moody's *Handbook of Common Stocks,* Winter 1978-79 Edition.

Comparative Summary of Characteristics of Reports

In this brief survey of the various types and forms of financial information available to the external investor, we have implicitly noted certain properties or characteristics of each of the reports. We have specifically commented on the timing of the release of the report, the scope of distribution, the comprehensiveness of the information contained in the report, and the formality of the report requirements. In Exhibit 18-3 these properties are summarized for each of the reports discussed. Although necessarily abbreviated, this comparative summary should provide a good introductory perspective on the corporate reporting process now in existence. We should note here that there is an abundant amount of other "nonaccounting" information about most listed corporations' activities and plans that is publicly available, and the external investor will often find this information relevant to the investment decision.

SOME CUSTOMARY WAYS OF RELATING CONTENT OF FINANCIAL REPORTS TO RESOURCE ALLOCATION DECISIONS

Now that we have briefly reviewed the types and sources of financial information that are made available to external decision makers through the corporate reporting process, we consider the manner in which this total package of information might be used by the decision maker. In our brief examination of this matter, we focus on the investment decision. This choice of emphasis is motivated by two factors. First, the investment decision is an important, pervasive, yet relatively definable kind of decision problem. And second, the information used in the analysis of investment alternatives typically includes a variety of measurements from the publicly available corporate annual report.[1] As a result, the investment decision problem illustrates the decision relevance of the interrelated set of information included in the financial statements. In contrast to this use of publicly available information, the distribution of benefits decisions are more often specified by some legal or regulatory authority such that the information is specifically designed in accordance with the objectives of the particular distributional process.

The Investment Decision Problem in Review

Prospective owners and creditors who supply capital to a business do so in return for expected future cash inflows. A creditor (e.g., the owner of a corporate bond) acquires contractual rights to specified future payments of interest and principal amounts. A purchaser of shares of corporate stock, on the other

---

[1] For similar reasons the Financial Accounting Standards Board also placed primary emphasis on the investment decision in the adoption of a set of objectives for financial reporting (*FASB Statement of Financial Accounting Concepts No. 1,* "Objectives of Financial Reporting by Business Enterprises").

Exhibit 18-3
COMPARATIVE SUMMARY OF CHARACTERISTICS OF REPORTS

Reports / Characteristics	Annual Financial Reports	Interim Financial Reports	SEC Reports	News Announcements	Commercial Financial Services
Timing of release	Annually	Quarterly for larger corporations	10-K annually, 10-Q quarterly; other reports (e.g., Form S-1) when specified economic activities occur	At intervals throughout year (usually at least quarterly)	Usually monthly or quarterly, plus special reports
Scope of distribution	Shareholders (generally available to public on request)	Shareholders	SEC offices (available to public on request)	Newswire services; financial press	Available by subscription (and in many libraries)
Comprehensiveness of information	Extensive	Somewhat summarized	Most comprehensive source of information	Highly abbreviated	Somewhat summarized
Formality of report requirements	Relatively formal (compliance with generally accepted accounting principles)	Less formal than annual report	Highly formal (requirements imposed by SEC)	Few formal requirements	Based on source data formality

hand, acquires the right to share proportionately with all other shareholders in the residual cash flows generated by the corporation. To choose to invest in a particular business, both the creditor and the owner will presumably want to assess the present value (adjusted appropriately for risk) of the rights that come from the investment and compare that present value with the amount they will have to pay to receive those rights. They will then compare the net present values of investments in various businesses in determining the investment or set of investments they will undertake.

The nature of the decision to invest in a business is simple in principle. In practice, however, it is a formidable challenge. The process of arriving at present values, as described in Chapter 2, begins with the task of specifying the cash flows expected from an investment in future periods. Of course other elements, such as selection of the appropriate time preference rate, are necessary as well. But the valuation of a particular investment opportunity cannot proceed without a projected stream of future cash flows on which to operate.

For the prospective owner, the task of projecting or forecasting future cash flows is quite open-ended. For the prospective creditor, the task is simplified somewhat, as the maximum cash flows from the investment are usually specified in a contract. On the other hand, in a world of uncertainty, both the creditor and the owner will want to assess the risk associated with expected future cash flows, because the greater the risk associated with a given expected future cash flow, the less it will be valued by either a creditor or an owner, other things equal. The necessity for risk assessment means that in addition to forecasting various potential future cash flows, thought must also be given to the likelihood that the forecast flows will or will not materialize. Thus investors face the task of looking into the future and making some fairly complex predictions or forecasts about the amounts and probabilities of the cash payments the enterprise will be able to make to them in fulfillment of their rights as owners or creditors.

The ultimate objective for the investor of this forecasting-analysis process is the selection of a portfolio of securities that has the optimum return to risk trade-off. A representative decision model for the investor therefore includes parameters (generally numerical measures) dealing with two major elements: (1) *expected return* (future cash flows), and (2) *expected risk*.

Estimating Investment Decision Parameters from Financial Statement Information

Use of information from corporate financial statements to estimate the two parameters of the investment decision is dependent upon the assumption that historical data are relevant to a meaningful formation of expectations. We have addressed this issue previously in developing the rationale for the conventional accounting model, but its importance to the investment decision problem justifies repetition here.

The notion that information about events and activities already experienced by an enterprise can be relevant to expectation formation is based upon an assumed continuity of events and activities engaged in by the enterprise. That is, although many aspects of an enterprise's activities (like its product lines, production processes, etc.) may change over time, many important aspects remain constant or change slowly. The immediate past provides a context in which to consider future possibilities. The further various future possibilities depart from the immediate past, the less credible or probable they will seem.

This idea of continuity of events was then applied to the enterprise as a generator of cash flows. Assuming that there is some continuity in the cash-generating process, a portrayal of the enterprise's present "performance" in that process will presumably be relevant to investors who are interested in future cash flows. Thus the conventional accounting performance measurement was developed in the context of representing the enterprise's long-run cash-generating ability. To the extent that these assumptions are valid, the financial statements obviously contain information relevant to the estimation of the expected return parameter. The estimation of the expected risk parameter is similarly dependent upon the assumption of the relevance of historical data. The particular data that are presumably useful to this estimation process will be discussed later in this section. In light of the recent requirement that larger companies must report certain replacement cost data, some limitations of the conventional accounting model may be overcome by incorporating this additional information into the analysis.

Before leaving the subject of using financial statement information as a basis for estimating the relevant decision parameters for the investment decision problem, we should briefly note recent developments in the finance literature suggesting possible limitations on this approach for the individual investor. In particular, the analysis of financial statements for an individual company is a manifestation of what is labeled "intrinsic value" analysis of investment opportunities. This same intrinsic value concept is also implicit in our categorization of the investment decision problem. A company that appears to be a good investment on the basis of an analysis of the information included in the financial statement is one whose intrinsic value is relatively high in relation to its current stock price, and a company that does not appear to be a desirable investment is one whose intrinsic value is low in relation to its current stock price. However, recent research on the efficiency of the capital markets suggests the possibility that the average individual investor *cannot* systematically identify investment opportunities that will enable him or her to earn consistently above-normal returns. That is, the research suggests that the prices established in the capital markets are already based on all available public information (which includes all publicly available financial statements), and individual investors can do no better than to invest in a diversified portfolio with an appropriate (to them) risk level (as defined by market indicators of risk) and earn the market return for that level of risk. In this context, the investor accepts market prices as reasonable estimates of value and abstains from analysis of individual investments for purposes of seeking "bargain purchases."

Whether this "price-taking" posture is actually optimal for a given investor, however, depends upon a number of factors, including the market in which the investment is traded and the individual's personal assessment of his or her ability to evaluate information vis-à-vis the aggregate class of investors in that market (i.e., whether the investor has a comparative advantage in this type of activity). It seems reasonable to conclude, therefore, that though intrinsic value analysis is not an activity that should be engaged in by everyone, those who have (or believe they have) superior skills in estimating the intrinsic values of securities will act accordingly.

Developing Financial Statistics From Financial Statements

Before considering the specific financial statistics that may be helpful in assessing the risk and return parameters for an investment alternative, we first need to consider some general properties of these financial statistics. The values (measurements in dollar terms) reflected in corporate financial reports represent in one sense merely "numbers" that have limited meaning and significance in and of themselves. Meaning and significance come from and depend upon an understanding of (1) the environmental context from which the numbers were drawn, (2) the relationship between the numbers and the underlying economic phenomena that are the real items of interest, (3) the relationship of any particular number or set of numbers to other numbers included in the statements, and (4) the relationships between the real economic phenomena that underlie the numerical relationships expressed in the statements.

Example 18-1

> The High Profit Corporation reported net income for 1980 of $100,000. This measure in itself does provide some information to the investor in that it suggests a potential level of cash-generating ability that is relevant to the investment decision. However, the investor is interested in a broader, more comprehensive, measure of the corporation's performance as a basis for predicting future performance. In particular, given the amount of investment that the High Profit Corporation had in its productive facilities for the period, does the $100,000 represent good or bad performance? Additionally, how does the $100,000 reported profit stand compared with previous profits that the firm has generated or with profits or productivity by other firms in the same industry?

The unanswered questions raised in Example 18-1 suggest two important requirements of the investor's interpretive process: (1) the need for some type of *scaling* of the reported, unadjusted "numbers," and (2) the need for base figures, or *standards*, indicating performance over time and by similar companies (industry standards).

Need for Scaling. The process of "scaling" the numbers reported in the financial statements is a process of relating one number to another number based upon a presumably important relationship between the numbers. In Example 18-1 the implicit relationship alluded to in the first question is the relationship, or ratio, between the net income for the year and the investment required to generate this return. By combining these two measures in the form of a ratio, the investor generates a new measure indicating an important relationship—return on investment. More will be said about this particular ratio and others later.

Need for Standards: Time and Industry. In addition to developing the ratios alluded to above, the investor engaging in financial statement analysis is interested in the relationship between numbers (or ratios) and some standard. Two standards are of general interest to investors—*time standards* and *industry standards*. Time standards merely call for the provision of the numbers (or ratios) from preceding time periods so that the investor can assess the progress of the firm in relationship to prior performance.

Example 18-2

> Assuming investment is constant, if the High Profit Corporation had reported profits of $60,000 and $80,000 in 1978 and 1979, respectively, the $100,000 profit reported in 1980 suggests a continued improvement in the performance of the corporation *relative to its past performance.* On the other hand, if the reported profits for the preceding years had been $140,000 and $120,000, the investor would probably assess the desirability of an investment in High Profit Corporation in a much different light.

Because time standards are important in evaluating the reported numbers for any particular time period, present accounting policy calls for the inclusion of data from the immediately prior period in corporate financial reports. In many instances a corporation also reports selected numbers from prior financial statements for a period of five or ten years. (Recall that NYSE listing requirements call for inclusion of a five-year summary in the annual report.)

The other class of standards that is frequently useful in evaluating the overall attractiveness of an investment alternative is based on the performance of other business enterprises. In some cases the standards are developed from the financial representations of all other corporations. More frequently, the standards represent norms developed from other corporations within the same industry.

Example 18-3

> If the scaling alluded to earlier produced a measure of return on investment of 10 percent ($100,000 net income divided by $1 million investment in production facilities), the investor still needs additional information regarding the level of performance implicit in this measure. If the average performance in this industry were an 8 percent return on investment, the investor might conclude that the management of High Profit Corporation was performing better than the industry norm. On the other hand, if the average return on investment in the industry were 12 percent, the particular investment alternative might not seem as desirable.

Because of the importance of industry norms, commercial financial services make them available (at a price) to interested investors.

Customary Statistical Measures (Indicators) for Decision Parameters

In analyzing the information provided in corporate financial reports, analysts have developed a number of statistical measures, or indicators, that they presumably use as a basis for reaching general estimates of the expected risk and return parameters. Rather than attempt to cover all of these various measures, which is better left to a more advanced course in accounting or finance, we will briefly consider a few of the more important indicators to illustrate the analysis procedure. These indicators will be grouped under the two decision parameters, risk and return, for purposes of exposition. However, the reader should be aware that some of the indicators often have implications for both of the decision parameters, and the specific way in which the various pieces of information are assembled and processed to arrive at estimates of the parameters is a complex and somewhat individualistic information-processing problem. The more competent the investor is in this processing of information, the more likely it is that financial statement analysis of investment alternatives will represent a profitable use of the investor's resources.

The various statistical measures will be illustrated using the data included in the simple financial statements reflected in Exhibit 18-4. Although these statements do not include data for preceding years, or draw upon the information contained in the statement of changes in financial position, they suffice for our exposition at this point. Similar types of analyses may be applied to the more complete information contained in the actual financial statements for United States Steel Corporation included in the Appendix to this chapter.

Indicators of Return. The investor's principal interest in analyzing the returns of various investment alternatives is the comparative return efficiency of the alternatives. Hence investors are interested in several different indicators of return efficiency. The set of general statistical measures of return efficiency that are reviewed here are (1) earnings per share and earnings yield, (2) net income to equity and/or assets, and (3) net income to sales.

EARNINGS PER SHARE (EPS) AND EARNINGS YIELD. One indication of potential return is the earnings that will accrue to the investor's benefit. Since the investor's interest in the corporation is typically reflected in terms of the number of shares he or she possesses relative to the total number of shares outstanding, an important measure of the performance of the company in terms of the investor's interest, or potential interest, is provided by scaling the income in terms of total number of shares outstanding:

$$\text{Earnings per share} = \frac{\text{Net income accruing to common stock}}{\text{Total shares of common stock outstanding}}$$

$$= \frac{\$390,000}{400,000}$$

$$= 97.5 \text{ cents per share}$$

EPS is the earnings attributable to each share of common stock, with the dividend requirements on any preferred stock (which does not share to any greater extent than the amount to which it has preference) deducted from net income in arriving at the income available to common-stock holders. Since the illustrative financial statements in Exhibit 18-4 do not include any outstanding preferred stock, no adjustment for dividend requirements on preferred stock is necessary in the calculation of earnings per share above.

The calculation of the earnings-per-share statistic is further complicated when the firm has a capital structure that includes stock options, or bonds and/or preferred stock that are convertible into common stock. In this circumstance the number of shares of common stock outstanding can increase, often substantially, should the holders of these convertible securities elect to exercise their conversion option. The issue this poses for the EPS calculation is whether or not the number of common shares "outstanding" in the denominator of the

Exhibit 18-4

A MERCHANDISING COMPANY

Statement of Financial Position
As of December 31, 1980

Assets

Current assets:			
Cash		$ 350,000	
Marketable securities at cost			
(market value, $542,000)		460,000	
Accounts receivable	$1,410,000		
Less allowance for bad debts	(70,000)	1,340,000	
Inventory (at lower of Fifo cost			
or market)		2,300,000	$4,450,000
Property, plant, and equipment:			
Land		$ 300,000	
Buildings	$ 750,000		
Store equipment	375,000		
	$1,125,000		
Less accumulated depreciation	(200,000)	925,000	1,225,000
Total assets			$5,675,000

Liabilities and Shareholders' Equity

Current liabilities:			
Accounts payable		$1,400,000	
Accrued expenses payable		420,000	
Federal income taxes payable		140,000	$1,960,000
Long-term liabilities:			
Long-term notes, 8% interest,			
due 1984			1,500,000
Total liabilities			$3,460,000
Shareholders' equity:			
Common stock, $1 par value;			
authorized 1,000,000 shares, issued			
and outstanding 400,000 shares		$ 400,000	
Paid-in capital in excess of par value			
of common stock		900,000	
Retained earnings		915,000	
Total shareholders' equity			2,215,000
Total liabilities and shareholders' equity			$5,675,000

A MERCHANDISING COMPANY

Income Statement
For Year Ended December 31, 1980

Sales		$11,500,000
Expenses:		
Cost of merchandise sold	$6,800,000	
Depreciation expense	80,000	
Selling and administrative expenses	3,700,000	
Interest expense	120,000	10,700,000
Net income before federal income tax		$ 800,000
Federal income tax expense		410,000
Net income		$ 390,000

ratio should be adjusted to reflect the conversion possibility. Current accounting policy provides for such an adjustment, but in a two-stage process. If, at date of issuance, the convertible security is determined to derive a "significant" portion of its market value from its conversion feature, it is considered a "common-stock equivalent" and the common shares that would be issued upon conversion are added to the common shares actually outstanding in all future calculations of an EPS statistic labeled "primary earnings per share." If a convertible security at date of issuance does not meet the test of a common-stock equivalent, then the potentially issuable common shares will never be included in the calculation of primary earnings per share. Hence the primary earnings-per-share statistic represents a type of upper bound on earnings per share generated for the period, as it is presumed to be unlikely that fewer shares of common stock will be outstanding in the future. But the convertible securities that are not classified as common-stock equivalents at the date they are issued may nonetheless be converted at some future date. Therefore a second earnings-per-share statistic, labeled "fully diluted earnings per share," is also calculated. In this calculation all the outstanding convertible securities are assumed to be converted into common stock, and the number of common shares that would be issued is added to the common shares actually outstanding in the denominator of the EPS ratio. The "fully diluted earnings per share" represents a type of lower bound on the firm's ability to generate earnings per common share outstanding, as it seems unlikely that any more shares would be outstanding based upon the current capital structure. Application of these general principles involves many detailed operational rules, including specific tests for determining common-stock equivalents, procedures for modifying the numerator of the ratio consistent with the assumptions made in the denominator, and so forth. Examination of these rules is left to a more advanced course in accounting. It is sufficient for our purposes to note that for firms with a complex capital structure, the income statement will include the calculated values for both primary earnings per share and fully diluted earnings per share. (See Note 12, page 738)

To relate EPS more directly to the decision parameter of interest—expected return—EPS may be divided by the price of a share of stock. The resulting statistical measure represents the current "earnings yield" on the required monetary investment. Whether this potential yield needs to be further adjusted depends upon the dividend policy of the corporation and the investor's attitude toward the relative desirability of "paid out" and "retained" earnings.

NET INCOME TO EQUITY AND/OR ASSETS. As suggested in Example 18-1, the performance of a corporation is often judged in terms of the investment required to generate a particular return. Performance in this sense is an indicator of the average efficiency of capital employed by the firm.

This type of return indicator is calculated by dividing income for the period by the firm's capital investment. Two possible investment bases are customarily used: (1) total assets and (2) owners' equity (net assets). (Note: Since the purpose of return indicators is to depict the efficiency of capital utilized *during* the period, the average levels of total assets or owners' equity may be preferred as bases. However, recognizing this possible preference, we will use the end-of-period figures from Exhibit 18-4 for simplicity of exposition.) When the total value of assets deployed is used as the investment base, the return measure presumably reflects the percentage return that the corporation is able to generate on its total asset commitment, *regardless of the source of the investment* (i.e., whether from creditors or owners). This general measure of earning power is important in assessing the performance of two or more companies that have different mixes of debt and owners' equity.

The ratio of return to total assets is calculated as follows:

$$\text{Return on assets} = \frac{\text{Net income} + \text{Interest expense}}{\text{Total assets}}$$

$$= \frac{\$390,000 + \$120,000}{\$5,675,000}$$

$$= 9\%$$

Since return on assets is a measure that is intended to be independent of the source of funds, the relevant measure of return should be independent of the cost of the various types of financing. The interest expense of $120,000 on the long-term notes is therefore added back to the net income for the year of $390,000 to arrive at the return figure included in the numerator. We have not attempted here to adjust for the income tax effect of interest expense, although a more precise calculation would do so.

In addition to the firm's ability to generate a return on its total asset base, investors are also interested in the return residual (after payments to creditors) accruing to them as holders of common stock. In this case the denominator of the return-on-investment ratio is the value of owners' equity (net assets), and in the numerator the return accruing to this group is net income for the year. Note that in contrast to the return-on-assets ratio, we essentially exclude the value of assets supplied (in the past) by creditors from the denominator and the interest paid to the creditors from the numerator.

The ratio of return to owners' equity is calculated for the illustrative data as follows:

$$\text{Return on owners' equity} = \frac{\text{Net income}}{\text{Owners' equity}}$$

$$= \frac{\$390,000}{\$2,215,000}$$

$$= 17.6\%$$

This measure of return reflects the scaled return accruing to shareholders on their contributed capital, after payments to other sources of funds. It is larger than the return on assets because the return on total assets (9 percent) is larger than the cost of borrowed capital. This phenomenon is known as the *leverage effect*.

NET INCOME TO SALES. Another indicator of a firm's return efficiency is the ratio of net income for the year to total sales. This indicates the amount of profit that is generated from each dollar of sales. In the example, this is calculated as follows:

$$\text{Net income to sales} = \frac{\text{Net income}}{\text{Sales}}$$

$$= \frac{\$390,000}{\$11,500,000}$$

$$= 3.4\%$$

For every dollar of sales, the expenses of producing this revenue amount to approximately 96.6 cents, and the residual return accruing to the owners of the business is 3.4 cents.

Whether a particular return for a dollar of sales is good or bad depends, of course, upon the total volume of sales that a firm generates, and also the investment required to generate this level of sales. This particular statistic, net income to sales, can be related to the return on investment (say, investment by owners) through the following relationship:

$$\text{Return on owners' equity} = \frac{\text{Net income}}{\text{Sales}} \times \frac{\text{Sales}}{\text{Owners' equity}}$$

$$= \frac{\$390,000}{\$11,500,000} \times \frac{\$11,500,000}{\$2,215,000}$$

$$= 3.4\% \times 5.19$$

$$= 17.6\%$$

The reasoning behind this expanded equation is that the second of the two ratios on the right-hand side of the equation indicates the number of times that the total owners' investment "turns over" during the year. Thus, if the firm earns 3.4 percent on each dollar of sales, and the total investment of the owners is in a sense "realized," or turned over, approximately five times per year, the total return on owners' equity is roughly five times the return on sales. Obviously, for firms that turn over total investment frequently (such as the grocery-chain industry), a lower profit per dollar of sales can be sustained while generating a reasonably good return on total investment. On the other hand, a firm that has a slow turnover of investment (such as a jewelry retailer) may require a higher return on each dollar of sales in order to maintain a reasonable return on investment.

Indicators of Risk. The set of general statistical measures used to estimate expected risk includes the following: (1) current and acid-test ratios, (2) debt-equity ratio, and (3) times interest earned.

CURRENT AND ACID-TEST RATIOS. An obviously important indicator of the potential riskiness of a particular investment is the company's short-term solvency, or ability to meet its financial obligations in the immediate future. Two different ratios are often used as indicators of an enterprise's short-term solvency: (1) the current ratio and (2) the acid-test (or quick assets) ratio.

The current ratio is determined in the following manner:

$$\text{Current ratio} = \frac{\text{Current assets}}{\text{Current liabilities}}$$

$$= \frac{\$4,450,000}{\$1,960,000}$$

$$= 2.27:1$$

This ratio sugggests that for each $1.00 of current liabilities, there are $2.27 in current assets to "back it up." Presumably, the larger this ratio is, the less the risk of default and bankruptcy or takeover by the creditors (other things being equal).

The current assets in the numerator of the current ratio include, of course, the total value of inventories. And, in many cases, inventories are not readily available for settlement of liabilities. Therefore a more stringent indicator of the short-term solvency of a corporation is determined by including only cash, marketable securities, and accounts receivable in the assets available to satisfy the current liabilities. This group of assets is often referred to as quick assets, that is, they are susceptible to fairly quick conversion into cash without any substantial loss in value. The acid-test ratio is determined as follows:

$$\text{Acid-test ratio} = \frac{\text{Quick assets}}{\text{Current liabilities}}$$

$$= \frac{\$2,150,000}{\$1,960,000}$$

$$= 1.10:1$$

This ratio suggests that for each $1.00 of current liabilities, there are $1.10 in quick assets available to satisfy it.

DEBT-EQUITY RATIO. Another indication of the relative riskiness of a corporation is provided by the relationship between funds provided by creditors and funds provided by owners. Obviously, the higher the percentage of assets provided by creditors, the potentially more risky the investment is in terms of susceptibility to insolvency. For our example, the debt-equity ratio is computed as follows:

$$\text{Debt-equity ratio} = \frac{\text{Total liabilities}}{\text{Total liabilities and owners' equity}}$$

$$= \frac{\$3,460,000}{\$5,675,000}$$

$$= 61\%$$

Creditors of all types therefore supply approximately 61 percent of the assets for this corporation, and the owners supply approximately 39 percent.

Since the current liabilities may fluctuate in amount and may not represent, in a sense, a permanent capitalization, we may choose to exclude them from creditor-supplied funds. In this case we obtain a measure of the firm's *long-term capitalization:*

Long-term notes	$1,500,000	40%
Common equity	$2,215,000	60%
	$3,715,000	100%

The debt-equity ratio, or alternatively the long-term capitalization of the firm, may be important in an overall assessment of the riskiness of the particular investment to shareholders (or additional creditors whose claims would be subordinated to present creditors). It is also an indicator of potential return on investment. The larger the amount of funds supplied by creditors, the potentially larger the return that will accrue to the owners (in good times) from the leverage effect. Thus, in assessing a firm's debt-equity ratio, the investor is confronted with a trade-off between the risk of having additional debt and the potentially high return on a smaller investment by the owners.

TIMES INTEREST EARNED. A final indicator of the risk of a particular investment that we examine is the extent to which interest requirements are covered by net income. Presumably, the larger the income (before interest expense) in relationship to contractual interest requirements, the smaller the possibility that the firm will be unable to meet its legal obligation to make interest payments as they come due. On the other hand, if income (before interest expense) is not much larger (if as large) than its interest obligations, there is a greater chance of insolvency, and thus a higher degree of general riskiness.

This measure is determined as follows:

$$\text{Times interest earned} = \frac{\text{Before-tax income} + \text{Interest expense}}{\text{Interest expense}}$$

$$= \frac{\$800,000 + \$120,000}{\$120,000}$$

$$= 7.67$$

Thus the required interest payments are covered by earnings amounting to roughly eight times the dollar amount of the interest requirement.

SOME LIMITATIONS OF FINANCIAL RATIOS. We could continue to develop other relationships between measures included in the financial statements, but the ratios covered illustrate the way in which the total package of financial information can be used to develop estimates of the required decision parameters. One point of importance that should be kept firmly in mind is that each of the measures is essentially evaluated in a *ceteris paribus* mode. That is, the interpretation of any single statistic in terms of evaluating its desirability or lack of desirability is based upon the assumption that all other measures are held constant. In point of fact, whether a higher or a lower value is desirable for any single statistic is a function of the values for all other financial statistics and all other sources of information about the enterprise as well.

Another point of extreme importance is the effect of conventional valuation policy on the degree of fidelity between financial ratios and the underlying economic relationships of interest. Present-day financial reports contain mixtures of unexpired (or undischarged) original transaction values of assets and liabilities. Such values impose additional limitations on the usefulness of ratios in at least two respects: (1) current exchange values may better relate to the intended information of a particular ratio—for example, the average efficiency of capital employed in a business might be measured better by the ratio of market-value-based net income to total assets than by the ratio of the counterpart conventional measures, and (2) the dollars of various original transaction values (established in exchanges at various times in the past) do not represent the same economic sacrifice as time passes and the general level of prices changes.

These and other limitations on the use of statistics based on present-day financial reports (brought out in the next section) serve to emphasize again the complex information-processing problem faced by investors in arriving at assessments of the expected returns and risk associated with investments in business enterprises.

THE COMPARABILITY QUESTION

An implicit issue in the analysis of the financial statements (and financial statistics or ratios) of several investment alternatives is the comparability of the data over time and between firms. Comparisons with both the past and with other firms generally are used in analyzing any particular company's data. Indeed, between-firm comparisons are thought to be at the heart of assessing the relative values of alternative investment opportunities. Whether or not actual comparisons are useful, however, is another matter—depending on the comparability of the accounting methods used by each firm and the particular situation.

Comparability Over Time

Comparability *over time* (i.e., stability in whatever relationship exists between accounting data and economic phenomena of interest) is enhanced through the application of the same accounting policies each year. Accordingly, present accounting policy includes a principle, referred to as the *consistency principle,* that urges the use of the same accounting policies by a given firm from one time period to the next (assuming circumstances have not changed). In those instances when an accounting method is changed, the consistency principle calls for prominent disclosure in the financial statements of the existence of the change and the dollar impact on affected items in the statements. Thus, although the corporation may choose among the alternative accounting policies available for valuing its resources and obligations, one can assume that the choices have been consistently applied over time unless a specific indication of a change is noted. And when such a change is made, some (if not always totally adequate) data are provided to facilitate the modifications necessary for the investor to reconstruct time-comparability standards.

Comparability Between Firms

The question of comparability between firms is unfortunately not as well settled as that of comparability over time. Different firms in different industries, and in many cases within the same industries, use different accounting methods to value similar resources. The resulting mixture of valuation bases and measurement rules creates a serious problem for the investor in comparing the financial status and operating performance of different companies. One obvious solution to this problem is for appropriate policy makers (FASB or SEC) to require the uniform application of one approved set of accounting methods—either by all companies or within particular industries.

Notwithstanding its intuitive appeal, this solution also has its drawbacks. Although many measurement problems and situations appear to be similar, they are not in most cases identical. Hence there may be merit in allowing management some flexibility in choosing the accounting policies to be used in best representing the financial status of the firm. At present, the trade-off between the advantages and disadvantages of uniformity and flexibility has been resolved in favor of substantial, albeit not unlimited, flexibility for management. Accordingly, the external decision maker must adapt to this situation when making cross-sectional (between companies) comparisons.

Present Adaptations to Absence of Cross-Sectional Comparability

In seeking comparability across companies (cross-sectional comparability), the external decision maker or financial analyst may wish to make some types of adjustments to the data included in the various financial reports. To facilitate this adjustment process, certain actions have been taken by accounting policy-making bodies. First, "full disclosure" of all material facts has long been a tenet of accounting and, not unimportantly, a legal requirement embodied in the Securities Acts of 1933 and 1934. Additionally, the interpretation of what constitutes material, relevant information has been increasingly broadened by the FASB and the SEC, and the investor now receives a larger amount of supplementary information which may be helpful in reconciling differences in accounting methods between firms.

A second adaptation to the need for cross-sectional comparability is the elimination of some alternative accounting policies. While the accounting profession, and the business community, do not seem prepared at this time to accept *uniform* accounting methods, there is considerable consensus that the number of acceptable alternatives should be reduced. To the extent that a reduction of alternatives is achieved, the investor's adjustment process is obviously simplified, as there will be fewer discrepancies in accounting policies between firms.

As long as management continues to have some flexibility in choosing the accounting policies to be used in preparing financial reports, however, it seems reasonable that investors will want some type of independent review of management's choices. This independent review is provided by the independent certified public accountant. The manner in which the review is undertaken, and some of the standards employed by the auditor, are the subject of the next chapter. Suffice it to say at this point that the auditing process is an important and integral part of the corporate financial reporting process.

APPENDIX: ILLUSTRATIVE FINANCIAL STATEMENTS FROM UNITED STATES STEEL CORPORATION

Section A: Financial Statements from 1978 Annual Report to Shareholders

**Management's Report—
Independent Accountant's Report**

Management's Report—

The Corporation believes that the accompanying consolidated financial statements of United States Steel Corporation and Subsidiary Companies have been prepared in conformity with generally accepted accounting principles and necessarily include some amounts that are based on best judgments and estimates. The financial information displayed in other sections of this Annual Report is consistent with that in the consolidated financial statements.

The Corporation seeks to assure the objectivity and integrity of its financial records by careful selection of its managers, by organizational arrangements that provide an appropriate division of responsibility and by communications programs aimed at assuring that its policies and methods are understood throughout the organization.

The Corporation has established a comprehensive formalized system of internal accounting controls designed to provide reasonable assurance that assets are safeguarded and as to the reliability of its financial records. Appropriate management monitors the system for compliance, and the internal auditors independently measure its effectiveness and recommend possible improvements thereto. In addition, as part of their examination of the consolidated financial statements, the Corporation's independent public accountants, who are elected by the stockholders, review and test the internal accounting controls on a selective basis to establish a basis of reliance thereon in determining the nature, extent and timing of audit tests to be applied.

The Board of Directors pursues its oversight role in the area of financial reporting and internal accounting control through its Audit Committee. This committee, composed solely of non-management directors, regularly meets (jointly and separately) with the independent public accountants, management and internal auditors to monitor the proper discharge by each of its responsibilities relative to internal accounting controls and consolidated financial statements.

BD Smith
Vice President and Comptroller

WB Thomas
Executive Vice President—
Accounting and Finance

600 GRANT STREET
PITTSBURGH, PENNSYLVANIA 15219
412-355-6000

February 13, 1979

To the Stockholders of
United States Steel Corporation:

In our opinion, the accompanying Consolidated Balance Sheet and related Statements of Income and Income Reinvested in Business and Statement of Changes in Financial Position present fairly the financial position of United States Steel Corporation and Subsidiary Companies at December 31, 1978 and December 31, 1977 and the results of operations and changes in financial position for the years then ended, in conformity with generally accepted accounting principles consistently applied. Our examinations of these statements were made in accordance with generally accepted auditing standards and accordingly included such tests of the accounting records and such other auditing procedures as we considered necessary in the circumstances.

Price Waterhouse & Co.

Summary of Principal Accounting Policies

Principles applied in consolidation — Majority-owned subsidiaries are consolidated, except for leasing and finance companies.

Investments — Investments in leasing and finance companies are at U. S. Steel's equity in the net assets plus advances to such companies. Investments in other companies, in which U. S. Steel has significant influence in the management and control, are also accounted for by the equity method. Marketable equity securities are at the lower of cost or market and other investments are at cost.

Inventories — Since 1941, the cost of inventories has been determined primarily under the last-in, first-out (LIFO) method which, in the aggregate, is lower than market.

Income recognition — Sales and related cost of sales are included in income when goods are shipped or services are rendered to the customer, except those related to construction projects which are accounted for on the completed contract method.

Property, plant and equipment — Generally, depreciation is computed on the straight-line method, based on estimated useful lives (usually those established under Guideline and Asset Depreciation Range systems). For the most part, depreciation expense is related to rates of operation, within a limited range.

Depletion of the cost of mineral properties is computed on the unit of production method based on estimated mineral reserves of the particular property.

For disposition of a plant or a major facility within a plant, the resultant gain or loss is reflected in income. Proceeds from other sales of facilities depreciated on a group basis are credited to the depreciation reserve. When facilities depreciated on an individual basis are sold, the difference between the selling price and the undepreciated cost is included in income.

Expenditures for renewals and betterments are capitalized. Costs of repairs and maintenance are expensed.

Mineral exploration and development — General prospecting costs are charged to expense as incurred. Exploration and development costs of domestic projects (except oil and gas) are expensed as incurred, but when it is determined to be a commercially feasible project, such exploration costs are capitalized. Domestic oil and gas and foreign exploration and development costs are capitalized as incurred. When a project is determined commercially unfeasible, these costs are expensed.

Pensions — Non-contributory pension provisions of the U. S. Steel Plan for Employee Pension Benefits cover substantially all employees and, in addition, participating salaried employees are also covered by the contributory pension provisions.

Pension costs under this plan are determined by an independent actuary based upon an acceptable actuarial method and various actuarial factors which, from time-to-time, are adjusted in light of actual experience. Pension costs reflect current service and a 25-year amortization of unfunded past service. The funding policy provides that payments to the pension trusts shall be equal to the minimum funding requirements of ERISA plus additional amounts which may be approved from time-to-time.

Insurance — U. S. Steel self-insures risks for property and casualty losses except for catastrophic casualty exposures and where insurance is required by law or contract. Costs resulting from self-insured losses are charged against income upon occurrence.

Deferred income taxes — These taxes result from recognizing certain items of income and expense in the consolidated financial statements in different years than they are recognized for income tax purposes.

Investment credit — For 1968 and thereafter, investment tax credits have been recognized in income in the year earned. Deferred investment credits for 1967 and prior years were fully amortized in 1977.

Consolidated Statements of Income and Income Reinvested in Business

	(In millions)	
	1978	1977
SALES	$11,049.5	$9,609.9
OPERATING COSTS		
Cost of sales (excludes items shown below)	9,046.4	7,944.5
Selling, general and administrative expenses	372.4	349.5
Pensions, insurance and other employee benefits	693.6	572.1
Wear and exhaustion of facilities	435.6	372.0
State, local and miscellaneous taxes	215.4	196.3
	10,763.4	9,434.4
OPERATING INCOME	286.1	175.5
Interest, dividends and other income *(Note 21)*	155.3	81.2
Interest and other financing costs *(Note 21)*	(191.4)	(154.8)
INCOME BEFORE TAXES ON INCOME	250.0	101.9
Provision (credit) for estimated United States and foreign income taxes *(Note 17)*		
Current	6.7	(98.3)
Deferred	1.3	62.3
	8.0	(36.0)
INCOME	$ 242.0	$ 137.9
Income Per Common Share [in dollars] *(Note 12)*		
Primary	$ 2.85	$ 1.66
Fully diluted	$ 2.78	$ 1.66

INCOME REINVESTED IN BUSINESS		
Balance at beginning of year	$ 3,412.7	$3,457.2
Income	242.0	137.9
	3,654.7	3,595.1
Less—Dividends on common stock $1.60 and $2.20 per share	135.9	182.4
Balance at end of year	$ 3,518.8	$3,412.7

Consolidated Balance Sheet

	(In millions) December 31	
	1978	1977
ASSETS		
Current Assets:		
Cash *(Note 1)*..	**$ 377.6**	$ 273.4
Marketable securities, at cost (approximates market)................	**338.4**	425.5
Receivables, less allowance for doubtful accounts of $15.2 and $13.0...	**1,433.9**	1,086.6
Inventories *(Note 2)*...	**1,257.0**	1,254.8
Total Current Assets..	**3,406.9**	3,040.3
Long-term receivables and other investments, less estimated losses of $32.3 and $31.0 *(Note 3)*...	**748.1**	745.3
Property, plant and equipment, less accumulated depreciation of $7,208.6 and $6,817.3 *(Note 4)*....................................	**5,975.0**	5,724.2
Operating parts and supplies..	**113.8**	116.9
Costs applicable to future periods...................................	**292.5**	287.7
Total Assets..	**$10,536.3**	$9,914.4
LIABILITIES		
Current Liabilities:		
Notes payable *(Note 5)*...	**$ 163.8**	$ 167.9
Accounts payable..	**827.7**	651.1
Payroll and benefits payable...	**638.0**	558.8*
Accrued taxes *(Note 6)*...	**339.1**	230.4
Long-term debt due within one year *(Note 7)*.......................	**74.5**	82.1
Total Current Liabilities......................................	**2,043.1**	1,690.3*
Long-term debt, less unamortized discount *(Note 7)*...................	**2,194.5**	2,300.2
Deferred income taxes..	**416.8**	445.8
Deferred credits and other liabilities...................................	**100.9**	86.4*
Preferred stock of consolidated subsidiary *(Note 8)*...................	**500.0**	250.0
Total Liabilities...	**5,255.3**	4,772.7
OWNERSHIP EVIDENCED BY		
Common stock (par value $1 per share, authorized 150,000,000 shares) outstanding—85,567,163 shares and 84,169,399 shares, stated at $20 per share *(Note 10)*...	**1,711.3**	1,683.4
Capital in excess of stated value *(Note 10)*..........................	**70.0**	61.1
Net unrealized loss on marketable equity securities *(Note 3)*..........	**(19.1)**	(15.5)
Income reinvested in business.......................................	**3,518.8**	3,412.7
Total Ownership..	**5,281.0**	5,141.7
Total Liabilities and Ownership...............................	**$10,536.3**	$9,914.4

*Reflects reclassification of long-term occupational injury and disease liabilities.

Statement of Changes in Consolidated Financial Position

	(In millions)	
	1978	1977
ADDITIONS TO WORKING CAPITAL		
Income	$ 242.0	$ 137.9
Add—Wear and exhaustion of facilities	435.6	372.0
Deferred taxes on income	(27.3)	47.1
Funds from operations	650.3	557.0
Increases in long-term debt due after one year	226.5	577.5
Proceeds from sales of common stock	36.8	72.7
Proceeds from sales and salvage of plant and equipment	22.6	71.2
Issuance of preferred stock of consolidated subsidiary	250.0	250.0
Total additions	1,186.2	1,528.4
DEDUCTIONS FROM WORKING CAPITAL		
Expended for plant and equipment	667.8	864.7
Increases in investments and long-term receivables	2.8	10.1
Dividends paid on common stock	135.9	182.4
Decreases in long-term debt due after one year	332.2	237.2
Increases in costs applicable to future periods	4.8	47.3
Miscellaneous deductions (Net)	28.9	5.9*
Total deductions	1,172.4	1,347.6
INCREASE IN WORKING CAPITAL	$ 13.8	$ 180.8*

ANALYSIS OF INCREASE (DECREASE) IN WORKING CAPITAL

WORKING CAPITAL AT BEGINNING OF YEAR	$1,350.0	$1,169.2*
Cash and marketable securities	17.1	138.3
Receivables, less allowance for doubtful accounts	347.3	243.1
Inventories	2.2	(132.3)
Notes payable	4.1	(23.4)
Accounts payable	(176.6)	(28.3)
Payroll and benefits payable	(79.2)	(29.9)*
Accrued taxes	(108.7)	44.6
Long-term debt due within one year	7.6	(31.3)
INCREASE IN WORKING CAPITAL	13.8	180.8*
WORKING CAPITAL AT END OF YEAR	$1,363.8	$1,350.0*

*Reflects reclassification of long-term occupational injury and disease liabilities.

Notes to Financial Statements

1. CASH—Included in cash are interest-bearing, short-term time deposits of $312.4 million and $217.4 million at December 31, 1978 and December 31, 1977, respectively.

2. INVENTORIES—

	(In millions)	
	December 31	
	1978	1977
Raw materials	$ **169.2**	$ 401.0
Semi-finished products	**511.7**	372.6
Finished products	**337.1**	263.4
Supplies and sundry items	**206.9**	212.5
Construction contracts in progress	**183.5**	126.6
Less invoices rendered	**(151.4)**	(121.3)
Total	**$1,257.0**	$1,254.8

Under the LIFO method, current acquisition costs are estimated to exceed the inventory value at December 31, 1978 as shown above by approximately $1,929 million.

Included in Cost of sales and Income before taxes on income are estimated credits of $124.5 million in 1978 and $76.0 million in 1977 from LIFO inventory liquidations. In 1978, the pool-by-pool basis of calculating the effects of LIFO liquidations was refined to more realistically measure the difference between estimated replacement costs and LIFO values. Inventory quantity liquidations are a common and frequent occurrence in U. S. Steel and generally result from planned inventory programs to support changes in process technology, customer product specifications and market conditions, and because of the discontinuance of product lines.

The net of construction contracts in progress less invoices rendered includes $43.5 million in 1978 and $12.1 million in 1977 related to contracts for which cumulative costs exceed invoices rendered and $(11.4) million in 1978 and $(6.8) million in 1977 applicable to contracts for which cumulative invoices rendered exceed cumulative costs.

3. LONG-TERM RECEIVABLES AND OTHER INVESTMENTS—

	(In millions)	
	December 31	
	1978	1977
Receivables due after one year, less reserve of $1.1 and $4.5	**$104.2**	$116.0
Trusteed funds for environmental improvements	**283.8**	214.3
Other trusteed funds and statutory deposits	**38.9**	89.7
Investments:		
Wholly owned leasing and finance companies—equity method	**42.7**	39.6
Partnership interests	**24.5**	18.5
Other partially owned companies—		
Equity method	**184.0**	179.9
Cost method, less reserve of $28.8 and $24.2	**37.4**	53.2
Other	**32.6**	34.1
Total	**$748.1**	$745.3

Income from investments accounted for by the equity method amounted to $15.6 million in 1978 and $14.7 million in 1977 and dividends received in 1978 and 1977 were $6.3 million and $5.4 million, respectively. Geographic areas and industries in which equity companies operate are shown on page 21.

Investments in partially owned companies (cost method) include marketable equity securities of $7.1 million for 1978 and $13.2 million for 1977. Cost exceeded market value by $27.4 million in 1978 and $22.1 million for 1977. This amount has been credited to the investment and the unrealized loss, net of deferred tax, reflected in stockholders' equity.

Guarantees by U. S. Steel of the liabilities of other companies, most of which are accounted for by the equity method, were $205.7 million at December 31, 1978 and $187.5 million at December 31, 1977.

4. PROPERTY, PLANT AND EQUIPMENT—

	(In millions)	
	December 31	
	1978	1977
Land	$ **293.1**	$ 283.9
Buildings	**1,451.4**	1,419.7
Machinery & equipment	**11,342.5**	10,819.9
Capital leases—machinery & equipment	**96.6**	18.0
Total (at cost)	**13,183.6**	12,541.5
Less accumulated depreciation:		
Buildings	**703.6**	667.5
Machinery & equipment	**6,469.0**	6,148.8
Capital leases—machinery & equipment	**36.0**	1.0
Total	**7,208.6**	6,817.3
Net	**$ 5,975.0**	$ 5,724.2

Depreciable lives are the midpoint lives under the IRS Asset Depreciation Range System: machinery and equipment—primary metals—18 years, mining—10 years, chemicals—11 years, etc. Building lives average 40 years.

In 1977, U. S. Steel adopted Financial Accounting Standard No. 13 for lease transactions and agreements entered into after January 1, 1977. In 1978, pre-1977 capital leases existing at December 31, 1978 were also capitalized. This retroactive application of FAS No. 13 increased Property, plant and equipment $56.3 million, accumulated depreciation $31.5 million, Long-term debt due within one year $8.1 million and Long-term debt $20.4 million. The cumulative effect reduced income before taxes by $3.7 million in 1978. Prior years were not restated due to immateriality. The amortization of capital leases is included in Wear and exhaustion of facilities.

Notes to Financial Statements (continued)

5. NOTES PAYABLE—Notes payable (principally demand basis) were to banks and had average interest rates at year-end of 10.2% for 1978 and 6.9% for 1977.

	($ millions)	
	1978	1977
Maximum aggregate amount at any month-end	**$167.4**	$167.9
Weighted daily average:		
Borrowing	**$164.0**	$157.8
Interest rate*	**8.0%**	5.9%

*Computed by relating interest expense to average daily borrowing.

6. ACCRUED TAXES—Details of accrued taxes at December 31, were as follows:

	(In millions)	
	1978	1977
Income taxes—Current	**$243.4**	$153.8
—Deferred	**(47.5)**	(48.2)
Other taxes	**143.2**	124.8
Total	**$339.1**	$230.4

7. LONG-TERM DEBT—A summary of long-term debt, except for leasing and finance companies, outstanding at December 31, is as follows:

	Interest rates	Years of maturity	(In millions)	
			1978	1977
United States Steel Corporation				
Sinking Fund Debentures (callable)	4	1983	**$ 54.9**	$ 69.8
Sinking Fund Debentures (callable)	4½	1986	**74.0**	93.5
Sinking Fund Debentures (callable)	7¾	2001	**130.5**	150.0
Subordinated Debentures (callable) (sinking fund began 1976)	4⅝	1996	**437.6**	520.3
Convertible Subordinated Debentures (callable) (a)	5¾	2001	**384.9**	400.0
Obligations relating to Industrial Development and Environmental Improvement Bonds	4¹/₁₀-7⅝	1979-2008	**602.3**	457.3
Notes payable to others (b)	7⅜- 8¼	1979-1995	**262.0**	268.0
Mortgages, purchase money obligations and contracts	0 -10¼	1979-2002	**21.7**	37.3
Capital lease obligations		1979-2007	**46.4**	17.1
Consolidated subsidiaries				
Obligations relating to Industrial Development Bonds	5½- 8½	1979-1987	**67.4**	68.7
Railroads First Mortgage Bonds (callable)	2⅞- 3	1979-1996	**7.2**	7.8
Notes payable to banks	3 -12¹/₃	1979-1989	**135.2**	187.6
Notes payable to others (c)	7¾	1981-1985	**—**	20.1
Swiss franc bonds	5½	1983-1987	**—**	50.3
Mortgages, purchase money obligations and contracts	5¾-11¾	1979-1999	**39.7**	50.3
Capital lease obligations		1979-1988	**19.2**	.5
Total (d)			**2,283.0**	2,398.6
Less unamortized discount (e)			**14.0**	16.3
			2,269.0	2,382.3
Less amount due within one year			**74.5**	82.1
Long-term debt due after one year			**$2,194.5**	$2,300.2

U. S. Steel has no immediate plans of utilizing $250 million of existing bank lines of credit.

(a) Convertible into common stock at $62.75 per share. Sinking fund begins 1987. In 1978, $15.1 million were repurchased.

(b) Includes $100 million 8¼% note which matures 1986-1995 and a $150 million 7⅜% note which matures 1985-1987, both of which were privately placed in 1977 with financial institutions.

(c) On November 30, 1978, U. S. Steel entered into an agreement with a third party to assume the principal, interest and prepayment obligations of notes payable to others in 1981-1985 at a cost of $2.8 million. U. S. Steel is contingently liable until the third party discharges the assumed obligation in January, 1981.

(d) Required payments of long-term debt for the years 1980-1983 are $50.3 million, $58.7 million, $81.1 million, and $125.0 million.

(e) Unamortized discount (principally on 4⅝% Subordinated Debentures) is being amortized over the lives of the related debt.

Notes to Financial Statements (continued)

8. PREFERRED STOCK OF CONSOLIDATED SUBSIDIARY—Quebec Cartier Mining Company (QCM) has outstanding, at December 31, 1978, 5,000,000 shares of U. S. $100 par, non-voting, floating rate, cumulative preferred stock. Two and one-half million of these shares were issued in 1977 and a like amount in 1978. This financing allowed QCM to replace substantial amounts of its existing long-term debt at a lower carrying cost and also to provide financing for current expenditures.

Shares may be tendered by the holders at specified series installment dates from 1982 through 1985 and are redeemable at any time by QCM. U. S. Steel has agreed that upon the happening of certain stated events, it will, upon tender by any holder, purchase such shares at par plus 200% of accrued and unpaid dividends.

Quarterly dividends, charged to Interest and other financing costs, were paid based on annual floating rates ranging from 4.71% to 5.52% in 1978 and 4.25% to 4.42% in 1977.

9. PREFERRED STOCK—U. S. Steel is authorized to issue 20,000,000 shares of preferred stock, without par value. At December 31, 1978, none of this stock had been issued.

10. COMMON STOCK—At December 31, 1978 the status of authorized shares of common stock reserved for specific purposes was as follows:

	Shares reserved	Shares issued
Conversion of convertible subordinated debentures	6,374,502	—
Dividend reinvestment plan	3,000,000	2,191,993
Savings fund plan	4,000,000	2,120,977
1976 stock option incentive plan	3,000,000	—
Total	16,374,502	4,312,970

Shares issued at market prices under the Corporation's Dividend Reinvestment Plan were 851,262 in 1978 and 735,046 in 1977. Reserved shares purchased by the Savings Fund Plan were 546,502 in 1978 and 1,228,158 in 1977. The decrease in 1978 Savings Fund Plan purchases of reserved shares was the result of purchasing shares on the open market commencing in May 1978. As a result of the above issuances, capital in excess of stated value increased by $8.9 million in 1978 and $33.4 million in 1977.

11. STOCK OPTION INCENTIVE PLAN—The 1976 Stock Option Incentive Plan was approved by stockholders on May 3, 1976. Under this plan, the Compensation Committee of the Board of Directors may grant to key management employees options to purchase, in the aggregate up to 3,000,000 shares, unissued or reacquired common stock at not less than 100% of market value at date of grant. Options are exercisable after one year, but not to exceed ten years, from date of grant. The Compensation Committee may authorize the surrender of the right to exercise an option or portion thereof in exchange for an amount of stock and/or cash equal to the excess of the fair market value at the time of surrender over the aggregate option price of such shares. Unoptioned shares available at December 31, 1978 were 1,352,600 and at December 31, 1977 were 1,887,000. No options have been exercised or surrendered through 1978. Transactions during 1978 and 1977 were as follows:

	Number Shares	Option Price Per Share	Value at Date of Grant (In millions)
Shares under option 12/31/76	559,000	$ 53.50	$29.9
Granted 6/28/77	564,000	38.8125	21.9
Canceled in 1977	(10,000)	38.8125-53.50	(.5)
Shares under option 12/31/77	1,113,000	38.8125-53.50	$51.3
Granted 5/30/78	543,900	28.875	15.7
Canceled in 1978	(9,500)	28.875 -53.50	(.4)
Shares under option 12/31/78	1,647,400	28.875 -53.50	$66.6

The market price per share at date options became exercisable in 1978 was 26⅜ and in 1977 was 42⅜.

12. INCOME PER COMMON SHARE—Primary income per common share is based on the weighted average number of common shares outstanding which were 84,961,076 in 1978 and 83,011,299 in 1977.

Fully diluted income per share assumes full conversion of the 5¾% convertible subordinated debentures outstanding. In 1978, the income for computation of primary income per share was adjusted by $11.6 million for assumed reduction of interest and other related costs of these debentures. The weighted average number of shares used to compute fully diluted income per share was 91,095,738. In 1977, the conversion of these convertible debentures was excluded from computation of fully diluted income per share because of anti-dilutive effects.

13. PENSION COSTS—Pension costs for the U. S. Steel Plan were $331.7 million in 1978 and $234.5 million in 1977, respectively. The increase in costs resulted principally from the increase in non-contributory pension benefits negotiated in 1977 and from actuarial losses incurred since the last triennial valuation which primarily resulted from heavier than anticipated early

Notes to Financial Statements (continued)

retirements and from less than anticipated appreciation of trust assets.

Pension trust assets for the U. S. Steel Plan are valued for actuarial purposes on a 5-year moving average of quarterly market values for quoted securities and at estimated current value for other assets. The actuarially computed value of vested benefits as estimated at December 31, 1978 exceeded the average value of trust assets by approximately $1.0 billion. The unfunded accrued liability (past service) was approximately $1.2 billion at December 31, 1978.

In addition, for certain other employees, U. S. Steel made payments of approximately $32 million in 1978 and $29 million in 1977 to multi-employer retirement benefit plans and to other pension plans qualified under the laws of the countries involved.

14. INDUSTRY SEGMENT & GEOGRAPHIC AREA INFORMATION (in millions)

By Industry Segment:

	\multicolumn{6}{c}{SALES}		
	To Unaffiliated Customers		Between Segments		Total		Operating Income	
	1978	1977	1978	1977	1978	1977	1978	1977
Steel Manufacturing	$ 8,535.8	$7,352.0	$ 453.0	$ 383.6	$ 8,988.8	$ 7,735.6	$ 33.4	$(45.0)
Chemicals	763.1	664.5	44.7	35.4	807.8	699.9	21.0	32.7
Resource Development	271.1	242.1	124.9	143.4	396.0	385.5	25.1	26.3
Fabricating & Engineering and Other	1,305.7	1,215.4	230.6	243.9	1,536.3	1,459.3	80.2	80.5
Domestic Transportation & Utility Subsidiaries	173.8	135.9	374.7	310.4	548.5	446.3	119.9	71.3
Adjustments and Eliminations	—	—	(1,227.9)	(1,116.7)	(1,227.9)	(1,116.7)	6.5	9.7
Total Consolidated	$11,049.5	$9,609.9	$ —	$ —	$11,049.5	$ 9,609.9	$286.1	$175.5

	Identifiable Assets		Wear and Exhaustion		Capital Expenditures			
	1978	1977	1978	1977	1978	1977		
Steel Manufacturing	$ 5,869.2	$5,616.3	$ 319.9	$ 268.4	$ 398.2	$ 604.9		
Chemicals	457.3	353.6	23.6	17.5	100.0	67.5		
Resource Development	1,085.7	1,057.8	41.3	38.0	54.1	65.0		
Fabricating & Engineering and Other	896.7	769.3	32.0	32.1	30.8	33.4		
Domestic Transportation & Utility Subsidiaries	713.1	630.2	19.5	16.4	84.7	93.9		
Corporate Assets and Adjustments	1,514.3	1,487.2	(.7)	(.4)	—	—		
Total Consolidated	$10,536.3	$9,914.4	$ 435.6	$ 372.0	$ 667.8	$ 864.7		

By Geographic Area:

	\multicolumn{6}{c}{SALES}		
	To Unaffiliated Customers		Transfers Between Geographic Areas		Total	
	1978	1977	1978	1977	1978	1977
United States (Domestic)	$10,642.6	$9,205.5	$ 15.6	$ 13.1	$10,658.2	$ 9,218.6
Foreign:						
North America excluding U.S.	259.5	254.2	122.6	145.0	382.1	399.2
Other	147.4	150.2	5.5	3.6	152.9	153.8
Adjustments & Eliminations	—	—	(143.7)	(161.7)	(143.7)	(161.7)
Total Consolidated	$11,049.5	$9,609.9	$ —	$ —	$11,049.5	$ 9,609.9

	Operating Income		Identifiable Assets			
	1978	1977	1978	1977		
United States (Domestic)	$ 245.5	$ 105.7	$ 7,943.9	$ 7,404.1		
Foreign:						
North America excluding U.S.	40.8	56.6	947.5	909.8		
Other	(.2)	3.5	130.6	113.3		
Corporate Assets, Adjustments & Eliminations	—	9.7	1,514.3	1,487.2		
Total Consolidated	$ 286.1	$ 175.5	$10,536.3	$ 9,914.4		

Notes to Financial Statements (continued)

14. INDUSTRY SEGMENT & GEOGRAPHIC AREA INFORMATION (continued)

GENERAL—Intersegment sales and transfers, for the most part, are accounted for at commercial prices. Steel Manufacturing transfers of coal chemical by-products to the Chemicals segment reflect the current value of the raw by-product material as a replacement for purchased fuels plus the costs incurred to convert the raw material to the transferred product.

Operating income does not include profit or loss on the sale of investments and property, plant and equipment, equity in the income of unconsolidated investees, dividend and interest income on marketable securities and other outside investments, interest and other financing costs, income taxes and other items considered to be general corporate income or expense. Selling, general and administrative expenses have been allocated to segments.

Corporate assets consist largely of cash, notes receivable, marketable securities and other investments.

Export sales from domestic operations were not material. U. S. Steel has no single customer from which it derives 10 percent or more of its revenue.

STEEL MANUFACTURNG—Includes domestic iron ore, coal and limestone operations integrated with steel plants which produce and sell a wide range of steel mill products. Also included are the Great Lakes transportation operations, principally involving the movement of ore and limestone to steel plants, and the sales of steel mill products by a network of steel service centers across the United States and by export distributors. Some of the steel mill products are sold to other lines of business of U. S. Steel for further processing and fabrication into such products as drums, bridges and buildings.

CHEMICALS—Includes the production and marketing of various industrial and coal chemicals, polystyrene resins and agricultural chemicals.

RESOURCE DEVELOPMENT—Includes the operation of both domestic and foreign businesses, either wholly or majority-owned. These involve certain iron ore, coal, uranium and other mineral properties; the development of commercial outlets for currently owned mineral resources considered as excess to U. S. Steel's requirements, either by outright sale or development, the activities of the ocean transportation companies; and the search for and development of new mineral and energy reserves.

FABRICATING & ENGINEERING AND OTHER—Includes the fabrication and erection of structural steel for buildings, bridges, storage tanks and other structures and the fabrication of barges, ship sections, transmission towers, large diameter pipe and a variety of standard fabricated steel products; the manufacture and marketing of gas and oil field drilling and pumping equipment, shipping containers, electrical cable and products for residential housing; the production of cement; and technology licensing, engineering and consulting services. Also includes real estate and miscellaneous operations.

DOMESTIC TRANSPORTATION & UTILITY SUBSIDIARIES—Includes domestic barge lines, gas utility companies and common carrier railroads. These subsidiaries, operating autonomously, serve the general public including U. S. Steel and charge for their services on the basis of rates filed with and approved by regulatory agencies as applicable or by contract rates.

15. LEASE COMMITMENTS

At December 31, 1978, U. S. Steel's present value of net minimum capital lease payments and future minimum operating lease payments was:

	(In millions)	
	Capital Leases	Operating Leases
1979	$17.4	$ 40.3
1980	14.7	33.5
1981	11.4	29.1
1982	8.8	21.9
1983	8.2	20.5
Later years	35.7	116.2
Sublease rentals (decrease)	—	(3.9)
Total minimum lease payments	96.2	$257.6
Less: Imputed interest costs	30.6	
Present value of net minimum lease payments included in long-term debt	$65.6	

As to operating leases, approximately 60% of such rentals involve vessel charters, 21% railway equipment leases and the balance covers a variety of facilities and equipment. Most long-term vessel charters and railway equipment leases include purchase options.

Total rental expense for operating leases amounted to $91.0 million in 1978 and $90.8 million in 1977 including reduction of sublease rentals of $1.0 million each

Notes to Financial Statements (continued)

year. The noncancelable lease portion amounted to $62.1 million in 1978 and $59.5 million in 1977 of which $57.8 million and $52.5 million, respectively, represented minimum rentals.

16. CAPITAL AUTHORIZATIONS — At December 31, 1978, the estimated amount required to complete authorized projects for property, plant and equipment was $1,045.0 million.

17. TAX PROVISION — The provision (credit) for estimated United States and foreign taxes on income was:

	(In millions)	
	1978	1977
Currently payable (refundable):		
U.S. Federal		
Current year	$ 20.8	$ 8.5
Investment credit carryback	—	(22.8)
Operating loss carryback effects	(34.9)	(102.8)
Adjustment of prior years	(1.9)	—
	(16.0)	(117.1)
U.S. State and Local	8.0	3.7
Foreign	14.7	15.1
Total	6.7	(98.3)
Deferred:		
U.S. Federal	(1.3)	58.4
U.S. State and Local	2.0	2.5
Foreign	.6	1.4
Total	1.3	62.3
Total provision (credit)	$ 8.0	$ (36.0)

Timing differences increased (decreased) the deferred tax provision as follows:

	(In millions)	
	1978	1977
Depreciation	$ 107.3	$ 89.2
Investment credit	(119.9)	(51.8)
Interest costs	24.7	(7.8)
Unremitted earnings of foreign consolidated subsidiaries	2.3	7.8
Intercompany profit in inventory	3.9	4.6
Minimum income tax adjustment	—	13.7
Adjustment of prior years	(24.5)	—
Other	7.5	6.6
Total deferred tax provision	$ 1.3	$ 62.3

The primary reasons for the difference between the basic Federal income tax (FIT) rate of 48% and the effective tax rates are as follows:

	Percent of income before taxes	
	1978	1977
Basic Federal Income Tax rate:	48.0%	48.0%
Increase (decrease) in rate resulting from:		
Investment credit	(32.5)	(73.2)
Excess wear and exhaustion	(10.5)	(30.3)
Unremitted earnings of certain foreign subsidiaries	3.9	(12.9)
Minimum income tax	4.9	21.7
Foreign income taxes	2.2	7.1
State and local income taxes after FIT benefit	2.2	3.5
Adjustment of prior years	(10.6)	—
Other	(4.4)	.8
Effective tax rate	3.2%	(35.3)%

Investment credits recognized and $6.8 million amortization in 1977 of the pre-1968 investment credit reduced the provisions for taxes on income by $81.2 million in 1978 and $74.5 million in 1977.

The U.S. income tax liabilities for all tax years prior to 1957 have been paid. The 1957-1960 tax years are settled except for two issues on which the Tax Court rendered decisions in 1977, one in favor of the Corporation and the other partially in favor of the Corporation. After entry of the Court's judgment in this case, payment will be required in 1979 of approximately $16 million in tax and about an equal amount of interest. The Corporation believes $14 million of this tax assessment is not proper and expects to request review by the U.S. Court of Appeals for the Second Circuit. The government may also file an appeal which, if successful, would require the payment of an additional $16.3 million in tax. The liabilities for the years 1961-1963 have been settled except for one issue involving $10 million tax for which a refund claim has been submitted to the U.S. Court of Claims. The tax years 1964-1972 are in various stages of audit or administrative review. The Corporation has made adequate provision for income taxes and any interest which may become payable on account of those years not yet settled.

U.S. income taxes have not been provided on unremitted earnings of certain foreign subsidiaries, as these earnings are considered to be permanently invested by the subsidiaries. On a consolidated basis, these earnings totaled $96.2 million through 1978.

Notes to Financial Statements (continued)

18. CONTINGENCIES—Many uncertainties exist concerning the capital requirements of and operating costs associated with the implementation of environmental and similar laws. These government-imposed requirements stem from various legislative enactments including the Water Pollution Control Act, the Clean Air Act, the Resource Conservation and Recovery Act, the Toxic Substances Control Act, the Occupational Safety and Health Act, the Coal Mine Health and Safety Act, and the Surface Mining Reclamation and Enforcement Act. In some instances, regulations have not been issued, performance standards have not been established, and equipment requirements have not been defined. In other instances, the laws have been amended to the extent that facilities which had been installed to comply with then-existing laws will require further investment. In still other areas, administrative or judicial proceedings are pending to clarify or establish the extent and type of facilities or facility modifications required for compliance.

Broad-based estimates by the Corporation, in many cases without detailed engineering or other support, indicate authorization of expenditures for bringing into compliance with the above-mentioned legislative requirements those existing facilities which are currently expected to be economically operational ranging from $1,350 million to $1,800 million through 1983 (in 1978 dollars) assuming (a) only minor changes in operating procedures, (b) no process changes and (c) compliance by all Corporation facilities with such environmental and other laws and regulations, as presently enforced. The economics of the required investment may dictate that certain facilities be abandoned instead of modified to comply with the requirements. The substantial sums which will be required for these non-income generating expenditures may well restrict the ability of the Corporation to continue to modernize and expand its facilities. To preclude a negative impact upon the Corporation's earnings in future years, the costs associated with compliance with all these regulations will have to be recovered through cost-covering price increases, market conditions permitting.

The outcome of pending and potential administrative and judicial proceedings, as well as future legislative and regulatory changes, will be significant factors in determining the specific amount of expenditures required for this purpose and the periods of time for achieving legislatively established goals. Federal laws and regulations provide for the assessment of substantial civil penalties for noncompliance with environmental requirements under specified circumstances. It is not possible at this time to estimate the specific amount of such penalties that might be assessed against U. S. Steel or the outcome of any pending or future proceeding in which penalties are sought. However, it is not anticipated that the outcome of such proceedings should result in a material adverse effect upon the consolidated net worth of U. S. Steel.

19. SEC REPLACEMENT COST REQUIREMENTS (Unaudited)—Inflation continues to increase both production costs and capital spending requirements. Depreciation allowances based on the historical costs of existing facilities are inadequate to support the increasing capital requirements for replacements, modernization, and environmental control facilities at the higher current costs of the new facilities. These added costs, which at present can only be recovered through depreciation over many future years, are in effect currently taxed as if they were profits. The result is the taxing away of much of the capital needed to meet the steadily rising costs of inflation. U. S. Steel's annual report on Form 10-K filed with the Securities and Exchange Commission contains quantitative replacement cost information in accordance with SEC Accounting Series Release 190; however, these data do not provide a basis for adjusting reported net income or balance sheet values. The replacement costs required do not measure either the erosion in value of the dollar from inflation or the current value of the facilities presently in place. They represent only the estimated current costs of a hypothetical total replacement of productive capabilities at specified dates, which could be substantially offset over the years by the lower operating costs of the more efficient replacement facilities. The required assumptions ignore the fact that the normal process of replacements necessarily takes place over a period of many years with continuing technological advance and changing economic conditions.

Notes to Financial Statements (continued)– S.E.C. Matters

USS

20. QUARTERLY FINANCIAL DATA (Unaudited)–

(In millions except per share data)

	1978				1977			
	4th Qtr.	**3rd Qtr.**	**2nd Qtr.**	**1st Qtr.**	4th Qtr.	3rd Qtr.	2nd Qtr.	1st Qtr.
Sales	**$2,955.4**	**$2,788.0**	**$2,878.2**	**$2,427.9**	$2,448.6	$2,359.1	$2,565.1	$2,237.1
Cost of sales	**2,379.7**	**2,265.9**	**2,284.0**	**2,116.8**	2,075.8	1,949.7	2,060.7	1,858.3
Provision (credit) for income taxes	**29.0**	**(9.0)**	**21.0**	**(33.0)**	(26.0)	(22.0)	6.0	6.0
Income (loss)	**94.6**	**88.8**	**117.3**	**(58.7)**	9.0	25.2	76.3	27.4
Per share data								
Primary income	**$ 1.11**	**$ 1.04**	**$ 1.38**	**$ (.70)**	$ .11	$ .30	$ .91	$ .33
Fully diluted income	**1.07**	**1.00**	**1.32**	**(.70)**(a)	.11(a)	.30(a)	.88	.33(a)
Dividends paid	**.40**	**.40**	**.40**	**.40**	.55	.55	.55	.55
Price range of common stock (b)								
–Low	**21⅛**	**25**	**24⅞**	**25**	28	27	38	43⅞
–High	**28⅜**	**30¼**	**30⅝**	**32⅞**	32½	40	49⅝	50

(a) Conversion of convertible debentures excluded from fully diluted computation because of anti-dilutive effects.

(b) Composite Tape.

21. OTHER ITEMS–*Operating costs:* Maintenance and repairs of plant and equipment totaled $1,417.8 million in 1978 and $1,195.2 million in 1977.

Research and development costs totaled $52.5 million in 1978 and $49.8 million in 1977.

Interest, dividends and other income: Gains resulting from the repurchase of debt securities, primarily to satisfy sinking fund requirements, amounted to $35.6 million in 1978 and $2.2 million in 1977. In 1978, a profit of $11.7 million was realized from the sale of U. S. Steel's investment in FLO-CON Systems, Inc. In 1977, a nominal profit from the disposition of plants and investments included a $22.1 million loss resulting from the sale of Bahama Cement Company, a wholly owned foreign subsidiary.

Interest and other financing costs: Expenses included in this account were as follows:

	1978	1977
Interest on debt	**$157.5**	$137.2
Preferred stock dividend of QCM (See Note 8)	**22.1**	4.5
Foreign exchange losses related to debt	**9.1**	10.9
Other	**2.7**	2.2
Total	**$191.4**	$154.8

Other: The aggregate foreign exchange loss included in income was $16.1 million in 1978 and $13.5 million in 1977.

SECURITIES AND EXCHANGE COMMISSION MATTERS

As previously reported in filings with the Securities and Exchange Commission (SEC), in 1977 the SEC ordered a private investigation of U. S. Steel to determine the adequacies under the Federal securities laws of U. S. Steel's disclosures relating to environmental matters. While there have been extensive discussions concerning settlement, as of the date of this report the matter remains unresolved and the investigation is still pending. Stockholders will be informed concerning resolution of the matter.

Receipts and Their Disposition in 1978

	Dollars per Employee	Dollars per Man-Hour
Receipts from customers—The public	$66,933	$35.38
Disposed of as follows:		
Employment costs—U. S. Steel's direct employment	$27,169	$14.36
Products and services bought—Provides employment by suppliers and by their suppliers in turn	33,146	17.52
Wear and exhaustion—Provides employment by suppliers of new plants and equipment and by their suppliers in turn	2,639	1.39
Taxes—Provides revenue for governments	1,353	.72
Interest—Compensation for savings loaned	1,160	.61
Dividends—Compensation for savings invested	823	.44
Income reinvested in business	643	.34
Total	$66,933	$35.38

Stockholders and Shares—Common Stock December 31, 1978

Registered in name of:	Holders	Shares
Individuals—		
Women	96,047	11,814,465
Men	69,051	14,013,968
Joint Accounts	68,104	10,371,082
Total Individuals	233,202	36,199,515
Nominees, Brokers & Others	25,037	49,367,648
Total	258,239	85,567,163

No individual held of record as much as one-tenth of one percent of the common stock. Stock registered in the name of nominees, brokers and others is owned by insurance companies; charitable, religious and educational organizations of many types; pension funds; investment companies; trustees, custodians and estates; and others, including many individuals.

U. S. Steel's Principal Direct and Indirect Ownership Interests—Unconsolidated Companies December 31, 1978

Company	Country	% Ownership	Activity
Percy Wilson Mortgage and Finance Corp.	United States	100%	Mortgage Banking
U. S. Steel Credit Corp.	United States	100%	Leasing & Finance
Terninoss Acciai Inossidabili, S.p.A.	Italy	50%	Stainless Steel Products
Minerales Ordaz, C.A.	Venezuela	49%	Partially Reduced Iron Ore Briquettes
Oresteel Investments (Pty.) Ltd.	South Africa	49%	Holding Company—Mining
P.T. Pacific Nikkel Indonesia	Indonesia	48%	Nickel & Cobalt Exploration & Development
Prieska Copper Mines (Pty.) Ltd.	South Africa	46%	Copper & Zinc Concentrates
Feralloys Ltd.	South Africa	45%	Ferromanganese & Ferrochrome
Compagnie Miniere de l'Ogooue	Gabon	44%	Manganese Ore
Northern Tier Pipeline Co.	United States	40%	Crude Oil Pipeline
Zuari Agro Chemicals, Ltd.	India	36%	Fertilizer
Altos Hornos de Vizcaya, S.A.	Spain	27%	Steel Products
Associated Manganese Mines of South Africa, Ltd.	South Africa	20%	Manganese & Iron Ores
Sidbec-Normines, Inc.	Canada	8%	Iron Ore Mining & Concentrating

Section B: Replacement Cost Disclosure in 1978 Annual Report to the SEC

UNITED STATES STEEL CORPORATION
ESTIMATED REPLACEMENT COST INFORMATION
(Unaudited)

By Accounting Series Release 190 (ASR 190) issued in 1976, the Securities and Exchange Commission established a new rule requiring disclosure of the estimated current cost of replacing total inventory and productive capacity at year-end, the depreciated net replacement cost of fixed assets, and the effects of the assumed replacements on depreciation and cost of sales.

The Commission acknowledged that the new rule is a limited one and does not measure either the effects of inflation or the current value of all assets and liabilities. The rule does not cover the value of monetary assets and liabilities or the gains or losses that accrue from holding such assets and liabilities during inflationary periods. The cost of funds that may be required for replacements is not comprehended by the rule, nor are the effects of income taxes, including the investment tax credit.

The required estimate of the current cost of replacing productive capacity does not represent the future actual replacements nor the replacement expenditures that will take place over a period of many years. The required estimate of depreciated net replacement cost cannot be construed to represent the current value of the assets now owned, since the replacement facilities would, for the most part, differ materially in technology and efficiency from the assets presently in place. Moreover, the assumption of currently replacing total present capacity with new assets is unrealistic, since complete replacement at any single point in time would not be economical and would only be undertaken step-by-step when and if future technological and other developments would financially justify the expenditures. This is particularly true with respect to replacing the facilities recently installed or modernized for the latest technological developments, as well as older facilities presently operative at relatively high levels of efficiency.

Investors and analysts are cautioned against simplistic use of the data. The disclosure requirements were not designed to provide a basis for adjusting net income and balance sheet values. In addition, due to widely varying subjective judgments and assumptions, as well as different factual circumstances involved, the data are not comparable among companies and are inherently subject to errors of estimation. Because of the substantial conceptual and implemental problems that have not been resolved by ASR 190, the following required data have been assembled and are presented solely to comply with the existing rules of the Commission.

Inventories

For LIFO inventories, current acquisition costs were applied to year-end inventory quantities. Non-LIFO inventories are reflected at current actual cost. This estimate of current replacement cost, which excludes the cost reduction of own-produced inventories that would result from the more efficient replacement facilities, is more than double the historical cost amount reflected in the balance sheet. Sufficient calculations of cost benefits were made to establish that cost reduction from facility replacements would be substantial. This subject is further discussed under Cost of Sales.

Property, Plant and Equipment

The current replacement cost disclosure requirements comprehend all fixed assets (plus certain leased facilities) except land, construction in process and mineral resources. The replacement cost estimates, which are three to four times the historical costs reflected in the balance sheet, are necessarily tentative and subject to future modification. It is believed that these estimated replacement costs (new), required by ASR 190, would exceed the costs of maintaining some portion of capacity by the renovation of existing facilities. The extent to which lower cost replacement opportunities might evolve for such renovation, or for further consolidating existing plants into larger scale plants over the years, is not comprehended because of currently unknown future conditions.

For the most part, the gross property, plant and equipment replacement costs were estimated by the use of functional prices, utilizing present day technology and recognizing current environmental requirements. The costs of recent facility installations were updated to current price levels, and engineering project estimates were utilized for other facilities including the normal complement of support facilities such as in-plant utili-

UNITED STATES STEEL CORPORATION
ESTIMATED REPLACEMENT COST INFORMATION (continued)
(Unaudited)

ties, transportation and maintenance equipment. These estimates, compiled in terms of cost per unit of capacity of type of operation, were applied to the productive capacities of facilities comprising over 90% of the estimated gross replacement cost. The historical costs of the remaining miscellaneous fixed assets currently in use were indexed by year of acquisition to present price levels. As required by ASR 190, net depreciated replacement cost was calculated based on the estimated gross replacement cost adjusted for the expired portion of the currently estimated total service potential of present facilities.

Cost of Sales

This replacement cost estimate represents the historical cost of products and services sold adjusted to a replacement cost basis for the LIFO inventories used and reduced for the rental cost of leased facilities that were capitalized in developing fixed asset replacement costs. The resultant amount, not adjusted to reflect the productivity and efficiency gains that would be realized from the use of new facilities, is approximately the same as the historical costs reflected in the income statement.

It would be entirely impractical to currently fully engineer and evaluate the eventual replacement of the Corporation's entire productive capacity, since future product markets and plant locations are unknown. The timing of such replacements would necessarily extend far into the realm of undeterminable future technology and economic conditions. However, sufficient calculations of cost benefits were made to determine that they would be substantial. Based on studies that have been made, U. S. Steel management believes that the cost savings from completely replacing present capacity over the years would at least offset the additional depreciation from the significantly increased investment.

Depreciation (Wear and Exhaustion of Facilities)

The estimated replacement cost depreciation, based upon the required determinations, is approximately double the historical costs reflected in the income statement. In accordance with ASR 190, this estimate is based on the economic lives and the straight-line method used in calculating historical cost depreciation, thus excluding any depreciation for fully depreciated investments. It was calculated by (a) dividing the estimated gross replacement cost by the comparable historical gross cost indexed to a current price level, and then (b) multiplying the result by the price indexed historical depreciation for the investment currently being depreciated.

If all assumed replacement facilities were currently being depreciated based on the presently estimated service potential of existing facilities, replacement cost depreciation could be three to four times the historical costs reflected in the income statement. The estimated service potential of existing assets reflects a long period of history during which cash flow from profits and depreciation allowances was inadequate to provide and attract the funds necessary to keep pace with technological advances. Depreciation allowances based on the historical costs of existing facilities have been and continue to be inadequate to support the increasing capital requirements for replacements, modernization and environmental control facilities at the higher current costs of the new facilities. These added costs, which at present can only be recovered through depreciation over many future years, are in effect currently taxed as if they were profits. The result is the taxing away of much of the capital needed to meet the steadily rising costs of inflation.

As previously stated, the estimated cost of replacing existing capacity, and consequently the estimated depreciation, is necessarily subject to future modification. Depending upon future conditions which may materially affect the magnitude and timing of replacement expenditures and thus the service potential of the assets involved, replacement cost depreciation could be either higher or lower than the above indicated range.

UNITED STATES STEEL CORPORATION
ESTIMATED REPLACEMENT COST INFORMATION (continued)
(Unaudited)

Summary of Replacement Cost Data

	(In billions)					
	Assets Subject to Replacement Cost Disclosure				Total Amount Per Financial Statements	
	Estimated Replacement Cost		Present Recorded Cost			
	1978	1977	1978	1977	1978	1977
AT YEAR-END						
Inventories	$ 3.2	$ 2.8	$ 1.3	$ 1.3	$ 1.3	$ 1.3
Property, Plant and Equipment						
Gross	$45.4	$41.3	$12.4	$11.4	$13.2	$12.5
Net	15.3	14.1	5.3	4.7	6.0	5.7
FOR THE YEAR						
Cost of Sales	$ 9.1	$ 8.0	$ 9.0	$ 7.9	$ 9.0	$ 7.9
Depreciation (Wear & Exhaustion of Facilities)	$ .9	$ .8	$ .4	$ .4	$ .4	$ .4

Mineral Resources (Other than Oil and Gas)

Expenditures for acquiring mineral rights, leases or properties; exploration activities; and development of mineral bodies in 1978 and 1977 include $80 million and $60 million, respectively, charged to consolidated income. In addition, expenditures of $10 million were capitalized in 1978 and an insignificant amount was capitalized in 1977. The Corporation's consolidated balance sheet at December 31, 1978 included $225 million and at December 31, 1977 included $235 million (restated) in land and deferred amounts, both carried at net value, for these types of expenditures. The current year amortization of such capitalized costs was $20 million in 1978 and $10 million in 1977. Excluded from development expenditures were plant and equipment assets which U. S. Steel management normally associates to the mining of these minerals and which others might treat as development assets. These have been considered as productive capacity and included in assets subject to replacement cost disclosure.

The majority of domestic reserves of iron ore, coal and limestone were purchased or leased prior to 1940 while Canadian iron ore reserve mining rights were obtained primarily in the late 1950's and the 1960's. Present mineral reserves are sufficient to support operations in the foreseeable future.

Conclusion

The required replacement cost data do not reflect all of the effects of inflation on the Corporation's income whether favorable or unfavorable. U. S. Steel management has endeavored over the years to modify selling prices to maintain a reasonable return on equity when permitted by markets, competitive conditions and governmental restrictions. The current relationship of costs, selling prices and net income reflects changing economic conditions, including the effects of inflation. The effects of inflation are not measured by either historical costs or by the replacement cost requirements of ASR 190. U. S. Steel management continues to caution that the replacement cost data required by ASR 190 provides no basis for adjusting reported net income and balance sheet values.

Questions for Review and Discussion

18-1. Define or explain:
    a. Annual financial report
    b. "Notes" to financial statements
    c. Interim financial report
    d. 10-K, 10-Q, and S-1
    e. News announcements
    f. Commercial financial services
    g. Expected return
    h. Expected risk
    i. Intrinsic value analysis
    j. Scaling
    k. Industry standards
    l. Consistency principle

18-2. Interim financial reports are typically considered less reliable and more abbreviated than annual financial reports. Why then might the investor find interim reports useful in evaluating investment alternatives?

18-3. What is the usual relationship between a company's annual report and the company's 10-K report which it files with the SEC?

18-4. Rank the financial information reports provided by a company (annual report, etc.) according to the following criteria:
    a. Level of detail (comprehensiveness)
    b. Scope of distribution
    c. Formality or rigidity of reporting requirements
    d. Frequency of release

18-5. What are the major elements in a representative decision model for an investor?

18-6. "*Expected* return is a crucial parameter of the investment decision. Accounting reports are historical in nature. Therefore, accounting reports are useless in the investment decision." Comment.

18-7. "Since it is impossible for the average investor to earn an above-average return on investments, brokerage houses can provide no useful financial information to the potential investor." Comment.

18-8. The meaning and significance of "numbers" reflected in corporate financial reports depend upon an understanding of several different variables and relationships. Enumerate these critical factors.

18-9. Why is it important to "scale" the reported numbers in corporate financial reports?

18-10. What are the two main classes of "standards" used in interpreting financial statements, and how are they useful?

18-11. What are accountants or financial analysts attempting to measure or describe when they calculate various financial statistics? Are the financial statistics sufficient for this task, or is additional information necessary?

18-12. What usually is the *minimum* number of years for which financial data are included in a company's annual report? Why is this a minimum (i.e., why not include data only for the current year)?

18-13. What are the major classifications of financial statistics? Are these sets mutually exclusive? Why or why not?

18-14. The naive interpretation of many financial statistics implies that "higher is better, lower is worse." However, such a sweeping generalization is incorrect. For example, a high current ratio may imply an unwarranted buildup in inventory, and the buildup in inventory may be a sign of an unfavorable situation in the future.

For each of the following statistics, give an example, if possible, of a high value that might *not* be interpreted favorably (or might have *unfavorable* connotations as well as a favorable interpretation):
  a. EPS
  b. Return on assets
  c. Return on owners' equity
  d. Net income to sales
  e. Current ratio
  f. Acid-test ratio
  g. Debt-equity ratio
  h. Times interest earned

18-15. "The problem of comparability between firms would be settled if a national uniform set of accounts were required for all industrial corporations (similar to the set of accounts prescribed by the Federal Power Commission for utilities under its jurisdiction)." Comment.

Exercises

18-1. Analyzing Financial Statements. Using the financial statements from the United States Steel Corporation 1978 annual report included in the Appendix:
  1. Calculate the statistical indicators of return and risk for 1977 and 1978.
  2. What major decisions or actions by U.S. Steel Corporation during 1978 are highlighted by the statement of changes in financial position?
  3. Based upon the numerical measures developed in number 1, and any other background information on the company or the industry you might be familiar with, evaluate the company's financial status and prospects.
  4. Comment briefly on any accounting policies chosen by the company that you feel are, or may be, important to take into consideration when evaluating the company as an investment opportunity.

18-2. Using Replacement Cost Information in Analyzing Financial Statements. Using United States Steel Corporation's 1978 financial statements and 10-K replacement cost disclosures (both reproduced in the

Appendix to this chapter):
1. Calculate the statistical indicators of return and risk for 1978, using replacement-cost-based values for income, total assets, and owners' equity. (Note: For statistics involving net income, make one calculation using replacement-cost-based current operating income and a second calculation using replacement-cost-based net income. See Chapter 14.)
2. Evaluate the changes in the statistical indicators produced by using the replacement cost values.

18-3. Computing Financial Statistics. Condensed financial statements for Standard Corporation follow.

	(000s omitted)	
	1979	1980
Cash	$ 20	$ 15
Marketable securities	10	5
Accounts receivable	30	40
Inventory	50	70
Plant and equipment (net of depreciation)	290	370
	$400	$500
Current liabilities	$ 60	$ 80
Long-term debt	100	170
Owners' equity (10,000 shares outstanding)	240	250
	$400	$500
Sales		$480
Expenses:		
Cost of sales		320
Selling and administrative		70
Depreciation		20
Interest		10
Federal income taxes		30
		450
Net income for 1980		$ 30

Compute the financial statistics that may be used to evaluate the expected return and risk parameters for Standard Corporation. Where the measures refer only to balance sheet relationships, calculate the statistics for both 1979 and 1980.

18-4. Effect of Financial Leverage. Conservative Appliances, Inc., and Highly Leveraged Appliances Company both manufacture and distribute home appliances. Each company has total assets of $1 million, but Highly Leveraged Appliances Company has outstanding debt (current and long-term) of $700,000, while Conservative Appliances, Inc., has no outstanding debt. The annual interest cost incurred by Highly Leveraged Appliances Company amounts to $50,000. For two consecutive years, the two companies earned the following rates of return on total assets (before considering interest expense):

Year	Return on Assets
19X1	10%
19X2	6%

Required:

1. Determine the net income for each company for each of the two years.
2. Determine the return on owners' equity for each company for each of the two years.
3. Explain the reason for the variation in performance (as measured by return on owners' equity) over the two years for the two companies, given that both earned the same return on assets deployed.
4. What factor(s) would be critical in choosing between the two companies as investment alternatives (assuming the price was the same)?

18-5. Relationship between Return on Owners' Equity and Net Income to Sales. For each independent case that follows, calculate the amount or percentage for each item with a question mark.

Case	Sales	Net Income	Owners' Equity	Net Income to Sales (Percent)	"Investment" Turnover	Percent Return on Owners' Equity
1	$20,000	$ 2,000	$10,000	?	?	?
2	40,000	?	30,000	25	?	?
3	50,000	?	?	1	10	?
4	?	15,000	?	?	0.8	15
5	?	8,000	?	5	?	40
6	30,000	6,000	?	?	0.5	?
7	?	?	50,000	?	2	10
8	?	?	25,000	4	?	20
9	60,000	?	20,000	?	?	10
10	?	5,000	?	5	4	?

18-6. Effect of Transactions on Current and Acid-Test Ratios. The current asset and liability sections from a corporate balance sheet follow.

Current assets:	
Cash	$ 150,000
Marketable securities	125,000
Accounts receivable	175,000
Inventory	500,000
Prepaid expenses	50,000
	$1,000,000
Current liabilities:	
Accounts payable	300,000
Estimated federal income taxes payable	60,000
Accrued liabilities	40,000
	$ 400,000

For each of the following *independent* transactions, indicate whether the current ratio and the acid-test ratio would be *increased, decreased,* or *unaffected* after the transaction.
  a. Collected $75,000 on account from customers.
  b. Paid $80,000 on account to suppliers.
  c. Borrowed $100,000 on a 90-day note.
  d. Paid the federal income tax liability.
  e. Sold the marketable securities for $125,000.
  f. Purchased new equipment for the plant costing $200,000, and signed a 180-day installment contract with the seller.
  g. Purchased inventory of $100,000 on account.
  h. Purchased inventory of $100,000 for cash.
  i. Purchased $50,000 marketable securities for cash.
  j. Recognized expense of $20,000 from the prepaid expense account.

18-7. Evaluating Long-Term Capitalization Structures. C. Madelyn Panozzo, chief executive officer of the Madpan Corporation, is studying alternative means of financing a new 100 percent-owned subsidiary that is being set up to market a new soft drink. The total investment required is $2 million, and the return on assets (before interest costs) is expected to range between 5 percent and 15 percent.

Three alternative financing plans are under consideration:

	Long-Term Debt	Common Stock
Plan I	80%	20%
Plan II	50	50
Plan III	20	80

The interest rate on long-term debt issued by the subsidiary will be 10 percent. Whichever plan is selected, Madpan Corporation will furnish the total funds for the common stock and will therefore be a 100 percent owner of the equity interest in the subsidiary.

Required:

1. To evaluate these financing alternatives, Ms. Panozzo asks you to prepare a schedule that depicts net income, return on owners' equity, and times interest earned for each plan, assuming a return on assets (before interest) of
  (a) 5 percent
  (b) 10 percent
  (c) 15 percent
  Ignore the effect of income taxes in your solution.

2. Comment on the risk-return trade-off in the alternative financing plans.

18-8. Interpreting Changes in Accounting Methods. In a recent annual report of the National Cash Register Company, the following note dealing with changes in accounting methods appeared:

> [For many years] the Company had used the LIFO (last-in, first-out) basis for valuing most domestic inventories. Effective January 1, 19X2, the FIFO (first-in, first-out) method of inventory valuation was adopted for inventories previously valued on the LIFO basis. This results in a more uniform valuation method throughout the Company and makes the financial statements with respect to inventory valuation comparable with those of the other major United States business equipment manufacturers. As a result of adopting the FIFO method, the net loss for 19X2 is approximately $4,565,000 ($.20 per share) less than it would have been on a LIFO basis. The financial statements for prior years have been retroactively restated for this change and, as a result, earnings retained for use in the business have been increased by $25,297,000 as of January 1, 19X1. Also, the 19X1 income statement has been restated resulting in an increase in net income of $847,000 ($.04 per share). Inventories at December 31, 19X1 are stated higher by $50,276,000 than they would have been had the LIFO method been continued.
>
> Beginning with 19X2 additions, the Company changed its method of computing depreciation on rental equipment and on property, plant and equipment in the United States from the sum-of-the-years digits method to the straight-line method while continuing the former method for assets acquired prior to 19X2. This change in depreciation method was made to bring the company in line with general accounting practices in the business equipment industry. Concurrent with the change in depreciation method, for additions after January 1, 19X2 the Company reduced the estimated useful life of rental equipment from 6 to 5 years and changed the estimated useful lives of certain other fixed assets. The effect of the change in depreciation method was to reduce the net loss after tax for the year 19X2 by approximately $2,400,000 ($.11 per share), while the effect of the change in useful lives was not significant.

Required:

1. What reason(s) does NCR give to support the changes in accounting methods? Are there any other reasons you think might have motivated the changes?
2. What effect do the changes have on the comparability over time of the NCR statements? Is there sufficient information provided to allow the statement user to reconstruct this comparability element?
3. What effect do the changes have on cross-sectional comparability?
4. With respect to the change in inventory method:
   (a) Was income (loss) higher or lower in 19X2 as a result of the change? How much?
   (b) Was there any effect on income of prior years? How much?
   (c) What do you suppose was the reason for the rather large difference in the amount of the effects of the change on income (loss) in 19X1 and 19X2?
   (d) What do you think the effect of the change will be on future years' income?

(e) What was the effect of the change on the value of the inventory in the balance sheet?
(f) What effect would the change have on the financial statistics used to estimate NCR's risk and return parameters?

5. With respect to the changes in depreciation method:
   (a) What two distinct changes were made?
   (b) Was income (loss) higher or lower in 19X2 as a result of the changes? How much? Did both changes contribute to this effect?
   (c) Was there any effect on income of prior years? How much?
   (d) What was the effect of the changes on the value of the rental equipment and the property, plant, and equipment in the 19X2 balance sheet? What will be the effect in the future?

18-9. Using Risk and Return Indicators. Based on (1) the partial information appearing in the following balance sheet, (2) the "additional information" given, and (3) the definitions of the various return and risk indicators described in the chapter, determine the amounts of the missing numbers. Ignore income taxes.

PARTIAL INFORMATION, INCORPORATED

Balance Sheet
As of December 31, 1980

Assets

Cash	$ 2,000,000
Accounts receivable	2,000,000
Marketable securities	?
Prepaid expenses	1,000,000
Inventory	?
Total current assets	$?
Plant and equipment (net)	?
Total assets	$?

Liabilities and Stockholders' Equity

Accounts payable	$?
Wages payable	1,500,000
Taxes payable	1,000,000
Total current liabilities	$?
6% Bonds payable	10,000,000
Total liabilities	$?
Stockholders' equity:	
Common stock, $1 stated value, 10,000,000 shares authorized; ___?___ outstanding	$?
Paid in excess over stated value	8,000,000
Retained earnings	?
Total stockholders' equity	$?
Total liabilities and stockholders' equity	$?

Additional Information:

Expenses	$16,000,000
Times interest earned	7⅔
Current ratio	2:1
Debt-to-equity ratio	2:3
Acid-test ratio	1.2:1
Earnings per share	.50
Permanent capital: ¼ long-term debt; ¾ stockholders' equity	

18-10. Comparative Financial Ratios under Alternative Valuation Bases. Following are the statement of income, the statement of assets, and the statement of capital (the last two together making up the traditional balance sheet) from a recent annual report of Indiana Telephone Corporation. The column B figures are based on the column A figures *adjusted* for changes in the general price level.

Required:

1. Calculate the statistical indicators of risk and return described in the chapter, based on the 19X1 column A and column B figures.

2. Are there any significant differences between the column A and column B indicators? Are the differences in predictable directions, that is, would they be the same (or tend to be the same) for all businesses?

3. Indiana Telephone is a regulated company. Its rates are set by the Public Service Commission of Indiana at a level expected to ensure that the company recovers its investment plus a fair return on that investment. In petitioning the commission for rate changes, would the company prefer to use the column A or the column B based indicators of the return on investment earned in the past? Explain your answer.

INDIANA TELEPHONE CORPORATION (cont.)

Statement of Income

	Column A Historical Cost		Column B Historical Cost Restated for Changes in Purchasing Power of Dollar	
	19X1	19X0	19X1	19X0
Operating Revenues:				
Local service	$ 5,744,356	$5,384,154	$ 5,788,990	$ 5,695,270
Toll service	4,852,156	4,350,496	4,889,858	4,601,883
Miscellaneous	304,522	234,979	306,888	248,557
Total operating revenues	10,901,034	9,969,629	10,985,736	10,545,710
Operating Expenses:				
Depreciation provision	1,943,551	1,541,560	2,497,078	2,026,211
Maintenance	1,486,495	1,427,487	1,505,457	1,523,311
Traffic	1,226,906	1,157,565	1,237,139	1,224,453
Commercial	511,661	449,104	515,637	475,054
General and administrative	1,055,318	1,170,198	1,068,682	1,278,407
State, local, and miscellaneous federal taxes	912,601	648,996	919,692	686,497
Federal income taxes:				
Currently payable	1,132,500	1,127,087	1,141,300	1,192,215
Deferred until future years	315,800	295,000	318,254	312,047
Deferred investment tax credit (net)	9,708	(14,997)	3,262	(21,018)
Total operating expenses	8,594,540	7,802,000	9,206,501	8,697,177
Operating Income	2,306,494	2,167,629	1,779,235	1,848,533
Income Deductions:				
Interest on funded debt	651,195	659,567	656,255	697,679
Other deductions	36,828	21,355	40,229	24,583
Interest charged to construction (credit)	(63,905)	(30,442)	(64,402)	(32,201)
Other income (credit)	(95,974)	(98,759)	(96,720)	(104,466)
Gain from retirement of long-term debt through operation of sinking fund (credit)	(15,192)	(15,865)	(15,310)	(16,781)
Price level gain from retirement of long-term debt (credit)	—	—	(61,137)	(55,175)
Gain from retirement of preferred stock through operation of sinking fund (credit)	(5,055)	(5,515)	(5,094)	(5,834)
Price level gain from retirement of preferred stock (credit)	—	—	(12,908)	(12,029)
Price level loss from other monetary items	—	—	87,508	118,125
Total income deductions	507,897	530,341	528,421	613,901
Net Income	1,798,597	1,637,288	1,250,814	1,234,632
Preferred stock dividends applicable to the period	96,209	97,541	96,957	103,178
Earnings Applicable to Common Stock	$ 1,702,388	$1,539,747	$ 1,153,857	$ 1,131,454
Earnings per Common Share	$ 3.49	$ 3.16	$ 2.37	$ 2.32
Book Value per Share	$ 21.45	$ 18.29	$ 20.19	$ 18.14
Stations in Service at End of Year	75,015	72,569	75,015	72,569

INDIANA TELEPHONE CORPORATION (cont.)

Statement of Assets—December 31, 19X1

	Column A *Historical Cost*	*Column B Historical Cost Restated for Changes in Purchasing Power of Dollar*
Telephone Plant, at original cost:		
In service	$32,681,923	$41,791,787
Less—Accumulated depreciation	10,598,883	14,354,244
	22,083,040	27,437,543
Plant under construction	1,568,243	1,580,428
	23,651,283	29,017,971
Working Capital:		
Current assets—		
Cash	679,475	679,475
Temporary cash investments accumulated for construction—at cost, which approximates market	3,074,351	3,074,351
Accounts receivable, less reserve	1,220,555	1,220,555
Materials and supplies	531,855	536,583
Prepayments	71,059	71,611
	5,577,295	5,582,575
Current liabilities—		
Sinking fund obligations	162,000	162,000
Accounts payable	635,552	635,552
Advance billings	315,647	315,647
Dividends payable	23,886	23,886
Federal income taxes	242,393	242,393
Other accrued taxes	600,190	600,190
Other current liabilities	713,455	713,455
	2,693,123	2,693,123
Net working capital	2,884,172	2,889,452
Other:		
Debt expense being amortized	201,810	260,266
Other deferred charges	49,616	57,566
Deferred federal income taxes	(1,273,254)	(1,390,176)
Unamortized investment tax credit being amortized over the useful lives of related property	(391,778)	(472,321)
	(1,413,606)	(1,544,665)
Total Investment in Telephone Business	$25,121,849	$30,362,758

INDIANA TELEPHONE CORPORATION (cont.)

Statement of Capital—December 31, 19X1

	Column A Historical Cost		Column B Historical Cost Restated for Changes in Purchasing Power of Dollar	
	Amount	Ratio	Amount	Ratio
First Mortgage Sinking Fund Bonds:				
Series 1, 3%	$ 770,000		$ 770,000	
Series 2, $3\frac{3}{8}$%	390,000		390,000	
Series 3, $3\frac{7}{8}$%	410,000		410,000	
Series 4, $3\frac{3}{4}$%	935,000		935,000	
Series 5, $4\frac{1}{4}$%	870,000		870,000	
Series 6, $5\frac{3}{8}$%	1,840,000		1,840,000	
Series 7, $4\frac{3}{4}$%	1,995,000		1,995,000	
Series 8, $4\frac{3}{4}$%	2,910,000		2,910,000	
Series 9, $6\frac{1}{2}$%	2,940,000		2,940,000	
Less—Current sinking funds	(142,000)		(142,000)	
Total first mortgage sinking fund bonds	12,918,000	51%	12,918,000	43%
Preferred Stock (no maturity):				
Cumulative, sinking fund, par value $100 per share, 30,000 shares authorized of which 10,000 are unissued:				
Series 4.80%	240,000		240,000	
Series 4.80%	242,900		242,900	
Series $5\frac{1}{4}$%	333,400		333,400	
Series 5%	256,900		256,900	
Series $6\frac{1}{8}$%	686,000		686,000	
Less—Current sinking funds	(20,000)		(20,000)	
Total preferred stock	1,739,200	7%	1,739,200	6%
Common Shareholders' Interest:				
Common stock, no par value, authorized 500,000 shares, issued 492,086 shares	4,251,785		6,474,592	
Retained earnings	6,295,365		3,500,069	
	10,547,150		9,974,661	
Less—Treasury stock, 4,336 shares, at cost	(5,192)		(7,882)	
Stock discount and expense	(77,309)		(121,103)	
Total common shareholders' interest	10,464,649	42%	9,845,676	32%
Unrealized Effects of Price Level Changes	—	—	5,859,882	19%
Total Investment in Telephone Business	$25,121,849	100%	$30,362,758	100%

The Audit Function in Financial Reporting 19

Most of the discussion in the earlier chapters of this book is built on the premise that accounting is an information specialization. This point is established in Chapter 1. Subsequent chapters demonstrate how decision-relevant accounting information is in fact produced within the contemporary corporate financial reporting environment. Now we address the question of the general reliability of reported accounting information. In so doing, our focus shifts from aspects of quantity and types of information to quality of information.

Quality of information generally is improved when completely independent and competent outside experts review it and attest to its reliability, fairness, and other aspects of quality. Investors have a big stake in such attestation, since they can make decisions with better expected outcomes if they have relatively better information available. The public interest is also involved. If incomplete, unreliable, or even misleading financial information is furnished to investors so that they enter into (sell off) investments that they would not otherwise have undertaken (disposed of), the public interest is affected in the sense that the level of capital formation in the economy may decrease. Moreover, scarce resources may be misdirected into socially less desirable channels or inefficient processes.

Example 19-1

Three brothers have invested all of their resources in the purchase of a parcel of land suitable for a shopping center development. They have borrowed from banks for purposes of surveying the land, acquiring architectural layouts, and installing streets, utilities, and parking lots.

To secure building construction loans, they have approached Jack Ehrlich to invest $75,000 in their venture. In return, Mr. Ehrlich would receive a one-third equity interest in Brothers Three, Ltd., a company to be formed if the additional investment is made.

Before Mr. Ehrlich is willing to invest, he would like to know the full investment history of the venture. Financial statements attested to by competent outside experts would be relatively more reliable than any furnished by the three brothers themselves, since they have a direct self-interest in having Mr. Ehrlich make the investment.

Striving for a high degree of financial information reliability is, of course, not limited to the information needs of investors. Enterprise managements likewise require reliable financial information for managerial decision making. For instance, decisions about lines of credit extended to customers depend on good data about accounts receivable collections. Product line profitability must be measured in part by reliable costing procedures.

Internal Revenue agents examine financial information provided by taxpayers with a view to detecting errors and omissions (intentional and unintentional) and, therefore, increasing its reliability for federal income tax collection purposes. The General Accounting Office of the federal government helps to ensure the reliability of financial information compiled and furnished by federal government departments and agencies.

The Soviet system uses financial reviewers (i.e., auditors) as extensively as do market-based systems, even though its reviewers are government employees and not independent professionals as in the case of, let us say, Anglo-American practices. Moreover, financial review activities are as old as accounting itself. They were present in the ancient tax collection systems of Babylonia and Egypt as well as in the extensive trading systems of the Middle Ages. In the Western countries, independent auditors established themselves as separately recognized professionals in Scotland during the 1860s.

Auditing today is as complex as the financial systems of the enterprises that it serves. Due to this complexity and in keeping with the emphasis adopted for this book, the remaining discussion in this chapter is limited to the branch of auditing concerned with financial reporting to third parties by private enterprises.

Role of Auditing

Independent auditors (CPAs) perform an attest function aimed primarily at establishing and maintaining the integrity of financial information. As review specialists, they can accomplish this function in an economically efficient manner. The objective of their typical examinations (audits) of financial statements is the expression of an opinion (attestation) on the so-called fairness with which the financial statements present financial position and results of operations of an enterprise. The auditors' reports are the medium through which they express their opinions or, if circumstances require, disclaim professional opinions.

Audit Reports. In an audit report, the auditor states whether his examination has been made in accordance with generally accepted auditing standards. In turn, these standards require him to attest whether, in his opinion, the financial statements are presented in conformity with generally accepted accounting principles and whether such principles have been consistently applied in the preparation of the financial statements of the current period in relation to those of the preceding period.

The CPA profession, with concurrence from the SEC, has adopted the following standard form of an independent auditor's report which is used when an examination reveals no reservations about the adequacy of the financial statements under audit:

> We have examined the balance sheet of X Company as of December 31, 19—, and the related statements of income and retained earnings and the statement of changes in financial position for the year then ended. Our examination was made in accordance with generally accepted auditing standards, and accordingly included such tests of the accounting records and such other auditing procedures as we considered necessary in the circumstances.
>
> In our opinion, the aforementioned financial statements present fairly the financial position of X Company at December 31, 19—, and the results of its operations and the changes in its financial position for the year then ended, in conformity with generally accepted accounting principles applied on a basis consistent with that of the preceding year.

Responsibility for Financial Statements. While the professional literature establishes that the independent auditor is solely responsible for his report on the financial statements, it is equally emphatic in pointing out that enterprise management has the responsibility for the production and preparation of proper financial statements. Thus it is management's responsibility to adopt sound accounting policies, to maintain adequate and effective systems of accounts, to safeguard enterprise assets, and to devise control systems that will accomplish these objectives.

At all times the financial statements remain representations of enterprise management and as such are an implicit and integral part of management's responsibility. No one should know an enterprise better than its management. Consequently, management is usually in the best position to choose procedures and policies and ultimately financial statement formats that will most fairly report a company's financial position and results of operations to third parties. Both the AICPA and the FEI (Financial Executives Institute) have issued formal recommendations to the effect that "management reports" about the responsibility of management for the form and content of financial statements should accompany all formally issued (published) financial reports.

The auditor's responsibility with respect to financial statements is therefore secondary. He cannot issue an unqualified audit report on a set of financial statements unless these statements represent actual business transactions and events and conform to established accounting principles. The London *Economist* once called the auditor's responsibility a "watchdog function." Later on in the chapter we describe how this function is performed.

Effects of Independent Audits. Treatises have been written on behavioral effects produced when auditors perform audit activities in a client's office. Company accounting personnel often feel uneasy when the independent auditors are around. That is, auditing produces what might be called a "report card" effect. Jobs get done with fewer errors, and system improvements are constantly sought because of the periodic report card prepared by the independent auditors. Some observers feel that this effect may even prevent some contemplated frauds or lesser irregularities by employees. However, the typical financial audit review is not intended to *guarantee* fraud detection. This is discussed at greater length in a later section.

Another consequence of auditing relates to producing valid and reliable financial information efficiently. As pointed out in earlier paragraphs of this chapter, management clearly knows the most about the business enterprise and understands its strengths and weaknesses best. Therefore management usually is and should be most efficient in preparing financial representations about the firm.

Unfortunately, however, management also has a direct interest in the representations made. If things are not going well, then management, in its own interest, might make biased representations. Such biases might even shade into misrepresentations or dishonesty. From the point of view of management, occasional presentation of biased financial information may be a perfectly logical step to take in terms of survival of the company, availability of ready borrowing capacity, or a strong product image with consumers. Knowing that independent audit procedures will eventually test their financial representations, managements are probably less prone to make deliberately or intentionally biased judgments and estimates than would otherwise be the case.

Efficiency Provided by Independent Audits. Despite report card effects within enterprises, outside users of financial information want additional assurances about its validity and reliability. Here is where the full impact of the economics of auditing enters the picture. If users of financial information had to obtain and verify this information item by item and user by user, an immensely costly process would unnecessarily be repeated over and over.

As it stands, division of responsibilities produces significant efficiencies. Management is most efficient in preparing and offering financial representations needed by outsiders. The independent auditing function helps to ensure that these representations are by and large free of bias and "present fairly . . . in conformity with generally accepted accounting principles applied on a basis consistent with that of the preceding year." Thus we have an economically more efficient information process both for the providers and for the users of the information.

Moreover, independent auditing has spawned many techniques and procedures that might be described as self-auditing devices. Internal control, defined later in this chapter, is a good illustration. To some degree all modern business enterprises employ systems of checks and balances and exception reports. Also, many companies have sizable internal audit staffs. Internal auditors not only audit many aspects of enterprise operations on a continuous basis for the information of top management, but their work is often utilized by independent auditors. Internal audit results thus become part of the evidence needed in forming evaluative judgments about the integrity of the system and the records on which the financial statements are based.

Auditing in a Changing World

We mentioned earlier that professional auditing had its genesis in Scotland during the middle of the nineteenth century. As British railroad, insurance, and other investments moved to North America, independent auditors moved with them initially to protect large British investor interests. The antecedents of North American professional accounting are therefore British.

Until the late 1940s, auditing was viewed as a process of examining the documentation supporting recorded transactions and verifying their classification in financial statements. This approach to auditing has been characterized as "auditing the books."

Internal Control Emphasis. In 1949 a committee of the AICPA issued a special report containing a comprehensive statement on the significance of internal control to the auditing process. In this statement *internal control* is defined as follows:

> Internal control comprises the plan of organization and all of the coordinated methods and measures adopted within a business to safeguard its assets, check the accuracy and reliability of its accounting data, promote operational efficiency, and encourage adherence to prescribed managerial policies. This definition possibly is broader than the meaning sometimes attributed to the term. It recognizes that a system of internal control extends beyond those matters which relate directly to the functions of the accounting and financial departments.

Soon after the special report, independent auditors began to place greater reliance on internal control considerations. At the beginning of an audit process, they now carefully evaluate a company's internal control system. If internal controls operate well, the system is likely to produce reasonably complete and accurate financial data. In turn, such data are a good starting point for reliable financial statements. On the other hand, the financial data base of an enterprise is not very dependable when internal controls are either weak or absent altogether.

1977 Foreign Corrupt Practices Act. During the early 1970s it was discovered that unauthorized payments were being made by U.S.-based multinational companies to foreign customers and suppliers. The resulting furor gave rise to passage of the federal Foreign Corrupt Practices Act. This act consists of two major parts. First, it renders illegal (and therefore subject to criminal prosecution) any "under-the-table" or otherwise unauthorized payments. And second, it places stringent and direct responsibility on the managements of corporations under the jurisdiction of the SEC to institute and operate comprehensive systems of internal control so as to preclude the possibility of unauthorized use or disbursement of corporate assets. The latter requirement extends to *all* corporate activities—domestic and foreign.

Example 19-2

> After the Brothers Three, Ltd., Shopping Center is built, rents and fees are collected from different occupants according to a wide variety of individual contracts. The controller's department of the Shopping Center has established the following internal control procedures, among others, to correspond to recognized internal control principles.

Procedure	Why Done	Principle
1. The receptionist prepares and mails all bank deposits as checks are received. The bookkeeper reconciles each monthly bank statement to the company's cash records.	To avoid misuse of funds received (as can occur when the same individual who receives funds also controls the records) and ensure timely bank deposits.	A plan of organization that provides appropriate segregation of functional responsibilities among employees.
2. Each advertising allowance made to tenant stores is individually authorized by the controller.	To control total amount of allowances granted and prevent kickbacks.	A system of authorization and recording procedures adequate to provide reasonable accounting control over assets, liabilities, revenues, and expenses.
3. New construction activities are recorded in accounts clearly separated from repair and maintenance accounts.	To ensure appropriate accounting classifications and control repair and maintenance operations.	Sound practices to be followed in the performance of duties and functions of each of the organizational departments.
4. The job description for the controller's position requires that appointees hold a CPA certificate.	To seek best possible job performance within budgeted salary range.	A degree of quality of personnel commensurate with responsibilities.

If an internal control system is found to be highly effective, independent audit procedures can be curtailed. With a well-functioning internal control system, relatively less extensive tests or samples may be required to supply the auditor with needed evidential matter directly supporting representations in the financial statements because he can rely more readily on the quality of the data produced by the system. On the other hand, a weak system of internal control generally dictates more extensive auditing procedures to provide sufficient evidence for an adequate evaluation of data quality and opinion formulation on the financial statements under audit.

Auditing Framework

When the independent auditor begins an audit assignment, he assumes that (1) the internal control system of the enterprise is appropriate and effective; (2) generally accepted accounting principles have been applied in all accounting processes underlying the financial statements; (3) the generally accepted accounting principles utilized have been applied consistently between the current and the prior periods; and (4) there is an adequate amount of informative financial disclosure in the financial statements and footnotes. Evidence gathering and its evaluation enable the auditors to reject or confirm these *a priori* assumptions. We are thus in a position to define *auditing*.

Auditing. The analytical process of gathering sufficient evidential matter on a test or sampling basis to enable a competent professional to express an opinion as to whether a given set of financial statements meets established standards of financial reporting.

Now we can enumerate the major steps of the auditing process: (1) become acquainted with the firm—its environment and its accounting, personnel, production, marketing, and other systems; (2) review and evaluate the management and the accounting control system in operation; (3) gather evidential matter on the integrity of the system; (4) gather further evidence related to the representations made in the financial statements; and (5) formulate a judgment opinion on the basis of the evidence available.

Getting Acquainted. Auditing is an analytical process applied to everyday business situations. Hence it is closely related to existing business practices. Without firsthand knowledge of the nature of these practices and their larger setting, the auditor would have to rely exclusively on available financial data. This would jeopardize both audit efficiency and effectiveness. Therefore a getting-acquainted phase (which usually includes a visit to a client's facilities and certain analytical preliminary tests and inquiries) initiates the typical audit process. The likely activities of this phase are described later in Example 19-6. While "getting-acquainted" preliminaries to the conduct of an audit are standard procedures today, they were quite novel prior to 1965. Initially such procedures were described as the "business approach to auditing."

Control System Review. We have already described the nature of internal control and its relationship to the auditing process. As was pointed out earlier, the auditor's evaluation of the control systems operating within the enterprise has a direct influence on the scope of the examination he undertakes and the nature of the tests he conducts. However, even though preliminary evaluation of control systems is an essential ingredient of planning the audit scope, we must remember that eventually *both the system and the data* it produces are covered by the audit process.

Example 19-3

> The Brothers Three Shopping Center has leased space to Mr. Hines, who operates a quality restaurant named The Duncan Inn located within it. Lease payments are based on a minimum monthly amount sufficient to cover taxes and insurance on the building plus a graduated percentage of the restaurant's gross sales to diners and bar patrons. No percentage payments are due on catering services.
>
> Bar and restaurant receipts of The Duncan Inn are collected in cash and from credit card billings. A select few patrons have the privilege of open credit with monthly billings.
>
> In planning the initial audit of The Duncan Inn's financial statements, a CPA finds that virtually no internal control exists over cash bar receipts. Hence tests covering cash bar receipts are scheduled more comprehensively than those extending to credit card sales.

Evidential Matter. Evidential matter supporting financial statements consists of the underlying accounting data and all corroborating information available to the auditor. The auditor tests underlying accounting data by analysis and review, retracing some of the procedural steps followed in the original accounting process and reconciling the events with the information reported.

The auditor's evidential material is the result of tests, selected observations, and statistical sampling where large compilations of data are involved. The auditor must always balance the natural desire for more evidential matter to support an opinion against the costliness and social usefulness of completely reconstructing the underlying data and processes that produced the financial statements. One key justification for independent audits, as we have seen, is the economy that results from producing expert opinion-based judgments from limited but reliable evidential matter.

Example 19-4

> Among tests covering cash bar receipts of The Duncan Inn, the CPA determined what the expected average ratios should be between liquor used, average number of individual drinks per bottle of liquor, and the price structure of drinks served. Making appropriate allowances for credit card sales, the CPA was then able to make a reasonable estimate of cash bar receipts for the period under audit. The estimate of the cash bar receipts constitutes evidential matter for purposes of the audit. (Note that the foregoing test has physical and financial dimensions. A purely financial test would be to subtract cash restaurant receipts from total bank deposits to arrive at cash bar receipts. In an actual engagement, an auditor might have undertaken both types of tests.)

Professional Judgment. The object of an independent audit, as we have noted, is to express a professional opinion on a set of financial statements. Rendering such an opinion is a matter of judgment. Professional evaluation of audit evidence gathered is therefore a key function of the independent auditor. The AICPA's *Statement on Auditing Standards No. 1* (paragraph 330.02), 1973, puts it into the following context:

> Most of the independent auditor's work in formulating his opinion on financial statements consists of obtaining and examining evidential matter. The measure of the validity of such evidence for audit purposes lies in the judgment of the auditor; in this respect audit evidence differs from legal evidence, which is circumscribed by rigid rules.

The foregoing statement can be rephrased to say that judgment of *what* evidential matter should be obtained and *how* it is to be interpreted permits confirmation or rejection of the assumption that the financial statements examined are in conformity with established financial reporting standards. There is no way in which the individual auditor's judgment can be completely eliminated from the attest function—despite a concerted effort by the profession to evolve more quantitative standards for the types of evidence that will support a given audit opinion.

Standards and Procedures. AICPA literature carefully distinguishes between auditing standards and auditing procedures:

> Auditing standards differ from auditing procedures in that procedures relate to acts to be performed, whereas standards deal with measures of the quality of performance of those acts and the objective to be obtained by the use of the procedures undertaken.

Exhibit 19-1 lists the ten generally accepted auditing *standards* which are binding upon most CPAs performing an independent audit. The binding force of these standards is established by (1) AICPA membership and the corresponding requirement to observe its Code of Professional Ethics, or (2) state

CPA licensing requirements, which might have built these standards into a state accountancy statute, or (3) regulatory enforcement of these standards by administrative agencies like the SEC. It is noteworthy that the CPA profession itself sets the standards by which it conducts its independent audit activities.

Exhibit 19-1   GENERALLY ACCEPTED AUDITING STANDARDS

General Standards

1. The examination is to be performed by a person or persons having adequate technical training and proficiency as an auditor.
2. In all matters relating to the assignment an independence in mental attitude is to be maintained by the auditor or auditors.
3. Due professional care is to be exercised in the performance of the examination and the preparation of the report.

Standards of Field Work

1. The work is to be adequately planned and assistants, if any, are to be properly supervised.
2. There is to be a proper study and evaluation of the existing internal control as a basis for reliance thereon and for the determination of the resultant extent of the tests to which auditing procedures are to be restricted.
3. Sufficient competent evidential matter is to be obtained through inspection, observation, inquiries, and confirmations to afford a reasonable basis for an opinion regarding the financial statements under examination.

Standards of Reporting

1. The report shall state whether the financial statements are presented in accordance with generally accepted principles of accounting.
2. The report shall state whether such principles have been consistently observed in the current period in relation to the preceding period.
3. Informative disclosures in the financial statements are to be regarded as reasonably adequate unless otherwise stated in the report.
4. The report shall either contain an expression of opinion regarding the financial statements, taken as a whole, or an assertion to the effect that an opinion cannot be expressed. When an over-all opinion cannot be expressed, the reasons therefor should be stated. In all cases where an auditor's name is associated with financial statements the report should contain a clear-cut indication of the character of the auditor's examination, if any, and the degree of responsibility he is taking.

Auditing procedures are less clearly established, because the nature, substance, and importance of any single procedure varies with the circumstances.

No two companies or no two transactions are completely alike. Consequently, few auditing procedures have been officially established, as the following AICPA statement indicates (from *Audits by Certified Public Accountants*):

> Each audit discloses circumstances which require differences to a greater or lesser degree in the auditing procedures that should be employed, the manner in which they should be used, and the extent to which they should be applied. Among the reasons for their differences in requirements are that (1) significant variations exist in the nature and scope of the operations of companies in different industrial or commercial groups, or even of companies within the same group or classification; (2) the degree of effectiveness of the internal control varies among companies; (3) even within a single company the operating and accounting problems frequently change from year to year; and (4) the amount of detail to be included in the financial statements varies. In new engagements, there may be the additional problem of making an appropriate review of the important transactions of prior years and determining the nature and extent of the accounting procedures and internal control in effect.
>
> These differences make it apparent that it is impossible to lay down specific procedures which could be applied satisfactorily in all cases. Often there is a choice of procedures, any of which would be satisfactory in a given situation. Here, as elsewhere in accounting and auditing, there must be an exercise of judgment based upon experience and upon a clear view of the objective of providing a sound basis for an informed, professional opinion.

From time to time the AICPA issues formal *Statements on Auditing Standards* (formerly known as *Statements on Auditing Procedure*). These standards serve as guidelines for the work of independent auditors. In the words of the AICPA's Auditing Standards Executive Committee (*Statement on Auditing Standards No. 1*, p. 205):

> Such statements [on auditing standards], covering recommended auditing procedures, represent the opinion of the Committee on the particular matters recited therein. While it is true that circumstances alter cases . . . such pronouncements point the general direction in which conclusions might be expected to lie under circumstances not radically different; while they [the standards] do not preempt the independent auditor's judgment, they do guide his judgment.

An Audit Engagement

Some audit engagements are so large that the CPA firm responsible for the audit may assign one or more of its partners full time to the particular client. In turn, each partner would be working with several audit managers, each of whom would be responsible for a number of supervising accountants and staff accountants working under supervision. In contrast, the independent audit needed by the local university YWCA for purposes of continued allocations from the United Way Fund may require no more than two hours of a supervising accountant's time. The vast majority of independent audit engagements fall between these two extremes. Auditors typically visit company offices for relatively short periods of time. Usually, small teams of auditors perform an engagement.

Start of an Engagement. Most independent audit engagements begin as a consequence of (1) legal requirements, (2) referrals by head offices of companies or home offices of large international CPA firms, or (3) suggestions from attorneys, bankers, or other businesspersons.

Example 19-5

When Mr. Hines, owner of The Duncan Inn, realized that his restaurant was highly profitable, he discussed with his banker the possibility of a large loan for the purpose of building The Second Duncan Inn. The banker suggested an independent audit of the Hines Company's financial statements as a condition for the loan. Furthermore, three to five years hence the Hines Company, which owns The Duncan Inn and would be the owner of The Second Duncan Inn, might offer some of its stock for sale to the public. This could require registration with the SEC and therefore audited financial statements. To explore the possibility of an independent audit for his company, Mr. Hines makes an appointment with Jonathan Lee, a partner in the CPA firm of MacLean & Co.

Mr. Hines comes to the meeting with two sets of financial statements prepared by his bookkeeper—one for the year just ended and one for the preceding year. After short introductory amenities, Mr. Hines comes right to the point by asking how much it will cost to have the two sets of financial statements audited by MacLean & Co. Mr. Lee explains that his firm has an hourly billing rate for each staff classification and that Mr. Hines's company would be billed for the exact number of hours spent on the audit at an appropriate billing rate for each auditor. Mr. Lee then estimates a range for the probable cost of an annual audit for Mr. Hines's company.

The estimate satisfies Mr. Hines and he agrees to appoint MacLean & Co. as his company's auditors. (This is possible, since Mr. Hines is at present the sole stockholder.) In further discussion it is agreed that retroactive audits are difficult and costly to undertake and that therefore the engagement will begin now so that the first audited financial statements can be produced a year from now. Based upon these various understandings, Mr. Lee drafts an appropriate engagement letter for Mr. Hines's signature. The appointment of MacLean & Co. as independent auditors of the Hines Company becomes official with the execution of the engagement letter. The engagement letter also spells out the services to be performed, and responsibilities to be undertaken, by MacLean & Co., along with the necessary cooperation and access to records to be provided by Hines.

Planning Audit Activities. Once an engagement is agreed upon, many different planning procedures take place. Within a CPA firm, appropriate staff assignments are necessary. Dates for the auditors' visit must be agreed upon and needed documents and information made available. Personal introductions and tours of facilities are another type of essential preliminary.

As established earlier in this chapter, a comprehensive evaluation of a company's internal control system is a significant determinant of the types and amounts of evidential matter needed for a given audit. The effectiveness of other organizational and operational controls must also be considered.

Example 19-6

Continuing the case of Example 19-5, an initial visit from two MacLean & Co. auditors is scheduled almost immediately. The purpose of the initial visit is to gather facts about the Hines Company in general and collect data concerning its various control systems.

During the visit, the auditors acquaint themselves with all management personnel of the company, its physical facilities, and a long list of such relevant information as membership on the board of directors, name and address of the company's attorneys, and copies of governmental and tax reports filed. Some desk space is arranged for the auditors, and they begin their first assignment. The task is finished in two days. Evidence gathered is recorded in audit working papers and standard review questionnaires which MacLean & Co. uses.

Setting of a Regular Audit Examination. Independent auditors always keep in mind that their primary purpose is the expression of an opinion on the fairness of representations in financial statements. Hence it is not surprising to find that each audit step and each audit test is a building block toward the final expression of a professional opinion.

For example, what are some things an auditor would wish to know about sales revenues appearing in the financial statements of the Hines Company? A partial list might include the following:

1. Have actual revenues been recorded *properly* and *completely?* Tests like the one described in Example 19-4 help to answer this question. The auditor begins with evidence of products or services provided to customers and compares the corresponding amount of revenue with the amount recorded.

2. Were reported revenues earned in the *period* for which they are reported? In this connection the auditor performs so-called cutoff tests, making sure that all December sales, for instance, are recorded in December and not carried forward to January. Improper cutoffs of revenues and/or expenses represent misallocations of reported net income between successive periods.

3. Do accounts receivable shown at year-end reflect *bona fide receivables* and are they *collectible?* Correctness is tested by direct correspondence with debtors to confirm outstanding balances. Analysis of subsequent actual payments received helps to establish whether any bad accounts were among the receivables listed. Overstatement of receivables may again overstate reported net income (because of insufficient provision for uncollectibles) as well as financial position amounts and ratios.

With an appreciation of what is needed to achieve fair presentation in financial statements, an auditor can evaluate an individual company situation and the state of its control systems for purposes of setting scope and depth of needed audit examinations. In determining which aspects of an accounting system should be tested and in what fashion, the auditor typically relies on guidelines available in the professional literature. These help him to arrive at his own judgments in given circumstances. Exhibit 19-2 contains a "Guide to Audit Programs and Procedures" for sales and receivables of a larger company. Similar guides are available for other financial statement categories. Evidential matter produced by following such guides provides at least a minimum basis for the eventual expression of a professional opinion on the financial statements under audit.

Exhibit 19-2

GUIDE TO AUDIT PROGRAMS AND PROCEDURES—SALES AND RECEIVABLES

Review, test, and record explanations for significant fluctuations in sales and sales-related accounts noted in comparing current results with budgets, forecasts, prior periods, industry data

Evaluate overall reasonableness of recorded sales and related amounts by reviewing available marketing data:
    Reconcile volume, activity, statistical or dollar reports to regulatory agencies or others with recorded amounts
    Reconcile internal sales and shipping reports with recorded amounts
    Compute an estimate of sales using production or shipping data and average sales prices. Summarize sales by major contracts and reconcile to control account balances (consider confirming major transactions with customers)

Evaluate and test internal accounting controls over sales and receivables—sales order entry, credit, shipping, billing, accounts receivable ledger controls, general ledger controls

Review and test general ledger accounts for entries to sales, receivables and related control accounts from controlled accounting journals—investigate entries from other sources

Summarize observations and conclusions on types and levels of management controls over granting and monitoring of credit

Circularize receivables

Evaluate and test adequacy of provisions for doubtful accounts, returns and allowances, warranties and guaranties, discounts and renegotiation liabilities

Evaluate and test period cutoffs of sales and sales-related transactions

Review and test all nontrade receivables

On initial examinations, determine work required to substantiate balances at beginning of period

Review appropriateness and consistency of accounting principles and methods for recording sales and receivables

Determine existence and appropriate accounting treatment or disclosure of:
    Sales recognized under percentage-of-completion method
    Consignment sales
    Sales to affiliates
    Long-term sales contracts or other delayed billing arrangements
    Unusual or adverse sales commitments

Review appropriateness of proposed disclosure of:
    Revenues by operating, nonoperating, and nonrecurring categories
    Receivables by type (trade, installment, affiliate, employee, officer, other) and by due date (current vs. noncurrent)
    Revenue recognition basis
    Pledged or discounted receivables

Summarize conclusions as to whether all material elements of sales, receivables, and related accounts have met the financial statement objectives

---

Audit Completion and Reporting. The tests and other necessary procedures that are included in an audit are documented in a set of audit working papers. The AICPA recommends that audit working papers include or show the following:

1. Data sufficient to demonstrate that the financial statements or other information upon which the auditor is reporting were in agreement with (or reconciled with) the client's records.

2. That the engagement had been planned, such as by use of work programs, and that the work of any assistants was supervised and reviewed, indicating observance of the first standard of fieldwork. (See Exhibit 19-1.)

3. That the client's system of internal control was reviewed and evaluated in determining the extent of the tests to which auditing procedures were restricted, indicating observance of the second standard of fieldwork.

4. The auditing procedures followed and tests performed in obtaining evidential matter, indicating observance of the third standard of fieldwork. The record in these respects may take various forms, including memoranda, checklists, work programs, and schedules and would generally permit reasonable identification of the work done by the author.

5. How exceptions and unusual matters, if any, disclosed by the independent auditor's procedures were resolved or treated.

6. Appropriate commentaries prepared by the auditor indicating his conclusions concerning significant aspects of the engagement.

Working papers are reviewed by managers and partners of the CPA firm conducting the audit. Eventually, a partner signs an appropriate auditor's report on behalf of his firm.

Example 19-7

Let us assume that all necessary fieldwork is now completed on the first annual audit of Hines Company. The supervising accountant on the engagement completes the working papers and sends them to his manager for review. Thereafter, a number of accounting adjustments are suggested to Mr. Hines and his bookkeeper so that the financial statements will be brought into conformity with generally accepted accounting principles. The representatives of the Hines Company agree, and the financial statements are adjusted accordingly.

At this point, Mr. Lee reviews all of the working papers that have been prepared, as well as the drafted financial statements and footnotes. Mr. Lee asks quite a few questions of the audit manager and receives satisfactory answers so that he feels justified in signing the auditor's opinion on the Hines Company financial statements. Copies of the statements and the opinion are then mailed to Mr. Hines as the sole shareholder. A statement (bill) for professional auditing services rendered by MacLean & Co. is sent to the company as well.

Special Auditing Tools and Techniques

The case just described is highly simplified to acquaint the reader with the essential steps in conducting an audit. Engagements for large clients are enormously more complicated and often involve large-scale coordination between client locations and subsidiaries not only across North America but in many overseas countries as well. In addition, auditors rely on some rather sophisticated techniques in conducting large-scale engagements. Three of these techniques are described briefly in the following paragraphs.

Flowcharts. A quick and comprehensive way of understanding, but more importantly reviewing, the information system of a client company is to flowchart all or parts of it. Flows of documents and document storage are quickly apparent from flowcharts, and weaknesses in information systems can be detected and analyzed by an expert. A flowchart used to describe an auditor's summary of a client's payroll procedures by Robert M. Rennie in an article appearing in the March 1965 edition of *The Quarterly* (a publication of Touche Ross & Co.) is reproduced in Exhibit 19-3.

Statistical Sampling. Where the sets of documents constituting evidential matter are relatively large and homogeneous, statistical sampling can be applied to good advantage. This is most likely to apply to auditing procedures involving invoices payable to creditors, accounts receivable from customers, inventories, and payroll applications. By using statistical sampling in these areas, the auditor is often able to reduce the number of documents actually examined and at the same time control the precision and the confidence level. As a result, statistical sampling may reduce audit costs to clients.

Computer-assisted Auditing Procedures. Another sophisticated auditing technique is the use of computers in the auditing process. Among the more simple tests in this connection is deliberate processing of nonsensical or impossible transactions to determine the client company's computer system's reaction. For instance, if a payroll program would process a monthly payroll check exceeding, let us say, $500,000, then the internal control of the system is weak. It should reject any wage payment exceeding reasonable maximum amounts.

Computer audit software packages are increasingly efficient in expediting audit tests and procedures. The larger CPA firms have developed such software packages, which use the client's own computing equipment to perform predetermined test and check functions on the client's computerized information systems and records. These packages have enabled auditors to audit "with the computer" rather than "around" the computer.

Detection of Errors and Irregularities (Including Fraud)

In the course of an ordinary examination, the independent auditor is aware that the possibility of errors in the client's records or the possibility of irregularities such as fraud may exist. Financial statements may be misstated as a result of errors, defalcations, or deliberate misrepresentations by management. The auditor recognizes that errors or irregularities, if sufficiently material, will affect his opinion about the financial statements. Therefore his examination, made in accordance with generally accepted auditing standards, includes reasonable procedures designed to detect material errors or irregularities. If errors or irregularities are discovered the auditor has several responsibilities, which include the following: (1) to notify the appropriate officers and/or board members and (2) to assess the implications of the discovery for the remainder of planned audit procedures and the rendering of an opinion on the client's financial statements.

However, the ordinary examination for the purpose of expressing an opinion on financial statements is *not primarily* designed to disclose defalcations or fraud, although their discovery may result. Thus, although the discovery of deliberate misrepresentations by management is closely associated with the

Exhibit 19-3
FLOWCHART OF WEEKLY FACTORY PAYROLL PROCEDURES

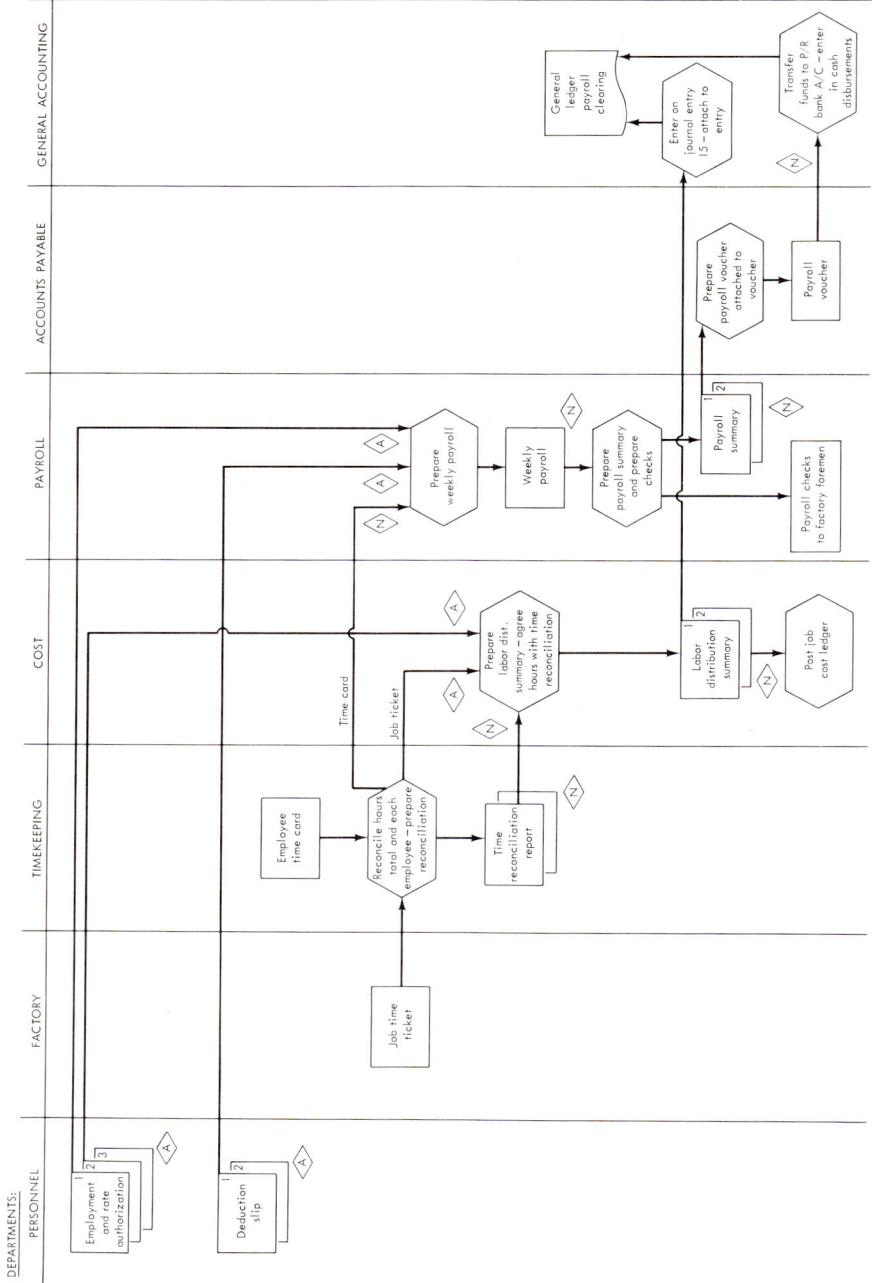

objectives of an ordinary examination, such an examination cannot be relied upon to guarantee their discovery.

If an objective of an independent auditor's examination were the discovery of all fraud, the audit would have to be extended to a point where its cost might be prohibitive. Even then the auditor could probably not give assurance that all types of fraud had been detected or that none existed, because items such as unrecorded transactions, forgeries, and collusive fraud would not necessarily be uncovered. Therefore, reliance for the prevention and detection of fraud is placed principally upon an adequate accounting system with appropriate built-in controls.

In the course of an ordinary examination, the independent auditor may find specific circumstances that lead him to suspect that fraud may exist. Disclosure is made to proper representatives of the enterprise (probably the board of directors or one of its members) together with a recommendation for further action. The auditor must also decide whether the possible fraud might be of such magnitude as to affect his opinion on the financial statements. If the opinion could be affected, a special investigation becomes necessary.

Example 19-8

Lisa Young is a third-year staff auditor in a large public accounting firm. As a member of an audit team, she was performing examinations of the financial records of a large pulp mill. Her specific assignment was to check truck-weighing tickets so that the recorded amounts of trucked-in raw material (logs) could be established as a reliable basis for the cost of the pulp manufactured. No log inventory was kept at the pulp mill; all logs were fed directly into the shredding machinery as delivered.

Checking weighing tickets was not a particularly exciting task for Lisa. They all seemed to be in order, with serial numbers properly accounted for and authorization initials appearing on each. After she had established the totals for the month she was checking, she wondered what the daily usage rate was. After she had computed that amount, she was struck by the fact that the plant superintendent had quoted a total capacity for the shredding machinery which was below the actual volume she had calculated.

Lisa then checked her findings with the auditor in charge of the team. They both went over the calculations and found that indeed the reported amount of logs delivered could not have been used by the available shredding capacity. Since the most important cost item of the pulp mill was affected, the partner in charge of the audit was contacted and brought into the picture immediately.

Since there existed the possibility of fraud at the plant superintendent's level, top production management at corporate headquarters was informed of the suspected irregularity. The corporate vice-president in charge of production then confronted the plant superintendent, who was both surprised and embarrassed. An unobtrusive surveillance system was then put into effect over the scale master. Telescopic scale readings were compared with imprinted weighing tickets. Over the course of several days, it was discovered that the scale master was in collusion with three driver-operators. He advanced his scales from actual readings by as much as 10 to 20 percent on individual loads being delivered. The copies of weighing tickets which remained with the truck operators even had the fictitious weight differential noted!

Over a three-year period, the company had paid for approximately 20 percent more than it should have on the logs it had purchased from those operators. If better internal control over the scale master had been in effect (job rotation, required vacations, direct observation by supervisor), the defalcation might not have occurred. Lisa Young's role in discovering it was a result of alertness combined with audit procedures that were designed with an awareness that such a defalcation was a possibility. However, Lisa might not have become suspicious if the plant superintendent had not quoted the plant's shredding capacity *accurately.* Had the superintendent been in collusion with the scale master, the defalcation might not have been discovered.

Professional Independence

Ideally, CPAs ought to be completely independent when they perform audits related to financial statements. The second general auditing standard listed in Exhibit 19-1 requires that in all respects related to the audit of financial statements an independence of mental attitude is to be maintained. Public confidence in independent auditors' reports would be impaired if there were evidence that independence was actually lacking. It might also be impaired by the existence of circumstances that reasonable people would believe likely to influence independence. To be independent, the auditor must be intellectually honest. To be recognized as independent, he must be free from any obligation to or interest in the client, its management, or its owners. Through the AICPA's *Code of Professional Ethics* (which has been written into local law by many state legislatures), the profession guards itself against public presumption of a loss of independence. The code requires that CPAs acting as independent auditors must avoid situations that may lead outsiders to doubt their independence.

The requirement for complete independence creates several dilemmas for the CPA. One dilemma is *economic.* Since managements often directly pay auditors' fees, an economic relationship necessarily exists between the auditor and "the auditee." The creation of audit committees among corporate boards of directors as the boards' conduits to their independent auditors has alleviated but not eliminated the dilemma. When board audit committees exist, auditors have an opportunity to become more independent of a company's top operating management. The New York Stock Exchange requires that all companies whose securities are listed on the NYSE have audit committees consisting of outside board members. The SEC and the AICPA strongly recommend audit committees—at least for companies subject to SEC jurisdiction.

Another dilemma is *behavioral.* Mental attitudes are difficult to change through laws and codes of ethics. Despite all outward appearances of independence, the behavioral makeup of some persons simply precludes a consistent and pervasive mental attitude of independence on their part. Some CPA licensing rules and continuing professional education requirements for license renewals again mitigate this dilemma without eliminating it.

SEC Influence. We pointed out earlier that the SEC administers the Securities Acts which provide for the adequate and accurate disclosure of all material facts relating to financial information filed by companies with the Agency. The SEC believes that an auditor's independence is fundamental in implementing the purposes of the Securities Acts. Most filings of financial statements with the SEC must include an independent auditor's report on such statements.

On July 5, 1972, the SEC issued Accounting Series Release No. 126 entitled "Guidelines and Examples of Situations Involving the Independence of Accountants." The following examples are taken directly from this SEC release. Examples 1 and 2 deal with family relationships, while Example 3 addresses the question of an outside interest. Other situations, like performing EDP or bookkeeping services for a client, becoming a client's creditor, or having other business or occupational conflicting interests, may affect independence as well.

1. An accountant has a sister-in-law whose husband is a 40 percent stockholder of a company. There is no other business connection between the company, the stockholder, the accountant, or his wife. Conclusion: *Independence is adversely affected because of the family relationship between the accountant and a major stockholder in a client company.*

2. The father of a partner in a public accounting firm was the chairman of the board and chief executive officer of a client company. The accounting firm had approximately 400 general partners and had offices throughout the U.S. The client was a large and diverse company with many consolidated subsidiaries. The partner's office was located over 500 miles from the client's home offices and the partner was totally isolated from the audit engagement. This situation and the independence issue involved were presented to and reviewed by the company's board of directors. This body, which performs the functions typically delegated to an audit committee of directors, decided that, if the son would not be involved in the audit in any way, his association with the accounting firm would not be incompatible with the independence relationship. Conclusion: *No question of independence was raised under these circumstances.*

3. A partner in an accounting firm is a member of an investment club. The club owns stock in a company which is a client of the accounting firm. Neither the number nor the value of the shares purchased is material to the club or the company. Conclusion: *The firm's independence would be adversely affected as a result of the partner's interest in the investment club. In this regard, an investment club does not stand on the same footing as the mutual fund, because the former is comprised of relatively few members, and each member plays an active part in the selection of investments.*

Changing Nature. Professional independence is really a system of various trade-offs. The appropriate balance changes as social patterns change. For instance, British auditors may still serve on boards of directors of companies they audit. German and Swiss audit companies are in many cases owned by large banks (which affects independence when audit clients are also bank customers). Thus economic, social, legal, and behavioral forces must be balanced against each other at a given point in time and space to arrive at a workable concept of professional independence. Obviously, such a balance (or equilibrium point) must necessarily shift in response to changing conditions if the social usefulness of professional independence is to be maintained.

Social Setting of the Attest Function

Various court cases have extended the professional liability of independent auditors to third parties. Growing economic complexity of industrialized society has brought in its wake a clearly discernible extension of the traditional boundaries of the attest function. Auditing of public sector agencies and programs has become a steadily growing activity.

Third-party Liabilities. With regard to potential auditor liabilities to third parties, several hundred well-publicized legal actions have been brought during the recent past. Bar Chris Construction Corporation (1968), Memorex Corporation (1970), Penn Central Company (1970), and Four Seasons Nursing Homes (1971) are among the widely noted earlier cases. Legal entanglements are still pending on more recent ones.

In the Bar Chris action, the suing bondholders did not accuse the underwriters, auditors, or outside directors of trying to *deceive* them or anyone else *intentionally.* But were the auditors nevertheless liable for the demonstrably incorrect information that management had distributed? *Yes,* ruled U.S. District Court Judge Edward C. McLean, because they had *not* made a *reasonable effort* to check the facts.

Civil negligence charges by stockholders against independent auditors characterize the suit involving the Yale Express System, Inc. A failing internal control system led to a reported net income for 1963 of $1.1 million, which upon later review resulted in a change to a loss approximating $1.9 million. In the Westec Corporation case, certain accounting procedures were drawn into question. Nine months after reporting 1965 earnings of $4.9 million and assets of $56 million, Westec Corporation went into bankruptcy.

The Continental Vending Machine Corporation case produced criminal convictions against some auditors. Illegal funds transfers and other irregularities involving Continental's president were not properly reported in the audited financial statements, which had shown $250,000 cash as an asset when in fact a cash deficit of more than $1 million should have been reported. Continental went into receivership in 1963.

Most observers seem to agree that the trend toward greater third-party responsibility for auditors will continue.

Broader Applications of Auditing. Aside from naming independent auditors as codefendants in suits brought by the SEC (under the U.S. Securities Acts), other administrative agencies, individual business enterprises, or class actions by stockholders and creditors, new developments are likely with regard to using the auditor's professional expertise more broadly. This appears certain to occur in such matters as greater emphasis on the auditing function prior to proposed business combinations or mergers, audit coverage of business forecasts by enterprise managements, and heavier audit requirements in regulatory activities like direct foreign investment control or domestic price and wage control. Also, the field of the so-called social audit can be expected to open up in the next decade or two. Social auditing concerns the social impact of business enterprises in such areas as work environment, noise and air pollution, inefficient use of natural resources, and minimum performance and safety standards for consumer products.

Public Sector Developments. Auditing can also be expected to extend its traditional boundaries in the public sector. The General Accounting Office, which is the auditing watchdog of the U.S. Congress, increasingly engages in "performance" audits—an audit function addressed more to the effectiveness of a particular agency or program management than to its financial affairs and conditions. It is noteworthy that in 1972 the GAO published a body of audit standards applicable to all forms of governmental organizations and activities.[1] These standards are intended to apply to government and private auditors alike when audit work is performed in the public sector.

Aside from the GAO, most large federal cabinet-level departments and state governments maintain growing audit agencies of their own. These auditors, while internal to the respective organizations, typically have the power to publish their findings without jeopardy and are able to deliver their reports and recommendations to the highest management levels of the organizations they serve. Large audit organizations of this type are found in the Department of Defense and the Department of Health, Education, and Welfare. State auditors and their staffs are similarly organized, even though in some states the state auditor is publicly elected and therefore subject to at least some influence from political pressures.

The CPA Profession

CPAs perform most of the independent audits of financial statements in the United States. According to Professor Howard Stettler of the University of Kansas, the annual growth rate of the number of CPAs in the United States has been around 6 percent since 1930. This compares with growth rates of less than 2 percent per year for the United States population as a whole and for the professional groups of physicians and surgeons, and lawyers.

CPA certificates, along with state licenses to practice as independent auditors, are issued by the individual states and territories. The issuing agency is normally a State Board of Accountancy. Typical prerequisites for a CPA certificate include (1) a baccalaureate degree from an accredited college or university, (2) passing of the Uniform CPA Examination, which is a rigorous two-and-a-half-day examination covering accounting practice, accounting theory, auditing, and commercial law, (3) practical experience under the supervision of a CPA, (4) domonstrated knowledge of local professional ethics statutes, and (5) satisfactory personal references. A number of jurisdictions now require specified periodic amounts of continuing education as a condition for renewal of the license to practice as a CPA.

Professional CPA organizations include the AICPA and the State Societies of CPAs. However, membership in these two types of organizations is not compulsory for practicing CPAs. The AICPA acts as the advocate of the profession vis-à-vis government, industry, and the financial community. In connection with the attest function, it establishes guidelines and standards for "generally

---

[1] U.S. General Accounting Office, *Standards for Audit of Governmental Organizations, Programs, Activities & Functions* (Washington, D.C.: The Comptroller General of the United States, 1972).

accepted" auditing. It also conducts research and professional development activities on a wide scale. Furthermore, it prepares and administers the Uniform CPA Examination twice each year.

State Societies of CPAs are predominantly concerned with local or regional matters. They seek to safeguard professional interests in state legislatures, support state boards of accountancy in their various activities, and conduct scores of professional seminars and continuing education programs. Quite often they also operate speakers' bureaus, assist local social programs and charitable organizations, and encourage public professional involvement.

Questions for Review and Discussion

19-1. Define the following:
   a. Audit reports
   b. Internal control
   c. Auditing
   d. Auditing standards

19-2. What is the objective of audits of financial statements of enterprises by independent professional accountants?

19-3. Who has primary responsibility for the preparation of financial statements? Why?

19-4. Explain how independent audits generally provide economies in the production of reasonably reliable corporate financial reports.

19-5. What is the relationship between an internal control system of an enterprise and the scope of an audit of financial statements performed by independent auditors?

19-6. What are the typical prerequisites for obtaining a CPA certificate?

19-7. The standard audit report makes a number of representations about audit performance and financial statement characteristics. List and explain briefly three additional items that a standard audit report might refer to.

19-8. Differentiate between a transactions approach and a business approach to auditing corporate financial statements.

19-9. Why do auditing procedures that independent auditors actually use differ from year to year and from company to company?

19-10. What kinds of things do independent auditors typically want to accomplish on an initial visit to the offices of a new client?

19-11. List three things that independent auditors might want to know in forming an opinion about the liabilities listed in a company's statement of financial position.

19-12. What is the relationship between detection of fraud and an audit of financial statements for the purpose of expressing an independent opinion thereon?

19-13. Why is the SEC concerned with professional auditor independence?

19-14. Find the description of a recent third-party liability suit involving independent auditors (from the *Wall Street Journal* or another financial newspaper) and explain concisely the charge against the auditors.

19-15. Is the professional audit function limited to private enterprises? If not, how and where else does it operate?

Exercises

19-1. Flowchart Preparation. Enrollment in and ultimate completion of a course of study at a college or university involve a series of actions constituting a system, which may be better understood when represented in flowchart form. Design a flowchart of the system for enrolling in and completing the course for which you are studying this chapter. Restrict your flowchart to fifteen stages or less and include only those stages in which you are personally involved.

19-2. Internal Control System Design. Jerry Mander is chairman of the "Committee to Reelect Stan the Man as State Governor." The committee has its own offices and a large number of workers. All campaign workers are regarded as having high dedication and integrity. Nevertheless, Jerry is concerned about the control over the handling of donations.

Potential donors are listed in a directory kept at the committee's offices. Each day Phil E. Buster (Jerry's second-in-command) allocates several names from the list to each of his campaign workers. They then visit the prospective donors and, if possible, collect a check or cash from them. No donations are ever received by mail. At the end of the day the campaign workers return to the offices and hand Phil their collections, which he places in a safe. Periodically, the contents of the safe are deposited in the committee's checking account. Devise an effective but simple internal control system for the solicitation and receipt of donations.

19-3. Professional Independence Case Analysis. For each of the following cases, state whether the independence of the auditor concerned is adversely affected, and give brief reasons for your answer:
   a. A partner in an accounting firm is the trustee of the estate of a deceased friend and administers the estate on behalf of the friend's children. A material portion of the value of the estate consists of stocks of a company that is a client of his accounting firm.
   b. A partner in a public accounting firm is a member of a tennis club of which his brother is president. The club has raised a relatively large amount of funds to finance the eventual construction of additional courts and social facilities. Most of these funds have been invested temporarily in common stocks. Half the total investment has been made in a company that is a client of the accounting firm.
   c. A manufacturing company employs a small firm to handle most of its advertising activities. Without the revenue generated by this association, the advertising firm could not remain in business. The owner of the advertising firm has a son who is a

partner in an accounting firm. The manufacturing company is a client of the accounting firm.

d. A partner in an accounting firm has not completed repayment of a large loan made by a bank. The money had been borrowed to enable payment of damages resulting from a car accident involving a member of the partner's family. The bank has now appointed his firm as its auditors. The partner will not be involved in the audit of the bank, and he now resides in a state in which the bank has no branches.

19-4. Conflict of Interest Resolution. Some have claimed that a reasonable degree of independence is rarely maintained by CPAs, chiefly because remuneration of the CPA comes from clients. However, there is little evidence of agreement on possible alternatives to the present practices. Three possible alternatives may be—

a. Appointment of independent auditors and negotiation of scope of services and fees by an "audit committee" composed of nonmanagement members of the board of directors, or

b. A requirement that companies change their auditors fairly frequently, for example, every three years, or

c. Performance of the attest function by a governmental body.

Required:

Critically evaluate each of the above alternatives.

19-5. Physical Inventory Program. You are an audit manager in a large accounting firm. One of the clients for whose audit you are responsible is the Diaper Distributors Company. The company purchases fully completed and packaged diapers from major suppliers and arranges their distribution throughout the state. You are now developing an audit program for the verification of inventories. The company's inventories will be counted on December 31, 19X5, and you intend that your staff auditors will be present on that day at all locations where inventory counting is to be undertaken. From past experience you know that a substantial quantity of inventories will be in transit between locations on that day. For example, inventory from the head office warehouse will leave by truck on December 30 and will not reach the company's regional warehouse until January 2, 19X6.

Required:

Draw up an audit program that will ensure that no inventories on hand or in transit are counted twice or omitted altogether from the inventory records compiled in the count.

19-6. Marketable Securities Audit. A large company holds a substantial number of bonds and stocks in other companies. The stocks and bonds are kept in a safe at the company's offices, with the exception of some that are kept at the bank. Ignoring the problems of valuation of the stocks and bonds, how would you verify their existence? That they are actually owned by the company? How would you ensure that dividends and interest have been recorded properly?

19-7. Leased Equipment Audit. Hubert's Hirings specializes in the leasing of construction equipment—compressors, welders, pneumatic drills, and bulldozers. On any given day, approximately 75 percent of its lease equipment will not be in the company's yards, but out on lease to customers of Hubert's Hirings. Design an audit program to verify the existence of the equipment shown on the company's records at any given time.

19-8. Accounts Receivable Analysis. Debts due from customers, that is, accounts receivable, normally constitute a significant portion of an enterprise's total assets. How would you audit accounts receivable? What steps would you take to ensure that they have not been overstated due to inadequacies in the recognition of potentially uncollectible accounts?

19-9. Contingent Liability Procedure. When an individual is being sued, or guarantees repayment of loans made to others by his local bank, he has a contingent liability, that is, he may have to pay out money if a certain future event occurs. Likewise companies may have contingent liabilities which should be disclosed to stockholders. How would you approach the problem of satisfying yourself that the company you are auditing has no undisclosed contingent liabilities?

19-10. Reasons for Internal Control Weaknesses. After their interim audit of a small company, the auditors sent their client a letter, listing weaknesses in the client's system of internal control. Among the weaknesses were the following:
    a. Checks and cash are accumulated for three or four days before being deposited.
    b. The cashier (who handles all cash receipts) has access to the accounts receivable ledger from which monthly statements are prepared.
    c. The person responsible for preparing the bank deposit and depositing funds at the bank also prepares the bank reconciliation.
    d. Persons who are authorized to sign checks for payment of accounts payable do not cancel the supporting documentary evidence (e.g., invoices).
    e. There is no rotation of employees' duties, nor are annual vacations compulsory.

Required:

Give a brief explanation of why each of these facts involves an internal control weakness.

19-11. Fraud Discovery. Yecch Breakfast Foods Company is a small family business which specializes in breakfast cereals. Its financial statements have never been audited by a CPA. To the owner's chagrin, he eventually finds that—
    a. Bags of spices which ostensibly filled a large portion of his warehouse were arranged in hollow stacks. In some cases, bags

were found to be filled with sand. In addition, the quality (and hence the cost) of many of the spices actually in stock was inferior to the quality specified in the company records.

    b. The company accountant occasionally pocketed receipts from customers which had arrived by mail. He would then sign a credit note for the amount, so that the balance of the statement eventually mailed to the customer would be in accordance with the customer's records. To Yecch Breakfast Foods Company, the credit note indicated that the client had received a reduction in the amount due because goods delivered to him were spoiled on arrival.

    c. The company accountant had also sold some of the company's marketable securities for $10,000. When the stock market price of these securities subsequently dropped, he replaced them at a cost of $4,000. No records of the transactions were made in the company's books, and the accountant retained the $6,000 net proceeds for himself.

Although examinations by independent auditors are not specifically designed to discover fraud, it is possible that their presence and their procedures might have prevented or more quickly disclosed these defalcations. For each of the above examples of fraud, indicate how the independent auditor might have detected it during the course of a normal audit examination.

19-12. Audit Committee Duties. The chapter text briefly mentions audit committees of corporate boards of directors as communication channels for the potential concerns of independent auditors. Using your own imagination and library resources available to you, develop a list of ten likely duties that could be assigned to an audit committee of a corporate board of directors.

19-13. Audit Committee Decision Making. After a highly successful career, Arthur Stanwood retires as senior financial executive of Y Corporation. An intensive executive search procedure reveals that the best candidate for the resulting job opening is the CPA firm partner who has been in charge of the Y Corporation independent audit for the past eight years. Should Y Corporation hire the partner "away" from his firm? Since the partner necessarily has had a close relationship with his firm's audit staff, would this create any difficulties if he were employed? In case of his employment, should Y Corporation change CPA firms?

Required:

Write a short essay in response to the questions posed.

19-14. International Audit Activities. Assume that you are a partner in a medium-sized CPA firm that does not have offices outside North America. One of your clients has acquired several subsidiary companies in Europe and the Far East, whose business volume is important in relation to total consolidated sales, net income, and assets. The client proposes that local audit firms be employed to perform independent audits of the subsidiary companies in question.

Required:

Draft a short memorandum to the client outlining the conditions precedent to your acceptance of the work and opinions of foreign auditors.

19-15. Qualified Reports of Independent Auditors. Sometimes CPA auditors have reservations about the results of their audit activities and thus issue so-called qualified reports. Utilizing the resources of your closest library, make a copy of a qualified report of an independent auditor and state why the qualification occurred.

Index

Accomplishment, value-added concept and, 84, 271, 596–99
Account analysis approach, 199–201
Accounting:
  accrual, 117
  basic concepts of, 266–69
  business enterprise, external parties and, 267
  choosing alternative models of, 628–32
    social choice problem, 628–29
    traditional criteria, 630–31
  constant dollar, 638–39
  conventional, 83–84
    changing prices and, 499–501
    conservatism in applying, 163–64
    framework, 104–12, 159
    income measurement, 147–68
    investment decision perspective, 72–91
    objectivity and, 167
    performance measurement, 83–91
    performance measurement and changing prices, 505
    relevance of, 165
    uncertainty in measurement, 162–63
    valuation, 108–9
  current cost, 639–40
  defined, 3, 6
  external users of, 6
  financial, 6–7
  information, 4–6
  as information specialization, 17
    conditions necessary for, 17, 266
  for income taxes, 436–44
  for long-term noncancelable leases, 444–53
  market-value, present status of, 612
  for parent companies and subsidiaries:
    consolidation, 465–72
    equity method, 459–65
    pooling-of-interests method, 472–74
    purchase method, 472–74
  price-level, 495–524
  transactions (events) approach, 125–27
Accounting cycle, 127–28, 241–45
Accounting equation, 109, 225
Accounting policy:
  capital market institutions and, 673–709
  government regulation of, historical perspective on, 682–85
Accounting practice (*see* Accounting policy)
Accounting Principles Board (APB), 207, 452, 685, 689, 690
Accounting-processing function, categories of, 230, 233
Accounting subsystems:
  acquisitions and payments, 249
  capital acquisition and repayment, 249

788 INDEX

Accounting subsystems (cont.)
  flowchart of credit sales and collections, 251
  inventory, 249
  payroll, 249
  related operations and, 248-50
  sales and collections, 248
Accounts:
  permanent, 240
  revenue and expense, 240
  temporary, 229-30
Accounts payable, defined, 114
Accretion, defined, 282 (*see also* Value-added concept)
Accrual accounting, 117
Accruals, 117, 239
Acid test:
  ratio, 725-26
Acquisitions, bona fide, 249
Adjustments, 117-20
  end-of-period, 237-39
AICPA (*see* American Institute of Certified Public Accountants)
Alternative costing methods, 353
American Accounting Association, 686
American Institute of Certified Public Accountants (AICPA), 3-4, 207
  auditing procedures and standards of, 606-7, 685, 686, 688-89, 761-63, 766-68, 776, 779
Amortization, defined, 366
APB (*see* Accounting Principles Board)
Assets:
  acquisition of, 110
  attributes of, 633, 634-35
  defined, 106, 149
  intangible, 365-67
    amortization of, 366
    estimated useful life and, 366
    examples of, 365
    treatment of, 365
  long-lived, 162
    depreciation methods for, 360-64
    disposal of, 367-68
    valuation of and related expense recognition, 358-67
  market values of, 599
  monetary:
    defined, 106
    valuing, 107
  net, 152
  nonmonetary:
    defined, 106
    replacement cost model and, 551
  price level:
    adjustment of, 502, 515
    valuing, 107-8
  original transaction cost, 108
  original transaction value, 108
  valuation of, in conventional accounting, 106-9

Attestation, 776 (*see also* Auditing)
Auditing:
  defined, 764
  engagements for, 768-72
  error detection, 773-76
  financial reporting and, 759-80
  framework of, 764-68
    control system review and, 765
    evidential matter, 765-66
    professional judgment and, 766
    standards and procedures and, 766-67
  fraud detection, 773-76
  independent auditors and, 762
  internal control and, 763
  irregularities, detection of, 773-76
  professional independence and, 776-79
  role of, 760-62
  tools and techniques, 772-73
    computer-assisted auditing procedures, 773
    flowcharts, 772-73
    statistical sampling, 773
Auditors (*see* Certified Public Accountants)
Available cash, and disposable wealth, 160-63
Average cost method of inventory cost assignment, 349-51

Bad debt(s):
  estimating, 302-3
  financial position, effect of, 302
  treatment of, 304-5
Bad debt loss, 301
Balance, defined, 228
Balance of the asset, defined, 361
Balance sheet, 121-22, 461, 504 (*see also* Statement of financial position)
  characteristics of, 121-22
  consolidated:
    at acquisition, 467-69
    subsequent to acquisition, 469-72
"Balloon payment" bonds, 396
Benefit, prepayment for, 111-12
Blough, Carman G., 686, 687
Bond discount, defined, 391
Bond premium, defined, 391
Bonds:
  conversion provisions, 420
  distinction between stock and, 419
  face value of, 391, 400
  market interest rate, 391
  maturity date of, 391
  present value of, 397
  redemption provisions, 420
  sinking fund provisions, 420
  stated interest rate, 391
  treatment of, 399-400
  types of, 419-20
Bookkeeping:
  debit-credit convention, 225-26, 233

Bookkeeping (cont.)
  general ledger, 231, 243
    characteristics, 223-24
    closing entries, 240
    end-of-period adjustments, 237-39
    general journal, 224-27
    income statement, 239
    preparing permanent accounts, 240
    preparing statement of financial position, 240-41
    preparing statements of changes in financial position, 241
    recording and posting transactions, 237
    temporary (period-related or nominal) accounts, 229-30
    terminating (closing) revenue and expense accounts, 240
    transactions entries, 232, 237
    traditional format, 224
Book value, defined, 362
Borrowing, 416-21
  influencing factors of, 416-17
  long-term, 417
  methods of, 418-21
    accounts receivable financing, 418-19
    corporate bonds, 419-20
    inventory financing, 420
    mortgage, 420
    notes, 420-21
    series bonds, 421
    short-term loans, 421
  secured, 418-21
  short-term, 417
  unsecured, 418-21
Business enterprises:
  alternative reporting possibilities and, 75
  cash-generating ability of, 79, 80
  comparative features of types of, 21
  corporation, 20-22
  decision making and, 22-25, 266-67
  distribution of benefits, 24
  and enterprise function, 17-19
  impact in economic life, 18
  investments and, 73-75
  in market economy, 17
  as net cash producer, 73-74
  operating sequence of, 74
  original investment in, 110
  partnerships, 20
  past performance:
    measures of, 79-83
    related to future cash flow, 79
    relevance of in forecasting, 78-79
  proprietorships, 19-20
  as reservoir of cash, 545
  as reservoir of physical resources, 546
  role of management and investor forecasting, 75-78
  sources of funds and, 678
  valuation of, 76-78

Capital:
  defined, 8
  demand and, 676
  financial concept of, 638
  formation of:
    adequacy of funds for, 679-80
    in market economy, 675-78
  physical concept of, 545-46
Capitalization, leases and, 445
Capital maintenance concept, 636-37
Capital market:
  accounting policy-making process and, 673-709
  defined, 676-77
  intermediaries and, 677
  participants and transactions and, 677
Carrying value:
  defined, 390
  of liabilities, 398
Cash:
  as exchange medium, 165
  as "eye of the needle," 188
  pivotal role of, 188
  provided by operations, 204
Cash discounts, treatment of, 318
Cash dividends, 408, 409
Cash flow, 37-38
  as measure of performance:
    advantages, 80
    disadvantages, 80
    expected, 56-57
    net operating, 80
Cash inadequacy, 203
Cash receipts and revenue, 84
Certainty equivalent approach, 57
Certified Public Accountant (CPA), 760, 779-80
Common denominator (see Common index of merit)
Common index of merit, 11
Common stock, 405-6
Common unit, money value as, 496
Comparative values approach, to accounting, 125-27
Completed contract method, of revenue recognition, 276-81
Compound interest, 42
Computer-assisted audits, 773
Conservatism:
  concept of, 163-64
  defined, 163
  effects of excessive, 164
Constraints, defined, 10
Consumer Price Index for All Urban Consumers, 576
Consumption postponement, 675-76
Contra-asset account, defined, 119
Contributed capital, distinction between earned and, 405
Conventional accounting (see Accounting, conventional)

790 INDEX

Conventional accounting (cont.)
Conversion right, defined, 407
Convertible bond, defined, 420
Corporate bonds, 419-20
Corporate securities markets (*see* Securities markets, corporate)
Corporations, characteristics, 20-22
Cost:
  expired, 109
  recording of, 104
  unexpired, 109
Cost allocation process, 238
Cost or market method of valuation, 354-55, 454-57
Cost principle, 338, 352
  defined, 86, 340
  expense recognition and, 86, 340-44
Cost recovery method, of revenue recognition, 308
CPA (*see* Certified Public Accountant)
Creditors:
  ability to satisfy, 606-7
  defined, 419, 715
  rights of, 23-24
Current (acid-test) ratio, as risk indicator, 725-26
Current assets, defined, 188
Current benefits, distribution and, 267
Current cost, 633, 634
Current entry price (replacement cost):
  defined, 544
  money vs. physical capital, 545-48
  recognition of accounting model based on, 543-79
Current exchange price, defined, 544
Current exchange value, estimated, 342
Current exit price (value):
  attribute of assets and liabilities, 633-34
  defined, 544, 611, 633
  measurement of, 611
  recognition of accounting model based on, 543
Current liabilities, defined, 188-89
Current market-value model, of liability valuation, 402
Current operating income, replacement-cost-based, 548
Current prices, 521
Current ratio, as risk indicator, 725-26

Data gathering and processing, 245-48
Debentures, defined, 419
Debit-credit convention, 225-26, 233
Debt, retirement of, before maturity, 403
Debt-equity ratio, as indicator of risk, 726-27
Decision makers:
  external, 22, 23-24
  internal, 22-23
Decision making, 7-15

  business enterprises and, 22-25
  constraints and, 10
  corporate financial reports and, 715-28
  depreciation methods and, 364
  disposal of long-lived assets and, 367
  distribution of benefits and, 269
  economics of, 13
  enterprises and, 8
  evaluation of alternatives and, 10-12
  identification of problems and, 9-10
  information for, 266
    role of, 13
    usefulness of, 629
  information specialists and, 15-17
  investment (*see* Investment decisions)
  objectivity and, 630
  quantification of attributes, 12
  relevance and, 14, 629
  resource allocation dilemma and, 7-8
  stages in, 8
  statement of objectives, 9
  statistical measures (indicators) and, 720-28
  wealth distribution and, 160-62
Decision relevance, 629
  defined, 14
Decisions:
  distribution of current benefits and, 267
  external, classes of, 267
  risk-evaluation-related, 269
Declining-balance depreciation method, 361-63
Deferred costs, defined, 366
Depletion expense, 365
Depreciation, accumulated, 119
Depreciation methods:
  alternative, 363-64
  comparison of depreciation expense under alternative, 363
  decision making and, 364
  declining balance, 361-63
  straight-line, 118-19, 360
  sum-of-the-years digits, 360-61
Discount rate, 40
Disposable wealth:
  available cash vs., 160-63
  calculation of, 502-5
  changing prices and, 501-5
  conventional accounting measurement of, 149-53
  corporations and dividend distribution, 158
  criterion level and, 148, 158
  defined, 53
  Hicksian criterion for measuring, 149, 269, 503
  market values and measurement of, 269, 602-5
  net operating income as measure of, 149, 150

Disposable wealth (cont.)
  price-level-adjusted measure of, 550
  relationship with performance, 508
  replacement costs and, 565-68
  taxation and, 148
  valuation of, 149
Dividends:
  dates significant for, 408-9
  distribution decisions, 405
  legal considerations and, 158
  stock, 408-12
  uncertainty and policy on, 163
Double-declining-balance depreciation method, 362
Dr-Cr general ledger format, 224-25

Earned capital, contributed and, 405
Earnings per share (EPS), as indicator of return, 721-23
Economic units, transfer of funds between, 676
Effective interest approach to accounting for liabilities, 394-402
Effective interest rate:
  defined, 394
  of liabilities, 394
End-of-period adjustments, 238
Enterprise, defined, 8
Enterprise function, 18-19
Enterpriser, role of, 19
Entrepreneurial ability (*see* Enterprise)
Equity method, 460
Errors, detection of, 773-76
Events, recognition of, 112-14
Exchange price, defined, 544
Executory contract, defined, 444
Expected cash flow, 268
Expected exit value, 633, 634
Expected return, 717
Expected risk, 717
Expense(s) (*see also specific type of expenses*)
  defined, 85, 338, 593
  measurement, 338-45
  recognition, 86-87, 104
    asset valuation issues and, 337-72
    duality of asset and liability valuation, 344-45
    within financial position framework, 116-17
    inventory valuation and, 345-57
    long-lived assets, 358-68
    objective of, 338
    related equity valuation issues and, 387
    timing of, 338
Expired cost(s), 109
  defined, 340
External accounting, 6, 7
External parties, reports to. 711-15

FASB (*see* Financial Accounting Standards Board)
Federal Trade Commission (FTC), 284, 674, 684
FIFO (*see* First in, first out method)
Financial accounting, 6-7 (*see also specific topic*)
  data-processing system of, 245-48
  defined, 7
Financial Accounting Foundation (FAF), 685
Financial accounting information system, 222-52
Financial accounting models, 627-53
  alternatives and choice, 628-32
  classification of, 635-36
  comparison of, 640-53
  conventional model, 641-45
  current exit prices (market values), 593-612
  current market-value, 652-53
  market-value, 543
  price-level changes and, 495-524
  replacement cost, 543-79
  traditional criteria for choice, 629
Financial accounting policy:
  authority of, 686-91
  defined, 674
  eclectic approach to, 688
  effect of changes in business environment and, 689
  environmental influences on, 686-91
  formulation of, 269-71
  influences exerted on, 674
  legislation and, 674-75
  special interest groups and, 689
Financial accounting standards. See Financial accounting policy
Financial Accounting Standards Board (FASB), 270, 284, 452, 453, 521, 575, 576-77, 633, 637, 638, 686, 688, 689, 690
Financial accounting information system:
  flow chart, 247
Financial activities, defined, 187
Financial Analysts Federation, 686
Financial Executives Institute (FEI), 686, 761
Financial (money) capital, vs. physical capital, 545-53
Financial position, 105
  classification of activities, 187
  cumulative effect of events on, 112
  defined, 109
  direct effects of operation on, 188
  effects of investment and financing activities on, 187, 194
  end-of-period, 120-24
  enterprise and, 269
  and net operating income, 123-24

Financial position (cont.)
  relevance of, 121
  statement of cash flow, 124
  statements of changes in, 184–207, 242
Financial position worksheet, 112, 113
Financial ratios. *See* Indicators
Financial reports:
  annual, 711
  audit function and, 759–80
  characteristics of, 716
  content of, 710–30
  disclosure and, 682–85
  dissemination of, 710–30
  external parties and, 711–15
  independent auditors and, 762
  interim, 711–12
  public interest and, 681–82
  responsibility and, 761
  Securities Exchange Commission and, 712
Financial statement(s), 731–58
  comparability of data from, 728–30
  consolidated, 457, 465–72
  individuals and, 606–11
  restatement of prior year's and, 518–19
  scaling and, 719
  standards and, 719–20
    industry, 719
    performance, 720
    time, 719
  verifiability and, 167
Financial statement worksheet, 244
First in, first out (FIFO) method, 351–52
Fixed assets, examples of, 189
Flowchart(s), auditing and, 772–73
Flowchart, example of, 247
Flowchart symbols, 248
Forced liquidation, 611
Forecasting:
  future cash flows and, 74–75
  investor:
    impediments to, 75
    information needed from management and, 78–79
  management and, 76, 268
  relevance of past performance and, 78–79
Forecast statement, of resource flows, 187
Foreign Corrupt Practices Act (1977), 763
Franchising, characteristics of, 315
Franchisor, defined, 315
Fraud, auditor's detection of, 773–76
Free enterprise system, 17
Free market, 684
Funds, sources of, 189–90
Funds statement (*see* Statement of changes in financial position)
Future cash flows:
  forecasting, 74–75
  past performance, 79
Future value:
  of any amount, 43
  net present value and, 47–49
  of one dollar, 42
    table, 60
  relationship of present value and, 46

Gains (losses):
  defined, 153
  disposable wealth, and, 156
  events giving rise to, 153
  extraordinary, 154, 156
  income measurement and, 153
  offsetting, 153
  recognition of, 153–54
  unrealized holding, 553–56
Gains and losses, unrealized, 597–98
General ledger, 233–36
  accounts, 441
  defined, 227
General journal, 224–27, 232–33
  defined, 228
  entry format, 245
Generally accepted accounting principles (GAAP), 271
Generally accepted auditing standards (GAAS), 767
Great Depression, 682–83
Gross profit method, of estimating inventory, 370–72

Health, Education, and Welfare, Department of, 3
Hicks, J.R., 52
Hicksian income (*see* Disposable wealth)
Historical cost, 633, 634 (*see also* Original transaction cost)

Income:
  components of, 153
  determinants of, 54–55
  Hicksian concept of (*see* Disposable wealth)
  as long-run concept, 186
  as measure of resource flows, 185
  net, 157
  net operating, 123
  price-level-adjusted, 604
  reported, effect of inventory errors on, 357
  timing of, and market values, 598–99
  valuation and, 435–74
Income measurement:
  conventional accounting and, 147–68
  gains and losses and, 153–60
  net income, 157
  net operating income, 123, 157
  price-level adjusted, 514–15
Income measures, 653
Income statement(s), 123, 157, 185, 239, 462, 464, 466, 506, 560
  characteristics of, 122
  comparative, 438, 598, 599
  consolidated, 471

Income statement(s) (cont.)
   subsequent to acquisition, 469-72
   constructing, 122-23
   conventional accounting model, 547
   market-value-based, 602
   and working capital from operations, 198-201
   preparation of, 239-40
   replacement-cost model, 549
Income taxes:
   accounting for, 436-44
   assessments, 436-39
   comparative calculations and, 439
   corporate rate structure, 87, 436
   expense, 87
   gains (losses) and, 153
   matching principle and, 439-44
   as period costs, 439-40
   related revenue and expense and, 440
   treatment of, 442
Independence, professional, in auditing, 776-79
Index numbers, constructing, 497-98
Indicators:
   of return, 721-25
   of risk, 725-28
   limitations of, 727-28
Information, accounting:
   decision making, 13, 266
   decision-relevant, 267-69
   defined, 13
   dissemination of, 710-15
   economics of decisions and, 13-15
   external decisions and, 269
   financial services and, 713
   news announcements and, 713
   specialization in, 15-17
Information specialist, defined, 15
Installment sales method, of revenue recognition, 306-8
Intercorporate ownership, levels of accounting recognition and, 459
Interest expense:
   calculation of, 398
   measurement of, 396-401
   recognition of, 391, 393
Internal control:
   auditing and, 763
   defined, 763
Internal Revenue Code, 436, 437, 438
International Monetary Fund, 3
Inventory(ies):
   basic classes of, in manufacturing firms, 355
   estimating:
      from aggregate data, 355
      gross profit method, 370-72
   financing, 420
Inventory cost assignment:
   methods of, 348-55
      average cost method, 349-51
      first in, first out (FIFO), 351-52
      last in, first out (LIFO), 352-53
      lower of cost or market, 354-55
      specific identification, 348-49
Inventory valuation:
   assignment of cost and, 347-53
   departure from cost basis, 354-55
   methods of:
      periodic, 353
      perpetual, 353
   periodic vs. perpetual, 368-70
   physical quantity and, 346
   related expense recognition and, 345-57
Investment activities, defined, 187
Investment Advisors Act (1940), 675
Investment Company Act (1940), 675
Investment decisions, 23-24, 72-91, 267, 715-17
   alternate information for, 268
   alternative opportunities and, 41-42
   assumptions, 37
   consumption levels and, 41
   defined, 37
   estimating parameters and, 717-20
   expected cash flows and, 56-57
   financial accounting information and, 267-68
   financial statement information and, 717-20
   objective of, 36-37
   present value model for, 39-60
   problem of, 36-39
   risk and, 57-58
   simplified models of:
      net present value, 47-51
      present value, 39-47
      time preference and, 39-41
   uncertainty and, 55-56
   under certainty, 38-39
Investment opportunities, valuing, 73
Investments:
   business enterprises and, 73-75
   in corporate stock, accounting for, 454-74
   in other corporations, 459-74
      treatment of intercorporate, in marketable securities, 454-57
Investment tax credit, 692-94
Investors, defined, 267
Irregularities, detection of, in auditing, 773-76

Joint costs, 339
Joint products (goods and services), provision of:
   credit along with product, 309-13
   franchising services and product, 315-17
   warranty services and product, 313-15

Labor, defined, 8
Labor, U.S. Department of, 576
Labor costs, 249

"Labor-intensive" production process, 187
Land:
  defined, 8
  valuation of, 365
Last in, first out (LIFO) method, 352-53
Leases:
  accounting for, 451-53
  capitalization-financing treatment of, 445-59
  lessee and, 445
  lessor and, 445-56
  long-term noncancelable, 444-53
  realization principle and, 452
  short-term rental (operating), 450-51
Legal capital, defined, 409
Liability(ies), 387-404
  attributes of, 387, 633, 634-35
    from timing of cash flows perspective, 635
    from type of transaction perspective, 635
    from type of event perspective, 636
  basic characteristics of, 387-89
  carrying value of, 393, 398
  defined, 105, 149, 189
  disclosure of, 403-4
  effective interest approach to accounting for, 394-402
  effective interest rate of, 394-96
  examples, 106
  expenditure approach to accounting for, 389-94
  installment, 402-3
  monetary, 106, 107
  nonmonetary, 106, 107-8
  original transaction value, 108
  price-level changes and, 508-9
  third-party, 778
  valuation of, 401
    in conventional accounting, 106-9 401-2
    current market-value model, 402
LIFO (see Last in, first out method)
Long-lived assets:
  decision-making and, 367
  disposal of, 367-68
  examples of, 189
  expenditure to maintain and/or improve, 359
  intangible, 358-68
  measurement of benefits derived from, 359-63
    price-level changes and, 516-18
    recognition of gain or loss, 367
  tangible, 358-68
  uncertainty and, 162
  valuation at acquisition and, 358
Long-term liabilities, defined, 189
Losses. *See* Gains (losses)

Lower of cost or market method
  accounting for intercorporate ownership and, 460
  of inventory cost assignment, 354-55
  treatment of marketable securities and, 457

Management forecasts, 76-78, 268
Manufacturing costs, treatment of, 355
Manufacturing firm, inventory relationships in, 356
Market, as current replacement cost, 354
Marketable securities, intercorporate ownership, 454-57
Market economy:
  capital formation and, 675-78
  public interest and, 681-82
  role of money in, 37-38, 267
Market efficiency:
  primary, 680
  secondary, 681
Marketing activities, 187
Market value(s):
  measurement of disposable wealth and, 602-5
  measurement of firm's, 605
  recognition of:
    decision relevance and, 612
    limitations and, 612
  timing of income and, 598-99
  value-added concept and, 596-97
Market-value accounting, 612
Matching principle, 85-86, 116, 338-40, 390, 594
  causal relationships and, 338
  concept of, 338
  defined, 86, 338
  income taxes and, 439-44
Materiality, 359
Merchandise:
  obsolete or damaged, 355
  returns and allowances, 319-20
Moffat, Donald W., 416
Monetary assets:
  defined, 106
  price-level changes and, 508-9
  valuing, 107-8
Monetary gains (losses):
  calculation of, 509-12
  defined, 509
  Interpretation of, 512
Money values, use as common unit, 496
Monopolies, 25
Mortgage, defined, 420

National Association of Accountants, 686
National Bankruptcy Act (1938), 675
Net assets:

Net assets (cont.)
  defined, 152
  market-value-based relevance of, 605-11
Net cash flow vs. net operating income, 90-91
Net income:
  defined, 157
  to equity/assets, as return indicator, 723-24
  market-value-based, 602-3
  price-level adjusted, 512-15
  replacement-cost-based, 553
  to sales, as return indicator, 724-25
Net monetary gain (loss), 514
  estimating, 519-20
Net operating cash flow, defined, 80
Net operating income:
  defined, 89, 157
  disposable wealth and, 156
  dual role of, 156
  as index of periodic performance, 89
  as measure of disposable wealth, 149-53
  relationship to financial position, 123-24
Net present value (*see* Present value, net)
Net realizable values, defined, 611
New York Stock Exchange, 679, 776
Nominal accounts, 107
Nominal amounts, defined, 229
Noncancelable lease, defined, 453
Note, defined, 420

Objectivity, conventional accounting and, 167
"Operating cycle," 189
Operating income:
  defined, 507
  market-value-based, format for reporting, 600-602
  price-level adjusted, 506-8
  current, replacement-cost-based, 548
Operational efficiency, defined, 680
Operations:
  classification of activities, 187
  defined, 187
Opportunity rate, defined, 41
Original transaction cost, 108
Original transaction rate of interest, 401
Original transaction value:
  defined, 108, 340
  measurement of, 341
Owner's equity, 404-16
  classification of paid-in-capital, 405-8
  defined, 109, 189
  dividends on stock, 408-11
  earned and contributed capital, distinction between, 405
  as single residual calculation, 404
  sources of, 405, 415
  stock options, 412-14
  stock splits, 411-12
  treasury stock, 412
  valuation of, 109
Owners of record, 249

Paid-in-capital:
  classification of, 405-8
  defined, 158, 405
Partnerships, characteristics, 20
Par value, defined, 407
Patterns of benefits, from use of resources, 339
Percentage-of-completion method, of revenue recognition, 276-81
Performance, relationship with disposable wealth, 508
Performance index, 354
Performance measurement:
  advantages of revenue for, 85
  conventional accounting, 83-91
  market value and, 593-99
  periodic, 89-90
  price-level changes and, 505-7
  recognition of accomplishment and, 593-96
  replacement costs and, 568-70
Period expenses, 339
  product expenses vs., 87-89
Periodic accomplishment, measuring, 84
Periodic method, of inventory valuation, 353, 368, 369-70
Periodic performance, measurement of, 89-90
Period-related accounts (*see* Nominal accounts)
Perpetual method, of inventory valuation, 353, 368, 369-70
Physical capital, and financial (money) capital, 545-53
Pooling-of-interests method, of accounting, 472-74
Posting, defined, 228
Preferred stock:
  convertible, 407
  cumulative, 406
  non-cumulative, 406
  rights of owners of, 405
Present value:
  of any amount, 45
  concept of, 43-58
  defined, 44
  of expected cash flows, 633, 634
  and future value tables, 45-46
  Hicksian concept of income and, 52-55
  management forecasting and, 77
  methodology, 51-58, 268
  model, 312
  net:
    calculating, 47
    defined, 47

Present value (cont.)
  interpreting, 48-49
    as model for investment choice, 47-49
    time preference rate, sensitivity to, 51-52
  of one dollar, 45
    table, 59
  relationship of future value and, 46
  risk assessment and, 57-58
  uncertainty and, 55-57
  wealth maximization and, 51-52
Price-level accounting, 495-524
  present status of, 520-22
Price-level adjusted net income (disposable wealth), 503, 512-15
  defined, 512
Price-level adjusted operating income, 506, 514
  defined, 507
Price-level adjustments, replacement costs and, 570-72
Price-level changes:
  conventional accounting and, 499-501
  disposable wealth and, 501-5
  long-lived assets and, 515-18
  performance measurement and, 505-8
Price-level index, 497, 498
Proceeds of liability, defined, 388
Product expenses, 339
  period expenses vs., 87-89
Profits, intercompany, elimination of, 472
Proprietorships, 19-20
Public Utility Holding Company Act (1934), 675
Purchase method, of accounting, 472-74
Purchasing power, 546
  price-level indexes and comparative, 497-98
  relevance of changes in, 495-96

Rate of return, defined, 41
Ratios. *See* Indicators
Realization principle, 593-96
  defined, 84, 271
  leases and, 452
  revenue and, 83-84
  uncertainty and, 162
Realized gain (loss), 605
Realized holding gain (loss), 548-49
Related companies, 469
Relative reliability, of estimated current exchange values, 342
Replacement cost, information (unaudited), 577-79
Replacement cost(s), 165-66
  disposable wealth measurement and, 565-68
  performance measurement and, 568-70
  price-level adjustments and, 570-72
  reporting requirements and, 572-77

Replacement cost model, 543-79
  nominal dollars, 646-48
  units of purchasing power, 648-51
Residual beneficiaries:
  defined, 24
  enterprises and, 24
  sharers of, 24, 148
Resource allocation, dilemma over, 7-8
Resource flows, 184-207
  cash, 185-87
  forecast statements and, 187
  income, 185-87
  working capital, 185-87
Resources:
  allocation of, 266, 715-28
  classification, 8
  consumption of, 188
  examples of, 271
  natural, allocation of costs and, 365
  scarce, 7-8, 266
Retained earnings, 158, 405
Return indicators, 721-25
Revenue:
  defined, 83, 272, 593
  expense summary and, 240
  and realization principle, 83-84
  relationship of cash receipts and, 84
Revenue measurement, 271-81
  components of, 271
Revenue recognition, 265-87, 300-21
  completed contract method of, 276-81
  cost recovery method, 308
  discounts and, 317-19
  expanded historical-cost based, 284, 287
  forgiven billings, and, 320
  installment sales method, 306-8
  objective of, 271
  percentage-of-completion method of, 276-81
  point-of-sale interpretation, 272
  prior to delivery of goods and services, 273
  production and delivery of separable units and, 275-76
  production of salable commodities and, 274-75
  prolonged production on firm orders and, 276-81
  reporting business segments, 284
  returns and allowances and, 319-20
  sale-with-financing method, 312
  timing of, fundamental criteria, 271
  uncertainty of collection and, 300-308
  unresolved conceptual issues of, 281-83
  within financial position framework, 115-16
Ripley, William Z., 683, 686
Risk:
  assessment, 57
  defined, 57

Index 797

Risk (cont.)
    indicators, 725-28
    value and, 58

Sales, valid, 248
Scales, quantitative, 12
Scaling, 719
Securities Act (1933), 674, 683
SEC (see Securities and Exchange Commission)
Securities and Exchange Commission (SEC), 268, 284, 521, 572, 674, 684, 685, 688, 690, 712, 767, 776
Securities Exchange Act (1934), 674, 683
Securities markets, corporate, 678
    operational efficiency of, 680-81
    primary, 679
    secondary, 679
    social demands on, 678-82
    source of funds for enterprise, 678-79
Security Industry Association, 686
Serial bonds, 393
Series bonds, defined, 421
Service, prepayment for, 111-12
Short-term loans, defined, 421
Source documents, 245
Specific identification, method of inventory, 348-49
Standardized procedures, 246
Standards, need for, 719-20
Stated value, defined, 407
Statement of cash flow, 125
Statement of changes in financial position, 184-207, 242
Statement of financial position, 121-22, 186, 189, 559, 564
    components of, 190
    preparation, 240-41
Statement of objectives, defined, 9
Statement of retained earnings, 161
Static prices, 514
Statistical sampling, auditing and, 773
Stettler, Howard, 779
Stock:
    bonds and, distinction between, 419
    classes of, 405-6
    common, 405-6
    dividends on, 408-12
    par value, 407
    preferred, 406
    stated value, 407
Stock dividend(s), 409-11
Stock options, 412-14
Stock splits, 411-12
Straight-line method of depreciation, 360
Subsidiary journals, 245
Subsidiary ledger accounts, nonfinancial accounting application of, 246

Subsidiary ledgers, 246
Sum-of-the-years digits depreciation method, 360-61
Systems design, 249

T-account, 228
Tax allocation, interperiod, 440-43
Taxable income, 443
Temporary accounts (see Nominal accounts)
Term loan, defined, 421
Third party liabilities, 778
Time preference for money, 39-58
Time preference rate, 40-41
    use of, 40
Trade discounts, treatment of, 317
Transactions, recording and posting, 237
Transactions approach to accounting, 125-28
Transfer of funds, between economic units, 676
Treasury stock, 412
Trial balance(s), 243, 244
Trust Indenture Act (1939), 675

Uncertainty:
    adaptations to, 163-64
    defined, 13, 38, 55
    dividend policy and, 163
    implications of, 163-64
    lessening effects of, 13
    long-lived assets and, 162
    realization principle and, 162
Unexpired cost(s), 109, 340
Uniform CPA examination, 779, 780
Unrealized gains (losses), 597-98, 605

Valuation, 50-51
    defined, 50
    duality of asset and liability, 344-45
Value-added concept:
    accomplishment and, 84, 271, 596-99
    market values and, 596-97

Wealth:
    defined, 37
    disposable, 53, 147-49
    distribution, 160-62
    maximizing, 37
    present value and concept of, 49-51
Working capital, 190
    concept of, 188-91
    defined, 189
    from operations, 198-201
    sources, 192
        nonoperating, 194
    uses, 192
        nonoperating, 194
World Health Organization, 3

Fixed Assets

- Cost of Land = purchase price + insurance, legal fees ...
- Depreciation expense = f (depreciable base, useful life)

  ↓

  original acquisition cost − residual value

- Depreciation
  1. Straight line : YR : Dep Base : Rate : expense : Acc dep : BV
  2. Units of service :
  3. Accelerated methods :
     a) Declining balance
        - apply fixed depⁿ rate to declining BV   (rate usually double SL rate)

        YR   Beg BV   Dep Rate   Dep Ex   Acc Dep   Ending BV

     b) SOYD
        - apply decreasing dep rate to fixed depreciable base

        YR   Dep base   Dep rate   Dep Ex   Acc Dep   BV

- Cash flow = net cash receipts − taxes
            = net income + depreciation

- Disposal of asset

Cash	500	
Acc Depr	10 000	
Computer		10 400
gain on disposal		100

  } same at end or before end of life

  Asset exchange

  Fair market value method

Truck (cash + trade in)	13000	
Acc Depⁿ - computer	10 000	
Computer		10 400
Cash		11 000
Gain on exch		600

  Income tax method

New Computer (cash + BV)	11 400	
Acc Dep - old computer	10 000	
Old Computer		10 400
Cash		11 000

- Goodwill
  1) Capitalisation of X$ earnings
     - PV of company's X$ earnings
  3) Residual method
     - Δ (Purchase Price − F.M.V Net Assets)

     Adjusting entry

Amortization expense - goodwill	5000	
Goodwill		5000

Corporate Investments

ownership < 20%   cost method
20 < ownership < 50%   Equity method

Cost

		Equity	
Investment in B 1,500,000		Inv in B 1,500,000	
Cash 1,500,000		Cash 1,500,000	
No entry		Inv in B 150,000	
		Investment income 150,000	
Cash 45,000		Cash 45,000	
Dividend income 45,000		Investment in B 45,000	

I/S

Investment income   45,000   Investment income   150,000

B/S

Investment in B   1,500,000   Investment in B   1,605,000

Purchase vs Pooling

Purchase : CE at acquisition say does not change
           Goodwill at Δ (Purchase price − FMV F.A)

Pooling : simply add together B/S without adjustment to FMV

Exchange Gains & Losses

Transaction gain/loss   caused by physical change ⇒ cash flow effect
Translation gain/loss   caused by restatement   ⇒ no cash flow effect

Translation methods

⇒ accounting exposure
⇒ gain/loss measured by Δ OE (before & after)

	Current rate	Historical rate	Average Rate
current – non-current	Current assets – cash – A/R – Inv Current liabilities	Fixed assets L-T debt	Revenues Expenses (except depⁿ – historical)
monetary – non monetary	Monetary assets – cash – A/R Monetary liabilities – ST payables – LT debt	Non monetary – Inv – F.A.	Revenues Expenses (except depⁿ)
Temporal	as for m/n-m but if inventory stated at market include in monetary assets		
Current	everything		

LIABILITIES : DEFERRED TAXES : LEASES : DEFEASANCE

Credit terms
- least expensive: net 30
- most expensive: 2/10 net 30 |——10——|——+2%——|——20——|

Purchase Discount

Gross Method

Purchases:
- Purchases   1000
-    A/P   1000

If discount taken:
- A/P   1000
-    P. Disc   20
-    Cash   980

If discount not taken:
- A/P   1000
-    Cash   1000

Net Method

- Purchases   980
-    A/P   980

- A/P   980
-    Cash   980

- A/P   980
- Disc Loss   20
-    Cash   1000

Notes Payable

Add-on Method
a) proceed of loan = face value
b) interest is calculated on F.V.

e.g. 1000 borrowed, 12 month, 10% N/P

To record borrowing:
- Cash   1000
-    N/P   1000

Adjusting entry:
- Interest expense   100
-    I/P   100

To record repayment:
- Interest payable   100
- N/P   1000
-    Cash   1100

Discount Method
a) Proceeds of loan < face value
b) interest expense = Δ loan proceeds & maturity value

1000 borrowed, one yr, non-interest bearing note (10%) is given

- Cash   900
- Discount on N/P   100
-    N/P   1000

- Interest expense   100
-    Discount on N/P   100

- N/P   1000
-    Cash   1000

Nominal rate = stated rate
Effective rate = annual interest / loan proceeds

BONDS

AT PAR

Issue:
- Cash   1,000,000
-    B/P   1,000,000

Interest expense:
- Interest expense   30,000
-    Cash   30,000